SOCIAL
ETHICS

SOCIAL ETHICS

Morality and Social Policy
Second Edition

THOMAS A. MAPPES
Frostburg State College

JANE S. ZEMBATY
University of Dayton

McGRAW-HILL BOOK COMPANY

New York | St. Louis | San Francisco | Auckland
Bogotá | Hamburg | Johannesburg | London | Madrid
Mexico | Montreal | New Delhi | Panama | Paris
São Paulo | Singapore | Sydney | Tokyo | Toronto

SOCIAL ETHICS
Morality and Social Policy

567890 HDHD 898765

This book was set in Souvenir Light by University Graphics, Inc.
The editors were Kaye Pace and Barry Benjamin;
the designer was Nicholas Krenitsky;
the production supervisor was Diane Renda.

Library of Congress Cataloging in Publication Data

Mappes, Thomas A.
    Social ethics.

    Includes bibliographies.
    1. Social ethics—Addresses, essays, lectures.
2. Ethics—Addresses, essays, lectures.   3. Social
policy—Addresses, essays, lectures.   4. Moral
conditions—Addresses, essays, lectures.
I. Zembaty, Jane S.   II. Title.
HM216.M27   1982   170   81-6025
ISBN 0-07-040121-7   AACR2

CONTENTS

CHAPTER 11: ANIMALS AND THE ENVIRONMENT   385

PREFACE

Is the death penalty a morally acceptable type of punishment? Is our human interest in eating meat sufficient to justify the way in which we raise and slaughter animals? Do affluent, technologically advanced nations have moral obligations to aid technologically underdeveloped countries? Is society justified in enacting laws which limit individual liberty in sexual matters?

The way we answer such moral questions and the social policies we adopt in keeping with our answers will directly affect our lives. It is not surprising, therefore, that discussions of these and other contemporary moral issues often involve rhetorical arguments whose intent is to elicit highly emotional, nonobjective responses. This book is designed to provide material which will encourage an objective study of some contemporary moral problems. To achieve this end, we have developed chapters which bring the central issues into clear focus, while allowing the supporting arguments for widely diverse positions to be presented by those who embrace them.

With the appearance of this second edition, we are confident that *teachability* will continue to be the most salient characteristic of *Social Ethics*. All of the editorial features employed in the first edition to enhance teachability have been retained in the second. An introduction to each chapter both sets the ethical issues and scans the various positions together with their supporting argumentation. Every selection is prefaced by a headnote which provides both biographical data on the author and a short statement of some of the key points or arguments to be found in the selection. Every selection is followed by questions whose purpose is to elicit further critical analysis and discussion. Finally, each chapter concludes with a short annotated bibliography designed to guide the reader in further research.

We have tried to provide readings that are free of unnecessary technical jargon and yet introduce serious moral argumentation. Further, in order to emphasize the connection of contemporary moral problems with matters of social policy, we have liberally incorporated relevant legal opinions. We have taken substantial editorial license by deleting almost all the numerous citations that usually attend legal writing in order to render the legal opinions maximally readable to the nonlegal eye. Those interested in further legal research can check the appropriate credit lines for the necessary bibliographical data to locate the cases in their original form.

We would be remiss not to express our indebtedness to all those whose work is reprinted in these pages. We are also indebted to Raymond M. Herbenick, Margaret Knapke, Christopher Brelje, Mark Wicclair, and Joy Kroeger Mappes for their helpful critical comments. Betty Hume, Linda McKinley, Carol Ruffing, Phyllis Bateson, and Shelley Drees deserve thanks for their help with manuscript preparation, and we continue to be grateful to the reference librarians at both the University of Dayton and Frostburg State College.

Thomas A. Mappes
Jane S. Zembaty

ABORTION

With the landmark abortion decision of the United States Supreme Court in *Roe v. Wade* (1973), restrictive abortion laws, except under narrowly defined conditions, have been ruled unconstitutional. Thus abortion is *legally* available and, unless opponents of abortion succeed in their efforts to have the Constitution amended, it seems that it will remain legally available. However, as reflected in the debate over a proposed constitutional amendment, the ethical (moral) acceptability of abortion remains a hotly contested issue. This chapter focuses attention on abortion as an ethical issue.

ABORTION: THE ETHICAL ISSUE

Discussions of the ethical acceptability of abortion often take for granted (1) an awareness of the various kinds of reasons that may be given for having an abortion and (2) a minimal sort of acquaintance with the biological development of a human fetus.

1. Reasons for Abortion

Why would a woman have an abortion? The following catalog, not meant to provide an exhaustive survey, is sufficient to indicate that there is a wide range of potential reasons for abortion.

(a) In certain extreme cases, if the fetus is allowed to develop normally and come to term, the mother herself will die.

(b) In other cases it is not the mother's life but her health, physical or mental, that will be severely endangered if the pregnancy is allowed to continue.

(c) There are also cases in which the pregnancy will probably, or surely, produce a severely deformed child.

(d) There are others in which the pregnancy is the result of rape or incest.[1]

(e) There are instances in which the mother is unmarried and there will be the social stigma of illegitimacy.

(f) There are other instances in which having a child, or having another child, will be an unbearable financial burden.

(g) Certainly common, and perhaps most common of all, are those instances in which having a child will interfere with the happiness of the woman, or the joint happiness of the parents, or even the joint happiness of a family unit that already includes children. Here there are almost endless possibilities. The woman may desire a professional career. A couple may be content and happy together and feel their relationship would be damaged by the intrusion of a child. Parents may have older children and not feel up to raising another child, etc.

2. The Biological Development of a Human Fetus

During the course of a human pregnancy, in the nine-month period from conception to birth, the product of conception undergoes a continual process of change and development.

---

[1]The expression "therapeutic abortion" suggests abortion for medical reasons. Accordingly, abortions corresponding to (a), (b), and (c) are usually said to be therapeutic. More problematically, abortions corresponding to (d) have often been identified as therapeutic. Perhaps it is presumed that pregnancies resulting from rape or incest are traumatic, thus a threat to mental health. Or perhaps calling such an abortion "therapeutic" is just a way of indicating that it is thought to be justifiable.

Conception takes place when a male germ cell (the spermatozoon) combines with a female germ cell (the ovum), resulting in a single cell (the single-cell zygote), which embodies the full genetic code, twenty-three pairs of chromosomes. The single-cell zygote soon begins a process of cellular division. The resultant multicell zygote, while continuing to grow and beginning to take shape, proceeds to move through the fallopian tube and then to undergo gradual *implantation* at the uterine wall. The unborn entity is formally designated a zygote up until the time that implantation is complete, almost two weeks after conception. Thereafter, until the end of the eighth week, roughly the point at which brain waves can be detected, the unborn entity is formally designated an *embryo*. It is in this embryonic period that organ systems and other human characteristics begin to undergo noticeable development. From the end of the eighth week until birth, the unborn entity is formally designated a *fetus*. (The term "fetus," however, is commonly used as a general term to designate the unborn entity, whatever its stage of development.) Two other points in the development of the fetus are especially noteworthy as relevant to discussions of abortion. First, somewhere between the twelfth and the sixteenth week *quickening* usually occurs. Quickening is the point at which the mother begins to feel the movements of the fetus. Second, somewhere between the twentieth and the twenty-eighth week the fetus reaches *viability,* the point at which it is capable of surviving outside the womb.

With the facts of fetal development in view, it may be helpful to indicate the various medical techniques of abortion. Early (first trimester) abortions are performed by "dilatation and curettage" (D & C) or, increasingly, by "uterine aspiration." The D & C features the stretching (dilatation) of the cervix and the scraping (curettage) of the inner walls of the uterus. The technique of uterine aspiration simply involves sucking the fetus out of the uterus by means of a tube connected to a suction pump. Later abortions require "saline injection" or a "hysterotomy" (a miniature cesarean section). In the former technique, a saline solution injected into the amniotic cavity induces labor, thus expelling the fetus.

A brief discussion of fetal development together with a cursory survey of various reasons for abortion has prepared the way for a formulation of the ethical issue of abortion in its broadest terms. *Up to what point of fetal development, if any, and for what reasons, if any, is abortion ethically acceptable?* Some hold that abortion is *never* ethically acceptable, or at most is acceptable only where abortion is necessary to save the life of the mother. This view is frequently termed the *conservative* view on abortion. Others hold that abortion is *always* ethically acceptable — at any point of fetal development and for any of the standard reasons. This view is frequently termed the *liberal* view on abortion. Still others are anxious to defend more *moderate* views, holding that abortion is ethically acceptable up to a certain point of fetal development *and/or* holding that some reasons provide a sufficient justification for abortion whereas others do not.

THE CONSERVATIVE VIEW AND THE LIBERAL VIEW

The *moral status* of the fetus has been a pivotal issue in discussions of the ethical acceptability of abortion. The concept of moral status is commonly explicated in terms of rights. On this construal, to say that a fetus has moral status is to say that the fetus has rights. What kinds of rights, if any, does the fetus have? Does it have the same rights as more visible humans, and thus *full moral status,* as conservatives typically contend? Does it have no rights, and thus *no (significant) moral status,* as liberals typically contend? (Or perhaps, as some moderates argue, does the fetus have a subsidiary or *partial moral status,* however this is to be conceptualized?) If the fetus has no rights, the liberal is prone to argue, then it does not have any more right to life than a piece of tissue such as an appendix, and an abortion is no more morally objectionable than an appendectomy. If the fetus has the same rights as any other human being, the conservative is prone to argue, then it has the same right to life as the latter, and an abortion, except perhaps when the mother's life is endangered, is as morally objectionable as any other murder.

Discussions of the moral status of the fetus often refer directly to the biological development of the fetus and pose the question: At what point in the continuous development of the fetus do we have a human life? In the context of such discussions, "human" implies full moral status, "nonhuman" implies no (significant) moral status, and any notion of partial moral status is systematically excluded. To distinguish the human from the nonhuman, to "draw the line," and to do so in a nonarbitrary way, is the central matter of concern. The *conservative* on abortion typically holds that the line must be drawn at conception. Usually the conservative argues that conception is the only point at which the line can be nonarbitrarily drawn. Against attempts to draw the line at points such as implantation, quickening, viability, or birth, considerations of continuity in the development of the fetus are pressed. The conservative is sometimes said to employ "slippery-slope arguments," that is, to argue that a line cannot be securely drawn anywhere along the path of fetal development. It is said that the line will inescapably slide back to the point of conception in order to find objective support. John T. Noonan argues in this fashion as he provides a defense of the conservative view in one of the selections in this chapter.

With regard to "drawing the line," the *liberal* typically contends that the fetus remains nonhuman even in its most advanced stages of development. The liberal, of course, does not mean to deny that a fetus is biologically a human fetus. Rather the claim is that the fetus is not human in any morally significant sense—it has no (significant) moral status. This point is often made in terms of the concept of personhood. Mary Anne Warren, who defends the liberal view on abortion in one of this chapter's selections, argues that the fetus is not a person. She also contends that the fetus bears so little resemblance to a person that it cannot be said to have a significant right to life. It is important to notice that, as Warren analyzes the concept of personhood, even a newborn baby is not a person. This conclusion, as might be expected, prompts Warren to a consideration of the moral justifiability of infanticide, an issue closely related to the problem of abortion.

Though the conservative view on abortion is most commonly predicated upon the straightforward contention that the fetus is a person from conception, there are at least two other lines of argument that have been advanced in its defense. One conservative, advancing what might be labeled the "presumption argument," writes:

> In being willing to kill the embryo, we accept responsibility for killing what we must admit *may* be a person. There is some reason to believe it is—namely the *fact* that it is a living, human individual and the inconclusiveness of arguments that try to exclude it from the protected circle of personhood.
> *To be willing to kill what for all we know could be a person is to be willing to kill it if it is a person.* And since we cannot absolutely settle if it is a person except by a metaphysical postulate, for all practical purposes we must hold that to be willing to kill the embryo is to be willing to kill a person.[2]

In accordance with this line of argument, though it may not be possible to conclusively show that the fetus is a person from conception, we must presume that it is. Another line of argument that has been advanced by some conservatives emphasizes the potential rather than the actual personhood of the fetus. Even if the fetus is not a person, it is said, there can be no doubt that it is a potential person. Accordingly, by virtue of its potential personhood, the fetus must be accorded a right to life. Mary Anne Warren, in response to this line of argument, argues that the potential personhood of the fetus provides no basis for the claim that it has a significant right to life.

---

[2]Germain Grisez, *Abortion: The Myths, the Realities, and the Arguments* (New York: Corpus Books, 1970), p. 306.

MODERATE VIEWS

The conservative and liberal views, as explicated, constitute two extreme poles on the spectrum of ethical views of abortion. Each of the extreme views is marked by a formal simplicity. The conservative proclaims abortion to be immoral, irrespective of the stage of fetal development and irrespective of alleged justifying reasons. The one exception, admitted by some conservatives, is the case in which abortion is necessary to save the life of the mother.[3] The liberal proclaims abortion to be morally acceptable, irrespective of the stage of fetal development.[4] Moreover, there is no need to draw distinctions between those reasons which are sufficient to justify abortion and those which are not. No justification is needed. The *moderate,* in vivid contrast to both the conservative and the liberal, is unwilling to sweepingly condemn or condone abortion. Some abortions are morally justifiable; some are morally objectionable. In some moderate views, the stage of fetal development is a relevant factor in the assessment of the moral acceptability of abortion. In other moderate views, the alleged justifying reason is a relevant factor in the assessment of the moral acceptability of abortion. In still other moderate views, both the stage of fetal development and the alleged justifying reason are relevant factors in the assessment of the moral acceptability of abortion.

Moderate views have been developed in accordance with the following clearly identifiable strategies:

1. Moderation of the Conservative View

One strategy for generating a moderate view presumes the typical conservative contention that the fetus has full moral status from conception. What is denied, however, is that we must conclude to the moral impermissibility of abortion in *all* cases. In one of this chapter's readings, Jane English attempts to moderate the conservative view in just this way. She argues that certain abortion cases may be assimilated to cases of self-defense. Thus, for English, on the presumption that the fetus from conception has full moral status, some reasons are sufficient to justify abortion whereas others are not.

2. Moderation of the Liberal View

A second strategy for generating a moderate view presumes the liberal contention that the fetus has no (significant) moral status even in the latest stages of pregnancy. What is denied, however, is that we must conclude to the moral permissibility of abortion in *all* cases. It might be said, in accordance with this line of thought, that even though abortion does not violate the rights of the fetus (which is presumed to have no rights), the practice of abortion

---

[3]One especially prominent conservative view is associated with the Roman Catholic Church. In accordance with Catholic moral teaching, the *direct* killing of innocent human life is forbidden. Hence, abortion is forbidden. Even if the mother's life is in danger, perhaps because her heart or kidney function is inadequate, abortion is impermissible. In two special cases, however, procedures resulting in the death of the fetus are allowable. In the case of an ectopic pregnancy, where the developing fetus is lodged in the fallopian tube, the fallopian tube may be removed. In the case of a pregnant woman with a cancerous uterus, the cancerous uterus may be removed. In these cases, the death of the fetus is construed as *indirect* killing, the foreseen but unintended by-product of a surgical procedure designed to protect the life of the mother. If the distinction between direct and indirect killing is a defensible one (and this is a controversial issue), it might still be suggested that the distinction is not rightly applied in the Roman Catholic view of abortion. For example, some critics contend that abortion may be construed as indirect killing, indeed an allowable form of indirect killing, in at least all cases where it is necessary to save the life of the mother. For one helpful exposition and critical analysis of the Roman Catholic position on abortion, see Daniel Callahan, *Abortion: Law, Choice and Morality* (New York: Macmillan, 1970), chap. 12, pp. 409–447.

[4]In considering the liberal contention that abortions are morally acceptable irrespective of the stage of fetal development, we should take note of an ambiguity in the concept of abortion. Does "abortion" refer merely to the termination of a pregnancy in the sense of detaching the fetus from the mother, or does "abortion" entail the death of the fetus as well? Whereas the abortion of a *previable* fetus entails its death, the "abortion" of a *viable* fetus, by means of hysterotomy (a miniature cesarean section), does not entail the death of the fetus and would seem to be tantamount to the birth of a baby. With regard to the "abortion" of a *viable* fetus, liberals can defend the woman's right to detach the fetus from her body without contending that the woman has the right to insist on the death of the child.

remains ethically problematic because of its negative social consequences. Such an argument seems especially forceful in the later stages of pregnancy, when the fetus increasingly resembles a newborn infant. It is argued that very late abortions have a brutalizing effect on those involved and, in various ways, lead to the breakdown of attitudes associated with respect for human life. Jane English, in an effort to moderate the liberal view, advances an argument of this general type. Even if the fetus is not a person, she holds, it is gradually becoming increasingly personlike. Appealing to a "coherence of attitudes," she argues that abortion demands more weighty justifying reasons in the later stages of pregnancy than it does in the earlier stages.

3. Moderation in "Drawing the Line"

A third strategy for generating a moderate view, in fact a whole range of moderate views, is associated with "drawing the line" discussions. Whereas the conservative typically draws the line between human (having full moral status) and nonhuman (having no moral status) at conception, and the liberal typically draws that same line at birth (or sometime thereafter), a moderate view may be generated by drawing the line somewhere between these two extremes. For example, the line might be drawn at implantation, at the point where brain activity begins, at quickening, at viability, etc. Whereas drawing the line at implantation would tend to generate a rather "conservative" moderate view, drawing the line at viability would tend to generate a rather "liberal" moderate view. Wherever the line is drawn, it is the burden of any such moderate view to show that the point specified is a nonarbitrary one. Once such a point has been specified, however, it might be argued that abortion is ethically acceptable before that point and ethically unacceptable after that point. Or further stipulations may be added in accordance with strategies (1) and (2) above.

4. Moderation in the Assignment of Moral Status

A fourth strategy for generating a moderate view is dependent upon assigning the fetus some sort of subsidiary or *partial moral status,* an approach taken by Daniel Callahan in one of this chapter's readings. It would seem that anyone who defends a moderate view based on the concept of partial moral status must first of all face the problem of explicating the nature of such partial moral status. A second and closely related problem is that of showing how the interests of those with partial moral status are to be weighed against the interests of those with full moral status.

Thomas A. Mappes

JUSTICE HARRY A. BLACKMUN

MAJORITY OPINION IN *ROE v. WADE*

Harry A. Blackmun, associate justice of the United States Supreme Court, is a graduate of Harvard Law School. After some fifteen years in private practice he became legal counsel to the Mayo Clinic (1950–1959). Justice Blackmun also served as United States circuit judge (1959–1970) before his appointment in 1970 to the Supreme Court.

In this case, a pregnant single woman, suing under the fictitious name of Jane Roe, challenged the constitutionality of the existing Texas criminal abortion law. According to the Texas Penal Code, the performance of an abortion, except to save the life of the mother, constituted a crime that was punishable by a prison sentence of two to five years. At the time this case was finally resolved by the Supreme Court, abortion legislation varied widely from state to state. Some states, principally New York, had already legalized abortion on demand. Most other states, however, had legalized various forms of therapeutic abortion but had retained some measure of restrictive abortion legislation.

Justice Blackmun, writing an opinion concurred in by six other justices, argues that a woman's decision to terminate a pregnancy is encompassed by a *right to privacy*—but only up to a certain point in the development of the fetus. As the right to privacy is not an absolute right, it must yield at some point to the state's legitimate interests. Justice Blackmun contends that the state has a legitimate interest in protecting the health of the mother and that this interest becomes compelling at approximately the end of the first trimester in the development of the fetus. He also contends that the state has a legitimate interest in protecting potential life and that this interest becomes compelling at the point of viability.

It is . . . apparent that at common law, at the time of the adoption of our Constitution, and throughout the major portion of the 19th century, abortion was viewed with less disfavor than under most American statutes currently in effect. Phrasing it another way, a woman enjoyed a substantially broader right to terminate a pregnancy than she does in most States today. At least with respect to the early stage of pregnancy, and very possibly without such a limitation, the opportunity to make this choice was present in this country well into the 19th century. Even later, the law continued for some time to treat less punitively an abortion procured in early pregnancy. . . .

Three reasons have been advanced to explain historically the enactment of criminal abortion laws in the 19th century and to justify their continued existence.

It has been argued occasionally that these laws were the product of a Victorian social concern to discourage illicit sexual conduct. Texas, however, does not advance this justification in the present case, and it appears that no court or commentator has taken the argument seriously. . . .

A second reason is concerned with abortion as a medical procedure. When most criminal abortion laws were first enacted, the procedure was a hazardous one for the woman. This was particularly true prior to the development of antisepsis. Antiseptic techniques, of course, were based on discoveries by Lister, Pasteur, and others first announced in 1867, but were not generally accepted and employed until about the turn of the century. Abortion mortality was high. Even after 1900, and perhaps until as late as the development of antibiotics in the 1940's, standard modern techniques such as dilatation and curettage were not nearly so safe as they are today. Thus it has been argued that a State's real concern in enacting a criminal abortion law was to protect the pregnant woman, that is, to restrain her from submitting to a procedure that placed her life in serious jeopardy.

Modern medical techniques have altered this situation. Appellants and various *amici* refer to medical data indicating that abortion in early pregnancy, that is, prior to the end of first trimester, although not without its risk, is now relatively safe. Mortality rates for women undergoing early abortions, where the procedure is legal, appear to be as low as or lower than the rates for normal childbirth. Consequently, any interest of the State in protecting the woman from an inherently hazardous procedure, except when it would be equally dangerous for her to forgo it, has largely disappeared. Of course, important state interests in the area of health and medical standards do remain. The State has a legitimate interest in seeing to it that abortion, like any other medical procedure, is performed under

United States Supreme Court. 410 U.S. 113 (1973).

circumstances that insure maximum safety for the patient. This interest obviously extends at least to the performing physician and his staff, to the facilities involved, to the availability of after-care, and to adequate provision for any complication or emergency that might arise. The prevalence of high mortality rates at illegal "abortion mills" strengthens, rather than weakens, the State's interest in regulating the conditions under which abortions are performed. Moreover, the risk to the woman increases as her pregnancy continues. Thus the State retains a definite interest in protecting the woman's own health and safety when an abortion is performed at a late stage of pregnancy.

The third reason is the State's interest—some phrase it in terms of duty—in protecting prenatal life. Some of the argument for this justification rests on the theory that a new human life is present from the moment of conception. The State's interest and general obligation to protect life then extends, it is argued, to prenatal life. Only when the life of the pregnant mother herself is at stake, balanced against the life she carries within her, should the interest of the embryo or fetus not prevail. Logically, of course, a legitimate state interest in this area need not stand or fall on acceptance of the belief that life begins at conception or at some other point prior to live birth. In assessing the State's interest, recognition may be given to the less rigid claim that as long as at least *potential* life is involved, the State may assert interests beyond the protection of the pregnant woman alone.

Parties challenging state abortion laws have sharply disputed in some courts the contention that a purpose of these laws, when enacted, was to protect prenatal life. Pointing to the absence of legislative history to support the contention, they claim that most state laws were designed solely to protect the woman. Because medical advances have lessened this concern, at least with respect to abortion in early pregnancy, they argue that with respect to such abortions the laws can no longer be justified by any state interest. There is some scholarly support for this view of original purpose. The few state courts called upon to interpret their laws in the late 19th and early 20th centuries did focus on the State's interest in protecting the woman's health rather than in preserving the embryo and fetus. . . .

The Constitution does not explicitly mention any right of privacy. In a line of decisions, however, going back perhaps as far as *Union Pacific R. Co. v. Botsford* (1891), the Court has recognized that a right of personal privacy, or a guarantee of certain areas or zones of privacy, does exist under the Constitution. In varying contexts the Court or individual Justices have indeed found at least the roots of that right in the First Amendment, . . . in the Fourth and Fifth Amendments . . . in the penumbras of the Bill of Rights . . . in the Ninth Amendment . . . or in the concept of liberty guaranteed by the first section of the Fourteenth Amendment. . . . These decisions make it clear that only personal rights that can be deemed "fundamental" or "implicit in the concept of ordered liberty," . . . are included in this guarantee of personal privacy. They also make it clear that the right has some extension to activities relating to marriage, . . . procreation, . . . contraception, . . . family relationships, . . . and child rearing and education. . . .

This right of privacy, whether it be founded in the Fourteenth Amendment's concept of personal liberty and restrictions upon state action, as we feel it is, or, as the District Court determined, in the Ninth Amendment's reservation of rights to the people, is broad enough to encompass a woman's decision whether or not to terminate her pregnancy. . . .

. . . [A]ppellants and some *amici* argue that the woman's right is absolute and that she is entitled to terminate her pregnancy at whatever time, in whatever way, and for whatever reason she alone chooses. With this we do not agree. Appellants' arguments that Texas either has no valid interest at all in regulating the abortion decision, or no interest strong enough to support any limitation upon the woman's sole determination, is unpersuasive. The Court's decisions recognizing a right of privacy also acknowledge that some state regulation in areas protected by that right is appropriate. As noted above, a state may properly assert important interests in safe-guarding health, in maintaining medical standards, and in protecting potential life. At some point in pregnancy, these respective interests become sufficiently compelling to sustain regulation of the factors that govern the abortion decision. The privacy right involved, therefore, cannot be said to be absolute. . . .

We therefore conclude that the right of personal privacy includes the abortion decision, but that this right is not unqualified and must be considered against important state interests in regulation.

We note that those federal and state courts that have recently considered abortion law challenges have reached the same conclusion. . . .

Although the results are divided, most of these courts have agreed that the right of privacy, however based, is broad enough to cover the abortion decision; that the right, nonetheless, is not absolute and is subject to some limitations; and that at some point the state interests as to protection of health, medical standards, and prenatal life, become dominant. We agree with this approach. . . .

The appellee and certain *amici* argue that the fetus is a "person" within the language and meaning of the Fourteenth Amendment. In support of this they outline at length and in detail the well-known facts of fetal development. If this suggestion of personhood is established, the appellant's case, of course, collapses, for the fetus' right to life is then guaranteed specifically by the Amendment. The appellant conceded as much on reargument. On the other hand, the appellee conceded on reargument that no case could be cited that holds that a fetus is a person within the meaning of the Fourteenth Amendment. . . .

All this, together with our observation, *supra*, that throughout the major portion of the 19th century prevailing legal abortion practices were far freer than they are today, persuades us that the word "person," as used in the Fourteenth Amendment, does not include the unborn. . . . Indeed, our decision in *United States v. Vuitch* (1971) inferentially is to the same effect, for we there would not have indulged in statutory interpretation favorable to abortion in specified circumstances if the necessary consequence was the termination of life entitled to Fourteenth Amendment protection.

. . . As we have intimated above, it is reasonable and appropriate for a State to decide that at some point in time another interest, that of health of the mother or that of potential human life, becomes significantly involved. The woman's privacy is no longer sole and any right of privacy she possesses must be measured accordingly.

Texas urges that, apart from the Fourteenth Amendment, life begins at conception and is present throughout pregnancy, and that, therefore, the State has a compelling interest in protecting that life from and after conception. We need not resolve the difficult question of when life begins. When those trained in the respective disciplines of medicine, philosophy, and theology are unable to arrive at any consensus, the judiciary, at this point in the development of man's knowledge, is not in a position to speculate as to the answer.

It should be sufficient to note briefly the wide divergence of thinking on this most sensitive and difficult question. There has always been strong support for the view that life does not begin until live birth. This was the belief of the Stoics. It appears to be the predominant, though not the unanimous, attitude of the Jewish faith. It may be taken to represent also the position of a large segment of the Protestant community, insofar as that can be ascertained; organized groups that have taken a formal position on the abortion issue have generally regarded abortion as a matter for the conscience of the individual and her family. As we have noted, the common law found greater significance in quickening. Physicians and their scientific colleagues have regarded that event with less interest and have tended to focus either upon conception or upon live birth or upon the interim point at which the fetus becomes "viable," that is, potentially able to live outside the mother's womb, albeit with artificial aid. Viability is usually placed at about seven months (28 weeks) but may occur earlier, even at 24 weeks. . . .

In areas other than criminal abortion the law has been reluctant to endorse any theory that life, as we recognize it, begins before live birth or to accord legal rights to the unborn except in narrowly defined situations and except when the rights are contingent upon live birth. . . . In short, the unborn have never been recognized in the law as persons in the whole sense.

In view of all this, we do not agree that, by adopting one theory of life, Texas may override the rights of the pregnant woman that are at stake. We repeat, however, that the State does have an important and legitimate interest in preserving and protecting the health of the pregnant woman, whether she be a resident of the State or a nonresident who seeks medical consultation and treatment there, and that it has still *another* important and legitimate interest in protecting the potentiality of human life. These interests are separate and distinct. Each grows in substantiality as the woman approaches term and, at a point during pregnancy, each becomes "compelling."

With respect to the State's important and legitimate interest in the health of the mother, the "compelling" point, in the light of present medical knowledge, is at approximately the end of the first trimester. This is so because of the now established medical fact . . . that until the end of the first trimester mortality in abortion is less than mortality in normal childbirth. It follows that, from and after this point, a State may regulate the abortion procedure to the extent that the regulation reasonably relates to the preservation and protection of maternal health. Examples of permissible state regulation in this area are requirements as to the qualifications of the person who is to perform the abortion; as to the licensure of that person; as to the facility in which the procedure is to be performed, that is, whether it must be a hospital or may be a clinic or some other place of less-than-hospital status; as to the licensing of the facility; and the like.

This means, on the other hand, that, for the period of pregnancy prior to this "compelling" point, the attending physician, in consultation with his patient, is free to determine, without regulation by the State, that in his medical judgment the patient's pregnancy should be terminated. If that decision is reached, the judgment may be effectuated by an abortion free of interference by the State.

With respect to the State's important and legitimate interest in potential life, the "compelling" point is at viability. This is so because the fetus then presumably has the capability of meaningful life outside the mother's womb. State regulation protective of fetal life after viability thus has both logical and biological justifications. If the State is interested in protecting fetal life after viability, it may go so far as to proscribe abortion during that period except when it is necessary to preserve the life or health of the mother. . . .

To summarize and repeat:

1. A state criminal abortion statute of the current Texas type, that excepts from criminality only a *life saving* procedure on behalf of the mother, without regard to pregnancy stage and without recognition of the other interests involved, is violative of the Due Process Clause of the Fourteenth Amendment.

(a) For the stage prior to approximately the end of the first trimester, the abortion decision and its effectuation must be left to the medical judgment of the pregnant woman's attending physician.

(b) For the stage subsequent to approximately the end of the first trimester, the State, in promoting its interest in the health of the mother, may, if it chooses, regulate the abortion procedure in ways that are reasonably related to maternal health.

(c) For the stage subsequent to viability the State, in promoting its interest in the potentiality of human life, may, if it chooses, regulate, and even proscribe, abortion except where it is necessary, in appropriate medical judgment, for the preservation of the life or health of the mother.

2. The State may define the term "physician," as it has been employed [here], to mean only a physician currently licensed by the State, and may proscribe any abortion by a person who is not a physician as so defined.

. . . The decision leaves the State free to place increasing restrictions on abortion as the period of pregnancy lengthens, so long as those restrictions are tailored to the recognized state interests. The decision vindicates the right of the physician to administer medical treatment according to his professional judgment up to the points where important state interests provide compelling justifications for intervention. Up to those points the abortion decision in all its aspects is inherently, and primarily, a medical decision, and basic responsibility for it must rest with the physician. If an individual practitioner abuses the privilege of exercising proper medical judgment, the usual remedies, judicial and intraprofessional, are available. . . .

QUESTIONS

1. Justice Blackmun contends that the state's legitimate interest in protecting the health of the mother becomes *compelling* at the end of the first trimester. Does the Court's choice of this particular point as "compelling" have any substantial justification, or is the choice fundamentally arbitrary?
2. Justice Blackmun contends that the state's legitimate interest in protecting potential life becomes *compelling* at the point of viability. Does the Court's choice of this particular point as "compelling" have any substantial justification, or is the choice fundamentally arbitrary?
3. Justice Blackmun *explicitly* disavows entering into philosophical speculation on the problem of the beginning of human life. To what extent could it be said that he *implicitly* takes a philosophical position on this problem?

JUSTICE BYRON R. WHITE

DISSENTING OPINION IN *ROE v. WADE*

Byron R. White, associate justice of the United States Supreme Court, first achieved national attention as an all-American football player at the University of Colorado. Thereupon he accepted a Rhodes scholarship for study at Oxford University (England). A graduate of Yale Law School, Justice White remained in private practice until 1960, served as United States deputy attorney general (1961–1962), and was appointed to the Supreme Court in 1962.

Justice White, writing an opinion concurred in by Justice Rehnquist, contends that the Court, in sanctioning the abortion of a pre-viable fetus for any reason whatever, has overstepped its legitimate bounds and manufactured a "new constitutional right for pregnant mothers." He maintains that there is no constitutional warrant for denying to the legislatures of the states the power to weigh the interests of the mother versus the interests of the fetus and to legislate accordingly.

At the heart of the controversy in these cases are those recurring pregnancies that pose no danger whatsoever to the life or health of the mother but are nevertheless unwanted for any one or more of a variety of reasons—convenience, family planning, economics, dislike of children, the embarrassment of illegitimacy, etc. The common claim before us is that for any one of such reasons, or for no reason at all, and without asserting or claiming any threat to life or health, any woman is entitled to an abortion at her request if she is able to find a medical advisor willing to undertake the procedure.

The Court for the most part sustains this position: During the period prior to the time the fetus becomes viable, the Constitution of the United States values the convenience, whim or caprice of the putative mother more than the life or potential life of the fetus; the Constitution, therefore, guarantees the right to an abortion as against any state law or policy seeking to protect the fetus from an abortion not prompted by more compelling reasons of the mother.

With all due respect, I dissent. I find nothing in the language or history of the Constitution to support the Court's judgment. The Court simply fashions and announces a new constitutional right for pregnant mothers and, with scarcely any reason or authority for its action, invests that right with sufficient substance to override most existing state abortion statutes. The upshot is that the people and the legislatures of the 50 States are constitutionally disentitled to weigh the relative importance of the continued existence and development of the fetus on the one hand against a spectrum of possible impacts on the mother on the other hand. As an exercise of raw judicial power, the Court perhaps has authority to do what it does today; but in my view its judgment is an improvident and extravagant exercise of the power of judicial review which the Constitution extends to this Court.

The Court apparently values the convenience of the pregnant mother more than the continued existence and development of the life or potential life which she carries. Whether or not I might agree with that marshalling of values, I can in no event join the Court's judgment because I find no constitutional warrant for imposing such an order of priorities on the people and legislatures of the States. In a sensitive area such as this, involving as it does issues over which reasonable men may easily and heatedly differ, I cannot accept the Court's exercise of its clear power of choice by interposing a constitutional barrier to state efforts to protect human life and by investing mothers and doctors with the constitutionally protected right to exterminate it. This issue, for the most part, should be left with the people and to the political processes the people have devised to govern their affairs.

It is my view, therefore, that the Texas statute is not constitutionally infirm because it denies abortions to those who seek to serve only their convenience rather than to protect their life or health. . . .

QUESTIONS

1. It has been suggested by some advocates of abortion on demand that the dissenting opinion of Justice White reveals an attitude of insensitivity to the personal significance of an unwanted pregnancy. Does Justice White's opinion manifest such an attitude?

United States Supreme Court. 410 U.S. 113 (1973).

2.   If the Court as a whole had agreed with Justice White, then there would have been no constitutional impediment to restrictive abortion laws. Constitutional grounds aside, would you favor restrictive or permissive legislation? To what extent and on what grounds?

JOHN T. NOONAN, JR.

AN ALMOST ABSOLUTE VALUE IN HISTORY

John T. Noonan, Jr., is professor of law at the University of California, Berkeley. His academic interests extend beyond matters of law to philosophical and theological issues, and his intellectual allegiance in this regard is with the Roman Catholic tradition. Among his books are *Contraception: A History of Its Treatment by the Catholic Theologians and Canonists* (1965), *The Morality of Abortion* (1970), and *Persons and Masks of the Law* (1976).

Noonan, defending the conservative view on abortion, immediately raises the question of how to determine the *humanity* of a being. In an updated version of the traditional theological view he contends that, if a being is conceived by human parents and thereby has a human genetic code, then that being is a *human being*. Conception is the point at which the nonhuman becomes the human. Noonan argues that other alleged criteria of humanity are inadequate. He also argues, primarily through an analysis of probabilities, that his own criterion of humanity is objectively based and nonarbitrary. Finally, Noonan contends, once the humanity of the fetus is recognized, we must judge abortion morally wrong, except in those rare cases where the mother's life is in danger.

The most fundamental question involved in the long history of thought on abortion is: How do you determine the humanity of a being? To phrase the question that way is to put in comprehensive humanistic terms what the theologians either dealt with as an explicitly theological question under the heading of "ensoulment" or dealt with implicitly in their treatment of abortion. The Christian position as it originated did not depend on a narrow theological or philosophical concept. It had no relation to theories of infant baptism. It appealed to no special theory of instantaneous ensoulment. It took the world's view on ensoulment as that view changed from Aristotle to Zacchia. There was, indeed, theological influence affecting the theory of ensoulment finally adopted, and, of course, ensoulment itself was a theological concept, so that the position was always explained in theological terms. But the theological notion of ensoulment could easily be translated into humanistic language by substituting "human" for "rational soul"; the problem of knowing when a man is a man is common to theology and humanism.

If one steps outside the specific categories used by the theologians, the answer they gave can be analyzed as a refusal to discriminate among human beings on the basis of their varying potentialities. Once conceived, the being was recognized as man because he had man's potential. The criterion for humanity, thus, was simple and all-embracing: if you are conceived by human parents, you are human.

The strength of this position may be tested by a review of some of the other distinctions offered in the contemporary controversy over legalizing abortion. Perhaps the most popular distinction is in terms of viability. Before an age of so many months, the fetus is not viable, that is, it cannot be removed from the mother's womb and live apart from her. To that extent, the life of the fetus is absolutely dependent on the life of the mother. This dependence is made the basis of denying recognition to its humanity.

There are difficulties with this distinction. One is that the perfection of artificial incubation may make the fetus viable at any time: it may be removed and artificially sustained. Experiments with animals already show that such a procedure is possible. This hypothetical extreme case relates to an actual difficulty: there is considerable elasticity to the idea of viability. Mere length of life is not an exact measure. The viability of the fetus depends on the extent of its anatomical and functional development. The weight and length of the fetus are better guides to the state of its development than age, but weight and length vary. Moreover, different racial groups have different ages at which their fetuses are viable. Some evidence, for example, suggests that Negro fetuses mature more quickly than white fetuses. If viability is the norm, the standard would vary with race and with many individual circumstances.

The most important objection to this approach is that dependence is not ended by viability. The fetus is still absolutely dependent on someone's care in order to continue existence; indeed a child of one or three or even five years of age is absolutely dependent on another's care for existence; uncared for, the older fetus or the younger child will die as surely as the early fetus detached from the mother. The unsubstantial lessening in dependence at viability does not seem to signify any special acquisition of humanity.

A second distinction has been attempted in terms of experience. A being who has had experience, has lived and suffered, who possesses memories, is more human than one who has not. Humanity depends on formation by experience. The fetus is thus "unformed" in the most basic human sense.

This distinction is not serviceable for the embryo which is already experiencing and reacting. The embryo is responsive to touch after eight weeks and at least at that point is experiencing. At an earlier stage the zygote is certainly alive and responding to its environment. The distinction may also be challenged by the rare case where aphasia has erased adult memory: has it erased humanity? More fundamentally, this distinction leaves even the older fetus or the younger child to be treated as an unformed inhuman thing. Finally, it is not clear why experience as such confers humanity. It could be argued that certain central experiences such as loving or learning are necessary to make a man human. But then human beings who have failed to love or to learn might be excluded from the class called man.

A third distinction is made by appeal to the sentiments of adults. If a fetus dies, the grief of the parents is not the grief they would have for a living child. The fetus is an unnamed "it" till birth, and is not perceived as personality until at least the fourth month of existence when movements in the womb manifest a vigorous presence demanding joyful recognition by the parents.

Yet feeling is notoriously an unsure guide to the humanity of others. Many groups of humans have had difficulty in feeling that persons of another tongue, color, religion, sex, are as human as they. Apart from reactions to alien groups, we mourn the loss of a ten-year-old boy more than the loss of his one-day-old brother or his 90-year-old grandfather. The difference felt and the grief expressed vary with the potentialities extinguished, or the experience wiped out; they do not seem to point to any substantial difference in the humanity of baby, boy, or grandfather.

Distinctions are also made in terms of sensation by the parents. The embryo is felt within the womb only after about the fourth month. The embryo is seen only at birth. What can be neither seen nor felt is different from what is tangible. If the fetus cannot be seen or touched at all, it cannot be perceived as man.

Yet experience shows that sight is even more untrustworthy than feeling in determining humanity. By sight, color became an appropriate index for saying who was a man, and the evil of racial discrimination was given foundation. Nor can touch provide the test; a being confined by sickness, "out of touch" with others, does not thereby seem to lose his humanity. To the extent that touch still has appeal as a criterion, it appears to be a survival of the old English idea of "quickening"—a possible mistranslation of the Latin *animatus* used in the canon law. To that extent touch as a criterion seems to be dependent on the Aristotelian notion of ensoulment, and to fall when this notion is discarded.

Finally, a distinction is sought in social visibility. The fetus is not socially perceived as human. It cannot communicate with others. Thus, both subjectively and objectively, it is not a member of society. As moral rules are rules for the behavior of members of society to each other, they cannot be made for behavior toward what is not yet a member. Excluded from the society of men, the fetus is excluded from the humanity of men.

By force of the argument from the consequences, this distinction is to be rejected. It is more subtle than that founded on an appeal to physical sensation, but it is equally dangerous in its implications. If humanity depends on social recognition, individuals or whole groups may be dehumanized by being denied any status in their society. Such a fate is fictionally portrayed in *1984* and has actually been the lot of many men in many societies. In the Roman empire, for example, condemnation to slavery meant the practical denial of most human rights; in the Chinese Communist world, landlords have been classified as enemies of the people and so treated as nonpersons by the state. Humanity does not depend on social recognition, though often the failure of society to recognize the prisoner, the alien, the heterodox as human has led to the destruction of human beings. Anyone conceived by a man and a woman is human. Recognition of this condition by society follows a real event in the objective order, however imperfect and halting the recognition. Any attempt to limit humanity to exclude some group runs the risk of furnishing authority and precedent for excluding other groups in the name of the consciousness or perception of the controlling group in the society.

A philosopher may reject the appeal to the humanity of the fetus because he views "humanity" as a secular view of the soul and because he doubts the existence of anything real and objective which can be identified as humanity. One answer to such a philosopher is to ask how he reasons about moral questions without supposing that there is a sense in which he and the others of whom he speaks are human. Whatever group is taken as the society which determines who may be killed is thereby taken as human. A second answer is to ask if he does not believe that there is a right and wrong way of deciding moral questions. If there is such a difference, experience may be appealed to: to decide who is human on the basis of the sentiment of a given society has led to consequences which rational men would characterize as monstrous.

The rejection of the attempted distinctions based on viability and visibility, experience and feeling, may be buttressed by the following considerations: Moral judgments often rest on distinctions, but if the distinctions are not to appear arbitrary fiat, they should relate to some real difference in probabilities. There is a kind of continuity in all life, but the earlier stages of the elements of human life possess tiny probabilities of development. Consider for example, the spermatozoa in any normal ejaculate: There are about 200,000,000 in any single ejaculate, of which one has a chance of developing into a zygote. Consider the oocytes which may become ova: there are 100,000 to 1,000,000 oocytes in a female infant, of which a maximum of 390 are ovulated. But once spermatozoon and ovum meet and the conceptus is formed, such studies as have been made show that roughly in only

20 percent of the cases will spontaneous abortion occur. In other words, the chances are about 4 out of 5 that this new being will develop. At this stage in the life of the being there is a sharp shift in probabilities, an immense jump in potentialities. To make a distinction between the rights of spermatozoa and the rights of the fertilized ovum is to respond to an enormous shift in possibilities. For about twenty days after conception the egg may split to form twins or combine with another egg to form a chimera, but the probability of either event happening is very small.

It may be asked, What does a change in biological probabilities have to do with establishing humanity? The argument from probabilities is not aimed at establishing humanity but at establishing an objective discontinuity which may be taken into account in moral discourse. As life itself is a matter of probabilities, as most moral reasoning is an estimate of probabilities, so it seems in accord with the structure of reality and the nature of moral thought to found a moral judgment on the change in probabilities at conception. The appeal to probabilities is the most commonsensical of arguments, to a greater or smaller degree all of us base our actions on probabilities, and in morals, as in law, prudence and negligence are often measured by the account one has taken of the probabilities. If the chance is 200,000,000 to 1 that the movement in the bushes into which you shoot is a man's, I doubt if many persons would hold you careless in shooting; but if the chances are 4 out of 5 that the movement is a human being's, few would acquit you of blame. Would the argument be different if only one out of ten children conceived came to term? Of course this argument would be different. This argument is an appeal to probabilities that actually exist, not to any and all states of affairs which may be imagined.

The probabilities as they do exist do not show the humanity of the embryo in the sense of a demonstration in logic any more than the probabilities of the movement in the bush being a man demonstrate beyond all doubt that the being is a man. The appeal is a "buttressing" consideration, showing the plausibility of the standard adopted. The argument focuses on the decisional factor in any moral judgment and assumes that part of the business of a moralist is drawing lines. One evidence of the nonarbitrary character of the line drawn is the difference of probabilities on either side of it. If a spermatozoon is destroyed, one destroys a being which had a chance of far less than 1 in 200 million of developing into a reasoning being, possessed of the genetic code, a heart and other organs, and capable of pain. If a fetus is destroyed, one destroys a being already possessed of the genetic code, organs, and sensitivity to pain, and one which had an 80 percent chance of developing further into a baby outside the womb who, in time, would reason.

The positive argument for conception as the decisive moment of humanization is that at conception the new being receives the genetic code. It is this genetic information which determines his characteristics, which is the biological carrier of the possibility of human wisdom, which makes him a self-evolving being. A being with a human genetic code is man.

This review of current controversy over the humanity of the fetus emphasizes what a fundamental question the theologians resolved in asserting the inviolability of the fetus. To regard the fetus as possessed of equal rights with other humans was not, however, to decide every case where abortion might be employed. It did decide the case where the argument was that the fetus should be aborted for its own good. To say a being was human was to say it had a destiny to decide for itself which could not be taken from it by another man's decision. But human beings with equal rights often come in conflict with each other, and some decision must be made as whose claims are to prevail. Cases of conflict involving the fetus are different only in two respects: the total inability of the fetus to speak for itself and the fact that the right of the fetus regularly at stake is the right to life itself.

The approach taken by the theologians to these conflicts was articulated in terms of "direct" and "indirect." Again, to look at what they were doing from outside their categories, they may be said to have been drawing lines or "balancing values." "Direct" and "indirect" are spatial metaphors; "line-drawing" is another. "To weigh" or "to balance" values is a metaphor of a more complicated mathematical sort hinting at the process which goes on in moral judgments. All the metaphors suggest that, in the moral judgments made, comparisons were necessary, that no value completely controlled. The principle of double effect was no doctrine fallen from heaven, but a method of analysis appropriate where two relative values were being compared. In Catholic moral theology, as it developed, life even of the innocent was not taken as an absolute. Judgments on acts affecting life issued from a process of weighing. In the weighing, the fetus was always given a value greater than zero, always a value separate and independent from its parents. This valuation was crucial and fundamental in all Christian thought on the subject and marked it off from any approach which considered that only the parents' interests needed to be considered.

Even with the fetus weighed as human, one interest could be weighed as equal or superior: that of the mother in her own life. The casuists between 1450 and 1895 were willing to weigh this interest as superior. Since 1895, that interest was given decisive weight only in the two special cases of the cancerous uterus and the ectopic pregnancy. In both of these cases the fetus itself had little chance of survival even if the abortion were not performed. As the balance was once struck in favor of the mother whenever her life was endangered, it could be so struck again. The balance reached between 1895 and 1930 attempted prudentially and pastorally to forestall a multitude of exceptions for interests less than life.

The perception of the humanity of the fetus and the weighing of fetal rights against other human rights constituted the work of the moral analysts. But what spirit animated their abstract judgments? For the Christian community it was the injunction of Scripture to love your neighbor as yourself. The fetus as human was a neighbor; his life had parity with one's own. The commandment gave life to what otherwise would have been only rational calculation.

The commandment could be put in humanistic as well as theological terms: Do not injure your fellow man without reason. In these terms, once the humanity of the fetus is perceived, abortion is never right except in self-defense. When life must be taken to save life, reason alone cannot say that a mother must prefer a child's life to her own. With this exception, now of great rarity, abortion violates the rational humanist tenet of the equality of human lives.

For Christians the commandment to love had received a special imprint in that the exemplar proposed of love was the love of the Lord for his disciples. In the light given by this example, self-sacrifice carried to the point of death seemed in the extreme situations not without meaning. In the less extreme cases, preference for one's own interests to the life of another seemed to express cruelty or selfishness irreconcilable with the demands of love.

QUESTIONS

1. Is conception an objectively based and nonarbitrary point at which to draw the line between the human and the nonhuman?

2. If you think that Noonan is wrong in drawing the line at conception, where would you draw the line? How would you answer the charge that the point you specify is an arbitrary one?

3. Consider the following argument: Let it be admitted that the fetus has full moral status from the moment of conception; nevertheless, abortion in the case of rape is morally justifiable because no person (in this case, the fetus) has the right to use another person's body, unless that right has been *freely* extended from the latter to the former. Is this argument successful in its effort to "moderate the conservative view?"

MARY ANNE WARREN

ON THE MORAL AND LEGAL STATUS OF ABORTION

Many Anne Warren is a philosopher who teaches at San Francisco State University. Feminist-related issues provide one focal point of her philosophical work. Among her published articles are "Secondary Sexism and Quota Hiring" and "Do Potential People Have Moral Rights?"

Warren, defending the liberal view on abortion, promptly distinguishes two senses of the term "human": (1) One is *human in the genetic sense* when one is a member of the biological species *Homo sapiens.* (2) One is *human in the moral sense* when one is a full-fledged member of the moral community. Warren attacks the presupposition underlying Noonan's argument against abortion—that the fetus is human in the moral sense. She contends that the moral community, the set of beings with full and equal moral rights, consists of all and only people (persons). (Thus she takes the concept of personhood to be equivalent to the concept of humanity in the moral sense.) After analyzing the concept of person, she concludes that a fetus is so unlike a person as to have no significant right to life. Nor, she argues, does the fetus's *potential* for being a person provide us any basis for ascribing to it any significant right to life. It follows, she contends, that a woman's right to obtain an abortion is absolute. Abortion is morally justified at any stage of fetal development. It also follows, she contends, that no legislation against abortion can be justified on the grounds of protecting the rights of the fetus. In a concluding postscript, Warren briefly assesses the moral justifiability of infanticide.

The question which we must answer in order to produce a satisfactory solution to the problem of the moral status of abortion is this: How are we to define the moral community, the set of beings with full and equal moral rights, such that we can decide whether a human fetus is a member of this community or not? What sort of entity, exactly, has the inalienable rights to life, liberty, and the pursuit of happiness? Jefferson attributed these rights to all *men*, and it may or may not be fair to suggest that he intended to attribute them *only* to men. Perhaps he ought to have attributed them to all human beings. If so, then we arrive, first, at Noonan's problem of defining what makes a being human, and, second, at the equally vital question which Noonan does not consider, namely, What reason is there for identifying the moral community with the set of all human beings, in whatever way we have chosen to define that term?

Reprinted from *The Monist,* vol. 57, no. 1 (January 1973), with the permission of the author and the publisher. "Postscript on Infanticide" reprinted with permission of the author from Richard Wasserstrom, ed., *Today's Moral Problems* (New York: Macmillan Publishing Co., 1975).

1. ON THE DEFINITION OF "HUMAN"

One reason why this vital second question is so frequently overlooked in the debate over the moral status of abortion is that the term "human" has two distinct, but not often distinguished, senses. This fact results in a slide of meaning, which serves to conceal the fallaciousness of the traditional argument that since (1) it is wrong to kill innocent human beings, and (2) fetuses are innocent human beings, then (3) it is wrong to kill fetuses. For if "human" is used in the same sense in both (1) and (2) then, whichever of the two senses is meant, one of these premises is question-begging. And if it is used in two different senses then of course the conclusion doesn't follow.

Thus, (1) is a self-evident moral truth,[1] and avoids begging the question about abortion, only if "human being" is used to mean something like "a full-fledged member of the moral community." (It may or may not also be meant to refer exclusively to members of the species *Homo sapiens*.) We may call this the *moral* sense of "human." It is not to be confused with what we will call the *genetic* sense, i.e., the sense in which *any* member of the species is a human being, and no member of any other species could be. If (1) is acceptable only if the moral sense is intended, (2) is non-question-begging only if what is intended is the genetic sense.

In "Deciding Who Is Human," Noonan argues for the classification of fetuses with human beings by pointing to the presence of the full genetic code, and the potential capacity for rational thought.[2] It is clear that what he needs to show, for his version of the traditional argument to be valid, is that fetuses are human in the moral sense, the sense in which it is analytically true that all human beings have full moral rights. But, in the absence of any argument showing that whatever is genetically human is also morally human, and he gives none, nothing more than genetic humanity can be demonstrated by the presence of the human genetic code. And, as we will see, the *potential* capacity for rational thought can at most show that an entity has the potential for *becoming* human in the moral sense.

2. DEFINING THE MORAL COMMUNITY

Can it be established that genetic humanity is sufficient for moral humanity? I think that there are very good reasons for not defining the moral community in this way. I would like to suggest an alternative way of defining the moral community, which I will argue for only to the extent of explaining why it is, or should be, self-evident. The suggestion is simply that the moral community consists of all and only *people*, rather than all and only human beings;[3] and probably the best way of demonstrating its self-evidence is by considering the concept of personhood, to see what sorts of entity are and are not persons, and what the decision that a being is or is not a person implies about its moral rights.

What characteristics entitle an entity to be considered a person? This is obviously not the place to attempt a complete analysis of the concept of personhood, but we do not need such a fully adequate analysis just to determine whether and why a fetus is or isn't a person. All we need is a rough and approximate list of the most basic criteria of personhood, and some idea of which, or how many, of these an entity must satisfy in order to properly be considered a person.

In searching for such criteria, it is useful to look beyond the set of people with whom we are acquainted, and ask how we would decide whether a totally alien being was a

---

[1] Of course, the principle that it is (always) wrong to kill innocent human beings is in need of many other modifications, e.g., that it may be permissible to do so to save a greater number of other innocent human beings, but we may safely ignore these complications here.
[2] John Noonan, "Deciding Who is Human," *Natural Law Forum,* 13 (1968), 135.
[3] From here on, we will use "human" to mean genetically human, since the moral sense seems closely connected to, and perhaps derived from, the assumption that genetic humanity is sufficient for membership in the moral community.

person or not. (For we have no right to assume that genetic humanity is necessary for personhood.) Imagine a space traveler who lands on an unknown planet and encounters a race of beings utterly unlike any he has ever seen or heard of. If he wants to be sure of behaving morally toward these beings, he has to somehow decide whether they are people, and hence have full moral rights, or whether they are the sort of thing which he need not feel guilty about treating as, for example, a source of food.

How should he go about making this decision? If he has some anthropological background, he might look for such things as religion, art, and the manufacturing of tools, weapons, or shelters, since these factors have been used to distinguish our human from our prehuman ancestors, in what seems to be closer to the moral than the genetic sense of "human." And no doubt he would be right to consider the presence of such factors as good evidence that the alien beings were people, and morally human. It would, however, be overly anthropocentric of him to take the absence of these things as adequate evidence that they were not, since we can imagine people who have progressed beyond, or evolved without ever developing, these cultural characteristics.

I suggest that the traits which are most central to the concept of personhood, or humanity in the moral sense, are, very roughly, the following:

1. consciousness (of objects and events external and/or internal to the being), and in particular the capacity to feel pain;

2. reasoning (the *developed* capacity to solve new and relatively complex problems);

3. self-motivated activity (activity which is relatively independent of either genetic or direct external control);

4. the capacity to communicate, by whatever means, messages of an indefinite variety of types, that is, not just with an indefinite number of possible contents, but on indefinitely many possible topics;

5. the presence of self-concepts, and self-awareness, either individual or racial, or both.

Admittedly, there are apt to be a great many problems involved in formulating precise definitions of these criteria, let alone in developing universally valid behavioral criteria for deciding when they apply. But I will assume that both we and our explorer know approximately what (1)–(5) mean, and that he is also able to determine whether or not they apply. How, then, should he use his findings to decide whether or not the alien beings are people? We needn't suppose that an entity must have *all* of these attributes to be properly considered a person; (1) and (2) alone may well be sufficient for personhood, and quite probably (1)–(3) are sufficient. Neither do we need to insist that any one of these criteria is *necessary* for personhood, although once again (1) and (2) look like fairly good candidates for necessary conditions, as does (3), if "activity" is construed so as to include the activity of reasoning.

All we need to claim, to demonstrate that a fetus is not a person, is that any being which satisfies *none* of (1)–(5) is certainly not a person. I consider this claim to be so obvious that I think anyone who denied it, and claimed that a being which satisfied none of (1)–(5) was a person all the same, would thereby demonstrate that he had no notion at all of what a person is—perhaps because he had confused the concept of a person with that of genetic humanity. If the opponents of abortion were to deny the appropriateness of these five criteria, I do not know what further arguments would convince them. We would probably have to admit that our conceptual schemes were indeed irreconcilably different, and that our dispute could not be settled objectively.

I do not expect this to happen, however, since I think that the concept of a person is one which is very nearly universal (to people), and that it is common to both proabortionists and antiabortionists, even though neither group has fully realized the relevance of this concept to the resolution of their dispute. Furthermore, I think that on reflection even the antiabortionists ought to agree not only that (1)–(5) are central to the concept of personhood, but also that it is a part of this concept that all and only people have full moral rights. The concept of a person is in part a moral concept; once we have admitted that x is a person we have recognized, even if we have not agreed to respect, x's right to be treated as a member of the moral community. It is true that the claim that x is a *human being* is more commonly voiced as part of an appeal to treat x decently than is the claim that x is a person, but this is either because "human being" is here used in the sense which implies personhood, or because the genetic and moral senses of "human" have been confused.

Now if (1)–(5) are indeed the primary criteria of personhood, then it is clear that genetic humanity is neither necessary nor sufficient for establishing that an entity is a person. Some human beings are not people, and there may well be people who are not human beings. A man or woman whose consciousness has been permanently obliterated but who remains alive is a human being which is no longer a person; defective human beings, with no appreciable mental capacity, are not and presumably never will be people; and a fetus is a human being which is not yet a person, and which therefore cannot coherently be said to have full moral rights. Citizens of the next century should be prepared to recognize highly advanced, self-aware robots or computers, should such be developed, and intelligent inhabitants of other worlds, should such be found, as people in the fullest sense, and to respect their moral rights. But to ascribe full moral rights to an entity which is not a person is as absurd as to ascribe moral obligations and responsibilities to such an entity.

3. FETAL DEVELOPMENT AND THE RIGHT TO LIFE

Two problems arise in the application of these suggestions for the definition of the moral community to the determination of the precise moral status of a human fetus. Given that the paradigm example of a person is a normal adult human being, then (1) How like this paradigm, in particular how far advanced since conception, does a human being need to be before it begins to have a right to life by virtue, not of being fully a person as of yet, but of being *like* a person? and (2) To what extent, if any, does the fact that a fetus has the *potential* for becoming a person endow it with some of the same rights? Each of these questions requires some comment.

In answering the first question, we need not attempt a detailed consideration of the moral rights of organisms which are not developed enough, aware enough, intelligent enough, etc., to be considered people, but which resemble people in some respects. It does seem reasonable to suggest that the more like a person, in the relevant respects, a being is, the stronger is the case for regarding it as having a right to life, and indeed the stronger its right to life is. Thus we ought to take seriously the suggestion that, insofar as "the human individual develops biologically in a continuous fashion . . . the rights of a human person might develop in the same way."[4] But we must keep in mind that the atttributes which are relevant in determining whether or not an entity is enough like a person to be regarded as having some of the same moral rights are no different from those which are relevant to determining whether or not it is fully a person—i.e., are no different from (1)–(5)—and

[4]Thomas L. Hayes, "A Biological View," *Commonweal*, 85 (March 17, 1967), 677–78; quoted by Daniel Callahan, *in Abortion: Law, Choice and Morality* (London: Macmillan & Co., 1970).

that being genetically human, or having recognizably human facial and other physical features, or detectable brain activity, or the capacity to survive outside the uterus, are simply not among these relevant attributes.

Thus it is clear that even though a seven- or eight-month fetus has features which make it apt to arouse in us almost the same powerful protective instinct as is commonly aroused by a small infant, nevertheless it is not significantly more personlike than is a very small embryo. It is *somewhat* more personlike; it can apparently feel and respond to pain, and it may even have a rudimentary form of consciousness, insofar as its brain is quite active. Nevertheless, it seems safe to say that it is not fully conscious, in the way that an infant of a few months is, and that it cannot reason, or communicate messages of indefinitely many sorts, does not engage in self-motivated activity, and has no self-awareness. Thus, in the *relevant* respects, a fetus, even a fully developed one, is considerably less personlike than is the average mature mammal, indeed the average fish. And I think that a rational person must conclude that if the right to life of a fetus is to be based upon its resemblance to a person, then it cannot be said to have any more right to life than, let us say, a newborn guppy (which also seems to be capable of feeling pain), and that a right of that magnitude could never override a woman's right to obtain an abortion, at any stage of her pregnancy.

There may, of course, be other arguments in favor of placing legal limits upon the stage of pregnancy in which an abortion may be peformed. Given the relative safety of the new techniques of artificially inducing labor during the third trimester, the danger to the woman's life or health is no longer such an argument. Neither is the fact that people tend to respond to the thought of abortion in the later stages of pregnancy with emotional repulsion, since mere emotional responses cannot take the place of moral reasoning in determining what ought to be permitted. Nor, finally, is the frequently heard argument that legalizing abortion, especially late in the pregnancy, may erode the level of respect for human life, leading, perhaps, to an increase in unjustified euthanasia and other crimes. For this threat, if it is a threat, can be better met by educating people to the kinds of moral distinctions which we are making here than by limiting access to abortion (which limitation may, in its disregard for the rights of women, be just as damaging to the level of respect for human rights).

Thus, since the fact that even a fully developed fetus is not personlike enough to have any significant right to life on the basis of its personlikeness shows that no legal restrictions upon the stage of pregnancy in which an abortion may be performed can be justified on the grounds that we should protect the rights of the older fetus, and since there is no other apparent justification for such restrictions, we may conclude that they are entirely unjustified. Whether or not it would be *indecent* (whatever that means) for a woman in her seventh month to obtain an abortion just to avoid having to postpone a trip to Europe, it would not, in itself, be *immoral*, and therefore it ought to be permitted.

4. POTENTIAL PERSONHOOD AND THE RIGHT TO LIFE

We have seen that a fetus does not resemble a person in any way which can support the claim that it has even some of the same rights. But what about its *potential*, the fact that if nurtured and allowed to develop naturally it will very probably become a person? Doesn't that alone give it at least some right to life? It is hard to deny that the fact that an entity is a potential person is a strong prima facie reason for not destroying it; but we need not conclude from this that a potential person has a right to life, by virtue of that potential. It may be that our feeling that it is better, other things being equal, not to destroy a potential person is better explained by the fact that potential people are still (felt to be) an invaluable resource, not to be lightly squandered. Surely, if every speck of dust were a potential person, we would be much less apt to conclude that every potential person has a right to become actual.

Still, we do not need to insist that a potential person has no right to life whatever. There may well be something immoral, and not just imprudent, about wantonly destroying potential people, when doing so isn't necessary to protect anyone's rights. But even if a potential person does have some prima facie right to life, such a right could not possibly outweigh the right of a woman to obtain an abortion, since the rights of any actual person invariably outweigh those of any potential person, whenever the two conflict. Since this may not be immediately obvious in the case of a human fetus, let us look at another case.

Suppose that our space explorer falls into the hands of an alien culture, whose scientists decide to create a few hundred thousand or more human beings, by breaking his body into its component cells, and using these to create fully developed human beings, with, of course, his genetic code. We may imagine that each of these newly created men will have all of the original man's abilities, skills, knowledge, and so on, and also have an individual self-concept, in short that each of them will be a bona fide (though hardly unique) person. Imagine that the whole project will take only seconds, and that its chances of success are extremely high, and that our explorer knows all of this, and also knows that these people will be treated fairly. I maintain that in such a situation he would have every right to escape if he could, and thus to deprive all of these potential people of their potential lives; for his right to life outweighs all of theirs together, in spite of the fact that they are all genetically human, all innocent, and all have a very high probability of becoming people very soon, if only he refrains from acting.

Indeed, I think he would have a right to escape even if it were not his life which the alien scientists planned to take, but only a year of his freedom, or, indeed, only a day. Nor would he be obligated to stay if he had gotten captured (thus bringing all these people-potentials into existence) because of his own carelessness, or even if he had done so deliberately, knowing the consequences. Regardless of how he got captured, he is not morally obligated to remain in captivity for *any* period of time for the sake of permitting any number of potential people to come into actuality, so great is the margin by which one actual person's right to liberty outweighs whatever right to life even a hundred thousand potential people have. And it seems reasonable to conclude that the rights of a woman will outweigh by a similar margin whatever right to life a fetus may have by virtue of its potential personhood.

Thus, neither a fetus's resemblance to a person, nor its potential for becoming a person provides any basis whatever for the claim that it has any significant right to life. Consequently, a woman's right to protect her health, happiness, freedom, and even her life,[5] by terminating an unwanted pregnancy, will always override whatever right to life it may be appropriate to ascribe to a fetus, even a fully developed one. And thus, in the absence of any overwhelming social need for every possible child, the laws which restrict the right to obtain an abortion, or limit the period of pregnancy during which an abortion may be performed, are a wholly unjustified violation of a woman's most basic moral and constitutional rights.[6]

POSTSCRIPT ON INFANTICIDE

Since the publication of this article, many people have written to point out that my argument appears to justify not only abortion, but infanticide as well. For a newborn infant is not significantly more personlike than an advanced fetus, and consequently it would seem

[5]That is, insofar as the death rate, for the woman, is higher for childbirth than for early abortion.
[6]My thanks to the following people, who were kind enough to read and criticize an earlier version of this paper: Herbert Gold, Gene Glass, Anne Lauterbach, Judith Thomson, Mary Mothersill, and Timothy Binkley.

that if the destruction of the latter is permissible so too must be that of the former. Inasmuch as most people, regardless of how they feel about the morality of abortion, consider infanticide a form of murder, this might appear to represent a serious flaw in my argument.

Now, if I am right in holding that it is only people who have a full-fledged right to life, and who can be murdered, and if the criteria of personhood are as I have described them, then it obviously follows that killing a new-born infant isn't murder. It does *not* follow, however, that infanticide is permissible, for two reasons. In the first place, it would be wrong, at least in this country and in this period of history, and other things being equal, to kill a new-born infant, because even if its parents do not want it and would not suffer from its destruction, there are other people who would like to have it, and would, in all probability, be deprived of a great deal of pleasure by its destruction. Thus, infanticide is wrong for reasons analogous to those which make it wrong to wantonly destroy natural resources, or great works of art.

Secondly, most people, at least in this country, value infants and would much prefer that they be preserved, even if foster parents are not immediately available. Most of us would rather be taxed to support orphanages than allow unwanted infants to be destroyed. So long as there are people who want an infant preserved, and who are willing and able to provide the means of caring for it, under reasonably humane conditions, it is *ceteris paribus*, wrong to destroy it.

But, it might be replied, if this argument shows that infanticide is wrong, at least at this time and in this country, doesn't it also show that abortion is wrong? After all, many people value fetuses, are disturbed by their destruction, and would much prefer that they be preserved, even at some cost to themselves. Furthermore, as a potential source of pleasure to some foster family, a fetus is just as valuable as an infant. There is, however, a crucial difference between the two cases: so long as the fetus is unborn, its preservation, contrary to the wishes of the pregnant woman, violates her rights to freedom, happiness, and self-determination. Her rights override the rights of those who would like the fetus preserved, just as if someone's life or limb is threatened by a wild animal, his right to protect himself by destroying the animal overrides the rights of those who would prefer that the animal not be harmed.

The minute the infant is born, however, its preservation no longer violates any of its mother's rights, even if she wants it destroyed, because she is free to put it up for adoption. Consequently, while the moment of birth does not mark any sharp discontinuity in the degree to which an infant possesses the right to life, it does mark the end of its mother's right to determine its fate. Indeed, if abortion could be performed without killing the fetus, she would never possess the right to have the fetus destroyed, for the same reasons that she has no right to have an infant destroyed.

On the other hand, it follows from my argument that when an unwanted or defective infant is born into a society which cannot afford and/or is not willing to care for it, then its destruction is permissible. This conclusion will, no doubt, strike many people as heartless and immoral; but remember that the very existence of people who feel this way, and who are willing and able to provide care for unwanted infants, is reason enough to conclude that they should be preserved.

QUESTIONS

1. Does Warren's analysis effectively undermine Noonan's conservative position on abortion?
2. Does the fetus, even if it is not an *actual* person, have a serious right to life on the grounds that it is a *potential* person?

3. Is a newborn infant a person? In any case, are there any circumstances in which infanticide would be morally permissible?

DANIEL CALLAHAN

ABORTION DECISIONS: PERSONAL MORALITY

Daniel Callahan, a philosopher, is the director of the Institute of Society, Ethics and the Life Sciences, usually called The Hastings Center. His numerous publications reflect an enduring concern with issues in biomedical ethics. He is, for example, the author of *Ethics and Population Limitation* (1971) and the coeditor of *Science, Ethics and Medicine* (1976). Callahan's principal work on the subject of abortion is *Abortion: Law, Choice and Morality* (1970), from which this selection is excerpted.

After declaring himself in support of permissive abortion legislation, Callahan proceeds to defend one kind of moderate view on the problem of the ethical acceptability of abortion. On the issue of the moral status of the fetus, he steers a middle course. He rejects the "tissue" theory, the view that the fetus has negligible moral status, on the grounds that such a theory is out of tune with both the biological evidence and a respect for the sanctity of human life. On the other hand, he contends that the fetus does not qualify as a person and thus rejects the view that the fetus has full moral status. His contention that the fetus is nevertheless an "important and valuable form of human life" can be understood as implying that the fetus has some kind of *partial* moral status.

In Callahan's view, a respect for the sanctity of human life should incline every woman to a strong initial (moral) bias against abortion. Yet, he argues, since a woman has duties to herself, her family, and her society, there may be circumstances in which such duties would override the prima facie duty not to abort. Callahan concludes by criticizing various efforts to dissolve the "moral tension" involved in abortion decisions.

The strength of pluralistic societies lies in the personal freedom they afford individuals. One is free to choose among religious, philosophical, ideological and political creeds; or one can create one's own highly personal, idiosyncratic moral code and view of the universe. Increasingly, the individual is free to ignore the morals, manners and mores of society. The only limitations are upon those actions which seem to present clear and present dangers to the common good, and even there the range of prohibited actions is diminishing as more and more choices are left to personal and private decisions. I have contended that, apart from some regulatory laws, abortion decisions should be left, finally, up to the women themselves. Whatever one may think of the morality of abortion, it cannot be established that it poses a clear and present danger to the common good. Thus society does not have the right decisively to interpose itself between a woman and the abortion she wants. It can only intervene where it can be shown that some of its own interests are at stake *qua* society. Regulatory laws of a minimal kind therefore seem in order, since in a variety of ways already mentioned society will be affected by the number, kind and quality of legal abortions. In short, with a few important stipulations, what I have been urging is tantamount to saying that abortion decisions should be private decisions. It is to accept, in principle, the contention of those who believe that, in a free, pluralistic society, the woman should be allowed to make her own moral choice on abortion and be allowed to implement that choice.

But pluralistic societies also lay a few traps for the unwary. It is not a large psychological step from saying that individuals should be left free to make up their own minds on some crucial moral issues (of which abortion is one) to an adoption of the view that one personal decision is as good as another, that any decision is a good one as long as it is honest or sincere, that a free decision equals a correct decision. However short the psychological step, the logical gap is very large. An absence of cant, hypocrisy and coercion may prepare the way for good personal decisions. But that is only to clean the room, and something must then be put in it. The hazard is that, once cleaned, it will be filled with capriciousness, sentimentality, a thinly disguised conformity to the reigning moral taste, or strongly felt but inadequately analyzed moral opinions. This is a particular danger in affluent pluralistic societies, heavily dominated by popular tastes, communication media and the absence of shared values. Philosophically, the view that all values are equally good and all private moral choices on a par is all but dead; but it still has a strong life at the popular level, where there is a tendency to act as if, once personal freedom is legally and socially achieved, moral questions cease to exist.

A considerable quantity of literature exists in the field of ethics concerned with such problems as subjective and objective values, the meaning and use of ethical principles and moral rules, the role of intentionality. That literature need not be reviewed here. But it is directly to the point to observe that a particular failing of the abortion-on-request literature is that it persistently scants the moral problem of how a woman, if granted the desired legal freedom to make her own decision about abortion, should go about making that decision. Up to a point, this deficiency is understandable. The immediate tactical problem has been to get the laws changed or repealed; that has been the burden of the public struggle, which has concentrated on statutes and legislators rather than on the moral contents and problems of personal decision-making. It is reasonable and legitimate to say that a woman should be left free to make the decision in the light of her own personal values; that is, I believe, the best legal solution. But it leaves totally untouched the question of how, once freedom is achieved, she ought to go about the personal business of forming a coherent, rational, sensitive moral perspective and opinion on abortion. After freedom, what then? Society may have no right to demand that a woman give it good reasons why she should have an abortion before permitting it. But this does not entail that the woman should not, as a morally responsible person, have good reasons to justify her desires or acts in her own eyes.

This is only to say that a solution of the legal problem is not the same as a solution to the moral problem. That the moral struggle is transferred from the public to the private sphere should not be taken to mean that the moral problem has been solved; only its public aspect, under a permissive law or a repeal of all laws, has been dealt with. The personal problem will remain.

Some women will be part of a religious group or ethical tradition which they freely choose and which can offer them something, possibly very much, in the way of helpful moral insight consistent with that tradition. The obvious course in that instance is for them to turn to their tradition to see what it has to offer them on the particular problem of abortion. But what of those who have no tradition to repair to or those who find their tradition wanting on this problem? One way or another, they will have to find some way of developing a set of ethical principles and moral rules to help them act responsibly, to justify their own conduct in their own eyes. To press the problem to a finer point, what ought they to think about as they try to work out their own views on abortion?

Only a few suggestions will be made here, taking the form of arguing for an ethic of personal responsibility which tries, in the process of decision-making, to make itself aware of a number of things. The biological evidence should be considered, just as the problem of methodology must be considered; the philosophical assumptions implicit in different uses of the word "human" need to be considered; a philosophical theory of biological analysis is required; the social consequences of different kinds of analyses and different meanings of the word "human" should be thought through; consistency of meaning and use should be sought to avoid *ad hoc* and arbitrary solutions.

It is my own conviction that the "developmental school" offers the most helpful and illuminating approach to the problem of the beginning of human life, avoiding, on the one hand, a too narrow genetic criterion of human life and, on the other, a too broad and socially dangerous social definition of the "human." Yet the kinds of problems which appear in any attempt to decide upon the beginning of life suggest that no one position can be either proved or disproved from biological evidence alone. It becomes a question of trying to do justice to the evidence while, at the same time, realizing that how the evidence is approached and used will be a function of one's way of looking at reality, one's moral policy, the values and rights one believes need balancing, and the type of questions one thinks need to be asked. At the very least, however, the genetic evidence for the uniqueness of zygotes and embryos (a uniqueness of a different kind than that of the uniqueness of sperm and ova), their potentiality for development into a human person, their early development of human characteristics, their genetic and organic distinctness from the organism of the mother, appear to rule out a treatment even of zygotes, much less the more developed stages of the conceptus, as mere pieces of "tissue," of no human significance or value. The "tissue" theory of the significance of the conceptus can only be made plausible by a systematic disregard of the biological evidence. Moreover, though one may conclude that a conceptus is only potential human life, in the process of continually actualizing its potential through growth and development, a respect for the sanctity of life, with its bias in favor even of undeveloped life, is enough to make the taking of such life a moral problem. There is a choice to be made and it is a moral choice. In the near future, it is likely that some kind of simple, safe abortifacient drug will be developed, which either prevents implantation or destroys the conceptus before it can develop. It will be tempting then to think that the moral dilemma has vanished, but I do not believe it will have.

It is possible to imagine a huge number of situations where a woman could, in good and sensitive conscience, choose abortion as a moral solution to her personal or social difficulties. But, at the very least, the bounds of morality are overstepped when either through a systematic intellectual negligence or a willful choosing of that moral solution most personally convenient, personal choice is deliberately made easy and problem-free. Yet it seems to me that a pressure in that direction is a growing part of the ethos of technological societies; it is easily possible to find people to reassure us that we need have no scruples about the way we act, whether the issue is war, the suppression of rebellion and revolution, discrimination against minorities or the use of technological advances. Pluralism makes possible the achieving of freer, more subtle moral thinking; but it is a possibility constantly endangered by cultural pressures which would simplify or dissolve moral doubts and anguish.

The question of abortion "indications" returns at the level of personal choice. I have contended that the advent of permissive laws should not mean a cessation of efforts to explore the problem of "indications." When a woman asks herself, as she ought, whether

her reasons for wanting an abortion are sound reasons—which presumes abortion is a serious enough moral issue to warrant the need to provide oneself with good reasons for choosing it—she will be asking herself about justifiable indications. Thus, transposed from the legal to the personal level, the kinds of concerns adumbrated in the earlier chapters on indications remain fully pertinent. It was argued in those chapters that, with the possible exception of exceedingly rare instances of a direct threat to the physical life of the mother, one cannot speak of general categories of abortion indications as *necessitating* an abortion. In a number of circumstances, abortion may be a wise and justifiable solution to a distressed pregnancy. But when the language of necessity is used, the implication is that no other conceivable alternative is available. It may be granted, willingly enough, that some set of practical circumstances in some (possibly very many) concrete cases may indicate that abortion is the only feasible option open. But these cases cannot readily be determined in advance, and, for that reason, it is necessary to say that no formal indication as such (e.g., a psychiatric indication) entails a necessary, predetermined choice in favor of abortion.

The word "indication" remains the best word, suggesting that a number of given circumstances will bring the possibility or desirability of abortion to the fore. But to escalate the concept of an indication into that of a required procedure is to go too far. Abortion is *one* way to solve the problem of an unwanted or hazardous pregnancy (physically, psychologically, economically or socially), but it is rarely the only way, at least in affluent societies (I would be considerably less certain about making the same statement about poor societies). Even in the most extreme cases—rape, incest, psychosis, for instance—alternatives will usually be available and different choices open. It is not necessarily the end of every woman's chance for a happy, meaningful life to bear an illegitimate child. It is not necessarily the automatic destruction of a family to have a seriously defective child born into it. It is not necessarily the ruination of every family living in overcrowded housing to have still another child. It is not inevitable that every immature woman would become even more so if she bore a child or another child. It is not inevitable that a gravely handicapped child can hope for nothing from life. It is not inevitable that every unwanted child is doomed to misery. It is not written in the essence of things, as a fixed law of human nature, that a woman cannot come to accept, love and be a good mother to a child who was initially unwanted. Nor is it a fixed law that she could not come to cherish a grossly deformed child. Naturally, these are only generalizations. The point is only that human beings are as a rule flexible, capable of doing more than they sometimes think they can, able to surmount serious dangers and challenges, able to grow and mature, able to transform inauspicious beginnings into satisfactory conclusions. Everything in life, even in procreative and family life, is not fixed in advance; the future is never wholly unalterable.

Yet the problem of personal question-asking must be pushed a step farther. The way the questions are answered will be very much determined by a woman's way of looking at herself and at life. A woman who has decided, as a personal moral policy, that nothing should be allowed to stand in the way of her own happiness, goals and self-interest will have no trouble solving the moral problem. For her, an unwanted pregnancy will, by definition, be a pregnancy to be terminated. But only by a Pickwickian use of words could this form of reasoning be called moral. It would preclude any need to consult the opinion of others, any need to examine the validity of one's own viewpoint, any need to, for instance, ask when human life begins, any need to interrogate oneself in any way, intellectually or morally; will and desire would be king.

Assuming, however, that most women would seek a broader ethical horizon than that of their exclusively personal self-interest, what might they think about when faced with an abortion decision? A respect for the sanctity of human life should, I believe, incline them toward a general and strong bias against abortion. Abortion is an act of killing, the violent, direct destruction of potential human life, already in the process of development. That fact should not be disguised, or glossed over by euphemism and circumlocution. It is not the destruction of a human person—for at no stage of its development does the conceptus fulfill the definition of a person, which implies a developed capacity for reasoning, willing, desiring and relating to others—but it is the destruction of an important and valuable form of human life. Its value and its potentiality are not dependent upon the attitude of the woman toward it; it grows by its own biological dynamism and has a genetic and morphological potential distinct from that of the woman. It has its own distinctive and individual future. If contraception and abortion are both seen as forms of birth limitation, they are distinctly different acts; the former precludes the possibility of a conceptus being formed, while the latter stops a conceptus already in existence from developing. The bias implied by the principle of the sanctity of human life is toward the protection of all forms of human life, especially, in ordinary circumstances, the protection of the right to life. That right should be accorded even to doubtful life; its existence should not be wholly dependent upon the personal self-interest of the woman.

Yet she has her own rights as well, and her own set of responsibilities to those around her; that is why she may have to choose abortion. In extreme situations of overpopulation, she may also have a responsibility for the survival of the species or of a people. In many circumstances, then, a decision in favor of abortion—one which overrides the right to life of that potential human being she carries within—can be a responsible moral decision, worthy neither of the condemnation of others nor of self-condemnation. But the bias of the principle of the sanctity of life is against a routine, unthinking employment of abortion; it bends over backwards not to take life and gives the benefit of the doubt to life. It does not seek to diminish the range of responsibility toward life—potential or actual—but to extend it. It does not seek the narrowest definition of life, but the widest and the richest. It is mindful of individual possibility, on the one hand, and of a destructive human tendency, on the other, to exclude from the category of "the human" or deny rights to those beings whose existence is or could prove burdensome to others.

The language used to describe abortion will have an important bearing on the sensitivities and imagination of those women who must make abortion decisions. Abortion can be talked about in the language of medical technology and technique—as, say, "a therapeutic procedure involving the emptying of the uterine contents." That language is neutral, clinical, unemotional. Or abortion can be talked about in the emotive language of relieving woman from suffering, or meeting the need for freedom among women, or saving a nation from a devastating overpopulation. Both kinds of language have their place, for abortion has more than one result and meaning and abortion can legitimately be talked about in more than one way. What is objectionable is a conscious manipulation of language to incite an irrational emotional response, to allay doubts or to mislead the imagination. Particularly misleading is one commonly employed mixture of rhetorical modes by advocates of abortion on request. That is the use of a detached, clinical language to describe the actual operation itself combined with an emotive rhetoric to evoke the personal and social goods which an abortion can bring about. Thus, when every effort is made to suggest that emotion and feeling are perfectly appropriate to describe the social and personal goals of abortion, but that a clinical language only is appropriate when the actual technique and medical objective of an abortion is described, then the moral imagination is being misled.

Any human act can be described in impersonal, technological language, just as any act can be described in emotive language. What is wanted is an equity in the language. It is fair enough and to the point to say that in many circumstances abortion will save a woman's health or her family. It only becomes misleading when the act itself, as distinguished from its therapeutic goal, is talked about in an entirely different way. For, abortion is not just an "emptying of the uterine contents." It is also an act of killing; there will be no abortion unless the conceptus is killed (or its further existence made impossible, which amounts to the same thing). If it is appropriate to evoke the imagination and elicit sympathy for those women in a distressed pregnancy who could be helped by abortion, it is no less appropriate to evoke the imagination about what actually occurs in an abortion "procedure."

Imagination should also come into play at another point. It is often argued by proponents of abortion that there is no need for a woman ever to take any chances in a distressed pregnancy, particularly in the instance of an otherwise healthy woman who, if she has an abortion on one occasion, could simply get pregnant again on another, more auspicious occasion. This might be termed the "replacement theory" of abortion indications: since fetus "x" can be replaced by fetus "y," then there is no reason why a woman should have any scruples about such a replacement. This way of conceiving the choices effectively dissolves them; it becomes important only to know whether a woman can get pregnant again when she wants to. But this strategy can be employed only at the price of convincing oneself that there is no difference whatever among embryos or fetuses, that they all have exactly the same potentiality. But even the sketchiest knowledge of the genetic uniqueness of each conceptus (save in the instance of monozygotic twins), and thus the different genetic potentialities of each, should raise doubts on that point. Yet, having said that, I would not want to deny that the possibility of a further pregnancy could have an important bearing on the moral reasoning of a woman whose present pregnancy was threatening. If, out of a sense of responsibility toward her present children or her present life situation, a woman decided that an abortion was the wisest, most moral course, then the possibility that she could become pregnant later, when these responsibilities would be less pressing, would be a pertinent consideration.

The goal of these remarks is to keep alive in the consciences of women who have an abortion choice a moral tension; and it is to hope that they will be willing to bear the pain and the uncertainty of having to make a moral choice. It is the automatic, unthinking and unimaginative personal solution of abortion questions which women themselves should be extremely wary of, either for or against an abortion. A woman can, with little trouble, find both people and books to reassure her that there is no problem about abortion at all; or people and books to convince her that she would be a moral monster if she chose abortion. A woman can choose in advance the views she will listen to and thus have her predispositions confirmed. Yet a willingness to keep alive a moral tension, and to be wary of precipitous solutions, presupposes two things. First, that the woman herself wants to do what is right, realizing that what is right may not always be that which is most convenient, most easy or most immediately apt to solve a pressing problem. It is simply not the case that what one wants to do, or would like to do, or is predisposed to do is necessarily the right thing to do. A willingness seriously to entertain that moral perception—which, of course, does not in itself imply a decision for or against an abortion—is one sign of moral seriousness.

Second, moral seriousness presupposes one is concerned with the protection and furthering of life. This means that, out of respect for human life, one bends over backwards not to eliminate human life, not to desensitize oneself to the meaning and value of potential life, not to seek definitions of the "human" which serve one's self-interest only. A desire to respect human life in all of its forms means, therefore, that one voluntarily imposes upon oneself a pressure against the taking of life; that one demands of oneself serious reasons for doing so, even in the case of a very early embryo; that one use not only the mind but also the imagination when a decision is being made; that one seeks not to evade the moral issues but to face them; that one searches out the alternatives and conscientiously entertains them before turning to abortion. A bias in favor of the sanctity of human life in all of its forms would include a bias against abortion on the part of women; it would be the last rather than the first choice when unwanted pregnancies occurred. It would be an act to be avoided if at all possible.

A bias of this kind, voluntarily imposed by a woman upon herself, would not trap her; for it is also part of a respect for the dignity of life to leave the way open for an abortion when other reasonable choices are not available. For she also has duties toward herself, her family and her society. There can be good reasons for taking the life even of a very late fetus; once that also is seen and seen as a counterpoise in particular cases to the general bias against the taking of potential life, the way is open to choose abortion. The bias of the moral policy implies the need for moral rules which seek to preserve life. But, as a policy which leaves room for choice — rather than entailing a fixed set of rules — it is open to flexible interpretation when the circumstances point to the wisdom of taking exception to the normal ordering of the rules in particular cases. Yet, in that case, one is not genuinely taking exception to the rules. More accurately, one would be deciding that, for the preservation or furtherance of other values or rights — species-rights, person-rights — a choice in favor of abortion would be serving the sanctity of life. That there would be, in that case, conflict between rights, with one set of rights set aside (reluctantly) to serve another set, goes without saying. A subversion of the principle occurs when it is made out that there is no conflict and thus nothing to decide.

QUESTIONS

1. Does Callahan's analysis effectively undermine both Noonan's conservative position and Warren's liberal position on abortion?

2. Consider an abortion that is secured for each of the following reasons: (1) to preserve the physical health of the mother, (2) to preserve the mental health of the mother, (3) to prevent the birth of a severely deformed child, (4) to eliminate the product of rape, (5) to prevent the birth of an illegitimate child, (6) to preserve the life-style of the mother. According to Callahan, the fetus is neither a "person" nor a "piece of tissue." Reasoning from this moderate point of view, in which of the above cases would abortion be morally justifiable?

JANE ENGLISH

ABORTION AND THE CONCEPT OF A PERSON

Jane English (1947–1978) was a philosopher whose life came to a tragic end, at the age of thirty-one, in a mountain-climbing accident on the Matterhorn. She had taught at the University of North Carolina, Chapel Hill, and had published such articles as "Justice between Generations" and "Sex Equality in Sports." She was also the editor of *Sex Equality* (1977) and the coeditor of *Feminism and Philosophy* (1977).

English begins by arguing that one of the central issues in the abortion debate, whether a fetus is a person, cannot be decisively resolved. However, she contends, whether we presume that the fetus is or is not a person, we must arrive at a moderate stance on the problem of abortion. In an effort to moderate the *conservative* view, English argues that it is unwarranted to conclude, from the presumption that the fetus is a person, that abortion is always morally impermissible. Reasoning on the basis of a self-defense model, she finds abortion morally permissible in many cases. In an effort to moderate the *liberal* view, English argues that it is unwarranted to conclude, from the presumption that the fetus is not a person, that abortion is always morally permissible. Even if the fetus is not a person, she argues, the similarity between a fetus and a baby is sufficient to make abortion problematic in the later stages of pregnancy.

The abortion debate rages on. Yet the two most popular positions seem to be clearly mistaken. Conservatives maintain that a human life begins at conception and that therefore abortion must be wrong because it is murder. But not all killings of humans are murders. Most notably, self defense may justify even the killing of an innocent person.

Liberals, on the other hand, are just as mistaken in their argument that since a fetus does not become a person until birth, a woman may do whatever she pleases in and to her own body. First, you cannot do as you please with your own body if it affects other people adversely.[1] Second, if a fetus is not a person, that does not imply that you can do to it anything you wish. Animals, for example, are not persons, yet to kill or torture them for no reason at all is wrong.

At the center of the storm has been the issue of just when it is between ovulation and adulthood that a person appears on the scene. Conservatives draw the line at conception, liberals at birth. In this paper I first examine our concept of a person and conclude that no single criterion can capture the concept of a person and no sharp line can be drawn. Next I argue that if a fetus is a person, abortion is still justifiable in many cases; and if a fetus is not a person, killing it is still wrong in many cases. To a large extent, these two solutions are in agreement. I conclude that our concept of a person cannot and need not bear the weight that the abortion controversy has thrust upon it.

I

The several factions in the abortion argument have drawn battle lines around various proposed criteria for determining what is and what is not a person. For example, Mary Anne Warren[2] lists five features (capacities for reasoning, self-awareness, complex communication, etc.) as her criteria for personhood and argues for the permissibility of abortion because a fetus falls outside this concept. Baruch Brody[3] uses brain waves. Michael Tooley[4] picks having-a-concept-of-self as his criterion and concludes that infanticide and abortion are justifiable, while the killing of adult animals is not. On the other side, Paul Ramsey[5] claims a certain gene structure is the defining characteristic. John Noonan[6] prefers conceived-of-humans and presents counterexamples to various other candidate criteria. For instance, he argues against viability as the criterion because the newborn and infirm would then be non-persons, since they cannot live without the aid of others. He rejects any cri-

Reprinted with permission of the publisher from the *Canadian Journal of Philosophy*, vol. 5, no. 2 (October 1975), pp. 233–243.
[1]We also have paternalistic laws which keep us from harming our own bodies even when no one else is affected. Ironically, anti-abortion laws were originally designed to protect pregnant women from a dangerous but tempting procedure.
[2]Mary Anne Warren, ''On the Moral and Legal Status of Abortion,'' *Monist* 57 (1973), p. 55.
[3]Baruch Brody, ''Fetal Humanity and the Theory of Essentialism,'' in Robert Baker and Frederick Elliston, eds., *Philosophy and Sex* (Buffalo, N.Y., 1975).
[4]Michael Tooley, ''Abortion and Infanticide,'' *Philosophy and Public Affairs* 2 (1971).
[5]Paul Ramsey, ''The Morality of Abortion,'' in James Rachels, ed., *Moral Problems* (New York, 1971).
[6]John Noonan, ''Abortion and the Catholic Church: A Summary History,'' *Natural Law Forum* 12 (1967), pp. 125–131.

terion that calls upon the sorts of sentiments a being can evoke in adults on the grounds that this would allow us to exclude other races as non-persons if we could just view them sufficiently unsentimentally.

These approaches are typical: foes of abortion propose sufficient conditions for personhood which fetuses satisfy, while friends of abortion counter with necessary conditions for personhood which fetuses lack. But these both presuppose that the concept of a person can be captured in a strait jacket of necessary and/or sufficient conditions.[7] Rather, "person" is a cluster of features, of which rationality, having a self concept and being conceived of humans are only part.

What is typical of persons? Within our concept of a person we include, first, certain biological factors: descended from humans, having a certain genetic makeup, having a head, hands, arms, eyes, capable of locomotion, breathing, eating, sleeping. There are psychological factors: sentience, perception, having a concept of self and of one's own interests and desires, the ability to use tools, the ability to use language or symbol systems, the ability to joke, to be angry, to doubt. There are rationality factors: the ability to reason and draw conclusions, the ability to generalize and to learn from past experience, the ability to sacrifice present interests for greater gains in the future. There are social factors: the ability to work in groups and respond to peer pressures, the ability to recognize and consider as valuable the interests of others, seeing oneself as one among "other minds," the ability to sympathize, encourage, love, the ability to evoke from others the responses of sympathy, encouragement, love, the ability to work with others for mutual advantage. Then there are legal factors: being subject to the law and protected by it, having the ability to sue and enter contracts, being counted in the census, having a name and citizenship, the ability to own property, inherit, and so forth.

Now the point is not that this list is incomplete, or that you can find counterinstances to each of its points. People typically exhibit rationality, for instance, but someone who was irrational would not thereby fail to qualify as a person. On the other hand, something could exhibit the majority of these features and still fail to be a person, as an advanced robot might. There is no single core of necessary and sufficient features which we can draw upon with the assurance that they constitute what really makes a person; there are only features that are more or less typical.

This is not to say that no necessary or sufficient conditions can be given. Being alive is a necessary condition for being a person, and being a U.S. Senator is sufficient. But rather than falling inside a sufficient condition or outside a necessary one, a fetus lies in the penumbra region where our concept of a person is not so simple. For this reason I think a conclusive answer to the question whether a fetus is a person is unattainable.

Here we might note a family of simple fallacies that proceed by stating a necessary condition for personhood and showing that a fetus has that characteristic. This is a form of the fallacy of affirming the consequent. For example, some have mistakenly reasoned from the premise that a fetus is human (after all, it is a human fetus rather than, say, a canine fetus), to the conclusion that it is a human. Adding an equivocation on "being," we get the fallacious argument that since a fetus is something both living and human, it is a human being.

Nonetheless, it does seem clear that a fetus has very few of the above family of characteristics, whereas a newborn baby exhibits a much larger proportion of them—and a two-year-old has even more. Note that one traditional anti-abortion argument has centered on pointing out the many ways in which a fetus resembles a baby. They emphasize

[7]Wittgenstein has argued against the possibility of so capturing the concept of a game, *Philosophical Investigations* (New York, 1958), §66–71.

its development ("It already has ten fingers . . .") without mentioning its dissimilarities to adults (it still has gills and a tail). They also try to evoke the sort of sympathy on our part that we only feel toward other persons ("Never to laugh . . . or feel the sunshine?"). This all seems to be a relevant way to argue, since its purpose is to persuade us that a fetus satisfies so many of the important features on the list that it ought to be treated as a person. Also note that a fetus near the time of birth satisfies many more of these factors than a fetus in the early months of development. This could provide reason for making distinctions among the different stages of pregnancy, as the U.S. Supreme Court has done.[8]

Historically, the time at which a person has been said to come into existence has varied widely. Muslims date personhood from fourteen days after conception. Some medievals followed Aristotle in placing ensoulment at forty days after conception for a male fetus and eighty days for a female fetus.[9] In European common law since the Seventeenth Century, abortion was considered the killing of a person only after quickening, the time when a pregnant woman first feels the fetus move on its own. Nor is this variety of opinions surprising. Biologically, a human being develops gradually. We shouldn't expect there to be any specific time or sharp dividing point when a person appears on the scene.

For these reasons I believe our concept of a person is not sharp or decisive enough to bear the weight of a solution to the abortion controversy. To use it to solve that problem is to clarify *obscurum per obscurius*.

II

Next let us consider what follows if a fetus is a person after all. Judith Jarvis Thomson's landmark article, "A Defense of Abortion,"[10] correctly points out that some additional argumentation is needed at this point in the conservative argument to bridge the gap between the premise that a fetus is an innocent person and the conclusion that killing it is always wrong. To arrive at this conclusion, we would need the additional premise that killing an innocent person is always wrong. But killing an innocent person is sometimes permissible, most notably in self defense. Some examples may help draw out our intuitions or ordinary judgments about self defense.

Suppose a mad scientist, for instance, hypnotized innocent people to jump out of the bushes and attack innocent passers-by with knives. If you are so attacked, we agree you have a right to kill the attacker in self defense, if killing him is the only way to protect your life or to save yourself from serious injury. It does not seem to matter here that the attacker is not malicious but himself an innocent pawn, for your killing of him is not done in a spirit of retribution but only in self defense.

How severe an injury may you inflict in self defense? In part this depends upon the severity of the injury to be avoided: you may not shoot someone merely to avoid having your clothes torn. This might lead one to the mistaken conclusion that the defense may only equal the threatened injury in severity; that to avoid death you may kill, but to avoid a black eye you may only inflict a black eye or the equivalent. Rather, our laws and customs seem to say that you may create an injury somewhat, but not enormously, greater than the injury to be avoided. To fend off an attack whose outcome would be as serious as rape, a severe beating or the loss of a finger, you may shoot; to avoid having your clothes torn, you may blacken an eye.

[8]Not because the fetus is partly a person and so has some of the rights of persons, but rather because of the rights of person-like non-persons. This I discuss in part III below.
[9]Aristotle himself was concerned, however, with the different question of when the soul takes form. For historical data, see Jimmye Kimmey, "How the Abortion Laws Happened," Ms.1 (April, 1973), pp. 48ff, and John Noonan, *loc. cit.*
[10]J. J. Thomson, "A Defense of Abortion," *Philosophy and Public Affairs* 1 (1971).

Aside from this, the injury you may inflict should only be the minimum necessary to deter or incapacitate the attacker. Even if you know he intends to kill you, you are not justified in shooting him if you could equally well save yourself by the simple expedient of running away. Self defense is for the purpose of avoiding harms rather than equalizing harms.

Some cases of pregnancy present a parallel situation. Though the fetus is itself innocent, it may pose a threat to the pregnant woman's well-being, life prospects or health, mental or physical. If the pregnancy presents a slight threat to her interests, it seems self defense cannot justify abortion. But if the threat is on a par with a serious beating or the loss of a finger, she may kill the fetus that poses such a threat, even if it is an innocent person. If a lesser harm to the fetus could have the same defensive effect, killing it would not be justified. It is unfortunate that the only way to free the woman from the pregnancy entails the death of the fetus (except in very late stages of pregnancy). Thus a self defense model supports Thomson's point that the woman has a right only to be freed from the fetus, not a right to demand its death.[11]

The self defense model is most helpful when we take the pregnant woman's point of view. In the pre-Thomson literature, abortion is often framed as a question for a third party: do you, a doctor, have a right to choose between the life of the woman and that of the fetus? Some have claimed that if you were a passer-by who witnessed a struggle between the innocent hypnotized attacker and his equally innocent victim, you would have no reason to kill either in defense of the other. They have concluded that the self defense model implies that a woman may attempt to abort herself, but that a doctor should not assist her. I think the position of the third party is somewhat more complex. We do feel some inclination to intervene on behalf of the victim rather than the attacker, other things equal. But if both parties are innocent, other factors come into consideration. You would rush to the aid of your husband whether he was attacker or attackee. If a hypnotized famous violinist were attacking a skid row bum, we would try to save the individual who is of more value to society. These considerations would tend to support abortion in some cases.

But suppose you are a frail senior citizen who wishes to avoid being knifed by one of these innocent hypnotics, so you have hired a bodyguard to accompany you. If you are attacked, it is clear we believe that the bodyguard, acting as your agent, has a right to kill the attacker to save you from a serious beating. Your rights of self defense are transferred to your agent. I suggest that we should similarly view the doctor as the pregnant woman's agent in carrying out a defense she is physically incapable of accomplishing herself.

Thanks to modern technology, the cases are rare in which pregnancy poses as clear a threat to a woman's bodily health as an attacker brandishing a switchblade. How does self defense fare when more subtle, complex and long-range harms are involved?

To consider a somewhat fanciful example, suppose you are a highly trained surgeon when you are kidnapped by the hypnotic attacker. He says he does not intend to harm you but to take you back to the mad scientist who, it turns out, plans to hypnotize you to have a permanent mental block against all your knowledge of medicine. This would automatically destroy your career which would in turn have a serious adverse impact on your family, your personal relationships and your happiness. It seems to me that if the only way you can avoid this outcome is to shoot the innocent attacker, you are justified in so doing. You are defending yourself from a drastic injury to your life prospects. I think it is no exaggeration to claim that unwanted pregnancies (most obviously among teenagers) often have such adverse life-long consequences as the surgeon's loss of livelihood.

Several parallels arise between various views on abortion and the self defense model.

---

[11] *Ibid.*, p.52.

Let's suppose further that these hypnotized attackers only operate at night, so that it is well known that they can be avoided completely by the considerable inconvenience of never leaving your house after dark. One view is that since you could stay home at night, therefore if you go out and are selected by one of these hypnotized people, you have no right to defend yourself. This parallels the view that abstinence is the only acceptable way to avoid pregnancy. Others might hold that you ought to take along some defense such as Mace which will deter the hypnotized person without killing him, but that if this defense fails, you are obliged to submit to the resulting injury, no matter how severe it is. This parallels the view that contraception is all right but abortion is always wrong, even in cases of contraceptive failure.

A third view is that you may kill the hypnotized person only if he will actually kill you, but not if he will only injure you. This is like the position that abortion is permissible only if it is required to save a woman's life. Finally we have the view that it is all right to kill the attacker, even if only to avoid a very slight inconvenience to yourself and even if you knowingly walked down the very street where all these incidents have been taking place without taking along any Mace or protective escort. If we assume that a fetus is a person, this is the analogue of the view that abortion is always justifiable, "on demand."

The self defense model allows us to see an important difference that exists between abortion and infanticide, even if a fetus is a person from conception. Many have argued that the only way to justify abortion without justifying infanticide would be to find some characteristic of personhood that is acquired at birth. Michael Tooley, for one, claims infanticide is justifiable because the really significant characteristics of person are acquired some time after birth. But all such approaches look to characteristics of the developing human and ignore the relation between the fetus and the woman. What if, after birth, the presence of an infant or the need to support it posed a grave threat to the woman's sanity or life prospects? She could escape this threat by the simple expedient of running away. So a solution that does not entail the death of the infant is available. Before birth, such solutions are not available because of the biological dependence of the fetus on the woman. Birth is the crucial point not because of any characteristics the fetus gains, but because after birth the woman can defend herself by a means less drastic than killing the infant. Hence self defense can be used to justify abortion without necessarily thereby justifying infanticide.

III

On the other hand, supposing a fetus is not after all a person, would abortion always be morally permissible? Some opponents of abortion seem worried that if a fetus is not a full-fledged person, then we are justified in treating it in any way at all. However, this does not follow. Non-persons do get some consideration in our moral code, though of course they do not have the same rights as persons have (and in general they do not have moral responsibilities), and though their interests may be overridden by the interests of persons. Still, we cannot just treat them in any way at all.

Treatment of animals is a case in point. It is wrong to torture dogs for fun or to kill wild birds for no reason at all. It is wrong Period, even though dogs and birds do not have the same rights persons do. However, few people think it is wrong to use dogs as experimental animals, causing them considerable suffering in some cases, provided that the resulting research will probably bring discoveries of great benefit to people. And most of us think it all right to kill birds for food or to protect our crops. People's rights are different from the consideration we give to animals, then, for it is wrong to experiment on people, even if others might later benefit a great deal as a result of their suffering. You might volunteer to be a subject, but this would be supererogatory; you certainly have a right to refuse to be a medical guinea pig.

But how do we decide what you may or may not do to non-persons? This is a difficult problem, one for which I believe no adequate account exists. You do not want to say, for instance, that torturing dogs is all right whenever the sum of its effects on people is good — when it doesn't warp the sensibilities of the torturer so much that he mistreats people. If that were the case, it would be all right to torture dogs if you did it in private, or if the torturer lived on a desert island or died soon afterward, so that his actions had no effect on people. This is an inadequate account, because whatever moral consideration animals get, it has to be indefeasible, too. It will have to be a general proscription of certain actions, not merely a weighing of the impact on people on a case-by-case basis.

Rather, we need to distinguish two levels on which consequences of actions can be taken into account in moral reasoning. The traditional objections to Utilitarianism focus on the fact that it operates solely on the first level, taking all the consequences into account in particular cases only. Thus Utilitarianism is open to "desert island" and "lifeboat" counterexamples because these cases are rigged to make the consequences of actions severely limited.

Rawls' theory could be described as a teleological sort of theory, but with teleology operating on a higher level.[12] In choosing the principles to regulate society from the original position, his hypothetical choosers make their decision on the basis of the total consequences of various systems. Furthermore, they are constrained to choose a general set of rules which people can readily learn and apply. An ethical theory must operate by generating a set of sympathies and attitudes toward others which reinforces the functioning of that set of moral principles. Our prohibition against killing people operates by means of certain moral sentiments including sympathy, compassion and guilt. But if these attitudes are to form a coherent set, they carry us further: we tend to perform supererogatory actions, and we tend to feel similar compassion toward person-like non-persons.

It is crucial that psychological facts play a role here. Our psychological constitution makes it the case that for our ethical theory to work, it must prohibit certain treatment of non-persons which are significantly person-like. If our moral rules allowed people to treat some person-like non-persons in ways we do not want people to be treated, this would undermine the system of sympathies and attitudes that makes the ethical system work. For this reason, we would choose in the original position to make mistreatment of some sorts of animals wrong in general (not just wrong in the cases with public impact), even though animals are not themselves parties in the original position. Thus it makes sense that it is those animals whose appearance and behavior are most like those of people that get the most consideration in our moral scheme.

It is because of "coherence of attitudes," I think, that the similarity of a fetus to a baby is very significant. A fetus one week before birth is so much like a newborn baby in our psychological space that we cannot allow any cavalier treatment of the former while expecting full sympathy and nurturative support for the latter. Thus, I think that anti-abortion forces are indeed giving their strongest arguments when they point to the similarities between a fetus and a baby, and when they try to evoke our emotional attachment to and sympathy for the fetus. An early horror story from New York about nurses who were expected to alternate between caring for six-week premature infants and disposing of viable 24-week aborted fetuses is just that — a horror story. These beings are so much alike that no one can be asked to draw a distinction and treat them so very differently.

Remember, however, that in the early weeks after conception, a fetus is very much unlike a person. It is hard to develop these feelings for a set of genes which doesn't yet

[12]John Rawls, *A Theory of Justice* (Cambridge, Mass., 1971), §3–4.

have a head, hands, beating heart, response to touch or the ability to move by itself. Thus it seems to me that the alleged "slippery slope" between conception and birth is not so very slippery. In the early stages of pregnancy, abortion can hardly be compared to murder for psychological reasons, but in the latest stages it is psychologically akin to murder.

Another source of similarity is the bodily continuity between fetus and adult. Bodies play a surprisingly central role in our attitudes toward persons. One has only to think of the philosophical literature on how far physical identity suffices for personal identity or Wittgenstein's remark that the best picture of the human soul is the human body. Even after death, when all agree the body is no longer a person, we still observe elaborate customs of respect for the human body; like people who torture dogs, necrophiliacs are not to be trusted with people.[13] So it is appropriate that we show respect to a fetus as the body continuous with the body of a person. This is a degree of resemblance to persons that animals cannot rival.

Michael Tooley also utilizes a parallel with animals. He claims that it is always permissible to drown newborn kittens and draws conclusions about infanticide.[14] But it is only permissible to drown kittens when their survival would cause some hardship. Perhaps it would be a burden to feed and house six more cats or to find other homes for them. The alternative of letting them starve produces even more suffering than the drowning. Since the kittens get their rights second-hand, so to speak, *via* the need for coherence in our attitudes, their interests are often overridden by the interests of full-fledged persons. But if their survival would be no inconvenience to people at all, then it is wrong to drown them, *contra* Tooley.

Tooley's conclusions about abortion are wrong for the same reason. Even if a fetus is not a person, abortion is not always permissible, because of the resemblance of a fetus to a person. I agree with Thomson that it would be wrong for a woman who is seven months pregnant to have an abortion just to avoid having to postpone a trip to Europe. In the early months of pregnancy when the fetus hardly resembles a baby at all, then, abortion is permissible whenever it is in the interests of the pregnant woman or her family. The reasons would only need to outweigh the pain and inconvenience of the abortion itself. In the middle months, when the fetus comes to resemble a person, abortion would be justifiable only when the continuation of the pregnancy or the birth of the child would cause harms— physical, psychological, economic or social—to the woman. In the late months of pregnancy, even on our current assumption that a fetus is not a person, abortion seems to be wrong except to save a woman from significant injury or death.

The Supreme Court has recognized similar gradations in the alleged slippery slope stretching between conception and birth. To this point, the present paper has been a discussion of the moral status of abortion only, not its legal status. In view of the great physical, financial and sometimes psychological costs of abortion, perhaps the legal arrangement most compatible with the proposed moral solution would be the absence of restrictions, that is, so-called abortion "on demand."

So I conclude, first, that application of our concept of a person will not suffice to settle the abortion issue. After all, the biological development of a human being is gradual. Second, whether a fetus is a person or not, abortion is justifiable early in pregnancy to avoid modest harms and seldom justifiable late in pregnancy except to avoid significant injury or death.[15]

---

[13]On the other hand, if they can be trusted with people, then our moral customs are mistaken. It all depends on the facts of psychology.

[14]*Op. cit.*, pp. 40, 60–6l.

[15]I am deeply indebted to Larry Crocker and Arthur Kuflik for their constructive comments.

QUESTIONS

1. Is English successful in her effort to moderate both the conservative view and the liberal view on abortion?

2. Is the following a justifiable criticism? In moderating the conservative view, English winds up with a rather "conservative" moderate view, whereas in moderating the liberal view, she winds up with a rather "liberal" moderate view. Therefore, she is not successful in showing that the problem of abortion can be effectively resolved without first establishing whether or not the fetus is a person.

SUGGESTED ADDITIONAL READINGS

ARMSTRONG, ROBERT L.: "The Right to Life." *Journal of Social Philosophy*, vol. 8, January 1977, pp. 13–19. Also reprinted in Thomas A. Mappes and Jane S. Zembaty, eds., *Biomedical Ethics*. New York: McGraw-Hill, 1981, pp. 432–438. Armstrong develops an interesting and somewhat distinctive moderate view on the morality of abortion. Though fetuses are not actual persons, he contends, they may be said to have a right to life on the basis of their potential personhood, but *only if* they have what he calls "real or serious" potentiality.

BRODY, BARUCH: "On the Humanity of the Foetus." In Robert L. Perkins, ed., *Abortion: Pro and Con.* Cambridge, Mass.: Schenkman, 1974, pp. 69–90. Brody critically examines the various proposals for "drawing the line" on the humanity of the fetus, ultimately suggesting that the most defensible view would draw the line at the point where fetal brain activity begins.

ENGELHARDT, H. TRISTRAM, JR.: "The Ontology of Abortion." *Ethics*, vol. 84, April 1974, pp. 217–234. Engelhardt focuses attention on the issue of "whether or to what extent the fetus is a person." He argues that, strictly speaking, a human person is not present until the later stages of infancy. However, he finds the point of viability significant in that, with viability, an infant can play the social role of "child" and thus be treated "as if it were a person."

FEINBERG, JOEL, ed.: *The Problem of Abortion.* Belmont, Calif.: Wadsworth, 1973. This excellent anthology features a wide range of articles on both the moral and the legal aspects of abortion.

GRISEZ, GERMAIN: *Abortion: The Myths, The Realities, and the Arguments.* New York: Corpus Books, 1970. Early chapters of this long book provide discussions of a number of factual and historical aspects of abortion. Grisez's conservative view on the morality of abortion appears in Chapter 6, "Ethical Arguments." Chapter 7, also notable, is entitled "Toward a Sound Public Policy."

HUMBER, JAMES M.: "Abortion: The Avoidable Moral Dilemma." *Journal of Value Inquiry,* vol. 9, Winter 1975, pp. 282–302. Humber, defending the conservative view on the morality of abortion, examines and rejects what he identifies as the major defenses of abortion. He also contends that proabortion arguments are typically so poor that they can only be viewed as "after-the-fact-rationalizations."

MAPPES, THOMAS A., and JANE S. ZEMBATY, eds.: *Biomedical Ethics.* New York: McGraw-Hill, 1981. Chapter 9 of this extensive anthology includes a subsection on fetal research, an issue closely related to the problem of abortion. Chapter 10 includes a subsection entitled "Prenatal Diagnosis and Selective Abortion."

NOONAN, JOHN T., JR., ed.: *The Morality of Abortion: Legal and Historical Perspectives.* Cambridge, Mass.: Harvard University Press, 1970. This book contains a series of readings representing various theological perspectives on abortion. The conservative view is prominent.

SUMNER, L. W.: "Toward a Credible View of Abortion." *Canadian Journal of Philosophy,* vol. 4, September 1974, pp. 163–181. Rejecting both the conservative and liberal views on the morality of abortion, Sumner develops a "more credible, because more moderate, alternative." Following a developmental approach, he holds that the moral status of the fetus increases as the fetus develops.

THOMSON, JUDITH JARVIS: "A Defense of Abortion." *Philosophy and Public Affairs,* vol. 1, Fall 1971, pp. 47–66. In this widely discussed article, Thomson attempts to "moderate the conservative view." For the sake of argument, she grants the premise that the fetus (from conception) is a person. Still, she argues, under certain conditions abortion remains morally permissible.

TOOLEY, MICHAEL: "Abortion and Infanticide." *Philosophy and Public Affairs,* vol. 2, Fall 1972, pp. 37–65. Tooley, in this landmark defense of the liberal view on the morality of abortion, investigates the question of what properties an organism must possess in order to qualify as having a serious right to life. On his analysis, neither a fetus nor an infant can be said to have a serious right to life, and thus both abortion and infanticide are ethically acceptable.

EUTHANASIA

2

Questions about the morality of euthanasia are not new but they are debated with a new intensity in contemporary times. Recent advances in biomedical technology have made it possible to prolong human life in ways undreamed of by past generations. As a result, it is not unusual to find individuals who have lived a long and useful life now permanently incapable of functioning in any recognizably human fashion. Biological life continues; but some find it tempting to say that human life, in any meaningful sense, has ceased. In one case the patient is in an irreversible coma, reduced to a vegetative existence. In another case the patient's personality has completely deteriorated. In still another case the patient alternates inescapably between excruciating pain and drug-induced stupor. In each of these cases, the quality of human life has deteriorated. There is no longer any capacity for creative employment, intellectual pursuits, or the cultivation of interpersonal relationships. In short, in each of these three cases life seems to have been rendered meaningless in the sense that the individual has lost all capacity for normal human satisfactions. In the first case there is simply no consciousness, which is a necessary condition for deriving satisfaction. In the second case consciousness has been dulled to such an extent that there is no longer any capacity for satisfaction. In the third case excruciating pain and sedation combine to undercut the possibility of satisfaction.

At the other end of the spectrum of life, we are confronted with the severely defective newborn child. In some tragic cases, a child seems to have no significant potential for meaningful human life. For example, an anencephalic child, one born with a partial or total absence of the brain, has no prospect for human life as we know it. Biomedical technology is sometimes sufficient to sustain or at least temporarily prolong the life of a severely defective newborn, depending on the particular nature of the child's medical condition, but one question commands attention: Is the child better off dead?

Religious people pray and nonreligious people hope that death will come quickly to themselves or to loved ones who are in the midst of terminal illnesses and forced to endure pain and/or indignity. The same attitudes often prevail in the face of severely defective newborns. The prevalence of these attitudes seems to support the view, however sad, that some human beings, by virtue of their medical condition, are better off dead. But if it is true that someone is better off dead, then mercy is on the side of death, and the issue of euthanasia comes to the fore. Euthanasia, in its various forms, is the focal point of discussion in this chapter.

THE MORAL JUSTIFIABILITY OF EUTHANASIA

Discussions of the moral justifiability of euthanasia often involve distinctions which are themselves controversial. Such distinctions include that between *ordinary* and *extraordinary* means of prolonging life, that between *killing* and *allowing to die,* and that between *active* and *passive* euthanasia. Indeed, the very concept of euthanasia is controversial. In accordance with a "narrow construal of euthanasia," euthanasia is equivalent to mercy *killing*. In this view, if a physician administers a lethal dose of a drug (on grounds of mercy), this act is a paradigm of euthanasia. If, on the other hand, a physician allows the patient to die by ceasing to employ "extraordinary means" (such as a respirator), this does not count as euthanasia. J. Gay-Williams in this chapter adopts a narrow construal of euthanasia. In contrast, on a "broad construal of euthanasia," the category of euthanasia encompasses both killing and allowing to die (on grounds of mercy). Those who adopt a broad construal of euthanasia often distinguish between active euthanasia, i.e., killing, and passive euthanasia, i.e., allowing to die. Though there seem to be clear cases of killing (e.g., the lethal dose) and clear cases of allowing to die (e.g., withdrawing a respirator), there are more troublesome cases as well. Suppose a physician administers pain medication with the knowledge that the patient's life will be shortened as a result. A case of killing? Suppose a physician discontinues "ordinary means" of treatment? A case of allowing to die? Sometimes it is even said that *withdrawing* extraordinary means of life support is active ("pulling the plug!'') in a way that *withholding* extraordinary means is not. And at a time when coronary bypass surgery and hemodialysis treatments are almost routine medical procedures, just what distinguishes ordinary means from extraordinary ones? Cost? Availability? The age of the patient?

There is one further distinction, relatively uncontroversial, that is prominent in discussions of euthanasia. *Voluntary* euthanasia proceeds with the (informed) consent of the person involved. *Involuntary* euthanasia proceeds without the consent of the individual involved because the individual is *incapable* of (informed) consent.[1] The possibility of involuntary euthanasia arises, for example, in the case of comatose adults, such as the much-discussed Karen Ann Quinlan.[2] It also arises in the case of individuals who are not comatose but who are considered *incompetent,* such as Earle N. Spring, whose case is included in this chapter. The most prominent variety of involuntary euthanasia, however, involves severely defective newborns. When the voluntary/involuntary distinction is combined with the active/passive distinction, four types of euthanasia result: (1) active voluntary euthanasia, (2) passive voluntary euthanasia, (3) active involuntary euthanasia, and (4) passive involuntary euthanasia.

A very common view on the morality of euthanasia, so common that it might justifiably be termed the "standard view," may be explicated as follows: Withholding or withdrawing extraordinary means of life support is morally acceptable (under certain specifiable conditions), but mercy killing is never morally acceptable. Those who operate in accordance with the narrow conception of euthanasia would express the standard view by saying that withholding or withdrawing extraordinary means of life support is morally acceptable, but euthanasia is never morally acceptable. J. Gay-Williams expresses the standard view in just this way in this chapter. Those who operate in accordance with the broad conception of euthanasia would express the standard view by saying that *passive euthanasia* is morally acceptable (under certain specifiable conditions), but *active euthanasia* is never morally acceptable. The standard view, as officially endorsed by the American Medical Association (AMA), is vigorously attacked by James Rachels in one of this chapter's

---

[1] It is often suggested that competent adults make a "living will" in order to express their wishes with regard to the treatment they would desire, should they become incompetent. In this way, it is thought, individual autonomy is fostered and others (e.g., physicians and family) can be relieved of the responsibility for making involuntary euthanasia decisions. One well-known example of a "living will" has been promulgated by the Euthanasia Educational Council. Addressed to all those who may be concerned, the statement reads as follows:

> Death is as much a reality as birth, growth, maturity and old age—it is the one certainty of life. If the time comes when I, _____, can no longer take part in decisions for my own future, let this statement stand as an expression of my wishes, while I am still of sound mind.

> If the situation should arise in which there is no reasonable expectation of my recovery from physical or mental disability, I request that I be allowed to die and not be kept alive by artificial means or "heroic measures." I do not fear death itself as much as the indignities of deterioration, dependence and hopeless pain. I, therefore, ask that medication be mercifully administered to me to alleviate suffering even though this may hasten the moment of death.

> This request is made after careful consideration. I hope you who care for me will feel morally bound to follow its mandate. I recognize that this appears to place a heavy responsibility upon you, but it is with the intention of relieving you of such responsibility and of placing it upon myself in accordance with my strong convictions, that this statement is made.

[2] In the Quinlan case, Joseph Quinlan, the father of comatose twenty-one-year-old Karen Ann Quinlan, sought to be appointed guardian of the person and property of his daughter. As guardian, he would then authorize the discontinuance of the mechanical respirator that was thought to be sustaining the vital life processes of his daughter. Judge Muir of the Superior Court of New Jersey decided against the request of Joseph Quinlan. *In re Quinlan,* 137 N.J. Super 227 (1975). Justice Hughes of the Supreme Court of New Jersey overturned the lower-court decision. *In re Quinlan,* 70 N.J. 10, 335 A. 2d 647 (1976).

readings. Thomas D. Sullivan accuses Rachels of misconstruing the sense behind the standard view. Sullivan offers a defense of the standard view. Rachels, in turn, criticizes Sullivan's reliance on the distinction between intentional and nonintentional terminations of life and the distinction between ordinary and extraordinary means of life support.

The withholding or withdrawing of extraordinary means of life support in the case of terminally ill patients is surely an established part of medical practice, as reflected in the AMA's official endorsement of the standard view. Moreover, several religious traditions explicitly acknowledge the morality of this practice. In addition, it is widely believed that a patient has the moral (and legal) right to refuse treatment, a right that would encompass the refusal of extraordinary means of life support. Thus, despite any difficulties that might be involved in specifying what counts as "extraordinary means" of life support, there is a substantial body of opinion, perhaps something close to a consensus view, maintaining the moral legitimacy of withholding or withdrawing extraordinary means of life support in the case of terminally ill patients. There is no such consensus view on the morality of mercy killing, which will be referred to here as "active euthanasia."

Those who argue for the moral legitimacy of active euthanasia emphasize considerations of humaneness. In the case of *voluntary* active euthanasia, the humanitarian appeal is often conjoined with an appeal to the primacy of individual freedom. Thus the case for the morality of voluntary active euthanasia incorporates two basic arguments: (1) It is cruel and inhumane to refuse the plea of a terminally ill person that his or her life be mercifully ended in order to avoid future suffering and indignity. (2) Individuals should be free to do as they choose as long as their actions do not result in harm to others. Since no one is harmed by terminally ill patients undergoing active euthanasia, their freedom to have their lives ended in this fashion should not be infringed.

Those who argue against the moral legitimacy of active euthanasia (in both its voluntary and involuntary forms) rest their case on one or both of the following strategies of argument: (1) They appeal to some "sanctity of life" principle to the effect that the intentional termination of (innocent) human life is always immoral. Sullivan advances this sort of argument in his defense of the standard view. (2) They advance arguments based on considerations of utility. On a *utilitarian view of morality,* actions and social policies should be judged right or wrong solely on the basis of their tendency to produce good or bad consequences. According to the *principle of utility,* that action or social practice is morally correct which in the circumstances will tend to produce the greatest possible balance of good over evil for members of the group affected. Opponents of active euthanasia advancing utilitarian arguments bring out the possible bad consequences of adopting active euthanasia as a social policy. Among the predicted bad consequences are premature deaths resulting from misdiagnosis and a lessening of respect for human life that might have extremely damaging consequences for society.

THE TREATMENT OF DEFECTIVE NEWBORNS

The well-established medical practice of allowing severely defective newborns to die, often identified as the practice of passive (involuntary) euthanasia, has recently made its way into the public consciousness. As a result, both the legality and the morality of this practice have been subjected to intense scrutiny. It is important to realize that "allowing to die," in this context, includes what most people would regard as the withholding of ordinary, not just extraordinary, medical treatment. For example, a severely defective newborn might be denied the antibiotics necessary to fight pneumonia, though the pneumonia is totally unrelated to the condition which renders the child severely defective.

The central moral question with regard to the treatment of defective newborns may be identified as follows: Under what conditions, if any, is it morally acceptable to allow a severely defective newborn to die? Two other closely related issues are also worthy of mention. The first has to do with the procedural question: Who should make the decision to treat or not treat?[3] It has sometimes been argued that the decision is a medical one, to be made by physicians. But the more common view is that the parents are the appropriate decision makers, as informed by consultation with physicians and (perhaps) as limited by boundaries set by society at large. The second issue worthy of mention has to do with the moral legitimacy of active euthanasia. If it is morally acceptable to allow a severely defective newborn to die, on grounds that the child is better off dead, then is it not also morally acceptable (perhaps morally preferable) to painlessly kill the child?

Broadly speaking, there are three different views on the moral acceptability of allowing severely defective newborns to die.

1. It is morally acceptable to allow a severely defective newborn to die if and only if there is no significant potential for a meaningful human existence. Defenders of this view are firmly committed to quality-of-life judgments, maintaining that certain newborn children are better off dead. Importantly, in this view, the cost of caring for severely defective newborns is considered an irrelevant factor in the decision to treat or not treat.

2. It is morally acceptable to allow a severely defective newborn to die if at least one of the following conditions is satisfied: (a) There is no significant potential for a meaningful human existence; (b) The emotional and/or financial hardship of caring for the severely defective newborn child would constitute a grave burden for the family. It is the introduction of the cost factor that distinguishes view (2) from view (1). Defenders of this second view, such as H. Tristram Engelhardt, Jr., in this chapter, often maintain that the newborn child does not have the status of personhood, thereby defending the legitimacy of the cost factor.

3. It is never morally acceptable to allow a severely defective newborn to die. Or, to put it somewhat more cautiously, it would never be morally acceptable to withhold treatment from a severely defective newborn unless it would be morally acceptable to withhold such treatment from a normal infant. That is, whatever treatment standard medical practice would dictate as appropriate for a normal infant must be provided for the severely defective newborn as well. In this view, it is usually presumed that a newborn child has the status of personhood and, however severely defective, has a right to life. Defenders of this view, such as Judge David G. Roberts in this chapter, often argue against the validity of quality-of-life judgments (as featured in both of the above views) as well as the validity of the cost factor (as featured exclusively in the second view).

Thomas A. Mappes and Jane S. Zembaty

---

[3]The same procedural question is raised in the case of incompetent adults, such as Earle N. Spring.

JUDGE CHRISTOPHER J. ARMSTRONG

OPINION IN THE *MATTER OF EARLE N. SPRING*

Christopher J. Armstrong is a graduate of Yale Law School. He was admitted to the bar in 1961 and appointed to the lifetime position of associate justice of the Massachusetts Appeals Court in 1972.

In January of 1979, the son and wife of Earle N. Spring petitioned a probate court for legal authorization to discontinue his life-prolonging medical treatment. (The son had earlier been appointed temporary guardian of his father, who was declared legally incompetent.) At that time Earle N. Spring, born in 1901, was suffering from "end-stage kidney disease" which required him to undergo hemodialysis three days a week, five hours a day. He was also diagnosed as suffering from "chronic organic brain syndrome or senility" and was completely confused and disoriented. Both the kidney disease and the senility were considered permanent and irreversible, and there was no prospect of a medical breakthrough that would provide a cure for either disease. The prognosis was that, without the dialysis treatment, Spring would die; with it he might survive for months or even years.

The probate court judge appointed a guardian for Spring, and the guardian opposed the cessation of treatment. The judge, however, rendered a judgment authorizing the discontinuance of further life-prolonging treatment. In response, the court-appointed guardian appealed the judgment to the Massachusetts Appeals Court. The higher court, whose reasoning appears here in the opinion of Judge Armstrong, upheld the judgment of the lower court. Though further legal moves were made by the court-appointed guardian, Spring died in April of 1980, more than a year after the initial petition was filed and prior to any final legal resolution.

Judge Armstrong affirms an individual's right to refuse life-prolonging treatment, barring some overriding state interest. If the individual is *legally incompetent,* however, the problem is to determine whether the incompetent person, if competent, would want life-prolonging treatment to be discontinued. Taking into account a host of factual considerations, Judge Armstrong affirms the finding of the probate court judge: Earle N. Spring, if competent, would wish to discontinue dialysis treatments. Judge Armstrong insists throughout that the judgment of Spring's family should be accorded substantial weight in determining what choice Spring, if competent, would make.

The general parameters of our law applicable to the giving or withholding of medical treatment in cases of incompetency were recently spelled out in *Superintendent of Belchertown State Sch. v. Saikewicz* (1977). . . .

The *Saikewicz* case held that a person does not through incompetency lose his right to be "free from nonconsensual invasion of his bodily integrity"; that "the substantive rights of the competent and the incompetent person are the same in regard to the right to decline potentially life-prolonging treatment"; and that the conceptual mechanism by which the right of the incompetent person to refuse medical treatment is to be effectuated is the doctrine of "substituted judgment," by which is meant the judgment that the incompetent person would himself make in the circumstances if he were competent to do so. "[T]he goal is to determine with as much accuracy as possible the wants and needs of the individual involved."

Massachusetts Appeals Court. Adv. Sh. (1979) 2469.

By the terms of this framework, the present case pivots on the finding made by the judge that, in these circumstances, the ward would wish to have the dialysis treatments discontinued. This finding did not rest on any expression of such an intention by the ward, and the guardian contended in the trial court that, absent such an expression of intent by the ward when he was competent, such a finding could not appropriately be made. The judge correctly rejected that contention: carried to a conclusion, it would largely stifle the very rights of privacy and personal dignity which the *Saikewicz* case sought to secure for incompetent persons. The essence of that case is that when a person becomes incompetent to formulate a lucid judgment he is not thereby stripped of the right of choice enjoyed by others in the making of treatment decisions. An expression of opinion by the patient when competent would obviously be of great assistance, especially where the expression indicates a contemplation or understanding of the circumstances later obtaining; but the right secured by the *Saikewicz* case is not conditioned on the patient's having had the presence of mind to formulate such an expression of his wishes when competent.

The judge's finding that the ward would wish to have dialysis terminated appears to have been determined in the light of eight subsidiary considerations: (1) the fact that he had led an active, robust, independent life; (2) the fact that he has fallen into a pitiable state of physical dependence and mental incapacity; (3) the fact that no improvement can be expected in his physical or mental condition, but only further deterioration; (4) the fact that dialysis treatments exact a significant toll in terms of frequency and duration of treatments and uncomfortable side effects; (5) the fact that the ward has no understanding of the nature and purpose of his treatments and cannot cooperate and does not reliably acquiesce in their administration; (6) the fact that his wife and son, with whom the ward had and has a very close relationship, feel that it would be his wish not to continue with dialysis in the present circumstances; (7) the fact that it is their wish that dialysis not be administered; and (8) the fact that the attending physician recommends against a continuation of dialysis treatments in these circumstances. We hold that, in light of these considerations, the judge's general finding that the ward would wish not to submit to further dialysis treatments was warranted by the evidence. . . .

Certain of the listed considerations require discussion. The guardian ad litem contends that the ward's condition of mental incapacity may not be appropriately taken into account without violating the principle stated in the *Saikewicz* case, that the "supposed ability of [the patient] . . . to appreciate or experience life has no place in the decision. . . ." We think that the guardian's contention involves a misapplication of that principle. In context, the court was making the important points that "the value of life under the law [has] no relation to intelligence or social position" and that the State's interest in the preservation of life is no less in the case of a profoundly mentally retarded person such as Joseph Saikewicz than it is in the case of one more gifted. That principle is of particular significance in applying the balancing test between the various State interests in the preservation of life and the interest of the individual "in avoiding significant, nonconsensual invasion of his bodily integrity." But a patient's mental condition will in certain circumstances be a relevant factor in determining whether he would elect, if competent to do so, to undergo an intrusive life-saving or life-prolonging treatment. "[T]he decision in cases such as this should be that which would be made by the incompetent person, if that person were competent, but taking into account the present and future incompetency of the individual as one of the factors which would necessarily enter into the decision-making process of the competent person." That statement seems fully in accord with common experience; it is hardly unusual to hear people observe that they would not wish to cling to life for long after their mental faculties have been taken from them. That point of view would not have been relevant in the case of Joseph Saikewicz, for he had known no other condition; but it can be appropriately considered in the case of one who has been reduced in a short time from a state of physical and mental vigor to one of total and irreversible dependence and incompetency, when the evidence generally suggests that that state of incompetency would be a factor which the patient would himself take into account in making a treatment decision if he were able to do so.

Another factor which should be touched on is the role of the family and the recommendation of the attending physician in applying the substituted judgment test. . . . It is evident that we are dealing with a close-knit family unit, with a long history of mutual love, concern and support. In such circumstances the decision of the family, particularly where that decision is in accord with the recommendation of the attending physician, is of particular importance, both as evidence of the decision the patient himself would make in the circumstances and, at a later stage of analysis, as a factor lending added weight to the patient's interest in privacy and personal dignity in the face of any countervailing State interests.

Probably the strongest factor which would, standing by itself, tend towards a contrary determination of the ward's wishes is the fact that, at a time when he was mentally competent (although subject to some degree of impairment), he himself consented to, or at least acquiesced in, the initiation of dialysis treatments. But conditions were different at that time. The ward could then understand the necessity for the treatments and the accompanying discomfort and cooperate in their administration. When the treatments were initiated, it was hoped that they would restore the ward's ability to enjoy a relatively normal existence, subject of course to the burden of lengthy and uncomfortable treatments far from home three times a week, but otherwise permitting him the pleasures of life with his family in familiar and comfortable surroundings. Unfortunately, this hope did not and cannot materialize; he is, and must remain, institutionalized, heavily sedated to restrain his hostile impulses, uncooperative towards his arduous maintenance program, insensible of his family and his situation. There now obtains a very different set of circumstances from those in which the decision to undertake dialysis was made; whether the present circumstances would influence the ward to make a different decision is obviously a question not of law but of fact, one which the trier of fact is in a position superior to that of an appellate court to resolve. . . .

It is thus established as a fact that it would be the ward's wish, if competent, to discontinue dialysis treatments. But because the ward is an incompetent person, towards whom the State stands in the relation of parens patriae, his "wish," as thus determined, is not necessarily decisive of the case. The general rule is that "[t]he constitutional right to privacy . . . is an expression of the sensitivity of individual free choice and self-determination as fundamental constituents of life. The value of life as so perceived is lessened not by a decision to refuse treatment, but by the failure to allow a competent human being the right of choice." . . . Where there is no occasion for State intervention in the treatment decision, "[t]he law protects [the patient's] right to make [his] own decision to accept or reject treatment, whether that decision is wise or unwise."

But the case law in this area recognizes several situations in which the State may intrude on an individual's freedom to consent or not consent, as he wishes, to medical treatment, and require that his right to refuse medical treatment be weighed in the balance against various countervailing State interests. . . .

[The] countervailing interests of the State . . . cannot overcome the right of private choice in the circumstances presented. The policy against suicide and the protection of innocent third parties are of no relevance. The ethics of the medical profession do not present a conflict: the doctor who is treating the ward supports the family's view that further treatment is inappropriate. The general State interest in the preservation of life—

most weighty where the patient, properly treated, can return to reasonable health, without great suffering, and a decision to avoid treatment would be aberrational—carries far less weight where the patient is approaching the end of his normal life span, where his afflictions are incapacitating, and where the best that medicine can offer is an extension of suffering. Such a case presents instead the recurrent and always difficult ethical problem: To what extent should aggressive medical treatments be administered to preserve life after life itself, for reasons beyond anyone's control, has become irreversibly burdensome?

The law does not furnish an answer to that question. It leaves the answer to the person whose life is involved, if that person is competent to make the decision for himself. Where the person is incompetent, the law intervenes, not to displace the traditional role of the family and the attending physician in weighing that question, but to protect the rights of the incompetent person by determining, as best it can, what his wish would be, and ensuring that that wish is carried out if it does not violate the policy of the State or the ethics of the medical profession. If the patient is fortunate enough to have close family, as does the ward in this case, and where they and the attending physician are at one in recommending a course of treatment, or non-treatment, as that which is in the best interests of the patient and which they feel he would choose, the law should and, we think, does accord their judgment substantial weight not only in determining what course of action the patient would himself choose in the circumstances if he were able to do so, but also in determining the appropriate resolution of conflicting interests. . . .

QUESTIONS

1. What kinds of considerations should be taken into account in deciding whether to discontinue the use of respirators or other life-sustaining apparatus or treatment? (a) The age of the patient? (b) The social responsibilities of the patient? (c) The need of others for the equipment? (d) The length of time the patient may live without the treatment or equipment? (e) The quality of the life the patient is living? Can you suggest any other possible considerations?
2. Who should decide when the use of life-sustaining treatment should be discontinued? The patients? The physicians? A hospital ethics committee? The immediate family? The courts?

J. GAY-WILLIAMS

THE WRONGFULNESS OF EUTHANASIA

J. Gay-Williams has requested that no biographical information be provided here.

Gay-Williams, who adopts a narrow construal of euthanasia, defines it as "intentionally taking the life of a presumably hopeless person." He refuses to use the expression "passive euthanasia" to describe actions that are labeled in this way by those who adopt a broad construal of euthanasia. Gay-Williams does not consider these latter actions morally unacceptable, but he does consider all actions falling in the category of euthanasia (as he defines it) morally unacceptable. (Thus, in effect, he defends the standard view on the morality of euthanasia.) He is opposed to euthanasia for three reasons: (1) It violates the natural inclination to preserve life and, therefore, goes against nature; (2) euthanasia may work against our own interest if we practice it or allow it to be practiced on us; and (3) accepting euthanasia as a practice may result in certain undesirable long-term consequences.

My impression is that euthanasia—the idea, if not the practice—is slowly gaining acceptance within our society. Cynics might attribute this to an increasing tendency to devalue human life, but I do not believe this is the major factor. The acceptance is much more likely to be the result of unthinking sympathy and benevolence. Well-publicized, tragic stories like that of Karen Quinlan elicit from us deep feelings of compassion. We think to ourselves, "She and her family would be better off if she were dead." It is an easy step from this very human response to the view that if someone (and others) would be better off dead, then it must be all right to kill that person.[1] Although I respect the compassion that leads to this conclusion, I believe the conclusion is wrong. I want to show that euthanasia is wrong. It is inherently wrong, but it is also wrong judged from the standpoints of self-interest and of practical effects.

Before presenting my arguments to support this claim, it would be well to define "euthanasia." An essential aspect of euthanasia is that it involves taking a human life, either one's own or that of another. Also, the person whose life is taken must be someone who is believed to be suffering from some disease or injury from which recovery cannot reasonably be expected. Finally, the action must be deliberate and intentional. Thus, euthanasia is intentionally taking the life of a presumably hopeless person. Whether the life is one's own or that of another, the taking of it is still euthanasia.

It is important to be clear about the deliberate and intentional aspect of the killing. If a hopeless person is given an injection of the wrong drug by mistake and this causes his death, this is wrongful killing but not euthanasia. The killing cannot be the result of accident. Furthermore, if the person is given an injection of a drug that is believed to be necessary to treat his disease or better his condition and the person dies as a result, then this is neither wrongful killing nor euthanasia. The intention was to make the patient well, not kill him. Similarly, when a patient's condition is such that it is not reasonable to hope that any medical procedures or treatments will save his life, a failure to implement the procedures or treatments is not euthanasia. If the person dies, this will be as a result of his injuries or disease and not because of his failure to receive treatment.

The failure to continue treatment after it has been realized that the patient has little chance of benefitting from it has been characterized by some as "passive euthanasia." This phrase is misleading and mistaken.[2] In such cases, the person involved is not killed (the first essential aspect of euthanasia), nor is the death of the person intended by the withholding of additional treatment (the third essential aspect of euthanasia). The aim may be to spare the person additional and unjustifiable pain, to save him from the indignities of hopeless manipulations, and to avoid increasing the financial and emotional burden on his family. When I buy a pencil it is so that I can use it to write, not to contribute to an increase in the gross national product. This may be the unintended consequence of my action, but it is not the aim of my action. So it is with failing to continue the treatment of a dying person. I

From Ronald Munson, *Intervention and Reflection: Basic Issues in Medical Ethics.* Copyright © 1979 by Wadsworth Publishing Company, Inc., Belmont, California 94002. Reprinted by permission of the publisher.
[1]For a sophisticated defense of this position see Philippa Foot, "Euthanasia," *Philosophy and Public Affairs,* vol. 6 (1977), pp. 85–112. Foot does not endorse the radical conclusion that euthanasia, voluntary and involuntary, is always right.
[2]James Rachels rejects the distinction between active and passive euthanasia as morally irrelevant in his "Active and Passive Euthanasia," *New England Journal of Medicine,* vol. 292, pp. 78–80. But see the criticism by Foot, pp. 100–103.

intend his death no more than I intend to reduce the GNP by not using medical supplies. His is an unintended dying, and so-called "passive euthanasia" is not euthanasia at all.

1. THE ARGUMENT FROM NATURE

Every human being has a natural inclination to continue living. Our reflexes and responses fit us to fight attackers, flee wild animals, and dodge out of the way of trucks. In our daily lives we exercise the caution and care necessary to protect ourselves. Our bodies are similarly structured for survival right down to the molecular level. When we are cut, our capillaries seal shut, our blood clots, and fibrogen is produced to start the process of healing the wound. When we are invaded by bacteria, antibodies are produced to fight against the alien organisms, and their remains are swept out of the body by special cells designed for clean-up work.

Euthanasia does violence to this natural goal of survival. It is literally acting against nature because all the processes of nature are bent towards the end of bodily survival. Euthanasia defeats these subtle mechanisms in a way that, in a particular case, disease and injury might not.

It is possible, but not necessary, to make an appeal to revealed religion in this connection.[3] Man as trustee of his body acts against God, its rightful possessor, when he takes his own life. He also violates the commandment to hold life sacred and never to take it without just and compelling cause. But since this appeal will persuade only those who are prepared to accept that religion has access to revealed truths, I shall not employ this line of argument.

It is enough, I believe, to recognize that the organization of the human body and our patterns of behavioral responses make the continuation of life a natural goal. By reason alone, then, we can recognize that euthanasia sets us against our own nature.[4] Furthermore, in doing so, euthanasia does violence to our dignity. Our dignity comes from seeking our ends. When one of our goals is survival, and actions are taken that eliminate that goal, then our natural dignity suffers. Unlike animals, we are conscious through reason of our nature and our ends. Euthanasia involves acting as if this dual nature—inclination towards survival and awareness of this as an end—did not exist. Thus, euthanasia denies our basic human character and requires that we regard ourselves or others as something less than fully human.

2. THE ARGUMENT FROM SELF-INTEREST

The above arguments are, I believe, sufficient to show that euthanasia is inherently wrong. But there are reasons for considering it wrong when judged by standards other than reason. Because death is final and irreversible, euthanasia contains within it the possibility that we will work against our own interest if we practice it or allow it to be practiced on us.

Contemporary medicine has high standards of excellence and a proven record of accomplishment, but it does not possess perfect and complete knowledge. A mistaken diagnosis is possible, and so is a mistaken prognosis. Consequently, we may believe that we are dying of a disease when, as a matter of fact, we may not be. We may think that we have no hope of recovery when, as a matter of fact, our chances are quite good. In such circumstances, if euthanasia were permitted, we would die needlessly. Death is final and the chance of error too great to approve the practice of euthanasia.

[3]For a defense of this view see J. V. Sullivan, "The Immorality of Euthanasia," in Marvin Kohl, ed., *Beneficent Euthanasia* (Buffalo, New York: Prometheus Books, 1975), pp. 34–44.
[4]This point is made by Ray V. McIntyre in "Voluntary Euthanasia: The Ultimate Perversion," *Medical Counterpoint*, vol. 2, pp. 26–29.

Also, there is always the possibility that an experimental procedure or a hitherto untried technique will pull us through. We should at least keep this option open, but euthanasia closes it off. Furthermore, spontaneous remission does occur in many cases. For no apparent reason, a patient simply recovers when those all around him, including his physicians, expected him to die. Euthanasia would just guarantee their expectations and leave no room for the "miraculous" recoveries that frequently occur.

Finally, knowing that we can take our life at any time (or ask another to take it) might well incline us to give up too easily. The will to live is strong in all of us, but it can be weakened by pain and suffering and feelings of hopelessness. If during a bad time we allow ourselves to be killed, we never have a chance to reconsider. Recovery from a serious illness requires that we fight for it, and anything that weakens our determination by suggesting that there is an easy way out is ultimately against our own interest. Also, we may be inclined towards euthanasia because of our concern for others. If we see our sickness and suffering as an emotional and financial burden on our family, we may feel that to leave our life is to make their lives easier.[5] The very presence of the possibility of euthanasia may keep us from surviving when we might.

3. THE ARGUMENT FROM PRACTICAL EFFECTS

Doctors and nurses are, for the most part, totally committed to saving lives. A life lost is, for them, almost a personal failure, an insult to their skills and knowledge. Euthanasia as a practice might well alter this. It could have a corrupting influence so that in any case that is severe doctors and nurses might not try hard enough to save the patient. They might decide that the patient would simply be "better off dead" and take the steps necessary to make that come about. This attitude could then carry over to their dealings with patients less seriously ill. The result would be an overall decline in the quality of medical care.

Finally, euthanasia as a policy is a slippery slope. A person apparently hopelessly ill may be allowed to take his own life. Then he may be permitted to deputize others to do it for him should he no longer be able to act. The judgment of others then becomes the ruling factor. Already at this point euthanasia is not personal and voluntary, for others are acting "on behalf of" the patient as they see fit. This may well incline them to act on behalf of other patients who have not authorized them to exercise their judgment. It is only a short step, then, from voluntary euthanasia (self-inflicted or authorized), to directed euthanasia administered to a patient who has given no authorization, to involuntary euthanasia conducted as part of a social policy.[6] Recently many psychiatrists and sociologists have argued that we define as "mental illness" those forms of behavior that we disapprove of.[7] This gives us license then to lock up those who display the behavior. The category of the "hopelessly ill" provides the possibility of even worse abuse. Embedded in a social policy, it would give society or its representatives the authority to eliminate all those who might be considered too "ill" to function normally any longer. The dangers of euthanasia are too great to all to run the risk of approving it in any form. The first slippery step may well lead to a serious and harmful fall.

I hope that I have succeeded in showing why the benevolence that inclines us to give approval of euthanasia is misplaced. Euthanasia is inherently wrong because it violates the nature and dignity of human beings. But even those who are not convinced by this must be persuaded that the potential personal and social dangers inherent in euthanasia are sufficient to forbid our approving it either as a personal practice or as a public policy.

[5]See McIntyre, p. 28.
[6]See Sullivan, "Immorality of Euthanasia," pp. 34–44, for a fuller argument in support of this view.
[7]See, for example, Thomas S. Szasz, *The Myth of Mental Illness*, rev. ed. (New York: Harper & Row, 1974).

Suffering is surely a terrible thing, and we have a clear duty to comfort those in need and to ease their suffering when we can. But suffering is also a natural part of life with values for the individual and for others that we should not overlook. We may legitimately seek for others and for ourselves an easeful death, as Arthur Dyck has pointed out.[8] Euthanasia, however, is not just an easeful death. It is a wrongful death. Euthanasia is not just dying. It is killing.

QUESTIONS

1. What is euthanasia? Is it always morally wrong?
2. Gay-Williams contends that "euthanasia as a policy is a slippery slope." Is the slippery-slope argument developed by Gay-Williams a substantial argument or a rhetorical "scare tactic" as it is sometimes alleged to be?

JAMES RACHELS

ACTIVE AND PASSIVE EUTHANASIA

James Rachels is dean of the school of humanities at the University of Alabama in Birmingham. As a philosopher who specializes in ethics, he is the author of such articles as "Why Privacy Is Important" and "On Moral Absolutism." He is also the editor of *Moral Problems: A Collection of Philosophical Essays* (1971, 3d ed., 1979) and *Understanding Moral Philosophy* (1976).

Rachels identifies the standard (conventional) view on the morality of euthanasia as the doctrine which permits passive euthanasia but rejects active euthanasia. He then argues that the conventional doctrine may be challenged for four reasons. First, active euthanasia is in many cases more humane than passive euthanasia. Second, the conventional doctrine leads to decisions concerning life and death on irrelevant grounds. Third, the doctrine rests on a distinction between killing and letting die that itself has no moral importance. Fourth, the most common arguments in favor of the doctrine are invalid.

The distinction between active and passive euthanasia is thought to be crucial for medical ethics. The idea is that it is permissible, at least in some cases, to withhold treatment and allow a patient to die, but it is never permissible to take any direct action designed to kill the patient. This doctrine seems to be accepted by most doctors, and it is endorsed in a statement adopted by the House of Delegates of the American Medical Association on December 4, 1973:

> The intentional termination of the life of one human being by another—mercy killing—is contrary to that for which the medical profession stands and is contrary to the policy of the American Medical Association.

[8]Arthur Dyck, "Beneficent Euthanasia and Benemortasia," Kohl, *op. cit.*, pp. 117–129.
Reprinted by permission from *The New England Journal of Medicine*, vol. 292, no. 2 (Jan. 9, 1975), pp. 78–80.

The cessation of the employment of extraordinary means to prolong the life of the body when there is irrefutable evidence that biological death is imminent is the decision of the patient and/or his immediate family. The advice and judgment of the physician should be freely available to the patient and/or his immediate family.

However, a strong case can be made against this doctrine. In what follows I will set out some of the relevant arguments, and urge doctors to reconsider their views on this matter.

To begin with a familiar type of situation, a patient who is dying of incurable cancer of the throat is in terrible pain, which can no longer be satisfactorily alleviated. He is certain to die within a few days, even if present treatment is continued, but he does not want to go on living for those days since the pain is unbearable. So he asks the doctor for an end to it, and his family joins in the request.

Suppose the doctor agrees to withhold treatment, as the conventional doctrine says he may. The justification for his doing so is that the patient is in terrible agony, and since he is going to die anyway, it would be wrong to prolong his suffering needlessly. But now notice this. If one simply withholds treatment, it may take the patient longer to die, and so he may suffer more than he would if more direct action were taken and a lethal injection given. This fact provides strong reason for thinking that, once the initial decision not to prolong his agony has been made, active euthanasia is actually preferable to passive euthanasia, rather than the reverse. To say otherwise is to endorse the option that leads to more suffering rather than less, and is contrary to the humanitarian impulse that prompts the decision not to prolong his life in the first place.

Part of my point is that the process of being "allowed to die" can be relatively slow and painful, whereas being given a lethal injection is relatively quick and painless. Let me give a different sort of example. In the United States about one in 600 babies is born with Down's syndrome. Most of these babies are otherwise healthy—that is, with only the usual pediatric care, they will proceed to an otherwise normal infancy. Some, however, are born with congenital defects such as intestinal obstructions that require operations if they are to live. Sometimes, the parents and the doctor will decide not to operate, and let the infant die. Anthony Shaw describes what happens then:

> . . . When surgery is denied [the doctor] must try to keep the infant from suffering while natural forces sap the baby's life away. As a surgeon whose natural inclination is to use the scalpel to fight off death, standing by and watching a salvageable baby die is the most emotionally exhausting experience I know. It is easy at a conference, in a theoretical discussion, to decide that such infants should be allowed to die. It is altogether different to stand by in the nursery and watch as dehydration and infection wither a tiny being over hours and days. This is a terrible ordeal for me and the hospital staff—much more so than for the parents who never set foot in the nursery.[1]

I can understand why some people are opposed to all euthanasia, and insist that such infants must be allowed to live. I think I can also understand why other people favor destroying these babies quickly and painlessly. But why should anyone favor letting "dehydration and infection wither a tiny being over hours and days?" The doctrine that says that a baby may be allowed to dehydrate and wither, but may not be given an injection that would end its life without suffering, seems so patently cruel as to require no further refutation. The strong language is not intended to offend, but only to put the point in the clearest possible way.

---

[1]A. Shaw: "Doctor, Do We Have a Choice?" *The New York Times Magazine*, Jan. 30, 1972, p. 54.

My second argument is that the conventional doctrine leads to decisions concerning life and death made on irrelevant grounds.

Consider again the case of the infants with Down's syndrome who need operations for congenital defects unrelated to the syndrome to live. Sometimes, there is no operation, and the baby dies, but when there is no such defect, the baby lives on. Now, an operation such as that to remove an intestinal obstruction is not prohibitively difficult. The reason why such operations are not performed in these cases is, clearly, that the child has Down's syndrome and the parents and doctor judge that because of that fact it is better for the child to die.

But notice that this situation is absurd, no matter what view one takes of the lives and potentials of such babies. If the life of such an infant is worth preserving, what does it matter if it needs a simple operation? Or, if one thinks it better that such a baby should not live on, what difference does it make that it happens to have an unobstructed intestinal tract? In either case, the matter of life and death is being decided on irrelevant grounds. It is the Down's syndrome, and not the intestines, that is the issue. The matter should be decided, if at all, on that basis, and not be allowed to depend on the essentially irrelevant question of whether the intestinal tract is blocked.

What makes this situation possible, of course, is the idea that when there is an intestinal blockage, one can "let the baby die," but when there is no such defect there is nothing that can be done, for one must not "kill" it. The fact that this idea leads to such results as deciding life or death on irrelevant grounds is another good reason why the doctrine should be rejected.

One reason why so many people think that there is an important moral difference between active and passive euthanasia is that they think killing someone is morally worse than letting someone die. But is it? Is killing, in itself, worse than letting die? To investigate this issue, two cases may be considered that are exactly alike except that one involves killing whereas the other involves letting someone die. Then, it can be asked whether this difference makes any difference to the moral assessments. It is important that the cases be exactly alike, except for this one difference, since otherwise one cannot be confident that it is this difference and not some other that accounts for any variation in the assessments of the two cases. So, let us consider this pair of cases:

In the first, Smith stands to gain a large inheritance if anything should happen to his six-year-old cousin. One evening while the child is taking his bath, Smith sneaks into the bathroom and drowns the child, and then arranges things so that it will look like an accident.

In the second, Jones also stands to gain if anything should happen to his six-year-old cousin. Like Smith, Jones sneaks in planning to drown the child in his bath. However, just as he enters the bathroom Jones sees the child slip and hit his head, and fall face down in the water. Jones is delighted; he stands by, ready to push the child's head back under if it is necessary, but it is not necessary. With only a little thrashing about the child drowns all by himself, "accidentally," as Jones watches and does nothing.

Now Smith killed the child, whereas Jones "merely" let the child die. That is the only difference between them. Did either man behave better, from a moral point of view? If the difference between killing and letting die were in itself a morally important matter, one should say that Jones's behavior was less reprehensible than Smith's. But does one really want to say that? I think not. In the first place, both men acted from the same motive, personal gain, and both had exactly the same end in view when they acted. It may be inferred from Smith's conduct that he is a bad man, although that judgment may be withdrawn or modified if certain further facts are learned about him—for example, that he is mentally deranged. But would not the very same thing be inferred about Jones from his conduct? And would not the same further considerations also be relevant to any modification of this judgment? Moreover, suppose Jones pleaded, in his own defense, "After all, I didn't do anything except just stand there and watch the child drown. I didn't kill him; I only let him die." Again, if letting die were in itself less bad than killing, this defense should have at least some weight. But it does not. Such a "defense" can only be regarded as a grotesque perversion of moral reasoning. Morally speaking, it is no defense at all.

Now, it may be pointed out, quite properly, that the cases of euthanasia with which doctors are concerned are not like this at all. They do not involve personal gain or the destruction of normal healthy children. Doctors are concerned only with cases in which the patient's life is of no further use to him, or in which the patient's life has become or will soon become a terrible burden. However, the point is the same in these cases: the bare difference between killing and letting die does not, in itself, make a moral difference. If a doctor lets a patient die, for humane reasons, he is in the same moral position as if he had given the patient a lethal injection for humane reasons. If his decision was wrong—if, for example, the patient's illness was in fact curable—the decision would be equally regrettable no matter which method was used to carry it out. And if the doctor's decision was the right one, the method used is not in itself important.

The AMA policy statement isolates the crucial issue very well; the crucial issue is "the intentional termination of the life of one human being by another." But after identifying this issue, and forbidding "mercy killing," the statement goes on to deny that the cessation of treatment is the intentional termination of a life. This is where the mistake comes in, for what is the cessation of treatment, in these circumstances, if it is not "the intentional termination of the life of one human being by another?" Of course it is exactly that, and if it were not, there would be no point to it.

Many people will find this judgment hard to accept. One reason, I think, is that it is very easy to conflate the question of whether killing is, in itself, worse than letting die, with the very different question of whether most actual cases of killing are more reprehensible than most actual cases of letting die. Most actual cases of killing are clearly terrible (think, for example, of all the murders reported in the newspapers), and one hears of such cases every day. On the other hand, one hardly ever hears of a case of letting die, except for the actions of doctors who are motivated by humanitarian reasons. So one learns to think of killing in a much worse light than of letting die. But this does not mean that there is something about killing that makes it in itself worse than letting die, for it is not the bare difference between killing and letting die that makes the difference in these cases. Rather, the other factors—the murderer's motive of personal gain, for example, contrasted with the doctor's humanitarian motivation—account for different reactions to the different cases.

I have argued that killing is not in itself any worse than letting die; if my contention is right, it follows that active euthanasia is not any worse than passive euthanasia. What arguments can be given on the other side? The most common, I believe, is the following:

"The important difference between active and passive euthanasia is that, in passive euthanasia, the doctor does not do anything to bring about the patient's death. The doctor does nothing, and the patient dies of whatever ills already afflict him. In active euthanasia, however, the doctor does something to bring about the patient's death: he kills him. The doctor who gives the patient with cancer a lethal injection has himself caused his patient's death; whereas if he merely ceases treatment, the cancer is the cause of the death."

A number of points need to be made here. The first is that it is not exactly correct to say that in passive euthanasia the doctor does nothing, for he does do one thing that is very important: he lets the patient die. "Letting someone die" is certainly different, in some respects, from other types of action—mainly in that it is a kind of action that one may perform by way of not performing certain other actions. For example, one may let a patient die by way of not giving medication, just as one may insult someone by way of not shaking his hand. But for any purpose of moral assessment, it is a type of action nonetheless. The decision to let a patient die is subject to moral appraisal in the same way that a decision to kill him would be subject to moral appraisal: it may be assessed as wise or unwise, compassionate or sadistic, right or wrong. If a doctor deliberately let a patient die who was suffering from a routinely curable illness, the doctor would certainly be to blame for what he had done, just as he would be to blame if he had needlessly killed the patient. Charges against him would then be appropriate. If so, it would be no defense at all for him to insist that he didn't "do anything." He would have done something very serious indeed, for he let his patient die.

Fixing the cause of death may be very important from a legal point of view, for it may determine whether criminal charges are brought against the doctor. But I do not think that this notion can be used to show a moral difference between active and passive euthanasia. The reason why it is considered bad to be the cause of someone's death is that death is regarded as a great evil—and so it is. However, if it has been decided that euthanasia— even passive euthanasia—is desirable in a given case, it has also been decided that in this instance death is no greater an evil than the patient's continued existence. And if this is true, the usual reason for not wanting to be the cause of someone's death simply does not apply.

Finally, doctors may think that all of this is only of academic interest—the sort of thing that philosophers may worry about but that has no practical bearing on their own work. After all, doctors must be concerned about the legal consequences of what they do, and active euthanasia is clearly forbidden by the law. But even so, doctors should also be concerned with the fact that the law is forcing upon them a moral doctrine that may well be indefensible, and has a considerable effect on their practices. Of course, most doctors are not now in the position of being coerced in this matter, for they do not regard themselves as merely going along with what the law requires. Rather, in statements such as the AMA policy statement that I have quoted, they are endorsing this doctrine as a central point of medical ethics. In that statement, active euthanasia is condemned not merely as illegal but as "contrary to that for which the medical profession stands," whereas passive euthanasia is approved. However, the preceding considerations suggest that there is really no moral difference between the two, considered in themselves (there may be important moral differences in some cases in their *consequences,* but, as I pointed out, these differences may make active euthanasia, and not passive euthanasia, the morally preferable option). So, whereas doctors may have to discriminate between active and passive euthanasia to satisfy the law, they should not do any more than that. In particular, they should not give the distinction any added authority and weight by writing it into official statements of medical ethics.

QUESTIONS

1. If you were a physician, what would you do when the parents of a baby with Down's syndrome decided against surgery? Would you let the baby slowly die from dehydration and starvation, or would you take some active step to end the baby's life? Would you take the case to court to force the surgery? How would you justify your decision?

2. Can you rewrite the two paragraphs Rachels cites from the AMA statement so that your version of the statement avoids Rachels's criticisms?

3. Active euthanasia is illegal in all fifty states. Should it be legalized under specified conditions?

THOMAS D. SULLIVAN

ACTIVE AND PASSIVE EUTHANASIA: AN IMPERTINENT DISTINCTION?

Thomas D. Sullivan is associate professor of philosophy at the College of St. Thomas in St. Paul, Minnesota. Primarily specializing in logic and metaphysics, he is the author of "Between Thoughts and Things: The Status of Meaning" and the coauthor of "Diffusiveness of Intention Principle: A Counter-Example."

Sullivan, responding directly to Rachels, offers a defense of the standard (traditional) view on the morality of euthanasia. Sullivan charges Rachels with misconstruing the sense behind the traditional view. On Sullivan's analysis, the traditional view is not dependent on the distinction between killing and letting die. Rather, it simply forbids the *intentional* termination of life, whether by killing or letting die. The cessation of *extraordinary* means, he maintains, is morally permissible because, though death is foreseen, it need not be intended.

Because of recent advances in medical technology, it is today possible to save or prolong the lives of many persons who in an earlier era would have quickly perished. Unhappily, however, it often is impossible to do so without committing the patient and his or her family to a future filled with sorrows. Modern methods of neurosurgery can successfully close the opening at the base of the spine of a baby born with severe myelomeningocoele, but do nothing to relieve the paralysis that afflicts it from the waist down or to remedy the patient's incontinence of stool and urine. Antibiotics and skin grafts can spare the life of a victim of severe and massive burns, but fail to eliminate the immobilizing contractions of arms and legs, the extreme pain, and the hideous disfigurement of the face. It is not surprising, therefore, that physicians and moralists in increasing number recommend that assistance should not be given to such patients, and that some have even begun to advocate the deliberate hastening of death by medical means, provided informed consent has been given by the appropriate parties.

The latter recommendation consciously and directly conflicts with what might be called the "traditional" view of the physician's role. The traditional view, as articulated, for example, by the House of Delegates of the American Medical Association in 1973, declared:

> The intentional termination of the life of one human being by another—mercy killing—is contrary to that for which the medical profession stands and is contrary to the policy of the American Medical Association.
>
> The cessation of the employment of extra-ordinary means to prolong the life of the body when there is irrefutable evidence that biological death is imminent is the decision of the patient and/or his immediate family. The advice and judgment of the physician should be freely available to the patient and/or his immediate family.

Basically this view involves two points: (1) that it is impermissible for the doctor or anyone else to terminate intentionally the life of a patient, but (2) that it is permissible in some

From *Human Life Review,* vol. III, no. 3 (Summer 1977), pp. 40–46. Reprinted with permission from The Human Life Foundation, Inc., 150 East 35th Street, New York, N.Y. 10016.

cases to cease the employment of "extraordinary means" of preserving life, even though the death of the patient is a foreseeable consequence.

Does this position really make sense? Recent criticism charges that it does not. The heart of the complaint is that the traditional view arbitrarily rules out all cases of intentionally acting to terminate life, but permits what is in fact the moral equivalent, letting patients die. This accusation has been clearly articulated by James Rachels in a widely-read article that appeared in a recent issue of the *New England Journal of Medicine,* entitled "Active and Passive Euthanasia."[1] By "active euthanasia" Rachels seems to mean *doing something* to bring about a patient's death, and by "passive euthanasia," not doing anything, i.e., just letting the patient die. Referring to the A.M.A. statement, Rachels sees the traditional position as always forbidding active euthanasia, but permitting passive euthanasia. Yet, he argues, passive euthanasia may be in some cases morally indistinguishable from active euthanasia, and in other cases even worse. To make his point he asks his readers to consider the case of a Down's syndrome baby with an intestinal obstruction that easily could be remedied through routine surgery. Rachels comments:

> I can understand why some people are opposed to all euthanasia, and insist that such infants must be allowed to live. I think I can also understand why other people favor destroying these babies quickly and painlessly. But why should anyone favor letting 'dehydration and infection wither a tiny being over hours and days?' The doctrine that says that a baby may be allowed to dehydrate and wither, but may not be given an injection that would end its life without suffering, seems so patently cruel as to require no further refutation.[2]

Rachels' point is that decisions such as the one he describes as "patently cruel" arise out of a misconceived moral distinction between active and passive euthanasia, which in turn rests upon a distinction between killing and letting die that itself has no moral importance.

> One reason why so many people think that there is an important moral difference between active and passive euthanasia is that they think killing someone is morally worse than letting someone die. But is it? . . . To investigate this issue, two cases may be considered that are exactly alike except that one involves killing whereas the other involves letting someone die. Then, it can be asked whether this difference makes any difference to the moral assessments. . . .
>
> In the first, Smith stands to gain a large inheritance if anything should happen to his six-year-old cousin. One evening while the child is taking his bath, Smith sneaks into the bathroom and drowns the child, and then arranges things so that it will look like an accident.
>
> In the second, Jones also stands to gain if anything should happen to his six-year-old cousin. Like Smith, Jones sneaks in planning to drown the child in his bath. However, just as he enters the bathroom Jones sees the child slip and hit his head, and fall face down in the water. Jones is delighted; he stands by, ready to push the child's head back under if it is necessary, but it is not necessary. With only a little thrashing about the child drowns all by himself, "accidentally," as Jones watches and does nothing.[3]

Rachels observes that Smith killed the child, whereas Jones "merely" let the child die. If there's an important moral distinction between killing and letting die, then, we should say that Jones' behavior from a moral point of view is less reprehensible than Smith's. But while the law might draw some distinctions here, it seems clear that the acts of Jones and

---

[1] *The New England Journal of Medicine*, vol. 292 (Jan. 9, 1975), pp. 78–80. [Reprinted, this volume, pp. 52–56.]
[2] *Ibid.,* pp. 78–79. [This volume, p. 53.]
[3] *Ibid.,* p. 79. [This volume, p. 54.]

Smith are not different in any important way, or, if there is a difference, Jones' action is even worse.

In essence, then, the objection to the position adopted by the A.M.A. of Rachels and those who argue like him is that it endorses a highly questionable moral distinction between killing and letting die, which, if accepted, leads to indefensible medical decisions. Nowhere does Rachels quite come out and say that he favors active euthanasia in some cases, but the implication is clear. Nearly everyone holds that it is sometimes pointless to prolong the process of dying and that in those cases it is morally permissible to let a patient die even though a few hours or days could be salvaged by procedures that would also increase the agonies of the dying. But if it is impossible to defend a general distinction between letting people die and acting to terminate their lives directly, then it would seem that active euthanasia also may be morally permissible.

Now what shall we make of all this? It *is* cruel to stand by and watch a Down's baby die an agonizing death when a simple operation would remove the intestinal obstruction, but to offer the excuse that in failing to operate we didn't *do* anything to bring about death is an example of moral evasiveness comparable to the excuse Jones would offer for his action of "merely" letting his cousin die. Furthermore, it is true that if someone is trying to bring about the death of another human being, then it makes little difference from the moral point of view if his purpose is achieved by action or by malevolent omission, as in the cases of Jones and Smith.

But if we acknowledge this, are we obliged to give up the traditional view expressed by the A.M.A. statement? Of course not. To begin with, we are hardly obliged to assume the Jones-like role Rachels assigns the defender of the traditional view. We have the option of operating on the Down's baby and saving its life. Rachels mentions that possibility only to hurry past it as if that is not what his opposition would do. But, of course, that is precisely the course of action most defenders of the traditional position would choose.

Secondly, while it may be that the reason some rather confused people give for upholding the traditional view is that they think killing someone is always worse than letting them die, nobody who gives the matter much thought puts it that way. Rather they say that killing someone is clearly morally worse than not killing them, and killing them can be done by acting to bring about their death or by refusing ordinary means to keep them alive in order to bring about the same goal.

What I am suggesting is that Rachels' objections leave the position he sets out to criticize untouched. It is worth noting that the jargon of active and passive euthanasia—and it is jargon—does not appear in the resolution. Nor does the resolution state or imply the distinction Rachels attacks, a distinction that puts a moral premium on overt behavior—moving or not moving one's parts—while totally ignoring the intentions of the agent. That no such distinction is being drawn seems clear from the fact that the A.M.A. resolution speaks approvingly of ceasing to use extra-ordinary means in certain cases, and such withdrawals might easily involve bodily movement, for example unplugging an oxygen machine.

In addition to saddling his opposition with an indefensible distinction it doesn't make, Rachels proceeds to ignore one that it does make—one that is crucial to a just interpretation of the view. Recall the A.M.A. allows the withdrawal of what it calls extra-ordinary means of preserving life; clearly the contrast here is with ordinary means. Though in its short statement those expressions are not defined, the definition Paul Ramsey refers to as standard in his book, *The Patient as Person,* seems to fit.

> Ordinary means of preserving life are all medicines, treatments, and operations, which offer a reasonable hope of benefit for the patient and which can be obtained and used without excessive expense, pain, and other inconveniences.

Extra-ordinary means of preserving life are all those medicines, treatments, and operations which cannot be obtained without excessive expense, pain, or other inconvenience, or which, if used, would not offer a reasonable hope of benefit.[4]

Now with this distinction in mind, we can see how the traditional view differs from the position Rachels mistakes for it. The traditional view is that the intentional termination of human life is impermissible, irrespective of whether this goal is brought about by action or inaction. Is the action or refraining *aimed at* producing a death? Is the termination of life *sought, chosen or planned?* Is the intention deadly? If so, the act or omission is wrong.

But we all know it is entirely possible that the unwillingness of a physician to use extra-ordinary means for preserving life may be prompted not by a determination to bring about death, but by other motives. For example, he may realize that further treatment may offer little hope of reversing the dying process and/or be excruciating, as in the case when a massively necrotic bowel condition in a neonate is out of control. The doctor who does what he can to comfort the infant but does not submit it to further treatment or surgery may foresee that the decision will hasten death, but it certainly doesn't follow from that fact that he intends to bring about its death. It is, after all, entirely possible to foresee that something will come about as a result of one's conduct without intending the consequence or side effect. If I drive downtown, I can foresee that I'll wear out my tires a little, but I don't drive downtown with the intention of wearing out my tires. And if I choose to forego my exercises for a few days, I may think that as a result my physical condition will deteriorate a little, but I don't omit my exercise with a view to running myself down. And if you have to fill a position and select Green, who is better qualified for the post than her rival Brown, you needn't appoint Mrs. Green with the intention of hurting Mr. Brown, though you may foresee that Mr. Brown will feel hurt. And if a country extends its general education programs to its illiterate masses, it is predictable the suicide rate will go up, but even if the public officials are aware of this fact, it doesn't follow that they initiate the program with a view to making the suicide rate go up. In general, then, it is not the case that all the foreseeable consequences and side effects of our conduct are necessarily intended. And it is because the physician's withdrawal of extraordinary means can be otherwise motivated than by a desire to bring about the predictable death of the patient that such action cannot categorically be ruled out as wrong.

But the refusal to use ordinary means is an altogether different matter. After all, what is the point of refusing assistance which offers reasonable hope of benefit to the patient without involving excessive pain or other inconvenience? How could it be plausibly maintained that the refusal is not motivated by a desire to bring about the death of the patient? The traditional position, therefore, rules out not only direct actions to bring about death, such as giving a patient a lethal injection, but malevolent omissions as well, such as not providing minimum care for the newborn.

The reason the A.M.A. position sounds so silly when one listens to arguments such as Rachels' is that he slights the distinction between ordinary and extra-ordinary means and then drums on cases where *ordinary* means are refused. The impression is thereby conveyed that the traditional doctrine sanctions omissions that are morally indistinguishable in a substantive way from direct killings, but then incomprehensibly refuses to permit quick and painless termination of life. If the traditional doctrine would approve of Jones' standing

---

[4]Paul Ramsey, *The Patient As Person* (New Haven and London: Yale University Press, 1970), p. 122. Ramsey abbreviates the definition first given by Gerald Kelly, S.J., *Medico-Moral Problems* (St. Louis, Mo.: *The Catholic Hospital Association,* 1958), p. 129.

by with a grin on his face while his young cousin drowned in a tub, or letting a Down's baby wither and die when ordinary means are available to preserve its life, it would indeed be difficult to see how anyone could defend it. But so to conceive the traditional doctrine is simply to misunderstand it. It is not a doctrine that rests on some supposed distinction between "active" and "passive euthanasia," whatever those words are supposed to mean, nor on a distinction between moving and not moving our bodies. It is simply a prohibition against intentional killing, which includes both direct actions and malevolent omissions.

To summarize—the traditional position represented by the A.M.A. statement is not incoherent. It acknowledges, or more accurately, insists upon the fact that withholding ordinary means to sustain life may be tantamount to killing. The traditional position can be made to appear incoherent only by imposing upon it a crude idea of killing held by none of its more articulate advocates.

Thus the criticism of Rachels and other reformers, misapprehending its target, leaves the traditional position untouched. That position is simply a prohibition of murder. And it is good to remember, as C. S. Lewis once pointed out:

> No man, perhaps, ever at first described to himself the act he was about to do as Murder, or Adultery, or Fraud, or Treachery. . . . And when he hears it so described by other men he is (in a way) sincerely shocked and surprised. Those others "don't understand." If they knew what it had really been like for him, they would not use those crude "stock" names. With a wink or a titter, or a cloud of muddy emotion, the thing has slipped into his will as something not very extraordinary, something of which, rightly understood in all of his peculiar circumstances, he may even feel proud.[5]

I fully realize that there are times when those who have the noble duty to tend the sick and the dying are deeply moved by the sufferings of their patients, especially of the very young and the very old, and desperately wish they could do more than comfort and companion them. Then, perhaps, it seems that universal moral principles are mere abstractions having little to do with the agony of the dying. But of course we do not see best when our eyes are filled with tears.

QUESTIONS

1. Is Sullivan correct in holding that the traditional position is "simply a prohibition of murder"?
2. Is the traditional view dependent on the distinction between killing and letting die (contra Sullivan)?
3. Would it be morally wrong for a physician to withdraw "extraordinary means" *with the explicit intention* of bringing about the death of a terminally ill patient who is in great pain? Would it always be morally wrong for a physician to withdraw "ordinary means"?

[5]C. S. Lewis, *A Preface to Paradise Lost* (London and New York: Oxford University Press, 1970), p. 126.

JAMES RACHELS

MORE IMPERTINENT DISTINCTIONS AND A DEFENSE OF ACTIVE EUTHANASIA

A biographical sketch of James Rachels is found on p. 52.

This selection falls into two major sections. In the first major section, Rachels responds to Sullivan; in the second, he develops arguments in support of the moral justifiability of active euthanasia. Rachels's response to Sullivan consists primarily of two additional arguments against the standard (traditional) view on the morality of euthanasia. Rachels contends, first, that the traditional view is mistaken because it depends on an indefensible distinction between intentional and nonintentional terminations of life. Next he contends that the traditional view is mistaken because it depends on an indefensible distinction between ordinary and extraordinary means of treatment. Rachels's defense of active euthanasia rests on two arguments—the argument from mercy and the argument from the golden rule.

Many thinkers, including almost all orthodox Catholics, believe that euthanasia is immoral. They oppose killing patients in any circumstances whatever. However, they think it is all right, in some special circumstances, to allow patients to die by withholding treatment. The American Medical Association's policy statement on mercy killing supports this traditional view. In my paper "Active and Passive Euthanasia"[1] I argued, against the traditional view, that there is in fact no moral difference between killing and letting die—if one is permissible, then so is the other.

Professor Sullivan[2] does not dispute my argument; instead he dismisses it as irrelevant. The traditional doctrine, he says, does not appeal to or depend on the distinction between killing and letting die. Therefore, arguments against that distinction "leave the traditional position untouched."

Is my argument really irrelevant? I don't see how it can be. As Sullivan himself points out,

> Nearly everyone holds that it is sometimes pointless to prolong the process of dying and that in those cases it is morally permissible to let a patient die even though a few hours or days could be salvaged by procedures that would also increase the agonies of the dying. But if it is impossible to defend a general distinction between letting people die and acting to terminate their lives directly, then it would seem that active euthanasia also may be morally permissible. (59)

But traditionalists like Professor Sullivan hold that active euthanasia—the direct killing of patients—is *not* morally permissible; so, if my argument is sound, their view must be mistaken. I cannot agree, then, that my argument "leaves the traditional position untouched."

However, I shall not press this point. Instead I shall present some further arguments

Reprinted from Thomas A. Mappes and Jane S. Zembaty, eds., *Biomedical Ethics* (New York: McGraw-Hill, 1981), pp. 355–359. Copyright © 1978 by James Rachels. Also from Tom Regan, ed., *Matters of Life and Death: New Introductory Essays in Moral Philosophy.* Copyright © 1980 by Random House, Inc. Reprinted by permission of Random House, Inc.
[1]"Active and Passive Euthanasia," *The New England Journal of Medicine,* vol. 292 (Jan. 9, 1975), pp. 78–80. [Reprinted, this volume, pp. 52–56.]
[2]"Active and Passive Euthanasia: An Impertinent Distinction?" *The Human Life Review,* vol. III (1977), pp. 40–46. Parenthetical references in the text are to this article [as reprinted in this volume, pp. 57–61.]

against the traditional position, concentrating on those elements of the position which Professor Sullivan himself thinks most important. According to him, what is important is, first, that we should never *intentionally* terminate the life of a patient, either by action or omission, and second, that we may cease or omit treatment of a patient, knowing that this will result in death, only if the means of treatment involved are *extraordinary*.

INTENTIONAL AND NONINTENTIONAL TERMINATION OF LIFE

We can, of course, distinguish between what a person does and the intention with which he does it. But what is the significance of this distinction for ethics?

> The traditional view [says Sullivan] is that the intentional termination of human life is impermissible, irrespective of whether this goal is brought about by action or inaction. Is the action or refraining *aimed at* producing a death? Is the termination of life *sought, chosen or planned?* Is the intention deadly? If so, the act or omission is wrong. (60)

Thus on the traditional view there is a very definite sort of moral relation between act and intention. An act which is otherwise permissible may become impermissible if it is accompanied by a bad intention. The intention makes the act wrong.

There is reason to think that this view of the relation between act and intention is mistaken. Consider the following example. Jack visits his sick and lonely grandmother, and entertains her for the afternoon. He loves her and his only intention is to cheer her up. Jill also visits the grandmother, and provides an afternoon's cheer. But Jill's concern is that the old lady will soon be making her will; Jill wants to be included among the heirs. Jack also knows that his visit might influence the making of the will, in his favor, but that is no part of his plan. Thus Jack and Jill do the very same thing—they both spend an afternoon cheering up their sick grandmother—and what they do may lead to the same consequences, namely influencing the will. But their intentions are quite different.

Jack's intention was honorable and Jill's was not. Could we say on that account that what Jack did was right, but what Jill did was wrong? No; for Jack and Jill did the very same thing, and if they did the same thing, we cannot say that one acted rightly and the other wrongly.[3] Consistency requires that we assess similar actions similarly. Thus if we are trying to evaluate their *actions,* we must say about one what we say about the other.

However, if we are trying to assess Jack's *character,* or Jill's, things are very different. Even though their actions were similar, Jack seems admirable for what he did, while Jill does not. What Jill did—comforting an elderly sick relative—was a morally good thing, but we would not think well of her for it since she was only scheming after the old lady's money. Jack, on the other hand, did a good thing *and* he did it with an admirable intention. Thus we think well, not only of what Jack did, but of Jack.

The traditional view, as presented by Professor Sullivan, says that the intention with which an act is done is relevant to determining whether the act is right. The example of Jack and Jill suggests that, on the contrary, the intention is not relevant to deciding whether the *act* is right or wrong, but instead it is relevant to assessing the character of the person who does the act, which is very different.

---

[3]It might be objected that they did not "do the same thing," for Jill manipulated and deceived her grandmother, while Jack did not. If their actions are described in this way, then it may seem that "what Jill did" was wrong, while "what Jack did" was not. However, this description of what Jill did incorporates her intention into the description of the act. In the present context we must keep the act and the intention separate, in order to discuss the relation between them. If they *cannot* be held separate, then the traditional view makes no sense.

Now let us turn to an example that concerns more important matters of life and death. This example is adapted from one used by Sullivan himself (60). A massively necrotic bowel condition in a neonate is out of control. Dr. White realizes that further treatment offers little hope of reversing the dying process and will only increase the suffering; so, he does not submit the infant to further treatment—even though he knows that this decision will hasten death. However, Dr. White does not seek, choose, or plan that death, so it is not part of his intention that the baby dies.

Dr. Black is faced with a similar case. A massively necrotic bowel condition in a neonate is out of control. He realizes that further treatment offers little hope of saving the baby and will only increase its suffering. He decides that it is better for the baby to die a bit sooner than to go on suffering pointlessly; so, with the intention of letting the baby die, he ceases treatment.

According to the traditional position, Dr. White's action was acceptable, but Dr. Black acted wrongly. However, this assessment faces the same problem we encountered before. Dr. White and Dr. Black did *the very same thing:* their handling of the cases was identical. Both doctors ceased treatment, knowing that the baby would die sooner, and both did so because they regarded continued treatment as pointless, given the infants' prospects. So how could one's action be acceptable and the other's not? There was, of course, a subtle difference in their *attitudes* toward what they did. Dr. Black said to himself, "I want this baby to die now, rather than later, so that it won't suffer more; so I won't continue the treatment." A defender of the traditional view might choose to condemn Dr. Black for this, and say that his character is defective (although I would not say that); but the traditionalist should not say that Dr. Black's *action* was wrong on that account, at least not if he wants to go on saying that Dr. White's action was right. A pure heart cannot make a wrong act right; neither can an impure heart make a right act wrong. As in the case of Jack and Jill, the intention is relevant, not to determining the rightness of actions, but to assessing the character of the people who act.

There is a general lesson to be learned here. The rightness or wrongness of an act is determined by the reasons for or against it. Suppose you are trying to decide, in this example, whether treatment should be continued. What are the reasons for and against this course of action? On the one hand, if treatment is ceased the baby will die very soon. On the other hand, the baby will die eventually anyway, even if treatment is continued. It has no chance of growing up. Moreover, if its life is prolonged, its suffering will be prolonged as well, and the medical resources used will be unavailable to others who would have a better chance of a satisfactory cure. In light of all this, you may well decide against continued treatment. But notice that there is no mention here of anybody's intentions. The intention you would have, if you decided to cease treatment, is not one of the things you need to consider. It is not among the reasons either for or against the action. That is why it is irrelevant to determining whether the action is right.

In short, a person's intention is relevant to an assessment of his character. The fact that a person intended so-and-so by his action may be a reason for thinking him a good or a bad person. But the intention is not relevant to determining whether the act itself is morally right. The rightness of the act must be decided on the basis of the objective reasons for or against it. It is permissible to let the baby die, in Sullivan's example, because of the facts about the baby's condition and its prospects—not because of anything having to do with anyone's intentions. Thus the traditional view is mistaken on this point.

ORDINARY AND EXTRAORDINARY MEANS OF TREATMENT

The American Medical Association policy statement says that life-sustaining treatment may sometimes be stopped if the means of treatment are "extraordinary"; the implication is that "ordinary" means of treatment may not be withheld. The distinction between ordinary and extraordinary treatments is crucial to orthodox Catholic thought in this area, and Professor Sullivan reemphasizes its importance: he says that, while a physician may sometimes rightly refuse to use extraordinary means to prolong life, "the refusal to use ordinary means is an altogether different matter." (60)

However, upon reflection it is clear that it is sometimes permissible to omit even very ordinary sorts of treatments.

> Suppose that a diabetic patient long accustomed to self-administration of insulin falls victim to terminal cancer, or suppose that a terminal cancer patient suddenly develops diabetes. Is he in the first case obliged to continue, and in the second case obliged to begin, insulin treatment and die painfully of cancer, or in either or both cases may the patient choose rather to pass into diabetic coma and an earlier death? ... What of the conscious patient suffering from painful incurable disease who suddenly gets penumonia? Or an old man slowly deteriorating who from simply being inactive and recumbent gets pneumonia: Are we to use antibiotics in a likely successful attack upon this disease which from time immemorial has been called "the old man's friend"?[4]

These examples are provided by Paul Ramsey, a leading theological ethicist. Even so conservative a thinker as Ramsey is sympathetic with the idea that, in such cases, life-prolonging treatment is not mandatory: the insulin and the antibiotics need not be used. Yet surely insulin and antibiotics are "ordinary" treatments by today's medical standards. They are common, easily administered, and cheap. There is nothing exotic about them. So it appears that the distinction between ordinary and extraordinary means does not have the significance traditionally attributed to it.

But what of the *definitions* of "ordinary" and "extraordinary" means which Sullivan provides? Quoting Ramsey, he says that

> Ordinary means of preserving life are all medicines, treatments, and operations, which offer a reasonable hope of benefit for the patient and which can be obtained and used without excessive expense, pain, and other inconveniences.
>
> Extra-ordinary means of preserving life are all those medicines, treatments, and operations which cannot be obtained without excessive expense, pain, or other inconvenience, or which, if used, would not offer a reasonable hope of benefit. (59–60)

Do these definitions provide us with a useful distinction—one that can be used in determining when a treatment is mandatory and when it is not?

The first thing to notice is the way the word "excessive" functions in these definitions. It is said that a treatment is extraordinary if it cannot be obtained without *excessive* expense or pain. But when is an expense "excessive"? Is a cost of $10,000 excessive? If it would save the life of a young woman and restore her to perfect health, $10,000 does not seem excessive. But if it would only prolong the life of Ramsey's cancer-stricken diabetic a short while, perhaps $10,000 is excessive. The point is not merely that what is excessive changes from case to case. The point is that what is excessive *depends on* whether it would be a good thing for the life in question to be prolonged.

Second, we should notice the use of the word "benefit" in the definitions. It is said that ordinary treatments offer a reasonable hope of *benefit* for the patient; and that treatments are extraordinary if they will not benefit the patient. But how do we tell if a treatment will benefit the patient? Remember that we are talking about life-prolonging treatments; the "benefit," if any, is the continuation of life. Whether continued life is a benefit

---

[4] *The Patient as Person* (New Haven: Yale University Press, 1970), pp. 115–116.

depends on the details of the particular case. For a person with a painful terminal illness, a temporarily continued life may not be a benefit. For a person in irreversible coma, such as Karen Quinlan, continued biological existence is almost certainly not a benefit. On the other hand, for a person who can be cured and resume a normal life, life-sustaining treatment definitely is a benefit. Again, the point is that in order to decide whether life-sustaining treatment is a benefit we must *first* decide whether it would be a good thing for the life in question to be prolonged.

Therefore, these definitions do not mark out a distinction that can be used to help us decide when treatment may be omitted. We cannot by using the definitions identify which treatments are extraordinary, and then use that information to determine whether the treatment may be omitted. For the definitions require that we must *already* have decided the moral questions of life and death *before* we can answer the question of which treatments are extraordinary!

We are brought, then, to this conclusion about the distinction between ordinary and extraordinary means. If we apply the distinction in a straightforward, commonsense way, the traditional doctrine is false, for it is clear that it is sometimes permissible to omit ordinary treatments. On the other hand, if we define the terms as suggested by Ramsey and Sullivan, the distinction is useless in practical decision-making. In either case, the distinction provides no help in formulating an acceptable ethic of letting die.

To summarize what has been said so far, the distinction between killing and letting die has no moral importance; on that Professor Sullivan and I agree. He, however, contends that the distinctions between intentional and nonintentional termination of life, and ordinary and extraordinary means, must be at the heart of a correct moral view. I believe that the arguments given above refute this view. Those distinctions are no better than the first one. The traditional view is mistaken.

In my original paper I did not argue in favor of active euthanasia. I merely argued that active and passive euthanasia are equivalent: *if* one is acceptable, so is the other. However, Professor Sullivan correctly inferred that I do endorse active euthanasia. I believe that it is morally justified in some instances and that at least two strong arguments support this position. The first is the argument from mercy; the second is the argument from the golden rule.

THE ARGUMENT FROM MERCY

Preliminary Statement of the Argument

The single most powerful argument in support of euthanasia is the argument from mercy. It is also an exceptionally simple argument, at least in its main idea, which makes one uncomplicated point. Terminal patients sometimes suffer pain so horrible that it is beyond the comprehension of those who have not actually experienced it. Their suffering can be so terrible that we do not like even to read about it or think about it; we recoil even from the descriptions of such agony. The argument from mercy says: Euthanasia is justified because it provides an end to *that*.

The great Irish satirist Jonathan Swift took eight years to die, while, in the words of Joseph Fletcher, "His mind crumbled to pieces."[5] At times the pain in his blinded eyes was so intense he had to be restrained from tearing them out with his own hands. Knives and other potential instruments of suicide had to be kept from him. For the last three years of his life, he could do nothing but sit and drool; and when he finally died it was only after convulsions that lasted thirty-six hours.

[5] *Morals and Medicine* (Boston: Beacon Press, 1960), p. 174.

Swift died in 1745. Since then, doctors have learned how to eliminate much of the pain that accompanies terminal illness, but the victory has been far from complete. So, here is a more modern example.

Stewart Alsop was a respected journalist who died in 1975 of a rare form of cancer. Before he died, he wrote movingly of his experiences as a terminal patient. Although he had not thought much about euthanasia before, he came to approve of it after rooming briefly with someone he called Jack:

> The third night that I roomed with Jack in our tiny double room in the solid-tumor ward of the cancer clinic of the National Institutes of Health in Bethesda, Md., a terrible thought occurred to me.
>
> Jack had a melanoma in his belly, a malignant solid tumor that the doctors guessed was about the size of a softball. The cancer had started a few months before with a small tumor in his left shoulder, and there had been several operations since. The doctors planned to remove the softball-sized tumor, but they knew Jack would soon die. The cancer had metastasized—it had spread beyond control.
>
> Jack was good-looking, about 28, and brave. He was in constant pain, and his doctor had pre-scribed an intravenous shot of a synthetic opiate—a pain-killer, or analgesic—every four hours. His wife spent many of the daylight hours with him, and she would sit or lie on his bed and pat him all over, as one pats a child, only more methodically, and this seemed to help control the pain. But at night, when his pretty wife had left (wives cannot stay overnight at the NIH clinic) and darkness fell, the pain would attack without pity.
>
> At the prescribed hour, a nurse would give Jack a shot of the synthetic analgesic, and this would control the pain for perhaps two hours or a bit more. Then he would begin to moan, or whimper, very low, as though he didn't want to wake me. Then he would begin to howl, like a dog.
>
> When this happened, either he or I would ring for a nurse, and ask for a pain-killer. She would give him some codeine or the like by mouth, but it never did any real good—it affected him no more than half an aspirin might affect a man who had just broken his arm. Always the nurse would explain as encour-agingly as she could that there was not long to go before the next intravenous shot—"Only about 50 minutes now." And always poor Jack's whimpers and howls would become more loud and frequent until at last the blessed relief came.
>
> The third night of this routine, the terrible thought occurred to me. "If Jack were a dog," I thought, "what would be done with him?" The answer was obvious: the pound, and chloroform. No human being with a spark of pity could let a living thing suffer so, to no good end.[6]

The NIH clinic is, of course, one of the most modern and best-equipped hospitals we have. Jack's suffering was not the result of poor treatment in some backward rural facility; it was the inevitable product of his disease, which medical science was powerless to prevent.

I have quoted Alsop at length not for the sake of indulging in gory details but to give a clear idea of the kind of suffering we are talking about. We should not gloss over these facts with euphemistic language, or squeamishly avert our eyes from them. For only by keeping them firmly and vividly in mind can we appreciate the full force of the argument from mercy: If a person prefers—and even begs for—death as the only alternative to lingering on *in this kind of torment,* only to die anyway after a while, then surely it is not immoral to help this person die sooner. As Alsop put it, "No human being with a spark of pity could let a living thing suffer so, to no good end."

The Utilitarian Version of the Argument

In connection with this argument, the utilitarians should be mentioned. They argue that actions and social policies should be judged right or wrong *exclusively* according to whether

---

[6]"The Right to Die with Dignity," *Good Housekeeping,* August 1974, pp. 69, 130.

they cause happiness or misery; and they argue that when judged by this standard, euthanasia turns out to be morally acceptable. The utilitarian argument may be elaborated as follows:

1. Any action or social policy is morally right if it serves to increase the amount of happiness in the world or to decrease the amount of misery. Conversely, an action or social policy is morally wrong if it serves to decrease happiness or to increase misery.

2. The policy of killing, at their own request, hopelessly ill patients who are suffering great pain, would decrease the amount of misery in the world. (An example could be Alsop's friend Jack.)

3. Therefore, such a policy would be morally right.

The first premise of this argument, (1), states the Principle of Utility, which is the basic utilitarian assumption. Today most philosophers think that this principle is wrong, because they think that the promotion of happiness and the avoidance of misery are not the *only* morally important things. Happiness, they say, is only one among many values that should be promoted: freedom, justice, and a respect for people's rights are also important. To take one example: People *might* be happier if there were no freedom of religion; for, if everyone adhered to the same religious beliefs, there would be greater harmony among people. There would be no unhappiness caused within families by Jewish girls marrying Catholic boys, and so forth. Moreover, if people were brainwashed well enough, no one would mind not having freedom of choice. Thus happiness would be increased. But, the argument continues, even if happiness *could* be increased this way, it would not be right to deny people freedom of religion, because people have a right to make their own choices. Therefore, the first premise of the utilitarian argument is unacceptable.

There is a related difficulty for utilitarianism, which connects more directly with the topic of euthanasia. Suppose a person is leading a miserable life—full of more unhappiness than happiness—but does *not* want to die. This person thinks that a miserable life is better than none at all. Now I assume that we would all agree that the person should not be killed; that would be plain, unjustifiable murder. Yet it *would* decrease the amount of misery in the world if we killed this person—it would lead to an increase in the balance of happiness over unhappiness—and so it is hard to see how, on strictly utilitarian grounds, it could be wrong. Again, the Principle of Utility seems to be an inadequate guide for determining right and wrong. So we are on shaky ground if we rely on *this* version of the argument from mercy for a defense of euthanasia.

Doing What Is in Everyone's Best Interests

Although the foregoing utilitarian argument is faulty, it is nevertheless based on a sound idea. For even if the promotion of happiness and avoidance of misery are not the *only* morally important things, they are still very important. So, when an action or a social policy would decrease misery, that is *a* very strong reason in its favor. In the cases of voluntary euthanasia we are now considering, great suffering is eliminated, and since the patient requests it, there is no question of violating individual rights. That is why, regardless of the difficulties of the Principle of Utility, the utilitarian version of the argument still retains considerable force.

I want now to present a somewhat different version of the argument from mercy, which is inspired by utilitarianism but which avoids the difficulties of the foregoing version by not making the Principle of Utility a premise of the argument. I believe that the following argument is sound and proves that active euthanasia *can* be justified:

1. If an action promotes the best interests of *everyone* concerned, and violates *no one's* rights, then that action is morally acceptable.

2. In at least some cases, active euthanasia promotes the best interests of everyone concerned and violates no one's rights.

3. Therefore, in at least some cases active euthanasia is morally acceptable.

It would have been in everyone's best interests if active euthanasia had been employed in the case of Stewart Alsop's friend Jack. First, and most important, it would have been in Jack's own interests, since it would have provided him with an easier, better death, without pain. (Who among us would choose Jack's death, if we had a choice, rather than a quick painless death?) Second, it would have been in the best interests of Jack's wife. Her misery, helplessly watching him suffer, must have been almost equal to his. Third, the hospital staff's best interest would have been served, since if Jack's dying had not been prolonged, they could have turned their attention to other patients whom they could have helped. Fourth, other patients would have benefited since medical resources would no longer have been used in the sad, pointless maintenance of Jack's physical existence. Finally, if Jack himself requested to be killed, the act would not have violated his rights. Considering all this, how can active euthanasia in this case be wrong? How can it be wrong to do an action that is merciful, that benefits everyone concerned, and that violates no one's rights?

THE ARGUMENT FROM THE GOLDEN RULE

"Do unto others as you would have them do unto you" is one of the oldest and most familiar moral maxims. Stated in just that way, it is not a very good maxim: Suppose a sexual pervert started treating others as he would like to be treated himself; we might not be happy with the results. Nevertheless, the basic idea behind the golden rule is a good one. The basic idea is that moral rules apply impartially to everyone alike; therefore, you cannot say that you are justified in treating someone else in a certain way unless you are willing to admit that that person would also be justified in treating *you* in that way if your positions were reversed.

Kant and the Golden Rule

The great German philosopher Immanuel Kant (1724–1804) incorporated the basic idea of the Golden Rule into his system of ethics. Kant argued that we should act only on rules that we are willing to have applied universally; that is, we should behave as we would be willing to have *everyone* behave. He held that there is one supreme principle of morality, which he called "the Categorical Imperative." The Categorical Imperative says:

> Act only according to that maxim by which you can at the same time will that it should become a universal law.[7]

Let us discuss what this means. When we are trying to decide whether we ought to do a certain action, we must first ask what general rule or principle we would be following if we did it. Then, we ask whether we would be willing for everyone to follow that rule, in similar

---

[7] *Foundations of the Metaphysics of Morals*, p. 422.

circumstances. (This determines whether "the maxim of the act"—the rule we would be following—can be "willed" to be "a universal law.") If we would not be willing for the rule to be followed universally, then we should not follow it ourselves. Thus, if we are not willing for others to apply the rule to *us,* we ought not apply it to *them.*

In the eighteenth chapter of St. Matthew's gospel there is a story that perfectly illustrates this point. A man is owed money by another, who cannot pay, and so he has the debtor thrown into prison. But he himself owes money to the king and begs that *his* debt be forgiven. At first the king forgives the debt. However, when the king hears how this man has treated the one who owed him, he changes his mind and "delivers him unto the tormentors" until he can pay. The moral is clear: If you do not think that others should apply the rule "Don't forgive debts!" to *you,* then you should not apply it to others.

The application of all this to the question of euthanasia is fairly obvious. Each of us is going to die someday, although most of us do not know when or how. But suppose you were told that you would die in one of two ways, and you were asked to choose between them. First, you could die quietly, and without pain, from a fatal injection. Or second, you could choose to die of an affliction so painful that for several days before death you would be reduced to howling like a dog, with your family standing by helplessly, trying to comfort you, but going through its own psychological hell. It is hard to believe that any sane person, when confronted by these possibilities, would choose to have a rule applied that would force upon him or her the second option. And if we would not want such a rule, which excludes euthanasia, applied to us, then we should not apply such a rule to others.

Implications for Christians

There is a considerable irony here. Kant [himself] was personally opposed to active euthanasia, yet his own Categorical Imperative seems to sanction it. The larger irony, however, is for those in the Christian Church who have for centuries opposed active euthanasia. According to the New Testament accounts, Jesus himself promulgated the Golden Rule as the supreme moral principle—"This is the Law and the Prophets," he said. But if this is the supreme principle of morality, then how can active euthanasia be always wrong? If I would have it done to me, how can it be wrong for me to do likewise to others?

R. M. Hare has made this point with great force. A Christian as well as a leading contemporary moral philosopher, Hare has long argued that "universalizability" is one of the central characteristics of moral judgment. ('Universalizability' is the name he gives to the basic idea embodied in both the Golden Rule and the Categorical Imperative. It means that a moral judgment must conform to universal principles, which apply to everyone alike, if it is to be acceptable.) In an article called "Euthanasia: A Christian View," Hare argues that Christians, if they took Christ's teachings about the Golden Rule seriously, would not think that euthanasia is always wrong. He gives this (true) example:

> The driver of a petrol lorry [i.e., a gas truck] was in an accident in which his tanker overturned and immediately caught fire. He himself was trapped in the cab and could not be freed. He therefore besought the bystanders to kill him by hitting him on the head, so that he would not roast to death. I think that somebody did this, but I do not know what happened in court afterwards.
>
> Now will you please all ask yourselves, as I have many times asked myself, what you wish that men should do to you if you were in the situation of that driver. I cannot believe that anybody who considered the matter seriously, as if he himself were going to be in that situation and had now to give instructions as to what rule the bystanders should follow, would say that the rule should be one ruling out euthanasia absolutely.[8]

[8]*Philosophic Exchange* (Brockport, New York), II:I (Summer 1975), p. 45.

We might note that *active* euthanasia is the only option here; the concept of passive euthanasia, in these circumstances, has no application. . . .

Professor Sullivan finds my position pernicious. In his penultimate paragraph he says that the traditional doctrine "is simply a prohibition of murder," and that those of us who think otherwise are confused, teary-eyed sentimentalists. But the traditional doctrine is not that. It is a muddle of indefensible claims, backed by tradition but not by reason.

QUESTIONS

1. Rachels asks, "How can it be wrong to do an action that is merciful, that benefits everyone concerned, and that violates no one's rights?" If you think that it can be wrong to perform such an action, what arguments would you offer against Rachels's argument from mercy?

2. Some people offer the following argument against euthanasia: It is always possible that a patient has been misdiagnosed or that a cure may be found for an apparently terminal illness; therefore, we can *never* be certain that a patient's condition is hopeless. Is this conclusion true? If so, does it lead to the further conclusion that euthanasia is morally wrong?

JUDGE DAVID G. ROBERTS

OPINION IN *MAINE MEDICAL CENTER v. HOULE*

Judge David G. Roberts, who received his law degree from Boston University, was admitted to the bar in 1956. He is presently one of four regional presiding justices of the Maine Superior Court.

On February 9, 1974, a son was born to Mr. and Mrs. Robert H. T. Houle. The child was deformed. His entire left side was malformed; he had no left eye, practically no left ear, and a deformed left hand; some of his vertebrae were not fused. In addition, the baby was afflicted with a tracheal esophageal fistula and could not be fed by mouth. Instead of going to his lungs, air leaked into his stomach; fluid from the stomach pushed up into the lungs. As his condition deteriorated, pneumonia set in, his reflexes became impaired, and because of poor circulation, severe brain damage was suspected. The fistula, which was the most immediate threat to his survival, is easily correctible by surgery. The parents refused to consent to the surgery, but several doctors at the Maine Medical Center took the case to court. Maine Superior Court Judge David G. Roberts ordered the surgery performed. Baby Houle died on February 24, 1974, following the court-ordered surgery.

For Judge Roberts a human being exists at the moment of live birth, and this human being is entitled to the fullest protection of the law, including the protection of the right to life. Quality-of-life judgments are irrelevant. Since the medical measures in question are not "heroic" ones, and the surgery is necessary for survival, the Houles have no right to withhold such treatment.

The testimony herein indicates that a male child was born to the defendants on February 9, 1974 at the Maine Medical Center. Medical examination by the hospital staff revealed the absence of a left eye, a rudimentary left ear with no ear canal, a malformed left thumb and a tracheal esophageal fistula. The latter condition prevented the ingestion of nourishment, necessitated intravenous feeding and allowed the entry of fluids into the infant's lungs leading to the development of pneumonia and other complications. The recommended medical treatment was surgical repair of the tracheal esophageal fistula to allow normal feeding and respiration. Prior to February 11, 1974, the child's father directed the attending physician not to conduct surgical repair of the fistula and to cease intravenous feeding.

By Temporary Restraining Order issued ex parte on February 11, 1974, this court authorized the continuance of such measures as might be medically dictated to maintain said child in a stable and viable condition and restrained the defendants from issuing any orders, which, in the opinion of the attending physician, would be injurious to the current medical situation of said child.

In the interim the child's condition has deteriorated. Periods of apnea have necessitated the use of a bag breathing device to artificially sustain respiration. Several convulsive seizures of unknown cause have occurred. Medications administered include gentimycin for the treatment of pneumonia and phenobarbitol to control convulsive seizures. Further medical evaluation indicates the lack of response of the right eye to light stimuli, the existence of some nonfused vertebrae and the virtual certainty of some brain damage resulting from anoxia. The most recent developments have caused the attending physician to form the opinion that all life supporting measures should be withdrawn. The doctor is further of the opinion that without surgical correction of the tracheal esophageal fistula the child will certainly die and that with surgical correction the child can survive but with some degree of permanent brain damage.

The court heard further testimony concerning the present posture of the mother's emotional condition and attitude toward the future survival of the child. Without disparaging the seriousness of the emotional impact upon the parent and without ignoring the difficulties which this court's decision may cause in the future, it is the firm opinion of this court that questions of permanent custody, maintenance and further care of the child are for the moment legally irrelevant.

Quite literally the court must make a decision concerning the life or death of a new born infant. Recent decisions concerning the right of the state to intervene with the medical and moral judgments of a prospective parent and attending physician may have cast doubts upon the legal rights of an unborn child; but at the moment of live birth there does exist a human being entitled to the fullest protection of the law. The most basic right enjoyed by every human being is the right to life itself.

Where the condition of a child does not involve serious risk of life and where treatment involves a considerable risk, parents as the natural guardians have a considerable degree of discretion and the courts ought not intervene. The measures proposed in this case are not in any sense heroic measures except for the doctor's opinion that probable brain damage has rendered life not worth preserving. Were it his opinion that life itself could not be preserved, heroic measures ought not be required. However, the doctor's qualitative evaluation of the value of the life to be preserved is not legally within the scope of his expertise.

In the court's opinion the issue before the court is not the prospective quality of the

Maine Superior Court. Docket No. 74-145 (1974).

life to be preserved, but the medical feasibility of the proposed treatment compared with the almost certain risk of death should treatment be withheld. Being satisfied that corrective surgery is medically necessary and medically feasible, the court finds that the defendants herein have no right to withhold such treatment and that to do so constitutes neglect in the legal sense. Therefore, the court will authorize the guardian ad litem to consent to the surgical correction of the tracheal esophageal fistula and such other normal life supportive measures as may be medically required in the immediate future. It is further ordered that Respondents are hereby enjoined until further order of this court from issuing any orders to Petitioners or their employees which, in the opinion of the attending physicians or surgeons would be injurious to the medical condition of the child.

The court will retain jurisdiction for the purpose of determining any further measures that may be required to be taken and eventually for the purpose of determining the future custody of the child should the court determine that it is appropriate to do so.

QUESTIONS

1. Some people argue that it is morally correct to allow a severely defective newborn to die *if and only if* there is no significant potential for a meaningful human existence. They would maintain that Baby Houle should not have been operated upon. Can you suggest any arguments to support such a position?
2. Is the newborn a *person*, with the full complement of rights belonging to persons?

H. TRISTRAM ENGELHARDT, JR.

ETHICAL ISSUES IN AIDING THE DEATH OF YOUNG CHILDREN

H. Tristram Engelhardt, Jr., who has both an M.D. and a Ph.D. in philosophy, holds a joint appointment as a professor in the departments of philosophy and community medicine and as a senior research scholar, Kennedy Institute, Center for Bioethics, Georgetown University. He is the author of *Mind-Body: A Categorical Relation* (1973) and has published numerous articles on issues in biomedical ethics and the philosophy of medicine. He has also served as an associate editor of the *Encyclopedia of Bioethics* (1978) and is coeditor (with Stuart F. Spicker) of a number of volumes called the *Philosophy and Medicine* series.

After reviewing the differences between the euthanasia of adults and the euthanasia of children, Engelhardt focuses attention on the status of children. In his view, young children are not persons in a strict sense. Rather, they are persons only in "a social sense," by virtue of their role in a family and society. Since young children "belong" to their parents, it is the parents who are the proper decision makers with regard to the treatment or nontreatment of severely defective newborns. Engelhardt finds it morally acceptable to allow a severely defective newborn to die when (1) it is unlikely that the child can attain a "good quality of life" (i.e., a developed personal life) and/or (2) it seems clear that providing continued care for the child would constitute a "severe burden" for the family. Engelhardt goes on to develop the concept of "the injury of continued existence," arguing that a child has a right not to have its life prolonged in those cases where life would be painful and futile. Thus, he maintains, allowing a severely defective newborn to die (in some cases) is not only *morally acceptable* but indeed *morally demanded*. In concluding, Engelhardt briefly discusses the justifiability of active euthanasia of severely defective newborns.

Euthanasia in the pediatric age group involves a constellation of issues that are materially different from those of adult euthanasia.[1] The difference lies in the somewhat obvious fact that infants and young children are not able to decide about their own futures and thus are not persons in the same sense that normal adults are. While adults usually decide their own fate, others decide on behalf of young children. Although one can argue that euthanasia is or should be a personal right, the sense of such an argument is obscure with respect to children. Young children do not have any personal rights, at least none that they can exercise on their own behalf with regard to the manner of their life and death. As a result, euthanasia of young children raises special questions concerning the standing of the rights of children, the status of parental rights, the obligations of adults to prevent the suffering of children, and the possible effects on society of allowing or expediting the death of seriously defective infants.

What I will refer to as the euthanasia of infants and young children might be termed by others infanticide, while some cases might be termed the withholding of extraordinary life-prolonging treatment. One needs a term that will encompass both death that results from active intervention and death that ensues when one simply ceases further therapy.[2] In using such a term, one must recognize that death is often not directly but only obliquely intended. That is, one often intends only to treat no further, not actually to have death follow, even though one knows death will follow.

Finally, one must realize that deaths as the result of withholding treatment constitute a significant proportion of neonatal deaths. For example, as high as 14 percent of children in one hospital have been identified as dying after a decision was made not to treat further, the presumption being that the children would have lived longer had treatment been offered.[3]

Even popular magazines have presented accounts of parental decisions not to pursue treatment.[4] These decisions often involve a choice between expensive treatment with little chance of achieving a full, normal life for the child and "letting nature take its course," with the child dying as a result of its defects. As this suggests, many of these problems are products of medical progress. Such children in the past would have died. The quandaries are in a sense an embarrassment of riches; now that one *can* treat such defective children, *must* one treat them? And, if one need not treat such defective children, may one expedite their death?

Reprinted with permission of the publisher from Marvin Kohl, ed., *Beneficent Euthanasia*. Copyright © 1975 by Prometheus Books.
[1] I am grateful to Laurence B. McCullough and James P. Morris for their critical discussion of this paper. They may be responsible for its virtues, but not for its shortcomings.
[2] I will use the term euthanasia in a broad sense to indicate a deliberately chosen course of action or inaction that is known at the time of decision to be such as will expedite death. This use of euthanasia will encompass not only positive or active euthanasia (acting in order to expedite death) and negative or passive euthanasia (refraining from action in order to expedite death), but acting and refraining in the absence of a direct intention that death occur more quickly. . . .
[3] Raymond S. Duff and A. G. M. Campbell, "Moral and Ethical Dilemmas in the Special-Care Nursery," *The New England Journal of Medicine*, 289 (Oct. 25, 1973), pp. 890–894.
[4] Roger Pell, "The Agonizing Decision of Joanne and Roger Pell," *Good Housekeeping* (January 1972), pp. 76–77, 131–135.

I will here briefly examine some of these issues. First, I will review differences that contrast the euthanasia of adults to euthanasia of children. Second, I will review the issue of the rights of parents and the status of children. Third, I will suggest a new notion, the concept of the "injury of continued existence," and draw out some of its implications with respect to a duty to prevent suffering. Finally, I will outline some important questions that remain unanswered even if the foregoing issues can be settled. In all, I hope more to display the issues involved in a difficult question than to advance a particular set of answers to particular dilemmas.

For the purpose of this paper, I will presume that adult euthanasia can be justified by an appeal to freedom. In the face of imminent death, one is usually choosing between a more painful and more protracted dying and a less painful or less protracted dying, in circumstances where either choice makes little difference with regard to the discharge of social duties and responsibilities. In the case of suicide, we might argue that, in general, social duties (for example, the duty to support one's family) restrain one from taking one's own life. But in the face of imminent death and in the presence of the pain and deterioration of a fatal disease, such duties are usually impossible to discharge and are thus rendered moot. One can, for example, picture an extreme case of an adult with a widely disseminated carcinoma, including metastases to the brain, who because of severe pain and debilitation is no longer capable of discharging any social duties. In these and similar circumstances, euthanasia becomes the issue of the right to control one's own body, even to the point of seeking assistance in suicide. Euthanasia is, as such, the issue of assisted suicide, the universalization of a maxim that all persons should be free, *in extremis,* to decide with regard to the circumstances of their death.

Further, the choice of positive euthanasia could be defended as the more rational choice: the choice of a less painful death and the affirmation of the value of a rational life. In so choosing, one would be acting to set limits to one's life in order not to live when pain and physical and mental deterioration make further rational life impossible. The choice to end one's life can be understood as a noncontradictory willing of a smaller set of states of existence for oneself, a set that would not include a painful death. As such, it would not involve a desire to destroy oneself. That is, adult euthanasia can be construed as an affirmation of the rationality and autonomy of the self.

The remarks above focus on the active or positive euthanasia of adults. But they hold as well concerning what is often called passive or negative euthanasia, the refusal of life-prolonging therapy. In such cases, the patient's refusal of life-prolonging therapy is seen to be a right that derives from personal freedom, or at least from a zone of privacy into which there are no good grounds for social intervention.[5]

Again, none of these considerations apply directly to the euthanasia of young children, because they cannot participate in such decisions. Whatever else pediatric, in particular neonatal, euthanasia involves, it surely involves issues different from those of adult euthanasia. Since infants and small children cannot commit suicide, their right to assisted suicide is difficult to pose. The difference between the euthanasia of young children and that of adults resides in the difference between children and adults. The difference, in fact, raises the troublesome question of whether young children are persons, or at least whether they are persons in the sense in which adults are. Answering that question will resolve in part at least the right of others to decide whether a young child should live or die and whether he should receive life-prolonging treatment.

---

[5]Norman L. Cantor, "A Patient's Decision To Decline Life-Saving Medical Treatment: Bodily Integrity Versus the Preservation of Life," *Rutgers Law Review,* 26 (Winter 1972), p. 239.

THE STATUS OF CHILDREN

Adults belong to themselves in the sense that they are rational and free and therefore responsible for their actions. Adults are *sui juris.* Young children, though, are neither self-possessed nor responsible. While adults exist in and for themselves, as self-directive and self-conscious beings, young children, especially newborn infants, exist for their families and those who love them. They are not, nor can they in any sense be, responsible for themselves. If being a person is to be a responsible agent, a bearer of rights and duties, children are not persons in a strict sense. They are, rather, persons in a social sense: others must act on their behalf and bear responsibility for them. They are, as it were, entities defined by their place in social roles (for example, mother-child, family-child) rather than beings that define themselves as persons, that is, in and through themselves. Young children live as persons in and through the care of those who are responsible for them and those responsible for them exercise the children's rights on their behalf. In this sense children belong to families in ways that most adults do not. They exist in and through their family and society.

Treating young children with respect has, then, a sense different from treating adults with respect. One can respect neither a newborn infant's or very young child's wishes nor its freedom. In fact, a newborn infant or young child is more an entity that is valued highly because it will grow to be a person and because it plays a social role as if it were a person.[6] That is, a small child is treated as if it were a person in social roles such as mother-child and family-child relationships, though strictly speaking the child is in no way capable of claiming or being responsible for the rights imputed to it. All the rights and duties of the child are exercised and "held in trust" by others for a future time and for a person yet to develop.

Medical decisions to treat or not to treat a neonate or small child often turn on the probability and cost of achieving that future status—a developed personal life. The usual practice of letting anencephalic children (who congenitally lack all or most of the brain) die can be understood as a decision based on the absence of the possibility of achieving a personal life. The practice of refusing treatment to at least some children born with meningomyelocele can be justified through a similar, but more utilitarian, calculus. In the case of anencephalic children one might argue that care for them as persons is futile since they will never be persons. In the case of a child with meningomyelocele, one might argue that when the cost of cure would likely be very high and the probable lifestyle open to attainment very truncated, there is not a positive duty to make a large investment of money and suffering. One should note that the cost here must include not only financial costs but also the anxiety and suffering that prolonged and uncertain treatment of the child would cause the parents.

This further raises the issue of the scope of positive duties not only when there is no person present in a strict sense, but when the likelihood of a full human life is also very uncertain. Clinical and parental judgment may and should be guided by the expected life-style and the cost (in parental and societal pain and money) of its attainment. The decision about treatment, however, belongs properly to the parents because the child belongs to them in a sense that it does not belong to anyone else, even to itself. The care and raising

[6]By "young child" I mean either an infant or child so young as not yet to be able to participate, in any sense, in a decision. A precise operational definition of "young child" would clearly be difficult to develop. It is also not clear how one would bring older children into such decisions. See, for example, Milton Viederman, "Saying 'No' to Hemodialysis: Exploring Adaptation," and Daniel Burke, "Saying 'No' to Hemodialysis: An Acceptable Decision," both in *The Hastings Center Report,* 4 (September 1974), pp. 8–10, and John E. Schowalter, Julian B. Ferholt, and Nancy M. Mann, "The Adolescent Patient's Decision To Die," *Pediatrics,* 51 (January 1973), pp. 97–103.

of the child falls to the parents, and when considerable cost and little prospect of reasonable success are present, the parents may properly decide against life-prolonging treatment.

The physician's role is to present sufficient information in a usable form to the parents to aid them in making a decision. The accent is on the absence of a positive duty to treat in the presence of severe inconvenience (costs) to the parents; treatment that is very costly is not obligatory. What is suggested here is a general notion that there is never a duty to engage in extraordinary treatment and that "extraordinary" can be defined in terms of costs. This argument concerns children (1) whose future quality of life is likely to be seriously compromised and (2) whose present treatment would be very costly. The issue is that of the circumstances under which parents would not be obliged to take on severe burdens on behalf of their children or those circumstances under which society would not be so obliged. The argument should hold as well for those cases where the expected future life would surely be of normal quality, though its attainment would be extremely costly. The fact of little likelihood of success in attaining a normal life for the child makes decisions to do without treatment more plausible because the hope of success is even more remote and therefore the burden borne by parents or society becomes in that sense more extraordinary. But very high costs themselves could be a sufficient criterion, though in actual cases judgments in that regard would be very difficult when a normal life could be expected.

The decisions in these matters correctly lie in the hands of the parents, because it is primarily in terms of the family that children exist and develop—until children become persons strictly, they are persons in virtue of their social roles. As long as parents do not unjustifiably neglect the humans in those roles so that the value and purpose of that role (that is, child) stands to be eroded (thus endangering other children), society need not intervene. In short, parents may decide for or against the treatment of their severely deformed children.

However, society has a right to intervene and protect children for whom parents refuse care (including treatment) when such care does not constitute a severe burden and when it is likely that the child could be brought to a good quality of life. Obviously, "severe burden" and "good quality of life" will be difficult to define and their meanings will vary, just as it is always difficult to say when grains of sand dropped on a table constitute a heap. At most, though, society need only intervene when the grains clearly do not constitute a heap, that is, when it is clear that the burden is light and the chance of a good quality of life for the child is high. A small child's dependence on his parents is so essential that society need intervene only when the absence of intervention would lead to the role "child" being undermined. Society must value mother-child and family-child relationships and should intervene only in cases where (1) neglect is unreasonable and therefore would undermine respect and care for children, or (2) where societal intervention would prevent children from suffering unnecessary pain.[7]

THE INJURY OF CONTINUED EXISTENCE
But there is another viewpoint that must be considered: that of the child or even the person that the child might become. It might be argued that the child has a right not to have its life prolonged. The idea that forcing existence on a child could be wrong is a difficult notion, which, if true, would serve to amplify the foregoing argument. Such an argument would

---

[7]I have in mind here the issue of physicians, hospital administrators, or others being morally compelled to seek an injunction to force treatment of the child in the absence of parental consent. In these circumstances, the physician, who is usually best acquainted with the facts of the case, is the natural advocate of the child.

allow the construal of the issue in terms of the perspective of the child, that is, in terms of a duty not to treat in circumstances where treatment would only prolong suffering. In particular, it would at least give a framework for a decision to stop treatment in cases where, though the costs of treatment are not high, the child's existence would be characterized by severe pain and deprivation.

A basis for speaking of continuing existence as an injury to the child is suggested by the proposed legal concept of "wrongful life." A number of suits have been initiated in the United States and in other countries on the grounds that life or existence itself is, under certain circumstances, a tort or injury to the living person.[8] Although thus far all such suits have ultimately failed, some have succeeded in their initial stages. Two examples may be instructive. In each case the ability to receive recompense for the injury (the tort) presupposed the existence of the individual, whose existence was itself the injury. In one case a suit was initiated on behalf of a child against his father alleging that his father's siring him out of wedlock was an injury to the child.[9] In another case a suit on behalf of a child born of an inmate of a state mental hospital impregnated by rape in that institution was brought against the state of New York.[10] The suit was brought on the grounds that being born with such historical antecedents was itself an injury for which recovery was due. Both cases presupposed that nonexistence would have been preferable to the conditions under which the person born was forced to live.

The suits for tort for wrongful life raise the issue not only of when it would be preferable not to have been born but also of when it would be *wrong* to cause a person to be born. This implies that someone should have judged that it would have been preferable for the child never to have had existence, never to have been in the position to judge that the particular circumstances of life were intolerable.[11] Further, it implies that the person's existence under those circumstances should have been prevented and that, not having been prevented, life was not a gift but an injury. The concept of tort for wrongful life raises an issue concerning the responsibility for giving another person existence, namely, the notion that giving life is not always necessarily a good and justifiable action. Instead, in certain circumstances, so it has been argued, one may have a duty *not* to give existence to another person. This concept involves the claim that certain qualities of life have a negative value, making life an injury, not a gift; it involves, in short, a concept of human accountability and responsibility for human life. It contrasts with the notion that life is a gift of God and thus similar to other "acts of God," (that is, events for which no man is accountable). The concept thus signals the fact that humans can now control reproduction and that where rational control is possible humans are accountable. That is, the expansion of human capabilities has resulted in an expansion of human responsibilities such that one must now decide when and under what circumstances persons will come into existence.

The concept of tort for wrongful life is transferable in part to the painfully compromised existence of children who can only have their life prolonged for a short, painful, and marginal existence. The concept suggests that allowing life to be prolonged under such circumstances would itself be an injury of the person whose painful and severely compromised existence would be made to continue. In fact, it suggests that there is a duty not to prolong life if it can be determined to have a substantial negative value for the person involved. Such issues are moot in the case of adults, who can and should decide for themselves. But small children cannot make such a choice. For them it is an issue of justifying

---

[8]G. Tedeschi, "On Tort Liability for 'Wrongful Life,'" *Israel Law Review,* 1 (1966), p. 513.
[9]*Zepeda v. Zepeda*: 41 Ill. App. 2d 240, 190 N.E. 2d 849 (1963).
[10]*Williams v. State of New York*: 46 Misc. 2d 824, 260 N.Y.S. 2d 953 (Ct. Cl., 1965).
[11]Torts: "Illegitimate Child Denied Recovery against Father for 'Wrongful Life,'" *Iowa Law Review,* 49 (1969), p. 1009.

prolonging life under circumstances of painful and compromised existence. Or, put differently, such cases indicate the need to develop social canons to allow a decent death for children for whom the only possibility is protracted, painful suffering.

I do not mean to imply that one should develop a new basis for civil damages. In the field of medicine, the need is to recognize an ethical category, a concept of wrongful continuance of existence, not a new legal right. The concept of injury for continuance of existence, the proposed analogue of the concept of tort for wrongful life, presupposes that life can be of a negative value such that the medical maxim *primum non nocere* ("first do no harm") would require not sustaining life.[12]

The idea of responsibility for acts that sustain or prolong life is cardinal to the notion that one should not under certain circumstances further prolong the life of a child. Unlike adults, children cannot decide with regard to euthanasia (positive or negative), and if more than a utilitarian justification is sought, it must be sought in a duty not to inflict life on another person in circumstances where that life would be painful and futile. This position must rest on the facts that (1) medicine now can cause the prolongation of the life of seriously deformed children who in the past would have died young and that (2) it is not clear that life so prolonged is a good for the child. Further, the choice is made not on the basis of costs to the parents or to society but on the basis of the child's suffering and compromised existence.

The difficulty lies in determining what makes life not worth living for a child. Answers could never be clear. It seems reasonable, however, that the life of children with diseases that involve pain and no hope of survival should not be prolonged. In the case of Tay-Sachs disease (a disease marked by a progressive increase in spasticity and dementia usually leading to death at age three or four), one can hardly imagine that the terminal stages of spastic reaction to stimuli and great difficulty in swallowing are at all pleasant to the child (even insofar as it can only minimally perceive its circumstances). If such a child develops aspiration pneumonia and is treated, it can reasonably be said that to prolong its life is to inflict suffering. Other diseases give fairly clear portraits of lives not worth living: for example, Lesch-Nyhan disease, which is marked by mental retardation and compulsive self-mutilation.

The issue is more difficult in the case of children with diseases for whom the prospects for normal intelligence and a fair lifestyle do exist, but where these chances are remote and their realization expensive. Children born with meningomyelocele present this dilemma. Imagine, for example, a child that falls within Lorber's fifth category (an IQ of sixty or less, sometimes blind, subject to fits, and always incontinent). Such a child has little prospect of anything approaching a normal life, and there is a good chance of its dying even with treatment.[13] But such judgments are statistical. And if one does not treat such children, some will still survive and, as John Freeman indicates, be worse off if not treated.[14] In such cases one is in a dilemma. If one always treats, one must justify extending the life of those who will ultimately die anyway and in the process subjecting them to the morbidity of multiple surgical procedures. How remote does the prospect of a good life have to be in order not to be worth great pain and expense?[15] It is probably best to decide, in the absence

---

[12]H. Tristram Engelhardt, Jr., "Euthanasia and Children: The Injury of Continued Existence," *The Journal of Pediatrics,* 83 (July 1973), pp. 170–171.

[13]John Lorber, "Results of Treatment of Myelomeningocele," *Developmental Medicine and Child Neurology,* 13 (1971), p. 286.

[14]John M. Freeman, "The Shortsighted Treatment of Myelomeningocele: A Long-Term Case Report," *Pediatrics,* 53 (March 1974), pp. 311–313.

[15]John M. Freeman, "To Treat or Not To Treat," John Freeman, ed., *Practical Management of Meningomyelocele* (Baltimore: University Park Press, 1974), p. 21.

of a positive duty to treat, on the basis of the cost and suffering to parents and society. But, as Freeman argues, the prospect of prolonged or even increased suffering raises the issue of active euthanasia.[16]

If the child is not a person strictly, and if death is inevitable and expediting it would diminish the child's pain prior to death, then it would seem to follow that, all else being equal, a decision for active euthanasia would be permissible, even obligatory. The difficulty lies with "all else being equal," for it is doubtful that active euthanasia could be established as a practice without eroding and endangering children generally, since, as John Lorber has pointed out, children cannot speak in their own behalf.[17] Thus, although there is no argument in principle against the active euthanasia of small children, there could be an argument against such practices based on questions of prudence. To put it another way, even though one might have a duty to hasten the death of a particular child, one's duty to protect children in general could override that first duty. The issue of active euthanasia turns in the end on whether it would have social consequences that refraining would not, on whether (1) it is possible to establish procedural safeguards for limited active euthanasia and (2) whether such practices would have a significant adverse effect on the treatment of small children in general. But since these are procedural issues dependent on sociological facts, they are not open to an answer within the confines of this article. In any event, the concept of the injury of continued existence provides a basis for the justification of the passive euthanasia of small children—a practice already widespread and somewhat established in our society—beyond the mere absence of a positive duty to treat.

CONCLUSION

Though the lack of certainty concerning questions such as the prognosis of particular patients and the social consequence of active euthanasia of children prevents a clear answer to all the issues raised by the euthanasia of infants, it would seem that this much can be maintained: (1) Since children are not persons strictly but exist in and through their families, parents are the appropriate ones to decide whether or not to treat a deformed child when (a) there is not only little likelihood of full human life but also great likelihood of suffering if the life is prolonged, or (b) when the cost of prolonging life is very great. Such decisions must be made in consort with a physician who can accurately give estimates of cost and prognosis and who will be able to help the parents with the consequences of their decision. (2) It is reasonable to speak of a duty not to treat a small child when such treatment will only prolong a painful life or would in any event lead to a painful death. Though this does not by any means answer all the questions, it does point out an important fact— that medicine's duty is not always to prolong life doggedly but sometimes is quite the contrary.

QUESTIONS

1. Should the emotional and/or financial hardships of caring for a severely defective newborn child be considered morally relevant when decisions are made about whether the child will be allowed to die?

2. Is it morally wrong to "force existence on a child"?

[16]John Lorber, "Selective Treatment of Myelomeningocele: To Treat or Not To Treat," *Pediatrics*, 53 (March 1974), pp. 307–308.
[17]Lorber, "Selective Treatment of Myelomeningocele," p. 308.

SUGGESTED ADDITIONAL READINGS

BEAUCHAMP, TOM L., and SEYMOUR PERLIN, eds.: *Ethical Issues in Death and Dying.* Englewood Cliffs, N.J.: Prentice-Hall, 1978. Chapter 4 of this book is entitled "Euthanasia and Natural Death." It includes subsections on "The Quinlan Case" and "Natural Death and Living Wills." Also noteworthy, in "A Reply to Rachels on Active and Passive Euthanasia" (pp. 246–258), Beauchamp suggests that rule-utilitarian considerations may provide a basis for defending the moral significance of the distinction between active and passive euthanasia.

DOWNING, A. B., ed.: *Euthanasia and the Right to Death: The Case for Voluntary Euthanasia.* New York: Humanities Press; London: Peter Owen, 1969. This collection of euthanasia articles is written from many perspectives—philosophical, humanitarian, sociological, legal, and medical. Especially noteworthy is an article by Antony Flew, "The Principle of Euthanasia." Flew constructs "a general moral case for the establishment of a legal right" to voluntary (active) euthanasia.

DUFF, RAYMOND S., and A. G. M. CAMPBELL: "Moral and Ethical Dilemmas in the Special-Care Nursery." *New England Journal of Medicine,* vol. 289, Oct. 25, 1973, pp. 890–894. This article, a frequent reference point in ethical discussions of the treatment of defective newborns, provides helpful descriptions of the ethical attitudes and actual practices associated with one hospital's special-care nursery. Duff and Campbell make clear that in actual practice some infants are allowed to die.

GRISEZ, GERMAIN, and JOSEPH BOYLE: *Life and Death with Liberty and Justice.* Notre Dame, Ind.: University of Notre Dame Press, 1979. Grisez and Boyle distinguish jurisprudential questions concerning euthanasia from ethical ones and devote most of the book to the former. In addition to euthanasia as such, they discuss assisted and unassisted suicide, the definition of death, killing in war and self-defense, and other related topics.

KOHL, MARVIN, ed.: *Beneficent Euthanasia.* Buffalo, N.Y.: Prometheus Books, 1975. This anthology includes a number of excellent articles on the moral aspects of euthanasia. Also included are articles that provide statements of various religious positions on euthanasia. Other articles address the medical and legal aspects of euthanasia.

———, ed.: *Infanticide and the Value of Life.* Buffalo, N.Y.: Prometheus Books, 1978. Composed exclusively of original papers, this anthology focuses on the morality of putting to death severely defective newborns. Related social, medical, and legal issues are also discussed. Moreover, the value of life is a recurrent theme in the collection.

MAPPES, THOMAS A., and JANE S. ZEMBATY, eds.: *Biomedical Ethics.* New York: McGraw-Hill, 1981. Chapter 8 of this anthology includes helpful material in subsections entitled "Passive Euthanasia and the Definition of Death" and "The Legalization of Voluntary (Active) Euthanasia." Of special interest are two selections in the subsection entitled "The Treatment of Defective Newborns." Richard A. McCormick (pp. 379–384) defends the view that it is morally acceptable to allow a severely defective newborn to die *if and only if* there is no significant potential for a meaningful human existence. John A. Robertson (pp. 391–397) argues that the undesirable consequences of treating a severely defective newborn cannot morally justify the decision to withhold ordinary medical treatment.

ROBERTSON, JOHN A., and NORMAN FOST: "Passive Euthanasia of Defective Newborn Infants: Legal Considerations." *Journal of Pediatrics,* vol. 88, 1976, pp. 883–889. Robertson and Fost are concerned to make clear that there are grounds upon which parents, physicians, and other health personnel might be held criminally liable for their part in allowing severely defective newborns to die. They also argue that parents should not be the decision makers, on the presumption that society will continue to tolerate the practice of allowing severely defective newborns to die. They maintain that parents are not sufficiently disinterested to be legitimate decision makers.

TRAMMELL, RICHARD L.: "Euthanasia and the Law." *Journal of Social Philosophy,* vol. 9, January 1978, pp. 14–18. Trammell contends that the legalization of voluntary positive (i.e., active) euthanasia would probably not "result in overall positive utility for the class of people eligible to choose." He emphasizes the unwelcome pressures that would be created by legalization.

VEATCH, ROBERT M.: *Death, Dying, and the Biological Revolution: Our Last Quest for Responsibility.* New Haven, Conn.: Yale University Press, 1976. Two chapters of this book are especially notable in the context of euthanasia discussions. Chapter 3 considers many of the prominent conceptual difficulties. Chapter 5 considers various public policy options. Chapters 1 and 2 are of related interest; they provide an extensive discussion of the definition of death.

THE DEATH PENALTY

3

Strong convictions are firmly entrenched on both sides of the death penalty controversy. From one side, we hear in forceful tones that "murderers deserve to die." We are also told, not infrequently by those in law enforcement, that society simply cannot do without the death penalty: "Without the death penalty to deter potential criminals, serious crime will run rampant." From the other side of the controversy, in tones of equal conviction, we are told that the death penalty is a cruel and barbarous practice, effectively serving no purpose that could not be equally well served by a more humane punishment. "How long," it is asked, "must we indulge this uncivilized and pointless lust for revenge?" In the face of such strongly held but opposed views, each of us is invited to confront an important ethical issue, the morality of the death penalty. Before approaching the death penalty in its ethical dimensions, however, it may prove helpful to briefly discuss its constitutional dimensions. Many of the considerations raised in discussions of the constitutionality of the death penalty parallel those raised in discussions of the morality of the death penalty.

THE CONSTITUTIONALITY OF THE DEATH PENALTY

The Eighth Amendment to the Constitution of the United States explicitly prohibits the infliction of "cruel and unusual" punishment. If the death penalty is a cruel and unusual punishment, it is unconstitutional. But is it cruel and unusual? In a landmark case, *Furman v. Georgia* (1972), the Supreme Court ruled that the death penalty was unconstitutional *as then administered.* The Court did not comprehensively rule, however, that the death penalty was unconstitutional *by its very nature.* Indeed, subsequent developments in the Court have made clear that the death penalty, when administered under certain circumstances, is not unconstitutional.

The decision reached in *Furman* was by a mere five-to-four majority. Importantly, there was a basic divergence of viewpoint among those who voted with the majority. Both Justice Marshall and Justice Brennan argued straightforwardly that the death penalty is a cruel and unusual punishment *by its very nature.* From this perspective it would not matter how much the procedures of its administration might be modified. It would still remain a cruel and unusual punishment. Among the reasons advanced to support this contention, two are especially noteworthy. (1) The death penalty is excessive in the sense of being unnecessary; lesser penalties are capable of serving the desired legislative purpose. (2) The death penalty is abhorrent to currently existing moral values.

The other three justices (Douglas, White, and Stewart) who voted with the majority did not commit themselves to the position that the death penalty is unconstitutional *by its very nature.* Leaving this underlying issue unresolved, they simply advanced the more guarded contention that the death penalty was unconstitutional *as then administered.* In their view, the death penalty was unconstitutional primarily because it was being administered in an arbitrary and capricious manner. The essence of their argument can be reconstructed in the following way. The death penalty in its contemporary setting is, as a common matter of course, inflicted at the discretion of a jury (or sometimes a judge). The absence of explicit standards to govern the decision between life and death allows a wide range of unchecked prejudice to operate freely under the heading of "discretion." For example, "discretion" seems to render blacks more prone than whites to the death penalty. Such standardless discretion violates not only the Eighth Amendment but also the Fourteenth Amendment, which guarantees "due process of law."

As matters developed in the wake of *Furman,* it was the Court's objection to *standardless discretion* that provided an opening for the many individual states still anxious to retain the death penalty as a viable component of their legal systems. These states were faced with the challenge of devising procedures for inflicting the death penalty which would not be open to the charge of standardless discretion. Two such approaches gained prominence. (1) Some states (e.g., North Carolina) moved to dissolve the objection of standardless discretion by simply making the death penalty *mandatory* for certain crimes. (2) Other states (e.g., Georgia) took an equally obvious approach to avoid the charge of standardless discretion. It consisted in the effort to establish standards that would provide guidance for the jury (or the judge) in deciding between life and death.

Subsequent developments have made clear that the second approach is constitutionally acceptable whereas the first is not. In *Woodson v. North Carolina* (1976), the Court ruled (though by a mere five-to-four majority) that mandatory death sentences are unconstitutional. In *Gregg v. Georgia* (1976), however, the Court ruled (with only Justice Marshall and Justice Brennan dissenting) that the death penalty is not unconstitutional when imposed at the discretion of a jury for the *crime of murder,*[1] so long as appropriate safeguards are provided against any arbitrary or capricious imposition. Most prominently, there must be explicit standards established for the guidance of jury deliberations. The attitude of the Court in this regard is made clear by Justices Stewart, Powell, and Stevens in their opinion in *Gregg v. Georgia* (1976), which appears in this chapter. Also appearing in this chapter is the dissenting opinion of Justice Marshall.

THE ETHICAL ISSUE

In any discussion of the morality of the death penalty, it is important to remember that the death penalty is a kind of punishment. Indeed, it is normally thought to be the most serious kind of punishment, hence the term "*capital* punishment." Most philosophers agree that punishment in general (as contrasted with capital punishment in particular) is a morally justified social practice. For one thing, however uneasy we might feel about inflicting harm on another person, it is hard to visualize a complex society managing to survive without an established legal system of punishment. However, to say that most philosophers agree that punishment in general is a morally justified social practice is not to say that there are no dissenters from this view. Some argue that it is possible to structure society in ways that would not necessitate commitment to a legal system of punishment as we know it. For example, might it not be that undesirable social behavior could be adequately kept in check by therapeutic treatment rather than by traditional kinds of punishment? Such a system would certainly have the advantage of being more humane, but it seems doubtful that present therapeutic techniques are adequate to the task. Perhaps future advances in the

---

[1] In *Gregg,* the Supreme Court considered only the constitutionality of imposing the death penalty for the *crime of murder.* In *Coker v. Georgia* (1977), 433 U.S. 584, the Court subsequently considered the constitutionality of imposing the death penalty for the *crime of rape.* Holding death to be a "grossly disproportionate" punishment for the crime of rape, the Court declared such an employment of the death penalty unconstitutional.

behavioral sciences will render such an alternative more plausible. If so, it may be that one day the whole practice of (nontherapeutic) punishment will have to be rejected on moral grounds. Still, for now, there is widespread agreement on the moral defensibility of punishment as an overall social practice. What stands out as an open and hotly debated ethical issue is whether or not the death penalty, as a distinctive kind of punishment, ought to continue to play a role in our legal system of punishment.

Those in favor of retaining the death penalty are commonly called *retentionists.* Retentionists differ among themselves regarding the kinds of cases in which they find it appropriate to employ the death penalty. They also differ among themselves regarding the supporting arguments they find acceptable. But anyone who supports the retention of the death penalty—for employment in whatever kinds of cases and for whatever reason—is by definition a retentionist. Those in favor of abolishing the death penalty are commonly called *abolitionists.* Abolitionists, by definition, refuse to support any employment of the death penalty. Like the retentionists, however, they differ among themselves concerning the supporting arguments they find acceptable.

There is one extreme, and not widely embraced, abolitionist line of thought. It is based on the belief that the sanctity of human life demands absolute nonviolence. On this view, killing of any kind, for any reason, is always and everywhere morally wrong. No one has the right to take a human life, not in self-defense, not in war, not in any circumstance. Thus, since the death penalty obviously involves a kind of killing, it is a morally unacceptable form of punishment and must be abolished. This general view, which is associated with the Quakers and other pacifists, has struck most moral philosophers as implausible. Can we really think that killing, when it is the only course that will save oneself from an unprovoked violent assault, is morally wrong? Can we really think that it would be morally wrong to kill a terrorist if that were the *only* possible way of stopping him or her from exploding a bomb in the midst of a kindergarten class? The defender of absolute nonviolence is sometimes inclined to argue at this point that violence will only breed violence. There may indeed be much truth in this claim. Still, most people would reject the view that such a claim adequately supports the contention that *all* killing is morally wrong, and if *some* killing is morally acceptable, perhaps the death penalty itself is morally acceptable. What arguments can be made on its behalf?

RETENTIONIST ARGUMENTS

Broadly speaking, arguments for the retention of the death penalty usually emphasize either (1) considerations of *justice* or (2) considerations of *social utility.* Those who emphasize considerations of justice typically develop their case along the following line: When the moral order is upset by the commission of some offense, it is only right that the disorder be rectified by punishment equal in intensity to the seriousness of the offense. This view is reflected in remarks such as "The scales of justice demand retribution" and "The offender must pay for the crime." Along this line, the philosopher Immanuel Kant (1724–1804) is famous for his unequivocal defense of the principle of retaliation. According to this principle, punishment is to be inflicted in a measure that will equalize the offense. And when the offense is murder, *only* capital punishment is sufficient to equalize it.

In one of this chapter's readings, Burton M. Leiser defends the retention of the death penalty on grounds of retributive justice. Hugo Adam Bedau, a prominent abolitionist, provides a contrasting point of view. Emphasizing the difficulties associated with interpreting and applying the principle of "a life for a life," Bedau argues that considerations of retributive justice cannot effectively support the retention of the death penalty.

Although the demand for retribution continues to play a prominent role in the overall case for the death penalty, many retentionists (and obviously abolitionists as well) have come to feel quite uneasy with the notion of imposing the death penalty "because the wrongdoer deserves it." Perhaps, at least to some extent, this uneasiness has been provoked by our growing awareness of the way in which social conditions, such as ghetto living, seem to spawn criminal activity. If so, then it seems we have arrived at a point of intersection with a venerable philosophical problem, the problem of "freedom and determinism."

Since considerations of social utility are commonly advanced in defense of the practice of punishment in general, it is not surprising to find that they are also commonly advanced in defense of retaining the death penalty. Utilitarianism, as a distinct school of moral philosophy, locates the primary justification of punishment in its social utility. Utilitarians acknowledge that punishment consists in the infliction of evil upon another person, but they hold that such evil is far outweighed by the future benefits that will accrue to society. Imprisonment, for example, might lead to such socially desirable effects as (1) *rehabilitation* of the criminal, (2) *incapacitation,* whereby we achieve temporary or permanent protection from the imprisoned criminal, and (3) *deterrence* of other potential criminals. When utilitarian considerations are recruited in support of the retention of the *death* penalty, it is clear that rehabilitation of the criminal can play no part in the case. But retentionists do frequently promote considerations of incapacitation and deterrence.

Accordingly, retentionists often appeal to considerations of incapacitation and argue that the death penalty is the only effective way to protect society from certain *violence-prone and irreformable* criminals. (Notice that an important difficulty here would be finding effective criteria for the recognition of those criminals who are truly "violence-prone and irreformable.") Life imprisonment, it is said, cannot assure society of the needed protection, because criminals such as these pose an imminent threat even to their prison guards and fellow inmates. Furthermore, escape is always possible. In one of this chapter's readings, Sidney Hook relies on considerations of incapacitation in defending the retention of the death penalty for employment in the case of certain twice-guilty murderers.

Many retentionists think, however, that the strongest case for the death penalty can be made not on grounds of protecting society from convicted criminals but rather on grounds of deterring potential criminals. Because of the intense fear that most people have of death, it is argued, the death penalty functions as a uniquely effective deterrent to serious crime. When this argument appears, the debate between retentionists and abolitionists focuses totally on a factual issue. Is the death penalty indeed a more substantial deterrent than life imprisonment? Facts and figures often seem to dominate this particular aspect of the debate, and it is by no means easy to discern the true state of affairs. One retentionist argument, advanced by Ernest van den Haag in this chapter, takes as its starting point our very uncertainty. If we are unsure whether or not the death penalty is a uniquely effective deterrent, he argues, we are morally obliged to risk needlessly eradicating the lives of convicted murderers rather than risking the lives of innocent people who might become future murder victims.

ABOLITIONIST ARGUMENTS

What can be said of the abolitionist case against the death penalty? Most abolitionists do not care to argue the extreme position, already discussed, of absolute nonviolence, yet they often do want to commit themselves seriously to the "sanctity of human life." They emphasize the inherent worth and dignity of each individual and insist that the taking of a human life, while perhaps sometimes morally permissible, is a very serious matter and not to be permitted in the absence of weighty overriding reasons. At face value, they argue, the death penalty is cruel and inhumane; and since retentionists have not succeeded in advancing substantial reasons in its defense, it must be judged a morally unacceptable practice. Against retentionist arguments based on retribution as a demand of justice, abolitionists frequently argue that the "demand of justice" is nothing but a mask for a barbarous vengeance. Against retentionist arguments based on considerations of social utility, they simply argue that other more humane punishments will serve equally well. Indeed, in the last selection of this chapter, Hugo Adam Bedau contends that any complete account of utilitarian considerations would probably favor abolition of the death penalty.

In addition to advancing a number of direct arguments against retentionist arguments, abolitionists also prominently incorporate into their overall case the following consideration. It is impossible to guarantee that mistakes will not be made in the administration of punishment. But this factor is especially important in the case of the death penalty, because only *capital* punishment is irrevocable. Thus, only the death penalty eradicates the possibility of compensating an innocent person wrongly punished.

Thomas A. Mappes

**JUSTICES
POTTER STEWART,
LEWIS F. POWELL, JR.,
and JOHN PAUL STEVENS**

OPINION IN *GREGG V. GEORGIA*

Potter Stewart, Lewis F. Powell, Jr., and John Paul Stevens are associate justices of the United States Supreme Court. Justice Stewart, a graduate of Yale Law School, spent some years in private practice, served as judge of the United States Court of Appeals, Sixth Circuit (1954–1958), and was appointed to the Supreme Court in 1958. Justice Powell, LL.B (Washington and Lee), LL.M (Harvard), practiced law in Richmond, Virginia, for nearly forty years prior to his appointment in 1971 to the Supreme Court. Justice Stevens, a graduate of Northwestern University School of Law, spent a number of years in private practice, served as judge of the United States Court of Appeals, Seventh Circuit (1970–1975), and was appointed to the Supreme Court in 1975.

The State of Georgia reacted to the Court's decision in *Furman v. Georgia* (1972) by drafting a death penalty statute calculated to avoid the Court's objection to "standardless discretion." Georgia's approach, in contrast to the approach of those states that made the death penalty mandatory for certain crimes, embodied an effort to specify standards that would guide a jury (or a judge) in deciding between the death penalty and life imprisonment. In this case, with only Justice Marshall and Justice Brennan dissenting, the Court upheld the constitutionality of imposing the death penalty for the crime of murder under the law of Georgia.

Justices Stewart, Powell, and Stevens initially consider the contention that the death penalty for the crime of murder is, under all circumstances, "cruel and unusual" punishment, thus unconstitutional. On their analysis, a punishment is "cruel and unusual" if it fails to accord with "evolving standards of decency." Moreover, even if a punishment does accord with contemporary values, it must still be judged "cruel and unusual" if it fails to accord with the "dignity of man," the "basic concept underlying the Eighth Amendment." They take this second stipulation to rule out "excessive" punishment, identified as (1) that which involves the unnecessary and wanton infliction of pain or (2) that which is grossly out of proportion to the severity of the crime. In the light of these considerations, Justices Stewart, Powell, and Stevens argue that the imposition of the death penalty for the crime of murder does not invariably violate the Constitution. They contend that legislative developments since *Furman* have made clear that the death penalty is acceptable to contemporary society. Moreover, they contend, the death penalty is not invariably "excessive": (1) It may properly be considered necessary to achieve two principal social purposes—retribution and deterrence. (2) When the death penalty is imposed for the crime of murder, it may properly be considered not disproportionate to the severity of the crime.

Turning their attention to the death sentence imposed under the law of Georgia in this case, Justices Stewart, Powell, and Stevens maintain that a carefully drafted statute, ensuring "that the sentencing authority is given adequate information and guidance," makes it possible to avoid imposing the death penalty in an arbitrary or capricious manner. The revised Georgia statutory system under which Gregg was sentenced to death, they conclude, does not violate the Constitution.

The issue in this case is whether the imposition of the sentence of death for the crime of murder under the law of Georgia violates the Eighth and Fourteenth Amendments.

I

The petitioner, Troy Gregg, was charged with committing armed robbery and murder. In accordance with Georgia procedure in capital cases, the trial was in two stages, a guilt stage and a sentencing stage. . . .

. . . The jury found the petitioner guilty of two counts of armed robbery and two counts of murder.

At the penalty stage, which took place before the same jury, . . . the trial judge instructed the jury that it could recommend either a death sentence or a life prison sentence on each count. . . . The jury returned verdicts of death on each count.

The Supreme Court of Georgia affirmed the convictions and the imposition of the death sentences for murder. . . . The death sentences imposed for armed robbery, however, were vacated on the grounds that the death penalty had rarely been imposed in Georgia for that offense. . . .

II

. . . The Georgia statute, as amended after our decision in *Furman v. Georgia* (1972), retains the death penalty for six categories of crime: murder, kidnaping for ransom or where the victim is harmed, armed robbery, rape, treason, and aircraft hijacking. . . .

III

We address initially the basic contention that the punishment of death for the crime of murder is, under all circumstances, "cruel and unusual" in violation of the Eighth and Fourteenth Amendments of the Constitution. In Part IV of this opinion, we will consider the sentence of death imposed under the Georgia statutes at issue in this case.

United States Supreme Court. 428 U.S. 153 (1976).

The Court on a number of occasions has both assumed and asserted the constitutionality of capital punishment. In several cases that assumption provided a necessary foundation for the decision, as the Court was asked to decide whether a particular method of carrying out a capital sentence would be allowed to stand under the Eighth Amendment. But until *Furman v. Georgia* (1972), the Court never confronted squarely the fundamental claim that the punishment of death always, regardless of the enormity of the offense or the procedure followed in imposing the sentence, is cruel and unusual punishment in violation of the Constitution. Although this issue was presented and addressed in *Furman,* it was not resolved by the Court. Four Justices would have held that capital punishment is not unconstitutional *per se;* two Justices would have reached the opposite conclusion; and three Justices, while agreeing that the statutes then before the Court were invalid as applied, left open the question whether such punishment may ever be imposed. We now hold that the punishment of death does not invariably violate the Constitution.

A

The history of the prohibition of "cruel and unusual" punishment already has been reviewed at length. The phrase first appeared in the English Bill of Rights of 1689, which was drafted by Parliament at the accession of William and Mary. The English version appears to have been directed against punishments unauthorized by statute and beyond the jurisdiction of the sentencing court, as well as those disproportionate to the offense involved. The American draftsmen, who adopted the English phrasing in drafting the Eighth Amendment, were primarily concerned, however, with proscribing "tortures" and other "barbarous" methods of punishment.

In the earliest cases raising Eighth Amendment claims, the Court focused on particular methods of execution to determine whether they were too cruel to pass constitutional muster. The constitutionality of the sentence of death itself was not at issue, and the criterion used to evaluate the mode of execution was its similarity to "torture" and other "barbarous" methods. . . .

But the Court has not confined the prohibition embodied in the Eighth Amendment to "barbarous" methods that were generally outlawed in the 18th century. Instead, the Amendment has been interpreted in a flexible and dynamic manner. The Court early recognized that "a principle to be vital must be capable of wider application than the mischief which gave it birth." Thus the Clause forbidding "cruel and unusual" punishments "is not fastened to the obsolete but may acquire meaning as public opinion becomes enlightened by a humane justice." . . .

It is clear from the foregoing precedents that the Eighth Amendment has not been regarded as a static concept. As Mr. Chief Justice Warren said, in an oftquoted phrase, "[t]he Amendment must draw its meaning from the evolving standards of decency that mark the progress of a maturing society." Thus, an assessment of contemporary values concerning the infliction of a challenged sanction is relevant to the application of the Eighth Amendment. As we develop below more fully, this assessment does not call for a subjective judgment. It requires, rather, that we look to objective indicia that reflect the public attitude toward a given sanction.

But our cases also make clear that public perceptions of standards of decency with respect to criminal sanctions are not conclusive. A penalty also must accord with "the dignity of man," which is the "basic concept underlying the Eighth Amendment." This means, at least, that the punishment not be "excessive." When a form of punishment in the abstract (in this case, whether capital punishment may ever be imposed as a sanction for murder) rather than in the particular (the propriety of death as a penalty to be applied to a specific defendant for a specific crime) is under consideration, the inquiry into "excessiveness" has two aspects. First, the punishment must not involve the unnecessary and wanton infliction of pain. Second, the punishment must not be grossly out of proportion to the severity of the crime.

B

Of course, the requirements of the Eighth Amendment must be applied with an awareness of the limited role to be played by the courts. This does not mean that judges have no role to play, for the Eighth Amendment is a restraint upon the exercise of legislative power. . . .

But, while we have an obligation to insure that constitutional bounds are not over-reached, we may not act as judges as we might as legislators. . . .

Therefore, in assessing a punishment selected by a democratically elected legislature against the constitutional measure, we presume its validity. We may not require the legislature to select the least severe penalty possible so long as the penalty selected is not cruelly inhumane or disproportionate to the crime involved. And a heavy burden rests on those who would attack the judgment of the representatives of the people.

This is true in part because the constitutional test is intertwined with an assessment of contemporary standards and the legislative judgment weighs heavily in ascertaining such standards. "[I]n a democratic society legislatures, not courts, are constituted to respond to the will and consequently the moral values of the people."

The deference we owe to the decisions of the state legislatures under our federal system is enhanced where the specification of punishments is concerned, for "these are peculiarly questions of legislative policy." Caution is necessary lest this Court become, "under the aegis of the Cruel and Unusual Punishment Clause, the ultimate arbiter of the standards of criminal responsibility . . . throughout the country." A decision that a given punishment is impermissible under the Eighth Amendment cannot be reversed short of a constitutional amendment. The ability of the people to express their preference through the normal democratic processes, as well as through ballot referenda, is shut off. Revisions cannot be made in the light of further experience.

C

In the discussion to this point we have sought to identify the principles and considerations that guide a court in addressing an Eighth Amendment claim. We now consider specifically whether the sentence of death for the crime of murder is a *per se* violation of the Eighth and Fourteenth Amendments to the Constitution. We note first that history and precedent strongly support a negative answer to this question.

The imposition of the death penalty for the crime of murder has a long history of acceptance both in the United States and in England. . . .

It is apparent from the text of the Constitution itself that the existence of capital punishment was accepted by the Framers. At the time the Eighth Amendment was ratified, capital punishment was a common sanction in every State. Indeed, the First Congress of the United States enacted legislation providing death as the penalty for specified crimes. . . .

For nearly two centuries, this Court, repeatedly and often expressly, has recognized that capital punishment is not invalid *per se*. . . .

Four years ago, the petitioners in *Furman* and its companion cases predicated their argument primarily upon the asserted proposition that standards of decency had evolved to the point where capital punishment no longer could be tolerated. The petitioners in those cases said, in effect, that the evolutionary process had come to an end, and that standards of decency required that the Eighth Amendment be construed finally as prohibiting capital punishment for any crime regardless of its depravity and impact on society. This view was accepted by two Justices. Three other Justices were unwilling to go so far; focusing on the procedures by which convicted defendants were selected for the death penalty rather than on the actual punishment inflicted, they joined in the conclusion that the statutes before the Court were constitutionally invalid.

The petitioners in the capital cases before the Court today renew the "standards of decency" argument, but developments during the four years since *Furman* have undercut substantially the assumptions upon which their argument rested. Despite the continuing debate, dating back to the 19th century, over the morality and utility of capital punishment, it is now evident that a large proportion of American society continues to regard it as an appropriate and necessary criminal sanction.

The most marked indication of society's endorsement of the death penalty for murder is the legislative response to *Furman*. The legislatures of at least 35 States have enacted new statutes that provide for the death penalty for at least some crimes that result in the death of another person. And the Congress of the United States, in 1974, enacted a statute providing the death penalty for aircraft piracy that results in death. These recently adopted statutes have attempted to address the concerns expressed by the Court in *Furman* primarily (i) by specifying the factors to be weighed and the procedures to be followed in deciding when to impose a capital sentence, or (ii) by making the death penalty mandatory for specified crimes. But all of the post-*Furman* statutes make clear that capital punishment itself has not been rejected by the elected representatives of the people. . . .

The jury also is a significant and reliable objective index of contemporary values because it is so directly involved. The Court has said that "one of the most important functions any jury can perform in making . . . a selection [between life imprisonment and death for a defendant convicted in a capital case] is to maintain a link between contemporary community values and the penal system." It may be true that evolving standards have influenced juries in recent decades to be more discriminating in imposing the sentence of death. But the relative infrequency of jury verdicts imposing the death sentence does not indicate rejection of capital punishment *per se*. Rather, the reluctance of juries in many cases to impose the sentence may well reflect the humane feeling that this most irrevocable of sanctions should be reserved for a small number of extreme cases. Indeed, the actions of juries in many States since *Furman* are fully compatible with the legislative judgments, reflected in the new statutes, as to the continued utility and necessity of capital punishment in appropriate cases. At the close of 1974 at least 254 persons had been sentenced to death since *Furman,* and by the end of March 1976, more than 460 persons were subject to death sentences.

As we have seen, however, the Eighth Amendment demands more than that a challenged punishment be acceptable to contemporary society. The Court also must ask whether it comports with the basic concept of human dignity at the core of the Amendment. Although we cannot "invalidate a category of penalties because we deem less severe penalties adequate to serve the ends of penology," the sanction imposed cannot be so totally without penological justification that it results in the gratuitous infliction of suffering.

The death penalty is said to serve two principal social purposes: retribution and deterrence of capital crimes by prospective offenders.[1]

In part, capital punishment is an expression of society's moral outrage at particularly offensive conduct. This function may be unappealing to many, but it is essential in an

---

[1]Another purpose that has been discussed is the incapacitation of dangerous criminals and the consequent prevention of crimes that they may otherwise commit in the future.

ordered society that asks its citizens to rely on legal processes rather than self-help to vindicate their wrongs.

> The instinct for retribution is part of the nature of man, and channeling that instinct in the administration of criminal justice serves an important purpose in promoting the stability of a society governed by law. When people begin to believe that organized society is unwilling or unable to impose upon criminal offenders the punishment they "deserve," then there are sown the seeds of anarchy—of self-help, vigilante justice, and lynch law. *Furman v. Georgia* (STEWART, J., concurring).

"Retribution is no longer the dominant objective of the criminal law," but neither is it a forbidden objective nor one inconsistent with our respect for the dignity of men. Indeed, the decision that capital punishment may be the appropriate sanction in extreme cases is an expression of the community's belief that certain crimes are themselves so grievous an affront to humanity that the only adequate response may be the penalty of death.

Statistical attempts to evaluate the worth of the death penalty as a deterrent to crimes by potential offenders have occasioned a great deal of debate. The results simply have been inconclusive. . . .

Although some of the studies suggest that the death penalty may not function as a significantly greater deterrent than lesser penalties, there is no convincing empirical evidence either supporting or refuting this view. We may nevertheless assume safely that there are murderers, such as those who act in passion, for whom the threat of death has little or no deterrent effect. But for many others, the death penalty undoubtedly is a significant deterrent. There are carefully contemplated murders, such as murder for hire, where the possible penalty of death may well enter into the cold calculus that precedes the decision to act. And there are some categories of murder, such as murder by a life prisoner, where other sanctions may not be adequate.

The value of capital punishment as a deterrent of crime is a complex factual issue the resolution of which properly rests with the legislatures, which can evaluate the results of statistical studies in terms of their own local conditions and with a flexibility of approach that is not available to the courts. Indeed, many of the post-*Furman* statutes reflect just such a responsible effort to define those crimes and those criminals for which capital punishment is most probably an effective deterrent.

In sum, we cannot say that the judgment of the Georgia Legislature that capital punishment may be necessary in some cases is clearly wrong. Considerations of federalism, as well as respect for the ability of a legislature to evaluate, in terms of its particular State, the moral consensus concerning the death penalty and its social utility as a sanction, require us to conclude, in the absence of more convincing evidence, that the infliction of death as a punishment for murder is not without justification and thus is not unconstitutionally severe.

Finally, we must consider whether the punishment of death is disproportionate in relation to the crime for which it is imposed. There is no question that death as a punishment is unique in its severity and irrevocability. When a defendant's life is at stake, the Court has been particularly sensitive to insure that every safeguard is observed. But we are concerned here only with the imposition of capital punishment for the crime of murder, and when a life has been taken deliberately by the offender,[2] we cannot say that the pun-

---

[2]We do not address here the question whether the taking of the criminal's life is a proportionate sanction where no victim has been deprived of life—for example, when capital punishment is imposed for rape, kidnaping, or armed robbery that does not result in the death of any human being.

ishment is invariably disproportionate to the crime. It is an extreme sanction, suitable to the most extreme of crimes.

We hold that the death penalty is not a form of punishment that may never be imposed, regardless of the circumstances of the offense, regardless of the character of the offender, and regardless of the procedure followed in reaching the decision to impose it.

IV

We now consider whether Georgia may impose the death penalty on the petitioner in this case.

A

While *Furman* did not hold that the infliction of the death penalty *per se* violates the Constitution's ban on cruel and unusual punishments, it did recognize that the penalty of death is different in kind from any other punishment imposed under our system of criminal justice. Because of the uniqueness of the death penalty, *Furman* held that it could not be imposed under sentencing procedures that created a substantial risk that it would be inflicted in an arbitrary and capricious manner. . . .

Furman mandates that where discretion is afforded a sentencing body on a matter so grave as the determination of whether a human life should be taken or spared, that discretion must be suitably directed and limited so as to minimize the risk of wholly arbitrary and capricious action.

It is certainly not a novel proposition that discretion in the area of sentencing be exercised in an informed manner. We have long recognized that "[f]or the determination of sentences, justice generally requires . . . that there be taken into account the circumstances of the offense together with the character and propensities of the offender." . . .

Jury sentencing has been considered desirable in capital cases in order "to maintain a link between contemporary community values and the penal system—a link without which the determination of punishment could hardly reflect 'the evolving standards of decency that mark the progress of a maturing society.'" But it creates special problems. Much of the information that is relevant to the sentencing decision may have no relevance to the question of guilt, or may even be extremely prejudicial to a fair determination of that question. This problem, however, is scarcely insurmountable. Those who have studied the question suggest that a bifurcated procedure—one in which the question of sentence is not considered until the determination of guilt has been made—is the best answer. . . . When a human life is at stake and when the jury must have information prejudicial to the question of guilt but relevant to the question of penalty in order to impose a rational sentence, a bifurcated system is more likely to ensure elimination of the constitutional deficiencies identified in *Furman*.

But the provision of relevant information under fair procedural rules is not alone sufficient to guarantee that the information will be properly used in the imposition of punishment, especially if sentencing is performed by a jury. Since the members of a jury will have had little, if any, previous experience in sentencing, they are unlikely to be skilled in dealing with the information they are given. To the extent that this problem is inherent in jury sentencing, it may not be totally correctible. It seems clear, however, that the problem will be alleviated if the jury is given guidance regarding the factors about the crime and the defendant that the State, representing organized society, deems particularly relevant to the sentencing decision. . . .

While some have suggested that standards to guide a capital jury's sentencing deliberations are impossible to formulate, the fact is that such standards have been developed. When the drafters of the Model Penal Code faced this problem, they concluded "that it is within the realm of possibility to point to the main circumstances of aggravation and of mitigation that should be weighed *and weighed against each other* when they are presented in a concrete case."[3] While such standards are by necessity somewhat general, they do provide guidance to the sentencing authority and thereby reduce the likelihood that it will impose a sentence that fairly can be called capricious or arbitrary. Where the sentencing authority is required to specify the factors it relied upon in reaching its decision, the further safeguard of meaningful appellate review is available to ensure that death sentences are not imposed capriciously or in a freakish manner.

In summary, the concerns expressed in *Furman* that the penalty of death not be imposed in an arbitrary or capricious manner can be met by a carefully drafted statute that ensures that the sentencing authority is given adequate information and guidance. As a general proposition these concerns are best met by a system that provides for a bifurcated proceeding at which the sentencing authority is apprised of the information relevant to the imposition of sentence and provided with standards to guide its use of the information.

We do not intend to suggest that only the above-described procedures would be permissible under *Furman* or that any sentencing system constructed along these general lines would inevitably satisfy the concerns of *Furman,* for each distinct system must be examined on an individual basis. Rather, we have embarked upon this general exposition to make clear that it is possible to construct capital-sentencing systems capable of meeting *Furman's* constitutional concerns.

B

We now turn to consideration of the constitutionality of Georgia's capital-sentencing procedures. In the wake of *Furman,* Georgia amended its capital punishment statute, but chose not to narrow the scope of its murder provisions. Thus, now as before *Furman,* in Georgia "[a] person commits murder when he unlawfully and with malice aforethought,

---

[3]The Model Penal Code proposes the following standards: "(3) Aggravating Circumstances.

"(a) The murder was committed by a convict under sentence of imprisonment.

"(b) The defendant was previously convicted of another murder or of a felony involving the use or threat of violence to the person.

"(c) At the time the murder was committed the defendant also committed another murder.

"(d) The defendant knowingly created a great risk of death to many persons.

"(e) The murder was committed while the defendant was engaged or was an accomplice in the commission of, or an attempt to commit, or flight after committing or attempting to commit robbery, rape or deviate sexual intercourse by force or threat of force, arson, burglary or kidnapping.

"(f) The murder was committed for the purpose of avoiding or preventing a lawful arrest or effecting an escape from lawful custody.

"(g) The murder was committed for pecuniary gain.

"(h) The murder was especially heinous, atrocious or cruel, manifesting exceptional depravity.

"(4) Mitigating Circumstances.

"(a) The defendant has no significant history of prior criminal activity.

"(b) The murder was committed while the defendant was under the influence of extreme mental or emotional disturbance.

"(c) The victim was a participant in the defendant's homicidal conduct or consented to the homicidal act.

"(d) The murder was committed under circumstances which the defendant believed to provide a moral justification or extenuation for his conduct.

"(e) The defendant was an accomplice in a murder committed by another person and his participation in the homicidal act was relatively minor.

"(f) The defendant acted under duress or under the domination of another person.

"(g) At the time of the murder, the capacity of the defendant to appreciate the criminality [wrongfulness] of his conduct or to conform his conduct to the requirements of law was impaired as a result of mental disease or defect or intoxication.

"(h) The youth of the defendant at the time of the crime." ALI Model Penal Code § 210.6 (Proposed Official Draft 1962).

either express or implied, causes the death of another human being." All persons convicted of murder "shall be punished by death or by imprisonment for life."

Georgia did act, however, to narrow the class of murderers subject to capital punishment by specifying 10 statutory aggravating circumstances, one of which must be found by the jury to exist beyond a reasonable doubt before a death sentence can ever be imposed. In addition, the jury is authorized to consider any other appropriate aggravating or mitigating circumstances. The jury is not required to find any mitigating circumstance in order to make a recommendation of mercy that is binding on the trial court, but it must find a *statutory* aggravating circumstance before recommending a sentence of death.

These procedures require the jury to consider the circumstances of the crime and the criminal before it recommends sentence. No longer can a Georgia jury do as Furman's jury did: reach a finding of the defendant's guilt and then, without guidance or direction, decide whether he should live or die. Instead, the jury's attention is directed to the specific circumstances of the crime: Was it committed in the course of another capital felony? Was it committed for money? Was it committed upon a peace officer or judicial officer? Was it committed in a particularly heinous way or in a manner that endangered the lives of many persons? In addition, the jury's attention is focused on the characteristics of the person who committed the crime: Does he have a record of prior convictions for capital offenses? Are there any special facts about this defendant that mitigate against imposing capital punishment (*e.g.*, his youth, the extent of his cooperation with the police, his emotional state at the time of the crime). As a result, while some jury discretion still exists, "the discretion to be exercised is controlled by clear and objective standards so as to produce non-discriminatory application."

As an important additional safeguard against arbitrariness and caprice, the Georgia statutory scheme provides for automatic appeal of all death sentences to the State's Supreme Court. That court is required by statute to review each sentence of death and determine whether it was imposed under the influence of passion or prejudice, whether the evidence supports the jury's finding of a statutory aggravating circumstance, and whether the sentence is disproportionate compared to those sentences imposed in similar cases.

In short, Georgia's new sentencing procedures require as a prerequisite to the imposition of the death penalty, specific jury findings as to the circumstances of the crime or the character of the defendant. Moreover, to guard further against a situation comparable to that presented in *Furman,* the Supreme Court of Georgia compares each death sentence with the sentences imposed on similarly situated defendants to ensure that the sentence of death in a particular case is not disproportionate. On their face these procedures seem to satisfy the concerns of *Furman.* No longer should there be "no meaningful basis for distinguishing the few cases in which [the death penalty] is imposed from the many cases in which it is not." . . .

V

The basic concern of *Furman* centered on those defendants who were being condemned to death capriciously and arbitrarily. Under the procedures before the Court in that case, sentencing authorities were not directed to give attention to the nature or circumstances of the crime committed or to the character or record of the defendant. Left unguided, juries imposed the death sentence in a way that could only be called freakish. The new Georgia sentencing procedures, by contrast, focus the jury's attention on the particularized nature of the crime and the particularized characteristics of the individual defendant. While the jury is permitted to consider any aggravating or mitigating circumstances, it must find and identify at least one statutory aggravating factor before it may impose a penalty of death. In this way the jury's discretion is channeled. No longer can a jury wantonly and freakishly impose the death sentence; it is always circumscribed by the legislative guidelines. In addition, the review function of the Supreme Court of Georgia affords additional assurance that the concerns that prompted our decision in *Furman* are not present to any significant degree in the Georgia procedure applied here.

For the reasons expressed in this opinion, we hold that the statutory system under which Gregg was sentenced to death does not violate the Constitution. Accordingly, the judgment of the Georgia Supreme Court is affirmed.

QUESTIONS

1. With regard to the imposition of the death penalty for the crime of murder, Justices Stewart, Powell, and Stevens write, "we cannot say that the punishment is invariably disproportionate to the crime." The Georgia statute under which Gregg was sentenced, however, retained the death penalty not only for the crime of murder but also for "kidnaping for ransom or where the victim is harmed, armed robbery, rape, treason, and aircraft hijacking." In your view, is the death penalty a disproportionate punishment for such crimes?

2. In footnote 3, we find a set of proposed model standards for the guidance of a jury in deciding whether a murderer warrants the death penalty or some lesser penalty, typically life imprisonment. Is the proposed set of aggravating circumstances (those whose presence should incline a jury toward the death penalty) defensible and complete? Is the proposed set of mitigating circumstances (those whose presence should incline a jury away from the death penalty) defensible and complete?

JUSTICE THURGOOD MARSHALL

DISSENTING OPINION IN *GREGG V. GEORGIA*

Thurgood Marshall, associate justice of the United States Supreme Court, is the first black ever to be appointed to the Supreme Court. Much of his distinguished private career was given over to providing legal counsel for groups dedicated to the advancement of civil rights. Justice Marshall also served as United States circuit judge (1961–1965) and United States solicitor general (1965–1967), before his appointment in 1967 to the Supreme Court.

Justice Marshall reaffirms the conclusion he had reached in *Furman v. Georgia* (1972): The death penalty is unconstitutional for two individually sufficient reasons. (1) It is excessive. (2) The American people, if fully informed, would consider it morally unacceptable. He insists that his conclusion in *Furman* has not been undercut by subsequent developments. Despite the fact that legislative activity since *Furman* would seem to indicate that the American people do not consider the death penalty morally unacceptable, Justice Marshall continues to maintain that the citizenry, *if fully informed,* would consider it morally unacceptable. At any rate, he maintains, the death penalty is unconstitutional because it is excessive, i.e., unnecessary to accomplish a legitimate legislative purpose. Neither deterrence nor retribution, the principal purposes asserted by Justices Stewart, Powell, and Stevens, can sustain the death penalty as nonexcessive in Justice Marshall's view. Since the available evidence does not show the death penalty to be a more effective deterrent than life imprisonment, he contends, the death penalty is not necessary to promote the goal of deterrence. Moreover, the death penalty is unnecessary to "further any legitimate notion of retribution." According to Justice Marshall, the notion that a murderer "deserves" death constitutes a denial of the wrongdoer's dignity and worth and thus is fundamentally at odds with the Eighth Amendment.

In *Furman v. Georgia* (1972) (concurring opinion), I set forth at some length my views on the basic issue presented to the Court in [this case]. The death penalty, I concluded, is a cruel and unusual punishment prohibited by the Eighth and Fourteenth Amendments. That continues to be my view.

I have no intention of retracing the "long and tedious journey" that led to my conclusion in *Furman*. My sole purposes here are to consider the suggestion that my conclusion in *Furman* has been undercut by developments since then, and briefly to evaluate the basis for my Brethren's holding that the extinction of life is a permissible form of punishment under the Cruel and Unusual Punishments Clause.

In *Furman* I concluded that the death penalty is constitutionally invalid for two reasons. First, the death penalty is excessive. And second, the American people, fully informed as to the purposes of the death penalty and its liabilities, would in my view reject it as morally unacceptable.

Since the decision in *Furman,* the legislatures of 35 States have enacted new statutes authorizing the imposition of the death sentence for certain crimes, and Congress has enacted a law providing the death penalty for air piracy resulting in death. I would be less than candid if I did not acknowledge that these developments have a significant bearing on a realistic assessment of the moral acceptability of the death penalty to the American people. But if the constitutionality of the death penalty turns, as I have urged, on the opinion of an *informed* citizenry, then even the enactment of new death statutes cannot be viewed as conclusive. In *Furman,* I observed that the American people are largely unaware of the information critical to a judgment on the morality of the death penalty, and concluded that if they were better informed they would consider it shocking, unjust, and unacceptable. A recent study, conducted after the enactment of the post-*Furman* statutes, has confirmed that the American people know little about the death penalty, and that the opinions of an informed public would differ significantly from those of a public unaware of the consequences and effects of the death penalty.

Even assuming, however, that the post-*Furman* enactment of statutes authorizing the death penalty renders the prediction of the views of an informed citizenry an uncertain basis for a constitutional decision, the enactment of those statutes has no bearing whatsoever on the conclusion that the death penalty is unconstitutional because it is excessive. An excessive penalty is invalid under the Cruel and Unusual Punishments Clause "even though popular sentiment may favor" it. The inquiry here, then, is simply whether the death penalty is necessary to accomplish the legitimate legislative purposes in punishment, or whether a less severe penalty—life imprisonment—would do as well.

The two purposes that sustain the death penalty as nonexcessive in the Court's view are general deterrence and retribution. In *Furman,* I canvassed the relevant data on the deterrent effect of capital punishment. The state of knowledge at that point, after literally centuries of debate, was summarized as follows by a United Nations Committee:

"It is generally agreed between the retentionists and abolitionists, whatever their opinions about the validity of comparative studies of deterrence, that the data which now exist show no correlation between the existence of capital punishment and lower rates of capital crime."

United States Supreme Court. 428 U.S. 153 (1976).

The available evidence, I concluded in *Furman,* was convincing that "capital punishment is not necessary as a deterrent to crime in our society." . . .

. . . The evidence I reviewed in *Furman* remains convincing, in my view, that "capital punishment is not necessary as a deterrent to crime in our society." The justification for the death penalty must be found elsewhere.

The other principal purpose said to be served by the death penalty is retribution. The notion that retribution can serve as a moral justification for the sanction of death finds credence in the opinion of my Brothers STEWART, POWELL, and STEVENS. . . . It is this notion that I find to be the most disturbing aspect of today's unfortunate [decision].

The concept of retribution is a multifaceted one, and any discussion of its role in the criminal law must be undertaken with caution. On one level, it can be said that the notion of retribution or reprobation is the basis of our insistence that only those who have broken the law be punished, and in this sense the notion is quite obviously central to a just system of criminal sanctions. But our recognition that retribution plays a crucial role in determining who may be punished by no means requires approval of retribution as a general justification for punishment. It is the question whether retribution can provide a moral justification for punishment — in particular, capital punishment — that we must consider.

My Brothers STEWART, POWELL, and STEVENS offer the following explanation of the retributive justification for capital punishment:

> The instinct for retribution is part of the nature of man, and channeling that instinct in the administration of criminal justice serves an important purpose in promoting the stability of a society governed by law. When people begin to believe that organized society is unwilling or unable to impose upon criminal offenders the punishment they "deserve," then there are sown the seeds of anarchy—of self-help, vigilante justice, and lynch law.

This statement is wholly inadequate to justify the death penalty. As my Brother BRENNAN stated in *Furman,* "[t]here is no evidence whatever that utilization of imprisonment rather than death encourages private blood feuds and other disorders." It simply defies belief to suggest that the death penalty is necessary to prevent the American people from taking the law into their own hands.

In a related vein, it may be suggested that the expression of moral outrage through the imposition of the death penalty serves to reinforce basic moral values — that it marks some crimes as particularly offensive and therefore to be avoided. The argument is akin to a deterrence argument, but differs in that it contemplates the individual's shrinking from antisocial conduct, not because he fears punishment, but because he has been told in the strongest possible way that the conduct is wrong. This contention, like the previous one, provides no support for the death penalty. It is inconceivable that any individual concerned about conforming his conduct to what society says is "right" would fail to realize that murder is "wrong" if the penalty were simply life imprisonment.

The foregoing contentions — that society's expression of moral outrage through the imposition of the death penalty pre-empts the citizenry from taking the law into its own hands and reinforces moral values — are not retributive in the purest sense. They are essentially utilitarian in that they portray the death penalty as valuable because of its beneficial results. These justifications for the death penalty are inadequate because the penalty is, quite clearly I think, not necessary to the accomplishment of those results.

There remains for consideration, however, what might be termed the purely retributive justification for the death penalty — that the death penalty is appropriate, not because of its beneficial effect on society, but because the taking of the murderer's life is itself morally good. Some of the language of the opinion of my Brothers STEWART, POWELL, and

STEVENS . . . appears positively to embrace this notion of retribution for its own sake as a justification for capital punishment. They state:

> [T]he decision that capital punishment may be the appropriate sanction in extreme cases is an expression of the community's belief that certain crimes are themselves so grievous an affront to humanity that the only adequate response may be the penalty of death.

They then quote with approval from Lord Justice Denning's remarks before the British Royal Commission on Capital Punishment:

> The truth is that some crimes are so outrageous that society insists on adequate punishment, because the wrong-doer deserves it, irrespective of whether it is a deterrent or not.

Of course, it may be that these statements are intended as no more than observations as to the popular demands that it is thought must be responded to in order to prevent anarchy. But the implication of the statements appears to me to be quite different — namely, that society's judgment that the murderer "deserves" death must be respected not simply because the preservation of order requires it, but because it is appropriate that society make the judgment and carry it out. It is this latter notion, in particular, that I consider to be fundamentally at odds with the Eighth Amendment. The mere fact that the community demands the murderer's life in return for the evil he has done cannot sustain the death penalty, for as JUSTICES STEWART, POWELL, and STEVENS remind us, "the Eighth Amendment demands more than that a challenged punishment be acceptable to contemporary society." To be sustained under the Eighth Amendment, the death penalty must "compor[t] with the basic concept of human dignity at the core of the Amendment;" the objective in imposing it must be "[consistent] with our respect for the dignity of [other] men." Under these standards, the taking of life "because the wrongdoer deserves it" surely must fail, for such a punishment has as its very basis the total denial of the wrongdoer's dignity and worth.

The death penalty, unnecessary to promote the goal of deterrence or to further any legitimate notion of retribution, is an excessive penalty forbidden by the Eighth and Fourteenth Amendments. I respectfully dissent from the Court's judgment upholding the [sentence] of death imposed upon the [petitioner in this case].

QUESTIONS

1. Is Justice Marshall correct in claiming that the American people, *if fully informed* about the death penalty, would consider it morally unacceptable?
2. Is the death penalty, as Justice Marshall claims, "unnecessary to promote the goal of deterrence or to further any legitimate notion of retribution"?

BURTON M. LEISER

RETRIBUTION AND THE LIMITS OF CAPITAL PUNISHMENT

Burton M. Leiser is professor and chairperson of the department of philosophy at Drake University. A specialist in ethics and the philosophy of law, he is the author of *Custom, Law, and Morality* (1969) and *Liberty, Justice, and Morals* (2d ed., 1979). In addition to his work in philosophy, Leiser has published articles in the fields of biblical criticism, religion, and archaeology.

Leiser, a retentionist, responds rather directly to Justice Marshall's contention that imposing the death penalty "because the wrongdoer deserves it" constitutes a denial of the wrongdoer's dignity and worth. Far from this being the case, Leiser contends, to impose the death penalty on grounds of retributive justice is to recognize and affirm the wrongdoer's worth and dignity as a human being who is accountable for his or her action. He proceeds to identify those crimes for which the death penalty is an appropriate punishment. According to Leiser, the death penalty is an appropriate punishment for certain kinds of murder but not for others. He also contends that the death penalty is an appropriate punishment for such serious crimes as terrorism, treason, kidnapping, and airplane hijacking.

RETRIBUTION

In his dissent in *Gregg* v. *Georgia,* Justice Marshall said that "it simply defies belief to suggest that the death penalty is necessary to prevent the American people from taking the law into their hands." He went on to assert that Lord Denning's contention that some crimes are so outrageous as to deserve the death penalty, regardless of its deterrent effects, is at odds with the Eighth Amendment. "The mere fact that the community demands the murderer's life for the evil he has done," he said, "cannot sustain the death penalty," for

> the Eighth Amendment demands more than that a challenged punishment be acceptable to contemporary society. To be sustained under the Eighth Amendment, the death penalty must [comport] with the basic concept of human dignity at the core of the Amendment; the objective in imposing it must be [consistent] with our respect for the dignity of [other] men. Under these standards, the taking of life "because the wrongdoer deserves it" surely must fail, for such a punishment has as its very basis the total denial of the wrongdoer's dignity and worth. The death penalty, unnecessary to promote the goal of deterrence or to further any legitimate notion of retribution, is an excessive penalty forbidden by the Eighth and Fourteenth Amendments.

But retributive justice does not deny the wrongdoer's worth and dignity. It assumes it, and makes no sense at all unless the wrongdoer is regarded as a human being capable of making his own decisions, acting upon his own volition, and deserving moral praise or blame for what he does. The death penalty is the ultimate condemnation, morally and legally, of a person who has, through his actions, demonstrated his utter contempt for human worth and dignity and for the most fundamental rules of human society. It is precisely because of a nation's belief in the dignity and worth of those who live under the protection of its laws and because of its adherence to the principle that human life is sacred that it may choose to employ the death penalty against those who have demonstrated their disregard of those principles. . . .

THE LIMITS OF CAPITAL PUNISHMENT

The death penalty has historically been employed for such diverse offenses as murder, espionage, treason, kidnapping, rape, arson, robbery, burglary, and theft. Except for the most serious crimes, it is now agreed that lesser penalties are sufficient.

The distinction between first- and second-degree murder [does] not permit fine lines to be drawn between (for example) murder for hire and the killing of a husband by his jealous wife. Most murders committed in the United States are of a domestic nature — spouses or other close relatives becoming involved in angry scenes that end in homicide. Such crimes, usually committed in the heat of a momentary passion, seem inappropriate for the supreme penalty. Although they are premeditated in the legal sense (for it takes no more than an instant for a person to form the intent that is necessary for the legal test to be satisfied), there seems to be a great difference between such crimes and those committed out of a desire for personal gain or for political motives, between a crime committed in an instant of overwrought emotion and one carefully charted and planned in advance. It is reasonable, therefore, to suggest that the vast majority of murders not be regarded as capital crimes, because the penalty may be disproportionate to the crime committed and because people caught up in such momentarily overwhelming passions are not likely to be deterred by thoughts of the possible consequences of their actions.

Only the most heinous offenses against the state and against individual persons seem to deserve the ultimate penalty. If the claim that life is sacred has any meaning at all, it must be that no man may deliberately cause another to lose his life without some compelling justification.

Such a justification appears to exist when individuals or groups employ wanton violence against others in order to achieve their ends, whatever those ends might be. However appealing the cause, however noble the motives, the deliberate, systematic destruction of innocent human beings is one of the gravest crimes any person can commit and may justify the imposition of the harshest available penalty, consistent with principles of humanity, decency, and compassion. Some penalties, such as prolonged torture, may in fact be worse than death, but civilized societies reject them as being too barbarous, too brutal, and too dehumanizing to those who must carry them out.

Perpetrators of such crimes as genocide (the deliberate extermination of entire peoples, racial, religious, or ethnic groups) clearly deserve a penalty no less severe than death. Those who perpetrate major war crimes, crimes against peace, or crimes against humanity, deliberately and without justification plunging nations into violent conflicts that entail widespread bloodshed or causing needless suffering on a vast scale, deserve nothing less than the penalty of death.

Because of the reckless manner in which they endanger the lives of innocent citizens and their clear intention to take human lives on a massive scale in order to achieve their ends, terrorists should be subject to the death penalty — particularly because no other penalty is likely to serve as a deterrent to potential terrorists.

Major crimes against the peace, security, and integrity of the state constitute particularly heinous offenses, for they shake the very foundations upon which civilization rests and endanger the lives, the liberties, and the fundamental rights of all the people who depend upon the state for protection. Treason, espionage, and sabotage, particularly during times of great danger (as in time of war), ought to be punishable by death.

Murder for personal gain and murder committed in the course of the commission of a felony that is being committed for personal gain or out of a reckless disregard for the lives or fundamental rights and interests of potential victims ought to be punishable by death.

Murder committed by a person who is serving a life sentence ought to be punishable by death, both because of the enormity of the crime and because no other penalty is likely to deter such crimes.

Any murder that is committed in a particularly vile, wanton, or malicious way ought to be punishable by death.

One of the principle justifications for the state's existence is the protection it offers those who come under its jurisdiction against violations of their fundamental rights. Those who are entrusted with the responsibility for carrying out the duties of administering the state's functions, enforcing its laws, and seeing that justice is done carry an onerous burden and are particularly likely to become the targets of hostile, malicious, or rebellious individuals or groups. Their special vulnerability entitles them to special protection. Hence, any person guilty of murdering a policeman, a fireman, a judge, a governor, a president, a lawmaker, or any other person holding a comparable position while that person is carrying out his official duties or because of the office he holds has struck at the very heart of government and thus at the foundations upon which the state and civilized society depend. The gravity of such a crime warrants imposition of the death penalty.

Because the threat of death is inherent in every act of kidnapping and airplane hijacking—for without such a threat the holding of a hostage would not have the terrorizing effect the perpetrator desires in order to achieve his aim of extorting money or political concessions from those to whom his threats are delivered—those who perpetrate such crimes may appropriately be subject to capital punishment.

But those who commit homicide in a momentary fit of anger or passion, in contrast to those who carefully plan acts as well as those who commit homicide under excusing or mitigating circumstances, may either be fully excused or given some lesser penalty.

From the fact that some persons who bring about the deaths of fellow humans do so under conditions that just and humane men would consider sufficient to justify either complete exculpation or penalties less than death, it does not follow that all of them do. If guilt is clearly established beyond a reasonable doubt under circumstances that guarantee a reasonable opportunity for the defendant to confront his accusers, to cross-examine witnesses, to present his case with the assistance of professional counsel, and in general to enjoy the benefits of due process of law; if in addition he has been given the protection of laws that prevent the use of torture to extract confessions and is provided immunity against self-incrimination; if those who are authorized to pass judgment find there were no excusing or mitigating circumstances; if he is found to have committed a wanton, brutal, callous murder or some other crime that is subversive of the very foundations of an ordered society; and if, finally, the representatives of the people, exercising the people's sovereign authority, have prescribed death as the penalty for that crime; then the judge and jury are fully justified in imposing that penalty, and the proper authorities are justified in carrying it out.

QUESTIONS

1. Does the imposition of the death penalty on retributive grounds, "because the wrongdoer deserves it," constitute a denial of the wrongdoer's dignity and worth?

2. Under what conditions, if any, does murder warrant the death penalty? Are there any other crimes which warrant the death penalty?

HUGO ADAM BEDAU

CAPITAL PUNISHMENT AND RETRIBUTIVE JUSTICE

Hugo Adam Bedau is professor of philosophy at Tufts University in Medford, Massachusetts. A past president of the American League to Abolish Capital Punishment, he has been for many years a prominent spokesperson for the abolitionist movement in the United States. He is the editor of *The Death Penalty in America* (rev. ed., 1967), the coeditor of *Capital Punishment in the United States* (1976), and the author of *The Courts, the Constitution, and Capital Punishment* (1977). Bedau is also the editor of *Civil Disobedience* (1969) and *Justice and Equality* (1971); he has written extensively in the areas of social, political, and legal philosophy.

Setting aside all considerations of social defense, Bedau argues that considerations of retributive justice do not effectively support the retention of the death penalty. After dismissing one principle of retributive justice (that crime should be punished) as neutral to the controversy over the death penalty, he focuses attention on a second principle of retributive justice (that the severity of a punishment should be proportional to the gravity of the offense). Though Bedau endorses this latter principle as an important principle of retributive justice, he contends that it need not be understood as implying the view that "the punishment of death best fits the crime of murder." Indeed, he argues, any literal-minded acceptance of the principle of retaliation (*lex talionis,* usually expressed as "a life for a life") is indefensible. In his view, not only is the abstract principle of "a life for a life" notoriously difficult to interpret and apply, it plays virtually no role in our actual system of criminal justice. At any rate, he contends, the principle of "a life for a life" will not suffice as an adequate basis for the retention of the death penalty. Bedau concludes with a discussion of the moral import of the fact that the death penalty is prone to be administered in an unfair (arbitrary or discriminatory) fashion. In the light of such administrative realities, he contends, the retention of the death penalty "does not enhance respect for human life; it cheapens and degrades it."

. . . There are two leading principles of retributive justice relevant to the capital-punishment controversy. One is the principle that crimes should be punished. The other is the principle that the severity of a punishment should be proportional to the gravity of the offense. (A corollary to the latter principle is the judgment that nothing so fits the crime of murder as the punishment of death.) Although these principles do not seem to stem from any concern over the worth, value, dignity, or rights of persons, they are moral principles of recognized weight and no discussion of the morality of capital punishment would be complete without them. Leaving aside all questions of social defense, how strong a case for capital punishment can be made on the basis of these principles? How reliable and persuasive are these principles themselves?

CRIME MUST BE PUNISHED

Given [a general rationale for punishment], there cannot be any dispute over this principle. In embracing it, of course, we are not automatically making a fetish of "law and order," in the sense that we would be if we thought that the most important single thing society can do with its resources is to punish crimes. In addition, this principle is not likely to be in dispute between proponents and opponents of the death penalty. Only those who completely oppose punishment for murder and other erstwhile capital crimes would appear to disregard this principle. Even defenders of the death penalty must admit that putting a convicted murderer in prison for years is a punishment of that criminal. The principle that crime must be punished is neutral to our controversy, because both sides acknowledge it and comply with it.

It is the other principle of retributive justice that seems to be a decisive one. Under the principle of retaliation, *lex talionis,* it must always have seemed that murderers ought to be put to death. Proponents of the death penalty, with rare exceptions, have insisted on this point, and it seems that even opponents of the death penalty must give it grudging assent. The strategy for opponents of the death penalty is to show either (a) that this principle is not really a principle of justice after all, or (b) that although it is, other principles outweigh or cancel its dictates. As we shall see, both these objections have merit.

IS MURDER ALONE TO BE PUNISHED BY DEATH?

Let us recall, first, that not even the Biblical world limited the death penalty to the punishment of murder. Many other nonhomicidal crimes also carried this penalty (e.g., kidnapping, witchcraft, cursing one's parents). In our own recent history, persons have been executed for aggravated assault, rape, kidnapping, armed robbery, sabotage, and espionage. It is not possible to defend any of these executions (not to mention some of the more bizarre capital statutes, like the one in Georgia that used to provide an optional death penalty for desecration of a grave) on grounds of just retribution. This entails that either such executions are not justified or that they are justified on some ground other than retribution. In actual practice, few if any defenders of the death penalty have ever been willing to rest their case entirely on the moral principle of just retribution as formulated in terms of "a life for a life." Kant seems to have been a conspicuous exception. Most defenders of the death penalty have implied by their willingness to use executions to defend limb and property, as well as life, that they did not place much value on the lives of criminals when compared to the value of both lives and things belonging to innocent citizens.

ARE ALL MURDERS TO BE PUNISHED BY DEATH?

Our society for several centuries has endeavored to confine the death penalty to some criminal homicides. Even Kant took a casual attitude toward a mother's killing of her illegitimate child. ("A child born into the world outside marriage is outside the law . . . , and consequently it is also outside the protection of the law.")[1] In our society, the development nearly 200 years ago of the distinction between first- and second-degree murder was an attempt to narrow the class of criminal homicides deserving of the death penalty. Yet those dead owing to manslaughter, or to any kind of unintentional, accidental, unpremeditated, unavoidable, unmalicious killing are just as dead as the victims of the most ghastly murder. Both the law in practice and moral reflection show how difficult it is to identify all and only

[1] Immanuel Kant, *The Metaphysical Elements of Justice* (1797), tr. John Ladd, p. 106.

the criminal homicides that are appropriately punished by death (assuming that any are). Individual judges and juries differ in the conclusions they reach. The history of capital punishment for homicides reveals continual efforts, uniformly unsuccessful, to identify before the fact those homicides for which the slayer should die. Benjamin Cardozo, a justice of the United States Supreme Court fifty years ago, said of the distinction between degrees of murder that it was

> . . . so obscure that no jury hearing it for the first time can fairly be expected to assimilate and understand it. I am not at all sure that I understand it myself after trying to apply it for many years and after diligent study of what has been written in the books. Upon the basis of this fine distinction with its obscure and mystifying psychology, scores of men have gone to their death.[2]

Similar skepticism has been registered on the reliability and rationality of death-penalty statutes that give the trial court the discretion to sentence to prison or to death. As Justice John Marshall Harlan of the Supreme Court observed a decade ago,

> Those who have come to grips with the hard task of actually attempting to draft means of channeling capital sentencing discretion have confirmed the lesson taught by history. . . . To identify before the fact those characteristics of criminal homicide and their perpetrators which call for the death penalty, and to express these characteristics in language which can be fairly understood and applied by the sentencing authority, appear to be tasks which are beyond present human ability.[3]

The abstract principle that the punishment of death best fits the crime of murder turns out to be extremely difficult to interpret and apply.

If we look at the matter from the standpoint of the actual practice of criminal justice, we can only conclude that "a life for a life" plays little or no role whatever. Plea bargaining (by means of which one of the persons involved in a crime agrees to accept a lesser sentence in exchange for testifying against the others to enable the prosecutor to get them all convicted), even where murder is concerned, is widespread. Studies of criminal justice reveal that what the courts (trial or appellate) decide on a given day is first-degree murder suitably punished by death in a given jurisdiction could just as well be decided in a neighboring jurisdiction on another day either as second-degree murder or as first-degree murder but without the death penalty. The factors that influence prosecutors in determining the charge under which they will prosecute go far beyond the simple principle of "a life for a life." Nor can it be objected that these facts show that our society does not care about justice. To put it succinctly, either justice in punishment does not consist of retribution, because there are other principles of justice; or there are other moral considerations besides justice that must be honored; or retributive justice is not adequately expressed in the idea of "a life for a life."

IS DEATH SUFFICIENTLY RETRIBUTIVE?

Given the reality of horrible and vicious crimes, one must consider whether there is not a quality of unthinking arbitrariness in advocating capital punishment for murder as the retributively just punishment. Why does death in the electric chair or the gas chamber or

---

[2] Benjamin Cardozo, "What Medicine Can Do for Law" (1928), reprinted in Margaret E. Hall, ed., *Selected Writings of Benjamin Nathan Cardozo* (1947), p. 204.
[3] *McGautha v. California*, 402 U.S. 183 (1971), at p. 204.

before a firing squad or on a gallows meet the requirements of retributive justice? When one thinks of the savage, brutal, wanton character of so many murders, how can retributive justice be served by anything less than equally savage methods of execution for the murderer? From a retributive point of view, the oft-heard exclamation, "Death is too good for him!" has a certain truth. Yet few defenders of the death penalty are willing to embrace this consequence of their own doctrine.

The reason they do not and should not is that, if they did, they would be stooping to the methods and thus to the squalor of the murderer. Where criminals set the limits of just methods of punishment, as they will do if we attempt to give exact and literal implementation to *lex talionis,* society will find itself descending to the cruelties and savagery that criminals employ. But society would be deliberately authorizing such acts, in the cool light of reason, and not (as is often true of vicious criminals) impulsively or in hatred and anger or with an insane or unbalanced mind. Moral restraints, in short, prohibit us from trying to make executions perfectly retributive. Once we grant the role of these restraints, the principle of "a life for a life" itself has been qualified and no longer suffices to justify the execution of murderers.

Other considerations take us in a different direction. Few murders, outside television and movie scripts, involve anything like an execution. An execution, after all, begins with a solemn pronouncement of the death sentence from a judge, is followed by long detention in maximum security awaiting the date of execution, various appeals, perhaps a final sanity hearing, and then "the last mile" to the execution chamber itself. As the French writer Albert Camus remarked,

> For there to be an equivalence, the death penalty would have to punish a criminal who had warned his victim of the date at which he would inflict a horrible death on him and who, from that moment onward, had confined him at his mercy for months. Such a monster is not encountered in private life.[4]

DIFFERENTIAL SEVERITY DOES NOT REQUIRE EXECUTIONS

What, then, emerges from our examination of retributive justice and the death penalty? If retributive justice is thought to consist in *lex talionis,* all one can say is that this principle has never exercised more than a crude and indirect effect on the actual punishments meted out. Other principles interfere with a literal and single-minded application of this one. Some murders seem improperly punished by death at all; other murders would require methods of execution too horrible to inflict; in still other cases any possible execution is too deliberate and monstrous given the nature of the motivation culminating in the murder. Proponents of the death penalty rarely confine themselves to reliance on this principle of just retribution and nothing else, since they rarely confine themselves to supporting the death penalty only for all murders.

But retributive justice need not be thought to consist of *lex talionis.* One may reject that principle as too crude and still embrace the retributive principle that the severity of punishments should be graded according to the gravity of the offense. Even though one need not claim that life imprisonment (or any kind of punishment other than death) "fits" the crime of murder, one can claim that this punishment is the proper one for murder. To do this, the schedule of punishments accepted by society must be arranged so that this mode of imprisonment is the most severe penalty used. Opponents of the death penalty need not reject this principle of retributive justice, even though they must reject a literal *lex talionis.*

[4]Albert Camus, *Resistance, Rebellion, and Death* (1961), p. 199.

EQUAL JUSTICE AND CAPITAL PUNISHMENT

During the past generation, the strongest practical objection to the death penalty has been the inequities with which it has been applied. As Supreme Court Justice William O. Douglas once observed, "One searches our chronicles in vain for the execution of any member of the affluent strata of this society."[5] One does not search our chronicles in vain for the crime of murder committed by the affluent. Every study of the death penalty for rape has confirmed that black male rapists (especially where the victim is a white female) are far more likely to be sentenced to death (and executed) than white male rapists. Half of all those under death sentence during 1976 and 1977 were black, and nearly half of all those executed since 1930 were black. All the sociological evidence points to the conclusion that the death penalty is the poor man's justice; as the current street saying has it, "Those without the capital get the punishment."

Let us suppose that the factual basis for such a criticism is sound. What follows for the morality of capital punishment? Many defenders of the death penalty have been quick to point out that since there is nothing intrinsic about the crime of murder or rape that dictates that only the poor or racial-minority males will commit it, and since there is nothing overtly racist about the statutes that authorize the death penalty for murder or rape, it is hardly a fault in the idea of capital punishment if in practice it falls with unfair impact on the poor and the black. There is, in short, nothing in the death penalty that requires it to be applied unfairly and with arbitrary or discriminatory results. It is at worst a fault in the system of administering criminal justice (and some, who dispute the facts cited above, would deny even this).

Presumably, both proponents and opponents of capital punishment would concede that it is a fundamental dictate of justice that a punishment should not be unfairly— inequitably or unevenly—enforced and applied. They should also be able to agree that when the punishment in question is the extremely severe one of death, then the requirement to be fair in using such a punishment becomes even more stringent. Thus, there should be no dispute in the death penalty controversy over these principles of justice. The dispute begins as soon as one attempts to connect these principles with the actual use of this punishment.

In this country, many critics of the death penalty have argued, we would long ago have got rid of it entirely if it had been a condition of its use that it be applied equally and fairly. In the words of the attorneys who argued against the death penalty in the Supreme Court during 1972, "It is a freakish aberration, a random extreme act of violence, visibly arbitrary and discriminatory—a penalty reserved for unusual application because, if it were usually used, it would affront universally shared standards of public decency."[6] It is difficult to dispute this judgment, when one considers that there have been in the United States during the past fifty years about half a million criminal homicides but only about 4,000 executions (all but 50 of which were of men).

We can look at these statistics in another way to illustrate the same point. If we could be assured that the 4,000 persons executed were the worst of the worst, repeated offenders without exception, the most dangerous murderers in captivity—the ones who had killed more than once and were likely to kill again, and the least likely to be confined in prison without imminent danger to other inmates and the staff— then one might accept half a million murders and a few thousand executions with a sense that rough justice had been done. But the truth is otherwise. Persons are sentenced to death and executed not

[5]*Furman v. Georgia*, 408 U.S. 238 (1972), at pp. 251–252.
[6]NAACP Legal Defense and Educational Fund, Brief for Petitioner in *Aikens v. California*, O.T. 1971, No. 68-5027, reprinted in Philip English Mackey, ed., *Voices Against Death: American Opposition to Capital Punishment, 1787–1975* (1975), p. 288.

because they have been found to be uncontrollably violent, hopelessly poor parole and release risks, or for other reasons. Instead, they are executed for entirely different reasons. They have a poor defense at trial; they have no funds to bring sympathetic witnesses to court; they are immigrants or strangers in the community where they were tried; the prosecuting attorney wants the publicity that goes with "sending a killer to the chair"; they have inexperienced or overworked counsel at trial; there are no funds for an appeal or for a transcript of the trial record; they are members of a despised racial minority. In short, the actual study of why particular persons have been sentenced to death and executed does not show any careful winnowing of the worst from the bad. It shows that the executed were usually the unlucky victims of prejudice and discrimination, the losers in an arbitrary lottery that could just as well have spared them as killed them, the victims of the disadvantages that almost always go with poverty. A system like this does not enhance respect for human life; it cheapens and degrades it. However heinous murder and other crimes are, the system of capital punishment does not compensate for or erase those crimes. It only tends to add new injuries of its own to the catalogue of our inhumanity to each other.

QUESTIONS

1. To what extent, if at all, should the principle of "a life for a life" be incorporated in our system of criminal justice?
2. Does the retention of the death penalty enhance respect for human life or, as Bedau claims, does it cheapen and degrade it?

SIDNEY HOOK

THE DEATH SENTENCE

Sidney Hook is now, after some forty years of teaching philosophy at New York University, professor emeritus. Much of his philosophical work has centered on various aspects of human freedom, often as related to social, political, and legal issues. His numerous publications include *Political Power and Personal Freedom* (1959), *The Paradoxes of Freedom* (1962), and *The Place of Religion in a Free Society* (1968).

Hook supports the retention of the death penalty for employment in two diverse cases. (1) Some criminal defendants, when sentenced to life imprisonment, may in fact prefer death. Their preference should be honored. (2) Some convicted murderers, having served one prison sentence, murder again. When such twice-guilty murderers are found to be sane, and when there is a reasonable probability that they will attempt to murder again, the death penalty should be imposed. In arguing for both (1) and (2), Hook attempts to turn humanitarian considerations, usually part of the abolitionist case, against the abolitionist. To resist (1), he argues, is to treat the convicted criminal in an inhumane way. Similarly, to resist (2) involves a posture of inhumanity. Do we not care about the lives of the murderer's future victims?

Since I am not a fanatic or absolutist, I do not wish to go on record as being categorically opposed to the death sentence in all circumstances. I should like to recognize two exceptions. A defendant convicted of murder and sentenced to life should be permitted to choose the death sentence instead. Not so long ago a defendant sentenced to life imprisonment made this request and was rebuked by the judge for his impertinence. I can see no valid grounds for denying such a request out of hand. It may sometimes be denied, particularly if a way can be found to make the defendant labor for the benefit of the dependents of his victim as is done in some European countries. Unless such considerations are present, I do not see on what reasonable ground the request can be denied, particularly by those who believe in capital punishment. Once they argue that life imprisonment is either a more effective deterrent or more justly punitive, they have abandoned their position.

In passing, I should state that I am in favor of permitting *any* criminal defendant, sentenced to life imprisonment, the right to choose death. I can understand why certain jurists, who believe that the defendant wants thereby to cheat the state out of its mode of punishment, should be indignant at the idea. They are usually the ones who believe that even the attempt at suicide should be deemed a crime — in effect saying to the unfortunate person that if he doesn't succeed in his act of suicide, the state will punish him for it. But I am baffled to understand why the absolute abolitionist, dripping with treacly humanitarianism, should oppose this proposal. I have heard some people actually oppose capital punishment in certain cases on the ground that: "Death is too good for the vile wretch! Let him live and suffer to the end of his days." But the absolute abolitionist should be the last person in the world to oppose the wish of the lifer, who regards this form of punishment as torture worse than death, to leave our world.

My second class of exceptions consists of those who having been sentenced once to prison for premeditated murder, murder again. In these particular cases we have evidence that imprisonment is not a sufficient deterrent for the individual in question. If the evidence shows that the prisoner is so psychologically constituted that, without being insane, the fact that he can kill again with impunity may lead to further murderous behavior, the court should have the discretionary power to pass the death sentence if the criminal is found guilty of a second murder.

In saying that the death sentence should be *discretionary* in cases where a man has killed more than once, I am *not* saying that a murderer who murders again is more deserving of death than the murderer who murders once. Bluebeard was not twelve times more deserving of death when he was finally caught. I am saying simply this: that in a sub-class of murderers, i.e., those who murder several times, there may be a special group of sane murderers who, knowing that they will not be executed, will not hesitate to kill again and again. For *them* the argument from deterrence is obviously valid. Those who say that there must be no exceptions to the abolition of capital punishment cannot rule out the existence of such cases on *a priori* grounds. If they admit that there is a reasonable probability that such murderers will murder again or attempt to murder again, a probability which usually grows with the number of repeated murders, and still insist they would *never* approve of capital punishment, I would conclude that they are indifferent to the lives of the human beings doomed, on their position, to be victims. What fancies itself as a humanitarian attitude is sometimes an expression of sentimentalism. The reverse coin of sentimentalism is often cruelty.

Our charity for all human beings must not deprive us of our common sense. Nor should our charity be less for the future or potential victims of the murderer than for the

Reprinted by permission of the author from "The Death Sentence," in Hugo Adam Bedau, ed., *The Death Penalty in America,* rev. ed. (Garden City, N.Y.: Doubleday, 1967).

murderer himself. There are crimes in this world which are, like acts of nature, beyond the power of men to anticipate or control. But not all or most crimes are of this character. So long as human beings are responsible and educable, they will respond to praise and blame and punishment. It is hard to imagine it but even Hitler and Stalin were once infants. Once you *can* imagine them as infants, however, it is hard to believe that they were already monsters in their cradles. Every confirmed criminal was once an amateur. The existence of confirmed criminals testifies to the defects of our education—where they can be reformed—and of our penology—where they cannot. That is why we are under the moral obligation to be intelligent about crime and punishment. Intelligence should teach us that the best educational and penological system is the one which prevents crimes rather than punishes them; the next best is one which punishes crime in such a way as to prevent it from happening again.

QUESTIONS

1. If you were condemned to life imprisonment, assuming no possibility of parole, would you prefer life or death?
2. With regard to his contention that a criminal sentenced to life imprisonment ought to be able to choose the death penalty instead, Hook has been accused of defending not the institution of capital punishment but a different institution, a sophisticated form of "supervised suicide." Is this a valid criticism?
3. Can the death penalty be defended, at least in some cases, solely on the grounds that it is necessary to incapacitate a dangerous convicted criminal? Or is life imprisonment sufficient to achieve this aim?

ERNEST van den HAAG

DETERRENCE AND UNCERTAINTY

Ernest van den Haag, in addition to maintaining a private practice in psychoanalysis, is adjunct professor of social philosophy at New York University. He also teaches at the New School for Social Research. He is the author of such works as *The Fabric of Society* (1957), *Political Violence and Civil Disobedience* (1972), and *Punishing Criminals: Concerning a Very Old and Painful Question* (1975).

The retentionist argument advanced by van den Haag is based on our uncertainty concerning the deterrent effect of the death penalty (whether or not it is a uniquely effective deterrent). According to his analysis, if we retain the death penalty, we run the risk of needlessly eradicating the lives of convicted murderers; perhaps the death penalty is *not* a uniquely effective deterrent. On the other hand, if we abolish the death penalty, we run the risk of innocent people becoming future murder victims; perhaps the death penalty *is* a uniquely effective deterrent. Faced with such uncertainty, van den Haag maintains, it is our moral obligation to retain the death penalty. "We have no right to risk additional future victims of murder for the sake of sparing convicted murderers."

. . . If we do not know whether the death penalty will deter others [in a uniquely effective way], we are confronted with two uncertainties. If we impose the death penalty, and achieve no deterrent effect thereby, the life of a convicted murderer has been expended in vain (from a deterrent viewpoint). There is a net loss. If we impose the death sentence and thereby deter some future murderers, we spared the lives of some future victims (the prospective murderers gain too; they are spared punishment because they were deterred). In this case, the death penalty has led to a net gain, unless the life of a convicted murderer is valued more highly than that of the unknown victim, or victims (and the non-imprisonment of the deterred non-murderer).

The calculation can be turned around, of course. The absence of the death penalty may harm no one and therefore produce a gain—the life of the convicted murderer. Or it may kill future victims of murderers who could have been deterred, and thus produce a loss—their life.

To be sure, we must risk something certain—the death (or life) of the convicted man, for something uncertain—the death (or life) of the victims of murderers who may be deterred. This is in the nature of uncertainty—when we invest, or gamble, we risk the money we have for an uncertain gain. Many human actions, most commitments—including marriage and crime—share this characteristic with the deterrent purpose of any penalization, and with its rehabilitative purpose (and even with the protective).

More proof is demanded for the deterrent effect of the death penalty than is demanded for the deterrent effect of other penalties. This is not justified by the absence of other utilitarian purposes such as protection and rehabilitation; they involve no less uncertainty than deterrence.[1]

Irrevocability may support a demand for some reason to expect more deterrence than revocable penalties might produce, but not a demand for more proof of deterrence, as has been pointed out above. The reason for expecting more deterrence lies in the greater severity, the terrifying effect inherent in finality. Since it seems more important to spare victims than to spare murderers, the burden of proving that the greater severity inherent in irrevocability adds nothing to deterrence lies on those who oppose capital punishment. Proponents of the death penalty need show only that there is no more uncertainty about it than about greater severity in general.

The demand that the death penalty be proved more deterrent than alternatives can not be satisfied any more than the demand that six years in prison be proved to be more deterrent than three. But the uncertainty which confronts us favors the death penalty as long as by imposing it we might save future victims of murder. This effect is as plausible as the general idea that penalties have deterrent effects which increase with their severity. Though we have no proof of the positive deterrence of the penalty, we also have no proof of zero, or negative effectiveness. I believe we have no right to risk additional future victims of murder for the sake of sparing convicted murderers; on the contrary, our moral obligation is to risk the possible ineffectiveness of executions. However rationalized, the opposite view appears to be motivated by the simple fact that executions are more subjected to social control than murder. However, this applies to all penalties and does not argue for the abolition of any.

Reprinted with permission of the publisher from the *Journal of Criminal Law, Criminology and Police Science,* vol. 60, no. 2 (1969).
[1]Rehabilitation or protection are of minor importance in our actual penal system (though not in our theory). We confine many people who do not need rehabilitation and against whom we do not need protection (e.g., the exasperated husband who killed his wife); we release many unrehabilitated offenders against whom protection is needed. Certainly rehabilitation and protection are not, and deterrence is, the main actual function of legal punishment, if we disregard nonutilitarian purposes.

QUESTIONS

1. If we are unsure whether or not the death penalty is a uniquely effective deterrent, does our uncertainty favor retention, abolition, or neither?

2. Is the life of a convicted murderer worth as much as the life of a potential murder victim?

HUGO ADAM BEDAU

CAPITAL PUNISHMENT AND SOCIAL DEFENSE

A biographical sketch of Hugo Adam Bedau is found on page 103.

As the starting point of his effort to determine whether considerations of social defense can effectively support the retention of the death penalty, Bedau distinguishes between preventing and deterring crime. The death penalty *prevents crime* to the extent that a murderer who would have committed subsequent crimes is permanenty incapacitated; it *deters crime* to the extent that other would-be murderers are frightened off by the example of the execution. In his view, not much of a case can be made for the retention of the death penalty based on considerations of crime prevention. With regard to deterrence, Bedau reads the available evidence as indicating that "the deterrence achieved by the death penalty for murder is not measurably greater than the deterrence achieved by long-term imprisonment." Accordingly, he contends, the retention of the death penalty cannot effectively be defended on the basis that it is a uniquely effective deterrent. After pointing out that the retention of the death penalty is attended by a number of social costs, he suggests that an extensive cost/benefit analysis would likely favor abolition of the death penalty. But what would follow regarding the morality of the death penalty, Bedau asks, *if* the death penalty were known to be a uniquely effective method of social defense? Even in the face of such knowledge, he maintains, there might still be other factual considerations ("costs") in the light of which opposition to the death penalty would remain morally responsible.

PREVENTING CRIME *VERSUS* DETERRING CRIME

The analogy [that may be drawn] between capital punishment and self-defense requires us to face squarely the empirical questions surrounding the preventive and deterrent effects of the death penalty. Let us distinguish first between preventing and deterring crime. Executing a murderer in the name of punishment can be seen as a crime-*preventive* measure just to the extent it is reasonable to believe that if the murderer had not been executed he or she would have committed other crimes (including, but not necessarily confined to, murder). Executing a murderer can be seen as a crime *deterrent* just to the extent it is reasonable to believe that by the example of the execution other persons are frightened off from committing murder. Any punishment can be a crime preventive without being a crime deterrent, and it can be a deterrent without being a preventive. It can also be both or neither. Prevention and deterrence are theoretically independent because they operate by different methods. Crimes can be prevented by taking guns out of the hands of criminals, by putting criminals behind bars, by alerting the public to be less careless and less prone to victimization, and so forth. Crimes can be deterred only by making would-be criminals frightened of being arrested, convicted, and punished for crimes—that is, making persons overcome their desire to commit crimes by a stronger desire to avoid the risk of being caught and punished.

THE DEATH PENALTY AS A CRIME PREVENTIVE

Capital punishment is unusual among penalties because its preventive effects limit its deterrent effects. The death penalty can never deter the executed person from further crimes. At most, it can prevent him or her from committing them. Popular discussions of the death penalty are frequently confused and misleading because they so often involve the assumption that the death penalty is a perfect and infallible deterrent so far as the executed criminal is concerned, whereas nothing of the sort is true. It is even an exaggeration to think that in any given case of execution the death penalty has proved to be an infallible crime preventive. What is obviously true is that once a person has been executed, it is physically impossible for him or her to commit any further crimes. But this does not prove that by executing a murderer society has in fact prevented any crimes. To prove this, one would need to know what crimes the executed criminal would have committed if he or she had not been executed and had been punished only in some less severe way (e.g., by imprisonment).

What is the evidence that the death penalty is an effective crime preventive? From the study of imprisonment, and parole and release records, it is clear that in general, if the murderers and other criminals who have been executed are like the murderers who were convicted but not executed, then (a) executing all convicted murderers would have prevented few crimes, but not many murders (less than one convicted murderer in a hundred commits another murder); and (b) convicted murderers, whether inside prison or outside after release, have at least as good a record of no further criminal activity as does any other class of convicted felon.

These facts show that the general public tends to overrate the danger and threat to public safety constituted by the failure to execute every murderer who is caught and convicted. While one would be in error to say that there is no risk such criminals will repeat their crimes—or similar ones—if they are not executed, one would be equally in error to say that by executing every convicted murderer we know that many horrible crimes will never be committed. All we know is that a few such crimes will never be committed; we do not know how many or by whom they would have been committed. (Obviously, if we did we could have prevented them.) This is the nub of the problem. There is no way to know in advance which if any of the incarcerated or released murderers will kill again. It is useful in this connection to remember that the only way to guarantee that no horrible crimes ever occur is to execute *everyone* who might conceivably commit such a crime. Similarly, the only way to guarantee that no convicted murderer ever commits another murder is to execute them all. No society has ever done this, and for 200 years our society has been moving steadily in the opposite direction.

These considerations show that our society has implicitly adopted an attitude toward the risk of murder rather like the attitude it has adopted toward the risk of fatality from other sources, such as automobile accidents, lung cancer, or drowning. Since no one knows when or where or upon whom any of these lethal events will befall, it would be too great an invasion of freedom to undertake the severe restrictions that alone would suffice to prevent any of them from occurring. It is better to take the risks and keep our freedom than to try to eliminate the risks altogether and lose our freedom in the process. Hence, we have lifeguards at the beach, but swimming is not totally prohibited; smokers are warned, but cigarettes are still legally sold; pedestrians may be given the right of way in a crosswalk, but marginally competent drivers are still allowed to operate motor vehicles. Some risk is therefore imposed on the innocent; in the name of our right to freedom, our other rights are not protected by society at all costs.

THE DEATH PENALTY AS A CRIME DETERRENT

Determining whether the death penalty is an effective deterrent is even more difficult than determining its effectiveness as a crime preventive. In general, our knowledge about how penalties deter crimes and whether in fact they do—whom they deter, from which crimes, and under what conditions—is distressingly inexact. Most people nevertheless are convinced that punishments do deter, and that the more severe a punishment is the better it will deter. For more than a generation, social scientists have studied the question of whether the death penalty is a deterrent and of whether it is a better deterrent than the alternative of imprisonment. Their verdict, while not unanimous, is fairly clear. Whatever may be true about the deterrence of lesser crimes by other penalties, the deterrence achieved by the death penalty for murder is not measurably greater than the deterrence achieved by long-term imprisonment. In the nature of the case, the evidence is quite indirect. No one can identify for certain any crimes that did not occur because the would-be offender was deterred by the threat of the death penalty and that would not have been deterred by a lesser threat. Likewise, no one can identify any crimes that did occur because the offender was not deterred by the threat of prison even though he would have been deterred by the threat of death. Nevertheless, such evidence as we have fails to show that the more severe penalty (death) is really a better deterrent than the less severe penalty (imprisonment) for such crimes as murder.

If the conclusion stated above is correct, and the death penalty and long-term imprisonment are equally effective (or ineffective) as deterrents to murder, then the argument for the death penalty on grounds of deterrence is seriously weakened. [An important moral principle] comes into play and requires us to reject the death penalty on moral grounds. This is the principle that unless there is a good reason for choosing a more rather than a less severe punishment for a crime, the less severe penalty is to be preferred. This principle obviously commends itself to anyone who values human life and who concedes that, all other things being equal, less pain and suffering is always better than more. Human life is valued in part to the degree that it is free of pain, suffering, misery, and frustration, and in particular that it is free of such experiences when they serve no purpose. If the death penalty is not a more effective deterrent than imprisonment, then its greater severity than imprisonment is gratuitous, purposeless suffering and deprivation.

A COST/BENEFIT ANALYSIS OF THE DEATH PENALTY

A full study of the costs and benefits involved in the practice of capital punishment would not be confined solely to the question of whether it is a better deterrent or preventive of murder than imprisonment. Any thoroughgoing utilitarian approach to the death-penalty controversy would need to examine carefully other costs and benefits as well, because maximizing the balance of social benefits over social costs is the sole criterion of right and wrong according to utilitarianism. Let us consider, therefore, some of the other costs and benefits to be calculated. Clinical psychologists have presented evidence to suggest that the death penalty actually incites some persons of unstable mind to murder others, either because they are afraid to take their own lives and hope that society will punish them for murder by putting them to death, or because they fancy that they, too, are killing with justification analogously to the justified killing involved in capital punishment. If such evidence is sound, capital punishment can serve as a counterpreventive or an incitement to murder, and these incited murders become part of its social cost. Imprisonment, however, has not been known to incite any murders or other crimes of violence in a comparable fashion. (A possible exception might be found in the imprisonment of terrorists, which has inspired other terrorists to take hostages as part of a scheme to force the authorities to release their imprisoned comrades.) The risks of executing the innocent are also part of the social cost. The historical record is replete with innocent persons indicted, convicted, sentenced, and occasionally legally executed for crimes they did not commit, not to mention the guilty persons unfairly convicted, sentenced to death, and executed on the strength of perjured testimony, fraudulent evidence, subornation of jurors, and other violations of the civil rights and liberties of the accused. Nor is this all. The high costs of a capital trial, of the inevitable appeals, the costly methods of custody most prisons adopt for convicts on "death row," are among the straightforward economic costs that the death penalty incurs. No scientifically valid cost/benefit analysis of capital punishment has ever been conducted, and it is impossible to predict exactly what such a study would show. Nevertheless, based on such evidence as we do have, it is quite possible that a study of this sort would favor abolition of all death penalties rather than their retention.

WHAT IF EXECUTIONS DID DETER?

From the moral point of view, it is quite important to determine what one should think about capital punishment if the evidence clearly showed that the death penalty is a distinctly superior method of social defense by comparison with less severe alternatives. Kantian moralists . . . would have no use for such knowledge, because their entire case for the morality of the death penalty rests on the way it is thought to provide just retribution, not on the way it is thought to provide social defense. For a utilitarian, however, such knowledge would be conclusive. Those who follow Locke's reasoning would also be gratified, because they defend the morality of the death penalty both on the ground that it is retributively just and on the ground that it provides needed social defense.

What about the opponents of the death penalty, however? To oppose the death penalty in the face of incontestable evidence that it is an effective method of social defense seems to violate the moral principle that where grave risks are to be run, it is better that they be run by the guilty than by the innocent. Consider in this connection an imaginary world in which by executing a murderer the victim is invariably restored to life, whole and intact, as though the murder had never occurred. In such a miraculous world, it is hard to see how anyone could oppose the death penalty on moral grounds. Why shouldn't a murderer die if that will infallibly bring the victim back to life? What could possibly be morally wrong with taking the murderer's life under such conditions? It would turn the death penalty into an instrument of perfect restitution, and it would give a new and better meaning to *lex talionis*, "a life for a life." The whole idea is fanciful, of course, but it shows better than anything else how opposition to the death penalty cannot be both moral and wholly unconditional. If opposition to the death penalty is to be morally responsible, then it must be conceded that there are conditions (however unlikely) under which that opposition should cease.

But even if the death penalty were known to be a uniquely effective social defense, we could still imagine conditions under which it would be reasonable to oppose it. Suppose that in addition to being a slightly better preventive and deterrent than imprisonment, executions also have a slight incitive effect (so that for every ten murders an execution prevents or deters, it also incites another murder). Suppose also that the administration of criminal justice in capital cases is inefficient, unequal, and tends to secure convictions of murderers who least "deserve" to be sentenced to death (including some death sentences and a few executions of the innocent). Under such conditions, it would still be reasonable to oppose the death penalty, because on the facts supposed more (or not fewer) innocent lives are being threatened and lost by using the death penalty than would be risked by abolishing it. It is important to remember throughout our evaluation of the deterrence controversy that we cannot ever apply the principle . . . that advises us to risk the lives of the guilty in order to save the lives of the innocent. Instead, the most we can do is weigh the risk for the general public against the execution of those who are *found* guilty by an imperfect system of criminal justice. These hypothetical factual assumptions illustrate the contingencies upon which the morality of opposition to the death penalty rests. And not only the morality of opposition; the morality of any defense of the death penalty rests on the same contingencies. This should help us understand why, in resolving the morality of capital punishment one way or the other, it is so important to know, as well as we can, whether the death penalty really does deter, prevent, or incite crime, whether the innocent really are ever executed, and whether any of these things are likely to occur in the future.

HOW MANY GUILTY LIVES IS ONE INNOCENT LIFE WORTH?

The great unanswered question that utilitarians must face concerns the level of social defense that executions should be expected to achieve before it is justifiable to carry them out. Consider three possible situations: (1) At the level of a hundred executions per year, each additional execution of a convicted murderer reduces the number of murder victims by ten. (2) Executing every convicted murderer reduces the number of murders to 5,000 victims annually, whereas executing only one out of ten reduces the number to 5,001. (3) Executing every convicted murderer reduces the murder rate no more than does executing one in a hundred and no more than a random pattern of executions does.

Many people contemplating situation (1) would regard this as a reasonable trade-off: The execution of each further guilty person saves the lives of ten innocent ones. (In fact, situation (1) or something like it may be taken as a description of what most of those who defend the death penalty on grounds of social defense believe is true.) But suppose that, instead of saving 10 lives, the number dropped to 0.5, i.e., one victim avoided for each two additional executions. Would that be a reasonable price to pay? We are on the road toward the situation described in situation (2), where a drastic 90 percent reduction in the number of persons executed causes the level of social defense to drop by only 0.0002 percent. Would it be worth it to execute so many more murderers at the cost of such a slight decrease in social defense? How many guilty lives is one innocent life worth? In situation (3), of course, there is no basis for executing all convicted murderers, since there is no gain in social defense to show for each additional murderer executed after the first out of each hundred murderers has been executed. How, then, should we determine which out of each hundred convicted murderers is the unlucky one to be put to death?

It may be possible, under a complete and thoroughgoing cost/benefit analysis of the death penalty, to answer such questions. But an appeal merely to the moral principle that if lives are to be risked then let it be the lives of the guilty rather than the lives of the innocent will not suffice. (We have already noticed, in [the previous section], that this abstract principle is of little use in the actual administration of criminal justice, because the police and the courts do not deal with the guilty as such but only with those *judged* guilty.) Nor will it suffice to agree that society deserves all the crime prevention and deterrence it can get by inflicting severe punishments. These principles are consistent with too many different policies. They are too vague by themselves to resolve the choice on grounds of social defense when confronted with hypothetical situations like those proposed above.

Since no adequate cost/benefit analysis of the death penalty exists, there is no way to resolve these questions from this standpoint at the present time. Moreover, it can be argued that we cannot have such an analysis without already establishing in some way or other the relative value of innocent lives versus guilty lives. Far from being a product of a cost/benefit analysis, this comparative evaluation of lives would have to be brought into any such analysis. Without it, no cost/benefit analysis can get off the ground. Finally, it must be noted that we have no knowledge at present that begins to approximate anything like the situation described above in (1), whereas it appears from the evidence we do have that we achieve about the same deterrent and preventive effects whether we punish murder by death or by imprisonment. Therefore, something like the situation in (2) or in (3) may be correct. If so, this shows that the choice between the two policies of capital punishment and life imprisonment for murder will probably have to be made on some basis other than social defense; on that basis the two polices are equivalent and therefore equally acceptable.

QUESTIONS

1. Are there any good reasons for believing that the death penalty is a uniquely effective deterrent?
2. Is Bedau correct in thinking that an extensive cost/benefit analysis of the death penalty would favor abolition?

SUGGESTED ADDITIONAL READINGS

BEDAU, HUGO ADAM, ed.: *The Death Penalty in America,* rev. ed. Garden City, N.Y.: Doubleday, 1967. This classic work is a general reader, reflecting all aspects of the contemporary discussion of the death penalty. It is especially noteworthy in providing a wealth of factual data which, even if now somewhat outdated, retains its reference value.

———, and C. M. PIERCE, eds.: *Capital Punishment in the United States.* New York: AMS Press, 1976. There is an extensive literature in social science dealing with the many factual issues associated with the death penalty controversy. This particular collection of material draws exclusively on that literature and provides a helpful point of entry to it.

BERNS, WALTER: *For Capital Punishment.* New York: Basic Books, 1979. In this book, which provides a broadly ranging discussion of issues relevant to the death penalty controversy, Berns insists that capital punishment can be effectively defended on grounds of retribution.

BLACK, CHARLES L., JR.: *Capital Punishment: The Inevitability of Caprice and Mistake.* New York: Norton, 1974. Black, in this short and most readable book, argues for abolition on the grounds that it is virtually impossible to eliminate arbitrariness and mistake from the numerous decisions that lead to the imposition of the death penalty.

CAMUS, ALBERT: *Reflections on the Guillotine: An Essay on Capital Punishment.* Translated by Richard Howard. Michigan City, Ind.: Fridtjof-Karla Press, 1959. In this lengthy essay, Camus provides a strong, partially literary indictment of the practice of capital punishment.

CONWAY, DAVID A.: "Capital Punishment and Deterrence: Some Considerations in Dialogue Form." *Philosophy and Public Affairs,* vol. 3, Summer 1974, pp. 431–443. Conway provides a lively dialogue between a retentionist (who supports the death penalty on grounds of deterrence) and an abolitionist. Of special interest is the abolitionist's reaction to the line of argument advanced by Ernest van den Haag in this chapter.

EZORSKY, GERTRUDE, ed.: *Philosophical Perspectives on Punishment.* Albany: State University of New York Press, 1972. This book is an excellent anthology on a wide range of general philosophical questions concerning punishment. There is a small section on capital punishment.

FEINBERG, JOEL, and HYMAN GROSS, eds.: *Philosophy of Law.* Encino, Calif.: Dickenson, 1975. Part 5 of this anthology provides a set of helpful readings on various philosophical aspects of punishment. Some explicit attention is paid to capital punishment.

GOLDBERG, STEVEN: "On Capital Punishment." *Ethics,* vol. 85, October 1974, pp. 67–74. Goldberg, ultimately sympathetic to retentionism, focuses on the difficulties involved in the factual question of whether or not the death penalty is a uniquely effective deterrent. An extensively revised version of this article appears under the title "Does Capital Punishment Deter?" in Richard A. Wasserstrom, ed., *Today's Moral Problems,* 2d ed. New York: Macmillan, 1979, pp. 538–551.

MC CAFFERTY, JAMES A., ed.: *Capital Punishment.* New York: Lieber-Atherton, 1972. This general anthology is especially useful because it includes several position papers that reflect the views (both retentionist and abolitionist) taken by people who are directly involved in the administration of criminal justice.

SEXUAL
EQUALITY

4

In 1848 the Seneca Falls Women's Convention issued a demand for sexual equality:

> We hold these truths to be self-evident: that all men and women are created equal; . . .
>   The history of mankind is a history of repeated injuries and usurpations on the part of man toward woman, having in direct object the establishment of an absolute tyranny over her.[1]

When this demand was issued, women in the United States were denied many legal rights now taken for granted. They could not vote, own property, enter into contracts, serve on juries, or enter most professions. To win these crucial legal rights, feminists fought a long and difficult battle.

By the late 1960s and early 1970s, when the contemporary wave of feminism was launched in the United States, women had long possessed many of the above-mentioned rights. In addition, various legal measures had been enacted in the early 1960s explicitly prohibiting sexually discriminatory employment practices. Two examples of such legislation are especially worth noting. (1) The *Equal Pay Act of 1963* asserted that men and women had to be given the same pay for doing equal work, i.e., work requiring equal skill, effort, and responsibility and performed under similar working conditions in the same establishment. (2) *Title VII of the Civil Rights Act of 1964* prohibited *any* discrimination in employment based on race, color, religion, *sex*, or national origin. Despite such legislative changes, however, when contemporary feminists began their battle in the 1960s and early 1970s, sexual discrimination was commonplace, especially in the economic sphere. Evidence presented at the 1969 Congressional Hearings on Equal Rights in Education and Employment supported the feminists' claim of wide-spread discrimination: (1) vocational counseling which directed girls into nursing and boys into engineering, space science, and computer technology; (2) gross differences between the median earnings of full-time employed men and women—men, $7,644; women, $4,457; (3) low percentages of women in the highest grades of civil service and high percentages of women in the lowest grades—one-tenth of 1 percent in the highest grades, 86 percent in the lowest grades; and (4) extremely small percentages of women in the most prestigious professions—only 9 percent of all full professors, 3.5 percent of all lawyers, 7 percent of all physicians, and 1 percent of all engineers were women.

More than ten years after these hearings, and after more than a decade of protest by contemporary feminists, women's economic status has changed very little. Recent U.S. Department of Labor statistics show, for example, that the earnings gap between men and women remained unchanged during the eleven-year interval between 1967 and 1978. Women's median income in *any* occupation is still much less than that of men, and there are still gross differences between the weekly median earnings of full-time employed men and women—men, $272; women, $166. These statistics also reveal that women continue to be clustered in the five lowest-paid occupations and to be underrepresented in the three highest ones.[2] Thus, it is obvious that ours is not as yet a sexually egalitarian society. *Should it be?* Contemporary feminists respond in the affirmative, of course, and condemn social practices which discriminate against women. They demand a sexually egalitarian society,

---

[1]Judith Hole and Ellen Levine, "The First Feminists," in Anne Koedt, Ellen Levine, and Anita Rapon, eds., *Radical Feminism* (New York: Quadrangle, 1973), p. 7.
[2]Janice Neipert and Earl F. Mellor, "Weekly and Hourly Earnings of U.S. Workers, 1967–78," *Monthly Labor Review* 102:6 (August 1979), pp. 31, 34, 35.

rejecting as sexist any society whose education, political, business, and social institutions systematically accord unequal treatment to the sexes. In contrast, some of the strongest opponents of the *Equal Rights Amendment* to the Constitution[3] argue for the rightness of sexually nonegalitarian institutions and practices. They oppose the ERA precisely because they believe it will result in the blanket egalitarian treatment of the sexes. *What does morality dictate on the issue?* Can a moral justification be given for sexually nonegalitarian institutions and practices?

THE PRINCIPLE OF EQUALITY

One way to determine whether or not a social practice is morally correct is to see if it is either permitted or required by the *principle of equality*.[4] According to that principle, equals must be treated as equals while unequals should be treated unequally, in proportion to their differences. This is a formal principle of justice attributed to Aristotle. But what constitutes equality or inequality? In what ways must two individuals be alike before we can claim that they must receive the same treatment? In what ways must two individuals differ before we can claim that they must be accorded unequal treatment?

The usual way of answering these questions is to say that the differences between individuals must be relevant to the treatment in question. If Joe Smith and John Doe both apply for a job as a lifeguard, a difference in their religious beliefs has no bearing on which of them should get the job. But if Joe is a nonswimmer and John an Olympic swimming champion, that difference between them *is relevant* to the treatment they receive in this case. So we can say that people are entitled to the same treatment when there are no differences between them which are relevant to the treatment in question. Sex may be relevant when a wet nurse is being hired. But it is not relevant when a choice is being made between competing accountants, though mathematical ability is relevant.

Note what has just been claimed: Sex is *not* a relevant characteristic when an accountant is being hired. If a qualified woman accountant is told that she cannot apply for an accounting position simply because of her sex, she is not receiving the same treatment as male accountants whose applications are accepted. When this happens, the principle of equality is clearly violated. This is a *moral* violation analogous to the *legal* violation of Title VII which occurs when a woman is discriminated against in employment.

The discussion so far has focused on that part of the principle of equality which states that equals must be treated equally. But some unequal treatment is also required or permitted by the principle of equality. Young children, for example, cannot be given the same rights and responsibilities as adults. A five-year-old cannot be expected to take on responsibilities such as voting or signing binding contracts. This kind of unequal treatment of young children and adults is required by the principle of equality, since young children differ from adults in relevant respects. They are incapable of exercising the rational capacities requisite for the assumption of the responsibilities at issue. To sum up, both institutional practices which treat equals equally and those which treat unequals unequally, in proportion to their differences, are morally correct according to the principle of equality. But when equals are treated unequally, the principle is clearly violated.

---

[3]The Equal Rights Amendment was approved by Congress in 1971 and submitted to the states for ratification. It asserts, "Equality of rights shall not be denied or abridged by the United States or by any State on account of sex."

[4]To say that a social practice is *required* by a moral principle is to say that we must institute such a practice if we are to act in a morally correct way. To say that it is *permitted* is to say that its institution will not violate the moral principle.

SEXUAL DIFFERENCES AND THE PRINCIPLE OF EQUALITY

Some who argue for sexually nonegalitarian institutions and practices maintain that these are in keeping with the principle of equality. In their view, there are important differences between the sexes which justify the claim that sex *should* be used as a criterion for according unequal political, economic, and social treatment to the sexes. What reasons do they offer to support their claim? In Aristotle's own case, the answer is simple. He claims that there are *inherent differences* between men and women. Men by nature have the capacity to rule, but women do not. For Aristotle, such differences are just as relevant in determining women's political status as mathematical ability is in determining who should be hired as an accountant in the example discussed above. Since women, according to Aristotle's theory of human nature, are not the equals of men in the relevant respects, unequal economic and political treatment of women is required by the principle of equality. Justice Joseph P. Bradley's opinion in *Bradwell v. Illinois,* reprinted in this chapter, echoes such reasoning.

Is is plausible to make an Aristotelian type of claim today? Consider the kinds of things you often hear people say: "No woman should ever be President of the United States. Women are too emotional for the job." "Women can't manage other women." Or consider this remark made to a woman student, "We expect women who come here to be competent, good students, but we don't expect them to be brilliant or original."[5] Note what all these examples have in common. The sex of an individual is seen as a relevant factor when the capacity of that individual to perform certain tasks is being judged. Sex is here considered a relevant factor because differences in sex are believed to be correlated with psychological differences—differences in cognitive capacity or emotional makeup. These psychological differences are assumed to be relevant to the roles in question. As a result of such beliefs about female psychological characteristics, women are often treated unequally by the institutions of society. Is this inequality of treatment consistent with the principle of equality? Some who claim it is argue in an Aristotelian way: There are psychological differences between the sexes and these are relevant to job performance. Furthermore, these differences are natural ones; that is, they are genetically caused. Therefore, some of the unequal treatment accorded women is in keeping with the principle of equality because women *by their very nature* are unequal to men in relevant ways.

Much that is written by those who, like John Stuart Mill in this chapter, argue for the *equal* economic, political, and social treatment of the sexes focuses on the *factual claims* used to support the above argument. Sometimes the existence of sexually related psychological differences is denied. The claim here is that even though we believe, for example, that most women are passive and most men aggressive, these beliefs are incorrect. Beliefs about male and female psychological differences acquired through cultural training leads us to dismiss the counterevidence (the many atypical cases we encounter) as "mere" exceptions to the rule. At other times, the following argument is made: Even if it is true that women are more passive and men more aggressive on the average, or men more mathematically inclined than women on the average, this does not prove that there are *natural* differences between the sexes relevant to society-assigned role differences. Rather, it is because society differentiates between male and female roles and trains individuals to conform to these roles that the sexes tend to develop different psychological characteristics. If there are in fact psychological differences between the sexes, then the differences are artificial and not natural. It is the traditional unequal treatment accorded to the sexes by

[5]Quoted in a statement made by Ann Sutherland Harris to the Congressional Hearings on Equal Rights in Education and Employment. This statement is included in Catharine R. Stimpson, ed., *Discrimination Against Women: Congressional Hearings on Equal Rights in Education and Employment* (New York: Bowker, 1973), p. 399.

educational and other socializing institutions that causes any psychological differences between them which might be relevant in denying women access to the most authoritative and prestigious positions in society. Thus, society's nonegalitarian treatment of the sexes is not based on any natural inequality between them. Rather, it is the unequal treatment of the sexes which produces the artificial psychological differences which are then used in attempts to justify the further nonegalitarian economic, social, and educational treatment of the sexes.

Some philosophers prescind from the whole discussion of the *causes* of the assumed psychological differences between the sexes and focus on a different question: Even if there are psychological differences between the sexes (natural or socially induced) and women *on the average* are more emotional and more passive than men as well as less capable *on the average* of abstract thought, is it morally correct to systematically deny some roles to *all* women simply because many women are incapable of filling them? According to the principle of equality, social practices resulting in the systematic exclusion of all the members of a group are not justified when the psychological differences are not universal. The principle of equality requires that each person be judged simply on the basis of individual merit and not on the basis of the "average" psychological makeup of that person's sexual group. On this line of argument, any unequal treatment advocated by ERA opponents would be sanctioned by the principle of equality only if the relevant psychological differences between the sexes were universal and not statistical.

OTHER ARGUMENTS FOR UNEQUAL TREATMENT

Some who argue for sexually nonegalitarian institutions and practices ignore or downplay the significance of the principle of equality. These defenders of unequal treatment begin by arguing that natural psychological differences between the sexes make *most* women relevantly different from males. On the basis of this claim, further claims are made. Steven Goldberg, in a reading in this chapter, maintains, for example, that there are differences in the hormonal makeup of the sexes which are responsible for differences in their aggression level. A nonegalitarian society is inevitable given this difference in aggressiveness. Even if some women are capable of competing with men, he continues, women on the whole will be better off in the long run if direct competition between the sexes is minimized. Others using this approach argue in a similar consequentialist vein. They give their own accounts of sexual differences. They then maintain that it is in the best interest of women, or in the best interest of society as a whole, to establish social institutions which will enforce and perpetuate sexual roles, even if enforcing sexual roles violates the principle of equality in individual cases and limits the freedom of individuals to develop any chosen personality or interest. Joyce Trebilcot in her first article in this chapter analyzes and evaluates all such claims.

SEXUAL EQUALITY AND MALE LIBERATION

Although the focus of discussion thus far has been on *women* and sexual equality, there is a growing literature which claims that *men*, too, will benefit if the old sexual stereotypes are abandoned. In fact, some "male liberationists," including Herb Goldberg in this chapter, argue that males can be liberated from destructive life-styles only if women become fully autonomous persons, rather than dependents whose well-being depends on men's acceptance of economic and other responsibilities.

If the old stereotypes are abandoned, what alternatives should we adopt in the interest of a sexually egalitarian society? Should all women be trained to be physically aggressive, for example? Should all men be trained to express their affections more freely than the traditional model would allow? The word "androgynous" is often used to describe the personality type which should replace the old masculine and feminine models. Formed from the Greek words for "man" *(andros)* and "woman" *(gyne)*, the word connotes a personality which contains all the positive characteristics traditionally called masculine as well as those traditionally called feminine. Does this mean that social institutions should mold people on this new model to the greatest extent possible? Or should these institutions simply encourage individuals to develop the personalities and interests with which they are most comfortable, even if some people will end up with one-sided personalities and interests? Joyce Trebilcot in a second article in this chapter considers both alternatives in an effort to determine which approach is morally most desirable.

Jane S. Zembaty

JUSTICE JOSEPH P. BRADLEY

CONCURRING OPINION IN *BRADWELL v. ILLINOIS*

Joseph P. Bradley (1813–1892) was appointed associate justice of the United States Supreme Court in 1868 by President Grant. While serving as an associate justice (1868–1892) he wrote opinions which are influential in United States constitutional law.

This case (1873) furnishes an example of the overt and, at one time, widely accepted unequal treatment of women. Myra Bradwell's application for a license to practice law was denied by the Illinois Supreme Court simply on the basis of sex. Her appeal to the Supreme Court of the United States was made and denied on constitutional grounds. In a concurring opinion which goes beyond the Constitution, Justice Bradley expresses the following opinion: There are natural differences between the sexes. These natural differences are recognized by civil law. The legislator has the prerogative to take such natural differences into consideration when he prescribes regulations governing the admission of persons to professions and fields requiring special skill and confidence.

I concur in the judgment of the court in this case, by which the judgment of the Supreme Court of Illinois is affirmed, but not for the reasons specified in the opinion just read. . . .

The claim that, under the fourteenth amendment of the Constitution, which declares that no State shall make or enforce any law which shall abridge the privileges and immunities of citizens of the United States, the statute law of Illinois, or the common law prevailing in that State, can no longer be set up as a barrier against the right of females to pursue any lawful employment for a livelihood (the practice of law included), assumes that it is one of the privileges and immunities of women as citizens to engage in any and every profession, occupation, or employment in civil life.

United States Supreme Court. 83 U.S. 130 (1873).

It certainly cannot be affirmed, as an historical fact, that this has ever been established as one of the fundamental privileges and immunities of the sex. On the contrary, the civil law, as well as nature herself, has always recognized a wide difference in the respective spheres and destinies of man and woman. Man is, or should be, woman's protector and defender. The natural and proper timidity and delicacy which belongs to the female sex evidently unfits it for many of the occupations of civil life. The constitution of the family organization, which is founded in the divine ordinance, as well as in the nature of things, indicates the domestic sphere as that which properly belongs to the domain and functions of womanhood. The harmony, not to say identity, of interests and views which belong, or should belong, to the family institution is repugnant to the idea of a woman adopting a distinct and independent career from that of her husband. So firmly fixed was this sentiment in the founders of the common law that it became a maxim of that system of jurisprudence that a woman had no legal existence separate from her husband, who was regarded as her head and representative in the social state and, notwithstanding some recent modifications of this civil status, many of the special rules of law flowing from and dependent upon this cardinal principle still exist in full force in most States. One of these is, that a married woman is incapable, without her husband's consent, of making contracts which shall be binding on her or him. This very incapacity was one circumstance which the Supreme Court of Illinois deemed important in rendering a married woman incompetent fully to perform the duties and trusts that belong to the office of an attorney and counsellor.

It is true that many women are unmarried and not affected by any of the duties, complications, and incapacities arising out of the married state, but these are exceptions to the general rule. The paramount destiny and mission of woman are to fulfil the noble and benign offices of wife and mother. This is the law of the Creator. And the rules of civil society must be adapted to the general constitution of things, and cannot be based upon exceptional cases.

The humane movements of modern society, which have for their object the multiplication of avenues for woman's advancement, and of occupations adapted to her condition and sex, have my heartiest concurrence. But I am not prepared to say that it is one of her fundamental rights and privileges to be admitted into every office and position, including those which require highly special qualifications and demanding special responsibilities. In the nature of things it is not every citizen of every age, sex, and condition that is qualified for every calling and position. It is the prerogative of the legislator to prescribe regulations founded on nature, reason, and experience for the due admission of qualified persons to professions and callings demanding special skill and confidence. This fairly belongs to the police power of the State; and, in my opinion, in view of the peculiar characteristics, destiny, and mission of woman, it is within the province of the legislature to ordain what offices, positions, and callings shall be filled and discharged by man, and shall receive the benefit of those energies and responsibilities, and that decision and firmness which are presumed to predominate in the sterner sex.

QUESTIONS

1. Are there any sound reasons for believing that there are inherent psychological differences between the sexes?
2. If there are inherent psychological differences between the sexes, are they relevant in assessing candidates for law school or for admission to the bar?

OPINION IN *FRONTIERO v. RICHARDSON*

William Brennan, associate justice of the United States Supreme Court, is a graduate of Harvard Law School. He maintained a private law practice in Newark, New Jersey, until 1949. He then served as superior court judge (1949–1950), appellate division judge (1950–1952), and justice of the Supreme Court of New Jersey (1952–1956). Justice Brennan was appointed to the United States Supreme Court in 1956.

A married woman Air Force officer, Sharron Frontiero, attempted to get increased benefits for her husband as a "dependent" under two statutes—37 U.S.C., sections 401 and 403, and 10 U.S.C., sections 1072 and 1076. Under these statutes, the wives of military servicemen were automatically considered dependents for purposes of obtaining increased quarters allowances and medical and dental benefits. Husbands of military servicewomen were not considered dependents under these statutes, however, *unless* they were in fact dependent on their wives for over one-half of their support. Since Sharon Frontiero's husband was not so dependent on her, her application for increased benefits was denied. The Frontieros sued Eliot Richardson (the Secretary of Defense) and others, contending that the statutes violated servicewomen's right to due process, making sex alone the basis for the assignment of different legal rights and duties. A lower court in Alabama ruled against the Frontieros. They appealed to the United States Supreme Court, which reversed the Alabama Court's decision, ruling that the challenged statutes violated rights covered by the Fifth Amendment.

In holding for the Frontieros, Justice Brennan maintains that classifications based on sex must be subjected to close judicial scrutiny because their relevance is inherently suspect. As Justice Brennan notes, legal classifications based on sex often have the effect of invidiously relegating all females to an inferior legal status, regardless of the actual capabilities of individual women. The result is that similars are treated dissimilarly on the basis of an irrelevant criterion. Justice Brennan dismisses the argument that administrative convenience *alone* can legitimate the use of sex as a classification in the assignment of legal rights and duties, holding that this would necessarily result in the dissimilar treatment of those similarly situated.

The question before us concerns the right of a female member of the uniformed services to claim her spouse as a "dependent" for the purposes of obtaining increased quarters allowances and medical and dental benefits on an equal footing with male members. Under these statutes, a serviceman may claim his wife as a "dependent" without regard to whether she is in fact dependent upon him for any part of her support. A servicewoman, on the other hand, may not claim her husband as a "dependent" under these programs unless he is in fact dependent upon her for over one-half of his support. Thus, the question for decision is whether this difference in treatment constitutes an unconstitutional discrimination against servicewomen in violation of the Due Process Clause of the Fifth Amendment. A three-judge District Court for the Middle District of Alabama, one judge dissenting, rejected this contention and sustained the constitutionality of the provisions of the statutes making this distinction. We noted probable jurisdiction. We reverse.

United States Supreme Court. 411 U.S. 677 (1973).

I

In an effort to attract career personnel through reenlistment, Congress established a scheme for the provision of fringe benefits to members of the uniformed services on a competitive basis with business and industry. Thus, a member of the uniformed services with dependents is entitled to an increased "basic allowance for quarters" and a member's dependents are provided comprehensive medical and dental care.

Appellant Sharron Frontiero, a lieutenant in the United States Air Force, sought increased quarters allowances, and housing and medical benefits for her husband, appellant Joseph Frontiero, on the ground that he was her "dependent." Although such benefits would automatically have been granted with respect to the wife of a male member of the uniformed service, appellant's application was denied because she failed to demonstrate that her husband was dependent on her for more than one-half of his support. Appellants then commenced this suit, contending that, by making this distinction, the statutes unreasonably discriminate on the basis of sex in violation of the Due Process Clause of the Fifth Amendment.[1] In essence, appellants asserted that the discriminatory impact of the statutes is twofold: first, as a procedural matter, a female member is required to demonstrate her spouse's dependency, while no such burden is imposed upon male members; and, second, as a substantive matter, a male member who does not provide more than one-half of his wife's support receives benefits, while a similarly situated female member is denied such benefits. Appellants therefore sought a permanent injunction against the continued enforcement of these statutes and an order directing the appellees to provide Lieutenant Frontiero with the same housing and medical benefits that a similarly situated male member would receive.

Although the legislative history of these statutes sheds virtually no light on the purposes underlying the differential treatment accorded male and female members, a majority of the three-judge District Court surmised that Congress might reasonably have concluded that, since the husband in our society is generally the "breadwinner" in the family—and the wife typically the "dependent" partner—"it would be more economical to require married female members claiming husbands to prove actual dependency than to extend the presumption of dependency to such members." Indeed, given the fact that approximately 99% of all members of the uniformed services are male, the District Court speculated that such differential treatment might conceivably lead to a "considerable saving of administrative expense and manpower."

II

At the outset, appellants contend that classifications based upon sex, like classifications based upon race, alienage, and national origin, are inherently suspect and must therefore be subjected to close judicial scrutiny. We agree and, indeed, find at least implicit support for such an approach in our unanimous decision only last Term in *Reed v. Reed* (1971).

In *Reed,* the Court considered the constitutionality of an Idaho statute providing that, when two individuals are otherwise equally entitled to appointment as administrator of an estate, the male applicant must be preferred to the female. Appellant, the mother of the deceased, and appellee, the father, filed competing petitions for appointment as administrator of their son's estate. Since the parties, as parents of the deceased, were members of the same entitlement class, the statutory preference was invoked and the father's petition was therefore granted. Appellant claimed that this statute, by giving a mandatory

[1]"[W]hile the Fifth Amendment contains no equal protection clause, it does forbid discrimination that is 'so unjustifiable as to be violative of due process.'"

preference to males over females without regard to their individual qualifications, violated the Equal Protection Clause of the Fourteenth Amendment.

The Court noted that the Idaho statute "provides that different treatment be accorded to the applicants on the basis of their sex; it thus establishes a classification subject to scrutiny under the Equal Protection Clause." Under "traditional" equal protection analysis, a legislative classification must be sustained unless it is "patently arbitrary" and bears no rational relationship to a legitimate governmental interest.

In an effort to meet this standard, appellee contended that the statutory scheme was a reasonable measure designed to reduce the workload on probate courts by eliminating one class of contests. Moreover, appellee argued that the mandatory preference for male applicants was in itself reasonable since "men [are] as a rule more conversant with business affairs than . . . women." Indeed, appellee maintained that "it is a matter of common knowledge, that women still are not engaged in politics, the professions, business or industry to the extent that men are." And the Idaho Supreme Court, in upholding the constitutionality of this statute, suggested that the Idaho Legislature might reasonably have "concluded that in general men are better qualified to act as an administrator than are women."

Despite these contentions, however, the Court held the statutory preference for male applicants unconstitutional. In reaching this result, the Court implicitly rejected appellee's apparently rational explanation of the statutory scheme, and concluded that, by ignoring the individual qualifications of particular applicants, the challenged statute provided "dissimilar treatment for men and women who are . . . similarly situated." The Court therefore held that, even though the State's interest in achieving administrative efficiency "is not without some legitimacy," "[t]o give a mandatory preference to members of either sex over members of the other, merely to accomplish the elimination of hearings on the merits, is to make the very kind of arbitrary legislative choice forbidden by the [Constitution]. . . ." This departure from "traditional" rational-basis analysis with respect to sex-based classifications is clearly justified.

There can be no doubt that our Nation has had a long and unfortunate history of sex discrimination. Traditionally, such discrimination was rationalized by an attitude of "romantic paternalism" which, in practical effect, put women, not on a pedestal, but in a cage. Indeed, this paternalistic attitude became so firmly rooted in our national consciousness that, 100 years ago, a distinguished Member of this Court was able to proclaim:

> "Man is, or should be, woman's protector and defender. The natural and proper timidity and delicacy which belongs to the female sex evidently unfits it for many of the occupations of civil life. The constitution of the family organization, which is founded in the divine ordinance, as well as in the nature of things, indicates the domestic sphere as that which properly belongs to the domain and functions of womanhood. The harmony, not to say identity, of interests and views which belong, or should belong, to the family institution is repugnant to the idea of a woman adopting a distinct and independent career from that of her husband. . . .
>
> " . . . The paramount destiny and mission of woman are to fulfil the noble and benign offices of wife and mother. This is the law of the Creator." *Bradwell v. State* (1873) (Bradley, J., concurring).

As a result of notions such as these, our statute books gradually became laden with gross, stereotyped distinctions between the sexes and, indeed, throughout much of the 19th century the position of women in our society was, in many respects, comparable to that of blacks under the pre-Civil War slave codes. Neither slaves nor women could hold office, serve on juries, or bring suit in their own names, and married women traditionally were denied the legal capacity to hold or convey property or to serve as legal guardians of their own children. And although blacks were guaranteed the right to vote in 1870, women were denied even that right—which is itself "preservative of other basic civil and political rights"—until adoption of the Nineteenth Amendment half a century later.

It is true, of course, that the position of women in America has improved markedly in recent decades. Nevertheless, it can hardly be doubted that, in part because of the high visibility of the sex characteristic, women still face pervasive, although at times more subtle, discrimination in our educational institutions, in the job market and, perhaps most conspicuously, in the political arena.

Moreover, since sex, like race and national origin, is an immutable characteristic determined solely by the accident of birth, the imposition of special disabilities upon the members of a particular sex because of their sex would seem to violate "the basic concept of our system that legal burdens should bear some relationship to individual responsibility. . . ." And what differentiates sex from such nonsuspect statuses as intelligence or physical disability, and aligns it with the recognized suspect criteria, is that the sex characteristic frequently bears no relation to ability to perform or contribute to society. As a result, statutory distinctions between the sexes often have the effect of invidiously relegating the entire class of females to inferior legal status without regard to the actual capabilities of its individual members.

We might also note that, over the past decade, Congress has itself manifested an increasing sensitivity to sex-based classifications. In Tit. VII of the Civil Rights Act of 1964, for example, Congress expressly declared that no employer, labor union, or other organization subject to the provisions of the Act shall discriminate against any individual on the basis of "race, color, religion, *sex,* or national origin." Similarly, the Equal Pay Act of 1963 provides that no employer covered by the Act "shall discriminate . . . between employees on the basis of *sex.*" And § 1 of the Equal Rights Amendment, passed by Congress on March 22, 1972, and submitted to the legislatures of the States for ratification, declares that "[e]quality of rights under the law shall not be denied or abridged by the United States or by any State on account of sex." Thus, Congress itself has concluded that classifications based upon sex are inherently invidious, and this conclusion of a coequal branch of Government is not without significance to the question presently under consideration.

With these considerations in mind, we can only conclude that classifications based upon sex, like classifications based upon race, alienage, or national origin, are inherently suspect, and must therefore be subjected to strict judicial scrutiny. Applying the analysis mandated by that stricter standard of review, it is clear that the statutory scheme now before us is constitutionally invalid.

III

The sole basis of the classification established in the challenged statutes is the sex of the individuals involved. Thus a female member of the uniformed services seeking to obtain housing and medical benefits for her spouse must prove his dependency in fact, whereas no such burden is imposed upon male members. In addition, the statutes operate so as to deny benefits to a female member, such as appellant Sharron Frontiero, who provides less than one-half of her spouse's support, while at the same time granting such benefits to a male member who likewise provides less than one-half of his spouse's support. Thus, to this extent at least, it may fairly be said that these statutes command "dissimilar treatment for men and women who are . . . similarly situated."

Moreover, the Government concedes that the differential treatment accorded men and women under these statutes serves no purpose other than mere "administrative convenience." In essence, the Government maintains that, as an empirical matter, wives in our society frequently are dependent upon their husbands, while husbands rarely are dependent upon their wives. Thus, the Government argues that Congress might reasonably have concluded that it would be both cheaper and easier simply conclusively to presume that wives of male members are financially dependent upon their husbands, while burdening female members with the task of establishing dependency in fact.

The Government offers no concrete evidence, however, tending to support its view that such differential treatment in fact saves the Government any money. In order to satisfy the demands of strict judicial scrutiny, the Government must demonstrate, for example, that it is actually cheaper to grant increased benefits with respect to *all* male members, than it is to determine which male members are in fact entitled to such benefits and to grant increased benefits only to those members whose wives actually meet the dependency requirement. Here, however, there is substantial evidence that, if put to the test, many of the wives of male members would fail to qualify for benefits. And in light of the fact that the dependency determination with respect to the husbands of female members is presently made solely on the basis of affidavits, rather than through the more costly hearing process, the Government's explanation of the statutory scheme is, to say the least, questionable.

In any case, our prior decisions make clear that, although efficacious administration of governmental programs is not without some importance, "the Constitution recognizes higher values than speed and efficiency." And when we enter the realm of "strict judicial scrutiny," there can be no doubt that "administrative convenience" is not a shibboleth, the mere recitation of which dictates constitutionality. On the contrary, any statutory scheme which draws a sharp line between the sexes, *solely* for the purpose of achieving administrative convenience, necessarily commands "dissimilar treatment for men and women who are . . . similarly situated," and therefore involves the "very kind of arbitrary legislative choice forbidden by the [Constitution]. . . ." We therefore conclude that, by according differential treatment to male and female members of the uniformed services for the sole purpose of achieving administrative convenience, the challenged statutes violate the Due Process Clause of the Fifth Amendment insofar as they require a female member to prove the dependency of her husband.

QUESTIONS

1. Can you suggest any valid legislative purposes which might be reasonably related to the assignment of different legal rights and duties to men and women? Explain.
2. According to Justice Brennan, "Women still face pervasive, although at times more subtle, discrimination in our educational institutions, on the job market and, perhaps most conspicuously, in the political arena." Is this true today? What evidence can you present to support your answer?

JOHN STUART MILL

THE SUBJECTION OF WOMEN

John Stuart Mill (1806–1873) is known primarily as an advocate of utilitarianism. Unlike most contemporary philosophers, Mill was not an academician. He had a successful career with the British East India Company and served one term as a member of Parliament. While a member of Parliament, Mill

submitted the first bill on the enfranchisement of women to the House of Commons. Mill's classic feminist work, *The Subjection of Women,* from which this selection is excerpted, was written late in his
career. Among his related works are *On Liberty* and *Utilitarianism.*

Mill is a proponent of sexual equality. He argues that sex is not a relevant occupational criterion. In Mill
we see one of the earliest arguments against the following claims: (1) The subordination of women to
men is natural. (2) It is based on natural differences between the sexes. Mill's arguments against these
claims are classic. He argues, first, that what is customary is usually accepted as natural and that no
attempt has ever been made to establish a society in which women were not subordinate to men. Second, he maintains that we cannot base claims about natural cognitive and other psychological differences between the sexes on the observation of men and women whose psychological makeup has
been affected by social institutions and practices which maintain the interests of society (that is, of
men). If you want to see what women can do, Mill says, look at the things they have done when they
have been given the opportunity to do them.

The object of this Essay is to explain, as clearly as I am able, the grounds of an opinion
which I have held from the very earliest period when I had formed any opinions at all on
social or political matters, and which, instead of being weakened or modified, has been
constantly growing stronger by the progress of reflection and the experience of life: That
the principle which regulates the existing social relations between the two sexes—the legal
subordination of one sex to the other—is wrong in itself, and now one of the chief hin-
drances to human improvement; and that it ought to be replaced by a principle of perfect
equality, admitting no power or privilege on the one side, nor disability on the other. . . .
      The generality of a practice is in some cases a strong presumption that it is, or at all
events once was, conducive to laudable ends. This is the case, when the practice was first
adopted, or afterward kept up, as a means to such ends, and was grounded on experience
of the mode in which they could be most effectually attained. If the authority of men over
women, when first established, had been the result of a conscientious comparison between
different modes of constituting the government of society; if, after trying various other
modes of social organization—the government of women over men, equality between the
two, and such mixed and divided modes of government as might be invented—it had been
decided, on the testimony of experience, that the mode in which women are wholly under
the rule of men, having no share at all in public concerns, and each in private being under
the legal obligation of obedience to the man with whom she has associated her destiny, was
the arrangement most conducive to the happiness and well-being of both; its general adoption might then be fairly thought to be some evidence that, at the time when it was adopted,
it was the best: though even then the considerations which recommended it may, like so
many other primeval social facts of the greatest importance, have subsequently, in the
course of ages, ceased to exist. But the state of the case is in every respect the reverse of
this. In the first place, the opinion in favor of the present system, which entirely subordi-
nates the weaker sex to the stronger, rests upon theory only; for there never has been trial
made of any other: so that experience, in the sense in which it is vulgarly opposed to
theory, cannot be pretended to have pronounced any verdict. And in the second place, the
adoption of this system of inequality never was the result of deliberation, or forethought,
or any social ideas, or any notion whatever of what conduced to the benefit of humanity or
the good order of society. It arose simply from the fact that from the very earliest twilight
of human society, every woman (owing to the value attached to her by men, combined with

Reprinted from the original edition published by Longmans, Green, Reades, and Dyer (London, 1869).

her inferiority in muscular strength) was found in a state of bondage to some man. Laws and systems of polity always begin by recognizing the relations they find already existing between individuals. They convert what was a mere physical fact into a legal right, give it the sanction of society, and principally aim at the substitution of public and organized means of asserting and protecting these rights, instead of the irregular and lawless conflict of physical strength. Those who had already been compelled to obedience became in this manner legally bound to it. Slavery, from being a mere affair of force between the master and the slave, became regularized and a matter of compact among the masters, who, binding themselves to one another for common protection, guaranteed by their collective strength the private possessions of each, including their slaves. In early times, the great majority of the male sex were slaves, as well as the whole of the female. And many ages elapsed, some of them ages of high cultivation, before any thinker was bold enough to question the rightfulness, and the absolute social necessity, either of the one slavery or of the other. By degrees such thinkers did arise: and (the general progress of society assisting) the slavery of the male sex has, in all the countries of the Christian Europe at least (though, in one of them, only within the last few years), been at length abolished, and that of the female sex has been gradually changed into a milder form of dependence. But this dependence, as it exists at present, is not an original institution, taking a fresh start from considerations of justice and social expediency — it is the primitive state of slavery lasting on, through successive mitigations and modifications occasioned by the same causes which have softened the general manners, and brought all human relations more under the control of justice and the influence of humanity. It has not lost the taint of its brutal origin. No presumption in its favor, therefore, can be drawn from the fact of its existence. . . . The *inequality of rights between men and women has no other source than the law of the strongest. . . .*

Some will object, that a comparison cannot fairly be made between the government of the male sex and the forms of unjust power which I have adduced in illustration of it, since these are arbitrary, and the effect of mere usurpation, while it on the contrary is natural. But was there ever any domination which did not appear natural to those who possessed it? There was a time when the division of mankind into two classes, a small one of masters and a numerous one of slaves, appeared, even to the most cultivated minds, to be a natural, and the only natural, condition of the human race. No less an intellect, and one which contributed no less to the progress of human thought, than Aristotle, held this opinion without doubt or misgiving; and rested it on the same premises on which the same assertion in regard to the dominion of men over women is usually based, namely, that there are different natures among mankind, free natures, and slave natures; that the Greeks were of a free nature, the barbarian races of Thracians and Asiatics of a slave nature. . . . The subjection of women to men being a universal custom, any departure from it quite naturally appears unnatural. But how entirely, even in this case, the feeling is dependent on custom, appears by ample experience. Nothing so much astonishes the people of distant parts of the world, when they first learn anything about England, as to be told that it is under a queen: the thing seems to them so unnatural as to be almost incredible. To Englishmen this does not seem in the least degree unnatural, because they are used to it; but they do feel it unnatural that women should be soldiers or members of Parliament. In the feudal ages, on the contrary, war and politics were not thought unnatural to women, because not unusual; it seemed natural that women of the privileged classes should be of manly character, inferior in nothing but bodily strength to their husbands and fathers. . . .

But, it will be said, the rule of men over women differs from all these others in not being a rule of force: it is accepted voluntarily; women make no complaint, and are consenting parties to it. In the first place a great number of women do not accept it. Ever since there have been women able to make their sentiments known by their writings (the only mode of publicity which society permits to them), an increasing number of them have recorded protests against their present social condition: . . .

All causes, social and natural, combined to make it unlikely that women should be collectively rebellious to the power of men. They are so far in a position different from all other subject classes, that their masters require something more from them than actual service. Men do not want solely the obedience of women, they want their sentiments. All men, except the most brutish desire to have, in the woman most nearly connected with them, not a forced slave but a willing one, not a slave merely, but a favorite. They have therefore put everything in practice to enslave their minds. The masters of all other slaves rely, for maintaining obedience, on fear, — either fear of themselves or religious fears. The masters of women wanted more than simple obedience, and they turned the whole force of education to effect their purpose. All women are brought up from the very earliest years in the belief that their ideal of character is the very opposite to that of man; not self-will and government by self-control, but submission and yielding to the control of others. All the moralities tell them that it is the duty of women, and all the current sentimentalities that it is their nature, to live for others, to make complete abnegation of themselves, and to have no life but in their affections. And by their affections are meant the only ones they are allowed to have — those to the men with whom they are connected, or to the children who constitute an additional and indefeasible tie between them and a man. When we put together three things — first, the natural attraction between opposite sexes; secondly, the wife's entire dependence on the husband, every privilege or pleasure she has being either his gift, or depending entirely on his will; and lastly, that the principal object of human pursuit, consideration, and all objects of social ambition, can in general be sought or obtained by her only through him, it would be a miracle if the object of being attractive to men had not become the polar star of feminine education and formation of character. And this great means of influence over the minds of women having been acquired, an instinct of selfishness made men avail themselves of it to the utmost as a means of holding women in subjection, by representing to them meekness, submissiveness, and resignation of all individual will into the hands of a man, as an essential part of sexual attractiveness. Can it be doubted that any of the other yokes which mankind have succeeded in breaking, would have subsisted till now if the same means had existed, and had been as sedulously used, to bow down their minds to it? . . .

The least that can be demanded is, that the question should not be considered as prejudged by existing fact and existing opinion, but open to discussion on its merits, as a question of justice and expediency; the decision on this, as on any of the other social arrangements of mankind, depending on what an enlightened estimate of tendencies and consequences may show to be most advantageous to humanity in general, without distinction of sex. And the discussion must be a real discussion, descending to foundations, and not resting satisfied with vague and general assertions. It will not do, for instance, to assert in general terms, that the experience of mankind has pronounced in favor of the existing system. Experience cannot possibly have decided between two courses, so long as there has only been experience of one. If it be said the the doctrine of the equality of the sexes rests only on theory, it must be remembered that the contrary doctrine also has only theory to rest upon. All that is proved in its favor by direct experience, is that mankind have been able to exist under it, and to attain the degree of improvement and prosperity which we now see; but whether that prosperity has been attained sooner, or is now greater, than it would have been under the other system, experience does not say. . . .

Neither does it avail anything to say that the *nature* of the two sexes adapts them to their present functions and position, and renders these appropriate to them. Standing on the ground of common sense and the constitution of the human mind, I deny that any one knows, or can know, the nature of the two sexes, as long as they have only been seen in their present relation to one another. If men had ever been found in society without women, or women without men, or if there had been a society of men and women in which the women were not under the control of the men, something might have been positively known about the mental and moral differences which may be inherent in the nature of each. What is now called the nature of women is an eminently artificial thing—the result of forced repression in some directions, unnatural stimulation in others. . . .

Of all difficulties which impede the progress of thought, and the formation of well-grounded opinions on life and social arrangements, the greatest is now the unspeakable ignorance and inattention of mankind in respect to the influences which form human character. Whatever any portion of the human species now are, or seem to be, such, it is supposed, they have a natural tendency to be: even when the most elementary knowledge of the circumstances in which they have been placed, clearly points out the causes that made them what they are. Because a cottier deeply in arrears to his landlord is not industrious, there are people who think that the Irish are naturally idle. Because constitutions can be overthrown when the authorities appointed to execute them turn their arms against them, there are people who think the French incapable of free government. Because the Greeks cheated the Turks, and the Turks only plundered the Greeks, there are persons who think that the Turks are naturally more sincere: and because women, as is often said, care nothing about politics except their personalities, it is supposed that the general good is naturally less interesting to women than to men. History, which is now so much better understood than formerly, teaches another lesson: if only by showing the extraordinary susceptibility of human nature to external influences, and the extreme variableness of those of its manifestations which are supposed to be most universal and uniform. . . .

Hence, in regard to that most difficult question, what are the natural differences between the two sexes—a subject on which it is impossible in the present state of society to obtain complete and correct knowledge—while almost everybody dogmatizes upon it, almost all neglect and make light of the only means by which any partial insight can be obtained into it. This is, an analytic study of the most important department of psychology, the laws of the influence of circumstances on character. For, however great and apparently ineradicable the moral and intellectual differences between men and women might be, the evidence of their being natural differences could only be negative. Those only could be inferred to be natural which could not possibly be artificial—the residuum, after deducting every characteristic of either sex which can admit of being explained from education or external circumstances. The profoundest knowledge of the laws of the formation of character is indispensable to entitle any one to affirm even that there is any difference, much more what the difference is, between the two sexes considered as moral and rational beings; and since no one, as yet, has that knowledge (for there is hardly any subject which, in proportion to its importance, has been so little studied), no one is thus far entitled to any positive opinion on the subject. Conjectures are all that can at present be made; conjectures more or less probable, according as more or less authorized by such knowledge as we yet have of the laws of psychology, as applied to the formation of character. . . .

One thing we may be certain of,—that what is contrary to women's nature to do, they never will be made to do by simply giving their nature free play. The anxiety of mankind to interfere in behalf of nature, for fear lest nature should not succeed in effecting its purpose, is an altogether unnecessary solicitude. What women by nature cannot do, it is quite superfluous to forbid them from doing. What they can do, but not so well as the men who are their competitors, competition suffices to exclude them from; since nobody asks for protective duties and bounties in favor of women; it is only asked that the present bounties and protective duties in favor of men should be recalled. If women have a greater natural inclination for some things than for others, there is no need of laws or social inculcation to make the majority of them do the former in preference to the latter. Whatever women's services are most wanted for, the free play of competition will hold out the strongest inducements to them to undertake. And, as the words imply, they are most wanted for the things for which they are most fit; by the apportionment of which to them, the collective faculties of the two sexes can be applied on the whole with the greatest sum of valuable result.

The general opinion of men is supposed to be, that the natural vocation of a woman is that of a wife and mother. I say, is supposed to be, because, judging from acts—from the whole of the present constitution of society—one might infer that their opinion was the direct contrary. They might be supposed to think that the alleged natural vocation of women was of all things the most repugnant to their nature; insomuch that if they are free to do anything else—if any other means of living, or occupation of their time and faculties, is open, which has any chance of appearing desirable to them—there will not be enough of them who will be willing to accept the condition said to be natural to them. If this is the real opinion of men in general, it would be well that it should be spoken out. I should like to hear somebody openly enunciating the doctrine (it is already implied in much that is written on the subject)—"It is necessary to society that women should marry and produce children. They will not do so unless they are compelled. Therefore it is necessary to compel them." The merits of the case would then be clearly defined. It would be exactly that of the slave-holders of South Carolina and Louisiana. "It is necessary that cotton and sugar should be grown. White men cannot produce them. Negroes will not, for any wages which we choose to give. *Ergo* they must be compelled.". . . Those who attempt to force women into marriage by closing all other doors against them, lay themselves open to a similar retort. If they mean what they say, their opinion must evidently be, that men do not render the married condition so desirable to women, as to induce them to accept it for its own recommendations. It is not a sign of one's thinking the boon one offers very attractive, when one allows only Hobson's choice, "that or none.". . .

On the other point which is involved in the just equality of women, their admissibility to all the functions and occupations hitherto retained as the monopoly of the stronger sex, . . . I believe that their disabilities elsewhere are only clung to in order to maintain their subordination in domestic life; . . . It is not sufficient to maintain that women on the average are less gifted than men on the average, with certain of the higher mental faculties, or that a smaller number of women than of men are fit for occupations and functions of the highest intellectual character. It is necessary to maintain that no women at all are fit for them, and that the most eminent women are inferior in mental faculties to the most mediocre of the men on whom those functions at present devolve. . . . Is there so great a superfluity of men fit for high duties, that society can afford to reject the service of any competent person? Are we so certain of always finding a man made to our hands for any duty or function of social importance which falls vacant, that we lose nothing by putting a ban upon one-half of mankind, and refusing beforehand to make their faculties available, however distinguished they may be? And even if we could do without them, would it be consistent with justice to refuse to them their fair share of honor and distinction, or to deny to them the equal moral right of all human beings to choose their occupation (short of injury to others) according to their own preferences, at their own risk? Nor is the injustice confined to them: it is shared by those who are in a position to benefit by their services. To ordain that any kind of persons shall not be physicians, or shall not be advocates, or shall not be members of Parliament, is to injure not them only, but all who employ physicians or advocates, or elect members of Parliament, and who are deprived of the stimulating effect of greater competition on the exertions of the competitors, as well as restricted to a narrower range of individual choice.

It will perhaps be sufficient if I confine myself, in the details of my argument, to functions of a public nature; since, if I am successful as to those, it probably will be readily granted that women should be admissible to all other occupations to which it is at all material whether they are admitted or not. . . .

. . . Any woman, who succeeds in an open profession, proves by that very fact that she is qualified for it. And in the case of public offices, if the political system of the country is such as to exclude unfit men, it will equally exclude unfit women: while if it is not, there is no additional evil in the fact that the unfit persons whom it admits may be either women or men. As long therefore as it is acknowledged that even a few women may be fit for these duties, the laws which shut the door on those exceptions cannot be justified by any opinion which can be held respecting the capacities of women in general. But, though this last consideration is not essential, it is far from being irrelevant. An unprejudiced view of it gives additional strength to the arguments against the disabilities of women, and reinforces them by high considerations of practical utility.

Let us at first make entire abstraction of all psychological considerations tending to show that any of the mental differences supposed to exist between women and men are but the natural effect of the differences in their education and circumstances, and indicate no radical difference, far less radical inferiority, of nature. Let us consider women only as they already are, or as they are known to have been; and the capacities which they have already practically shown. What they have done, that at least, if nothing else, it is proved that they can do. When we consider how sedulously they are all trained away from, instead of being trained toward, any of the occupations or objects reserved for men, it is evident that I am taking a very humble ground for them when I rest their case on what they have actually achieved. For, in this case, negative evidence is worth little, while any positive evidence is conclusive. It cannot be inferred to be impossible that a woman should be a Homer, or an Aristotle, or a Michael Angelo, or a Beethoven, because no woman has yet actually produced works comparable to theirs in any of those lines of excellence. This negative fact at most leaves the question uncertain, and open to psychological discussion. But it is quite certain that a woman can be a Queen Elizabeth, or a Deborah, or a Joan of Arc, since this is not inference, but fact. Now it is a curious consideration, that the only things which the existing law excludes women from doing, are the things which they have proved that they are able to do. There is no law to prevent a woman from having written all the plays of Shakespeare, or composed all the operas of Mozart. But Queen Elizabeth or Queen Victoria, had they not inherited the throne, could not have been intrusted with the smallest of the political duties, of which the former showed herself equal to the greatest. . . .

Is it reasonable to think that those who are fit for the greater functions of public office are incapable of qualifying themselves for the less? Is there any reason in the nature of things that the wives and sisters of princes should, whenever called on, be found as competent as the princes themselves to *their* business, but that the wives and sisters of statesmen, and administrators, and directors of companies, and managers of public institutions, should be unable to do what is done by their brothers and husbands? The real reason is plain enough; it is that princesses, being more raised above the generality of men by their rank than placed below them by their sex, have never been taught that it was improper for them to concern themselves with politics; but have been allowed to feel the liberal interest natural to any cultivated human being, in the great transactions which took place around them, and in which they might be called on to take a part. The ladies of reigning families are the only women who are allowed the same range of interests and freedoms of development as men; and it is precisely in their case that there is not found to be any inferiority. Exactly where and in proportion as women's capacities for government have been tried, in that proportion have they been found adequate. . . .

QUESTIONS

1.   Using Mill's arguments, what rebuttal could be given to Justice Bradley's claims?
2.   You are a member of an all-male legislative branch of government in a nation where women do not have the right to vote. Do you have the *moral* right to determine what is in the best interests of women?

STEVEN GOLDBERG

THE INEVITABILITY OF PATRIARCHY

Steven Goldberg teaches in the department of sociology at City College of the City University of New York. He is the only nonmedical fellow of the American Academy of Psychiatry and Neurology. Goldberg's articles include "Is Astrology a Science?" and "What Is Normal? Logical Aspects of the Question of Homosexual Behavior."

Goldberg defends the nonegalitarianism found in a patriarchy. He attacks the following basic assumption made by Mill and other feminists: There is no natural difference betweeen the sexes which makes a male-dominated society inevitable. Goldberg claims that there is such a difference—a hormonal one. Owing to hormonal differences, males are inherently more aggressive than females. This greater aggressiveness assures male domination of the high-status roles in society.

Moreover, Goldberg argues, if society does not socialize women away from competing with men, then most women will be condemned to failure and unhappiness. Given the innate aggression advantage of men over women, consider what would happen if society did not socialize women against competing with men for society's high-status positions. Some women would be aggressive enough to succeed. The vast majority would be failures, however, socialized to desire high-status positions but incapable of attaining them.

The view of man and woman in society that implicitly underlies all of the arguments of the feminists is this: there is nothing inherent in the nature of human beings or of society that necessitates that any role or task (save those requiring great strength or the ability to give birth) be associated with one sex or the other;[1] there is no natural order of things decreeing

Adapted from pp. 49, 51, 63, 81, 93, 105–109, 166–168 in *The Inevitability of Patriarchy* by Steven Goldberg. Copyright © 1973 by Steven Goldberg. By permission of William Morrow & Company.
[1] *It is time that we realized that the whole structure of male and female personality is entirely imposed by social conditioning.* All the possible traits of human personality have in this conditioning been *arbitrarily* assigned into two categories; thus aggression is masculine, passivity feminine. . . ." [Emphasis added]. (Kate Millett, *Barnard Alumnae.* Spring, 1970, p. 28.) This statement expresses the assumption which underpins all of Dr. Millett's *Sexual Politics* (New York: Doubleday, 1970).

that dyadic and social authority must be associated with men, nor is there any reason why it must be men who rule in *every* society. Patriarchy, matriarchy, and "equiarchy" are all equally possible and — while every society may invoke "the natural order of things" to justify its particular system — all the expectations we have of men and women are culturally determined and have nothing to do with any sort of basic male or female nature.[2]

There is nothing internally contradictory in such a hypothesis; indeed, it is an ideal place from which to begin an empirical investigation into the nature of man, woman, and society. However, the feminist does not use this as a heuristic first step but unquestioningly accepts it as true. . . .

Given the *seemingly* unlimited plasticity of human beings and the *seemingly* endless variety of their societal institutions, the universality of an institution alerts the objective investigator to the possibility that there is an underlying factor engendering universality and that, if this factor is inseparable from the general nature of society or of human biology, the institution, or some equivalent institutional channel for meeting the requirements of this factor may be inevitable. . . .

The only biological hypothesis included in this book states that those individuals whose male anatomy leads to a social identification as "male" have hormonal systems which generate a greater capacity for "aggression" (or a lower threshold for the release of "aggression" — for our purposes this is the same thing) than those individuals whose female anatomy leads to a social identification as "female" and that socialization and institutions conform to the reality of hormonal sexual differentiation and to the statistical reality of the "aggresion advantage" which males derive from their hormonal systems. . . .

The thesis put forth here is that the hormonal renders the social inevitable. . . .

I believe that in the past we have been looking in the wrong direction for the answer to the question of why every society rewards male roles with higher status than it does female roles (even when the male tasks in one society are the female tasks in another). While it is true that men are always in the positions of authority from which status tends to be defined, male roles are not given high status primarily *because* men fill these roles; men fill these roles because their biological aggression "advantage" can be manifested *in any non-child related area rewarded by high status in any society*. (Again: the line of reasoning used in this book demonstrates only that the biological factors we discuss would make the social institutions we discuss inevitable and does not preclude the existence of other forces also leading in the same direction; there may be a biologically based tendency for women to prefer male leadership, but there need not be for male attainment of leadership and high-status roles to be inevitable.) . . . This aggression "advantage" can be most manifested and can most enable men to reap status rewards *not* in those relatively homogeneous, collectivist primitive societies in which both male and female must play similar economic roles if the society is to survive or in the monarchy (which guarantees an occasional female

[2]The best presentation of the feminist assumption is unquestionably John Stuart Mill's *The Subjection of Women.* As an impassioned plea for women's rights Mill's essay is both moving and illuminating. As an attempt to explain the etiology of sexually differentiated behavior and institutions it is indefensible. One is tempted, given the fact that the author of the essay was Mill, to ascribe its inadequacies to the fact that little of the relevant anthropological evidence, and none of the relevant hormonal evidence, was available at the time. But the weakness of Mill's analysis is attributable even more to the fallacious reasoning that his preconceived conclusions demanded. For example, Mill argues that we can have no conception of the limits of possibility imposed by innate sexual differences, or even of whether such limits exist, because no society has been composed of one sex; thus he does not even attempt to explain why the conceptions of male and female held by his society are not reversed in any other society. Similarly Mill attempts to dismiss the possibility of the determinativeness of innate sexual differences by invoking the irrelevant fact that slave owners defended slavery with the invocation of physiological racial differences that do not exist; this fact is correct, of course, but it casts no more doubt on the likelihood that innate sexual differences are determinative to sexual differences in behavior and institutions than it does on the certainty that physiology is determinative to the ability to give birth. Mill's reasoning has been accepted without question by modern feminist writers.

leader); this biological factor will be given freest play in the complex, relatively individual-istic, bureaucratic, democratic society which, of necessity, must emphasize organizational authority and in which social mobility is relatively free of traditional barriers to advance-ment. There were more female heads of state in the first two-thirds of the sixteenth century than in the first two-thirds of the twentieth.

The mechanisms involved here are easily seen if we examine any roles that males have attained by channeling their aggression toward such attainment. We will assume for now that equivalent women could *perform* the tasks of roles as well as men if they could attain the roles.[3] Here we can speak of the corporation president, the union leader, the governor, the chairman of an association, or any other role or position for which aggression is a precondition for attainment. Now the environmentalist and the feminist will say that the fact that all such roles are nearly always filled by men is attributable not to male aggres-sion but to the fact that women have not been allowed to enter the competitive race to attain these positions, that they have been told that these positions are in male areas, and that girls are socialized away from competing with boys in general. Women *are* socialized in this way, but again we must ask why. If innate male aggression has nothing to do with male attainment of positions of authority and status in the political, academic, scientific, or financial spheres, if aggression has nothing to do with the reasons why *every* society social-izes girls away from those areas which are given high status and away from competition in general, then why is it never the *girls* in any society who are socialized toward these areas, why is it never the nonbiological roles played by women that have high status, why is it always boys who are told to compete, and why do women never "force" men into the low-status, nonmaternal roles that women play in every society?

These questions pose no problem if we acknowledge a male aggression that enables men to attain any nonbiological role given high status by any society. For one need merely consider the result of society's *not* socializing women away from competitions with men, from its *not* directing girls toward roles women are more capable of playing than are men or roles with status low enough that men will not strive for them. No doubt some women would be aggressive enough to succeed in competitions with men and there would be con-siderably more women in high-status positions than there are now. But most women would lose in such competitive struggles with men (because men have the aggression advantage) and so most women would be forced to live adult lives as failures in areas in which the society had *wanted them to succeed*. It is women, far more than men, who would never allow a situation in which girls were socialized in such a way that the vast majority of them were doomed to adult lifetimes of failure to live up to their own expectations. Now I have no doubt that there is a biological factor that gives women the desire to emphasize maternal and nurturance roles, but the point here is that we can accept the feminist assumption that there is no female propensity of this sort and still see that a society must socialize women away from roles that men will attain through their aggression. For if women did not develop an alternative set of criteria for success their sense of their own competence would suffer intolerably. It is undeniable that the resulting different values and expectations that are attached to men and women will tend to work against the aggressive woman while they

---

[3]I assume this for the present in order to demonstrate that these will be male roles even if women can *perform* these roles as well as men when they can attain them. It should be pointed out, however, that the line between attainment and performance is not always clear in a bureaucratic society or in leadership in any society; much of the *performance* of an executive or leader concerns his ability to maintain the authority which his position gives him. Therefore, it is possible that the greater innate male aggression, particularly when opposed to the lesser innate female aggression, leads to *performance* by the male which is superior to that of the female. This does not, of course, mean that the male at any level of the hierarchy has an advantage over the exceptional woman who was aggres-sive enough to attain a comparable position, but it might indicate that men in general have an innate advantage over women in general which is relevant to the *performance* of bureaucratic and leadership roles.

work for the man who is no more aggressive. But this is the unavoidable result of the fact that most men are more aggressive than most women so that this woman, who is as aggressive as the average man, but more aggressive than most women, is an exception. Furthermore, even if the sense of competence of each sex did not necessitate society's attaching to each sex values and expectations based on those qualities possessed by each sex, observation of the majority of each sex by the population would "automatically" lead to these values and expectations being attached to men and women.

SOCIALIZATION'S CONFORMATION TO BIOLOGICAL REALITY

Socialization is the process by which society prepares children for adulthood. The way in which its goals conform to the reality of biology is seen quite clearly when we consider the method in which testosterone generates male aggression (testosterone's serially developing nature). Preadolescent boys and girls have roughly equal testosterone levels, yet young boys are far more aggressive than young girls. Eva Figes has used this observation to dismiss incorrectly the possibility of a hormone-aggression association.[4] Now it is quite probable that the boy is more aggressive than the girl for a purely biological reason. . . . There is evidence of male-female differences in the behavior of infants shortly after birth (when differential socialization is not a plausible explanation of such differences). The fetal alteration of the boy's brain by the testosterone that was generated by his testes has probably left him far more sensitive to the aggression-related properties of the testosterone that is present during boyhood than the girl, who did not receive such alteration. But let us for the moment assume that this is not the case. This does not at all reduce the importance of the hormonal factor. For even if the boy is more aggressive than the girl only because the society allows him to be, the boy's socialization still flows from society's acknowledging biological reality. Let us consider what would happen if girls have the same innate aggression as boys and if a society did not socialize girls away from aggressive competitions. Perhaps half of the third-grade baseball team would be female. As many girls as boys would frame their expectations in masculine values and girls would develop not their feminine abilities but their masculine ones. During adolescence, however, the same assertion of the male chromosomal program that causes the boys to grow beards raises their testosterone level, and their potential for aggression, to a level far above that of the adolescent woman. If society did not teach young girls that beating boys at competitions was unfeminine (behavior inappropriate for a woman), if it did not socialize them away from the political and economic areas in which aggression leads to attainment, these girls would grow into adulthood with self-images based not on succeeding in areas for which biology has left them better prepared than men, but on competitions that most women could not win. If women did not develop feminine qualities as girls (assuming that such qualities do not spring automatically from female biology) then they would be forced to deal with the world in the aggressive terms of men. They would lose every source of power their feminine abilities now give them and they would gain nothing. . . .

The most crucial of the feminist fallacies involves the confusion of cause and function. We need not involve ourselves in a detailed discussion of causation here; a simple example should suffice. A jockey is small because biology made him that way. There may be an element of feedback here in that the jockey might well weigh more if society did not reward his weighing as little as possible, but the causation involved in the determination of his physical characteristics is certainly primarily biological. The function that his size plays in society, its manifestation in his role of jockey, is not biological, but society's putting his size

[4]Eva Figes, *Patriarchal Attitudes* (Greenwich, Conn.: Fawcett World, 1971), p. 8.

to use. Likewise, the economic functions that sexual differentiation requires do not cause the differentiation. The biological element of male aggression will manifest itself in any economic system. . . . Because the social and economic must conform to the biological, we can change any variable and patriarchy will not be diminished. Political rule is male whether the institutions relevant to private property, control of the means of production, and class stratification are as minimally present as is possible or as advanced as is found in any society. It is male whether a society is patrilineal, matrilineal, or bilateral; patrilocal, matrilocal, or neolocal; white, black, or heterogeneous; racist, separatist, or equalitarian; primitive, preindustrial, or technological; Shintoist, Catholic, or Zoroastrian; monarchical, totalitarian, or democratic; Spartan, Quaker, or Bourbon; ascetic, hedonist, or libertine. It makes no difference whether a society has a value system that specifically forbids women from entering areas of authority or, like Communist China, an ideological and political commitment to equal distribution of authority positions. One cannot "disprove" the inevitability of biological factors manifesting themselves by demonstrating the function that they serve in a political or economic system. No system could operate that did not conform to, and utilize, the reality that constitutes it. In short, . . . reasoning that concludes that men rule because of the nature of the political-economic system . . . ignores the reality that the possible varieties of political-economic systems are limited by, and must conform to, the nature of man.

QUESTIONS

1. Are social practices which accord unequal treatment to the sexes justified?
2. In *Sex Equality* (Englewood Cliffs, N.J.: Prentice Hall), p. 196, Jane English argues that the following reasoning parallels Goldberg's. "Height is determined by hormones and genes. In virtually all societies, the tall dominate over the short. Even if ten percent of the population were exceptions, this would be irrelevant. Therefore, we should condition short children to accept the dominance of the tall and not to strive for positions of power and leadership." English claims that if this conclusion does not follow from the premises about height, then Goldberg's conclusion does not follow from his analogous claims about sex. Is English correct?

JOYCE TREBILCOT

SEX ROLES: THE ARGUMENT FROM NATURE

Joyce Trebilcot is associate professor of philosophy at Washington University at St. Louis. Specializing in ethics and feminism, Trebilcot helped to establish a women's studies program at Washington University. Her articles include "Aprudentialism" and "Dr. Kenny's Perceptions."

Trebilcot examines and evaluates the following three arguments frequently given to support the claim that natural psychological differences between the sexes are relevant in deciding whether some roles in society should be assigned on the basis of sex. (1) The argument from inevitability. Since the alleged psychological differences between the sexes and the concomitant differences in behavior are inevitable, society will inevitably be structured to enforce sex roles. Therefore, sex roles are inevitable. (2) The argument from well-being. Because there are natural psychological differences between the sexes, members of each sex will be happier in certain roles than in others; the roles tending to promote happiness will differ according to sex. Thus, society should encourage individuals to make the right role choices so that happiness will be maximized. (3) The argument from efficiency. If there are natural differences in the capacities of the sexes to perform specified tasks, then, for the sake of efficiency, these tasks should be assigned to the sex with the greatest innate ability to perform them.

I am concerned here with the normative question of whether, in an ideal society, certain roles should be assigned to females and others to males. In discussions of this issue, a great deal of attention is given to the claim that there are natural psychological differences between the sexes. Those who hold that at least some roles should be sex roles generally base their view primarily on an appeal to such natural differences, while many of those advocating a society without sex roles argue either that the sexes do not differ in innate psychological traits or that there is no evidence that they do.[1] In this paper I argue that whether there are natural psychological differences between females and males has little bearing on the issue of whether society should reserve certain roles for females and others for males.

Let me begin by saying something about the claim that there are natural psychological differences between the sexes. The issue we are dealing with arises, of course, because there are biological differences among human beings which are bases for designating some as females and others as males. Now it is held by some that, in addition to biological differences between the sexes, there are also natural differences in temperament, interests, abilities, and the like. In this paper I am concerned only with arguments which appeal to these psychological differences as bases of sex roles. Thus, I exclude, for example, arguments that the role of jockey should be female because women are smaller than men or that boxers should be male because men are more muscular than women. Nor do I discuss arguments which appeal directly to the reproductive functions peculiar to each sex. If the physiological processes of gestation or of depositing sperm in a vagina are, apart from any psychological correlates they may have, bases for sex roles, these roles are outside the scope of the present discussion.

It should be noted, however, that virtually all those who hold that there are natural psychological differences between the sexes assume that these differences are determined primarily by differences in biology. According to one hypothesis, natural psychological differences between the sexes are due at least in part to differences between female and male nervous systems. As the male fetus develops in the womb, the testes secrete a hormone which is held to influence the growth of the central nervous system. The female fetus does not produce this hormone, nor is there an analogous female hormone which is significant at this stage. Hence it is suggested that female and male brains differ in structure, that this difference is due to the prenatal influence of testicular hormone, and that the difference in brains is the basis of some later differences in behavior.[2]

Reprinted from *Ethics,* vol. 85, no. 3 (April 1975), pp. 249–255, by permission of the University of Chicago Press. Copyright © 1975 by The University of Chicago.
[1]For support of sex roles, see, for example, Aristotle, *Politics,* book 1; and Erik Erikson, "Womanhood and the Inner Space," *Identity: Youth and Crisis* (New York: W.W. Norton & Co. 1968). Arguments against sex roles may be found, for example, in J. S. Mill, "The Subjection of Women," in Alice S. Rossi, ed., *Essays on Sex Equality: John Stuart Mill and Harriet Taylor Mill* (Chicago: University of Chicago Press, 1970); and Naomi Weisstein, "Psychology Constructs the Female," in Vivian Gornick and Barbara K. Moran, eds., *Women in Sexist Society* (New York: Basic Books, 1971).
[2]See John Money and Anke A. Ehrhardt, *Man and Woman, Boy and Girl* (Baltimore: Johns Hopkins Press, 1972).

A second view about the origin of allegedly natural psychological differences between the sexes, a view not incompatible with the first, is psychoanalytical. It conceives of feminine or masculine behavior as, in part, the individual's response to bodily structure. On this view, one's more or less unconscious experience of one's own body (and in some versions, of the bodies of others) is a major factor in producing sex-specific personality traits. The classic theories of this kind are, of course, Freud's; penis envy and the castration complex are supposed to arise largely from perceptions of differences between female and male bodies. Other writers make much of the analogies between genitals and genders: the uterus is passive and receptive, and so are females; penises are active and penetrating, and so are males.[3] But here we are concerned not with the etiology of allegedly natural differences between the sexes but rather with the question of whether such differences, if they exist, are grounds for holding that there should be sex roles.

That a certain psychological disposition is natural only to one sex is generally taken to mean in part that members of that sex are more likely to have the disposition, or to have it to a greater degree, than persons of the other sex. The situation is thought to be similar to that of height. In a given population, females are on the average shorter than males, but some females are taller than some males, as suggested by figure 1. The shortest

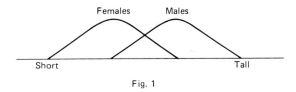

Females   Males

Short   Tall

Fig. 1

members of the population are all females, and the tallest are all males, but there is an area of overlap. For psychological traits, it is usually assumed that there is some degree of overlap and that the degree of overlap is different for different characteristics. Because of the difficulty of identifying natural psychological characteristics, we have of course little or no data as to the actual distribution of such traits.

I shall not undertake here to define the concept of role, but examples include voter, librarian, wife, president. A broad concept of role might also comprise, for example, being a joker, a person who walks gracefully, a compassionate person. The genders, femininity and masculinity, may also be conceived as roles. On this view, each of the gender roles includes a number of more specific sex roles, some of which may be essential to it. For example, the concept of femininity may be construed in such a way that it is necessary to raise a child in order to be fully feminine, while other feminine roles—teacher, nurse, charity worker—are not essential to gender. In the arguments discussed below, the focus is on sex roles rather than genders, but, on the assumption that the genders are roles, much of what is said applies, *mutatis mutandis,* to them.

A sex role is a role performed only or primarily by persons of a particular sex. Now if this is all we mean by "sex role," the problem of whether there should be sex roles must be dealt with as two separate issues: "Are sex roles a good thing?" and "Should society enforce sex roles?" One might argue, for example, that sex roles have value but that, even so, the demands of individual autonomy and freedom are such that societal institutions and

[3]For Freud, see, for example, "Some Psychological Consequences of the Anatomical Distinctions between the Sexes," in James Strachey, ed., *Sigmund Freud: Collected Papers* (New York: Basic Books, 1959), 5:186–97. See also Karl Stern, *The Flight from Woman* (New York: Farrar, Straus & Giroux, 1965), chap. 2; and Erikson.

practices should not enforce correlations between roles and sex. But the debate over sex roles is of course mainly a discussion about the second question, whether society should enforce these correlations. The judgment that there should be sex roles is generally taken to mean not just that sex-exclusive roles are a good thing, but that society should promote such exclusivity.

In view of this, I use the term "sex role" in such a way that to ask whether there should be sex roles is to ask whether society should direct women into certain roles and away from others, and similarly for men. A role is a sex role then (or perhaps an "institutionalized sex role") only if it is performed exclusively or primarily by persons of a particular sex *and* societal factors tend to encourage this correlation. These factors may be of various kinds. Parents guide children into what are taken to be sex-appropriate roles. Schools direct students into occupations according to sex. Marriage customs prescribe different roles for females and males. Employers and unions may refuse to consider applications from persons of the "wrong" sex. The media carry tales of the happiness of those who conform and the suffering of the others. The law sometimes penalizes deviators. Individuals may ridicule and condemn role crossing and smile on conformity. Societal sanctions such as these are essential to the notion of sex role employed here.

I turn now to a discussion of the three major ways the claim that there are natural psychological differences between the sexes is held to be relevant to the issue of whether there should be sex roles.

1. INEVITABILITY

It is sometimes held that if there are innate psychological differences between females and males, sex roles are inevitable. The point of this argument is not, of course, to urge that there should be sex roles, but rather to show that the normative question is out of place, that there will be sex roles, whatever we decide. The argument assumes first that the alleged natural differences between the sexes are inevitable; but if such differences are inevitable, differences in behavior are inevitable; and if differences in behavior are inevitable, society will inevitably be structured so as to enforce role differences according to sex. Thus, sex roles are inevitable.

For the purpose of this discussion, let us accept the claim that natural psychological differences are inevitable. We assume that there are such differences and ignore the possibility of their being altered, for example, by evolutionary change or direct biological intervention. Let us also accept the second claim, that behavioral differences are inevitable. Behavioral differences could perhaps be eliminated even given the assumption of natural differences in disposition (for example, those with no natural inclination to a certain kind of behavior might nevertheless learn it), but let us waive this point. We assume then that behavioral differences, and hence also role differences, between the sexes are inevitable. Does it follow that there must be sex roles, that is, that the institutions and practices of society must enforce correlations between roles and sex?

Surely not. Indeed, such sanctions would be pointless. Why bother to direct women into some roles and men into others if the pattern occurs regardless of the nature of society? Mill makes the point elegantly in *The Subjection of Women*: "The anxiety of mankind to interfere in behalf of nature, for fear lest nature should not succeed in effecting its purpose, is an altogether unnecessary solicitude."[4]

It may be objected that if correlations between sex and roles are inevitable, societal sanctions enforcing these correlations will develop because people will expect the sexes to

[4]Mill, p. 154.

perform different roles and these expectations will lead to behavior which encourages their fulfillment. This can happen, of course, but it is surely not inevitable. One need not act so as to bring about what one expects.

Indeed, there could be a society in which it is held that there are inevitable correlations between roles and sex but institutionalization of these correlations is deliberately avoided. What is inevitable is presumably not, for example, that every woman will perform a certain role and no man will perform it, but rather that most women will perform the role and most men will not. For any individual, then, a particular role may not be inevitable. Now suppose it is a value in the society in question that people should be free to choose roles according to their individual needs and interests. But then there should not be sanctions enforcing correlations between roles and sex, for such sanctions tend to force some individuals into roles for which they have no natural inclination and which they might otherwise choose against.

I conclude then that, even granting the assumptions that natural psychological differences, and therefore role differences, between the sexes are inevitable, it does not follow that there must be sanctions enforcing correlations between roles and sex. Indeed, if individual freedom is valued, those who vary from the statistical norm should not be required to conform to it.

2. WELL-BEING

The argument from well-being begins with the claim that, because of natural psychological differences between the sexes, members of each sex are happier in certain roles than in others, and the roles which tend to promote happiness are different for each sex. It is also held that if all roles are equally available to everyone regardless of sex, some individuals will choose against their own well-being. Hence, the argument concludes, for the sake of maximizing well-being there should be sex roles: society should encourage individuals to make "correct" role choices.

Suppose that women, on the average, are more compassionate than men. Suppose also that there are two sets of roles, "female" and "male," and that because of the natural compassion of women, women are happier in female than in male roles. Now if females and males overlap with respect to compassion, some men have as much natural compassion as some women, so they too will be happier in female than in male roles. Thus, the first premise of the argument from well-being should read: Suppose that, because of natural psychological differences between the sexes, *most* women are happier in female roles and *most* men in male roles. The argument continues: If all roles are equally available to everyone, some of the women who would be happier in female roles will choose against their own well-being, and similarly for men.

Now if the conclusion that there should be sex roles is to be based on these premises, another assumption must be added—that the loss of potential well-being resulting from societally produced adoption of unsuitable roles by individuals in the overlapping areas of the distribution is *less* than the loss that would result from "mistaken" free choices if there were no sex roles. With sex roles, some individuals who would be happier in roles assigned to the other sex perform roles assigned to their own sex, and so there is a loss of potential happiness. Without sex roles, some individuals, we assume, choose against their own well-being. But surely we are not now in a position to compare the two systems with respect to the number of mismatches produced. Hence, the additional premise required for the argument, that overall well-being is greater with sex roles than without them, is entirely unsupported.

Even if we grant, then, that because of innate psychological differences between the sexes members of each sex achieve greater well-being in some roles than in others, the argument from well-being does not support the conclusion that there should be sex roles. In our present state of knowledge, there is no reason to suppose that a sex role system which makes no discriminations within a sex would produce fewer mismatches between individuals and roles than a system in which all roles are open equally to both sexes.

3. EFFICIENCY

If there are natural differences between the sexes in the capacity to perform socially valuable tasks, then, it is sometimes argued, efficiency is served if these tasks are assigned to the sex with the greatest innate ability for them. Suppose, for example, that females are naturally better than males at learning foreign languages. This means that, if everything else is equal and females and males are given the same training in a foreign language, females, on the average, will achieve a higher level of skill than males. Now suppose that society needs interpreters and translators and that in order to have such a job one must complete a special training program whose only purpose is to provide persons for these roles. Clearly, efficiency is served if only individuals with a good deal of natural ability are selected for training, for the time and effort required to bring them to a given level of proficiency is less than that required for the less talented. But suppose that the innate ability in question is normally distributed within each sex and that the sexes overlap (see fig. 2). If we assume that a sufficient number of candidates can be recruited by considering

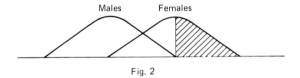

Fig. 2

only persons in the shaded area, they are the only ones who should be eligible. There are no men in this group. Hence, although screening is necessary in order to exclude nontalented women, it would be inefficient even to consider men, for it is known that no man is as talented as the talented women. In the interest of efficiency, then, the occupational roles of interpreter and translator should be sex roles; men should be denied access to these roles but women who are interested in them, especially talented women, should be encouraged to pursue them.

This argument is sound. That is, if we grant the factual assumptions and suppose also that efficiency for the society we are concerned with has some value, the argument from efficiency provides one reason for holding that some roles should be sex roles. This conclusion of course is only prima facie. In order to determine whether there should be sex roles, one would have to weigh efficiency, together with other reasons for such roles, against reasons for holding that there should not be sex roles. The reasons against sex roles are very strong. They are couched in terms of individual rights — in terms of liberty, justice, equality of opportunity. Efficiency by itself does not outweigh these moral values. Nevertheless, the appeal to nature, if true, combined with an appeal to the value of efficiency, does provide one reason for the view that there should be sex roles.

The arguments I have discussed here are not the only ones which appeal to natural psychological differences between the sexes in defense of sex roles, but these three arguments — from inevitability, well-being, and efficiency — are, I believe, the most common and the most plausible ones. The argument from efficiency alone, among them, provides a reason—albeit a rather weak reason—for thinking that there should be sex roles. I suggest, therefore, that the issue of natural psychological differences between women and men does not deserve the central place it is given, both traditionally and currently, in the literature on this topic.

It is frequently pointed out that the argument from nature functions as a cover, as a myth to make patriarchy palatable to both women and men. Insofar as this is so, it is surely worthwhile exploring and exposing the myth. But of course most of those who use the argument from nature take it seriously and literally, and this is the spirit in which I have dealt with it. Considering the argument in this way, I conclude that whether there should be sex roles does not depend primarily on whether there are innate psychological differences between the sexes. The question is, after all, not what women and men naturally are, but what kind of society is morally justifiable. In order to answer this question, we must appeal to the notions of justice, equality, and liberty. It is these moral concepts, not the empirical issue of sex differences, which should have pride of place in the philosophical discussion of sex roles.

QUESTIONS

1. Summarize Trebilcot's criticisms of the arguments based on appeals to well-being and inevitability. Are her criticisms well-taken?
2. If there are innate psychological differences between the sexes, should society enforce differentiated sex roles?
3. If there are innate psychological sexual differences, should society attempt to minimize such differences?

HERB GOLDBERG

FEMINISM AND MALE LIBERATION

Herb Goldberg, a clinical psychologist, is professor of psychology at the California State University. Goldberg, who also has a private practice, conducts workshops across the country. He has contributed to numerous professional journals, including *American Psychologist,* the *Journal of Abnormal Psychology,* and *Clinical Psychologist.* His books include *The New Male* (1979), from which this selection is taken, *The Hazards of Being Male* (1977), and *Creative Aggression,* with George R. Bach, (1975).

Goldberg argues that traditional gender roles are destructive for men. In his view men have paid a high price for the "control" and "power" they have traditionally exerted over women. He sees feminist attempts to turn women into autonomous, responsible decision makers as ultimately beneficial for men, as making male liberation possible. If the feminist movement falters, Goldberg argues, men should *insist* that women make the transition to become "total persons." If women do not become "total persons," he maintains, neither will men. Men can become "total persons" only if they are freed from the constraints imposed upon both sexes by traditional gender roles.

If men could see beyond feminist blaming and rage—rage that inevitably builds up in any party to a relationship who chronically assumes a passive-submissive role—the feminist movement could be regarded as simply a movement describing a new attitude. Primarily, it represents an insistence by women that they function as whole people, rather than feminine gender stereotypes. They are saying, "We refuse to relate like children anymore."

By doing this, the woman is shattering the man's fantasy of her as the weak, ethereal creature, the balancing opposite to his self-perceived animallike, selfish and destructive nature. It is hard for him to believe her when she communicates to him that she is not who and what he thinks she is.

He has come to need this fantasy of her in order to justify his own rigid, destructive style. Though it alienated him from other men, he saw himself as doing his performing, competitive and often destructive dances primarily for her. It is indeed disorienting and painful to have one's system of rationalization and justification pulled away, for now he too is faced with the psychologically threatening task of having to become a whole person rather than remaining a gender stereotype. . . .

The feminists would have us believe that men's satisfaction in . . . traditional relationships was in the control they supposedly had. He was the authoritarian thriving on her dependency and helplessness and her "need" for him. However, his was the kind of "power" and "control" that a parent gets in knowing a child won't leave as long as the child is unable to function and survive autonomously in the outside world. In marriage it is an expensive, exhausting form of control, contingent on the woman's remaining a child and relating in childlike fashion. The price for this is that he is endlessly under pressure to perform and drained constantly by responsibility. It is the sick parent who is distressed by a child's growing into maturity and autonomy. The healthy parent welcomes the easing of burdens and the pleasure of relating to the child as a capable adult person.

There are aspects of the way in which feminine changes have taken place that caused some men to react with resistance and justifiably with a sense of threat. So often what has been portrayed and labeled "men's lib" in the media, which in the minds of many people is a counterpart to feminism, amounts to a harried man rushing home from work to help with household chores such as vacuuming, washing dishes and cleaning or baby care. While there is nothing inherently wrong in the man's sharing in these responsibilities, compare that image of liberation with that of a woman emerging as an independent, assertive, sexual person who is redefining her role and her life to meet her needs for growth. In other words, while women's liberation has been depicted as a joyful, energetic freeing up and casting off of sex stereotypes and the onerous responsibilities that accompany them, "men's lib" has been depicted as the *addition* of responsibilities and onerous tasks to an already laden and pressured life and little else. No wonder the average man has resisted and reacted defensively.

In other words, what has been commonly described as "men's lib" is not liberation at all, but merely accommodation to women's changes. *What this means is that once again he is playing daddy, only this time, unlike in the traditional relationship where he got nurturance and support, the payoffs are almost nonexistent.* Changing would simply allow him to hang on to the relationship a little longer.

Authentic liberation means assertion, freeing up, breaking through gender barriers and refusing to continue playing self-denying and self-destructive games. It does not mean accommodation. For the man's liberation to be defined in terms of being a reinforcement and support for the woman while she goes through her changes is for him to be once again placed in the role of "strong man." His first assertive step must therefore be to reject that role with the realization that she is strong in her own right—indeed, *stronger* than he in many ways—and to transfer the focus of his energy toward finding ways that allow him to free up his own life from lethal and non-gratifying patterns.

Feminism was not born of or propelled by accommodation, but rather by a rejection of accommodating attitudes. The liberated woman is refusing to play nursemaid, housekeeper or "earth mother" anymore. It is time for the man, therefore, to reject the role demands on him to play superman: the unneeding, fearless, unemotional, independent, all-around strong man. Liberation for him would mean a reentry into the world of playfulness, intimacy, trusting relationships, emotions and caring, and a priority on fulfillment of *his* needs and *his* growth.

Until now, for many men the message of feminism has simply been that he has been a "bad boy," who must stop being a chauvinist. Nowhere has he been clearly informed or figured out what feminism *could* mean for him, i.e., no longer having to take responsibility for the woman. Furthermore, he could now also expect from her as much as he gave to her. It is no longer necessary for him to be exclusively responsible for courting, paying, performing, providing and deferring. In short, he no longer needs to put her on a pedestal, to hide his true self from her and to behave like a drone buzzing around a queen bee.

Clearly, the woman's role *before* feminism was psychologically disastrous for him. Because she repressed her autonomy, the burden of responsibility and decision making was placed on him. He was under constant pressure to produce and to be right. Her dependency may have engulfed and smothered him, but he couldn't acknowledge it. That would have meant being unmanly. Because it made him feel guilty to reject responsibility for her well-being, he could have no other relationships that might detract from the committment to "his" woman. Nor could he walk away from an unsatisfying job, because she counted on him. Whatever resentment he felt about all of this he had to repress or deny. To control these feelings, he behaved in an even more mechanical, detached way. This only brought him further criticism, as he was then attacked for not being sufficiently involved and human.

It was clearly a no-win situation. To be a man, he had to take on burdens that eventually overwhelmed and deadened him. If he rejected them, however, he felt guilty and considered that he was a failure. Alcoholism, television, work, cars and watching sports became his distraction and salvation. All were largely dehumanized activities. Often, too, he was chided for overindulging in them. So while her dependence on him may have given him a sense of "control," since he saw her as helpless and was therefore convinced that she would never leave him, from the psychological vantage point he paid a heavy price. . . .

The woman before feminist emergence . . . denied her aggression. Consequently, she resisted dealing directly with conflict and fighting on her own behalf. If she saw herself as injured or neglected, or if she sensed her husband's resentment or anger, she responded with tears or demonstrations of having been hurt. She presented herself as sensitive, fragile, weak and easily injured. In contrast, he was portrayed as the insensitive and hurtful one. He was ultimately responsible and therefore had to apologize. Fights had to be his fault, because she did not release her anger or aggression directly. She simply reacted to him and gained her power and control by acting helpless and maligned.

She gained her power indirectly also by making him feel guilty. Or she developed a repertoire of symptoms such as "nervousness," worry and fear. If he "misbehaved" by coming home late, looking at another woman, forgetting a birthday, making a hurtful remark and so on, she punished him by withdrawal of affection. The conflict, the differences, the causes of the difficulty were rarely dealt with or worked through directly. Nothing could ever be resolved, therefore, and there was little he could do but feel guilty and accept her demands.

In other, more damaging ways the repression of aggression was destructive to males. It is my belief that the resentment and rage a wife felt toward her husband over being "controlled" and "exploited" she displaced onto her son, toward whom she would over-react with excessive discipline, control, defensive overprotection and a punitive blocking of his sexuality and aggression. She reacted to her son as she might have wished to react to her husband but could not. The result of this, I believe, may partially explain the astoundingly disproportionate rates of problems experienced by young boys in comparison to young girls. Autism, hyperkinesis and stuttering all show rates several hundred percent higher for boys. Childhood schizophrenia is almost 50 percent higher.

According to government statistics in the early 1970s, admission to state and county mental hospitals for behavior disorders for boys in the five- to nine-year-old group was sixteen times greater than for girls.[1] Boys outnumbered girls five to one in this age group for admission for adjustive reactions.[2]

For residency in state and county mental hospitals, boys outnumbered girls by approximately ten to one for behavior disorders, and five to one for adjustive reactions.[3]

Psychologists Janet Hyde and Benjamin Rosenberg recently explored the myth of the demure little girl. With a broad sampling of females of all ages who were asked if they considered themselves tomboys when they were growing up or, for the younger girls, at present, over 60 percent said they either were or had been tomboys. These researchers found that "tomboyism is not so much abnormal as it is typical for girls." The image of the sweet, passive little girl sitting at home by her mother's side was, they concluded, a false stereotype.[4]

The woman before feminist emergence denied her assertiveness. When asked by the man what she wanted, what she liked or disliked, where she wanted to go and what she wanted to do, she frequently responded with a vague "It doesn't really matter," or "Whatever you want." She would go along with his choices but often react later with boredom or even resentment.

In the matter of sex, also, she rarely asserted herself. It was hard to determine what she really liked or disliked. She saw it as her job simply to please him. She waited for him to initiate and orchestrate the experience. Her resistances emerged as physical symptoms—headaches, fatigue, cramps and so on. Or she responded simply in lukewarm or passive fashion, which was also a powerful message of rejection. They were her indirect ways of saying the no she could not take conscious responsibility for.

Because she did not initiate sex or assert herself sexually, a "bad" sexual experience was blamed on *his* ignorance, insensitivity, poor timing and so on. In this regard he was caught in a bind. She would not clearly define her likes and dislikes, nor would she initiate sex. Consequently, he was groping in the dark, and when things went wrong, it was not possible to remedy them. She would not give him feedback or take responsibility and he could only blame himself.

Overall, with her autonomy, sexuality, aggression and assertiveness repressed or con-

[1] "Ratio of Male to Female Admissions to State and County Mental Hospitals by Age for Behavior Disorders and Adjustive Reactions, U.S., 1973," *National Institute of Mental Health Statistical Note* 115, Table 3, pp. 10–13.

[2] *Ibid.*

[3] "Ratio of Male to Female Residency in State and County Mental Hospitals by Age for Behavior Disorders and Adjustive Reactions, U.S., 1973," *National Institute of Mental Health Statistical Note* 115, Table 3, pp. 10–13.

[4] Janet S. Hyde and B. G. Rosenberg, "Tomboyism: Implications for Theories of Female Development"; paper presented at the Western Psychological Association Convention, San Francisco, Calif., April 1974.

sciously hidden, he was living out a part of a gender nightmare which he believed he was supposed to enjoy. After all, he was the master, he was told. The moment-to-moment reality of the situation, however, had to be excruciatingly unsatisfying, crazy-making and boring. He knew something was wrong, but there seemed to be no workable clues or ways to change things. It was a situation beyond his control.

Feminism has been a trauma for some men only because they have reacted defensively, trying to accommodate to the woman while being castigated for being exploiters and chauvinists. These were accusations he could not see beyond. While she was busy defining her new role, he was busy trying to adjust to it rather than redefining his. While she reexamined and rejected aspects of her roles as wife and mother and passive-supportive figure, he was unable to challenge the preconceptions and presumptions of his roles as father, husband, active dominator and so on.

Perhaps the single most valuable contribution of feminism has been the way it has chipped away at men's fantasies about women. Today it is the destructive woman, consciously or unconsciously intent on controlling, manipulating and exploiting men, who feeds on his regressive, pathetic desire to see himself as the dominant superman. In return for these false ego strokes, he assumes responsibility for her. As a result, his emergence out of the gender nightmare is aborted, and he remains a posturing caricature.

This hostile attitude was well expressed by one woman who responded with the following comment to a survey on attitudes and experiences regarding the roles of men and women in our society. She wrote:

"[If men learn that women are superior] we'll be stuck with a lot of sniveling little boys clinging to our skirts. It's better to let them think they're king of the castle, lean and depend on them, and continue to control and manipulate them as we always have."[5]

A man is in jeopardy if he fails to realize that the "fragile," "passive" woman of today is not "feminine" but repressed, and may well emerge as the angry woman of tomorrow who will turn the tables on him at a time when he may hardly be prepared or equipped to adapt to the changes. Such is the price of refusing to recognize what is.

The man who grasps the psychological meaning of feminism will be the man who can liberate himself from the destructive compulsion to perform and to assume all responsibility. He will be free to create a life-style that puts a focus on his own development as a person. This will mean an end to the all-consuming obsession with success, which has produced in him a defensive, distrustful stance toward the world such that all of his energies go toward protecting and proving himself. He will live not by the symbols of masculinity but by the measure of whether his life feels good and brings him in closer contact with himself and other people. Gone will be the days and the relationships that have drawn him into endless penis waving, muscle flexing and wallet flaunting in order to prove that he is worthy of love and respect.

Indeed, should the feminist movement falter, should the impetus toward female liberation be slowed by the regressive pull of old-time manipulative feminine role playing, men, out of the most self-caring of motives, must insist and facilitate woman's transition to the point where she relates and functions as a total person who is equally responsible, sexual, assertive and autonomous. The growth of men depends on the growth of women, and vice versa, in order for the sexes to experience the full potential of themselves and each other. To fall back into the sex-object, success-object way of relating may be a temporarily anxiety-reducing, even seemingly pleasant seduction because it is familiar ground, but the price will be the continuation of the destructive gender fantasy which perpetuates the annihilation of each other's full personhood.

[5]Carol Tavris, "Woman & Man," *Psychology Today*, March 1972, p. 58.

QUESTIONS

1.   Do you agree with Herb Goldberg's claim that traditional gender roles are destructive for males? What evidence would you cite to support your position?

2.   Is Goldberg correct when he states that "the growth of men depends on the growth of women, and vice versa"? Explain.

JOYCE TREBILCOT

TWO FORMS OF ANDROGYNISM

A biographical sketch of Joyce Trebilcot is found on page 140.

Trebilcot sees two opposing tendencies in the positions of those who advocate androgyny and relates these opposing tendencies to two versions of androgynism. One version of androgynism, which she labels *monoandrogynism,* holds that every individual should develop all the positive characteristics traditionally associated with both male and female roles. On this view, there is one ideal type that every "healthy person" should exemplify. The second version of androgynism, *polyandrogynism,* requires only that people be free to adopt any morally acceptable psychological characteristics and social roles which are in keeping with their wishes and inclinations, unbound by any stereotypical social expectations. Whereas polyandrogynism emphasizes freedom of choice, monoandrogynism limits individuals insofar as it prescribes one type of personality as the ideal one. Trebilcot attempts to determine which of these two versions of androgynism is more acceptable. She opts for the provisional adoption of polyandrogyny on the basis of arguments from freedom and from universal value.

Traditional concepts of women and men, of what we are and should be as females and males, of the implications of sex for our relationships to one another and for our places in society, are not acceptable. But what models, if any, should we adopt to replace them? In this paper I consider just two of the alternatives discussed in recent literature—two versions of androgynism.

In discussing these two views I follow the convention of distinguishing between sex (female and male) and gender (feminine and masculine). Sex is biological, whereas gender is psychosocial. Thus, for example, a person who is biologically female may be—in terms of psychological characteristics or social roles—feminine or masculine, or both.

Although what counts as feminine and masculine varies among societies and over time, I use these terms here to refer to the gender concepts traditionally dominant in our own society. Femininity, on this traditional view, has nurturing as its core: it centers on the image of woman as mother, as provider of food, warmth, and emotional sustenance. Masculinity focuses on mastery: it comprises the notion of man struggling to overcome obstacles, to control nature, and also the notion of man as patriarch or leader in society and the family.

Reprinted with permission of the publisher from the *Journal of Social Philosophy,* vol. VIII, no. 1 (January 1977), pp. 4–8.

The first form of androgynism to be discussed here takes the word "androgyny" literally, so to speak. In this word the Greek roots for man *(andros)* and woman *(gynē)* exist side by side. According to the first form of androgynism, both feminine and masculine characteristics should exist "side by side" in every individual: each woman and man should develop personality traits and engage in activities traditionally assigned to only one sex. Because this view postulates a single ideal for everyone, I call it monoandrogynism, or, for brevity, *M.*

Monoandrogynism, insofar as it advocates shared roles, is now official policy in a number of countries. For example, the Swedish government presented a report to the United Nations in 1968 specifying that in Sweden, "every individual, regardless of sex, shall have the same practical opportunities not only for education and employment but also fundamentally the same responsibility for his or her own financial support as well as shared responsibility for child upbringing and housework."[1]

Closer to home, Jessie Bernard, in her discussion of women's roles, distinguishes the one-role view, according to which woman's place is in the home; the two-role pattern, which prescribes a combination of the traditional housewife-mother functions and work outside the home; and what she calls the "shared-role ideology" which holds "that children should have the care of both parents, that all who benefit from the services supplied in the house-hold should contribute to them, and that both partners should share in supporting the household."[2]

Caroline Bird in her chapter "The Androgynous Life" writes with approval of role-sharing. She also suggests that the ideal person "combines characteristics usually attributed to men with characteristics usually attributed to women."[3]

The psychological dimension of *M* is stressed by Judith M. Bardwick. In her essay "Androgyny and Humanistic Goals, or Goodbye, Cardboard People," she discusses a view according to which the ideal or "healthy" person would have traits of both genders. "We would then expect," she says, "both nurturance and competence, openness and objectivity, compassion and competitiveness from both women and men, as individuals, according to what they were doing."[4]

The work of these and other writers provides the basis for a normative theory, *M,* which prescribes a single ideal for everyone: the person who is, in both psychological characteristics and social roles, both feminine and masculine.

The second form of androgynism shares with the first the principle that biological sex should not be a basis for judgments about the appropriateness of gender characteristics. It differs from the first, however, in that it advocates not a single ideal but rather a variety of options including "pure" femininity and masculinity as well as any combination of the two. According to this view, all alternatives with respect to gender should be equally available to and equally approved for everyone, regardless of sex. Thus, for example, a female might acceptably develop as a completely feminine sort of person, as both feminine and masculine in any proportion, or as wholly masculine. Because this view prescribes a variety of acceptable models, I call it polyandrogynism, or *P.*[5]

[1]Official Report to the United Nations on the Status of Women in Sweden, 1968. Quoted in Rita Liljeström, "The Swedish Model," in Georgene H. Seward and Robert C. Williamson, eds., *Sex Roles in Changing Society* (New York: Random House, 1970). p. 200.
[2]Jessie Bernard, *Women and the Public Interest* (Chicago: Aldine, 1971); and idem, *The Future of Marriage* (New York: Bantam Books, 1972). The quotation is from the latter book, p.279.
[3]Caroline Bird, *Born Female* (New York: Pocket Books, 1968), p. xi.
[4]Judith M. Bardwick, "Androgyny and Humanistic Goals, or Goodbye, Cardboard People," in Mary Louise McBee and Kathryn A. Blake, eds., *The American Woman: Who Will She Be?* (Beverly Hills, Calif.: Glencoe Press, 1974), p. 61.
[5]"Monoandrogynism" and "polyandrogynism" are perhaps not very happy terms, but I have been unable to find alternatives which are both descriptive and non-question-begging. In an earlier version of this paper I used "A₁" and "A₂" but these labels are not as perspicuous as "M" and "P." Mary Anne Warren in "The Ideal of Androgyny" (unpublished) refers to "the strong thesis" and "the weak thesis," but this terminology tends to prejudice judgment as to which view is preferable. Hence, I use "M" and "P."

Constantina Safilios-Rothschild supports *P* in her recent book *Women and Social Policy*. In this work she makes a variety of policy recommendations aimed at bringing about the liberation of both sexes. Liberation requires, she says, that individuals live "according to their wishes, inclinations, potentials, abilities, and needs rather than according to the prevailing stereotypes about sex roles and sex-appropriate modes of thought and behavior." Some persons, she adds, "might *choose* to behave according to their sex's stereotypic . . . patterns. But some women and some men may *choose,* if they are so inclined, to take options in some or all of the life sectors now limited to the opposite sex."[6]

Carolyn Heilbrun's work also suggests *P*. In *Toward a Recognition of Androgyny* she writes, "The ideal toward which I believe we should move is best described by the term 'androgyny.' This ancient Greek word . . . defines a condition under which the characteristics of the sexes, and the human impulses expressed by men and women, are not rigidly assigned. Androgyny seeks to liberate the individual from the confines of the appropriate." Androgyny suggests, Heilbrun says, "a full range of experience open to individuals who may, as women, be aggressive, as men, tender; it suggests a spectrum upon which human beings choose their places without regard to propriety or custom."[7]

This second form of androgynism focuses on a variety of options rather than on the single model of the part-woman/part-man (that is, of the androgyne in the classic sense). It is appropriate, however, to extend the term "androgynism" to apply to it; for, like *M,* it seeks to break the connection between sex and gender.

For both forms of androgynism, the postulated ideals are best construed so as to exclude aspects of traditional gender concepts which are morally objectionable. Femininity should not be taken to include, for example, weakness, foolishness, or incompetence. Similarly, tendencies such as those to authoritarianism and violence should be eliminated from the concept of masculinity. Most importantly, aspects of the gender concepts which prescribe female submissiveness and male domination (over women and over other men) must, on moral grounds, be excluded from both the single ideal advocated by *M* and the range of options recommended by *P*.

Either form of androgyny may, in the long run, lead to major changes in human attributes. It is often suggested that the androgyne is a person who is feminine part of the time and masculine part of the time. But such compartmentalization might be expected to break down, so that the feminine and masculine qualities would influence one another and be modified. Imagine a person who is at the same time and in the same respect both nurturant and mastery-oriented, emotional and rational, cooperative and competitive, and so on. I shall not undertake here to speculate on whether this is possible, or, if it is, on how such qualities might combine. The point is just that androgyny in the long run may lead to an integrating of femininity and masculinity that will yield new attributes, new kinds of personalities. The androgyne at this extreme would perhaps be not part feminine and part masculine, but neither feminine nor masculine, a person in whom the genders disappear.

I turn now to the question of which of these two forms of androgynism is more acceptable. I am not concerned here to evaluate these positions in relation to other alternatives (for example, to the traditional sexual constitution of society or to matriarchy).[8] For the sake of this discussion, I assume that either *M* or *P* is preferable to any alternative, and that the problem is only to decide between them. Let us first consider this problem not as abstract speculation, and not as a problem for some distant society, but rather as an

[6]Constantina Safilios-Rothschild, *Women and Social Policy* (Englewood Cliffs. N.J.: Prentice-Hall, 1974), p. 7; emphasis hers.
[7]Carolyn Heilbrun, *Toward a Recognition of Androgyny* (New York: Harper & Row, 1973), pp. 7–8.
[8]My current view is that we should work for the universal realization of women's values; but that is another paper. (For some arguments against the use of the term "androgyny" in feminist theory, see, for example, Mary Daly, "The Qualitative Leap beyond Patriarchal Religion," *Quest: A Feminist Quarterly,* vol. 1, no. 4 [Spring 1975], pp. 29ff.; and Janice Raymond, "The Illusion of Androgyny," *Quest, vol. 2, no. 1 [Summer 1975].)*

immediate issue for our own society. The question is then: Which form of androgynism is preferable as a guide to action for us here and now?

Suppose we adopt *M*. Our task then is to provide opportunities, encouragement, and perhaps even incentives for those who are now feminine to be also masculine, and conversely. Suppose, on the other hand, that we adopt *P*. Our task is to create an environment in which, without reference to sex, people choose among all (moral) gender alternatives. How can this best be accomplished? What is required, clearly, is that the deeply-entrenched normative connection between sex and gender be severed. Virtually everyone now, in formulating preferences for the self and in judging the appropriateness of gender characteristics for others, at least on some occasions takes it, consciously or otherwise, that the sex of the individual in question is a relevant consideration: that one is female tends to count in favor of a feminine trait and against a masculine one, and conversely. In order to break this connection, it must be shown that masculinity is acceptable for females and femininity for males. There must, then, be opportunities, encouragement, and perhaps even incentives for gender-crossing. But this is what is required by *M*. Hence, under present conditions, the two forms of androgynism prescribe the same course of action — that is, the promotion of gender-crossing.

The question "Which form of androgynism is preferable here and now?" then, is misconstrued. If one is an androgynist of either sort, what one must do now is seek to break the normative connection between sex and gender by bringing about gender-crossing. However, once the habit of taking sex as a reason for gender evaluation is overcome, or is at least much weaker and less widespread than it is today, then the two forms of androgynism do prescribe different courses of action. In particular, on *M* "pure" gender is condemned, but on *P* it is accepted. Let us consider, then, which version of androgynism is preferable for a hypothetical future society in which femininity and masculinity are no longer normatively associated with sex.

The major argument in favor of *P* is, of course, that because it stipulates a variety of acceptable gender alternatives it provides greater gender freedom than *M*. Now, freedom is a very high priority value, so arguments for *M* must be strong indeed. Let us consider, then, two arguments used to support *M* over *P*—one psychological, one ethical.

The psychological argument holds that in a society which is open with respect to gender, many people are likely to experience anxiety when faced with the need, or opportunity, to choose among different but equally acceptable gender models. Consider the words of Judith M. Bardwick:

> People need guidelines, directions that are agreed upon because they help each individual to know where one ought to go, how one can get there, and how far one is from one's goal. It is easier to sustain frustration that comes from knowing how far you are from your objective or what barriers are in your way than it is to sustain the anxiety that comes from not being sure about what you want to do or what others want you to do. It will be necessary, then, to develop new formulations by which people will guide their lives.[9]

Bardwick says that anxiety "comes from not being sure about what you want to do or what others want you to do." But in a society of the sort proposed by *P,* the notion that one should seek to please others in deciding among gender models would be rejected; ideally "what others want you to do" in such a society is to make your own decisions. Of course there is still the problem of not being sure about what *you* want to do. Presumably, under

[9]Bardwick, *op. cit.*, p. 50.

P, people would provide one another with help and support in finding suitable life-styles. Nevertheless, it could be that for some, choosing among alternatives would be anxiety-producing. On the other hand, under *M,* the lack of approved alternatives could produce frustration. Hence, the argument from anxiety should be paired with an argument from frustration. In *M,* socialization is designed to make everyone androgynous (in ways similar, perhaps, to those which have traditionally produced exclusive femininity and masculinity in our own society), and frustration is part of the cost. In *P,* socialization is directed toward enabling people to perceive, evaluate, and choose among alternatives, and there is a risk of anxiety. We are not now in a position to decide whether the frustration or the anxiety is worse, for there are no data on the numbers of people likely to suffer these emotions nor on the extent of the harm that they are likely to do. Hence, neither the argument from anxiety nor the argument from frustration is of any help in deciding between the two forms of androgynism.

I turn now to a more persuasive argument for *M,* one which claims that androgyny has universal value. This argument supports *M* not, as the argument from anxiety does, because *M* prescribes some norm or other, but rather because of the content of the norm. The argument holds that both traditional genders include qualities that have human value, qualities that it would be good for everyone to have. Among the elements of femininity, candidates for universal value are openness and responsiveness to needs and feelings, and being gentle, tender, intuitive, sensitive, expressive, considerate, cooperative, compassionate. Masculine qualities appealed to in this connection include being logical, rational, objective, efficient, responsible, independent, courageous. It is claimed, then, that there are some aspects of both genders (not necessarily all or only the ones I have mentioned) which are desirable for everyone, which we should value both in ourselves and in one another. But if there are aspects of femininity and masculinity which are valuable in this way — which are, as we might call them, virtues — they are *human* virtues, and are desirable for everyone. If Smith is a better person for being compassionate or courageous, then so is Jones, and never mind the sex of Smith or Jones. Hence, the argument concludes, the world envisioned by *M,* in which everyone or nearly everyone is both feminine and masculine, is one in which life for everyone is more rewarding than the world advocated by *P,* in which some people are of only one gender; therefore we should undertake to bring about *M.*

The argument claims, then, that both genders embody traits that it would be valuable for everyone to have. But how is this claim to be tested? Let us adopt the view that to say that something is valuable for everyone is, roughly, to say that if everyone were unbiased, well-informed, and thinking and feeling clearly, everyone would, in fact, value it. As things are now, it is difficult or impossible to predict what everyone would value under such conditions. But there is an alternative. We can seek to establish conditions in which people do make unbiased, informed, etc., choices, and see whether they then value both feminine and masculine traits.

But this reminds us, of course, of the program of *P. P* does not guarantee clear thought and emotional sensitivity, but it does propose an environment in which people are informed about all gender options and are unbiased with respect to them. If, in this context, all or most people, when they are thinking clearly, etc., tend to prefer, for themselves and others, both feminine and masculine virtues, we will have evidence to support the claim that androgyny has universal value. (In this case, *P* is likely to change into *M.*) On the other hand, if "pure" gender is preferred by many, we should be skeptical of the claim that androgyny has universal value. (In this case we should probably seek to preserve *P.*) It appears, then, that in order to discover whether *M* is preferable to *P,* we should seek to bring about *P.*

In summary, we have noted the argument from freedom, which supports P; arguments from anxiety and frustration, which are indecisive; and the argument from universal value, whose analysis suggests the provisional adoption of P. As far as I know, there are no additional major arguments which can plausibly be presented now for either side of the issue. Given, then, the problem of deciding between M and P without reference to other alternatives, my tentative conclusion is that because of the great value of freedom, and because in an atmosphere of gender-freedom we will be in a good position to evaluate the major argument for M (that is, the argument from the universal value of androgyny), P is preferable to M.

Of course all we have assumed about the specific nature of the hypothetical society for which we are making this judgment is that the connection between sex and gender would be absent, as would be the unacceptable components of traditional gender concepts, particularly dominance and submission. It might be, then, that particular social conditions would constitute grounds for supporting M rather than P. For example, if the society in question were hierarchical with leadership roles tightly held by the predominantly masculine individuals, and if leaders with feminine characteristics were more likely to bring about changes of significant value (for example, eliminating war or oppression), it could reasonably be argued that $M,$ in which everyone, including leaders, has both feminine and masculine characteristics, would be preferable to P. But such considerations are only speculative now.

QUESTIONS

1. Herb Goldberg, Trebilcot, and others are concerned with giving individuals the opportunity to develop into *autonomous* individuals. In your view, what characteristics are essential components of the auton-

2. In "Trebilcot on Androgynism" (*Journal of Social Philosophy*, 10 [May 1979], pp. 1-4) Mark Timmons and Wayne Wasserman argue that monoandrogyny is the ideal toward which all individuals should strive. In their view, it is this ideal which "most closely resembles our conception of the ideal *autonomous* moral agent," and, as such, should be adopted by our society as a universal ideal. Do you agree with Timmons and Wasserman? If yes, what arguments would you offer to counter those of Trebilcot?

SUGGESTED ADDITIONAL READINGS

DAVIDSON, KENNETH M., RUTH B. GINSBURG, and HERMA H. KAY, eds.: *Sex-Based Discrimination: Text, Cases, and Materials.* Minneapolis: West, 1974. This is a record and discussion of court cases centering on issues such as the inequality of the legal rights of men and women and the unequal treatment of the sexes in education.

ENGLISH, JANE, ed.: *Sex Equality.* Englewood Cliffs, N.J.: Prentice-Hall, 1977. The selections in this volume are divided into three sections. The first, "The Philosophical Background," contains selections from well-known philosophers such as Plato and John Locke. The second, "Contemporary Arguments," contains selections by contemporary philosophers. The last section, "The Popular Debate," provides readings by nonphilosophers. All the readings in the book focus on issues raised by the questions, "Are the sexes equal?" "Should they be?" Especially worth noting are Christine Pierce's "Natural Law Language and Women" and Naomi Weisstein's "Psychology Constructs the Female."

JAGGAR, ALISON M., and PAULA ROTHENBERG STRUHL, eds.: *Feminist Frameworks.* New York: McGraw-Hill, 1978. This book centers on alternative political theories about the nature of, origin of, and way to end women's oppression. It is divided into three parts. Part I, "The Problem," contains articles from various sources whose purpose is to show some of the problems in the areas of work, family, and sexuality which concern feminists. Part II, "Alternative Feminist Frameworks," presents the various theoretical accounts of the roots of women's oppression. In Part III, "Practice: The Implications of the Theories," the theories are applied to the problems raised in Part I.

OSBORNE, MARTHA LEE, ed.: *Woman in Western Thought.* New York: Random House, 1979. This anthology, which is arranged in historical sequence, contains selections from major philosophers dealing with their various concepts of women. The sequence begins with Plato and ends with Simone de Beauvoir. Each of the historical selections is followed by a contemporary piece dealing with some aspect of the preceding work.

Philosophical Forum 5 (Fall–Winter 1973–1974). This double issue is directed to the theme: "Women and Philosophy." It presents a number of philosophical approaches to the oppression and liberation of women. The articles are divided into three sections preceded by a discussion of the methodological issues involved. The three sections are (1) "Historical Critique"; (2) "Analysis: Critique of the Present"; (3) "What Is to Be Done? Contemporary Social, Ethical and Political Issues."

RESTAK, RICHARD M.: *The Brain: The Last Frontier.* Garden City, N.Y.: Doubleday, 1979. This is a very readable survey of recent attempts to combine brain science with behavioral science to provide a psychological explanation of how the physical functions of the human brain affect language, health, emotion, intelligence, and personality. Restak, a neurologist, discusses the cultural, moral, philosophical, and political implications of the recent psychobiological theories.

ROSSI, ALICE S., ed.: *The Feminist Papers.* New York: Bantam, 1974. This is a collection of feminist writings, most of them written in the eighteenth and nineteenth centuries. It is interesting as a history of feminist thought and feminist movements.

VETTERLING-BRAGIN, MARY, FREDERICK ELLISTON, and JANE ENGLISH, eds.: *Feminism and Philosophy.* Totowa, N.J.: Rowan and Littlefield, 1977. The articles in this collection examine some of the issues which concern many feminists: preferential hiring, sexism, abortion, rape, and marriage.

DISCRIMINATION AND REVERSE DISCRIMINATION

5

Prior to the 1960s and 1970s blatant racial discrimination was a fact of life for many minorities, especially blacks.[1] Many factors, including discrimination in housing, inferior education, and outright denial of access to most nonmenial positions as well as to union membership, kept the majority of blacks in the lowest economic strata of American society. Those who defended this discrimination as just often held that blacks differed inherently from whites in relevant respects. They sometimes pointed to the results of I.Q. and other psychometric tests to support their claim that blacks did not have the same cognitive abilities or psychological makeup as the members of preferred groups. Since the formal principle of justice, the principle of equality,[2] requires or permits the unequal treatment of unequals, practices discriminating against blacks were said by their defenders to be in keeping with that principle.

Those who condemned discrimination against blacks as unjust argued either that there were no such inherent differences between blacks and others or that, even if there were some kind of cognitive or other psychological differences, they were statistical and not universal.[3] In response to claims about differences in I.Q. test results among races and ethnic groups, for example, critics of racially discriminatory practices argued: (1) I.Q. tests are culturally biased; they tend to favor middle- and upper-class children, and many blacks come from the lower economic groups; and (2) no matter what the findings are about differences among groups, on the individual level many blacks score higher than many whites; and what the principle of equality requires is the equal treatment of equal *individuals.*

Today, many people agree that the racially discriminatory hiring, housing, and education practices of the past were morally wrong because they used race, an irrelevant criterion, as a basis for denying equality of treatment to blacks and others. Does it follow that using race as a criterion is *always arbitrary,* that is, that race is never a relevant criterion when hiring, housing, and education decisions are made? It is not immediately obvious that race is an arbitrary criterion in all such decisons. Peter Singer suggests in this chapter, for example, that there are cases in which individuals with a legitimate purpose in mind (e.g., maintaining a moderately profitable business) may seriously jeopardize that purpose by *not* discriminating. At the level of individual decisions, businessmen and landlords operating in a prejudiced society, one in which blacks as a group are in an economically inferior position, may risk losing their businesses and their property *if they do not* discriminate against blacks. Race in these sorts of cases may be economically relevant. Despite the economic risks, however, most of us would agree with Singer that racial discrimination is morally wrong when it functions to perpetuate the highly undesirable factors which apparently make race a relevant criterion. These factors include racial prejudice as well as the poverty of many blacks, which is itself largely the result of gross past injustices. Racial discrimination which functions to continue and perpetuate the results of past injustice can certainly be seen to be morally wrong. It remains possible, however, that some racial discrimination is morally correct. Race is often considered

---

[1]To say this is not to claim that discrimination against blacks and other minorities no longer exists. But prior to the legislation of the 1960s and 1970s it was both more blatant and less challenged.
[2]The principle of equality is discussed in the introduction to Chapter 4.
[3]The arguments on this issue are analogous to those presented in Chapter 4 regarding sexual differences.

a morally relevant criterion today, for example, in employment practices whose intent is to rectify wrongs resulting from past injustices.

It may seem strange to ask whether some cases of racial discrimination might be morally correct. But that is partly because the expression "racial discrimination" often carries a negative evaluative connotation. In trying to get clear on the issues discussed in this chapter, it is useful to follow Singer in distinguishing between the expressions "racism" and "racial discrimination."[4] We shall use "racist" in describing a racial classification which is morally unjustifiable. But we shall use "racial discrimination" in a morally neutral way to refer to racial classifications whose moral justifiability is an open question. This will make it easier to bring out some of the issues arising as a result of the past unjust treatment accorded certain groups in our society.

REVERSE DISCRIMINATION

Does society owe a debt to minority groups whose members have been systematically denied employment opportunities in the past? Must it rectify the wrongs resulting from past discriminatory quotas which effectively limited the access of minorities to the most desirable professions and graduate schools?[5] Just what is society's obligation in regard to groups whose past treatment has been grossly inconsistent with the principle of equality? One possible answer is that *compensation* is due to these groups for past injustices. This answer appeals to the *principle of compensatory justice*, which states that whenever an injustice has been committed, just compensation or reparation must be made to the injured parties. (The principle of compensatory justice is often invoked, for example, when the claim is made that American Indians must be compensated for the past unjust deprivation of land and water rights due to government exploitation.) Another possible answer, however, is that the primary issue is not *compensation* for past injustices but the *morally good consequences* to be produced for minority groups and/or society as a whole by *rectificatory* measures designed to eliminate the effects of past unjust discrimination. This answer appeals to the *principle of utility*, which states that an action or practice is morally correct if on balance it tends to produce more good consequences for the group affected than any alternative action or practice.

Affirmative Action

Compensatory or rectificatory measures take various forms. American Indians, for example, have sometimes been given financial reparation as compensation for past injustice. The measures giving rise to the greatest controversies, however, are the affirmative action programs adopted by businesses, educational institutions, and government agencies, primarily in response to government affirmative action policies. The intent of these policies is to eliminate the effects of past discrimination and to prevent future discrimination against blacks and other minorities.

Employers have responded to calls for affirmative action in various ways. Some have gone no further than to adopt practices of *passive nondiscrimination*. This simply requires that all decisions about hiring, promotion, etc., disregard race and sex. Here no attempt is made to compensate anyone for past injustices or to rectify some of the results of these injustices. The limitations of this approach are apparent when we realize the extent to which seniority systems perpetuate old discriminatory patterns. Other employers have adopted measures which more accurately fall under the heading "affirmative" action. Some of these employers simply make every effort to find minority applicants and to ensure that employment and promotion opportunities are highly visible. Here the pool of

[4]An analogous distinction can be made between "sexism" and "sexual discrimination."
[5]Even though women are not a numerical minority in our society, for purposes of convenience all further references to minorities in this introduction are also references to women (wherever relevant).

minority applicants may be enlarged, but decisions about hiring and promotion are usually made merely on the basis of qualifications, with no preference given to minorities. Other employers committed to affirmative action combine these sorts of affirmative action measures with *preferential treatment*. Here an attempt is made to do more than just expand the pool of minority applicants. Minority applicants are given preference in hiring and promotions. Some of those committed to affirmative action measures involving preferential treatment programs *establish hard quotas*. Unlike preferential treatment practices which do not involve some specific aimed-for numerical goal, hard quota preferential treatment programs specify some set number or proportion of minority applicants who must be hired or promoted. The hard quota approach is exemplified by the program at a Kaiser Aluminum plant which gave rise to the *U.S. Steelworkers v. Weber* case presented in this chapter.

Institutions of higher learning, law and medical schools, for example, have also attempted to establish affirmative action programs. They have developed admissions policies designed to get more minority applicants into their schools. Some of these programs have led to landmark lawsuits. A program at the University of Washington Law School, for example, which according to our above criteria would be classified as a preferential treatment program without hard quotas, led to the well-known *DeFunis v. Odegaard* case.[6] Another program, at the University of California at Davis Medical School, which would be classified as a *hard quota* preferential treatment program, resulted in the *University of California v. Bakke* case presented in this chapter.

In the DeFunis case, Marco DeFunis, a nonminority applicant, was denied admission to the University of Washington Law School's first-year law class in 1971. He filed a suit claiming that he had been unfairly discriminated against on the basis of race by the Admissions Committee of the Law School. Preferential treatment that year was accorded to blacks, American Indians, Chicanos, and Filipinos. The Law School had 150 available spaces in its first-year law class. There were 1,601 applicants. In order to enroll 150 students, 275 applicants were offered acceptances. Among the 275 who were accepted there were 37 minority applicants. Of these 37, 18 actually enrolled. The Law School Admission Test (LSAT) scores and Projected Grade Point Averages (PGAs) of almost all these minority applicants were lower than those of some of the rejected nonminority applicants. These nonminority applicants were denied admission simply because their PGAs and LSAT scores fell below a certain level. Minority applicants, however, whose scores fell even below the level of some rejected nonminority applicants were evaluated on the basis of other criteria and then admitted to the school.

The Supreme Court of the State of Washington ruled against DeFunis and argued as follows: (1) Racial classifications are not unconstitutional in themselves. A state university can take race and ethnic background into account when considering applicants. (2) If there is a compelling state interest which can be served only through the use of racial classifications, such use is acceptable. (3) The shortage of minority attorneys, and, therefore, also minority prosecutors, judges, and public officials, constitutes an undeniably compelling state interest. Although the case was appealed to the United States Supreme Court, the Court did not hand down a ruling. Since DeFunis had been attending the law school while the case was making its way through the courts and was then in his last year, the case was declared moot. The first university preferential treatment case decided by the United States Supreme Court was the Bakke case, mentioned above. The Court ruled in favor of Bakke, declaring Davis's hard quota approach constitutionally unacceptable. However, the Court also ruled that admissions policies can take race into account when evaluating individual applicants.

[6] *DeFunis v. Odegaard,* 82 Wash. 2d 11 (1973).

The Ethical Issues

Our primary concern here is not with legal or constitutional issues but with an important ethical question concerning the preferential treatment exemplified by these cases. Can the racial or sexual discrimination required by preferential treatment policies ever be morally justified, or is it always racist or sexist? Consider our earlier discussion of the principle of equality. We said that when two or more individuals compete for the same position, some of the characteristics are relevant to the position in question; other characteristics are not relevant. The principle of equality is violated whenever individuals are denied equal treatment simply on the basis of generally irrelevant characteristics such as sex or race. This is what seems to have happened to DeFunis and Bakke. They were not accorded the same treatment as the members of the favored minority groups. The unequal treatment given Bakke and DeFunis is sometimes called *reverse discrimination*. This label is used to describe actions or practices which discriminate against an individual or a group, on the basis of some normally irrelevant characteristic, *because* preference is being given to members of previously discriminated-against groups. In keeping with our earlier account of the principle of equality, reverse discrimination certainly seems to violate that principle. Thus, according to the principle of equality, preferential treatment practices productive of reverse discrimination appear to be morally wrong and, therefore, racist or sexist. However, as we noted earlier, the kind of compensatory or rectificatory measures exemplified by preferential treatment programs are held to be justified by other ethical principles — the principle of compensatory justice or the principle of utility. Thus, according to these principles, preferential treatment practices productive of reverse discrimination appear to be morally correct and, therefore, neither racist nor sexist. We seem to be faced with a moral dilemma.

One way of approaching this dilemma is to ask whether the injustices suffered by blacks and others in employment and education have made race and sex relevant criteria in these areas today. Those who call for *compensatory justice* argue that the present use of racial classifications is intended to "compensate" minorities by giving them things which were unjustly denied them in the past. Race and sex under these conditions, they maintain, can be perceived as *morally* relevant criteria, even though they are unrelated to job or school performance. On this approach, the principle of compensatory justice is invoked to justify the relevance of using sexual or racial criteria to distinguish equals from unequals. Both a black and a white male may show promise of having the same ability to perform a job, for example, but the black in addition merits compensation for past wrongs; in this respect the white is not his "equal." Judith Jarvis Thomson in this chapter offers a compensatory defense of preferential treatment.

Problems are raised for the compensatory approach by several considerations. (1) Those benefiting from preferential treatment may not have themselves suffered any unjust treatment. (2) Those losing out because of racial classifications may themselves have been severely disadvantaged economically and socially. (3) If compensatory justice requires preferential treatment for *individuals who have been treated unjustly in the past,* then race or sex is irrelevant. What is relevant is past unjust treatment; and individuals who have been treated unjustly belong to both sexes and to many different ethnic and racial groups. Robert Simon in this chapter discusses these considerations. A different line of attack against the compensatory approach utilizes an infinite regress argument: Suppose we are required to give preference today to individuals belonging to groups which were discriminated against in the past in order to compensate them for past inequality of treatment. Will we be required to give compensatory preferential treatment in the future to members of groups denied equality of treatment by today's compensatory programs? And what about the compensation due those treated unequally by those future programs, etc.? Still another attack against the compensatory approach comes from Lisa H. Newton, who maintains in this chapter that the use of any criteria other than merit or qualification in hiring or school admission is unjust because these are the *only* morally acceptable relevant characteristics.

In response to the above sorts of criticism, defenders of preferential treatment policies make two major moves, both involving utilitarian considerations. The first major move, exemplified by Richard Wasserstrom in this chapter, questions a major presumption underlying many of the attacks on preferential treatment programs — the presumption that the only morally relevant characteristics in hiring and school admittance are "pure qualifications." Wasserstrom and others argue that this presumption itself must be justified in some way, perhaps by a utilitarian appeal to consequences. But if this is the case, then it becomes relevant to consider the morally desirable consequences that preferential treatment programs are designed to bring about. The second major move, which also adopts a consequentialist approach, is represented by the kind of reasoning found in the DeFunis case, in the Weber case, and in the reasoning of those who denied Bakke admission to medical school. Here stress is placed on important social goods that will result from these programs. These goods include the demise of ongoing discrimination and, eventually, greater sexual and racial equality. Some who argue in this way concede that the principle of equality is violated by preferential treatment programs. As a result, some individuals are treated unjustly. Nonetheless, they argue, the good consequences produced by these programs will far outweigh the bad consequences, even though those bad consequences include the injustices resulting from reverse discrimination. An attempt to use consequentialist reasoning *against* preferential treatment programs is made by Lisa H. Newton when she speculates about the potential bad consequences of such programs.

If the ultimate justification offered in defense of preferential treatment and hard quota programs is a utilitarian one, then its defenders must pay special attention to *factual* issues. They must attempt to answer the following sorts of questions: Is racist and sexist discrimination still prevalent in our society? If it is, can we eliminate present discriminatory practices against minority applicants without using quota systems or other preferential treatment measures? Are racist and sexist attitudes so pervasive in our society that mandatory quota systems are required to eliminate continued discrimination against minorities? Are preferential treatment programs necessary to change institutions that perpetuate the results of past injustices? If they are, can only hard quota programs do the job?

Answers to such factual questions are important in evaluating the potential consequences of either adopting or not adopting preferential treatment programs. The answers given may help to determine the answer to the moral question: Is the sexual and racial discrimination built into preferential treatment programs in order to end racism and sexism and to promote greater sexual and racial equality itself racist or sexist, i.e., morally unjustified?

Jane S. Zembaty

PETER SINGER

IS RACIAL DISCRIMINATION ARBITRARY?

Peter Singer is a member of the philosophy department at LaTrobe University, Victoria, Australia. His books include *Animal Liberation* (1975) and *Practical Ethics* (1980). Singer's numerous published articles include "Anglin on the Obligation to Create Extra People" and "Killing Humans and Killing Animals."

Singer wants to bring out some of the reasons *why* racism is morally wrong. In order to avoid confusion, he begins by distinguishing between the expressions "racism" and "racial discrimination." He uses "racism" to describe practices, policies, laws, etc., which discriminate on the basis of race *and are morally wrong.* He uses "racial discrimination" as a morally neutral, simply descriptive expression to talk about discrimination based on race which *may or may not be morally justified.* Singer proceeds by presenting several examples of racial discrimination to illustrate his contention that racial discrimination is *not always* arbitrary; there may be reasons, especially economic ones, which underlie individual discriminatory acts. In discussing the examples, however, he points out the tremendous social costs resulting from some discriminatory practices—those practices which contribute to (1) the perpetuation of a cycle of racial discrimination and deprivation for the victims of discrimination, and (2) the social inequalities and racial divisiveness of society as a whole. Singer concludes by first invoking the moral principle of "equal consideration of interests" to show *why* racism is wrong and then applying that principle in a brief discussion of preferential treatment.

1. INTRODUCTION

There is nowadays wide agreement that racism is wrong. To describe a policy, law, movement or nation as "racist" is to condemn it. It may be thought that since we all agree that racism is wrong, it is unnecessary to speculate on exactly what it is and why it is wrong. This indifference to moral fundamentals could, however, prove dangerous. For one thing, the fact that most people agree today that racism is wrong does not mean that this attitude will always be so widely shared. Even if we had no fears for the future, though, we need to have some understanding of what it is about racism that is wrong if we are to handle satisfactorily all the problems we face today. For instance, there is the contentious issue of "reverse discrimination" or discrimination in favor of members of oppressed minority groups. It must be granted that a university which admits members of minority groups who do not achieve the minimum standard that others must reach in order to be admitted is discriminating on racial lines. Is such discrimination therefore wrong? . . .

First it is necessary to get our terms clear. "Racism" is, as I have said, a word which now has an inescapable evaluative force, although it also has some descriptive content. Words with these dual functions can be confusing if their use is not specified. People sometimes try to argue: "X is a case of racial discrimination, therefore X is racist; racism is wrong, therefore X is wrong." This argument may depend on an equivocation in the meaning of "racist," the term being used first in a morally neutral, descriptive sense, and secondly in its evaluative sense.

To avoid this kind of confusion, I shall accept the usual evaluative force of the term "racist" and reserve it for practices that are judged to be wrong. Thus we cannot pronounce a policy, law, etc., "racist" unless we have decided that it is wrong. "Racial discrimination" on the other hand I shall use in a descriptive, and morally neutral sense, so that to say that a policy or law discriminates racially is simply to point to the fact of discrimination based on race, leaving open the question of whether it can be justified. With this terminology it becomes possible to ask whether a given form of racial discrimination is racist; this is another way of asking whether it is justifiable.[1]

If we ask those who regard racial discrimination as wrong to say why it is wrong, it

---

[1]In popular usage, even the term "discrimination" is often used to suggest that the practice referred to is wrong; this is, of course, an abuse of language, for to discriminate is merely to distinguish, or differentiate, and we could hardly get along without doing that.

Reprinted with permission of the publisher from *Philosophia (Philosophical Quarterly of Israel),* vol. 8 (November 1978), pp. 185–203.

is commonly said that it is wrong to pick on race as a reason for treating one person differently from others, because race is irrelevant to whether a person should be given a job, the vote, higher education, or any benefits or burdens of this sort. The irrelevance of race, it is said, makes it quite arbitrary to give these things to people of one race while withholding them from those of another race. I shall refer to this account of what is wrong with racial discrimination as the "standard objection" to racial discrimination.

A sophisticated theory of justice can be invoked in support of this standard objection to racial discrimination. Justice requires, as Aristotle so plausibly said, that equals be treated equally and unequals be treated unequally. To this we must add the obvious proviso that the equalities or inequalities should be relevant to the treatment in question. Now when we consider things like employment, it becomes clear that the relevant inequalities between candidates for a vacant position are inequalities in their ability to carry out the duties of the position and, perhaps, inequalities in the extent to which they will benefit through being offered the position. Race does not seem to be relevant at all. Similarly with the vote, capacity for rational choice between candidates or policies might be held a relevant characteristic, but race should not be; and so on for other goods. It is hard to think of anything for which race in itself is a relevant characteristic, and hence to use race as a basis for discrimination is arbitrarily to single out an irrelevant factor, no doubt because of a bias or prejudice against those of a different race.[2]

As we shall see, this account of why racial discrimination is wrong is inadequate because there are many situations in which, from at least one point of view, the racial factor is by no means irrelevant, and therefore it can be denied that racial discrimination in these situations is arbitrary. . . .

2. EXAMPLES

I shall start by describing an example of racial discrimination which may at first glance seem to be an allowable exception to a general rule that racial discrimination is arbitrary and therefore wrong; and I shall then suggest that this case has parallels with other cases we may not be so willing to allow as exceptions.

Case 1

A film director is making a film about the lives of blacks living in New York's Harlem. He advertises for black actors. A white actor turns up, but the director refuses to allow him to audition, saying that the film is about blacks and there are no roles for whites. The actor replies that, with the appropriate wig and make-up, he can look just like a black; moreover he can imitate the mannerisms, gestures, and speech of Harlem blacks. Nevertheless the director refuses to consider him for the role, because it is essential to the director's conception of the film that the black experience be authentically portrayed, and however good a white actor might be, the director would not be satisfied with the authenticity of the portrayal.

The film director is discriminating along racial lines, yet he cannot be said to be discriminating arbitrarily. His discrimination is apt for his purpose. Moreover his purpose is a legitimate one. So the standard objection to racial discrimination cannot be made in this instance.

Racial discrimination may be acceptable in an area like casting for films or the theatre, when the race of a character in the film or play is important, because this is one of

---

[2]For a brief and clear statement of this idea of justice, see H. L. A. Hart, *The Concept of Law* (Clarendon Press, Oxford, 1961), pp. 156–8; see also Joel Feinberg, *Social Philosophy* (Prentice-Hall, Englewood Cliffs, N.J., 1973), ch.7.

the seemingly few areas in which a person's race is directly relevant to his capacity to perform a given task. As such, it may be thought, these areas can easily be distinguished from other areas of employment, as well as from areas like housing, education, the right to vote, and so on, where race has no relevance at all. Unfortunately there are many other situations in which race is not as totally irrelevant as this view assumes.

Case 2

The owner of a cake shop with a largely white and racially prejudiced clientele wishes to hire an assistant. The owner has no prejudice against blacks himself, but is reluctant to employ one, for fear that his customers will go elsewhere. If his fears are well-founded (and this is not impossible) then the race of a candidate for the position is, again, relevant to the purpose of the employer, which in this case is to maintain the profitability of his business.

What can we say about this case? We cannot deny the connection between race and the owner's purposes, and so we must recognize that the owner's discrimination is not arbitrary, and does not necessarily indicate a bias or prejudice on his part. Nor can we say that the owner's purpose is an illegitimate one, for making a profit from the sale of cakes is not generally regarded as wrong, at least if the amount of profit made is modest.

We can, of course, look at other aspects of the matter. We can object to the racial discrimination shown by customers who will search out shops staffed by whites only — such people do discriminate arbitrarily, for race is irrelevant to the quality of the goods and the proficiency of service in a shop — but is this not simply a fact that the shop owner must live with, however much he may wish he could change it? We might argue that by pandering to the prejudices of his customers, the owner is allowing those prejudices to continue unchallenged; whereas if he and other shopkeepers took no notice of them, people would eventually become used to mixing with those of another race, and prejudices would be eroded. Yet it is surely too much to ask an individual shop owner to risk his livelihood in a lone and probably vain effort to break down prejudice. Few of the most dedicated opponents of racism do as much. If there were national legislation which distributed the burden more evenly, by a general prohibition of discrimination on racial grounds (with some recognized exceptions for cases like casting for a film or play) the situation would be different. Then we could reasonably ask every shop owner to play his part. Whether there should be such legislation is a different question from whether the shop owner may be blamed for discriminating in the absence of legislation. I shall discuss the issue of legislation shortly, after we consider a different kind of racial discrimination that, again, is not arbitrary.

Case 3

A landlord discriminates against blacks in letting the accommodation he owns. Let us say that he is not so rigid as never to let an apartment to a black, but if a black person and a white person appear to be equally suitable as tenants, with equally good references and so on, the landlord invariably prefers the white. He defends his policy along the following lines:

> If more than a very small proportion of my tenants get behind in their rent and then disappear without paying the arrears, I will be out of business. Over the years, I have found that more blacks do this than whites. I admit that there are many honest blacks (some of my best tenants have been black) and many dishonest whites, but, for some reason I do not claim to understand, the odds on a white tenant defaulting are longer than on a black doing so, even when their references and other credentials appear equally good. In this business you can't run a full-scale probe of every prospective tenant—and if I tried I would be abused for invading privacy—so you have to go by the average rather than the individual. That is why blacks have to have better indications of reliability than whites before I will let to them.

Now the landlord's impression of a higher rate of default among blacks than among comparable whites may itself be the result of prejudice on his part. Perhaps in most cases when landlords say this kind of thing, there is no real factual basis to their allegations. People have grown up with racial stereotypes, and these stereotypes are reinforced by a tendency to notice occurrences which conform to the stereotype and to disregard those which conflict with it. So if unreliability is part of the stereotype of blacks held by many whites, they may take more notice of blacks who abscond without paying the rent than of blacks who are reliable tenants; and conversely they will take less notice of absconding whites and more of those whites who conform to their ideas of normal white behaviour.

If it is prejudice that is responsible for the landlord's views about black and white tenants, and there is no factual basis for his claims, then the problem becomes one of eliminating this prejudice and getting the landlord to see his mistake. This is by no means an easy task, but it is not a task for philosophers, and it does not concern us here, for we are interested in attempts to justify racial discrimination, and an attempted justification based on an inaccurate description of a situation can be rejected without raising the deeper issue of justification.

On the other hand, the landlord's impression of a higher rate of default among black tenants *could* be entirely accurate. (It might be explicable in terms of the different cultural and economic circumstances in which blacks are brought up.) Whether or not we think this likely, we need to ask what its implications would be for the justifiability of the racial discrimination exercised by the landlord. To refuse even to consider this question would be to rest all one's objections to the landlord's practice on the falsity of his claims, and thereby to fail to examine the possibility that the landlord's practice could be open to objection even if his impressions on tenant reliability are accurate.

If the landlord's impressions were accurate, we would have to concede, once again, that racial discrimination in this situation is not arbitrary; that it is, instead, relevant to the purposes of the landlord. We must also admit that these purposes—making a living from letting property that one owns—are not themselves objectionable, provided the rents are reasonable, and so on. Nor can we, this time, locate the origin of the problem in the prejudices of others, except insofar as the problem has its origin in the prejudices of those responsible for the conditions of deprivation in which many of the present generation of blacks grew up—but it is too late to do anything to alter those prejudices anyway, since they belong to previous generations.

We have now looked at three examples of racial discrimination, and can begin to examine the parallels and differences between them. Many people, as I have already said, would make no objection to the discriminatory hiring practice of the film director in the first of these cases. But we can now see that if we try to justify the actions of the film director in this case on the grounds that his purpose is a legitimate one and the discrimination he uses is relevant for his purpose, we will have to accept the actions of the cake-shop owner and the landlord as well. I suspect that many of those ready to accept the discriminatory practice in the first case will be much more reluctant about the other two cases. But what morally significant difference is there between them?

It might be suggested that the difference between them lies in the nature of what blacks are being deprived of, and their title to it. The argument would run like this: No-one has a right to be selected to act in a film; the director must have absolute discretion to hire whomsoever he wishes to hire. After all, no-one can force the director to make the film at all, and if he didn't make it, no-one would be hired to play in it; if he does decide to make it, therefore, he must be allowed to make it on his own terms. Moreover, since so few people ever get the chance to appear in a film, it would be absurd to hold that the director violates someone's rights by not giving him something which most people will never have anyway. On the other hand, people do have a right to employment, and to housing. To discriminate against blacks in an ordinary employment situation, or in the letting of accommodation, threatens their basic rights and therefore should not be tolerated.

Plausible as it appears, this way of distinguishing the first case from the other two will not do. Consider the first and second cases: almost everything that we have said about the film director applies to the cake-shop owner as well. No-one can force the cake-shop owner to keep his shop open, and if he didn't, no one would be hired to work in it. If in the film director's case this was a reason for allowing him to make the film on his own terms, it must be a reason for allowing the shop owner to run his shop on his own terms. In fact, such reasoning, which would allow unlimited discrimination in restaurants, hotels and shops, is invalid. There are plenty of examples where we would not agree that the fact that someone did not have to make an offer or provide an opportunity at all means that if he does do it he must be allowed to make the offer or provide the opportunity on his own terms. The United States Civil Rights Act of 1965 certainly does not recognize this line of argument, for it prohibits those offering food and lodgings to the public from excluding customers on racial grounds. We may, as a society, decide that we shall not allow people to make certain offers, if the way in which the offers are made will cause hardship or offense to others. In so doing we are balancing people's freedom to do as they please against the harm this may do to others, and coming down on the side of preventing harm rather than enlarging freedom. This is a perfectly defensible position, if the harm is sufficiently serious and the restriction of freedom not grave.[3]

Nor does it seem possible to distinguish the first and second cases by the claim that since so few people ever get the chance to appear in a film, no-one's rights are violated if they are not given something that most people will never have anyway. For if the number of jobs in cake shops was small, and the demand for such jobs high, it would also be true that few people would ever have the chance to work in a cake shop. It would be odd if such an increase in competition for the job justified an otherwise unjustifiable policy of hiring whites only. Moreover, this argument would allow a film director to discriminate on racial lines even if race was irrelevant to the roles he was casting; and that is quite a different situation from the one we have been discussing.

The best way to distinguish the situations of the film director and the shop owner is by reference to the nature of the employment offered, and to the reasons why racial discrimination in these cases is not arbitrary. In casting for a film about blacks, the race of the actor auditioning is intrinsically significant, independently of the attitudes of those connected with the film. In the case of hiring a shop assistant, race is relevant only because of the attitudes of those connected (as customers) with the shop; it has nothing to do with the selling of cakes in itself, but only with the selling of cakes to racially prejudiced customers. This means that in the case of the shop assistant we could eliminate the relevance of race if we could eliminate the prejudices of the customers; by contrast there is no way in which we could eliminate the relevance of the race of an actor auditioning for a role in a film about blacks, without altering the nature of the film. Moreover, in the case of the shop owner racial discrimination probably serves to perpetuate the very prejudices that make such discrimination relevant and (from the point of view of the owner seeking to maintain his profits) necessary. Thus people who can buy all their cakes and other necessities in shops staffed only by whites will never come into the kind of contact with comparable blacks which might break down their aversion to being served by blacks; whereas if shop

---

[3]See Feinberg, *op.cit.,* p. 78.

owners were to hire more blacks, their customers would no doubt become used to it and in time might wonder why they ever opposed the idea. (Compare the change of attitudes toward racial integration in the American South since the 1956 United States Supreme Court decision against segregated schools and subsequent measures against segregation were put into effect.[4])

Hence if we are opposed to arbitrary discrimination we have reason to take steps against racial discrimination in situations like Case 2, because such discrimination, while not itself arbitrary, both feeds on and gives support to discrimination by others which is arbitrary. In prohibiting it we would, admittedly, be preventing the employer from discriminating in a way that is relevant to his purposes; but if the causal hypothesis suggested in the previous paragraph is correct, this situation would only be temporary, and after some time the circumstances inducing the employer to discriminate racially would have been eliminated.

The case of the landlord presents a more difficult problem. If the facts he alleges are true his non-arbitrary reasons for discrimination against blacks are real enough. They do not depend on present arbitrary discrimination by others, and they may persist beyond an interval in which there is no discrimination. Whatever the roots of hypothetical racial differences in reliability as tenants might be, they would probably go too deep to be eradicated solely by a short period in which there was no racial discrimination.

We should recognize, then, that if the facts are as alleged, to legislate against the landlord's racially discriminatory practice is to impose a long-term disadvantage upon him. At the very least, he will have to take greater care in ascertaining the suitability of prospective tenants. Perhaps he will turn to data-collecting agencies for assistance, thus contributing to the growth of institutions that are threats, potential or actual, to our privacy. Perhaps, if these methods are unavailable or unavailing, the landlord will have to take greater losses than he otherwise would have, and perhaps this will lead to increased rents or even to a reduction in the amount of rentable housing available.

None of this forces us to conclude that we should not legislate against the landlord's racial discrimination. There are good reasons why we should seek to eliminate racial discrimination even when such discrimination is neither arbitrary in itself, nor relevant only because of the arbitrary prejudices of others. These reasons may be so important as to make the disadvantage imposed on the landlord comparatively insignificant.

An obvious point that can be made against the landlord is that he is judging people, at least in part, as members of a race rather than as individuals. The landlord does not deny that some black prospective tenants he turns away would make better tenants than some white prospective tenants he accepts. Some highly eligible black prospective tenants are refused accommodation simply because they are black. If the landlord assessed every prospective tenant as an individual this would not happen.

A similar point is often made in the debate over alleged differences between blacks and whites in America in whatever is measured by IQ tests. Even if, as Jensen and others

---

[4]"In most southern communities . . . the adjustment to public desegregation following the enactment of the 1964 Civil Rights Act was amazing." Lewis M. Killian, *White Southerners* (New York: Random House, 1970). Similar comments have been made by many other observers; for a more recent report, see *Time*, September 27, 1976, especially the favorable comments of Northern blacks who have recently moved to the South (p. 44). That contact with those of another race helps to reduce racial prejudice had been demonstrated as early as 1949, when a study of U.S. soldiers showed that the more contact white soldiers had with black troops, the more favorable were their attitudes to integration. See Samuel Stouffer *et al., The American Soldier: Adjustment During Army Life* (Princeton: Princeton University Press, 1949) p. 594. This finding was supported by a later study, "Project Clear," reported by Charles Moskos, Jr., "Racial Integration in the Armed Forces," *American Journal of Sociology,* vol. 72 (1966) pp. 132–48.

have suggested, there is a small inherited difference in IQ between blacks and whites, it is clear that this difference shows up only when we compare averages, and not when we compare individuals. Even if we accept the controversial estimates that the average IQ of American blacks is 15 points lower than the average IQ of American whites, there is still a tremendous amount of overlap between the IQs of blacks and whites, with many whites scoring lower than the majority of blacks. Hence the difference in averages between the races would be of limited significance. For any purpose for which IQ mattered — like entrance into higher levels of education — it would still be essential to consider each applicant individually, rather than as a member of a certain race.

There are plenty of reasons why in situations like admitting people to higher education or providing them with employment or other benefits we should regard people as individuals and not as members of some larger group. For one thing we will be able to make a selection better suited for our own purposes, for selecting or discarding whole groups of people will generally result in, at best, a crude approximation to the results we hope to achieve. This is certainly true in an area like education. On the other hand it must be admitted that in some situations a crude approximation is all that can be achieved anyway. The landlord claims that his situation is one of these, and that as he cannot reliably tell which individuals will make suitable tenants, he is justified in resorting to so crude a means of selection as race. Here we need to turn our attention from the landlord to the prospective black tenant.

To be judged merely as a member of a group when it is one's individual qualities on which the verdict should be given is to be treated as less than the unique individual that we see ourselves as. Even where our individual qualities would merit less than we receive as a member of a group — if we are promoted over better-qualified people because we went to the "right" private school — the benefit is usually less welcome than it would be if it had been merited by our own attributes. Of course in this case qualms are easily stilled by the fact that a benefit has been received, never mind how. In the contrary case, however, when something of value has been lost, the sense of loss will be compounded by the feeling that one was not assessed on one's own merits, but merely as a member of a group.

To this general preference for individual as against group assessment must be added a consideration arising from the nature of the group. To be denied a benefit because one was, say, a member of the Communist Party would be unjust and a violation of basic principles of political liberty, but if one has chosen to join the Communist Party, then one is, after all, being assessed for what one has done, and one can choose between living with the consequences of continued party membership or leaving the party.[5] Race, of course, is not something that one chooses to adopt or that one can ever choose to give up. The person who is denied advantages because of his race is totally unable to alter this particular circumstance of his existence and so may feel with added sharpness that his life is clouded, not merely because he is not being judged as an individual, but because of something over which he has no control at all. This makes racial discrimination peculiarly invidious.

So we have the viewpoint of the victim of racial discrimination to offset against the landlord's argument in favor, and it seems that the victim has more at stake and hence should be given preference, even if the landlord's reason for discrimination is nonarbitrary and hence in a sense legitimate. The case against racial discrimination becomes stronger still when we consider the long-term social effects of discrimination.

When members of a racial minority are overwhelmingly among the poorest members

---

[5]The situation is different if it is because of a past rather than a present political connection that one is subjected to disadvantages. Perhaps this is why the hounding of ex-communists in the McCarthy era was a particularly shameful episode in American history.

of a society, living in a deprived area, holding jobs low in pay and status, or no jobs at all, and less well educated than the average member of the community, racial discrimination serves to perpetuate a divided society in which race becomes a badge of a much broader inferiority. It is the association of race with economic status and educational disadvantages which in turn gives rise to the situation in which there could be a coloring of truth to the claim that race is a relevant ground for discriminating between prospective tenants, applicants for employment, and so on. Thus there is, in the end, a parallel between the situation of the landlord and the cake-shop owner, for both, by their discrimination, contribute to the maintenance of the grounds for claiming that this discrimination is non-arbitrary. Hence prohibition of such discrimination can be justified as breaking this circle of deprivation and discrimination. The difference between the situations, as I have already said, is that in the case of the cake-shop owner it is only a prejudice against contact with blacks that needs to be broken down, and experience has shown that such prejudices do evaporate in a relatively short period of time. In the case of the landlord, however, it is the whole social and economic position of blacks that needs to be changed, and while overcoming discrimination would be an essential part of this process it may not be sufficient. That is why, if the facts are as the landlord alleges them to be, prohibition of racial discrimination is likely to impose more of a long-term disadvantage on the landlord than on the shop owner — a disadvantage which is, however, outweighed by the costs of continuing the circle of racial discrimination and deprivation for those discriminated against; and the costs of greater social inequality and racial divisiveness for the community as a whole.

3. A BASIC PRINCIPLE

If our discussion of the three examples has been sound, opposition to racial discrimination cannot rely on the standard objection that racial discrimination is arbitrary because race is irrelevant to employment, housing, and other things that matter. While this very often will be true, it will not always be true. The issue is more complicated than that appealing formula suggests, and has to do with the effect of racial discrimination on its victims, and on society as a whole. Behind all this, however, there is a more basic moral principle, and at this more basic level the irrelevance of race and the arbitrariness of racial discrimination reappear and help to explain why racism is wrong. This basic moral principle is the principle of equal consideration of interests.

The principle of equal consideration of interests is easy to state, though difficult to apply. Bentham's famous "each to count for one and none for more than one" is one way of putting it, though not free from ambiguity; Sidgwick's formulation is more precise, if less memorable: "The good of any one individual is of no more importance, from the point of view (if I may say so) of the Universe, than the good of any other."[6] Perhaps the best way of explaining the effect of the principle is to follow C. I. Lewis's suggestion that we imagine ourselves living, one after the other, the lives of everyone affected by our actions; in this way we would experience all of their experiences as our own.[7] R. M. Hare's insistence that moral judgments must be universalizable comes to much the same thing, as he has pointed out.[8] The essence of the principle of equal consideration of interests is that we give equal weight in our moral deliberations to the like interests of all those affected by our actions. This means that if only X and Y would be affected by a possible act, and if X stands to

---

[6]Henry Sidgwick, *The Methods of Ethics* (Macmillan, London, 7th Edition, 1907), p. 382.
[7]C. I. Lewis, *Analysis of Knowledge and Valuation* (La Salle, 1946), p. 547; I owe this reference to R. M. Hare.
[8]See Hare, "Rules of War and Moral Reasoning," *Philosophy and Public Affairs,* vol. 1 (1972).

lose more than Y stands to gain (for instance, X will lose his job and find it difficult to get another, whereas Y will merely get a small promotion) then it is better not to do the act. We cannot, if we accept the principle of equal consideration of interests, say that doing the act is better, despite the facts described, because we are more concerned about Y than we are about X. What the principle is really saying is that an interest is an interest, whoever's interest it may be. . . .

. . . [T]he principle of equal consideration of interests does underpin the decisions we reached when considering the three more realistic examples of racial discrimination in the preceding section of this article. Although the principle is too general to allow the derivation of straightforward and indisputable conclusions from it in complex situations, it does seem that an impartial consideration of the interests of all involved would, for reasons already discussed, rule out discrimination by the shop owner and the landlord, though allowing that of the film director. Hence it is the arbitrariness of racial discrimination at the level of the principle of equal consideration of interests, rather than at the level of the particular decision of the person discriminating, that governs whether a given act of racial discrimination is justifiable.

This conclusion may be applied to other controversial cases. It suggests, for instance, that the problem of "reverse discrimination" or "compensatory discrimination" which arises when a university or employer gives preference to members of minority groups should be discussed by asking not whether racial discrimination is always and intrinsically wrong, but whether the proposal is, on balance, in the interests of all those affected by it. This is a difficult question, and not one that can be answered generally for all types of reverse discrimination. For instance, if white communities have a far better doctor-patient ratio than black communities because very few blacks are admitted to medical school and white doctors tend to work in white communities, there is a strong case for admitting some black candidates to medical school ahead of whites who are better qualified by the standard entry procedures, provided, of course, that the blacks admitted are not so poorly qualified as to be unable to become competent doctors. The case for separate and easier entry would be less strong in an area where there is no equivalent community need, for instance, in philosophy. Here much would depend on whether black students who would not otherwise have been admitted were able to make up ground and do as well as whites with higher ratings on standard entry procedures. If so, easier entry for blacks could be justified in terms of the conventional goal of admitting those students most likely to succeed in their course; taking into account a student's race would merely be a way of correcting for the failure of standard tests to allow for the disadvantages that face blacks in competing with whites on such tests. If, on the other hand, blacks admitted under easier entry in a field like philosophy did not do as well as the whites they displaced could have been expected to do, discrimination in their favor would be much harder to justify.[9] . . .

QUESTIONS

1. Are all racial classifications racist? Explain.
2. Can you suggest any morally acceptable criteria which should be used to distinguish morally acceptable racial classifications from "invidious" or "pernicious" ones?

---

[9]I am grateful to Robert Young for comments and criticism on this paper.

MAJORITY OPINION IN *UNITED STEELWORKERS V. WEBER*

████████   ████████

A biographical sketch of Justice William Brennan is found on page 125.

A 1974 agreement between the Kaiser Aluminum and Chemical Corporation (Kaiser) and United Steelworkers of America (USWA) included an affirmative action program designed to eliminate "conspicuous racial imbalance" in Kaiser's craft work forces. The hard quota preferential treatment program agreed upon required that in any particular plant 50 percent of the openings in in-plant craft-training programs be reserved for black employees until the percentage of black craft workers in the plant was commensurate with the percentage of blacks in the local labor force. When the plan was agreed upon in 1974, the percentage of black skilled-craft workers in the Gramercy, Louisiana, Kaiser plant was 1.83 percent, while the percentage of blacks in the local work force was 39 percent. Prior to that time, Kaiser had hired trained outsiders to fill craft openings. After the national agreement, Kaiser established a program to train production workers at its Gramercy plant to fill these openings. It was agreed that trainees were to be selected on the basis of seniority, but that at least 50 percent of those selected were to be black until the percentage of black skilled-craft workers in the plant approximated the percentage of blacks in the local labor force. During the first year of the plan's operation, six white and seven black trainees were selected, with the most junior black trainee having less seniority than several white workers who were denied admission to the program. One of these white workers, Brian F. Weber, instituted a class action against USWA and Kaiser, charging that he and other white production workers had been discriminated against in violation of Title VII of the 1964 Civil Rights Act. Title VII makes it unlawful to "discriminate . . . because of . . . race in admission to, or employment in, any program established to provide apprenticeship or other training." The lower courts ruled in favor of Weber, holding that *all* employment preferences based on race violated Title VII's prohibition against racial discrimination in employment. The United States Supreme Court ruled against Weber, holding that Title VII does *not* prohibit the kind of voluntary race-conscious affirmative action plans initiated at the Kaiser plant.

In this selection from the majority opinion, Justice Brennan argues that an act or practice can be within *the letter* of a statute and yet *not within* the statute because not within its spirit nor within the intention of its makers. What Justice Brennan wants to do, of course, is to distinguish between unacceptable racial classifications designed to segregate blacks from the rest of society and acceptable racial classifications designed to serve the morally desirable social purpose of integrating blacks into the mainstream of society. Justice Brennan argues that although a *literal* reading of Title VII would seem to forbid *all* racial discrimination in employment, the framers of the statute intended it to forbid only racial discrimination which works to perpetuate the old patterns of racial segregation and hierarchy. Justice Brennan's argument is a consequentialist one insofar as he distinguishes between acceptable and nonacceptable racial discrimination by appealing to the intended consequences of the discriminatory practice.

████████   ████████

Challenged here is the legality of an affirmative action plan—collectively bargained by an employer and a union—that reserves for black employees 50% of the openings in an in-plant craft-training program until the percentage of black craftworkers in the plant is com-

United States Supreme Court. 443 U.S. 193 (1979).

mensurate with the percentage of blacks in the local labor force. The question for decision is whether Congress, in Title VII of the Civil Rights Act of 1964, 78 Stat. 253, as amended, 42 U. S. C. § 2000e *et seq.,* left employers and unions in the private sector free to take such race-conscious steps to eliminate manifest racial imbalances in traditionally segregated job categories. We hold that Title VII does not prohibit such race-conscious affirmative action plans. . . .

I

We emphasize at the outset the narrowness of our inquiry. Since the Kaiser-USWA plan does not involve state action, this case does not present an alleged violation of the Equal Protection Clause of the Fourteenth Amendment. Further, since the Kaiser-USWA plan was adopted voluntarily, we are not concerned with what Title VII requires or with what a court might order to remedy a past proved violation of the Act. The only question before us is the narrow statutory issue of whether Title VII *forbids* private employers and unions from voluntarily agreeing upon bona fide affirmative action plans that accord racial preferences in the manner and for the purpose provided in the Kaiser-USWA plan. That question was expressly left open in *McDonald* v. *Santa Fe Trail Transp. Co.* (1976), which held, in a case not involving affirmative action, that Title VII protects whites as well as blacks from certain forms of racial discrimination.

Respondent argues that Congress intended in Title VII to prohibit all race-conscious affirmative action plans. Respondent's argument rests upon a literal interpretation of §§ 703 (a)[1] and (d)[2] of the Act. Those sections make it unlawful to "discriminate . . . because of . . . race" in hiring and in the selection of apprentices for training programs. Since, the argument runs, *McDonald* v. *Santa Fe Trail Transp. Co., supra,* settled that Title VII forbids discrimination against whites as well as blacks, and since the Kaiser-USWA affirmative action plan operates to discriminate against white employees solely because they are white, it follows that the Kaiser-USWA plan violates Title VII.

Respondent's argument is not without force. But it overlooks the significance of the fact that the Kaiser-USWA plan is an affirmative action plan voluntarily adopted by private parties to eliminate traditional patterns of racial segregation. In this context respondent's reliance upon a literal construction of §§ 703 (a) and (d) and upon *McDonald* is misplaced. It is a "familiar rule, that a thing may be within the letter of the statute and yet not within the statute, because not within its spirit, nor within the intention of its makers." The prohibition against racial discrimination in §§ 703 (a) and (d) of Title VII must therefore be read against the background of the legislative history of Title VII and the historical context from which the Act arose. Examination of those sources makes clear than an interpretation of the sections that forbade all race-conscious affirmative action would "bring about an end completely at variance with the purpose of the statute" and must be rejected.

Congress' primary concern in enacting the prohibition against racial discrimination in Title VII of the Civil Rights Act of 1964 was with "the plight of the Negro in our economy"

[1]Section 703(a), 42 U.S.C., § 2000e-2(a), provides: "(a) It shall be an unlawful employment practice for an employer—

"(1) to fail or refuse to hire or to discharge any individual, or otherwise to discriminate against any individual with respect to his compensation, terms, conditions, or privileges of employment, because of such individual's race, color, religion, sex, or national origin; or

"(2) to limit, segregate, or classify his employees or applicants for employment in any way which would deprive or tend to deprive any individual of employment opportunities or otherwise adversely affect his status as an employee, because of such individual's race, color, religion, sex, or national origin."

[2]Section 703 (d), 42 U. S. C. § 2000e-2 (d), provides: "It shall be an unlawful employment practice for any employer, labor organization, or joint labor-management committee controlling apprenticeship or other training or retraining, including on-the-job training programs to discriminate against any individual because of his race, color, religion, sex, or national origin in admission to, or employment in, any program established to provide apprenticeship or other training."

(remarks of Sen. Humphrey). Before 1964, blacks were largely relegated to "unskilled and semi-skilled jobs" (remarks of Sen. Humphrey); (remarks of Sen. Clark); (remarks of Sen. Kennedy). Because of automation the number of such jobs was rapidly decreasing (remarks of Sen. Humphrey); (remarks of Sen. Clark). As a consequence, "the relative position of the Negro worker [was] steadily worsening. In 1947 the nonwhite unemployment rate was only 64 percent higher than the white rate; in 1962 it was 124 percent higher" (remarks of Sen. Humphrey). Congress considered this a serious social problem. As Senator Clark told the Senate:

> "The rate of Negro unemployment has gone up consistently as compared with white unemployment for the past 15 years. This is a social malaise and a social situation which we should not tolerate. That is one of the principal reasons why the bill should pass."

Congress feared that the goals of the Civil Rights Act—the integration of blacks into the mainstream of American society—could not be achieved unless this trend were reversed. And Congress recognized that that would not be possible unless blacks were able to secure jobs "which have a future" (remarks of Sen. Clark). As Senator Humphrey explained to the Senate:

> "What good does it do a Negro to be able to eat in a fine restaurant if he cannot afford to pay the bill? What good does it do him to be accepted in a hotel that is too expensive for his modest income? How can a Negro child be motivated to take full advantage of integrated educational facilities if he has no hope of getting a job where he can use that education?"
>
> "Without a job, one cannot afford public convenience and accommodations. Income from employment may be necessary to further a man's education, or that of his children. If his children have no hope of getting a good job, what will motivate them to take advantage of educational opportunities?"

These remarks echoed President Kennedy's original message to Congress upon the introduction of the Civil Rights Act in 1963.

> "There is little value in a Negro's obtaining the right to be admitted to hotels and restaurants if he has no cash in his pocket and no job."

Accordingly, it was clear to Congress that "[t]he crux of the problem [was] to open employment opportunities for Negroes in occupations which have been traditionally closed to them," (remarks of Sen. Humphrey), and it was to this problem that Title VII's prohibition against racial discrimination in employment was primarily addressed.

It plainly appears from the House Report accompanying the Civil Rights Act that Congress did not intend wholly to prohibit private and voluntary affirmative action efforts as one method of solving this problem. The Report provides:

> "No bill can or should lay claim to eliminating all of the causes and consequences of racial and other types of discrimination against minorities. There is reason to believe, however, that national leadership provided by the enactment of Federal legislation dealing with the most troublesome problems *will create an atmosphere conducive to voluntary or local resolution of other forms of discrimination.*"

Given this legislative history, we cannot agree with respondent that Congress intended to prohibit the private sector from taking effective steps to accomplish the goal that Congress designed Title VII to achieve. The very statutory words intended as a spur or catalyst to cause "employers and unions to self-examine and to self-evaluate their employment practices and to endeavor to eliminate, so far as possible, the last vestiges of an unfortunate and ignominious page in this country's history" cannot be interpreted as an absolute prohibition against all private, voluntary, race-conscious affirmative action efforts to hasten the elimination of such vestiges.[3] It would be ironic indeed if a law triggered by a Nation's concern over centuries of racial injustice and intended to improve the lot of those who had "been excluded from the American dream for so long," (remarks of Sen. Humphrey), constituted the first legislative prohibition of all voluntary, private, race-conscious efforts to abolish traditional patterns of racial segregation and hierarchy.

Our conclusion is further reinforced by examination of the language and legislative history of § 703 (j) of Title VII.[4] Opponents of Title VII raised two related arguments against the bill. First, they argued that the Act would be interpreted to *require* employers with racially imbalanced work forces to grant preferential treatment to racial minorities in order to integrate. Second, they argued that employers with racially imbalanced work forces would grant preferential treatment to racial minorities, even if not required to do so by the Act (remarks of Sen. Sparkman). Had Congress meant to prohibit all race-conscious affirmative action, as respondent urges, it easily could have answered both objections by providing that Title VII would not require or *permit* racially preferential integration efforts. But Congress did not choose such a course. Rather Congress added § 703 (j) which addresses only the first objection. The section provides that nothing contained in Title VII "shall be interpreted to *require* any employer . . . to grant preferential treatment . . . to any group because of the race . . . of such . . . group on account of" a *de facto* racial imbalance in the employer's work force. The section does *not* state that "nothing in Title VII shall be interpreted to *permit*" voluntary affirmative efforts to correct racial imbalances. The natural inference is that Congress chose not to forbid all voluntary race-conscious affirmative action. . . .

Such a prohibition would augment the powers of the Federal Government and diminish traditional management prerogatives while at the same time impeding attainment of the ultimate statutory goals. In view of this legislative history and in view of Congress' desire to avoid undue federal regulation of private businesses, use of the word "require" rather than the phrase "require or permit" in § 703 (j) fortifies the conclusion that Congress did not intend to limit traditional business freedom to such a degree as to prohibit all voluntary, race-conscious affirmative action.

We therefore hold that Title VII's prohibition in §§ 703 (a) and (d) against racial discrimination does not condemn all private, voluntary, race-conscious affirmative action plans.

II

We need not today define in detail the line of demarcation between permissible and impermissible affirmative action plans. It suffices to hold that the challenged Kaiser-USWA

---

[3]The problem that Congress addressed in 1964 remains with us. In 1962, the nonwhite unemployment rate was 124% higher than the white rate (remarks of Sen. Humphrey). In 1978, the black unemployment rate was 129% higher. See Monthly Labor Review, U.S. Department of Labor, Bureau of Labor Statistics 78 (Mar. 1979).

[4]Section 703 (j) of Title VII, 42 U. S. C. § 2000e-2 (j), provides:

"Nothing contained in this title shall be interpreted to require any employer, employment agency, labor organization, or joint labor-management committee subject to this title to grant preferential treatment to any individual or to any group because of the race, color, religion, sex, or national origin of such individual or group on account of an imbalance which may exist with respect to the total number or percentage of persons of any race, color, religion, sex, or national origin employed by any employer, referred or classified for employment by any employment agency or labor organization, admitted to membership or classified by any labor organization, or admitted to, or employed in, any apprenticeship or other training program, in comparison with the total number or percentage of persons of such race, color, religion, sex, or national origin in any community, State, section, or other area, or in the available work force in any community, State, section, or other area."

affirmative action plan falls on the permissible side of the line. The purposes of the plan mirror those of the statute. Both were designed to break down old patterns of racial segregation and hierarchy. Both were structured to "open employment opportunities for Negroes in occupations which have been traditionally closed to them" (remarks of Sen. Humphrey).

At the same time, the plan does not unnecessarily trammel the interests of the white employees. The plan does not require the discharge of white workers and their replacement with new black hirees. Nor does the plan create an absolute bar to the advancement of white employees; half of those trained in the program will be white. Moreover, the plan is a temporary measure; it is not intended to maintain racial balance, but simply to eliminate a manifest racial imbalance. Preferential selection of craft trainees at the Gramercy plant will end as soon as the percentage of black skilled craftworkers in the Gramercy plant approximates the percentage of blacks in the local labor force.

We conclude, therefore, that the adoption of the Kaiser-USWA plan for the Gramercy plant falls within the area of discretion left by Title VII to the private sector voluntarily to adopt affirmative action plans designed to eliminate conspicuous racial imbalance in traditionally segregated job categories. Accordingly, the judgment of the Court of Appeals for the Fifth Circuit is reversed.

QUESTIONS

1. Assume the following facts are true about a particular factory:

(a) In the past the policy has been not to hire blacks for production work.

(b) For the last ten years or so, in response to civil rights legislation, both blacks and whites have been hired for the production line.

(c) A training policy such as the one at Kaiser has been instituted and seniority is the *sole criterion* for admission to the program. (Note that a greater number of years on the production line is *not* an indicator of a greater ability for skilled craft work.)

Is this policy fair to blacks who were unable to establish seniority rights because of past discriminatory policies?

2. Is racial discrimination whose intent is to rectify at least some of the results of past injustices morally acceptable?

JUDITH JARVIS THOMSON

PREFERENTIAL HIRING

Judith Jarvis Thomson is professor of philosophy in the department of linguistics and philosophy at Massachusetts Institute of Technology. Her areas of specialization are ethics, philosophy of action, and political philosophy. Thomson is the author of *Acts and Other Events* (1977) and numerous articles on normative issues, including "A Defense of Abortion," "Killing, Letting Die, and the Trolley Problem," and "The Right to Privacy."

Thomson argues in favor of some preferential hiring policies. Her discussion centers primarily on one kind of hiring decision—a hiring officer in a university, presented with several equally qualified candidates, uses race or sex as the deciding criterion and on this basis chooses a black or a woman. Thomson offers a *compensatory* argument to support the moral correctness of this decision. (1) Blacks and women who have been victims of social injustices have a right to compensatory amends. (2) Even blacks and women who have not been the direct victims of injustices suffer the consequences of the downgrading of other blacks and women—lack of self-confidence and lack of self-respect. Amends are due to them as well. (3) Amends to the first group are required by justice; amends to the second by common decency.

Many people are inclined to think preferential hiring an obvious injustice.[1] I should have said "feel" rather than "think": it seems to me the matter has not been carefully thought out, and that what is in question, really, is a gut reaction.

I am going to deal with only a very limited range of preferential hirings: that is, I am concerned with cases in which several candidates present themselves for a job, in which the hiring officer finds, on examination, that all are equally qualified to hold that job, and he then straightway declares for the black, or for the woman, because he or she *is* a black or a woman. And I shall talk only of hiring decisions in the universities, partly because I am most familiar with them, partly because it is in the universities that the most vocal and articulate opposition to preferential hiring is now heard—not surprisingly, perhaps, since no one is more vocal and articulate than a university professor who feels deprived of his rights.

I suspect that some people may say, Oh well, in *that* kind of case it's all right, what we object to is preferring the less qualified to the better qualified. Or again, What we object to is refusing even to consider the qualifications of white males. I shall say nothing at all about these things. I think that the argument I shall give for saying that preferential hiring is not unjust in the cases I do concentrate on can also be appealed to to justify it outside that range of cases. But I won't draw any conclusions about cases outside it. Many people do have that gut reaction I mentioned against preferential hiring in *any* degree or form; and it seems to me worthwhile bringing out that there is good reason to think they are wrong to have it. Nothing I say will be in the slightest degree novel or original. It will, I hope, be enough to set the relevant issues out clearly.

I

But first, something should be said about qualifications.

I said I would consider only cases in which the several candidates who present themselves for the job are equally qualified to hold it; and there plainly are difficulties in the way of saying precisely how this is to be established, and even what is to be established. Strictly academic qualifications seem at a first glance to be relatively straightforward: the hiring officer must see if the candidates have done equally well in courses (both courses they took, and any they taught), and if they are recommended equally strongly by their teachers, and if the work they submit for consideration is equally good. There is no denying that even these things are less easy to establish than first appears: for example, you may

[1]This essay is an expanded version of a talk given at the Conference on the Liberation of Female Persons, held at North Carolina State University at Raleigh, on March 26–28, 1973, under a grant from the S & H Foundation. I am indebted to James Thomson and the members of the Society for Ethical and Legal Philosophy for criticism of an earlier draft.

have a suspicion that Professor Smith is given to exaggeration, and that his "great student" is in fact less strong than Professor Jones's "good student"—but do you *know* that this is so? But there is a more serious difficulty still: as blacks and women have been saying, strictly academic indicators may themselves be skewed by prejudice. My impression is that women, white and black, may possibly suffer more from this than black males. A black male who is discouraged or down-graded for being black is discouraged or down-graded out of dislike, repulsion, a desire to avoid contact; and I suspect that there are very few teachers nowadays who allow themselves to feel such things, or, if they do feel them, to act on them. A woman who is discouraged or down-graded for being a woman is not discouraged or down-graded out of dislike, but out of a conviction she is not serious. . . .

II

. . . Suppose two candidates for a civil service job have equally good test scores, but that there is only one job available. We could decide between them by coin-tossing. But in fact we do allow for declaring for A straightway, where A is a veteran, and B is not.[2] It may be that B is a nonveteran through no fault of his own: perhaps he was refused induction for flat feet, or a heart murmur. That is, those things in virtue of which B is a nonveteran may be things which it was no more in his power to control or change than it is in anyone's power to control or change the color of his skin. Yet the fact is that B is not a veteran and A is. On the assumption that the veteran has served his country, the country owes him something. And it seems plain that giving him preference is a not unjust way in which part of that debt of gratitude can be paid.

And now, . . . we should turn to those debts which are incurred by one who wrongs another. It is here we find what seems to me the most powerful argument for the conclusion that the preferential hiring of blacks and women is not unjust.

I obviously cannot claim any novelty for this argument: it's a very familiar one. Indeed, not merely is it familiar, but so are a battery of objections to it. It may be granted that if we have wronged A, we owe him something: we should make amends, we should compensate him for the wrong done him. It may even be granted that if we have wronged A, we must make amends, that justice requires it, and that a failure to make amends is not merely callousness, but injustice. But (a) are the young blacks and women who are amongst the current applicants for university jobs amongst the blacks and women who were wronged? To turn to particular cases, it might happen that the black applicant is middle class, the son of professionals, and has had the very best in private schooling; or that the woman applicant is plainly the product of feminist upbringing and encouragement. Is it proper, much less required, that the black or woman be given preference over a white male who grew up in poverty, and has to make his own way and earn his encouragements? Again, (b), did we, the current members of the community, wrong any blacks or women? Lots of people once did; but then isn't it for them to do the compensating? That is, if they're still alive. For presumably nobody now alive owned any slaves, and perhaps nobody now alive voted against women's suffrage. And (c) what if the white male applicant for the job has never in any degree wronged any blacks or women? If so, *he* doesn't owe any debts to them, so why should *he* make amends to them?

These objections seem to me quite wrong-headed.

Obviously the situation for blacks and women is better than it was a hundred and fifty, fifty, twenty-five years ago. But it is absurd to suppose that the young blacks and women now of an age to apply for jobs have not been wronged. Large-scale, blatant, overt

---

[2]To the best of my knowledge, the analogy between veterans' preference and the preferential hiring of blacks has been mentioned in print only by Edward T. Chase, in a Letter to the Editor, *Commentary*, February 1973.

wrongs have presumably disappeared; but it is only within the last twenty-five years (perhaps the last ten years in the case of women) that it has become at all widely agreed in this country that blacks and women must be recognized as having, not merely this or that particular right normally recognized as belonging to white males, but all of the rights and respect which go with full membership in the community. Even young blacks and women have lived through down-grading for being black or female: they have not merely not been given that very equal chance at the benefits generated by what the community owns which is so firmly insisted on for white males, they have not until lately even been felt to have a right to it.

And even those who were not themselves down-graded for being black or female have suffered the consequences of the down-grading of other blacks and women: lack of self-confidence, and lack of self-respect. For where a community accepts that a person's being black, or being a woman, are right and proper grounds for denying that person full membership in the community, it can hardly be supposed that any but the most extraordinarily independent black or woman will escape self-doubt. All but the most extraordinarily independent of them have had to work harder — if only against self-doubt — than all but the most deprived white males, in the competition for a place amongst the best qualified.

If any black or woman has been unjustly deprived of what he or she has a right to, then of course justice does call for making amends. But what of the blacks and women who haven't actually been deprived of what they have a right to, but only made to suffer the consequences of injustice to other blacks and women? *Perhaps* justice doesn't require making amends to them as well; but common decency certainly does. To fail, at the very least, to make what counts as public apology to all, and to take positive steps to show that it is sincerely meant, is, if not injustice, then anyway a fault at least as serious as ingratitude.

Opting for a policy of preferential hiring may of course mean that some black or woman is preferred to some white male who as a matter of fact has had a harder life than the black or woman. But so may opting for a policy of veterans' preference mean that a healthy, unscarred, middle class veteran is preferred to a poor, struggling, scarred, nonveteran. Indeed, opting for a policy of setting who gets the job by having all equally qualified candidates draw straws may also mean that in a given case the candidate with the hardest life loses out. Opting for any policy other than hard-life preference may have this result.

I have no objection to anyone's arguing that it is precisely hard-life preference that we ought to opt for. If all, or anyway all of the equally qualified, have a right to an equal chance, then the argument would have to draw attention to something sufficiently powerful to override that right. But perhaps this could be done along the lines I followed in the case of blacks and women: perhaps it could be successfully argued that we have wronged those who have had hard lives, and therefore owe it to them to make amends. And then we should have in more extreme form a difficulty already present: how are these preferences to be ranked? shall we place the hard-lifers ahead of blacks? both ahead of women? and what about veterans? I leave these questions aside. My concern has been only to show that the white male applicant's right to an equal chance does not make it unjust to opt for a policy under which blacks and women are given preference. That a white male with a specially hard history may lose out under this policy cannot possibly be any objection to it, in the absence of a showing that hard-life preference is not unjust, and, more important, takes priority over preference for blacks and women.

Lastly, it should be stressed that to opt for such a policy is not to make the young white male applicants themselves make amends for any wrongs done to blacks and women. Under such a policy, no one is asked to give up a job which is already his; the job for which the white male competes isn't his, but is the community's, and it is the hiring officer who gives it to the black or woman in the community's name. Of course the white male is asked to give up his equal chance at the job. But that is not something he pays to the black or woman by way of making amends; it is something the community takes away from him in order that *it* may make amends.

Still, the community does impose a burden on him: it is able to make amends for its wrongs only by taking something away from him, something which, after all, we are supposing he has a right to. And why should *he* pay the cost of the community's amends-making?

If there were some appropriate way in which the community could make amends to its blacks and women, some way which did not require depriving anyone of anything he has a right to, then that would be the best course of action for it to take. Or if there were anyway some way in which the costs could be shared by everyone, and not imposed entirely on the young white male job applicants, then that would be, if not best, then any-way better than opting for a policy of preferential hiring. But in fact the nature of the wrongs done is such as to make jobs the best and most suitable form of compensation. What blacks and women were denied was full membership in the community; and nothing can more appropriately make amends for that wrong than precisely what will make them feel they now finally have it. And that means jobs. Financial compensation (the cost of which could be shared equally) slips through the fingers; having a job, and discovering you do it well, yield—perhaps better than anything else—that very self-respect which blacks and women have had to do without.

But of course choosing this way of making amends means that the costs are imposed on the young white male applicants who are turned away. And so it should be noticed that it is not entirely inappropriate that those applicants should pay the costs. No doubt few, if any, have themselves, individually, done any wrongs to blacks and women. But they have profited from the wrongs the community did. Many may actually have been direct benefi-ciaries of policies which excluded or down-graded blacks and women—perhaps in school admissions, perhaps in access to financial aid, perhaps elsewhere; and even those who did not directly benefit in this way had, at any rate, the advantage in the competition which comes of confidence in one's full membership, and of one's rights being recognized as a matter of course.

Of course it isn't only the young white male applicant for a university job who has benefited from the exclusion of blacks and women: the older white male, now comfortably tenured, also benefited, and many defenders of preferential hiring feel that he should be asked to share the costs. Well, presumably we can't demand that he give up his job, or share it. But it seems to me in place to expect the occupants of comfortable professorial chairs to contribute in some way, to make some form of return to the young white male who bears the cost, and is turned away. It will have been plain that I find the outcry now heard against preferential hiring in the universities objectionable; it would also be objec-tionable that those of us who are now securely situated should placidly defend it, with no more than a sigh of regret for the young white male who pays for it.

III

One final word: "discrimination." I am inclined to think we so use it that if anyone is con-victed of discriminating against blacks, women, white males, or what have you, then he is thereby convicted of acting unjustly. If so, and if I am right in thinking that preferential hiring in the restricted range of cases we have been looking at is *not* unjust, then we have two options: (a) we can simply reply that to opt for a policy of preferential hiring in those cases is not to opt for a policy of discriminating against white males, or (b) we can hope to get usage changed—e.g., by trying to get people to allow that there is discriminating against and discriminating against, and that some is unjust, but some is not.

Best of all, however, would be for that phrase to be avoided altogether. It's at best a blunt tool: there are all sorts of nice moral discriminations [*sic*] which one is unable to make while occupied with it. And that bluntness itself fits it to do harm: blacks and women are hardly likely to see through to what precisely is owed them while they are being accused of welcoming what is unjust.

QUESTIONS

1.   Thomson claims that even those women and blacks who have not themselves been downgraded for being women or blacks have "suffered the consequences" of such downgrading—lack of self-confidence and lack of self-respect." Is Thomson correct about this? What evidence supports your view?

2.   How have young white males benefited from the discrimination against blacks and women?

ROBERT SIMON

PREFERENTIAL HIRING: A REPLY TO JUDITH JARVIS THOMSON

Robert Simon is associate professor of philosophy at Hamilton College. He is coauthor with Norman Bowie of *The Individual and the Political Order: An Introduction to Social and Political Philosophy* (1977). His articles include "Preferential Treatment: For Groups or for Individuals?"; "Individual Rights and Benign Discrimination"; and "An Indirect Defense of the Merit Principle."

Simon agrees with Thomson that compensation is due to victims of social injustice. However, he argues, if preference in hiring is to be given to individuals injured by an unjust practice, it should be given to anyone so injured and not just to blacks or women. Racial and sexual classifications are irrelevant here. In fact, if preference is to be given to individuals who have been injured by social injustices, it might turn out that when two applicants (e.g., a white male and a black female) apply for a particular position, the person with a greater injury might be the white male. (Think of a white male from an economically deprived Appalachian family and a black woman from a prominent, economically upper-class family.) Simon raises other problems about the application of the principle of compensatory justice, when the compensation would seem to be owed to *groups* while the preferential hiring policies would "compensate" "arbitrarily selected" *members of the group.*

Judith Jarvis Thomson has recently defended preferential hiring of women and black persons in universities.[1] She restricts her defense of the assignment of preference to only those cases where candidates from preferred groups and their white male competitors are

[1] Judith Jarvis Thomson, "Preferential Hiring," *Philosophy & Public Affairs* 2, no. 4 (Summer 1973), 364–384.

Robert Simon, "Preferential Hiring: A Reply to Judith Jarvis Thomson," *Philosophy & Public Affairs* 3, no. 3 (Spring 1974). Copyright © 1974 by Princeton University Press. Excerpts reprinted by permission.

equally qualified, although she suggests that her argument can be extended to cover cases where the qualifications are unequal as well. The argument in question is compensatory; it is because of pervasive patterns of unjust discrimination against black persons and women that justice, or at least common decency, requires that amends be made.

While Thomson's analysis surely clarifies many of the issues at stake, I find it seriously incomplete. I will argue that even if her claim that compensation is due victims of social injustice is correct (as I think it is), it is questionable nevertheless whether preferential hiring is an acceptable method of distributing such compensation. This is so, even if, as Thomson argues, compensatory claims override the right of the white male applicant to equal consideration from the appointing officer. For implementation of preferential hiring policies may involve claims, perhaps even claims of right, other than the above right of the white male applicant. In the case of the claims I have in mind, the best that can be said is that where preferential hiring is concerned, they are arbitrarily ignored. If so, and if such claims are themselves warranted, then preferential hiring, while *perhaps* not unjust, is open to far more serious question than Thomson acknowledges.

A familiar objection to special treatment for blacks and women is that, if such a practice is justified, other victims of injustice or misfortune ought to receive special treatment too. While arguing that virtually all women and black persons have been harmed, either directly or indirectly, by discrimination, Thomson acknowledges that in any particular case, a white male may have been victimized to a greater extent than have the blacks or women with which he is competing. However, she denies that other victims of injustice or misfortune ought automatically to have priority over blacks and women where distribution of compensation is concerned. Just as veterans receive preference with respect to employment in the civil service, as payment for the service they have performed for society, so can blacks and women legitimately be given preference in university hiring, in payment of the debt owed them. And just as the former policy can justify hiring a veteran who in fact had an easy time of it over a nonveteran who made great sacrifices for the public good, so too can the latter policy justify hiring a relatively undeprived member of a preferred group over a more disadvantaged member of a nonpreferred group.

But surely if the reason for giving a particular veteran preference is that he performed a service for his country, that same preference must be given to anyone who performed a similar service. Likewise, if the reason for giving preference to a black person or to a woman is that the recipient has been injured due to an unjust practice, then preference must be given to anyone who has been similarly injured. So, it appears, there can be no relevant *group* to which compensation ought to be made, other than that made up of and only of those who have been injured or victimized.[2] Although, as Thomson claims, all blacks and women may be members of that latter group, they deserve compensation *qua* victim and not *qua* black person or woman.

There are at least two possible replies that can be made to this sort of objection. First, it might be agreed that anyone injured in the same way as blacks or women ought to receive compensation. But then, ''same way'' is characterized so narrowly that it applies to no one except blacks and women. While there is nothing logically objectionable about such a reply, it may nevertheless be morally objectionable. For it implies that a nonblack male who has been terribly injured by a social injustice has less of a claim to compensation than a black or woman who has only been minimally injured. And this implication may be morally unacceptable.

A more plausible line of response may involve shifting our attention from compen-

[2]This point also has been argued for recently by J. L. Cowen, ''Inverse Discrimination.'' *Analysis* 33, no. I (1972), 10–12.

sation of individuals to collective compensation of groups.[3] Once this shift is made, it can be acknowledged that as individuals, some white males may have stronger compensatory claims than blacks or women. But as compensation is owed the group, it is group claims that must be weighed, not individual ones. And surely, at the group level, the claims of black persons and women to compensation are among the strongest there are.

Suppose we grant that certain groups, including those specified by Thomson, are owed collective compensation. What should be noted is that the conclusion of concern here — that preferential hiring policies are acceptable instruments for compensating groups — does not directly follow. To derive such a conclusion validly, one would have to provide additional premises specifying the relation between collective compensation to groups and distribution of that compensation to individual members. For it does not follow from the fact that some group members are compensated that the group is compensated. Thus, if through a computer error, every member of the American Philosophical Association was asked to pay additional taxes, then if the government provided compensation for this error, it would not follow that it had compensated the Association. Rather it would have compensated each member *qua* individual. So what is required, where preferential hiring is concerned, are plausible premises showing how the preferential award of jobs to group members counts as collective compensation for the group.

Thomson provides no such additional premises. Moreover, there is good reason to think that if any such premises were provided, they would count against preferential hiring as an instrument of collective compensation. This is because although compensation is owed to the group, preferential hiring policies award compensation to an arbitrarily selected segment of the group; namely, those who have the ability and qualifications to be seriously considered for the jobs available. Surely, it is far more plausible to think that collective compensation ought to be equally available to all group members, or at least to all kinds of group members.[4] The claim that although compensation is owed collectively to a group, only a special sort of group member is eligible to receive it, while perhaps not incoherent, certainly ought to be rejected as arbitrary, at least in the absence of an argument to the contrary.

Accordingly, the proponent of preferential hiring faces the following dilemma. Either compensation is to be made on an individual basis, in which case the fact that one is black or a woman is irrelevant to whether one ought to receive special treatment, or it is made on a group basis, in which case it is far from clear that preferential hiring policies are acceptable compensatory instruments. Until this dilemma is resolved, assuming it can be resolved at all, the compensatory argument for preferential hiring is seriously incomplete at a crucial point.

QUESTIONS

1. What sorts of "collective compensation" could be given to women and blacks as *groups* rather than as individuals?
2. Is some kind of compensation morally due to individual victims of social injustices (regardless of race or sex)? If yes, what social injustices should be compensated for and what forms should such compensation take?

---

[3]Such a position has been defended by Paul Taylor, in his "Reverse Discrimination and Compensatory Justice," *Analysis* 33, no. 4 (1973), 177–182.
[4]Taylor would apparently agree, *ibid.*, 180.

LISA H. NEWTON

BAKKE AND DAVIS: JUSTICE, AMERICAN STYLE

Lisa H. Newton is professor of philosophy at Fairfield University. She has published numerous articles on political philosophy and philosophy of law, including "Reverse Discrimination as Unjustified" and "The Irrelevance of Religion in the Abortion Debate."

In this short essay, which first appeared as the nation awaited the decision of the Supreme Court in the Bakke case, Newton focuses on the quota system employed at the University of California Medical School at Davis. She attacks all preferential treatment programs as unjust for the following reasons (the first set appeals to justice; the second set, to consequences): (1) Those candidates who unjustly "lose out" because they do not belong to the preferred group are expected to make "reparations" for "wrongs" they did not commit; strict justice requires that the merit system be strictly applied. (2) The bad effects of quota systems will far outweigh any "social goods" produced.

The use of the special minority quota or "goal" to achieve a desirable racial mix in certain professions might appear to be an attractive solution to the problem of justice posed by generations of racial discrimination.[1] Ultimately, however, the quota solution fails. It puts an intolerable burden of injustice on a system strained by too much of that in the past, and prolongs the terrible stereotypes of inferiority into the indefinite future. It is a serious error to urge this course on the American people.

The quota system, as employed by the University of California's medical school at Davis or any similar institution, is unjust, for all the same reasons that the discrimination it attempts to reverse is unjust.[2] It diminishes the opportunities of some candidates for a social purpose that has nothing to do with them, to make "reparation" for acts they never committed. And "they" are no homogeneous "majority": as Swedish-Americans, Irish-Americans, Americans of Polish or Jewish or Italian descent, they can claim a past history of the same irrational discrimination, poverty and cultural deprivation that now plagues Blacks and Spanish-speaking individuals. In simple justice, all applicants (except, of course, the minority of WASPs!) should have access to a "track" specially constructed for their group, if any do. And none should. The salvation of every minority in America has been strict justice, the merit system strictly applied; the Davis quota system is nothing but a suspension of justice in favor of the most recent minorities, and is flatly unfair to all the others.

The quota system is generally defended by suggesting that a little bit of injustice is far outweighed by the great social good which will follow from it; the argument envisions a fully integrated society where all discrimination will be abolished. Such a result hardly seems likely. Much more likely, if ethnic quotas are legitimated by the Court in the Bakke Case, all the other ethnic minorities will promptly organize to secure special tracks of their own, including minorities which have never previously organized at all. In these days, the advantage of a medical education is sufficiently attractive to make the effort worthwhile. As elsewhere, grave political penalties will be inflicted on legislatures and institutions that

---

[1]See, for example, *The New York Times* editorial, "Reparation, American Style," June 19, 1977.
[2]See my "Reverse Discrimination as Unjustified," *Ethics* 83:308 (July, 1973).
Reprinted with permission of the author and the publisher from *National Forum (The Phi Kappa Phi Journal)*, vol. LVIII, no. 1 (Winter 1978), pp. 22–23.

attempt to ignore these interest groups. I give Davis, and every other desirable school in the country, one decade from a Supreme Court decision favorable to quotas, to collapse under the sheer administrative weight of the hundreds of special admissions tracks and quotas it will have to maintain.

But the worst effect of the quota system is on the minorities supposedly favored by it. In the past, Blacks were socially stereotyped as less intelligent than whites because disproportionately few Blacks could get into medical school; the stereotype was the result of the very racial discrimination that it attempted to justify. Under any minority quota system, ironically, that stereotype would be tragically reinforced. From the day the Court blesses the two-track system of admissions at Davis, the word is out that Black physicians, or those of Spanish or Asian derivation, are less qualified, just a little less qualified, than their "White-Anglo" counterparts, for they did not have to meet as strict a test for admission to medical school. And that judgment will apply, as the quota applies, on the basis of race alone, for we will have no way of knowing which Blacks, Spanish or Asians were admitted in a medical school's regular competition and which were admitted on the "special minority" track. The opportunity to bury their unfavorable ethnic stereotypes by clean and public success in strictly fair competition, an opportunity that our older ethnic groups seized enthusiastically, will be denied to these "special minorities" for yet another century.

In short, there are no gains, for American society or for groups previously disadvantaged by it, in quota systems that attempt reparation by reverse discrimination. The larger moral question of whether we should set aside strict justice for some larger social gain, does not have to be taken up in a case like this one, where procedural injustice produces only substantive harm for all concerned. Blacks, Hispanic and other minority groups which are presently economically disadvantaged will see real progress when, and only when, the American economy expands to make room for more higher status employment for all groups. The economy is not improved in the least by special tracks and quotas for special groups; on the contrary, it is burdened by the enormous weight of the nonproductive administrative procedure required to implement them. No social purpose will be served, and no justice done, by the establishment of such procedural monsters; we should hope that the Supreme Court will see its way clear to abolishing them once and for all.

QUESTIONS

1. Can you specify criteria for determining that a group had been sufficiently discriminated against in the past to warrant preferential treatment in the present?
2. If there were no affirmative action programs, do you believe that the *merit system would be strictly applied* in all hiring, promotions, etc., in the United States? If not, would "injustice" be rampant in hiring, etc.?

RICHARD WASSERSTROM

A DEFENSE OF PROGRAMS OF PREFERENTIAL TREATMENT

Richard Wasserstrom is professor of philosophy at the University of California at Santa Cruz. His books include *Morality and the Law* (1970) and *Philosophy and Social Issues: Five Studies* (1980). The latter volume includes an essay, "Preferential Treatment," which is a longer, more complete account of his views on the topic discussed here. Wasserstrom's many articles include "The Legal and Philosophical Foundations of the Right to Privacy" and "On Racism and Sexism."

In his limited defense of preferential treatment programs, Wasserstrom attacks two arguments frequently used to support the view that no matter what social goods they produce, preferential treatment programs are unfair or unjust. The two arguments at issue are the following: (1) One cannot consistently *condemn as immoral* past racial and sexual discriminatory quotas and exclusions which worked against blacks and women and *support as morally correct* present racial and sexual classifications which discriminate against white males. (2) Preferential treatment programs are wrong because race or sex are irrelevant when decisions are made about university employment and admissions; the only relevant factor is merit or qualification. Against (1) Wasserstrom argues that no inconsistency is involved in holding both views and gives reasons to show that quotas against blacks and women were pernicious while quotas favoring them are not. Against (2) he brings out a number of practical and theoretical difficulties faced by its proponents.

Many justifications of programs of preferential treatment depend upon the claim that in one respect or another such programs have good consequences or that they are effective means by which to bring about some desirable end, e.g., an integrated, equalitarian society. I mean by "programs of preferential treatment" to refer to programs such as those at issue in the *Bakke* case — programs which set aside a certain number of places (for example, in a law school) as to which members of minority groups (for example, persons who are nonwhite or female) who possess certain minimum qualifications (in terms of grades and test scores) may be preferred for admission to those places over some members of the majority group who possess higher qualifications (in terms of grades and test scores).

Many criticisms of programs of preferential treatment claim that such programs, even if effective, are unjustifiable because they are in some important sense unfair or unjust. In this paper I present a limited defense of such programs by showing that two of the chief arguments offered for the unfairness or injustice of these programs do not work in the way or to the degree supposed by critics of these programs.

The first argument is this. Opponents of preferential treatment programs sometimes assert that proponents of these programs are guilty of intellectual inconsistency, if not racism or sexism. For, as is now readily acknowledged, at times past employers, universities, and many other social institutions did have racial or sexual quotas (when they did not practice overt racial or sexual exclusion), and many of those who were most concerned to bring about the eradication of those racial quotas are now untroubled by the new programs which reinstitute them. And this, it is claimed, is inconsistent. If it was wrong to take race or sex

Reprinted with permission of the author and the publisher from *National Forum (The Phi Kappa Phi Journal)*, vol. LVIII, no. 1 (Winter 1978), pp. 15–18.

into account when blacks and women were the objects of racial and sexual policies and practices of exclusion, then it is wrong to take race or sex into account when the objects of the policies have their race or sex reversed. Simple considerations of intellectual consistency—of what it means to give racism or sexism as a reason for condemning these social policies and practices—require that what was a good reason then is still a good reason now.

The problem with this argument is that despite appearances, there is no inconsistency involved in holding both views. Even if contemporary preferential treatment programs which contain quotas are wrong, they are not wrong for the reasons that made quotas against blacks and women pernicious. The reason why is that the social realities do make an enormous difference. The fundamental evil of programs that discriminated against blacks or women was that these programs were a part of a larger social universe which systematically maintained a network of institutions which unjustifiably concentrated power, authority, and goods in the hands of white male individuals, and which systematically consigned blacks and women to subordinate positions in the society.

Whatever may be wrong with today's affirmative action programs and quota systems, it should be clear that the evil, if any, is just not the same. Racial and sexual minorities do not constitute the dominant social group. Nor is the conception of who is a fully developed member of the moral and social community one of an individual who is either female or black. Quotas which prefer women or blacks do not add to an already relatively overabundant supply of resources and opportunities at the disposal of members of these groups in the way in which the quotas of the past did maintain and augment the overabundant supply of resources and opportunities already available to white males.

The same point can be made in a somewhat different way. Sometimes people say that what was wrong, for example, with the system of racial discrimination in the South was that it took an irrelevant characteristic, namely race, and used it systematically to allocate social benefits and burdens of various sorts. The defect was the irrelevance of the characteristic used—race—for that meant that individuals ended up being treated in a manner that was arbitrary and capricious.

I do not think that was the central flaw at all. Take, for instance, the most hideous of the practices, human slavery. The primary thing that was wrong with the institution was not that the particular individuals who were assigned the place of slaves were assigned there arbitrarily because the assignment was made in virtue of an irrelevant characteristic, their race. Rather, it seems to me that the primary thing that was and is wrong with slavery is the practice itself—the fact of some individuals being able to own other individuals and all that goes with that practice. It would not matter by what criterion individuals were assigned; human slavery would still be wrong. And the same can be said for most if not all of the other discrete practices and institutions which comprised the system of racial discrimination even after human slavery was abolished. The practices were unjustifiable— they were oppressive—and they would have been so no matter how the assignment of victims had been made. What made it worse, still, was that the institutions and the supporting ideology all interlocked to create a system of human oppression whose effects on those living under it were as devastating as they were unjustifiable.

Again, if there is anything wrong with the programs of preferential treatment that have begun to flourish within the past ten years, it should be evident that the social realities in respect to the distribution of resources and opportunities make the difference. Apart from everything else, there is simply no way in which all of these programs taken together could plausibly be viewed as capable of relegating white males to the kind of genuinely oppressive status characteristically bestowed upon women and blacks by the dominant social institutions and ideology.

The second objection is that preferential treatment programs are wrong because they take race or sex into account rather than the only thing that does matter — that is, an individual's qualifications. What all such programs have in common and what makes them all objectionable, so this argument goes, is that they ignore the persons who are more qualified by bestowng a preference on those who are less qualified in virtue of their being either black or female.

There are, I think, a number of things wrong with this objection based on qualifications, and not the least of them is that we do not live in a society in which there is even the serious pretense of a qualification requirement for many jobs of substantial power and authority. Would anyone claim, for example, that the persons who comprise the judiciary are there because they are the most qualified lawyers or the most qualified persons to be judges? Would anyone claim that Henry Ford II is the head of the Ford Motor Company because he is the most qualified person for the job? Part of what is wrong with even talking about qualifications and merit is that the argument derives some of its force from the erroneous notion that we would have a meritocracy were it not for programs of preferential treatment. In fact, the higher one goes in terms of prestige, power and the like, the less qualifications seem ever to be decisive. It is only for certain jobs and certain places that qualifications are used to do more than establish the possession of certain minimum competencies.

But difficulties such as these to one side, there are theoretical difficulties as well which cut much more deeply into the argument about qualifications. To begin with, it is important to see that there is a serious inconsistency present if the person who favors "pure qualifications" does so on the ground that the most qualified ought to be selected because this promotes maximum efficiency. Let us suppose that the argument is that if we have the most qualified performing the relevant tasks we will get those tasks done in the most economical and efficient manner. There is nothing wrong in principle with arguments based upon the good consequences that will flow from maintaining a social practice in a certain way. But it is inconsistent for the opponent of preferential treatment to attach much weight to qualifications on this ground, because it was an analogous appeal to the good consequences that the opponent of preferential treatment thought was wrong in the first place. That is to say, if the chief thing to be said in favor of strict qualifications and preferring the most qualified is that it is the most efficient way of getting things done, then we are right back to an assessment of the different consequences that will flow from different programs, and we are far removed from the considerations of justice or fairness that were thought to weigh so heavily against these programs.

It is important to note, too, that qualifications — at least in the educational context — are often not connected at all closely with any plausible conception of social effectiveness. To admit the most qualified students to law school, for example — given the way qualifications are now determined — is primarily to admit those who have the greatest chance of scoring the highest grades at law school. This says little about efficiency except perhaps that these students are the easiest for the faculty to teach. However, since we know so little about what constitutes being a good, or even successful lawyer, and even less about the correlation between being a very good law student and being a very good lawyer, we can hardly claim very confidently that the legal system will operate most effectively if we admit only the most qualified students to law school.

To be at all decisive, the argument for qualifications must be that those who are the most qualified deserve to receive the benefits (the job, the place in law school, etc.) because they are the most qualified. The introduction of the concept of desert now makes it an objection as to justice or fairness of the sort promised by the original criticism of the programs. But now the problem is that there is no reason to think that there is any strong sense of "desert" in which it is correct that the most qualified deserve anything.

Let us consider more closely one case, that of preferential treatment in respect to admission to college or graduate school. There is a logical gap in the inference from the claim that a person is most qualified to perform a task, e.g., to be a good student, to the conclusion that he or she deserves to be admitted as a student. Of course, those who deserve to be admitted should be admitted. But why do the most qualified deserve anything? There is simply no necessary connection between academic merit (in the sense of being the most qualified) and deserving to be a member of a student body. Suppose, for instance, that there is only one tennis court in the community. Is it clear that the two best tennis players ought to be the ones permitted to use it? Why not those who were there first? Or those who will enjoy playing the most? Or those who are the worst and, therefore, need the greatest opportunity to practice? Or those who have the chance to play least frequently?

We might, of course, have a rule that says that the best tennis players get to use the court before the others. Under such a rule the best players would deserve the court more than the poorer ones. But that is just to push the inquiry back one stage. Is there any reason to think that we ought to have a rule giving good tennis players such a preference? Indeed, the arguments that might be given for or against such a rule are many and varied. And few if any of the arguments that might support the rule would depend upon a connection between ability and desert.

Someone might reply, however, that the most able students deserve to be admitted to the university because all of their earlier schooling was a kind of competition, with university admission being the prize awarded to the winners. They deserve to be admitted because that is what the rule of the competition provides. In addition, it might be argued, it would be unfair now to exclude them in favor of others, given the reasonable expectations they developed about the way in which their industry and performance would be rewarded. Minority-admission programs, which inevitably prefer some who are less qualified over some who are more qualified, all possess this flaw.

There are several problems with this argument. The most substantial of them is that it is an empirically implausible picture of our social world. Most of what are regarded as the decisive characteristics for higher education have a great deal to do with things over which the individual has neither control nor responsibility: such things as home environment, socioeconomic class of parents, and, of course, the quality of the primary and secondary schools attended. Since individuals do not deserve having had any of these things vis-à-vis other individuals, they do not, for the most part, deserve their qualifications. And since they do not deserve their abilities they do not in any strong sense deserve to be admitted because of their abilities.

To be sure, if there has been a rule which connects, say, performance at high school with admission to college, then there is a weak sense in which those who do well at high school deserve, for that reason alone, to be admitted to college. In addition, if persons have built up or relied upon their reasonable expectations concerning performance and admission, they have a claim to be admitted on this ground as well. But it is certainly not obvious that these claims of desert are any stronger or more compelling than the competing claims based upon the needs of or advantages to women or blacks from programs of preferential treatment. And as I have indicated, all rule-based claims of desert are very weak unless and until the rule which creates the claim is itself shown to be a justified one. Unless one has a strong preference for the status quo, and unless one can defend that preference, the practice within a system of allocating places in a certain way does not go very far at all in showing that that is the right or the just way to allocate those places in the future.

A proponent of programs of preferential treatment is not at all committed to the view that qualifications ought to be wholly irrelevant. He or she can agree that, given the existing structure of any institution, there is probably some minimal set of qualifications without which one cannot participate meaningfully within the institution. In addition, it can be granted that the qualifications of those involved will affect the way the institution works and the way it affects others in the society. And the consequences will vary depending upon the particular institution. But all of this only establishes that qualifications, in this sense, are relevant, not that they are decisive. This is wholly consistent with the claim that race or sex should today also be relevant when it comes to matters such as admission to college or law school. And that is all that any preferential treatment program—even one with the kind of quota used in the *Bakke* case—has ever tried to do.

I have not attempted to establish that programs of preferential treatment are right and desirable. There are empirical issues concerning the consequences of these programs that I have not discussed, and certainly not settled. Nor, for that matter, have I considered the argument that justice may permit, if not require, these programs as a way to provide compensation or reparation for injuries suffered in the recent as well as distant past, or as a way to remove benefits that are undeservedly enjoyed by those of the dominant group. What I have tried to do is show that it is wrong to think that programs of preferential treatment are objectionable in the centrally important sense in which many past and present discriminatory features of our society have been and are racist and sexist. The social realities as to power and opportunity do make a fundamental difference. It is also wrong to think that programs of preferential treatment are in any strong sense either unjust or unprincipled. The case for programs of preferential treatment could, therefore, plausibly rest both on the view that such programs are not unfair to white males (except in the weak, rule-dependent sense described above) and on the view that it is unfair to continue the present set of unjust—often racist and sexist—institutions that comprise the social reality. And the case for these programs could rest as well on the proposition that, given the distribution of power and influence in the United States today, such programs may reasonably be viewed as potentially valuable, effective means by which to achieve admirable and significant social ideals of equality and integration.

QUESTIONS

1. Wasserstrom's tennis court analogy has been severely criticized. Examine the analogy. What are its weaknesses? What are its strengths?
2. What criteria should be used in selecting candidates for professional schools?

JUSTICE LEWIS F. POWELL, JR.

OPINION IN *UNIVERSITY OF CALIFORNIA v. BAKKE*

A biographical sketch of Justice Lewis F. Powell, Jr., is found on page 87.

Allen Bakke, a white male, applied for admission to the University of California at Davis Medical School. The school, which had a hard quota preferential treatment admissions policy favoring minority students, had set aside 16 of its 100 places in the first-year class for those students. Admission was denied to Bakke, but it was granted to minority students whose college grade-point averages (GPA) and scores on the Medical College Admission Test (MCAT) were much lower than Bakke's. The trial court ruled that Bakke was a victim of *invidious* racial discrimination, and the Supreme Court of the State of California upheld that decision. The justices of the United States Supreme Court were divided four-to-four on the major issues in the case, with Justice Powell providing the decisive vote. Justice Powell sided with Chief Justice Warren E. Burger, Justice Potter Stewart, Justice William H. Rehnquist, and Justice John Paul Stevens in holding that the admissions program which resulted in Bakke's rejection was unlawful. With them he ruled that Bakke must be admitted to the medical school. But Justice Powell sided with Justice William J. Brennan, Justice Byron R. White, Justice Thurgood Marshall, and Justice Harry A. Blackmun in holding that colleges and universities *can* consider race as a factor in the admissions process.

In this excerpt from Justice Powell's opinion, the Court rejects "quotas" or "goals" drawn on the basis of race or ethnic status and holds that such quotas are not legitimated *simply* by their benign purposes. Justice Powell insists that the meaning of the equal protection clause of the Constitution cannot depend on transitory considerations which change with the ebb and flow of political forces. Justice Powell then proceeds to examine the purported purposes of the special admissions program at Davis to see if the program's racial classification is constitutionally permissible. In its previous rulings the Court had held that in "order to justify the use of a suspect classification a State must show that its purpose or interest is both constitutionally permissible and substantial, and that its use of the classification is 'necessary . . . to the accomplishment' of its purpose or the safeguarding of its interest." Justice Powell maintains that the Davis program is not constitutionally permissible; but he concludes that other admissions programs, such as Harvard's, which take race into account but treat each applicant as an individual in the admissions process, are constitutionally acceptable.

I

Over the past 30 years, this Court has embarked upon the crucial mission of interpreting the Equal Protection Clause with the view of assuring to all persons "the protection of equal laws," in a Nation confronting a legacy of slavery and racial discrimination. Because the landmark decisions in this area arose in response to the continued exclusion of Negroes from the mainstream of American society, they could be characterized as involving discrimination by the "majority" white race against the Negro minority. But they need not be read as depending upon that characterization for their results. It suffices to say that "[o]ver the years, this Court has consistently repudiated '[d]istinctions between citizens solely because of their ancestry' as being 'odious to a free people whose institutions are founded upon the doctrine of equality.'"

Petitioner urges us to adopt for the first time a more restrictive view of the Equal Protection Clause and hold that discrimination against members of the white "majority" cannot be suspect if its purpose can be characterized as "benign." The clock of our liberties, however, cannot be turned back to 1868. It is far too late to argue that the guarantee of equal protection to *all* persons permits the recognition of special wards entitled to a degree of protection greater than that accorded others. "The Fourteenth Amendment is not directed solely against discrimination due to a 'two-class theory'—that is, based upon differences between 'white' and Negro."

Once the artificial line of a "two-class theory" of the Fourteenth Amendment is put aside, the difficulties entailed in varying the level of judicial review according to a perceived "preferred" status of a particular racial or ethnic minority are intractable. The concepts of "majority" and "minority" necessarily reflect temporary arangements and political judgments. . . . [T]he white "majority" itself is composed of various minority groups, most of

United States Supreme Court. 438 U.S. 265 (1978).

which can lay claim to a history of prior discrimination at the hands of the State and private individuals. Not all of these groups can receive preferential treatment and corresponding judicial tolerance of distinctions drawn in terms of race and nationality, for then the only "majority" left would be a new minority of white Anglo-Saxon Protestants. There is no principled basis for deciding which groups would merit "heightened judicial solicitude" and which would not. Courts would be asked to evaluate the extent of the prejudice and consequent harm suffered by various minority groups. Those whose societal injury is thought to exceed some arbitrary level of tolerability then would be entitled to preferential classifications at the expense of individuals belonging to other groups. Those classifications would be free from exacting judicial scrutiny. As these preferences began to have their desired effect, and the consequences of past discrimination were undone, new judicial rankings would be necessary. The kind of variable sociological and political analysis necessary to produce such rankings simply does not lie within the judicial competence — even if they otherwise were politically feasible and socially desirable.

Moreover, there are serious problems of justice connected with the idea of preference itself. First, it may not always be clear that a so-called preference is in fact benign. Courts may be asked to validate burdens imposed upon individual members of a particular group in order to advance the group's general interest. Nothing in the Constitution supports the notion that individuals may be asked to suffer otherwise impermissible burdens in order to enhance the societal standing of their ethnic groups. Second, preferential programs may only reinforce common stereotypes holding that certain groups are unable to achieve success without special protection based on a factor having no relationship to individual worth. Third, there is a measure of inequity in forcing innocent persons in respondent's position to bear the burdens of redressing grievances not of their making.

By hitching the meaning of the Equal Protection Clause to these transitory considerations, we would be holding, as a constitutional principle, that judicial scrutiny of classifications touching on racial and ethnic background may vary with the ebb and flow of political forces. Disparate constitutional tolerance of such classifications well may serve to exacerbate racial and ethnic antagonisms rather than alleviate them. Also, the mutability of a constitutional principle, based upon shifting political and social judgments, undermines the chances for consistent application of the Constitution from one generation to the next, a critical feature of its coherent interpretation. In expounding the Constitution, the Court's role is to discern "principles sufficiently absolute to give them roots throughout the community and continuity over significant periods of time, and to lift them above the level of the pragmatic political judgments of a particular time and place."

If it is the individual who is entitled to judicial protection against classifications based upon his racial or ethnic background because such distinctions impinge upon personal rights, rather than the individual only because of his membership in a particular group, then constitutional standards may be applied consistently. Political judgments regarding the necessity for the particular classification may be weighed in the constitutional balance, but the standard of justification will remain constant. This is as it should be, since those political judgments are the product of rough compromise struck by contending groups within the democratic process. When they touch upon an individual's race or ethnic background, he is entitled to a judicial determination that the burden he is asked to bear on that basis is precisely tailored to serve a compelling governmental interest. The Constitution guarantees that right to every person regardless of his background. . . .

II

We have held that in "order to justify the use of a suspect classification, a State must show that its purpose or interest is both constitutionally permissible and substantial, and that its use of the classification is 'necessary . . . to the accomplishment' of its purpose or the safeguarding of its interest." The special admissions program purports to serve the purposes of: (i) "reducing the historic deficit of traditionally disfavored minorities in medical schools and in the medical profession"; (ii) countering the effects of societal discrimination; (iii) increasing the number of physicians who will practice in communities currently underserved; and (iv) obtaining the educational benefits that flow from an ethnically diverse student body. It is necessary to decide which, if any, of these purposes is substantial enough to support the use of a suspect classification.

A

If petitioner's purpose is to assure within its student body some specified percentage of a particular group merely because of its race or ethnic origin, such a preferential purpose must be rejected not as insubstantial but as facially invalid. Preferring members of any one group for no reason other than race or ethnic origin is discrimination for its own sake. This the Constitution forbids.

B

The State certainly has a legitimate and substantial interest in ameliorating, or eliminating where feasible, the disabling effects of identified discrimination. The line of school desegregation cases, commencing with *Brown v. Board of Education* (1954) attests to the importance of this state goal and the commitment of the judiciary to affirm all lawful means toward its attainment. In the school cases, the States were required by court order to redress the wrongs worked by specific instances of racial discrimination. That goal was far more focused than the remedying of the effects of "societal discrimination," an amorphous concept of injury that may be ageless in its reach into the past.

We have never approved a classification that aids persons perceived as members of relatively victimized groups at the expense of other innocent individuals in the absence of judicial, legislative, or administrative findings of constitutional or statutory violations. After such findings have been made, the governmental interest in preferring members of the injured groups at the expense of others is substantial, since the legal rights of the victims must be vindicated. In such a case, the extent of the injury and the consequent remedy will have been judicially, legislatively, or administratively defined. Also, the remedial action usually remains subject to continuing oversight to assure that it will work the least harm possible to other innocent persons competing for the benefit. Without such findings of constitutional or statutory violations, it cannot be said that the government has any greater interest in helping one individual than in refraining from harming another. Thus, the government has no compelling justification for inflicting such harm.

Petitioner does not purport to have made, and is in no position to make, such findings. Its broad mission is education, not the formulation of any legislative policy or the adjudication of particular claims of illegality. . . . [I]solated segments of our vast governmental structures are not competent to make those decisions, at least in the absence of legislative mandates and legislatively determined criteria. Before relying upon these sorts of findings in establishing a racial classification, a governmental body must have the authority and capability to establish, in the record, that the classification is responsive to identified discrimination. Lacking this capability, petitioner has not carried its burden of justification on this issue.

Hence, the purpose of helping certain groups whom the faculty of the Davis Medical School perceived as victims of "societal discrimination" does not justify a classification that imposes disadvantages upon persons like respondent, who bear no responsibility for whatever harm the beneficiaries of the special admissions program are thought to have suffered.

To hold otherwise would be to convert a remedy heretofore reserved for violations of legal rights into a privilege that all institutions throughout the Nation could grant at their pleasure to whatever groups are perceived as victims of societal discrimination. That is a step we have never approved.

C

Petitioner identifies, as another purpose of its program, improving the delivery of health-care services to communities currently underserved. It may be assumed that in some situations a State's interest in facilitating the health care of its citizens is sufficiently compelling to support the use of a suspect classification. But there is virtually no evidence in the record indicating that petitioner's special admissions program is either needed or geared to promote that goal. The court below addressed this failure of proof:

> "The University concedes it cannot assure that minority doctors who entered under the program, all of whom expressed an 'interest' in practicing in a disadvantaged community, will actually do so. It may be correct to assume that some of them will carry out this intention, and that it is more likely they will practice in minority communities than the average white doctor. Nevertheless, there are more precise and reliable ways to identify applicants who are genuinely interested in the medical problems of minorities than by race. An applicant of whatever race who has demonstrated his concern for disadvantaged minorities in the past and who declares that practice in such a community is his primary professional goal would be more likely to contribute to alleviation of the medical shortage than one who is chosen entirely on the basis of race and disadvantage. In short, there is no empirical data to demonstrate that any one race is more selflessly socially oriented or by contrast that another is more selfishly acquisitive."

Petitioner simply has not carried its burden of demonstrating that it must prefer members of particular ethnic groups over all other individuals in order to promote better health-care delivery to deprived citizens. Indeed, petitioner has not shown that its preferential classification is likely to have any significant effect on the problem.

D

The fourth goal asserted by petitioner is the attainment of a diverse student body. This clearly is a constitutionally permissible goal for an institution of higher education. Academic freedom, though not a specifically enumerated constitutional right, long has been viewed as a special concern of the First Amendment. The freedom of a university to make its own judgments as to education includes the selection of its student body.

Ethnic diversity, however, is only one element in a range of factors a university properly may consider in attaining the goal of a heterogeneous student body. Although a university must have wide descretion in making the sensitive judgments as to who should be admitted, constitutional limitations protecting individual rights may not be disregarded. Respondent urges—and the courts below have held—that petitioner's dual admissions program is a racial classification that impermissibly infringes his rights under the Fourteenth Amendment. As the interest of diversity is compelling in the context of a university's admissions program, the question remains whether the program's racial classification is necessary to promote this interest.

III

A

It may be assumed that the reservation of a specified number of seats in each class for individuals from the preferred ethnic groups would contribute to the attainment of considerable ethnic diversity in the student body. But petitioner's argument that this is the only effective means of serving the interest of diversity is seriously flawed. In a most fundamental sense the argument misconceives the nature of the state interest that would justify consideration of race or ethnic background. It is not an interest in simple ethnic diversity, in which a specified percentage of the student body is in effect guaranteed to be members of selected ethnic groups, with the remaining percentage an undifferentiated aggregation of students. The diversity that furthers a compelling state interest encompasses a far broader array of qualifications and characteristics of which racial or ethnic origin is but a single though important element. Petitioner's special admissions program, focused *solely* on ethnic diversity, would hinder rather than further attainment of genuine diversity.

Nor would the state interest in genuine diversity be served by expanding petitioner's two-track system into a multitrack program with a prescribed number of seats set aside for each identifiable category of applicants. Indeed, it is inconceivable that a university would thus pursue the logic of petitioner's two-track program to the illogical end of insulating each category of applicants with certain desired qualifications from competition with all other applicants.

The experience of other university admissions programs, which take race into account in achieving the educational diversity valued by the First Amendment, demonstrates that the assignment of a fixed number of places to a minority group is not a necessary means toward that end. An illuminating example is found in the Harvard College program:

"In recent years Harvard College has expanded the concept of diversity to include students from disadvantaged economic, racial and ethnic groups. Harvard College now recruits not only Californians or Louisianans but also blacks and Chicanos and other minority students. . . .

"In practice, this new definition of diversity has meant that race has been a factor in some admission decisions. When the Committee on Admissions reviews the large middle group of applicants who are 'admissible' and deemed capable of doing good work in their courses, the race of an applicant may tip the balance in his favor just as geographic origin or a life spent on a farm may tip the balance in other candidates' cases. A farm boy from Idaho can bring something to Harvard College that a Bostonian cannot offer. Similarly, a black student can usually bring something that a white person cannot offer. . . .

"In Harvard college admissions the Committee has not set target-quotas for the number of blacks, or of musicians, football players, physicists or Californians to be admitted in a given year. . . . But that awareness [of the necessity of including more than a token number of black students] does not mean that the Committee sets a minimum number of blacks or of people from west of the Mississippi who are to be admitted. It means only that in choosing among thousands of applicants who are not only 'admissible' academically but have other strong qualities, the Committee, with a number of criteria in mind, pays some attention to distribution among many types and categories of students."

In such an admissions program, race or ethnic background may be deemed a "plus" in a particular applicant's file, yet it does not insulate the individual from comparison with all other candidates for the available seats. The file of a particular black applicant may be examined for his potential contribution to diversity without the factor of race being decisive when compared, for example, with that of an applicant identified as an Italian-American if the latter is thought to exhibit qualities more likely to promote beneficial educational pluralism. Such qualities could include exceptional personal talents, unique work or service experience, leadership potential, maturity, demonstrated compassion, a history of overcoming disadvantage, ability to communicate with the poor, or other qualifications deemed important. In short, an admissions program operated in this way is flexible enough to consider all pertinent elements of diversity in light of the particular qualifications of each applicant, and to place them on the same footing for consideration, although not necessarily according them the same weight. Indeed, the weight attributed to a particular quality may vary from year to year depending upon the "mix" both of the student body and the applicants for the incoming class.

This kind of program treats each applicant as an individual in the admissions process. The applicant who loses out on the last available seat to another candidate receiving a "plus" on the basis of ethnic background will not have been foreclosed from all consideration for that seat simply because he was not the right color or had the wrong surname. It would mean only that his combined qualifications, which may have included similar nonobjective factors, did not outweigh those of the other applicant. His qualifications would have been weighed fairly and competitively, and he would have no basis to complain of unequal treatment under the Fourteenth Amendment.

It has been suggested that an admissions program which considers race only as one factor is simply a subtle and more sophisticated — but no less effective — means of according racial preference than the Davis program. A facial intent to discriminate, however, is evident in petitioner's preference program and not denied in this case. No such facial infirmity exists in an admissions program where race or ethnic background is simply one element — to be weighed fairly against other elements — in the selection process. "A boundary line," as Mr. Justice Frankfurter remarked in another connection, "is none the worse for being narrow." And a court would not assume that a university, professing to employ a facially nondiscriminatory admissions policy, would operate it as a cover for the functional equivalent of a quota system. In short, good faith would be presumed in the absence of a showing to the contrary in the manner permitted by our cases.

B

In summary, it is evident that the Davis special admissions program involves the use of an explicit racial classification never before countenanced by this Court. It tells applicants who are not Negro, Asian, or Chicano that they are totally excluded from a specific percentage of the seats in an entering class. No matter how strong their qualifications, quantitative and extracurricular, including their own potential for contribution to educational diversity, they are never afforded the chance to compete with applicants from the preferred groups for the special admissions seats. At the same time, the preferred applicants have the opportunity to compete for every seat in the class.

The fatal flaw in petitioner's preferential program is its disregard of individual rights as guaranteed by the Fourteenth Amendment. Such rights are not absolute. But when a State's distribution of benefits or imposition of burdens hinges on ancestry or the color of a person's skin or ancestry, that individual is entitled to a demonstration that the challenged classification is necessary to promote a substantial state interest. Petitioner has failed to carry this burden. For this reason, that portion of the California court's judgment holding petitioner's special admissions program invalid under the Fourteenth Amendment must be affirmed.

C

In enjoining petitioner from ever considering the race of any applicant, however, the courts below failed to recognize that the State has a substantial interest that legitimately may be served by a properly devised admissions program involving the competitive consideration of race and ethnic origin. For this reason, so much of the California court's judgment as enjoins petitioner from any consideration of the race of any applicant must be reversed.

QUESTIONS

1. Are there any morally good reasons for having two sets of criteria for judging applicants to institutions of higher learning?

2. It is sometimes claimed that discrimination *against* women and blacks will *not be* eliminated unless policies are adopted which produce "reverse discrimination." (a) Is this claim *factually* correct? What evidence do you have to support your answer? (b) If it is correct, does this provide good grounds for the justification of such policies?

SUGGESTED ADDITIONAL READINGS

BEAUCHAMP, TOM L.: "The Justification of Reverse Discrimination." In William T. Blackstone and Robert Heslep, eds., *Social Justice and Preferential Treatment* (Athens: University of Georgia Press, 1976). Beauchamp offers a utilitarian argument in favor of policies productive of reverse discrimination in hiring. He proffers "factual evidence" to support his claim that such policies are a necessary means to achieve a morally desirable end— the demise of the continued discrimination against women and blacks.

COHEN, MARSHALL, THOMAS NAGEL, and THOMAS SCANLON, eds.: *Equality and Preferential Treatment.* Princeton: Princeton University Press, 1977. This is an excellent collection of articles which, with one exception, originally appeared in different volumes of *Philosophy and Public Affairs.* The authors include Thomas Nagel, George Sher, Ronald Dworkin, Owen M. Fiss, and Alan H. Goldman. The readings also include longer versions of two articles reprinted in this chapter—those of Judith Jarvis Thomson and Robert Simon. Ronald Dworkin's article, which was not originally published in *Philosophy and Public Affairs,* is especially interesting insofar as Dworkin compares and contrasts the issues raised by two important legal decisions—the first dealing with a 1945 admittance policy which denied a black man admittance to the University of Texas Law School, the second with a 1971 admissions policy which worked to keep a white male (DeFunis) out of the University of Washington Law School.

EZORSKY, GERTRUDE: "Hiring Women Faculty." *Philosophy and Public Affairs,* vol. 7, Fall 1977, pp. 82–91. Ezorsky contends that neither departmental advertising for women faculty nor requirements for hiring women according to "availability ratio" are sufficient to remedy sex discrimination in college. She suggests that preferential goals are necessary to remedy the situation.

GROSS, BARRY R., ed.: *Reverse Discrimination.* Buffalo, N.Y.: Prometheus Books, 1977. This anthology includes some well-known articles on the topic, including those of Sidney Hook, Lisa H. Newton, Bernard Boxhill, and Alan H. Goldman. The large collection of articles is organized into three sections, labeled "Facts and Polemics," "The Law," and "Value."

HELD, VIRGINIA: "Reasonable Progress and Self-Respect." *The Monist,* vol. 57, January 1973, pp. 12–27. Held focuses on two questions: How long is it reasonable to expect the victims of past discrimination to wait for a redress of their wrongs? What reasonable rate of progress would not involve a loss of self-respect?

KATZNER, LOUIS: "Is the Favoring of Women and Blacks in Employment and Educational Opportunities Justified?" In Joel Feinberg and Hyman Gross, eds., *Philosophy of Law* (Encino, Calif.: Dickenson, 1975), pp. 291–296. Katzner's argument for the justification of reverse discrimination is based on the claim that the obligation to compensate for past wrongs justifies present policies productive of reverse discrimination.

SHER, GEORGE: "Reverse Discrimination, the Future, and the Past." *Ethics,* vol. 90, October 1979, pp. 81–87. Sher analyzes and criticizes some of the "forward-looking arguments" made to support preferential treatment programs.

THALBERG, IRVING: "Justification of Institutional Racism." *Philosophical Forum* (Boston), vol. 3, Winter 1972, pp. 243–264. Thalberg criticizes the arguments of those who oppose the kinds of changes which, on his view, are necessary to equalize the economic and political status of blacks.

SEXUAL MORALITY

6

Individuals are described as having "loose morals" when their *sexual* behavior is out of line with what is considered morally appropriate. But assessments of what is morally appropriate sexual behavior vary enormously. Conventionalists consider sex morally appropriate only within the bounds of marriage. Some conventionalists even insist that there are substantial moral restrictions on sex *within marriage;* they are committed to the principle that sexual activity may not take place in a way that cuts off the possibility of procreation. More liberal thinkers espouse various degrees of permissiveness. Some would allow a full and open promiscuity; some would not. Some would allow homosexual behavior; some would not. In this chapter, various views on the topic of sexual morality are investigated.

CONVENTIONAL SEXUAL MORALITY

According to conventional sexual morality, sex is morally legitimate only within the bounds of marriage; nonmarital sex is immoral. The category of *nonmarital sex* applies to any sexual relation other than that between marriage partners. Thus it includes sexual relations between single people as well as adulterous sexual relations. Both religious and nonreligious arguments are advanced in support of conventional sexual morality, but our concern here is with the nonreligious arguments that are advanced in its defense.

One common defense of the traditional convention that sex is permissible only within the bounds of marriage is based on considerations of *social utility.* It takes the following form: A stable family life is absolutely essential for the proper raising of children and the consequent welfare of society as a whole. But the limitation of sex to marriage is a necessary condition of forming and maintaining stable family units. The availability of sex within marriage will reinforce the loving relationship between husband and wife, the *exclusive* availability of sex within marriage will lead most people to get married and to stay married, and the unavailability of extramarital sex will keep the marriage strong. Therefore, the convention that sex is permissible only within the bounds of marriage is solidly based on considerations of social utility.

This argument is attacked in many ways. Sometimes it is argued that stable family units are not really so essential. More commonly, it is argued that the availability of nonmarital sex does not really undercut family life. Whereas adultery might very well undermine a marital relationship, it is argued, premarital sex often prepares one for marriage. At any rate, it is pointed out, people continue to marry even after they have had somewhat free access to sexual relations.

Another prominent defense of conventional sexual morality is intimately bound up with *natural law theory,* an approach to ethics that is historically associated with the medieval philosopher and theologian Thomas Aquinas (1225–1274). The fundamental principle of natural law theory may be expressed in rather rough form as follows: Actions are morally appropriate insofar as they accord with our nature and end as human beings and morally inappropriate insofar as they fail to accord with our nature and end as human beings. With regard to sexual morality, Aquinas argues as follows:

> . . . the emission of semen ought to be so ordered that it will result in both the production of the proper offspring and in the upbringing of this offspring.

It is evident from this that every emission of semen, in such a way that generation cannot follow, is contrary to the good for man. And if this be done deliberately, it must be a sin. Now, I am speaking of a way from which, *in itself,* generation could not result; such would be any emission of semen apart from the natural union of male and female. For which reason, sins of this type are called *contrary to nature.* . . .

Likewise, it must also be contrary to the good for man if the semen be emitted under conditions such that generation could result but the proper upbringing would be prevented. . . .

Now, it is abundantly evident that the female in the human species is not at all able to take care of the upbringing of offspring by herself, since the needs of human life demand many things which cannot be provided by one person alone. Therefore, it is appropriate to human nature that a man remain together with a woman after the generative act, and not leave her immediately to have such relations with another woman, as is the practice with fornicators. . . .

Now, we call this society *matrimony.* Therefore, matrimony is natural for man, and promiscuous performance of the sexual act, outside matrimony, is contrary to man's good. For this reason, it must be a sin.[1]

According to Aquinas, procreation is the natural purpose or end of sexual activity. Accordingly, sexual activity is morally legitimate only when it accords with this fundamental aspect of human nature. Since sex is for the purpose of procreation, and since the proper upbringing of children can occur only within the framework of marriage, nonmarital sex violates the natural law; it is thereby immoral. In this way, then, Aquinas constructs a defense of conventional sexual morality.

Notice, however, that Aquinas is also committed to substantial restrictions on marital sex itself. Since procreation is the natural purpose or end of sexual activity, he contends, any sexual act that cuts off the possibility of procreation is "contrary to nature." It follows that such practices as oral intercourse, anal intercourse, "mutual masturbation," and the use of artificial birth control are illicit, even within marriage. Of course, Aquinas also condemns masturbation and homosexual intercourse as "contrary to nature," but the immorality of these practices can also be understood, on his view, as following from his rejection of nonmarital sex.

One common criticism of Aquinas's point of view on sexual morality centers on his insistence that sexual activity must not frustrate its natural purpose — procreation. Granted, it is said, procreation is in a biological sense the "natural" purpose of sex. Still, the argument goes, it is not clear that sexual activity cannot legitimately serve other important human purposes. Why cannot sex legitimately function as a means for the expression of love? Why, for that matter, cannot sex legitimately function simply as a source of intense (recreational) pleasure?

In contemporary times, Aquinas's point of view on sexual morality is continually reaffirmed in the formal teaching of the Roman Catholic Church. In the 1968 papal encyclical *Humanae Vitae,* artificial birth control is once again identified as immoral, a violation of the natural law: "Each and every marriage act must remain open to the transmission of life."[2] In a more recent Vatican document, reprinted in this chapter, the natural law framework of Aquinas is equally apparent: "The deliberate use of the sexual faculties outside of normal conjugal relations essentially contradicts its finality." "Homosexual acts are disordered by their very nature." "Masturbation is an intrinsically and seriously disordered act."

[1]Thomas Aquinas, *On the Truth of the Catholic Faith,* Book Three, "Providence," Part II, trans. Vernon J. Bourke (New York: Doubleday, 1956).
[2]*Humanae Vitae* (1968), section 11. This encyclical is widely reprinted. See, for example, Robert Baker and Frederick Elliston, eds., *Philosophy and Sex* (Buffalo, N.Y.: Prometheus Books, 1975), pp. 131–149.

THE EXTREME LIBERAL VIEW

In vivid contrast to conventional sexual morality is an approach to sexual morality that might be identified as the *extreme liberal* view. The extreme liberal rejects as unfounded the conventionalist claim that nonmarital sex is immoral. Also rejected is the related claim (of some conventionalists) that sex is immoral if it cuts off the possibility of procreation. Nor is the extreme liberal willing to accept the claim (defended by some nonconventionalists) that *sex without love* is immoral. It is typical of the extreme liberal to insist that sexual activity is simply one type of human activity, subject to moral appraisal in the same way that any other human activity is subject to moral appraisal, by reference to relevant general moral rules or principles. Accordingly, it is argued, the way to construct a correct account of sexual morality is simply to work out whatever implications well-established general moral rules or principles have in the area of sexual behavior.

In this vein, since it is widely acknowledged that the infliction of personal harm is morally objectionable, *some* sexual activity may be identified as immoral simply because it involves one person inflicting harm on another. The seduction of a minor who does not even know "what it's all about," for example, is morally objectionable on the grounds that the minor will almost inevitably be psychologically harmed. Rape, of course, is a moral outrage, in no small part because it typically involves the infliction of both physical and psychological harm. Its immorality, however, can also be established by reference to another widely acknowledged general moral principle, roughly the moral principle that persons ought not to "use" other persons.

Since the domain of sexual interaction seems to offer ample opportunity for the "using" of another person, the concept of using is worthy of special attention in this context. We are concerned, of course, only with that sense of the word "using" according to which using is plausibly thought to be morally objectionable. On one possible construal, a person is used (sexually) if the requirement of *voluntary informed consent* (to sexual interaction) is not fulfilled. In rape, a person is used because the person's consent is entirely bypassed. Children, it can be argued, are *inescapably used* since, even if they "consent" to sexual interaction, they are incapable of *informed* consent. Sometimes a person is used through deception: "I told her that I loved her and would like to marry her." In such a case, consent to sexual intercourse is voluntary (freely given) but not truly *informed.* False information has been advanced; consent has been given under false pretenses; a person has been manipulated through deception. A person can also be used if consent, however informed, is *coerced* (not "freely" given, not fully voluntary): "I told him that if he refused to have sexual intercourse with me, I would tell his parents that he smokes marijuana." Through coercion, one person bends another to his or her own sexual will.

Is nonmarital sex immoral? Is sex that cuts off the possibility of procreation immoral? Is sex without love immoral? According to the extreme liberal, *no* sexual activity is immoral unless some well-established general moral rule or principle is transgressed. Does one's sexual activity involve the production of personal harm to another? Does it involve the using of another? Does it involve promise-breaking or deception, two other commonly recognized grounds of moral condemnation?[3] If the answer to these questions is no, the extreme liberal maintains, then the sexual activity in question is perfectly acceptable from a moral point of view.

According to the extreme liberal, then, we must conclude that nonmarital sex is, in many cases, morally acceptable. There may be present between sexual partners some degree of mutual affection or love, or there may be present merely a mutual desire to

---

[3]Though deception plays a role in the account of using suggested above, it may also be considered an independent ground of moral condemnation.

attain sexual satisfaction. The sexual interaction may be heterosexual or homosexual. Perhaps there is no interaction at all; the sexual activity may be masturbation. But what about the morality of adultery, an especially noteworthy type of nonmarital sex? As the marriage bond is usually understood, the extreme liberal might respond, there is present in cases of adultery a distinctive ground of moral condemnation. If marriage involves a pledge of sexual exclusivity, as is typically the case, then adulterous behavior seems to involve a serious breaking of trust. However, the extreme liberal would insist, if marriage partners have entered upon a so-called open marriage, where there has been no pledge of sexual exclusivity, then this special ground of moral condemnation evaporates.

In one of this chapter's readings, Raymond A. Belliotti advances and defends an analysis of sexual morality that clearly reflects an extreme liberal point of view. He emphasizes the contractual nature of sexual interaction and maintains that sexual interaction is morally objectionable if and only if it involves (1) deception, (2) promise-breaking, or (3) exploitation. If the extreme liberal approach to sexual morality is correct, however, it is nevertheless important to recognize (as Belliotti explicitly does) that a particular sexual involvement may very well be morally acceptable and yet unwise or imprudent, i.e., not in a person's best long-term interests. An individual, for example, might very well decide to steer clear of casual sex, not because it is immoral but because of a personal assessment that it is not productive of personal happiness.

THE SEX WITH LOVE APPROACH
There is one additional point of view on sexual morality that is sufficiently common to warrant explicit recognition. One may, after all, find conventional sexual morality unwarranted and yet be inclined to stop short of granting moral approval to the "promiscuity" that is found morally acceptable on the extreme liberal view. This intermediate point of view can be identified as the *sex with love* approach. Defenders of this approach typically insist that sex without love reduces a humanly significant activity to a merely mechanical performance, which in turn leads to the disintegration (fragmentation) of the human personality. They differ among themselves, however, as to whether the love necessary to warrant a sexual relationship must be an *exclusive* love or whether it may be a *nonexclusive* love. Those who argue that it must be exclusive nevertheless grant that *successive* sexual liaisons are not objectionable. Those who argue that the love may be nonexclusive necessarily presume that a person is capable of simultaneously loving several persons. On their view, even *simultaneous* love affairs are not objectionable. Whether exclusive or nonexclusive love is taken to be the relevant standard, proponents of the sex with love approach usually argue that their view allows for sexual freedom in a way that avoids the alleged dehumanizing effects of mere promiscuity. Where sex and love remain united, it is argued, there is no danger of dehumanization and psychological disintegration. The extreme liberal might respond: If psychological disintegration is a justifiable fear, which can be doubted, such a consideration shows not that sex without love is immoral but only that it is imprudent.

HOMOSEXUALITY, MORALITY, AND THE LAW
Is homosexual behavior immoral? While the advocate of conventional sexual morality vigorously condemns it, the extreme liberal typically maintains that homosexual behavior is no more immoral in itself than heterosexual behavior. There are, however, a substantial number of people who reject conventional sexual morality but nevertheless remain morally opposed to homosexual behavior. Are such people correct in thinking that homosexual

behavior is morally problematic in a way that heterosexual behavior is not? A homosexual, in the most generic sense, is a person (male or female) whose dominant sexual preference is for a person of the same sex. In common parlance, however, the term "homosexual" is often taken to designate a male, whereas the term "lesbian" is used to designate a female. It is apparently true that male homosexual behavior occasions a higher degree of societal indignation than female homosexual behavior, but it is implausible to believe that there is any morally relevant difference between the two.

There is no lack of invective against the homosexual and against homosexual behavior. For example, the following comments are often made: (1) "Homosexual behavior is repulsive and highly offensive." (2) "Homosexuality as a way of life is totally given over to promiscuity and is little susceptible of enduring human relationships." (3) "Homosexuals make the streets unsafe for our children." (4) "Homosexuality is a perversion, a sin against nature." (5) "If homosexual behavior is tolerated, the stability of family life will be threatened and the social fabric will be undermined." It is important to assess the extent to which such claims support the view that homosexual behavior is morally objectionable. With regard to (1), it may in fact be true that many people find homosexual behavior repulsive and offensive, but it is also true that many people find eating liver repulsive and offensive, and no one thinks that this fact establishes the conclusion that eating liver is morally objectionable. With regard to (2), it may be true that homosexuality is typically a promiscuous way of life, but it can be argued that society's attitude toward homosexuality is responsible for making stable homosexual relationships impossible. With regard to (3), it may be true that *some* homosexuals prey upon children, and surely this is morally reprehensible, but still we find ourselves left with the more typical case in which homosexual relations take place between consenting adults.

Arguments (4) and (5), in contrast to the other three, correlate with arguments already identified in our earlier discussion of conventional sexual morality. The "unnaturalness argument" (4), of course, is typically applied not only against homosexual behavior but also against other "perversions," such as masturbation, oral-genital sex practices, etc. In one of this chapter's selections, Burton M. Leiser critically analyzes and rejects the "unnaturalness argument" as it applies to homosexual behavior. Argument (5) is reminiscent of the argument that conventional sexual morality can be firmly based on considerations of *social utility*. Defenders of (5), however, need not be committed to a full-scale rejection of nonmarital sex. Some moral opposition to homosexual behavior derives, it is clear, from those who explicitly reject conventional sexual morality. Whereas nonmarital *heterosexual* behavior does not pose a serious threat to social well-being, they argue, homosexual behavior does pose a serious threat.

One of the central goals of the "gay liberation" movement is to achieve the decriminalization of homosexual behavior *between consenting adults in private*. Presently, however, homosexual behavior (even between consenting adults in private) remains a criminal offense in a majority of the states. These states have statutes that are often referred to as sodomy statutes. In the law, "sodomy" is roughly synonymous with "unnatural sex practices" or "crimes against nature." Accordingly, sodomy statutes typically prohibit both oral and anal intercourse, as well as other "crimes against nature," such as bestiality, i.e., sexual intercourse with animals. Though sodomy statutes apply to heterosexuals as well as homosexuals, they are usually enforced only against (male) homosexuals. The constitutionality of sodomy statutes is at issue in a court case presented in this chapter, *Doe v. Commonwealth's Attorney for City of Richmond* (1975). In addition to constitutional questions, sodomy statutes also raise important questions about the wisdom and the ethical justification of laws that criminalize sexual conduct *between consenting adults in private*. For one thing, such laws seem, at least in part, to be designed to "enforce" conventional sexual morality. This is a dimension, however, that is more fully discussed in conjunction with the topic of pornography in Chapter 7.

Thomas A. Mappes

VATICAN DECLARATION ON SOME QUESTIONS OF SEXUAL ETHICS

The title of this document is sometimes translated from the Latin as "Declaration on Certain Questions Concerning Sexual Ethics." The document itself was issued by the Sacred Congregation for the Doctrine of the Faith. It was approved by Pope Paul VI and first released for publication on January 15, 1976.

In this declaration, traditional Roman Catholic teaching is explicitly reaffirmed with regard to certain matters of sexual ethics. Both religious arguments (appeals to revealed truth) and philosophical arguments are advanced. (The philosophical arguments are developed within the framework of a natural law theory of ethics.) According to the document, there is an objective and unchanging moral order. Moral principles (including the principles of sexual morality) "have their origin in human nature itself." Accordingly, these principles may be known in two complementary ways: (1) through reason alone, via rational reflection on human nature, or (2) through divine revelation. After briefly explicating the natural law foundation of the traditional view that exercise of the sexual function is appropriate only within the marriage relationship, the document proceeds to reaffirm the immorality of premarital sex, homosexual behavior, and masturbation.

INTRODUCTION

Importance of Sexuality

1. The human person, according to the scientific disciplines of our day, is so deeply influenced by his sexuality that this latter must be regarded as one of the basic factors shaping human life. The person's sex is the source of the biological, psychological and spiritual characteristics which make the person male or female, and thus are extremely important and influential in the maturation and socialization of the individual. It is easy to understand, therefore, why matters pertaining to sex are frequently and openly discussed in books, periodicals, newspapers and other communications media.

Meanwhile, moral corruption is on the increase. One of the most serious signs of this is the boundless exaltation of sex. In addition, with the help of the mass media and the various forms of entertainment, sex has even invaded the field of education and infected the public mind.

Reprinted with permission from *The Pope Speaks,* vol. 21, no. 1 (1976), pp. 60–68. Copyright © Publications Office, United States Catholic Conference, Washington, D.C.

In this situation, some educators, teachers and moralists have been able to contribute to a better understanding and vital integration of the special values and qualities proper to each sex. Others, however, have defended views and ways of acting which are in conflict with the true moral requirements of man, and have even opened the door to a licentious hedonism.

The result is that, within a few years' time, teachings, moral norms and habits of life hitherto faithfully preserved have been called into doubt, even by Christians. Many today are asking what they are to regard as true when so many current views are at odds with what they learned from the Church.

Occasion for This Declaration

2. In the face of this intellectual confusion and moral corruption the Church cannot stand by and do nothing. The issue here is too important in the life both of the individual and of contemporary society.[1]

Bishops see each day the ever increasing difficulties of the faithful in acquiring sound moral teaching, especially in sexual matters, and of pastors in effectively explaining that teaching. The bishops know it is their pastoral duty to come to the aid of the faithful in such a serious matter. Indeed, some outstanding documents have been published on the subject by some bishops and some episcopal conferences. But, since erroneous views and the deviations they produce continue to be broadcast everywhere, the Sacred Congregation for the Doctrine of the Faith in accordance with its role in the universal Church[2] and by mandate of the Supreme Pontiff, has thought it necessary to issue this Declaration.

I. GENERAL CONSIDERATIONS

The Sources of Moral Knowledge

3. The men of our day are increasingly persuaded that their dignity and calling as human beings requires them to use their minds to discover the values and powers inherent in their nature, to develop these without ceasing and to translate them into action, so that they may make daily greater progress.

When it comes to judgments on moral matters, however, man may not proceed simply as he thinks fit. "Deep within, man detects the law of conscience — a law which is not self-imposed but which holds him to obedience. . . . For man has in his heart a law written by God. To obey it is the very dignity of man; according to it he will be judged."[3]

To us Christians, moreover, God has revealed his plan of salvation and has given us Christ, the Savior and sanctifier, as the supreme and immutable norm of life through his teaching and example. Christ himself has said: "I am the light of the world. No follower of mine shall ever walk in darkness; no, he shall possess the light of life."[4]

The authentic dignity of man cannot be promoted, therefore, except through adherence to the order which is essential to his nature. There is no denying, of course, that in the history of civilization many of the concrete conditions and relationships of human life have changed and will change again in the future but every moral evolution and every manner of life must respect the limits set by the immutable principles which are grounded in the constitutive elements and essential relations proper to the human person. These elements and relations are not subject to historical contingency.

[1] See Vatican II, *Pastoral Constitution on the Church in the World of Today,* no. 47: *Acta Apostolicae Sedis* 58 (1966) 1067 [*The Pope Speaks* XI, 289–290].
[2] See the Apostolic Constitution *Regimini Ecclesiae universae* (August 15, 1967), no. 29: *AAS* 59 (1967) 897 [*TPS* XII, 401–402].
[3] *Pastoral Constitution on the Church in the World of Today,* no. 16: *AAS* 58 (1966) 1037 [*TPS* XI, 268].
[4] *Jn* 8, 12.

The basic principles in question can be grasped by man's reason. They are contained in "the divine law—eternal, objective and universal—whereby God orders, directs and governs the entire universe and all the ways of the human community by a plan conceived in wisdom and love. God has made man a participant in this law, with the result that, under the gentle disposition of divine Providence, he can come to perceive ever more fully the truth that is unchanging."[5] This divine law is something we can know.

The Principles of Morality Are Perennial

4. Wrongly, therefore, do many today deny that either human nature or revealed law furnishes any absolute and changeless norm for particular actions except the general law of love and respect for human dignity. To justify this position, they argue that both the so-called norms of the natural law and the precepts of Sacred Scripture are simply products of a particular human culture and its expressions at a certain point in history.

But divine revelation and, in its own order, natural human wisdom show us genuine exigencies of human nature and, as a direct and necessary consequence, immutable laws which are grounded in the constitutive elements of human nature and show themselves the same in all rational beings.

Furthermore, the Church was established by Christ to be "the pillar and bulwark of truth."[6] With the help of the Holy Spirit she keeps a sleepless watch over the truths of morality and transmits them without falsification. She provides the authentic interpretation not only of the revealed positive law but also of "those principles of the moral order which have their origin in human nature itself"[7] and which relate to man's full development and sanctification. Throughout her history the Church has constantly maintained that certain precepts of the natural law bind immutably and without qualification, and that the violation of them contradicts the spirit and teaching of the Gospel.

The Fundamental Principles of Sexual Morality

5. Since sexual morality has to do wth values which are basic to human and Christian life, the general doctrine we have been presenting applies to it. In this area there are principles and norms which the Church has always unhesitatingly transmitted as part of her teaching, however opposed they might be to the mentality and ways of the world. These principles and norms have their origin, not in a particular culture, but in knowledge of the divine law and human nature. Consequently, it is impossible for them to lose their binding force or to be called into doubt on the grounds of cultural change.

These principles guided Vatican Council II when it provided advice and directives for the establishment of the kind of social life in which the equal dignity of man and woman will be respected, even while the differences between them also are preserved.[8]

In speaking of the sexual nature of the human being and of the human generative powers, the Council observes that these are "remarkably superior to those found in lower grades of life."[9] Then it deals in detail with the principles and norms which apply to human

---

[5] *Declaration on Religious Freedom,* no. 3: *AAS* 58 (1966) 931 [*TPS* XI, 86].

[6] *1 Tm* 3, 15.

[7] *Declaration on Religious Freedom,* no. 14: *AAS* 58 (1966) 940 [*TPS* XI, 93]. See also Pius XI, Encyclical *Casti Connubii* (December 31, 1930): *AAS* 22 (1930) 579–580; Pius XII, Address of November 2, 1954 *AAS* 46 (1954) 671–672 [*TPS* I, 380–381]; John XXIII, Encyclical *Mater et Magistra* (May 25, 1961), no. 239: *AAS* 53 (1961) 457 [*TPS* VII, 388]; Paul VI, Encyclical *Humanae Vitae* (July 25, 1968), no. 4: *AAS* 60 (1968) 483 [*TPS* XIII, 331–332].

[8] See Vatican II, *Declaration on Christian Education,* nos. 1 and 8: *AAS* 58 (1966) 729–730, 734–736 [*TPS* XI, 201–202, 206–207]; *Pastoral Constitution on the Church in the World of Today,* nos. 29, 60, 67: *AAS* 58 (1966) 1048–1049, 1080–1081, 1088–1089 [*TPS* XI, 276–277, 299–300, 304–305].

[9] *Pastoral Constitution on the Church in the World of Today,* no. 51: *AAS* 58 (1966) 1072 [*TPS* XI, 293].

sexuality in the married state and are based on the finality of the function proper to marriage.

In this context the Council asserts that the moral goodness of the actions proper to married life, when ordered as man's true dignity requires, "does not depend only on a sincere intention and the evaluating of motives, but must be judged by objective standards. These are drawn from the nature of the human person and of his acts, and have regard for the whole meaning of mutual self-giving and human procreation in the context of true love."[10]

These last words are a brief summation of the Council's teaching (previously set forth at length in the same document[11]) on the finality of the sexual act and on the chief norm governing its morality. It is respect for this finality which guarantees the moral goodness of the act.

The same principle, which the Church derives from divine revelation and from her authentic interpretation of the natural law, is also the source of her traditional teaching that the exercise of the sexual function has its true meaning and is morally good only in legitimate marriage.[12]

Limits of this Declaration

6. It is not the intention of this declaration to treat all abuses of the sexual powers nor to deal with all that is involved in the practice of chastity but rather to recall the Church's norms on certain specific points, since there is a crying need of opposing certain serious errors and deviant forms of behavior.

II. SPECIFIC APPLICATIONS

Premarital Relations

7. Many individuals at the present time are claiming the right to sexual union before marriage, at least when there is a firm intention of marrying and when a love which both partners think of as already conjugal demands this further step which seems to them connatural. They consider this further step justified especially when external circumstances prevent the formal entry into marriage or when intimate union seems necessary if love is to be kept alive.

This view is opposed to the Christian teaching that any human genital act whatsoever may be placed only within the framework of marriage. For, however firm the intention of those who pledge themselves to each other in such premature unions, these unions cannot guarantee the sincerity and fidelity of the relationship between man and woman, and, above all, cannot protect the relationship against the changeableness of desire and determination.

Yet, Christ the Lord willed that the union be a stable one and he restored it to its original condition as founded in the difference between the sexes. "Have you not read that at the beginning the Creator made them male and female and declared, 'For this reason a man shall leave his father and mother and cling to his wife and the two shall become as one'? Thus they are no longer two but one flesh. Therefore, let no man separate what God has joined."[13]

[10] *Loc. cit.*; see also no. 49: *AAS* 58 (1966) 1069–1070 [*TPS* XI, 291–292].
[11] See *Pastoral Constitution on the Church in the World of Today*, nos. 49–50: *AAS* 58 (1966) 1069–1072 [*TPS* XI, 291–293].
[12] The present Declaration does not review all the moral norms for the use of sex, since they have already been set forth in the encyclicals *Casti Connubii* and *Humanae Vitae*.
[13] *Mt* 19, 4–6.

St. Paul is even more explicit when he teaches that if unmarried people or widows cannot be continent, they have no alternative but to enter into a stable marital union: "It is better to marry than to be on fire."[14] For, through marriage the love of the spouses is taken up into the irrevocable love of Christ for his Church,[15] whereas unchaste bodily union[16] defiles the temple of the Holy Spirit which the Christian has become. Fleshly union is illicit, therefore, unless a permanent community of life has been established between man and woman.

Such has always been the Church's understanding of and teaching on the exercise of the sexual function.[17] She finds, moreover, that natural human wisdom and the lessons of history are in profound agreement with her.

Experience teaches that if sexual union is truly to satisfy the requirements of its own finality and of human dignity, love must be safeguarded by the stability marriage gives. These requirements necessitate a contract which is sanctioned and protected by society; the contract gives rise to a new state of life and is of exceptional importance for the exclusive union of man and woman as well as for the good of their family and the whole of human society. Premarital relations, on the other hand, most often exclude any prospect of children. Such love claims in vain to be conjugal since it cannot, as it certainly should, grow into a maternal and paternal love; or, if the pair do become parents, it will be to the detriment of the children, who are deprived of a stable environment in which they can grow up in a proper fashion and find the way and means of entering into the larger society of men.

Therefore, the consent of those entering into marriage must be externally manifested, and this in such a way as to render it binding in the eyes of society. The faithful, for their part, must follow the laws of the Church in declaring their marital consent; it is this consent that makes their marriage a sacrament of Christ.

Homosexuality

8. Contrary to the perennial teaching of the Church and the moral sense of the Christian people, some individuals today have, on psychological grounds, begun to judge indulgently or even simply to excuse homosexual relations for certain people.

They make a distinction which has indeed some foundation: between homosexuals whose bent derives from improper education or a failure of sexual maturation or habit or bad example or some similar cause and is only temporary or at least is not incurable; and homosexuals who are permanently such because of some innate drive or a pathological condition which is considered incurable.

The propensity of those in the latter class is — it is argued — so natural that it should be regarded as justifying homosexual relations within a sincere and loving communion of life which is comparable to marriage inasmuch as those involved in it deem it impossible for them to live a solitary life.

Objective Evil of Such Acts

As far as pastoral care is concerned, such homosexuals are certainly to be treated with understanding and encouraged to hope that they can some day overcome their difficulties

---

[14] *1 Cor* 7, 9.

[15] See *Eph* 5, 25–32.

[16] Extramarital intercourse is expressly condemned in *1 Cor* 5, 1; 6, 9; 7, 2; 10, 8; *Eph* 5, 5–7; *1 Tm* 1, 10; *Heb* 13, 4; there are explicit arguments given in *1 Cor* 6, 12–20.

[17] See Innocent IV, Letter *Sub Catholicae professione* (March 6, 1254) (*DS* 835); Pius II, Letter *Cum sicut accepimus* (November 14, 1459) (*DS* 1367); Decrees of the Holy Office on September 24, 1665 (*DS* 2045) and March 2, 1679 (*DS* 2148); Pius XI, Encyclical *Casti Connubii* (December 31, 1930): *AAS* 22 (1930) 538–539.

and their inability to fit into society in a normal fashion. Prudence, too, must be exercised in judging their guilt. However, no pastoral approach may be taken which would consider these individuals morally justified on the grounds that such acts are in accordance with their nature. For, according to the objective moral order homosexual relations are acts deprived of the essential ordination they ought to have.

In Sacred Scripture such acts are condemned as serious deviations and are even considered to be the lamentable effect of rejecting God.[18] This judgment on the part of the divinely inspired Scriptures does not justify us in saying that all who suffer from this anomaly are guilty of personal sin but it does show that homosexual acts are disordered by their very nature and can never be approved.

Masturbation

9. Frequently today we find doubt or open rejection of the traditional Catholic teaching that masturbation is a serious moral disorder. Psychology and sociology (it is claimed) show that masturbation, especially in adolescents, is a normal phase in the process of sexual maturation and is, therefore, not gravely sinful unless the individual deliberately cultivates a solitary pleasure that is turned in upon itself ("ipsation"). In this last case, the act would be radically opposed to that loving communion between persons of different sexes which (according to some) is the principal goal to be sought in the use of the sexual powers.

This opinion is contrary to the teaching and pastoral practice of the Catholic Church. Whatever be the validity of certain arguments of a biological and philosophical kind which theologians sometimes use, both the magisterium of the Church (following a constant tradition) and the moral sense of the faithful have unhesitatingly asserted that masturbation is an intrinsically and seriously disordered act.[19] The chief reason for this stand is that, whatever the motive, the deliberate use of the sexual faculty outside of normal conjugal relations essentially contradicts its finality. In such an act there is lacking the sexual relationship which the moral order requires, the kind of relationship in which "the whole meaning of mutual self-giving and human procreation" is made concretely real "in the context of true love."[20] Only within such a relationship may the sexual powers be deliberately exercised.

Even if it cannot be established that Sacred Scripture condemns this sin under a specific name, the Church's tradition rightly understands it to be condemned in the New Testament when the latter speaks of "uncleanness" or "unchasteness" or the other vices contrary to chastity and continence.

Sociological research can show the relative frequency of this disorder according to places, types of people and various circumstances which may be taken into account. It thus provides an array of facts. But facts provide no norm for judging the morality of human acts.[21] The frequency of the act here in question is connected with innate human weakness

---

[18]*Rom* 1:24–27: "In consequence, God delivered them up in their lusts to unclean practices; they engaged in the mutual degradation of their bodies, these men who exchanged the truth of God for a lie and worshiped and served the creature rather than the Creator—blessed be he forever, amen! God therefore delivered them to disgraceful passions. Their women exchanged natural intercourse for unnatural, and the men gave up natural intercourse with women and burned with lust for one another. Men did shameful things with men, and thus received in their own persons the penalty for their perversity." See also what St. Paul says of sodomy in *1 Cor* 6, 9; *1 Tm* 1, 10.

[19]See Leo IX, Letter *Ad splendidum nitentes* (1054) (*DS* 687–688); Decree of the Holy Office on March 2, 1679 (*DS* 2149); Pius XII, Addresses of October 8, 1953: *AAS* 45 (1953) 677–678, and May 19, 1956: *AAS* 48 (1956) 472–473.

[20]*Pastoral Constitution on the Church in the World of Today*, no. 51: *AAS* 58 (1966) 1072 [*TPS* XI, 293].

[21]See Paul VI, Apostolic Exhortation *Quinque iam anni* (December 8, 1970): *AAS* 63 (1971) 102 [*TPS* XV, 329]: "If sociological surveys are useful for better discovering the thought patterns of the people of a particular place, the anxieties and needs of those to whom we proclaim the word of God, and also the oppositions made to it by modern reasoning through the widespread notion that outside science there exists no legitimate form of knowledge, still the conclusions drawn from such surveys could not of themselves constitute a determining criterion of truth."

deriving from original sin, but also with the loss of the sense of God, with the moral corruption fostered by the commercialization of vice, with the unbridled license to be found in so many books and forms of public entertainment and with the forgetfulness of modesty, which is the safeguard of chastity.

In dealing with masturbation, modern psychology provides a number of valid and useful insights which enable us to judge more equitably of moral responsibility. They can also help us understand how adolescent immaturity (sometimes prolonged beyond the adolescent years) or a lack of psychological balance or habits can affect behavior, since they may make an action less deliberate and not always a subjectively serious sin. But the lack of serious responsibility should not be generally presumed; if it is, there is simply a failure to recognize man's ability to act in a moral way.

In the pastoral ministry, in order to reach a balanced judgment in individual cases account must be taken of the overall habitual manner in which the person acts, not only in regard to charity and justice, but also in regard to the care with which he observes the precept of chastity in particular. Special heed must be paid to whether he uses the necessary natural and supernatural helps which Christian asceticism recommends, in the light of long experience, for mastering the passions and attaining virtue. . . .

QUESTIONS

1. Is it plausible to maintain that unchanging moral principles "have their origin in human nature itself"? Is it plausible to maintain this especially with regard to principles of sexual morality?
2. Is masturbation immoral?

RAYMOND A. BELLIOTTI

A PHILOSOPHICAL ANALYSIS OF SEXUAL ETHICS

Raymond A. Belliotti is a philosopher who has taught at Virginia Commonwealth University and is presently attending Harvard Law School. Among his published articles are "Machiavelli and Machiavellianism," "Contributing to Famine Relief and Sending Poisoned Food," and "Do Dead Human Beings Have Rights?"

Belliotti advances and defends what he terms a "secular" analysis of sexual ethics; religious considerations are excluded as irrelevant. He contends that sexual interactions have a contractual basis and argues that they are morally objectionable if and only if they involve (1) deception, (2) promise-breaking, or (3) exploitation, i.e., treating another *merely* as a means to one's own ends. Applying his overall analysis to various sexual activities, he reaches the following set of conclusions: (1) Rape is intrinsically immoral. (2) Bestiality, i.e., sexual intercourse with an animal, is intrinsically immoral. (3) Necrophilia, i.e., sexual intercourse with a corpse, is usually but not necessarily immoral. (4) Incest is immoral if it involves a child but otherwise is not necessarily immoral. (5) Promiscuity and adultery are immoral only if they involve deception, promise-breaking, or exploitation.

I shall advance and defend what can be labeled a secular analysis of sexual ethics. As a secular analysis it shall make no appeal to religious considerations; it shall, in fact, consider religious factors irrelevant to the analysis. In doing so it should be obvious that the account will seem unsatisfactory to fervent religious believers.

I

I begin with what I take to be a fundamental ethical maxim: it is morally wrong for someone to treat another merely as a means to his own ends. Immanuel Kant first formulated the maxim in this way,[1] but I think it can be considered uncontroversially true by most, if not all, moral thinkers. We often speak disparagingly of a person who "uses" or "exploits" another. What do we mean by this? It seems that we are suggesting that the former is morally culpable because he has treated the latter in a way that is morally wrong for one human to treat another. The culpable individual has "objectified" his victim; he has treated the other as an object to be manipulated and used, much as we might utilize a tool. One of the worst things that one person can do to another is to recognize the other as something less than human or as something less than the other really is: to recognize the other, not as an end in himself, but rather as an object to be used merely as a means to the user's ends. If we believe, and I think we do, that each person has an intrinsic worth and value which demands that we treat all others as subjects of experience and as being as fully human as ourselves, then we are following the general pattern of Kant's ethical maxim.

Notice that the maxim does not state that we cannot treat others as a means to our ends. It only states that we cannot *merely* treat the other in this way. We often need others to fulfill our goals, but immorality occurs only if we treat them merely as a means to these goals and not as an equal subject of experience.

So in all our human interactions we have a moral obligation to treat others as more than just means to our ends. This obligation becomes even more important when considering sexual interactions since very important feelings, desires, and drives are involved.

The second stage of the argument concerns the nature of sexual interactions. I contend that the nature of these interactions is contractual and involves the important notion of reciprocity. When two people voluntarily consent to interact sexually they create obligations to each other based on their needs and expectations. Every sexual encounter has as its base the needs, desires, and drives of the individuals involved. That we choose to interact sexually is an acknowledgement that none of us is totally self-sufficient. We interact with others in order to fulfill certain desires which we cannot fulfill by ourselves. This suggests that the basis of the sexual encounter is contractual; i.e., it is a voluntary agreement on the part of both parties to satisfy the expectations of the other.

Some might recoil at the coldness of such an analysis. Is the sexual encounter as business-like a contract as the relationship between two corporations or the agreements one makes with his insurance agent? Of course it is not. Very important feelings of intimacy are involved which make the consenting parties emotionally vulnerable. But all this shows is that the sexual contract may well be the most important agreement that one makes from an emotional standpoint; it does not show that the interaction itself is not contractual. The contractual basis of the sexual interaction involves the notion of a voluntary agreement founded on the expectations of fulfillment of reciprocal needs.

The final stage of the argument consists of two acknowledgements: (1) That voluntary contracts are such that the parties are under a moral obligation, other things being equal,

[1]Immanuel Kant, *Foundations of the Metaphysics of Morals,* L. W. Beck, trans. (Indianapolis, Indiana: Library of Liberal Arts Press), p. 87.
Reprinted with permission of the publisher from the *Journal of Social Philosophy,* vol. X, no. 3 (September 1979), pp. 8–11.

to fulfill that which they agreed upon, and (2) that promise-breaking and deception are, other things equal, immoral actions. The acknowledgement of the second makes the recognition of the first redundant, since the non-fulfillment of one's contractual duties is a species of promise-breaking. Ordinarily we feel that promise-breaking and deception are paradigm cases of immoral actions, since they involve violations of moral duties, and often, explicit or implicit lying. If it is true that sexual interactions entail contractual relationships then any violation of that which one has voluntarily consented to perform is morally wrong, since it involves promise-breaking and the non-fulfillment of the moral duty to honor one's voluntary agreements.

It is clear, then, that both parties must perform that which they voluntarily contracted to do for the other, unless the other agrees to the non-performance of the originally agreed upon action. Although sexual contracts are not as formal or explicit as corporation agreements, the rule of thumb should be the concept of reasonable expectation. If a woman smiles at me and agrees to have a drink I cannot reasonably assume, at least at this point, that she has agreed to spend the weekend with me. On the other hand if she did agree to share a room and bed with me for the weekend I could reasonably assume that she had agreed to have sexual intercourse with me. Although all examples are not clearcut, in general, the notion of reasonable expectation should guide us here. If there is any doubt concerning whether or not someone has agreed to perform a certain sexual act with another, I would suggest that the doubting party simply ask the other and make the contract more explicit. In lieu of this, prudence dictates that we be cautious in assuming what the other has offered, and when in doubt assume nothing until a more explicit overture has been made.

The conclusion of the argument is that sex is immoral if and only if it involves deception, promise-breaking, and/or the treatment of the other merely as a means to one's own ends.

II

The results of this analysis can now be applied to various sexual activities.

(1) *Rape* is intrinsically immoral because it involves the involuntary participation of one of the parties. Since the basis of the sexual encounter is contractual it should be clear that any coercion or force renders the interaction immoral; contracts are not validly consummated if one of the parties is compelled to agree by force or fraud. An interesting question concerns whether it is possible for a husband to rape his wife. I tend to think that this is possible. Some contend that the marriage contract allows both parties unrestricted sexual access to the other, and that, therefore, rape cannot occur in a marital situation. Others define rape as a sexual interaction which occurs when one individual forcibly uses another and the parties are not married to each other. But I think of rape as any case of forcibly using another in a sexual encounter without the other's consent. Under this definition it would be possible for a man to rape his wife, and in doing so commit an immoral act.

(2) *Bestiality* is intrinsically immoral because it too involves the involuntary participation of one of the parties. No non-human animal is capable of entering into a valid sexual contract with a human; as such all cases of bestiality can be considered instances of animal rape. A critic might argue that bestiality is only a form of sex with an object since only a non-human animal is involved. Kant, himself, felt that animals could be used merely as a means to the ends of humans.[2] But this is mistaken from a moral point of view. Animals, unlike objects, have interests, desires, and are capable of experiencing pleasure and pain;

[2] *Ibid.*

i.e., they are sentient beings. As sentient beings their interests ought to be taken into account. As it seems clear that the interests of non-human animals are not advanced by being used as sexual objects by humans, it also seems clear that to do so cannot be morally justified. The differences between mere objects, which can be legitimately used merely as means to human ends, and non-human animals, who are sentient beings, are obvious. To use or totally objectify the latter is morally wrong; although probably less wrong than the use or objectification of other human beings.[3]

(3) *Necrophilia* is immoral since it also involves the involuntary participation of one of the parties. The corpse cannot voluntarily enter into a contract with a living human; hence cases of necrophilia can be considered instances of the rape of dead humans. Now it may seem that corpses *are* mere objects; certainly they cannot feel pleasure and pain. But are they mere objects in the sense that rocks, stones, and desks are objects? The corpse was once a sentient being and it may still be the case that even as a corpse it has interests. This may seem absurd at first glance. But we really acknowledge this very fact by honoring death bed promises made to the dying, by taking care when handling and displaying the bodies of the dead, and by being careful not to defame maliciously the reputations of dead people. Don't we feel that there is a difference between being buried with dignity and being hung and mutilated after we die?[4] Wouldn't we prefer the former? And the reason we would involves the fact that no *mere* object is involved, but rather a human corpse.

There are imaginable instances in which necrophilia would not be immoral. Suppose the will of man X contains a clause stipulating that "anyone wishing to use my corpse for sexual purposes between the hours of 7-9 P.M. on Thursdays at the Greenmount Cemetery may do so." As long as X made the stipulation rationally and sincerely[5] my analysis would consider sexual acts performed on the appointed day and time as not immoral; the law, however, might take a dimmer view of this activity.

(4) *Incest* is immoral when it involves a child who cannot be considered capable of entering into a contractual relationship. Children cannot know the ramifications of a sexual interaction with their parent(s); hence they cannot be thought of as fully responsible agents. Any contract, sexual or otherwise, can only be legitimately consummated with fully responsible parties.

Incest would also be immoral if the parties knowingly conceived a child with the likelihood of genetic defect, since this is an act which would contribute to the needless misery of another.

But there are times when incest is not immoral. Suppose a 50 year old father and his 30 year old daughter voluntarily agree, rationally and sincerely, to a sexual interaction. Both parties are fully responsible agents knowing the ramifications of their actions, and employ proper birth control methods to eliminate the possibility of conceiving a defective child, or engage in a sexual act in which no child could possibly be conceived. This, repugnant though it may seem, would not be an immoral act.

(5) *Promiscuity and adultery* are immoral only if they involve promise-breaking, deceit, or exploitation. Promise-breaking and deceit can occur in a number of ways: one party may deceive another concerning his real feelings for the other; he may break prom-

---

[3]This raises the interesting issue of whether other ways that humans treat animals are morally justified. A strong case can be made that eating meat and using animals for clothes are immoral.

[4]This was in fact the reason that Italian partisans thought that subjecting Mussolini to degradation after he was dead was in a sense *harming* Mussolini. They assumed that he still possessed certain interests which could be harmed by the indignities they inflicted upon him.

[5]By "rationally" and "sincerely" I only mean that the individual is not under the influence of hallucinogens and is not joking. The individual must be of sound mind. I do not mean by "rationally" that the individual is making the best decision, all things considered.

ises to his spouse in order that he might be with the other; he may explicitly lie in order to sustain the two relationships. In romantic triangles of this nature, immorality can occur from the actions of any of the parties in relation to the two other parties.

Some would argue that the nature of the marriage contract itself entails that *any* extramarital encounter on the part of either party is immoral (i.e., it involves promise-breaking) since one provision of the marriage contract is sexual exclusivity. But under my analysis the parties to the marriage contract may legitimately amend the contract at any time, and an extramarital sexual encounter need not be immoral as long as both marital partners agree prior to the encounter that it is permissible. If the marriage relationship is construed as a voluntary reciprocal contract the partners are free to amend its provisions insofar as they can both agree on the alterations involved.

III

The religious argument against many of the aforementioned sexual activities is often straightforward:

(A)   If an action is a violation of God's law then it is immoral.
(B)   X breaks the law of God.
    X is an immoral action.

Substitute the acts in question for X and we see the essence of the religious argument against these acts. For the believer a supernatural being, possessing certain qualities, has created us and set down a variety of laws. To transgress these laws is to violate morality, since the ultimate lawgiver has set forth the basis for morality in these laws. All the believer need do is point to the relevant biblical scripture or the relevant source of these laws to show that certain acts are immoral. These acts are seen as *intrinsically* immoral, regardless of whether promise-breaking, deception, or exploitation are involved. Surely these latter factors are viewed as immoral, but even if they do not occur the action in question is still immoral because it violates the law of God. Violating the law of God is considered a sufficient condition for an act to be immoral by the religious believer.

Of course to someone who does not believe in any supernatural being or to one who believes in a supernatural being of a radically different nature from the Christian God, this argument is not convincing. Without a religious conviction premise (A) is vacuous.

Yet it is true that many non-believers share the believer's convictions regarding the immorality of certain of the sexual practices we have considered. Why is this so? I think that an important reason is that many religious convictions about practical moral issues have become imbedded into our considered moral judgments. Because of the influence and historical power of Christianity throughout the ages certain beliefs about the immorality of particular actions became an integral part of our moral education and customs. Hence many nonbelievers still think that adultery, promiscuity, etc. are morally pernicious even though they deny the existence of the Christian God. Under my analysis, however, these actions are not immoral (presupposing no promise-breaking, deception, or exploitation) once belief in the Christian God is abrogated. Once sexual interactions are viewed as being contractual and reciprocal we have a basis for judging their morality independent of any reliance upon the laws of a supernatural being.

IV

The results of my analysis are in certain cases more liberal than conventional moralists (e.g., adultery, promiscuity, necrophilia, and incest are not immoral if certain conditions pertain), and in other cases more conservative (e.g., "teasing" without the intention to fulfill that which the other reasonably can be expected to think was offered is immoral, since it involves the nonfulfillment of that which the other could reasonably be expected to think was agreed upon).

It must be pointed out that to state that a certain act is not immoral does not entail that it is advisable to pursue. I have argued that under certain conditions these acts are not immoral, but I would certainly advise against most, if not all, of these actions. Often these actions still are offensive to our tastes, not in our best long term interests, and may be psychologically harmful. Because our most important feelings and emotions are involved in sexual interactions we must be cautious about engaging in certain acts which may be damaging in the long run. Just as we should be careful in agreeing to *any* voluntary contract involving a reciprocal exchange of goods and services, we should be most careful before agreeing upon what may be our most important kind of contract. The sexual contract is one in which our most valuable intangible commodities are at stake; in fact our self-esteem may well be on the line. And although we may freely enter into certain sexual contracts it is important to know the ramifications and long range effects to our own interests and the interests of others.

The purpose of this essay, then, is not to endorse or encourage certain of the sexual practices mentioned, but rather to show that the basis of our secular aversion to them often cannot be the notion of morality.

QUESTIONS

1. Is Belliotti correct in claiming that sexual interactions are morally objectionable *only if* they involve deception, promise-breaking, or exploitation?
2. What is promiscuity? Is it immoral?
3. Is prostitution immoral?

BURTON M. LEISER

HOMOSEXUALITY AND THE "UNNATURALNESS ARGUMENT"

A biographical sketch of Burton M. Leiser is found on page 100.

Leiser critiques an argument which is often advanced to show the immorality of homosexual behavior: Homosexual behavior is unnatural and therefore immoral. On Leiser's analysis, an adequate "unnaturalness argument" would have to provide the following: (1) a clearly specified sense of "unnatural" according to which homosexual behavior is rightly identified as unnatural; (2) substantiation for thinking that the unnaturalness of homosexual behavior is linked with the production of harm and is thus a ground of moral condemnation. Leiser analyzes four possible senses that proponents of the argument might attribute to "unnatural." Finding that each suggestion fails to satisfy one or both of the conditions necessary to sustain the argument, he concludes that the argument must be rejected.

[The alleged "unnaturalness" of homosexuality] raises the question of the meaning of *nature, natural,* and similar terms. Theologians and other moralists have said that [homosexual acts] violate the "natural law," and that they are therefore immoral and ought to be prohibited by the state.

The word *nature* has a built-in ambiguity that can lead to serious misunderstandings. When something is said to be "natural" or in conformity with "natural law" or the "law of nature," this may mean either (1) that it is in conformity with the descriptive laws of nature, or (2) that it is not artificial, that man has not imposed his will or his devices upon events or conditions as they exist or would have existed without such interference.

1. THE DESCRIPTIVE LAWS OF NATURE

The laws of nature, as these are understood by the scientist, differ from the laws of man. The former are purely descriptive, whereas the latter are prescriptive. When a scientist says that water boils at 212° Fahrenheit or that the volume of a gas varies directly with the heat that is applied to it and inversely with the pressure, he means merely that as a matter of recorded and observable fact, pure water under standard conditions always boils at precisely 212° Fahrenheit and that as a matter of observed fact, the volume of a gas rises as it is heated and falls as pressure is applied to it. These "laws" merely *describe* the manner in which physical substances *actually behave.* They differ from municipal and federal laws in that they *do not prescribe behavior.* Unlike manmade laws, natural laws are not passed by any legislator or group of legislators; they are not proclaimed or announced; they impose no obligation upon anyone or anything; their "violation" entails no penalty, and there is no reward for "following" them or "abiding by" them. When a scientist says that the air in a tire "obeys" the laws of nature that "govern" gases, he does *not* mean that the air, having been informed that it *ought* to behave in a certain way, behaves appropriately under the right conditions. He means, rather, that as a matter of fact, the air in a tire *will* behave like all other gases. In saying that Boyle's law "governs" the behavior of gases, he means merely that gases do, as a matter of fact, behave in accordance with Boyle's law, and that Boyle's law enables one to predict accurately what will happen to a given quantity of a gas as its pressure is raised; he does *not* mean to suggest that some heavenly voice has proclaimed that all gases should henceforth behave in accordance with the terms of Boyle's law and that a ghostly policeman patrols the world, ready to mete out punishments to any gases that "violate" the heavenly decree. In fact, according to the scientist, it does not make sense to speak of a natural law being violated. For if there were a true exception to a so-called law of nature, the exception would require a change in the description of those phenomena, and the "law" would have been shown to be no law at all. The laws of nature are revised as scientists discover new phenomena that require new refinements in their descriptions of the way things actually happen. In this respect they differ fundamentally from human laws, which are revised periodically by legislators who are not so interested in *describing* human behavior as they are in *prescribing* what human behavior *should* be.

2. THE ARTIFICIAL AS A FORM OF THE UNNATURAL

On occasion when we say that something is not natural, we mean that it is a product of human artifice. My typewriter is not a natural object, in this sense, for the substances of which it is composed have been removed from their natural state — the state in which they existed before men came along — and have been transformed by a series of chemical and physical and mechanical processes into other substances. They have been rearranged into a whole that is quite different from anything found in nature. In short, my typewriter is an artificial object. In this sense, the clothing that I wear as I lecture before my students is not natural, for it has been transformed considerably from the state in which it was found in nature; and my wearing of clothing as I lecture before my students is also not natural, in this sense, for in my natural state, before the application of anything artificial, before any human interference with things as they are, I am quite naked. Human laws, being artificial conventions designed to exercise a degree of control over the natural inclinations and propensities of men, may in this sense be considered to be unnatural.

Now when theologians and moralists speak of homosexuality, contraception, abortion, and other forms of human behavior as being unnatural, and say that for that reason such behavior must be considered to be wrong, in what sense are they using the word *unnatural*? Are they saying that homosexual behavior and the use of contraceptives are contrary to the scientific laws of nature, are they saying that they are artificial forms of behavior, or are they using the terms *natural* and *unnatural* in some third sense?

They cannot mean that homosexual behavior (to stick to the subject presently under discussion) violates the laws of nature in the first sense, for, as we have pointed out, in *that* sense it is impossible to violate the laws of nature. Those laws, being merely descriptive of what actually does happen, would have to *include* homosexual behavior if such behavior does actually take place. Even if the defenders of the theological view that homosexuality is unnatural were to appeal to a statistical analysis by pointing out that such behavior is not normal from a statistical point of view, and therefore not what the laws of nature require, it would be open to their critics to reply that any descriptive law of nature must account for and incorporate all statistical deviations, and that the laws of nature, in this sense, do not *require anything*. These critics might also note that the best statistics available reveal that about half of all American males engage in homosexual activity at some time in their lives, and that a very large percentage of American males have exclusively homosexual relations for a fairly extensive period of time; from which it would follow that such behavior is natural, for them, at any rate, in this sense of the word *natural*.

If those who say that homosexual behavior is unnatural are using the term *unnatural* in the second sense, it is difficult to see why they should be fussing over it. Certainly nothing is intrinsically wrong with going against nature (if that is how it should be put) in this sense. That which is artificial is often far better than what is natural. Artificial homes seem, at any rate, to be more suited to human habitation and more conducive to longer life and better health than caves and other natural shelters. There are distinct advantages to the use of such unnatural (i.e. artificial) amenities as clothes, furniture, and books. Although we may dream of an idyllic return to nature in our more wistful moments, we would soon discover, as Thoreau did in his attempt to escape from the artificiality of civilization, that needles and thread, knives and matches, ploughs and nails, and countless other products of human artifice are essential to human life. We would discover, as Plato pointed out in the *Republic,* that no man can be truly self-sufficient. Some of the by-products of industry are less than desirable; but neither industry itself, nor the products of industry, are intrinsically evil, even though both are unnatural in this sense of the word.

Interference with nature is not evil in itself. Nature, as some writers have put it, must be tamed. In some respects man must look upon it as an enemy to be conquered. If nature were left to its own devices, without the intervention of human artifice, men would be consumed with disease, they would be plagued by insects, they would be chained to the places where they were born with no means of swift communication or transport, and they would suffer the discomforts and the torments of wind and weather and flood and fire with no practical means of combating any of them. Interfering with nature, doing battle with nature, using human will and reason and skill to thwart what might otherwise follow from the conditions that prevail in the world, is a peculiarly human enterprise, one that can hardly be condemned merely because it does what is not natural.

Homosexual behavior can hardly be considered to be unnatural in this sense. There is nothing "artificial" about such behavior. On the contrary, it is quite natural, in this sense, to those who engage in it. And even if it were not, even if it were quite artificial, this is not in itself a ground for condemning it.

It would seem, then, that those who condemn homosexuality as an unnatural form of behavior must mean something else by the word *unnatural,* something not covered by either of the preceding definitions. A third possibility is this:

3. ANYTHING UNCOMMON OR ABNORMAL IS UNNATURAL

If this is what is meant by those who condemn homosexuality on the ground that it is unnatural, it is quite obvious that their condemnation cannot be accepted without further argument. For the fact that a given form of behavior is uncommon provides no justification for condemning it. Playing viola in a string quartet is no doubt an uncommon form of human behavior. I do not know what percentage of the human race engages in such behavior, or what percentage of his life any given violist devotes to such behavior, but I suspect that the number of such people must be very small indeed, and that the total number of man-hours spent in such activity would justify our calling that form of activity uncommon, abnormal (in the sense that it is statistically not the kind of thing that people are ordinarily inclined to do), and therefore unnatural, in this sense of the word. Yet there is no reason to suppose that such uncommon, abnormal behavior is, by virtue of its uncommonness, deserving of condemnation or ethically or morally wrong. On the contrary, many forms of behavior are praised precisely because they are so uncommon. Great artists, poets, musicians, and scientists are "abnormal" in this sense; but clearly the world is better off for having them, and it would be absurd to condemn them or their activities for their failure to be common and normal. If homosexual behavior is wrong, then, it must be for some reason other than its "unnaturalness" in this sense of the word.

4. ANY USE OF AN ORGAN OR AN INSTRUMENT THAT IS CONTRARY TO ITS PRINCIPAL PURPOSE OR FUNCTION IS UNNATURAL

Every organ and every instrument—perhaps even every creature—has a function to perform, one for which it is particularly designed. Any use of those instruments and organs that is consonant with their purposes is natural and proper, but any use that is inconsistent with their principal functions is unnatural and improper, and to that extent, evil or harmful. Human teeth, for example, are admirably designed for their principal functions—biting and chewing the kinds of food suitable for human consumption. But they are not particularly well suited for prying the caps from beer bottles. If they are used for the latter purpose, which is not natural to them, they are liable to crack or break under the strain. The abuse of one's teeth leads to their destruction and to a consequent deterioration in one's overall health. If they are used only for their proper function, however, they may continue to serve well for many years. Similarly, a given drug may have a proper function. If used in the furtherance of that end, it can preserve life and restore health. But if it is abused, and employed for purposes for which it was never intended, it may cause serious harm and even death. The natural uses of things are good and proper, but their unnatural uses are bad and harmful.

What we must do, then, is to find the proper use, or the true purpose, of each organ in our bodies. Once we have discovered that, we will know what constitutes the natural use of each organ, and what constitutes an unnatural, abusive, and potentially harmful employment of the various parts of our bodies. If we are rational, we will be careful to confine our behavior to our proper functions and to refrain from unnatural behavior. According to those philosophers who follow this line of reasoning, the way to discover the "proper" use of any organ is to determine what it is peculiarly suited to do. The eye is suited for seeing, the ear for hearing, the nerves for transmitting impulses from one part of the body to another, and so on.

What are the sex organs peculiarly suited to do? Obviously, they are peculiarly suited to enable men and women to reproduce their own kind. No other organ in the body is capable of fulfilling that function. It follows, according to those who follow the natural-law line, that the "proper" or "natural" function of the sex organs is reproduction, and that strictly speaking, any use of those organs for other purposes is unnatural, abusive, potentially harmful, and therefore wrong. The sex organs have been given to us in order to enable us to maintain the continued existence of mankind on this earth. All perversions — including masturbation, homosexual behavior, and heterosexual intercourse that deliberately frustrates the design of the sexual organs — are unnatural and bad. As Pope Pius XI once said, "Private individuals have no other power over the members of their bodies than that which pertains to their natural ends."

But the problem is not so easily resolved. Is it true that every organ has one and only one proper function? A hammer may have been designed to pound nails, and it may perform that particular job best. But it is not sinful to employ a hammer to crack nuts if I have no other more suitable tool immediately available. The hammer, being a relatively versatile tool, may be employed in a number of ways. It has no one "proper" or "natural" function. A woman's eyes are well adapted to seeing, it is true. But they seem also to be well adapted to flirting. Is a woman's use of her eyes for the latter purpose sinful merely because she is not using them, at that moment, for their "primary" purpose of seeing? Our sexual organs are uniquely adapted for procreation, but that is obviously not the only function for which they are adapted. Human beings may — and do — use those organs for a great many other purposes, and it is difficult to see why any *one* use should be considered to be the only proper one. The sex organs, for one thing, seem to be particularly well adapted to give their owners and others intense sensations of pleasure. Unless one believes that pleasure itself is bad, there seems to be little reason to believe that the use of the sex organs for the production of pleasure in oneself or in others is evil. In view of the peculiar design of these organs, with their great concentration of nerve endings, it would seem that they were designed (if they *were* designed) with that very goal in mind, and that their use for such purposes would be no more unnatural than their use for the purpose of procreation.

Nor should we overlook the fact that human sex organs may be and are used to express, in the deepest and most intimate way open to man, the love of one person for another. Even the most ardent opponents of "unfruitful" intercourse admit that sex does serve this function. They have accordingly conceded that a man and his wife may have intercourse even though she is pregnant, or past the age of child bearing, or in the infertile period of her menstrual cycle.

Human beings are remarkably complex and adaptable creatures. Neither they nor their organs can properly be compared to hammers or to other tools. The analogy quickly breaks down. The generalization that a given organ or instrument has one and only one proper function does not hold up, even with regard to the simplest manufactured tools, for, as we have seen, a tool may be used for more than one purpose — less effectively than one especially designed for a given task, perhaps, but "properly" and certainly not *sinfully*. A woman may use her eyes not only to see and to flirt, but also to earn money—if she is, for example, an actress or a model. Though neither of the latter functions seems to have been a part of the original "design," if one may speak sensibly of *design* in this context, of the eye, it is difficult to see why such a use of the eyes of a woman should be considered sinful, perverse, or unnatural. Her sex organs have the unique capacity of producing ova and nurturing human embryos, under the right conditions; but why should any other use of those organs, including their use to bring pleasure to their owner or to someone else, or to manifest love to another person, or even, perhaps, to earn money, be regarded as perverse, sinful, or unnatural? Similarly, a man's sexual organs possess the unique capacity of causing the generation of another human being, but if a man chooses to use them for pleasure, or for the expression of love, or for some other purpose—so long as he does not interfere with the rights of some other person—the fact that his sex organs do have their unique capabilities does not constitute a convincing justification for condemning their other uses as being perverse, sinful, unnatural, or criminal. If a man "perverts" himself by wiggling his ears for the entertainment of his neighbors instead of using them exclusively for their "natural" function of hearing, no one thinks of consigning him to prison. If he abuses his teeth by using them to pull staples from memos—a function for which teeth were clearly not designed—he is not accused of being immoral, degraded, and degenerate. The fact that people *are* condemned for using their sex organs for their own pleasure or profit, or for that of others, may be more revealing about the prejudices and taboos of our society than it is about our perception of the true nature or purpose or "end" (whatever that might be) of our bodies.

To sum up, then, the proposition that any use of an organ that is contrary to its principal purpose or function is unnatural assumes that organs *have* a principal purpose or function, but this may be denied on the ground that the purpose or function of a given organ may vary according to the needs or desires of its owner. It may be denied on the ground that a given organ may have more than one principal purpose or function, and any attempt to call one use or another the only natural one seems to be arbitrary, if not questionbegging. Also, the proposition suggests that what is unnatural is evil or depraved. This goes beyond the pure description of things, and enters into the problem of the evaluation of human behavior, which leads us to the fifth meaning of "natural."

5. THAT WHICH IS NATURAL IS GOOD, AND WHATEVER IS UNNATURAL IS BAD

When one condemns homosexuality or masturbation or the use of contraceptives on the ground that it is unnatural, one implies that whatever is unnatural is bad, wrongful, or perverse. But as we have seen, in some senses of the word, the unnatural (i.e., the artificial) is often very good, whereas that which is natural (i.e., that which has not been subjected to human artifice or improvement) may be very bad indeed. Of course, interference with nature may be bad. Ecologists have made us more aware than we have ever been of the dangers of unplanned and uninformed interference with nature. But this is not to say that *all* interference with nature is bad. Every time a man cuts down a tree to make room for a home for himself, or catches a fish to feed himself or his family, he is interfering with nature. If men did not interfere with nature, they would have no homes, they could eat no fish, and, in fact, they could not survive. What, then, can be meant by those who say that whatever is natural is good and whatever is unnatural is bad? Clearly, they cannot have intended merely to reduce the word *natural* to a synonym of *good, right,* and *proper,* and *unnatural* to a synonym of *evil, wrong, improper, corrupt,* and *depraved.* If that were all they had intended to do, there would be very little to discuss as to whether a given form of behavior might be proper even though it is not in strict conformity with someone's views of what is natural; for *good* and *natural* being synonyms, it would follow inevitably that whatever is good must be natural, and vice versa, by definition. This is certainly not what the opponents of homosexuality have been saying when they claim that homosexuality, being unnatural, is evil. For if it were, their claim would be quite empty. They would be saying merely that homosexuality, being evil, is evil—a redundancy that could as easily be reduced to the simpler assertion that homosexuality is evil. This assertion, however, is not an argument. Those who oppose homosexuality and other sexual "perversions" on the ground that they are "unnatural" are saying that there is some objectively identifiable quality in such behavior that is unnatural; and that that quality, once it has been identified by some kind of scientific observation, can be seen to be detrimental to those who engage in such behavior, or to those around them; and that *because* of the harm (physical, mental, moral, or spiritual) that results from engaging in any behavior possessing the attribute of unnaturalness, such behavior must be considered to be wrongful, and should be discouraged by society. "Unnaturalness" and "wrongfulness" are not synonyms, then, but different concepts. The problem with which we are wrestling is that we are unable to find a meaning for *unnatural* that enables us to arrive at the conclusion that homosexuality is unnatural or that if homosexuality is unnatural, it is therefore wrongful behavior. We have examined four common meanings of *natural* and *unnatural,* and have seen that none of them performs the task that it must perform if the advocates of this argument are to prevail. Without some more satisfactory explanation of the connection between the wrongfulness of homosexuality and its alleged unnaturalness, the argument must be rejected.

QUESTIONS

1. Can the "unnaturalness argument" be developed in a way that avoids Leiser's criticisms?
2. Is homosexual behavior immoral? If so, on what grounds?

JUDGE ALBERT V. BRYAN

MAJORITY OPINION IN *DOE v. COMMONWEALTH'S ATTORNEY FOR CITY OF RICHMOND*

Albert V. Bryan is judge of the U.S. Court of Appeals, Fourth Circuit. A graduate of the University of Virginia Law School, he was admitted to the Virginia bar in 1920 and maintained a private practice in Alexandria, Virginia, prior to becoming a judge in 1947.

In this case, two anonymous homosexuals brought an action before a three-judge District Court in Richmond, Virginia. They sought to have the Virginia statute making sodomy a crime declared unconstitutional. In a two-to-one decision, the District Court upheld the constitutionality of the statute. The case was subsequently appealed to the United States Supreme Court, but in 1976, by a vote of six-to-three, the Court refused to hear arguments and summarily affirmed the lower-court ruling. Laws similar to the Virginia statute at issue here presently exist in a majority of the states.

In the majority opinion of the District Court, Judge Bryan contends that Virginia's sodomy statute, inasmuch as it applies to homosexuals (even those who are *consenting adults* engaged in *private* behavior), is not unconstitutional. The constitutionally guaranteed right of privacy, in his view, is applicable to sexual behavior only within a marriage relationship, not without. Moreover, he insists, a legitimate state interest underlies Virginia's sodomy statute.

Virginia's statute making sodomy a crime is unconstitutional, each of the male plaintiffs aver, when it is applied to his active and regular homosexual relations with another *adult male, consensually* and *in private*. They assert that local State officers threaten them with prosecution for violation of this law, that such enforcement would deny them their Fifth and Fourteenth Amendments' assurance of due process, the First Amendment's protection of their rights of freedom of expression, the First and Ninth Amendments' guarantee of privacy, and the Eighth Amendment's forbiddance of cruel and unusual punishments. A declaration of the statute's invalidity in the circumstances is prayed as well as an injunction against its enforcement. Defendants are State prosecuting officials and they take issue with the plaintiffs' conclusions. With no conflict of fact present, the validity of this enactment becomes a question of law.

So far as relevant, the Code of Virginia, 1950, as amended, provides:

"§ 18.1-212. Crimes against nature.—If any person shall carnally know in any manner any brute animal, or carnally know any male or female person by the anus or by or with the mouth, or voluntarily submit to such carnal knowledge, he or she shall be guilty of a felony and shall be confined in the penitentiary not less than one year nor more than three years."

Our decision is that on its face and in the circumstances here it is not unconstitutional. No judgment is made upon the wisdom or policy of the statute. It is simply that we cannot say that the statute offends the Bill of Rights or any other of the Amendments and the wisdom or policy is a matter for the State's resolve.

I.

Precedents cited to us as *contra* rest exclusively on the precept that the Constitution condemns State legislation that trespasses upon the privacy of the incidents of marriage, upon the sanctity of the home, or upon the nurture of family life. This and only this concern has been the justification for nullification of State regulation in this area. Review of plaintiffs' authorities will reveal these as the principles underlying the referenced decisions.

In *Griswold v. Connecticut* (1965), plaintiffs' chief reliance, the Court has most recently announced its views on the question here. Striking down a State statute forbidding the use of contraceptives, the ruling was put on the right of marital privacy—held to be one of the specific guarantees of the Bill of Rights—and was also put on the sanctity of the home and family. Its thesis is epitomized by the author of the opinion, Mr. Justice Douglas, in his conclusion:

"We deal with a right of privacy older than the Bill of Rights—older than our political parties, older than our school system. Marriage is a coming together for better or for worse, hopefully enduring and intimate to the degree of being sacred. It is an association that promotes a way of life, not causes; a harmony in living, not political faiths; a bilateral loyalty, not commercial or social projects. Yet it is an association for as noble a purpose as any involved in our prior decisions."

United States District Court, E.D. Virginia. 403 F. Supp. 1199 (1975).

That *Griswold* is premised on the right of privacy and that homosexual intimacy is denunciable by the State is unequivocally demonstrated by Mr. Justice Goldberg in his concurrence in his adoption of Mr. Justice Harlan's dissenting statement in *Poe v. Ullman* (1961):

"Adultery, *homosexuality* and the like are sexual intimacies *which the State forbids* . . . but the intimacy of husband and wife is necessarily an essential and accepted feature of the institution of marriage, an institution which the State not only must allow, but which always and in every age it has fostered and protected. *It is one thing when the State exerts its power either to forbid extramarital sexuality . . .* or to say who may marry, but it is quite another when, having acknowledged a marriage and the intimacies inherent in it, it undertakes to regulate by means of the criminal law the details of that intimacy." (Emphasis added.)

Equally forceful is the succeeding paragraph of Justice Harlan:

"In sum, even though the State has determined that the use of contraceptives is as iniquitous as any act of extra-marital sexual immorality, the intrusion of the whole machinery of the criminal law into the very heart of marital privacy, requiring husband and wife to render account before a criminal tribunal of their uses of that intimacy is surely *a very different thing indeed from punishing those who establish intimacies which the law has always forbidden and which can have no claim to social protection.*" (Emphasis added.)

Justice Harlan's words are nonetheless commanding merely because they were written in dissent. To begin with, as heretofore observed, they were authentically approved in *Griswold*. Moreover, he was not differing with the majority there on the merits of the substantive case but only as to the procedural reason of its dismissal. At all events, the Justice's exegesis is that of a jurist of widely acknowledged superior stature and weighty whatever its context.

With his standing, what he had further to say in *Poe v. Ullman* is worthy of high regard. On the plaintiffs' effort presently to shield the practice of homosexuality from State incrimination by according it immunity when committed in private as against public exercise, the Justice said this:

"Indeed to attempt a line between public behavior and that which is purely consensual or solitary would be to withdraw from community concern a range of subjects with which every society in civilized times has found it necessary to deal. The laws regarding marriage which provide both when the sexual powers may be used and the legal and societal context in which children are born and brought up, as well as *laws forbidding adultery, fornication and homosexual practices which express the negative of the proposition,* confining sexuality to lawful marriage, form a pattern so deeply pressed into the substance of our social life that any Constitutional doctrine in this area must build upon that basis." (Accent added.)

Again:

"Thus, I would not suggest that *adultery, homosexuality, fornication and incest are immune* from criminal enquiry, *however privately practiced.* So much has been explicitly recognized in acknowledging the State's rightful concern for its people's moral welfare. . . . But not to discriminate between what is involved in this case and either the traditional offenses against good morals or crimes which, though they may be committed anywhere, *happen to have been committed or concealed in the home,* would entirely misconceive the argument that is being made." (Accent added.)

Many states have long had, and still have, statutes and decisional law criminalizing conduct depicted in the Virginia legislation.

II.

With no authoritative judicial bar to the proscription of homosexuality — since it is obviously no portion of marriage, home or family life — the next question is whether there is any ground for barring Virginia from branding it as criminal. If a State determines that punishment therefor, even when committed in the home, is appropriate in the promotion of morality and decency, it is not for the courts to say that the State is not free to do so. In short, it is an inquiry addressable only to the State's Legislature.

Furthermore, if the State has the burden of proving that it has a legitimate interest in the subject of the statute or that the statute is rationally supportable, Virginia has completely fulfilled this obligation. Fundamentally, the State action is simply directed to the suppression of crime, whether committed in public or in private. Both instances . . . are within the reach of the police power.

Moreover, to sustain its action, the State is not required to show that moral delinquency actually results from homosexuality. It is enough for upholding the legislation to establish that the conduct is likely to end in a contribution to moral delinquency. Plainly, it would indeed be impracticable to prove the actuality of such a consequence, and the law is not so exacting.

If such a prospect or expectation was in the mind of the General Assembly of Virginia, the prophecy proved only too true in the occurrences narrated in *Lovisi v. Slayton* (EDVa. 1973, now on appeal in the Fourth Circuit). The graphic outline by the District Judge there describes just such a sexual orgy as the statute was evidently intended to punish. The Lovisis, a married couple, advertised their wish "to meet people" and in response a man came to Virginia to meet the Lovisis on several occasions. In one instance the three of them participated in acts of fellatio. Photographs of the conduct were taken by a set camera and the acts were witnessed by the wife's daughters, aged 11 and 13. The pictures were carried by them to school.

Although a questionable law is not removed from question by the lapse of any prescriptive period, the longevity of the Virginia statute does testify to the State's interest and its legitimacy. It is not an upstart notion; it has ancestry going back to Judaic and Christian law. The immediate parentage may be readily traced to the Code of Virginia of 1792. All the while the law has been kept alive, as evidenced by periodic amendments, the last in the 1968 Acts of the General Assembly of Virginia.

In sum, we believe that the sodomy statute, so long in force in Virginia, has a rational basis of State interest demonstrably legitimate and mirrored in the cited decisional law of the Supreme Court. Indeed, the Court has treated as free of infirmity a State law with a background similar to the Virginia enactment in suit.

The prayers for a declaratory judgment and an injunction invalidating the sodomy statute will be denied.

QUESTIONS

1. Though he finds the Virginia sodomy statute not unconstitutional, Judge Bryan says, "No judgment is made upon the wisdom or policy of the statute." As a matter of social policy, is such a law well advised?
2. Some states retain statutes making both fornication and adultery criminal actions. As a matter of social policy, would these states be well advised to decriminalize such actions?

DISSENTING OPINION IN *DOE v. COMMONWEALTH'S ATTORNEY FOR CITY OF RICHMOND*

Robert R. Merhige, Jr., is judge of the U.S. District Court, Richmond, Virginia. He is a graduate of the University of Richmond Law School, was admitted to the Virginia bar in 1942, and maintained a private practice in Richmond until 1967, when he was appointed judge.

In his dissenting opinion, Judge Merhige rejects Judge Bryan's claim that the right of privacy is applicable to sexual behavior only within a marriage relationship. According to Judge Merhige, the right of privacy is applicable to all sexual behavior (whether heterosexual or homosexual) between consenting adults in private. Accordingly, he contends, state restrictions on private consensual sex acts between adults are justified only if a compelling state interest can validly be asserted. Thus, in his view, since there is no evidence that homosexual acts between consenting adults in private cause socially significant harm, Virginia's sodomy statute is unconstitutional.

. . . Regretfully, . . . my views as to the constitutionality of the statute in question, as it applies to consenting adults acting in the privacy of their homes, [do not conform with those of the majority].

In my view, in the absence of any legitimate interest or rational basis to support the statute's application we must, without regard to our own proclivities and reluctance to judicially bar the state proscription of homosexuality, hold the statute as it applies to the plaintiffs to be violative of their rights under the Due Process Clause of the Fourteenth Amendment to the Constitution of the United States. The Supreme Court decision in *Griswold v. Connecticut* (1965), is, as the majority points out, premised on the right of privacy, but I fear my brothers have misapplied its precedential value through an apparent overadherence to its factual circumstances.

The Supreme Court has consistently held that the Due Process Clause of the Fourteenth Amendment protects the right of individuals to make personal choices, unfettered by arbitrary and purposeless restraints, in the private matters of marriage and procreation. I view those cases as standing for the principle that every individual has a right to be free from unwarranted governmental intrusion into one's decisions on private matters of intimate concern. A mature individual's choice of an adult sexual partner, in the privacy of his or her own home, would appear to me to be a decision of the utmost private and intimate concern. Private consensual sex acts between adults are matters, absent evidence that they are harmful, in which the state has no legitimate interest.

To say, as the majority does, that the right of privacy, which every citizen has, is limited to matters of marital, home or family life is unwarranted under the law. Such a contention places a distinction in marital-nonmarital matters which is inconsistent with current Supreme Court opinions and is unsupportable.

In my view, the reliance of the majority on Mr. Justice Harlan's dissenting statement in *Poe v. Ullman* (1961) is misplaced. An analysis of the cases indicates that in 1965 when *Griswold,* which invalidated a statute prohibiting the use of contraceptives by married couples, was decided, at least three of the Court, relying primarily on Mr. Justice Harlan's

United States District Court, E.D. Virginia. 403 F. Supp. 1199 (1975).

dissent in *Poe v. Ullman,* and Mr. Justice Harlan himself, would not have been willing to attach the right of privacy to homosexual conduct. In my view, *Griswold* applied the right of privacy to its particular factual situation. That the right of privacy is not limited to the facts of *Griswold* is demonstrated by later Supreme Court decisions. After *Griswold,* by virtue of *Eisenstadt v. Baird* (1972), the legal viability of a marital-nonmarital distinction in private sexual acts if not eliminated, was at the very least seriously impaired. In *Eisenstadt,* the Court declined to restrict the right of privacy in sexual matters to married couples:

> Yet the marital couple is not an independent entity with a mind and heart of its own, but an association of two individuals each with a separate intellectual and emotional makeup. If the right of privacy means anything, it is the right of the *individual,* married or single, to be free from unwarranted governmental intrusion into matters so fundamentally affecting a person as the decision whether to bear or beget a child.

In significantly diminishing the importance of the marital-nonmarital distinction, the Court to a great extent vitiated any implication that the state can, as suggested by Mr. Justice Harlan in *Poe v. Ullman,* forbid extra-marital sexuality, and such implications are no longer fully accurate.

> It is one thing when the State exerts its power either to forbid extra-marital sexuality altogether, or to say who may marry, but it is quite another when, having acknowledged a marriage and the intimacies inherent in it, it undertakes to regulate by means of the criminal law the details of that intimacy. (Harlan J., dissenting).

Griswold, in its context, applied the right of privacy in sexual matters to the marital relationship. *Eisenstadt,* however, clearly demonstrates that the right to privacy in sexual relationships is not limited to the marital relationship. Both *Roe v. Wade* (1973) and *Eisenstadt* cogently demonstrate that intimate personal decisions or private matters of substantial importance to the well-being of the individuals involved are protected by the Due Process Clause. The right to select consenting adult sexual partners must be considered within this category. The exercise of that right, whether heterosexual or homosexual, should not be proscribed by state regulation absent compelling justification.

This approach does not unqualifiedly sanction personal whim. If the activity in question involves more than one participant, as in the instant case, each must be capable of consenting, and each must in fact consent to the conduct for the right of privacy to attach. For example, if one of the participants in homosexual contact is a minor, or force is used to coerce one of the participants to yield, the right will not attach. Similarly, the right of privacy cannot be extended to protect conduct that takes place in publicly frequented areas. However, if the right of privacy does apply to specific courses of conduct, legitimate state restriction on personal autonomy may be justified only under the compelling state interest test.

Plaintiffs are adults seeking protection from the effects of the statute under attack in order to engage in homosexual relations in private. Viewing the issue as we are bound to, as Mr. Justice Blackmun stated in *Roe v. Wade,* "by constitutional measurement, free of emotion and predilection," it is my view that they are entitled to be protected in their right to privacy by the Due Process Clause.

The defendants, represented by the highest legal officer of the state, made no tender of any evidence which even impliedly demonstrated that homosexuality causes society any significant harm. No effort was made by the defendants to establish either a rational basis or a compelling state interest so as to justify the proscription of § 8.1–212 of the Code of Virginia, presently under attack. To suggest, as defendants do, that the prohibition of homosexual conduct will in some manner encourage new heterosexual marriages and pre- vent the dissolution of existing ones is unworthy of judicial response. In any event, what we know as men is not forgotten as judges—it is difficult to envision any substantial number of heterosexual marriages being in danger of dissolution because of the private sexual activities of homosexuals.

On the basis of this record one can only conclude that the sole basis of the proscrip- tion of homosexuality was what the majority refers to as the promotion of morality and decency. As salutary a legislative goal as this may be, I can find no authority for intrusion by the state into the private dwelling of a citizen. *Stanley v. Georgia* (1969) teaches us that socially condemned activity, excepting that of demonstrable external effect, is and was intended by the Constitution to be beyond the scope of state regulation when conducted within the privacy of the home. "The Constitution extends special safeguards to the privacy of the home. . . ." Whether the guarantee of personal privacy springs from the First, Fourth, Fifth, Ninth, the penumbra of the Bill of Rights, or, as I believe, in the concept of liberty guaranteed by the first section of the Fourteenth Amendment, the Supreme Court has made it clear that fundamental rights of such an intimate facet of an individual's life as sex, absent circumstances warranting intrusion by the state, are to be respected. My broth- ers, I respectfully suggest, have by today's ruling misinterpreted the issue—the issue cen- ters not around morality or decency, but the constitutional right of privacy.

I respectfully note my dissent.

QUESTIONS

1. Opponents of the decriminalization of sodomy sometimes argue as follows: It is necessary that homo- sexual behavior, even between consenting adults in private, be considered a criminal offense; toleration of homosexual behavior would lead to long-term consequences disastrous for society. Is this a sound argument?
2. Constitutional considerations aside, would a state be well advised, as a matter of social policy, to decriminalize *all* sexual behavior between consenting adults in private?

SUGGESTED ADDITIONAL READINGS

ATKINSON, RONALD: *Sexual Morality.* New York: Harcourt, Brace & World, 1965. In this book Atkinson treats many aspects of sexual morality, concentrating on an analysis of the arguments that can be offered in support of the various positions.

BAKER, ROBERT, and FREDERICK ELLISTON: *Philosophy & Sex.* Buffalo, N.Y.: Prometheus, 1975. Two sec- tions of this very helpful anthology are especially relevant. One section is entitled "Sex and Morality," the other is entitled "The Morality of Marriage." Of related interest is "The Logic of Deviation," a section dealing with the concept of sexual perversion.

BARNHART, J. E., and MARY ANN BARNHART: "Marital Faithfulness and Unfaithfulness." *Journal of Social Philosophy,* vol. 4, April 1973, pp. 10–15. The Barnharts argue that we should recognize the legitimacy of dif- ferent marriage styles, including a marriage style that incorporates extramarital sex.

BERTOCCI, PETER A.: *Sex, Love, and the Person.* New York: Sheed & Ward, 1967. Bertocci emphasizes con- siderations of personal development and constructs a defense of conventional sexual morality.

CAMERON, PAUL: "A Case Against Homosexuality." *Human Life Review,* vol. 4, Summer 1978, pp. 17–49. As a psychologist, Cameron introduces empirical data about homosexuality. He contends that homosexuality is an undesirable life-style and argues against the liberalization of social policy (regarding homosexuality).

LEISER, BURTON M.: *Liberty, Justice and Morals,* 2d ed. New York: Macmillan, 1979. Chapter 2 of this book deals with homosexuality. In the course of constructing a case against criminal sanctions, Leiser analyzes the arguments commonly made in support of the condemnation of homosexual behavior.

RUSSELL, BERTRAND: *Marriage and Morals.* New York: Liveright, 1929. This highly readable statement against conventional sexual morality, by one of the most famous philosophers of our time, is now slightly dated but still worthy of attention.

VANNOY, RUSSELL: *Sex Without Love: A Philosophical Exploration.* Buffalo, N.Y.: Prometheus, 1980. Vannoy defends sex without love: "I conclude, therefore, that on the whole, sex with a humanistic non-lover is far preferable to sex with an erotic lover." Both Chapter 1, "Sex with Love vs. Sex without Love" (pp. 7–29), and Chapter 4, "Types of Sexual Philosophy: A Summary" (pp. 118–127), are especially relevant to the topic of sexual morality.

WASSERSTROM, RICHARD: "Is Adultery Immoral?" In Richard Wasserstrom, ed., *Today's Moral Problems,* 2d ed. New York: Macmillan, 1979. This helpful article investigates the various arguments that can plausibly be made in support of the claim that adultery is immoral. Wasserstrom's analysis is especially valuable in focusing attention on the presuppositions of such arguments.

WELLMAN, CARL: *Morals & Ethics.* Glenview, Ill.: Scott, Foresman, 1975. Chapter 5 of this book provides a highly readable analysis of the arguments that may be given for and against the moral acceptability of premarital sex.

WHITELEY, C. H., and W. N. WHITELEY: *Sex and Morals.* New York: Basic Books, 1967. This book as a whole is useful, but Chapter 5, on "Unfruitful Sex," is especially germane. In this chapter, the Whiteleys examine the morality of masturbation, homosexual behavior, and other types of sexual activity that cut off the possibility of procreation.

PORNOGRAPHY AND CENSORSHIP

7

In 1967, the Congress of the United States, labeling the traffic in obscene and pornographic materials "a matter of national concern," established the Commission on Obscenity and Pornography. This advisory commission, whose members were appointed by the President in January of 1968, was charged with initiating a thorough study of obscenity and pornography and, on the basis of such a study, submitting recommendations for the regulation of obscene and pornographic materials. In September of 1970 the Commission transmitted its final report to the President and to the Congress. Its fundamental recommendation was that all legislation prohibiting the sale, exhibition, or distribution of sexual materials to *consenting adults* be repealed. However, the Commission recommended the continuation of legislation intended to protect nonconsenting adults from being confronted with sexually explicit material through public displays and unsolicited mailings. It also recommended the continuation of legislation prohibiting the commercial distribution of certain sexual material to juveniles. The Commission based its fundamental recommendation largely, though not exclusively, on its central factual finding: There is no evidence to support the contention that exposure to explicit sexual materials plays a significant role in the causation of either social harms (via antisocial behavior) or individual harms (such as severe emotional disturbance).

The report of the Commission on Obscenity and Pornography was unwelcome in many quarters. To begin with, only twelve of the Commission's eighteen members voted in support of its fundamental recommendation. In fact, the report itself features a substantial minority report that questions the factual findings as well as the recommendations of the Commission. President Richard Nixon contended that the report was completely unsatisfactory. Many members of Congress were also displeased, and there was a substantial public outcry that the conclusions of the Commission were "morally bankrupt." As a result, there has been little movement to implement its fundamental recommendation.

The developments just described encourage us to pose, as the central issue of this chapter, the following ethical question: Is a government justified in limiting the access of consenting adults to pornographic materials?

LIBERTY-LIMITING PRINCIPLES

Laws limiting the access of consenting adults to pornographic materials, like all laws, inevitably involve limitation of individual liberty. Accordingly, one way of approaching our central question is to take notice of the kinds of grounds that may be advanced to justify the limitation of individual liberty. Four suggested liberty-limiting principles are especially noteworthy:[1]

1. The harm principle—Individual liberty is justifiably limited to prevent *harm to others.*

---

[1]Joel Feinberg's discussion of such principles served as a guide for the formulations adopted here. *Social Philosophy* (Englewood Cliffs, N.J.: Prentice-Hall, 1973), chap. 2.

2. The principle of legal paternalism—Individual liberty is justifiably limited to prevent *harm to self.*

3. The principle of legal moralism—Individual liberty is justifiably limited to prevent *immoral behavior.*

4. The offense principle—Individual liberty is justifiably limited to prevent *offense to others.*

The *harm principle* is the most widely accepted liberty-limiting principle. Few will dispute that the law is within its proper bounds when it restricts actions whereby one person causes harm to others. (The category of *harm to others* is understood as encompassing not only personal injury but also damage to the general welfare of society.) What remains a lively source of debate is whether any, or all, of the other suggested principles are legitimate liberty-limiting principles. According to John Stuart Mill (1806–1873), only the harm principle is a legitimate liberty-limiting principle. A short excerpt from his famous essay *On Liberty* appears in this chapter. Though Mill need not be read as unsympathetic to the offense principle, he clearly and vigorously rejects both the principle of legal paternalism and the principle of legal moralism.

According to the *principle of legal paternalism,* the law may justifiably be invoked to prevent self-harm, and thus "to protect individuals from themselves."[2] Supporters of this principle think that the law rightfully serves much as a benevolent parent who limits his or her child's liberty in order to save the child from harm. Some, of course, often in the spirit of Mill, hotly contest the legitimacy of the principle of legal paternalism. It is said, for example, that government does not have the right to meddle in the private life of its citizens. Though there is little doubt that there are presently numerous paternalistic features in our legal system, their justifiability remains a disputed issue. The widespread law that requires motorcyclists to wear protective headgear is one apparent example of a paternalistic law.

According to the *principle of legal moralism,* the law may justifiably be invoked to prevent immoral behavior or, as it is often expressed, to "enforce morals." Such things as kidnapping, murder, and fraud are undoubtedly immoral, but there would seem to be no need to appeal to the principle of legal moralism to justify laws against them. An appeal to the harm principle already provides a widely accepted independent justification. As a result, the principle of legal moralism usually comes to the fore only when so-called victimless crimes are under discussion. Is it justifiable to legislate against homosexual relations, gambling, and smoking marijuana simply on the grounds that such activities are thought to be morally unacceptable? There are many such laws, and presumably they are intended to enforce conventional morality, but some people continue to call for their repeal on the grounds that the principle of legal moralism is an unacceptable liberty-limiting principle. To accept the principle of legal moralism, in Mill's words, is tantamount to permitting a "tyranny of the majority."

According to the *offense principle,* the law may justifiably be invoked to prevent "offensive" behavior in public. "Offensive" behavior is understood as behavior that causes shame, embarrassment, discomfort, etc., to be experienced by onlookers. The offense principle, unlike the other principles discussed above, is not ordinarily advanced to justify laws that would limit the access of *consenting* adults to pornographic materials. The offense

---

[2]In Chapter 8, it will prove helpful to introduce a second paternalistic principle, the principle of *extreme* paternalism. According to this liberty-limiting principle, individual liberty is justifiably limited to *benefit* the individual.

principle, however, is sometimes advanced to justify laws that protect *nonconsenting* adults from "offensive" displays of pornography.

THE CASE FOR CENSORSHIP
Arguments in support of laws that would limit the access of consenting adults to pornographic materials can conveniently be organized in terms of the liberty-limiting principles upon which they are based.

1. Arguments Based on the Harm Principle
It is often alleged that exposure to pornography is a direct cause of crime. It is thought, on this view, that exposure to pornography is a significant causal factor in sex-related crimes such as rape. Defenders of this thesis often argue for their claim by citing examples where a person is exposed to pornographic material and subsequently commits a sex-related crime. Such examples, however, fail to establish that the crime, which *follows* exposure to pornography, is a *causal result* of exposure to pornography. Indeed, the Commission on Obscenity and Pornography reported that there is no evidence to support such a causal connection. Since the harm principle is a widely accepted liberty-limiting principle, a formidable argument for censorship would emerge if a causal connection between the use of pornography and antisocial behavior were ever to be demonstrated.

A second line of argument based on the harm principle emphasizes the alleged disastrous effects of the widespread exposure to pornography on the overall welfare of society. It is said, for example, that society will become obsessed with impersonal expressions of sexuality, that love will disappear, and that children entering such a society will be psychologically deprived. It has even been suggested that unlimited access to pornographic materials might eventually culminate in the total decay of order and civilization. "What is at stake is civilization and humanity, nothing less."[3] According to a closely related line of thought, pornography functions to break down the feelings of shame associated with sex and thereby represents a serious threat to democracy.

> To live together requires rules and a governing of the passions, and those who are without shame will be unruly and unreliable; having lost the ability to restrain themselves by observing the rules they collectively give themselves, they will have to be ruled by others. Tyranny is the natural and inevitable mode of government for the shameless and the self-indulgent who have carried liberty beyond any restraint.[4]

In the face of harm-principle arguments to the effect that widespread exposure to pornography will (in the long run) produce very dire consequences for society, two responses are commonly made: (1) The anticipated dire effects will not in fact occur. (2) The anticipated effects are so speculative as not to constitute a "clear and present danger."

2. Arguments Based on the Principle of Legal Paternalism
It is often said that those exposed to pornography will be harmed by such exposure. They will, it is thought, develop or reinforce emotional problems; they will render themselves incapable of love and other human relationships necessary for a happy and satisfying life. In a more abstract and possibly rhetorical version of this argument, it is alleged that fre-

[3]Irving Kristol, "Pornography, Obscenity, and the Case for Censorship," *The New York Times Magazine*, March 28, 1971, p. 113.
[4]Walter Berns, "Pornography vs. Democracy: The Case for Censorship," *Public Interest*, vol. 22, Winter 1971, p. 13.

quent exposure to pornography "depersonalizes" or "dehumanizes," and presumably such effects are at least in a broad sense harmful to the individual. Arguments based on the principle of legal paternalism are answered in two ways: (1) The alleged self-harm does not occur. (2) Regardless of the truth or falsity of the claim of self-harm, the principle of legal paternalism is not an acceptable liberty-limiting principle.

3. Arguments Based on the Principle of Legal Moralism

It is frequently claimed that there is a widespread consensus to the effect that pornography is morally repugnant. Inasmuch as the principle of legal moralism seems to allow a community to enforce its moral convictions, it follows that the access of consenting adults to pornographic materials may rightfully be restricted. Arguments thus based on the principle of legal moralism are answered in two ways: (1) The alleged consensus of moral opinion is nonexistent. (2) Regardless of the truth or falsity of the claim of an existing moral consensus, the principle of legal moralism is not an acceptable liberty-limiting principle.

The morality of pornography is an important ethical issue in its own right. To a large extent, of course, one's moral assessment of pornography will be a function of one's views on sexual morality in general. In one of this chapter's selections, Charles H. Keating, Jr., argues on rather traditional grounds that pornography is clearly immoral. Because Keating takes his view to be the consensus view of society, and because he explicitly endorses the principle of legal moralism, he is a vigorous proponent of censorship. Ann Garry, in this chapter's final selection, also discusses the morality of pornography. From a feminist perspective, she contends that most contemporary pornography is morally objectionable on the grounds that it is degrading to women. Garry, however, in contrast to Keating, is reluctant to call for censorship.

THE CASE AGAINST CENSORSHIP

The overall case against laws limiting the access of consenting adults to pornographic materials usually takes the following direction: The principle of legal paternalism is an unacceptable liberty-limiting principle; the government has no business meddling in the private affairs of its citizens since such meddling is likely to produce more harm than it prevents. The principle of legal moralism is also an unacceptable liberty-limiting principle; to enforce the moral views of the majority is, in effect, to allow a "tyranny of the majority." A government can rightfully legislate against the private activity of consenting adults only on the grounds that such activity is *harmful to others*. At the present time, however, there is no evidence that the access of consenting adults to pornographic materials presents a "clear and present danger." Thus, censorship is unwarranted.

It is sometimes further argued by opponents of censorship, in conjunction with the claim that pornography has no socially damaging consequences, that it is positively beneficial to those exposed to it and to society as a whole. Here it is said, for example, that exposure to pornography can aid normal sexual development, that it can invigorate sexual relationships, and that it can provide a socially harmless release from sexual tension. Such considerations are developed by G. L. Simons in one of the readings in this chapter.

Thomas A. Mappes

MAJORITY OPINION IN *PARIS ADULT THEATRE I v. SLATON*

Warren Burger is chief justice of the United States Supreme Court. Admitted to the Minnesota bar in 1931, he then spent a number of years in private practice, while simultaneously serving on the faculty of the Mitchell College of Law in St. Paul. Chief Justice Burger also served as assistant attorney general (1953–1956) and as judge of the U.S. Court of Appeals, District of Columbia Circuit (1956–1969). In 1969 he was appointed to the Supreme Court.

The state of Georgia sought an injunction against the showing of two films—*It All Comes Out in the End* and *Magic Mirror*—by the Paris Adult Theatres I and II (Atlanta). The state claimed that the films were obscene under the relevant Georgia standards. The trial court refused to grant the injunction, holding that the showing of the films could be prohibited only if it were proved that they were shown to minors or nonconsenting adults. The Supreme Court of Georgia reversed the decision of the trial court, and the Supreme Court of the United States upheld the reversal, though by a mere five-to-four majority.

In Chief Justice Burger's majority opinion, he argues that there are legitimate state interests at stake in the state regulation of consenting adults' access to obscene material. According to Chief Justice Burger, such interests include the maintenance of a decent society, the tone of commerce in large cities, and "possibly" the public safety. Chief Justice Burger acknowledges that there is no conclusive proof of a connection between obscene material and antisocial behavior, but he nevertheless considers the belief in such a connection to be a reasonable one. In arguing that state regulation of obscene material is constitutionally acceptable, he emphasizes two points: (1) State regulation of obscene material in no way violates the constitutionally protected right to privacy. (2) State regulation of obscene material is not tantamount to restricting the communication of ideas and thus does not violate the First Amendment.

We categorically disapprove the theory, apparently adopted by the trial judge, that obscene, pornographic films acquire constitutional immunity from state regulation simply because they are exhibited for consenting adults only. This holding was properly rejected by the Georgia Supreme Court. Although we have often pointedly recognized the high importance of the state interest in regulating the exposure of obscene materials to juveniles and unconsenting adults, this Court has never declared these to be the only legitimate state interests permitting regulation of obscene material. The States have a long-recognized legitimate interest in regulating the use of obscene material in local commerce and in all places of public accommodation, as long as these regulations do not run afoul of specific constitutional prohibitions. "In an unbroken series of cases extending over a long stretch of this Court's history, it has been accepted as a postulate that 'the primary requirements of decency may be enforced against obscene publications.'"

In particular, we hold that there are legitimate state interests at stake in stemming the tide of commercialized obscenity, even assuming it is feasible to enforce effective safeguards against exposure to juveniles and to the passerby. Rights and interests "other than those of the advocates are involved." These include the interest of the public in the quality

United States Supreme Court. 413 U.S. 49 (1973).

of life and the total community environment, the tone of commerce in the great city centers, and, possibly, the public safety itself. The Hill-Link Minority Report of the Commission on Obscenity and Pornography indicates that there is at least an arguable correlation between obscene material and crime. Quite apart from sex crimes, however, there remains one problem of large proportions aptly described by Professor Bickel:

> It concerns the tone of the society, the mode, or to use terms that have perhaps greater currency, the style and quality of life, now and in the future. A man may be entitled to read an obscene book in his room, or expose himself indecently there. . . . We should protect his privacy. But if he demands a right to obtain the books and pictures he wants in the market and to foregather in public places—discreet, if you will, but accessible to all—with others who share his tastes, *then to grant him his right is to affect the world about the rest of us, and to impinge on other privacies.* Even supposing that each of us can, if he wishes, effectively avert the eye and stop the ear (which, in truth, we cannot), what is commonly read and seen and heard and done intrudes upon us all, want it or not.
> 22 The Public Interest 25, 25–26 (Winter, 1971). (Emphasis supplied.)

As Chief Justice Warren stated there is a "right of the Nation and of the States to maintain a decent society. . . ."

But, it is argued, there is no scientific data which conclusively demonstrates that exposure to obscene materials adversely affects men and women or their society. It is urged on behalf of the petitioner that, absent such a demonstration, any kind of state regulation is "impermissible." We reject this argument. It is not for us to resolve empirical uncertainties underlying state legislation, save in the exceptional case where that legislation plainly impinges upon rights protected by the Constitution itself. Mr. Justice Brennan, speaking for the Court in *Ginsberg v. New York* (1968), said "We do not demand of legislatures 'scientifically certain criteria of legislation.' " Although there is no conclusive proof of a connection between antisocial behavior and obscene material, the legislature of Georgia could quite reasonably determine that such a connection does or might exist. . . .

If we accept the unprovable assumption that a complete education requires the reading of certain books, and the well nigh universal belief that good books, plays, and art lift the spirit, improve the mind, enrich the human personality and develop character, can we then say that a state legislature may not act on the corollary assumption that commerce in obscene books, or public exhibitions focused on obscene conduct, have a tendency to exert a corrupting and debasing impact leading to antisocial behavior? "Many of these effects may be intangible and indistinct, but they are nonetheless real." Mr. Justice Cardozo said that all laws in Western civilization are "guided by a robust common sense. . . ." The sum of experience, including that of the past two decades, affords an ample basis for legislatures to conclude that a sensitive, key relationship of human existence, central to family life, community welfare, and the development of human personality, can be debased and distorted by crass commercial exploitation of sex. Nothing in the Constitution prohibits a State from reaching such a conclusion and acting on it legislatively simply because there is no conclusive evidence or empirical data.

It is argued that individual "free will" must govern, even in activities beyond the protection of the First Amendment and other constitutional guarantees of privacy, and that Government cannot legitimately impede an individual's desire to see or acquire obscene plays, movies, and books. We do indeed base our society on certain assumptions that people have the capacity for free choice. Most exercises of individual free choice—those in politics, religion, and expression of ideas—are explicitly protected by the Constitution. Totally unlimited play for free will, however, is not allowed in ours or any other society. We have just noted, for example, that neither the First Amendment nor "free will" precludes States from having "blue sky" laws to regulate what sellers of securities may write or publish about their wares. Such laws are to protect the weak, the uninformed, the unsuspecting, and the gullible from the exercise of their own volition. Nor do modern societies leave disposal of garbage and sewage up to the individual "free will," but impose regulation to protect both public health and the appearance of public places. States are told by some that they must await a "laissez faire" market solution to the obscenity-pornography problem, paradoxically "by people who have never otherwise had a kind word to say for laissez-faire," particularly in solving urban, commercial, and environmental pollution problems.

The States, of course, may follow such a "laissez faire" policy and drop all controls on commercialized obscenity, if that is what they prefer, just as they can ignore consumer protection in the market place, but nothing in the Constitution *compels* the States to do so with regard to matters falling within state jurisdiction. . . .

It is asserted, however, that standards for evaluating state commercial regulations are inapposite in the present context, as state regulation of access by consenting adults to obscene material violates the constitutionally protected right to privacy enjoyed by petitioners' customers. Even assuming that petitioners have vicarious standing to assert potential customers' rights, it is unavailing to compare a theatre, open to the public for a fee, with the private home of *Stanley v. Georgia* (1969) and the marital bedroom of *Griswold v. Connecticut* (1965). This Court, has, on numerous occasions, refused to hold that commercial ventures such as a motion-picture house are "private" for the purpose of civil rights litigation and civil rights statutes. The Civil Rights Act of 1964 specifically defines motion-picture houses and theatres as places of "public accommodation" covered by the Act as operations affecting commerce.

Our prior decisions recognizing a right to privacy guaranteed by the Fourteenth Amendment included "only those personal rights that can be deemed 'fundamental' or 'implicit in the concept of ordered liberty.'" This privacy right encompasses and protects the personal intimacies of the home, the family, marriage, motherhood, procreation, and child rearing. Nothing, however, in this Court's decisions intimates that there is any "fundamental" privacy right "implicit in the concept of ordered liberty" to watch obscene movies in places of public accommodation.

If obscene material unprotected by the First Amendment in itself carried with it a "penumbra" of constitutionally protected privacy, this Court would not have found it necessary to decide *Stanley* on the narrow basis of the "privacy of the home," which was hardly more than a reaffirmation that "a man's home is his castle." Moreover, we have declined to equate the privacy of the home relied on in *Stanley* with a "zone" of "privacy" that follows a distributor or a consumer of obscene materials wherever he goes. The idea of a "privacy" right and a place of public accommodation are, in this context, mutually exclusive. Conduct or depictions of conduct that the state police power can prohibit on a public street does not become automatically protected by the Constitution merely because the conduct is moved to a bar or a "live" theatre stage, any more than a "live" performance of a man and woman locked in a sexual embrace at high noon in Times Square is protected by the Constitution because they simultaneously engage in a valid political dialogue.

It is also argued that the State has no legitimate interest in "control [of] the moral content of a person's thoughts," and we need not quarrel with this. But we reject the claim that the State of Georgia is here attempting to control the minds or thoughts of those who patronize theatres. Preventing unlimited display or distribution of obscene material, which by definition lacks any serious literary, artistic, political, or scientific value as communication, is distinct from a control of reason and the intellect. Where communication of ideas, protected by the First Amendment, is not involved, nor the particular privacy of the home protected by *Stanley*, nor any of the other "areas or zones" of constitutionally protected privacy, the mere fact that, as a consequence, some human "utterances" or "thoughts" may be incidentally affected does not bar the State from acting to protect legitimate state interests. The fantasies of a drug addict are his own and beyond the reach of government, but government regulation of drug sales is not prohibited by the Constitution.

Finally, petitioners argue that conduct which directly involves "consenting adults" only has, for that sole reason, a special claim to constitutional protection. Our Constitution establishes a broad range of conditions on the exercise of power by the States, but for us to say that our Constitution incorporates the proposition that conduct involving consenting adults only is always beyond state regulation, that is a step we are unable to take. Commercial exploitation of depictions, descriptions, or exhibitions of obscene conduct on commercial premises open to the adult public falls within a State's broad power to regulate commerce and protect the public environment. The issue in this context goes beyond whether someone, or even the majority, considers the conduct depicted as "wrong" or "sinful." The States have the power to make a morally neutral judgment that public exhibition of obscene material, or commerce in such material, has a tendency to injure the community as a whole, to endanger the public safety, or to jeopardize in Chief Justice Warren's words, the States' "right . . . to maintain a decent society."

To summarize, we have today reaffirmed the basic holding of *Roth v. United States* (1957) that obscene material has no protection under the First Amendment. We have directed our holdings, not at thoughts or speech, but at depiction and description of specifically defined sexual conduct that States may regulate within limits designed to prevent infringement of First Amendment rights. We have also reaffirmed the holdings of *United States v. Reidel* (1971) and *United States v. Thirty-Seven Photographs* (1971) that commerce in obscene material is unprotected by any constitutional doctrine of privacy. In this case we hold that the States have a legitimate interest in regulating commerce in obscene material and in regulating exhibition of obscene material in places of public accommodation, including so-called "adult" theatres from which minors are excluded. In light of these holdings, nothing precludes the State of Georgia from the regulation of the allegedly obscene materials exhibited in Paris Adult Theatre I or II, provided that the applicable Georgia law, as written or authoritatively interpreted by the Georgia courts, meets the First Amendment standards set forth in *Miller v. California* (1973). . . .

QUESTIONS

1. To what extent, if at all, does the opinion of Chief Justice Burger reveal a commitment to the principle of legal moralism and/or the principle of legal paternalism?

2. Chief Justice Burger contends that state regulation of obscene material is not tantamount to restricting the communication of ideas and thus does not violate the First Amendment. Is this a defensible position?

DISSENTING OPINION IN *PARIS ADULT THEATRE I v. SLATON*

A biographical sketch of Justice William Brennan is found on page 125.

Justice Brennan acknowledges that there may be a class of material—obscene material—that in itself is not protected by the First Amendment guarantee of free speech. He argues, however, that it is impossible to specifically define "obscenity," and, as a result, that state efforts to totally suppress obscene material inevitably lead to the erosion of protected speech, thus infringing on the First Amendment. Likewise, he contends, such state efforts inevitably infringe on the Fourteenth Amendment and generate "costly institutional harms." He analyzes the interests of the state in suppressing obscene material and concludes that such interests are not sufficient to "justify the substantial damage to constitutional rights and to this nation's judicial machinery."

Our experience since *Roth v. United States* (1957) requires us not only to abandon the effort to pick out obscene materials on a case-by-case basis, but also to reconsider a fundamental postulate of *Roth*: that there exists a definable class of sexually oriented expression that may be totally suppressed by the Federal and State Governments. Assuming that such a class of expression does in fact exist, I am forced to conclude that the concept of "obscenity" cannot be defined with sufficient specificity and clarity to provide fair notice to persons who create and distribute sexually oriented materials, to prevent substantial erosion of protected speech as a by-product of the attempt to suppress unprotected speech, and to avoid very costly institutional harms. Given these inevitable side-effects of state efforts to suppress what is assumed to be *unprotected* speech, we must scrutinize with care the state interest that is asserted to justify the suppression. For in the absence of some very substantial interest in suppressing such speech, we can hardly condone the ill-effects that seem to flow inevitably from the effort. . . .

Because we assumed—incorrectly, as experience has proven—that obscenity could be separated from other sexually oriented expression without significant costs either to the First Amendment or to the judicial machinery charged with the task of safeguarding First Amendment freedoms, we had no occasion in *Roth* to probe the asserted state interest in curtailing unprotected, sexually oriented speech. Yet as we have increasingly come to appreciate the vagueness of the concept of obscenity, we have begun to recognize and articulate the state interests at stake. Significantly, in *Redrup v. New York* (1967), where we set aside findings of obscenity with regard to three sets of material, we pointed out that

[i]n none of the cases was there a claim that the statute in question reflected a specific and limited state concern for juveniles. In none was there any suggestion of an assault upon individual privacy by publication in a manner so obtrusive as to make it impossible for an unwilling individual to avoid exposure to it. And in none was there evidence of the sort of 'pandering' which the Court found significant in *Ginzburg v. United States* (1966).

United States Supreme Court. 413 U.S. 49 (1973).

The opinions in *Redrup* and *Stanley v. Georgia* (1969) reflected our emerging view that the state interests in protecting children and in protecting unconsenting adults may stand on a different footing from the other asserted state interests. . . .

But whatever the strength of the state interests in protecting juveniles and unconsenting adults from exposure to sexually oriented materials, those interests cannot be asserted in defense of the holding of the Georgia Supreme Court in this case. That court assumed for the purposes of its decision that the films in issue were exhibited only to persons over the age of 21 who viewed them willingly and with prior knowledge of the nature of their contents. And on that assumption the state court held that the films could still be suppressed. The justification for the suppression must be found, therefore, in some independent interest in regulating the reading and viewing habits of consenting adults.

At the outset it should be noted that virtually all of the interests that might be asserted in defense of suppression, laying aside the special interests associated with distribution to juveniles and unconsenting adults, were also posited in *Stanley v. Georgia* where we held that the State could not make the "mere private possession of obscene material a crime." That decision presages the conclusions I reach here today.

In *Stanley* we pointed out that "[t]here appears to be little empirical basis for" the assertion that "exposure to obscene materials may lead to deviant sexual behavior or crimes of sexual violence." In any event, we added that "if the State is only concerned about printed or filmed materials inducing antisocial conduct, we believe that in the context of private consumption of ideas and information we should adhere to the view that '[a]mong free men, the deterrents ordinarily to be applied to prevent crime are education and punishment for violations of the law. . . .'"

Moreover, in *Stanley* we rejected as "wholly inconsistent with the philosophy of the First Amendment," the notion that there is a legitimate state concern in the "control [of] the moral content of a person's thoughts," and we held that a State "cannot constitutionally premise legislation on the desirability of controlling a person's private thoughts." That is not to say, of course, that a State must remain utterly indifferent to—and take no action bearing on—the morality of the community. The traditional description of state police power does embrace the regulation of morals as well as the health, safety, and general welfare of the citizenry. And much legislation—compulsory public education laws, civil rights laws, even the abolition of capital punishment—are grounded at least in part on a concern with the morality of the community. But the State's interest in regulating morality by suppressing obscenity, while often asserted, remains essentially unfocused and ill-defined. And, since the attempt to curtail unprotected speech necessarily spills over into the area of protected speech, the effort to serve this speculative interest through the suppression of obscene material must tread heavily on rights protected by the First Amendment.

In *Roe v. Wade* (1973), we held constitutionally invalid a state abortion law, even though we were aware of

> the sensitive and emotional nature of the abortion controversy, of the vigorous opposing views, even among physicians, and of the deep and seemingly absolute convictions that the subject inspires. One's philosophy, one's experiences, one's exposure to the raw edges of human existence, one's religious training, one's attitudes toward life and family and their values, and the moral standards one establishes and seeks to observe, are all likely to influence and to color one's thinking and conclusions about abortion.

Like the proscription of abortions, the effort to suppress obscenity is predicated on unprovable, although strongly held, assumptions about human behavior, morality, sex, and religion. The existence of these assumptions cannot validate a statute that substantially undermines the guarantees of the First Amendment, any more than the existence of similar assumptions on the issue of abortion can validate a statute that infringes the constitutionally protected privacy interests of a pregnant woman.

If, as the Court today assumes, "a state legislature may . . . act on the . . . assumption that . . . commerce in obscene books, or public exhibitions focused on obscene conduct, have a tendency to exert a corrupting and debasing impact leading to antisocial behavior," then it is hard to see how state-ordered regimentation of our minds can ever be forestalled. For if a State may, in an effort to maintain or create a particular moral tone, prescribe what its citizens cannot read or cannot see, then it would seem to follow that in pursuit of that same objective a State could decree that its citizens must read certain books or must view certain films. However laudable its goal—and that is obviously a question on which reasonable minds may differ—the State cannot proceed by means that violate the Constitution. . . .

Recognizing these principles, we have held that so-called thematic obscenity— obscenity which might persuade the viewer or reader to engage in "obscene" conduct—is not outside the protection of the First Amendment:

> It is contended that the State's action was justified because the motion picture attractively portrays a relationship which is contrary to the moral standards, the religious precepts, and the legal code of its citizenry. This argument misconceives what it is that the Constitution protects. Its guarantee is not confined to the expression of ideas that are conventional or shared by a majority. It protects advocacy of the opinion that adultery may sometimes be proper, no less than advocacy of socialism or the single tax. And in the realm of ideas it protects expression which is eloquent no less than that which is unconvincing. *Kingsley Int'l Pictures Corp. v. Regents* (1959).

Even a legitimate, sharply focused state concern for the morality of the community cannot, in other words, justify an assault on the protections of the First Amendment. Where the state interest in regulation of morality is vague and ill-defined, interference with the guarantees of the First Amendment is even more difficult to justify.

In short, while I cannot say that the interests of the State—apart from the question of juveniles and unconsenting adults—are trivial or nonexistent, I am compelled to conclude that these interests cannot justify the substantial damage to constitutional rights and to this Nation's judicial machiney that inevitably results from state efforts to bar the distribution even of unprotected material to consenting adults. I would hold, therefore, that at least in the absence of distribution to juveniles or obtrusive exposure to unconsenting adults, the First and Fourteenth Amendments prohibit the state and federal governments from attempting wholly to suppress sexually oriented materials on the basis of their allegedly "obscene" contents. Nothing in this approach precludes those governments from taking action to serve what may be strong and legitimate interests through regulation of the manner of distribution of sexually oriented material.

QUESTIONS

1. Is it impossible, as Justice Brennan believes, to specifically define "obscenity," or can a workable definition be advanced and defended?

2. Is "substantial damage to constitutional rights and to this nation's judicial machinery" the inevitable outcome of state efforts to suppress obscene material?

3. To what extent, if at all, does the opinion of Justice Brennan reveal a commitment to the principle of legal moralism?

JOHN STUART MILL

THE HARM PRINCIPLE

A biographical sketch of John Stuart Mill is found on page 129.

In this excerpt from his classic work *On Liberty* (1859), Mill contends that society is warranted in restricting individual liberty only if an action is harmful to others, never because an action in one way or another is harmful to the person who performs the action. He clearly rejects both the principle of legal paternalism and the principle of legal moralism. Mill argues on utilitarian grounds for an exclusive adherence to the harm principle, holding that society will be better off by tolerating all expressions of individual liberty that involve no harm to others, rather than by "compelling each to live as seems good to the rest." While alluding to offenses against decency, he makes it clear that certain actions may be exclusively "self-harming" when done in private and yet, when done in public, may constitute an offense against others.

The object of this Essay is to assert one very simple principle, as entitled to govern absolutely the dealings of society with the individual in the way of compulsion and control, whether the means used be physical force in the form of legal penalties, or the moral coercion of public opinion. That principle is, that the sole end for which mankind are warranted, individually or collectively, in interfering with the liberty of action of any of their number, is self-protection. That the only purpose for which power can be rightfully exercised over any member of a civilized community, against his will, is to prevent harm to others. His own good, either physical or moral, is not a sufficient warrant. He cannot rightfully be compelled to do or forbear because it will be better for him to do so, because it will make him happier, because, in the opinions of others, to do so would be wise, or even right. These are good reasons for remonstrating with him, or reasoning with him, or persuading him, or entreating him, but not for compelling him, or visiting him with any evil in case he do otherwise. To justify that, the conduct from which it is desired to deter him, must be calculated to produce evil to some one else. The only part of the conduct of any one, for which he is amenable to society, is that which concerns others. In the part which merely concerns himself, his independence is, of right, absolute. Over himself, over his own body and mind, the individual is sovereign.

It is, perhaps, hardly necessary to say that this doctrine is meant to apply only to human beings in the maturity of their faculties. We are not speaking of children, or of young persons below the age which the law may fix as that of manhood and womanhood. Those who are still in a state to require being taken care of by others, must be protected against their own actions as well as against external injury. . . .

There is a sphere of action in which society, as distinguished from the individual, has, if any, only an indirect interest; comprehending all that portion of a person's life and conduct which affects only himself, or if it also affects others, only with their free, voluntary, and undeceived consent and participation. When I say only himself, I mean directly, and in the first instance: for whatever affects himself, may affect others *through* himself; and the objection which may be grounded on this contingency, will receive consideration in the sequel. This, then, is the appropriate region of human liberty. It comprises, first, the inward

Reprinted from the original edition of *On Liberty* (London, 1859).

domain of consciousness; demanding liberty of conscience, in the most comprehensive sense; liberty of thought and feeling; absolute freedom of opinion and sentiment on all subjects, practical or speculative, scientific, moral, or theological. The liberty of expressing and publishing opinions may seem to fall under a different principle, since it belongs to that part of the conduct of an individual which concerns other people; but, being almost of as much importance as the liberty of thought itself, and resting in great part on the same reasons, is practically inseparable from it. Secondly, the principle requires liberty of tastes and pursuits; of framing the plan of our life to suit our own character; of doing as we like, subject to such consequences as may follow; without impediment from our fellow-creatures, so long as what we do does not harm them, even though they should think our conduct foolish, perverse, or wrong. Thirdly, from this liberty of each individual, follows the liberty, within the same limits, of combination among individuals; freedom to unite, for any purpose not involving harm to others: the persons combining being supposed to be of full age, and not forced or deceived.

No society in which these liberties are not, on the whole, respected, is free, whatever may be its form of government; and none is completely free in which they do not exist absolute and unqualified. The only freedom which deserves the name, is that of pursuing our own good in our own way, so long as we do not attempt to deprive others of theirs, or impede their efforts to obtain it. Each is the proper guardian of his own health, whether bodily, or mental and spiritual. Mankind are greater gainers by suffering each other to live as seems good to themselves, than by compelling each to live as seems good to the rest. . . .

Again, there are many acts which, being directly injurious only to the agents themselves, ought not to be legally interdicted, but which, if done publicly, are a violation of good manners, and coming thus within the category of offences against others, may rightfully be prohibited. Of this kind are offences against decency; on which it is unnecessary to dwell, the rather as they are only connected indirectly with our subject, the objection to publicity being equally strong in the case of many actions not in themselves condemnable, nor supposed to be so. . . .

QUESTIONS

1. Would Mill find permissible laws restricting the access of consenting adults to pornography? Would Mill find permissible laws restricting the access of minors to pornography? Would Mill find permissible laws prohibiting pornographic billboards? Explain.
2. Is it true, as Mill claims, that "Mankind are greater gainers by suffering each other to live as seems good to themselves, than by compelling each to live as seems good to the rest?"
3. Are those who are exposed to pornography themselves harmed by such exposure? If so, is the fact of self-harm sufficient to justify laws that limit the access of consenting adults to pornographic materials?

BURTON M. LEISER

THE EFFECTS OF OBSCENITY

A biographical sketch of Burton M. Leiser is found on page 100.

Leiser reviews the findings of the Commission on Obscenity and Pornography in regard to the effects of "erotic materials." He suggests that the minority report of the Commission may embody several fallacies of causal reasoning. Cautiously assessing the available evidence, Leiser concludes that we simply do not know, at this date, whether or not erotic materials have socially undesirable effects.

If no satisfactory definition of *obscenity* has thus far been developed, it cannot be for lack of effort. When the nine justices on a single court cannot arrive at a single definition that they can work with, but consistently come up with as many as seven or eight separate views on the meaning of the term in a given case, it is obvious that the problem is not only a difficult one, but that it has serious practical consequences. For the student who is interested in studying the effects of obscene materials, such a state of affairs must be most disconcerting; for if no definition of the key term can be found, then it is impossible to inquire meaningfully into the effects of obscene materials, because there is no way to distinguish such materials from those that are not obscene.

Until quite recently no sustained scientific research had been done in this area. But the Commission on Obscenity and Pornography, armed with a $2 million appropriation from Congress, was able to initiate a number of studies that have started to provide some answers to some of the most troublesome questions.

Instead of attempting to define *obscenity*, the commission chose to discuss "erotic materials," without passing moral or legal judgment on them. The problem, then, was to determine what effects erotic materials of various sorts have upon people in a variety of contexts.

Some of the research findings can be dismissed as trivial. Surveys, for example, revealed that at least half the population believes that explicit sexual materials provide information about sex, and that more than half of all police chiefs believe that obscene materials contribute to juvenile delinquency. They have also found that erotic materials cause sexual arousal in many males and females and that females are not as aroused by material designed to arouse male homosexuals as they are by material depicting heterosexual conduct.

Other findings, however, are more important for our purposes. The commission's studies concluded that a significant number of persons increased their masturbatory activity after exposure to erotic materials. Persons who reported increased rates of intercourse were generally those who were already experienced and had established sexual partners. In general, the commission concluded, any such increase in sexual activity tended to be temporary and was not significantly different from the kind of sexual behavior in which the individual had engaged prior to his or her exposure to the erotic materials. Erotic dreams, sexual fantasies, and conversation about sexual matters all tended to increase after exposure to such materials. Some married couples reported more agreeable relations and greater willingness to discuss sexual matters after such exposure than before.

One might have expected delinquent youth to have more and earlier exposure to erotic materials than nondelinquent youth. Both of these expectations turn out to be ill founded, according to the commission. Both delinquent and nondelinquent youth have wide exposure to such materials.

According to the commission's report, there is no statistical correlation between sex crimes and exposure to erotic materials. Although the United States has experienced a significant increase in arrests for rape during the past decade of relaxed restrictions on erotic material, arrests for juvenile sex crimes decreased during the same period. In Denmark there was a notable decrease in sex crimes after Danish law was changed to permit virtually unrestricted access to erotic materials.

The commission's overall conclusion was that "empirical research designed to clarify the question has found no evidence to date that exposure to explicit sexual materials plays a significant role in the causation of delinquent or criminal behavior among youth or adults. The commission cannot conclude that exposure to erotic materials is a factor in the causation of sex crime or sex delinquency."[1]

Other authorities had earlier come to much the same conclusion, but without the benefit of the extensive studies sponsored by the commission.

This is not the place for a detailed summary or evaluation of the commission's report or the data on which it based its findings. It is appropriate to note, however, that several members of the commission protested its findings, and wrote a minority report that contained the following major disagreements with it: A number of studies available to the commission were ignored or underrated by it in its final report. Thus, one research team found that there was a definite correlation between juvenile exposure to pornography and precocious heterosexual and deviant sexual behavior. Another study found that there was a direct relation between the frequency with which adolescents saw movies depicting sexual intercourse and the extent to which the adolescents themselves engaged in premarital sexual intercourse. In a third study it was found that "the rapists were the group reporting the highest 'excitation to masturbation' rates by pornography both in the adult (80%) as well as teen (90%) years." The dissenters add, "Considering the crime they were imprisoned for, this suggests that pornography (with accompanying masturbation) did not serve adequately as a catharsis [as some researchers have suggested it might], prevent a sex crime, or 'keep them off the streets.'" The same study reported that 80 per cent of prisoners who had had experience with erotica reported that they "wished to try the act" they had witnessed in the erotic films they had seen, and when asked whether they *had* followed through, between 30 and 38 per cent replied that they had. In still another study, 39 per cent of sex offenders reported that "pornography had something to do with their committing the offense" of which they were convicted.[2]

In addition, the minority accused the majority of being biased, of suppressing evidence, of misinterpreting statistics and conclusions of researchers, and of misrepresentation.

No attempt will be made here to analyze these findings. However, a number of venerable fallacies may have been perpetrated in them. One, known by its Latin description, *post hoc ergo propter hoc*, consists of supposing that because one phenomenon follows another, the later phenomenon must be caused by the earlier one. But this is not necessarily the case. I know a man who begins to eat his lunch every day promptly after the whistle at the steel mill blows; but the blowing of the whistle is not the cause of his eating, or even of his eating at that particular time. He eats at that time because that happens to be the beginning of his lunch hour. Nor, contrary to David Hume's opinion, is the fact that one

[1] *The Report of the Commission on Obscenity and Pornography* (New York: Bantam Books, 1970), p. 32.
[2] *Ibid.*, Part IV, pp. 443 ff.

phenomenon regularly accompanies another evidence that the one is necessarily the cause of, or caused by, the other. They may both be caused by some unknown third factor. Thus, in the cases before us, both the delinquent behavior and the reading of erotica may have been caused by some other factors in the lives of the adolescents who were surveyed; there is no way, with the information presently available, to show that the erotic material caused the delinquent behavior. Nor is the fact that some sex criminals report that they read pornographic books or saw pornographic films prior to the commission of their crimes an unequivocal indication that the pornography contributed to their criminal behavior. For one thing, they may have been seeking some excuse for their behavior or a scapegoat on whom to fasten the guilt. It would be useful if a rapist could claim that he is really not to blame for his crime. The man who should be in jail, he might claim, is the one who published the obscene book he read just before he raped his victim, or the governor who signed the liberalized censorship law, or the Supreme Court Justice who removed the ban on it. But this will not do at all, because so many persons read the same pornographic works and do not commit sex crimes.

This is not to say that there is *no* causal connection between erotic literature and sexual behavior. It is to suggest merely that the answers are not in yet, and that even such research as is presently available must be approached with considerable caution.

Thus far, one must conclude that available evidence does not support the thesis that erotic materials have socially undesirable effects upon the people who are exposed to them, but it does not support the thesis that such materials do *not* have such effects either.

QUESTIONS

1. Suppose a man sexually assaulted a small girl shortly after you happened to see him leave a pornographic-film theatre. Would you then be justified in concluding that exposure to pornographic materials is a cause of crime?

2. Consider the following suggestion: Even though there is presently no proof that exposure to pornography is causally linked with socially undesirable behavior, we had better take the path of caution and limit the access of consenting adults to pornographic materials. Is this a defensible position?

CHARLES H. KEATING, JR.

PORNOGRAPHY AND THE PUBLIC MORALITY

Charles H. Keating, Jr., is a lawyer whose private practice is based in Cincinnati, Ohio. He is legal counsel to the Citizens for Decent Literature, Inc., an organization which he founded in 1956. Keating, who served as a member of the Commission on Obscenity and Pornography, vigorously dissented from the findings of the majority. This short selection is taken from his extensive dissenting statement.

Keating characterizes pornography as a form of prostitution; it provides sexual pleasure for a price. In his view, which he identifies as "the traditional Judeo-Christian ethic," any form of impersonal sexual activity is debasing, a violation of human dignity. The use of pornography is immoral, he contends, because it involves the pursuit of pleasure for its own sake, thereby excluding "the higher purposes and values to which pleasure is attached." In vivid contrast to John Stuart Mill, Keating explicitly endorses the principle of legal moralism. Even if it were admitted that access to pornographic material plays no significant role in the causation of social or individual harms, he insists, anti-pornography laws are justified. In his view, the need to protect the public morality is not only the historical reason for anti-pornography laws but also a sufficient justification for them.

███████████

. . . I cannot undertake consideration of the subject of pornography without commenting on its underlying philosophical and moral basis.

For those who believe in God, in His absolute supremacy as the Creator and Lawgiver of life, in the dignity and destiny which He has conferred upon the human person, in the moral code that governs sexual activity—for those who believe in these "things," no argument against pornography should be necessary.

Though the meaning of pornography is generally understood, reference is seldom made to the root meaning of the term itself. This seems important to me. The Greeks had a word for it, for many "its." And the Greek word for pornography is highly significant. It comes from two Greek words, in fact: "prostitute" and "write." So, the dictionary defines pornography as "originally a description of prostitutes and their trade."

Pornography is not merely associated in this historical sense with prostitution, but it is actually a form of prostitution because it advertises and advocates "sex for sale," pleasure for a price.

The use of sexual powers is intimately bound up with both love and life, not merely with the momentary satisfaction of desire. Only a person is capable of love, but any of the lower forms of animal life can experience pleasure as a mere sense reaction. A person is much more than a body, and any form of sexual activity which is impersonal, which uses the body alone for pleasure, violates the integrity of the person and thereby reduces him to the level of an irrational and irresponsible animal.

The traditional Judeo-Christian ethic does not condemn pleasure as an evil in itself; it does condemn the pursuit of pleasure for its own sake, as an end rather than a means, deliberately excluding the higher purposes and values to which pleasure is attached. Everybody knows that the appetite for food makes the necessity of eating more palatable, more pleasurable. To eat to live is rational, sound procedure; to live to eat is an abuse of a basically good thing. The same is true of the sex drive. It serves the individual and the common good of the human race, only when it is creative, productive, when it ministers to love and life. When, however, it serves only itself, it becomes a perversion, actually an antisocial force disruptive and eventually destructive of all love and life. Every word by which the organs of sex are designated bears out this statement: genital, generative, reproductive, procreative. Love is always fruitful of lasting good; mere pleasure is of its nature transitory, barren, the only residue likely to be unhappy, remorseful memories. This thought could be amplified and graphically illustrated.

Those who speak in defense of sexual morality are accused of making sex "dirty." It's the other way around. The defenders of pornography are guilty of degrading sex. Marcel Proust, French novelist *(Sodom and Gomorrah),* described the effect of his early reading of erotica upon himself: "Oh stream of hell that undermined my adolescence." Literature is a better reflection of life than is scientific opinion; and I am certain that the testimony of men like Proust could be multiplied if someone took the time to assemble the sources.

Reprinted from the "Statement of Charles H. Keating, Jr.," in *The Report of the Commission on Obscenity and Pornography* (Washington, D.C.: U.S. Government Printing Office, 1970).

No, the state cannot legislate virtue, cannot make moral goodness by merely enacting law; but the state can and does legislate against vices which publicly jeopardize the virtue of people who might prefer to remain virtuous. If it is not the proper function of law to offer citizens such protection, then what is it? . . .

EFFECTS OF PORNOGRAPHY

We should begin by saying the law is clear. The law founded in reason and common sense recognizes obscenity as intrinsically evil and does not demand the "clear and present danger" test so ardently advocated by [Commission on Obscenity and Pornography] Chairman Lockhart and the American Civil Liberties Union. The law, rather, proscribes pornography on the basis of the public good—protecting public health and welfare, public decency, and morality, a condition absolutely essential to the well-being of the nation. . . .

One can consult all the experts he chooses, can write reports, make studies, etc., but the fact that obscenity corrupts lies within the common sense, the reason, and the logic of every man. . . .

If man is affected by his environment, by circumstances of his life, by reading, by instruction, by anything, he is then certainly affected by pornography. The mere nature of pornography makes it impossible for pornography to effect good. Therefore, it must necessarily effect evil. Sexual immorality, more than any other causative factor, historically speaking, is the root cause of the demise of all great nations and all great peoples. (Ref. Toynbee: Moral decay from within destroyed most of the world's great civilizations.) . . .

The Commission majority bases their recommended repeal of all federal and state laws that "prohibit consensual distribution of sexual material to adults" on the statement that "extensive empirical investigation, both by the Commission and by others, provides no evidence that exposure to or use of explicit sexual materials play a significant role in the causation of social or individual harms such as crime, delinquency, sexual or nonsexual deviancy or severe emotional disturbances."

While it is a fact that a significant percentage of nationally recognized psychiatric authorities and many law enforcement officials at all levels of jurisdiction would disagree with that statement, the important point I want to make here is that the reasons for obscenity laws are *not* contained in the statement. Obscenity laws have existed historically in recognition of the need to protect the *public morality*. . . .

I submit that never in the history of modern civilization have we seen more obvious evidence of a decline in public morality than we see today. Venereal disease is at epidemic proportions and literally out of control in many large urban centers—despite medicine. Illegitimacy statistics are skyrocketing—despite the pill and other contraceptive devices—and despite the relatively easy access to abortion. Both of these social statistics reflect a promiscuous attitude toward sex which is no doubt contributed to by many factors—but certainly one factor has to be the deluge of pornography which is screaming at young people from records, motion picture screens, newsstands, the United States mail and their peer groups.

To say that pornography has no effect is patently ridiculous. I submit that if pornography does *not* affect a person—that person has a problem. Pornography is intended to arouse the sexual appetite—one of the most volatile appetites of human nature. Once that appetite is aroused, it will seek satisfaction—and the satisfaction sought—without proper moral restraints—is often reflected in the social statistics discussed above. . . .

In addition to the social problems of venereal disease and illegitimacy, it is also of the very nature of obscenity to degrade sex and distort the role that sex plays in a normal life. There is no way to measure the terrible effects that pornography has had and is having on marital infidelity that is reflected in divorce statistics, abortions, suicide and other social problems that further reflect the decline in public morality. . . .

QUESTIONS

1. Is pornography immoral?
2. Is there a widespread consensus in American society to the effect that pornography is morally repugnant? If so, is the existence of such a consensus sufficient to justify laws that limit the access of consenting adults to pornographic materials?
3. Is the principle of legal moralism an acceptable liberty-limiting principle?

G. L. SIMONS

IS PORNOGRAPHY BENEFICIAL?

G. L. Simons, an Englishman, is an author whose principal works center on various aspects of human sexuality. His books include *A History of Sex* (1970), *A Place for Pleasure, The History of the Brothel* (1975), and *Pornography without Prejudice* (1972), from which this selection is excerpted.

Emphasizing that individual liberty is justifiably limited only when there is clear evidence that an activity produces significant harm, Simons constructs a case against censorship. In a more positive vein, he actively defends easy access to pornography. In the first place, he argues, pornography provides pleasure without producing significant harms; moreover, pornography is socially beneficial. Simons cites evidence in support of the view that pornography can aid normal sexual development. He also contends that pornography can provide "sex by proxy" for lonely and deprived people. Finally, he contends, with regard to an especially important aspect of "sex by proxy," it is at least plausible to think that the availability of pornography provides release for sexual desires that might otherwise be released through socially harmful behavior.

It is not sufficient, for the objectors' case, that they demonstrate that some harm has flowed from pornography. It would be extremely difficult to show that pornography had *never* had unfortunate consequences, but we should not make too much of this. Harm has flowed from religion, patriotism, alcohol and cigarettes without this fact impelling people to demand abolition. The harm, if established, has to be weighed against a variety of considerations before a decision can be reached as to the propriety of certain laws. Of the British Obscenity Laws the Arts Council Report comments[1] that "the harm would need to be both indisputable and very dire indeed before it could be judged to outweigh the evils and anomalies inherent in the Acts we have been asked to examine."

[1] *The Obscenity Laws,* André Deutsch, 1969, p. 33.

The onus therefore is upon the anti-pornographers to demonstrate not only that harm is caused by certain types of sexual material but that the harm is considerable: if the first is difficult the second is necessarily more so, and the attempts to date have not been impressive. It is even possible to argue that easily available pornography has a number of benefits. Many people will be familiar with the *catharsis* argument whereby pornography is said to cut down on delinquency by providing would-be criminals with substitute satisfactions. This is considered later but we mention it here to indicate that access to pornography may be socially beneficial in certain instances, and that where this is possible the requirement for anti-pornographers to *justify* their objections must be stressed.

The general conclusion[2] of the U.S. Commission was that no adequate proof had been provided that pornography was harmful to individual or society—"if a case is to be made out against 'pornography' [in 1970] it will have to be made on grounds other than demonstrated effects of a damaging personal or social nature." . . .

The heresy (to some ears) that pornography is harmless is compounded by the even greater impiety that it may be beneficial. Some of us are managing to adjust to the notion that pornography is unlikely to bring down the world in moral ruin, but the idea that it may actually do good is altogether another thing. When we read of Professor Emeritus E. T. Rasmussen, a pioneer of psychological studies in Denmark, and a government adviser, saying that there is a possibility "that pornography can be beneficial," many of us are likely to have *mixed* reactions, to say the least. In fact this thesis can be argued in a number of ways.

The simplest approach is to remark that people enjoy it. This can be seen to be true whether we rely on personal testimony or the most respectable index of all in capitalist society—"preparedness to pay." The appeal that pornography has for many people is hardly in dispute, and in a more sober social climate that would be justification enough. Today we are not quite puritan enough to deny that *pleasure* has a worthwhile place in human life: not many of us object to our food being tasty or our clothes being attractive. It was not always like this. In sterner times it was *de rigueur* to prepare food without spices and to wear the plainest clothes. The cult of puritanism reached its apotheosis in the most fanatical asceticism, where it was fashionable for holy men to wander off into a convenient desert and neglect the body to the point of cultivating its lice as "pearls of God." In such a bizarre philosophy pleasure was not only condemned in its sexual manifestations but in all areas where the body could conceivably take satisfaction. These days we are able to countenance pleasure in most fields but in many instances still the case for *sexual* pleasure has to be argued.

Pleasure is not of course its own justification. If it clearly leads to serious malaise, early death, or the *dis*pleasure of others, then there is something to be said against it. But the serious consequences have to be demonstrated: it is not enough to condemn certain forms of pleasurable experience on the grounds of *possible* ill effect. With such an approach *any* human activity could be censured and freedom would have no place. In short, if something is pleasurable and its bad effects are small or nonexistent then it is to be encouraged: opposition to such a creed should be recognized as an unwholesome antipathy to human potential. Pleasure is a good except where it is harmful (and where the harmfulness is *significant*). . . .

That pornography is enjoyable to many people is the first of the arguments in its favour. In any other field this would be argument enough. It is certainly sufficient to justify many activities that have—unlike a taste for pornography—demonstrably harmful con-

[2] *The Report of the Commission on Obscenity and Pornography,* Part Three, II, Bantam Books, 1970, p. 169.

sequences. Only in a sexually neurotic society could a tool for heightening sexual enjoyment be regarded as reprehensible and such as to warrant suppression by law. The position is well summarized[3] in the *first* of the Arts Council's twelve reasons for advocating the repeal of the Obscenity Publications Acts:

"It is not for the State to prohibit private citizens from choosing what they may or may not enjoy in literature or art unless there were incontrovertible evidence that the result would be injurious to society. There is no such evidence."

A further point is that availability of pornography may *aid*, rather than frustrate normal sexual development. Thus in 1966, for example, the New Jersey Committee for the Right to Read presented the findings of a survey conducted among nearly a thousand psychiatrists and psychologists of that state. Amongst the various personal statements included was the view that "sexually stimulating materials" might help particular people develop a normal sex drive.[4] In similar spirit, Dr. John Money writes[5] that pornography "may encourage normal sexual development and broadmindedness," a view that may not sound well to the anti-pornographers. And even in circumstances where possible dangers of pornography are pointed out conceivable good effects are sometimes acknowledged. In a paper issued[6] by The Danish Forensic Medicine Council it is pointed out that neurotic and sexually shy people may, by reading pornographic descriptions of normal sexual activity, be freed from some of their apprehension regarding sex and may thereby attain a freer and less frustrated attitude to the sexual side of life. . . .

One argument in favour of pornography is that it can serve as a substitute for actual sexual activity involving another person or other people. This argument has two parts, relating as it does to (1) people who fantasize over *socially acceptable* modes of sexual involvement, and (2) people who fantasize over types of sexual activity that would be regarded as illegal or at least immoral. The first type relates to lonely and deprived people who for one reason or another have been unable to form "normal" sexual contacts with other people; the second type are instances of the much quoted *catharsis* argument.

One writer notes[7] that pornography can serve as a substitute for both the knowledge of which some people have been deprived and the pleasure in sexual experience which they have not enjoyed. One can well imagine men or women too inhibited to secure sexual satisfaction with other adults and where explicit sexual material can alleviate some of their misery. It is facile to remark that such people should seek psychiatric assistance or even "make an effort": the factors that prevent the forming of effective sexual liaisons are just as likely to inhibit any efforts to seek medical or other assistance. Pornography provides *sex by proxy*, and in such usage it can have a clear justification.

It is also possible to imagine circumstances in which men or women—for reasons of illness, travel or bereavement—are unable to seek sexual satisfaction with spouse or other loved one. Pornography can help here too. Again it is easy to suggest that a person abstain from sexual experience, or, if having *permanently* lost a spouse, seek out another partner. Needless to say such advice is often quite impractical—and the alternative to pornography may be prostitution or adultery. Montagu notes that pornography can serve the same pur-

---

[3] *The Obscenity Laws,* André Deutsch, 1969, p. 35.
[4] Quoted by Isadore Rubin, "What Should Parents Do About Pornography?" *Sex in the Adolescent Years,* Fontana, 1969, p. 202.
[5] John Money, contribution to "Is Pornography Harmful to Young Children?" *Sex in the Childhood Years,* Fontana, 1971, p. 181–5.
[6] Paper from The Danish Forensic Medicine Council to The Danish Penal Code Council, published in The Penal Code Council Report on Penalty for Pornography, Report No. 435, Copenhagen, 1966, pp. 78–80, and as appendix to *The Obscenity Laws,* pp. 120–4.
[7] Ashley Montagu, "Is Pornography Harmful to Young Children?" *Sex in the Childhood Years,* Fontana, 1971, p. 182.

pose as "dirty jokes," allowing a person to discharge harmlessly repressed and unsatisfied sexual desires.

In this spirit, Mercier (1970) is quoted by the U.S. Commission:

" . . . it is in periods of sexual deprivation—to which the young and the old are far more subject than those in their prime—that males, at any rate, are likely to reap psychological benefit from pornography."

And also Kenneth Tynan (1970):

"For men on long journeys, geographically cut off from wives and mistresses, pornography can act as a portable memory, a welcome shortcut to remembered bliss, relieving tension without involving disloyalty."

It is difficult to see how anyone could object to the use of pornography in such circumstances, other than on the grounds of a morbid anti-sexuality.

The *catharsis argument* has long been put forward to suggest that availability of pornography will neutralize "aberrant" sexual tendencies and so reduce the incidence of sex crime or clearly immoral behaviour in related fields. (Before evidence is put forward for this thesis it is worth remarking that it should not be necessary to demonstrate a *reduction* in sex crime to justify repeal of the Obscenity Laws. It should be quite sufficient to show that an *increase* in crime will not ensue following repeal. We may even argue that a small increase may be tolerable if other benefits from easy access to pornography could be shown: but it is no part of the present argument to put this latter contention.)

Many psychiatrists and psychologists have favoured the catharsis argument. Chesser, for instance, sees[8] pornography as a form of voyeurism in which—as with sado-masochistic material—the desire to hurt is satisfied passively. If this is so and the analogy can be extended we have only to look at the character of the voyeur—generally furtive and clandestine—to realize that we have little to fear from the pornography addict. Where consumers are preoccupied with fantasy there is little danger to the rest of us. Karpman (1959), quoted by the U.S. Commission, notes that people reading "salacious literature" are less likely to become sexual offenders than those who do not since the reading often neutralizes "aberrant sexual interests." Similarly the Kronhausens have argued that "these 'unholy' instruments" may be a safety-valve for the sexual deviate and potential sex offender. And Cairns, Paul and Wishner (1962) have remarked that *obscene materials* provide a way of releasing strong sexual urges without doing harm to others.

It is easy to see the plausibility of this argument. The popularity of all forms of sexual literature—from the superficial, *sexless*, sentimentality of the popular women's magazine to the clearest "hard-core" porn—has demonstrated over the ages the perennial appetite that people have for fantasy. To an extent, a great extent with many single people and frustrated married ones, the fantasy constitutes an important part of the sex-life. The experience may be vicarious and sterile but it self-evidently fills a need for many individuals. If literature, as a *symbol* of reality, can so involve human sensitivities it is highly likely that when the sensitivities are *distorted* for one reason or another the same sublimatory function can occur: the "perverted" or potentially criminal mentality can gain satisfaction, as does the lonely unfortunate, in *sex by proxy*. If we wanted to force the potential sex criminal on to the streets in search of a human victim perhaps we would do well to deny him his sublimatory substitutes: deny him fantasy and he will be forced to go after the real thing. . . .

[8]Eustace Chesser, *The Human Aspects of Sexual Deviation,* Arrow Books, 1971, p. 39.

The importance of this possibility should be fully faced. If a causal connection *does* exist between availability of pornographic material and a *reduction* in the amount of sex crime—and the evidence is wholly consistent with this possibility rather than its converse— then people who deliberately restrict pornography by supporting repressive legislation are prime architects of sexual offences against the individual. The anti-pornographers would do well to note that their anxieties may be driving them into a position the exact opposite of the one they explicitly maintain—their commitment to reduce the amount of sexual delinquency in society.

The most that the anti-pornographers can argue is that at present the evidence is inconclusive. . . . But if the inconclusive character of the data is once admitted then the case for repressive legislation falls at once. For in a *free* society, or one supposedly aiming after freedom, social phenomena are, like individuals, innocent until proven guilty—and an activity will be permitted unless there is clear evidence of its harmful consequences. This point was well put—in the specific connection with pornography—by Bertrand Russell, talking[9] when he was well over 90 to Rupert Crawshay-Williams.

After noting how people beg the question of causation in instances such as the Moors murders (where the murders and the reading of de Sade *may* have a common cause), Russell ("Bertie") said that on the whole he disapproved of sadistic pornography being available. But when Crawshay-Williams put the catharsis view, that such material might provide a harmless release for individuals who otherwise may be dangerous, Russell said at once—"Oh, well, if that's true, then I don't see that there is anything against sadistic pornography. In fact it should be encouraged. . . ." When it was stressed that there was no preponderating evidence either way Russell argued that we should fall back on an overriding principle—"in this case the principle of free speech."

Thus in the absence of evidence of harm we should be permissive. Any other view is totalitarian. . . .

If human enjoyment *per se* is not to be condemned then it is not too rash to say that we *know* pornography does good. We can easily produce our witnesses to testify to experiencing pleasure. If in the face of this—and no other favourable argument—we are unable to demonstrate a countervailing harm, then the case for easy availability of pornography is unassailable. If, in such circumstances, we find some people unconvinced it is futile to seek out further empirical data. Once we commit ourselves to the notion that the evil nature of something is axiomatic we tacitly concede that evidence is largely irrelevant to our position. If pornography never fails to fill us with predictable loathing then statistics on crime, or measured statements by careful specialists, will not be useful: our reactions will stay the same. But in this event we would do well to reflect on what our emotions tell us of our own mentality. . . .

QUESTIONS

1. Is pornography of genuine benefit to society?
2. Consider the following claim: Seeking access to pornographic materials is not in a person's best self-interest because the immediate pleasure that pornography provides is far outweighed by its detrimental impact on the person in the long run. Is this a defensible position?
3. If the access of consenting adults to pornographic materials were left totally unregulated, what would be the long-term impact on the general welfare? Would the results, on balance, be desirable or undesirable?

[9]Rupert Crawshay-Williams, *Russell Remembered,* Oxford University Press, 1970, p. 144.

ANN GARRY

PORNOGRAPHY AND RESPECT FOR WOMEN

Ann Garry is associate professor of philosophy at California State University, Los Angeles. Her areas of specialization are philosophy of mind and feminism, and her published articles include "Mental Images" and "Why Are Love and Sex Philosophically Interesting?"

Writing from a feminist perspective, Garry presents a moral assessment of pornography. In her view, pornography is morally objectionable to the extent that it "exemplifies and recommends behavior that violates the moral principle to respect persons." After an extensive discussion of the notion of treating women as sex objects, Garry concludes that most pornography (as it presently exists) is morally objectionable. Since most pornography treats women as sex objects, she contends, it degrades women and thereby violates the moral principle to respect persons. Still, she argues, it is possible to visualize the production of nonsexist, nondegrading, hence morally acceptable pornography.

Pornography, like rape, is a male invention, designed to dehumanize women, to reduce the female to an object of sexual access, not to free sensuality from moralistic or parental inhibition. . . . Pornography is the undiluted essence of anti-female propaganda.

Susan Brownmiller, *Against Our Will: Men, Women and Rape*[1]

It is often asserted that a distinguishing characteristic of sexually explicit material is the degrading and demeaning portrayal of the role and status of the human female. It has been argued that erotic materials describe the female as a mere sexual object to be exploited and manipulated sexually. . . . A recent survey shows that 41 percent of American males and 46 percent of the females believe that "sexual materials lead people to lose respect for women." . . . Recent experiments suggest that such fears are probably unwarranted.

Presidential Commission on
Obscenity and Pornography[2]

The kind of apparent conflict illustrated in these passages is easy to find in one's own thinking as well. For example, I have been inclined to think that pornography is innocuous and to dismiss "moral" arguments for censoring it because many such arguments rest on an assumption I do not share—that sex is an evil to be controlled. At the same time I believe that it is wrong to exploit or degrade human beings, particularly women and others who are especially susceptible. So if pornography degrades human beings, then even if I would oppose its censorship I surely cannot find it morally innocuous.

In an attempt to resolve this apparent conflict I discuss three questions: Does pornography degrade (or exploit or dehumanize) human beings? If so, does it degrade women in ways or to an extent that it does not degrade men? If so, must pornography degrade women, as Brownmiller thinks, or could genuinely innocuous, nonsexist pornography exist? Although much current pornography does degrade women, I will argue that it is possible to have nondegrading, nonsexist pornography. However, this possibility rests on our making certain fundamental changes in our conceptions of sex and sex roles. . . .

[1] (New York: Simon and Schuster, 1975), p. 394.
[2] *The Report of the Commission on Obscenity and Pornography* (Washington, D.C., 1970), p. 201.
This article first appeared in *Social Theory and Practice*, vol. 4 (Summer 1978), pp. 395–421. It is reprinted here, by permission of the author, as it appears in *Philosophy and Women*, edited by Sharon Bishop and Majorie Weinzweig (Belmont, Calif.: Wadsworth, 1979).

I

The . . . argument I will consider [here] is that pornography is morally objectionable, not because it leads people to show disrespect for women, but because pornography itself exemplifies and recommends behavior that violates the moral principle to respect persons. The content of pornography is what one objects to. It treats women as mere sex objects "to be exploited and manipulated" and degrades the role and status of women. In order to evaluate this argument, I will first clarify what it would mean for pornography itself to treat someone as a sex object in a degrading manner. I will then deal with three issues central to the discussion of pornography and respect for women: how "losing respect" for a woman is connected with treating her as a sex object; what is wrong with treating someone as a sex object; and why it is worse to treat women rather than men as sex objects. I will argue that the current content of pornography sometimes violates the moral principle to respect persons. Then, in [the concluding part] of this paper, I will suggest that pornography need not violate this principle if certain fundamental changes were to occur in attitudes about sex.

To many people, including Brownmiller and some other feminists, it appears to be an obvious truth that pornography treats people, especially women, as sex objects in a degrading manner. And if we omit "in a degrading manner," the statement seems hard to dispute: How could pornography *not* treat people as sex objects?

First, is it permissible to say that either the content of pornography or pornography itself degrades people or treats people as sex objects? It is not difficult to find examples of degrading content in which women are treated as sex objects. Some pornographic films convey the message that all women really want to be raped, that their resisting struggle is not to be believed. By portraying women in this manner, the content of the movie degrades women. Degrading women is morally objectionable. While seeing the movie need not cause anyone to imitate the behavior shown, we can call the content degrading to women because of the character of the behavior and attitudes it recommends. The same kind of point can be made about films (or books or TV commercials) with other kinds of degrading, thus morally objectionable, content—for example, racist messages.

The next step in the argument is to infer that, because the content or message of pornography is morally objectionable, we can call pornography itself morally objectionable. Support for this step can be found in an analogy. If a person takes *every* opportunity to recommend that men rape women, we would think not only that his recommendation is immoral but that he is immoral too. In the case of pornography, the objection to making an inference from recommended behavior to the person who recommends is that we ascribe predicates such as 'immoral' differently to people than to films or books. A film vehicle for an objectionable message is still an object independent of its message, its director, its producer, those who act in it, and those who respond to it. Hence one cannot make an unsupported inference from "the content of the film is morally objectionable" to "the film is morally objectionable." Because the central points in this paper do not depend on whether pornography itself (in addition to its content) is morally objectionable, I will not try to support this inference. (The question about the relation of content to the work itself is, of course, extremely interesting; but in part because I cannot decide which side of the argument is more persuasive, I will pass.[3]) Certainly one appropriate way to evaluate pornography is in terms of the moral features of its content. If a pornographic film exemplifies and recommends morally objectionable attitudes or behavior, then its content is morally objectionable.

[3]In order to help one determine which position one feels inclined to take, consider the following statement: It is morally ojectionable to write, make, sell, act in, use, and enjoy pornography; in addition, the content of pornography is immoral; however, pornography itself is not morally objectionable. If this statement seems extremely problematic, then one might well be satisfied with the claim that pornography is degrading because its content is.

Let us now turn to the first of our three questions about respect and sex objects: What is the connection between losing respect for a woman and treating her as a sex object? Some people who have lived through the era in which women were taught to worry about men "losing respect" for them if they engaged in sex in inappropriate circumstances find it troublesome (or at least amusing) that feminists — supposedly "liberated" women — are outraged at being treated as sex objects, either by pornography or in any other way. The apparent alignment between feminists and traditionally "proper" women need not surprise us when we look at it more closely.

The "respect" that men have traditionally believed they have for women — hence a respect they can lose — is not a general respect for persons as autonomous beings; nor is it respect that is earned because of one's personal merits or achievements. It is respect that is an outgrowth of the "double standard." Women are to be respected because they are more pure, delicate, and fragile than men, have more refined sensibilities, and so on. Because some women clearly do not have these qualities, thus do not deserve respect, women must be divided into two groups — the good ones on the pedestal and the bad ones who have fallen from it. One's mother, grandmother, Sunday School teacher, and usually one's wife are "good" women. The appropriate behavior by which to express respect for good women would be, for example, not swearing or telling dirty jokes in front of them, giving them seats on buses, and other "chivalrous" acts. This kind of "respect" for good women is the same sort that adolescent boys in the back seats of cars used to "promise" not to lose. Note that men define, display, and lose this kind of respect. If women lose respect for women, it is not typically a loss of respect for (other) women as a class but a loss of self-respect.

It has now become commonplace to acknowledge that, although a place on the pedestal might have advantages over a place in the "gutter" beneath it, a place on the pedestal is not at all equal to the place occupied by other people (i.e., men). "Respect" for those on the pedestal was not respect for whole, full-fledged people but for a special class of inferior beings.

If a person makes two traditional assumptions — that (at least some) sex is dirty and that women fall into two classes, good and bad — it is easy to see how that person might think that pornography could lead people to lose respect for women or that pornography is itself disrespectful to women. Pornography describes or shows women engaging in activities inappropriate for good women to engage in — or at least inappropriate for them to be seen by strangers engaging in. If one sees these women as symbolic representatives of all women, then all women fall from grace with these women. This fall is possible, I believe, because the traditional "respect" that men have had for women is not genuine, whole-hearted respect for full-fledged human beings but half-hearted respect for lesser beings, some of whom they feel the need to glorify and purify.[4] It is easy to fall from a pedestal. Can we imagine 41 percent of men and 46 percent of women answering "yes" to the question, "Do movies showing men engaging in violent acts lead people to lose respect for men?"?

Two interesting asymmetries appear. The first is that losing respect for men as a class (men with power, typically Anglo men) is more difficult than losing respect for women or ethnic minorities as a class. Anglo men whose behavior warrants disrespect are more likely to be seen as exceptional cases than are women or minorities (whose "transgressions" may be far less serious). Think of the following: women are temptresses; Blacks cheat the welfare system; Italians are gangsters; but the men of the Nixon administration are excep-

---

[4]Many feminists point this out. One of the most accessible references is Shulamith Firestone, *The Dialectic of Sex: The Case for the Feminist Revolution* (New York: Bantam, 1970), especially pp. 128–32.

tions—Anglo men as a class did not lose respect because of Watergate and related scandals.

The second asymmetry concerns the active and passive roles of the sexes. Men are seen in the active role. If men lose respect for women because of something "evil" done by women (such as appearing in pornography), the fear is that men will then do harm to women—not that women will do harm to men. Whereas if women lose respect for male politicians because of Watergate, the fear is still that male politicians will do harm, not that women will do harm to male politicians. This asymmetry might be a result of one way in which our society thinks of sex as bad—as harm that men do to women (or to the person playing a female role, as in a homosexual rape). Robert Baker calls attention to this point in "'Pricks' and 'Chicks': A Plea for 'Persons'." [5] Our slang words for sexual intercourse— 'fuck', 'screw', or older words such as 'take' or 'have'—not only can mean harm but have traditionally taken a male subject and a female object. The active male screws (harms) the passive female. A "bad" woman only tempts men to hurt her further.

It is easy to understand why one's proper grandmother would not want men to see pornography or lose respect for women. But feminists reject these "proper" assumptions: good and bad classes of women do not exist; and sex is not dirty (though many people believe it is). Why then are feminists angry at the treatment of women as sex objects, and why are some feminists opposed to pornography?

The answer is that feminists as well as proper grandparents are concerned with respect. However, there are differences. A feminist's distinction between treating a woman as a full-fledged person and treating her as merely a sex object does not correspond to the good-bad woman distinction. In the latter distinction, "good" and "bad" are properties applicable to groups of women. In the feminist view, all women are full-fledged people— some, however, are treated as sex objects and perhaps think of themselves as sex objects. A further difference is that, although "bad" women correspond to those thought to deserve treatment as sex objects, good women have not corresponded to full-fledged people; only men have been full-fledged people. Given the feminist's distinction, she has no difficulty whatever in saying that pornography treats women as sex objects, not as full-fledged people. She can morally object to pornography or anything else that treats women as sex objects.

One might wonder whether any objection to treatment as a sex object implies that the person objecting still believes, deep down, that sex is dirty. I don't think so. Several other possibilities emerge. First, even if I believe intellectually and emotionally that sex is healthy, I might object to being treated *only* as a sex object. In the same spirit, I would object to being treated *only* as a maker of chocolate chip cookies or *only* as a tennis partner, because only one of my talents is being valued. Second, perhaps I feel that sex is healthy, but it is apparent to me that you think sex is dirty; so I don't want you to treat me as a sex object. Third, being treated as any kind of object, not just as a sex object, is unappealing. I would rather be a partner (sexual or otherwise) than an object. Fourth, and more plausible than the first three possibilities, is Robert Baker's view mentioned above. Both (i) our traditional double standard of sexual behavior for men and women and (ii) the linguistic evidence that we connect the concept of sex with the concept of harm point to what is wrong with treating women as sex objects. As I said earlier, 'fuck' and 'screw', in their traditional uses, have taken a male subject, a female object, and have had at least two meanings: harm and have sexual intercourse with. (In addition, a prick is a man who harms people ruthlessly; and a motherfucker is so low that he would do something very

---

[5] In Richard Wasserstrom, ed., *Today's Moral Problems* (New York: Macmillan, 1975), pp. 152–71; see pp. 167–71. Also in Robert Baker and Frederick Elliston, eds., *Philosophy and Sex* (Buffalo, N.Y.: Prometheus Books, 1975).

narmful to his own dear mother.)[6] Because in our culture we connect sex with harm that men do to women, and because we think of the female role in sex as that of harmed object, we can see that to treat a woman as a sex object is automatically to treat her as less than fully human. To say this does not imply that no healthy sexual relationships exist; nor does it say anything about individual men's conscious intentions to degrade women by desiring them sexually (though no doubt some men have these intentions). It is merely to make a point about the concepts embodied in our language.

Psychoanalytic support for the connection between sex and harm comes from Robert J. Stoller. Stoller thinks that sexual excitement is linked with a wish to harm someone (and with at least a whisper of hostility). The key process of sexual excitement can be seen as dehumanization (fetishization) in fantasy of the desired person. He speculates that this is true in some degree of everyone, both men and women, with "normal" or "perverted" activities and fantasies.[7]

Thinking of sex objects as harmed objects enables us to explain some of the first three reasons why one wouldn't want to be treated as a sex object: (1) I may object to being treated only as a tennis partner, but being a tennis partner is not connected in our culture with being a harmed object; and (2) I may not think that sex is dirty and that I would be a harmed object; I may not know what your view is; but what bothers me is that this is the view embodied in our language and culture.

Awareness of the connection between sex and harm helps explain other interesting points. Women are angry about being treated as sex objects in situations or roles in which they do not intend to be regarded in that manner — for example, while serving on a committee or attending a discussion. It is not merely that a sexual role is inappropriate for the circumstances; it is thought to be a less fully human role than the one in which they intended to function.

Finally, the sex-harm connection makes clear why it is worse to treat women as sex objects than to treat men as sex objects, and why some men have had difficulty understanding women's anger about the matter. It is more difficult for heterosexual men than for women to assume the role of "harmed object" in sex; for men have the self-concept of sexual agents, not of passive objects. This is also related to my earlier point concerning the difference in the solidity of respect for men and for women; respect for women is more fragile. Despite exceptions, it is generally harder for people to degrade men, either sexually or nonsexually, than to degrade women. Men and women have grown up with different patterns of self-respect and expectations regarding the extent to which they deserve and will receive respect or degradation. The man who doesn't understand why women do not want to be treated as sex objects (because he'd sure like to be) would not think of himself as being harmed by that treatment; a woman might.[8] Pornography, probably more than any other contemporary institution, succeeds in treating men as sex objects.

Having seen that the connection between sex and harm helps explain both what is wrong with treating someone as a sex object and why it is worse to treat a woman in this

---

[6]Baker, in Wasserstrom, *Today's Moral Problems*, pp. 168–169.

[7]"Sexual Excitement," *Archives of General Psychiatry* 33 (1976): 899–909, especially p. 903. The extent to which Stoller sees men and women in different positions with respect to harm and hostility is not clear. He often treats men and women alike, but in *Perversion: The Erotic Form of Hatred* (New York: Pantheon, 1975), pp. 89–91, he calls attention to differences between men and women especially regarding their responses to pornography and lack of understanding by men of women's sexuality. Given that Stoller finds hostility to be an essential element in male-oriented pornography, and given that women have not responded readily to such pornography, one can speculate about the possibilities for women's sexuality: their hostility might follow a different scenario; they might not be as hostile, and so on.

[8]Men seem to be developing more sensitivity to being treated as sex objects. Many homosexual men have long understood the problem. As women become more sexually aggressive, some heterosexual men I know are beginning to feel treated as sex objects. A man can feel that he is not being taken seriously if a woman looks lustfully at him while he is holding forth about the French judicial system or the failure of liberal politics. Some of his most important talents are not being properly valued.

way, I want to use the sex-harm connection to try to resolve a dispute about pornography and women. Brownmiller's view, remember, was that pornography is "the undiluted essence of anti-female propaganda" whose purpose is to degrade women. Some people object to Brownmiller's view by saying that, since pornography treats both men and women as sex objects for the purpose of arousing the viewer, it is neither sexist, antifemale, nor designed to degrade women; it just happens that degrading of women arouses some men. How can this dispute be resolved?

Suppose we were to rate the content of all pornography from most morally objectionable to least morally objectionable. Among the most objectionable would be the most degrading—for example, "snuff" films and movies which recommend that men rape women, molest children and puppies, and treat nonmasochists very sadistically.

Next we would find a large amount of material (probably most pornography) not quite so blatantly offensive. With this material it is relevant to use the analysis of sex objects given above. As long as sex is connected with harm done to women, it will be very difficult not to see pornography as degrading to women. We can agree with Brownmiller's opponent that pornography treats men as sex objects, too, but we maintain that this is only pseudoequality: such treatment is still more degrading to women.[9]

In addition, pornography often exemplifies the active/passive, harmer/harmed object roles in a very obvious way. Because pornography today is male-oriented and is supposed to make a profit, the content is designed to appeal to male fantasies. Judging from the content of the most popular legally available pornography, male fantasies still run along the lines of stereotypical sex roles—and, if Stoller is right, include elements of hostility. In much pornography the women's purpose is to cater to male desires, to service the man or men. Her own pleasure is rarely emphasized for its own sake; she is merely allowed a little heavy breathing, perhaps in order to show her dependence on the great male "lover" who produces her pleasure. In addition, women are clearly made into passive objects in still photographs showing only close-ups of their genitals. Even in movies marketed to appeal to heterosexual couples, such as *Behind the Green Door,* the woman is passive and undemanding (and in this case kidnapped and hypnotized as well). Although many kinds of specialty magazines and films are gauged for different sexual tastes, very little contemporary pornography goes against traditional sex roles. There is certainly no significant attempt to replace the harmer/harmed distinction with anything more positive and healthy. In some stag movies, of course, men are treated sadistically by women; but this is an attempt to turn the tables on degradation, not a positive improvement.

What would cases toward the least objectionable end of the spectrum be like? They would be increasingly less degrading and sexist. The genuinely nonobjectionable cases would be nonsexist and nondegrading; but commercial examples do not readily spring to mind.[10] The question is: Does or could any pornography have nonsexist, nondegrading content?

[9]I don't agree with Brownmiller that the purpose of pornography is to dehumanize women, rather it is to arouse the audience. The differences between our views can be explained, in part, by the points from which we begin. She is writing about rape; her views about pornography grow out of her views about rape. I begin by thinking of pornography as merely depicted sexual activity, though I am well aware of the male hostility and contempt for women that it often expresses. That pornography degrades women and excites men is an illustration of this contempt.

[10]Virginia Wright Wexman uses the film *Group Marriage* (Stephanie Rothman, 1973) as an example of "more enlightened erotica." Wexman also asks the following questions in an attempt to point out sexism in pornographic films:

> Does it [the film] portray rape as pleasurable to women? Does it consistently show females nude but present men fully clothed? Does it present women as childlike creatures whose sexual interests must be guided by knowing experienced men? Does it show sexually aggressive women as castrating viragos? Does it pretend that sex is exclusively the prerogative of women under twenty-five? Does it focus on the physical aspects of lovemaking rather than the emotional ones? Does it portray women as purely sexual beings? ("Sexism of X-rated Films," *Chicago Sun-Times,* 28 March 1976.)

II

I want to start with the easier question: Is it possible for pornography to have nonsexist, morally acceptable content? Then I will consider whether any pornography of this sort currently exists.

Imagine the following situation, which exists only rarely today: Two fairly conventional people who love each other enjoy playing tennis and bridge together, cooking good food together, and having sex together. In all these activities they are free from hang-ups, guilt, and tendencies to dominate or objectify each other. These two people like to watch tennis matches and old romantic movies on TV, like to watch Julia Child cook, like to read the bridge column in the newspaper, and like to watch pornographic movies. Imagine further that this couple is not at all uncommon in society and that nonsexist pornography is as common as this kind of nonsexist sexual relationship. This situation sounds fine and healthy to me. I see no reason to think that an interest in pornography would disappear in these circumstances. People seem to enjoy watching others experience or do (especially do well) what they enjoy experiencing, doing, or wish they could do themselves. We do not morally object to people watching tennis on TV; why would we object to these hypothetical people watching pornography?

Can we go from the situation today to the situation just imagined? In much current pornography, people are treated in morally objectionable ways. In the scene just imagined, however, pornography would be nonsexist, nondegrading, morally acceptable. The key to making the change is to break the connection between sex and harm. If Stoller is right, this task may be impossible without changing the scenarios of our sexual lives—scenarios that we have been writing since early childhood. (Stoller does not indicate whether he thinks it possible for adults to rewrite their scenarios or for social change to bring about the possibility of new scenarios in future generations.) But even if we believe that people can change their sexual scenarios, the sex-harm connection is deeply entrenched and has widespread implications. What is needed is a thorough change in people's deep-seated attitudes and feelings about sex roles in general, as well as about sex and roles in sex (sexual roles). Although I cannot even sketch a general outline of such changes here, changes in pornography should be part of a comprehensive program. Television, children's educational material, and nonpornographic movies and novels may be far better avenues for attempting to change attitudes; but one does not want to take the chance that pornography is working against one.

What can be done about pornography in particular? If one wanted to work within the current institutions, one's attempt to use pornography as a tool for the education of male pornography audiences would have to be fairly subtle at first; nonsexist pornography must become familiar enough to sell and be watched. One should realize too that any positive educational value that nonsexist pornography might have may well be as short-lived as most of the effects of pornography. But given these limitations, what could one do?

Two kinds of films must be considered. First is the short film with no plot or character development, just depicted sexual activity in which nonsexist pornography would treat men and women as equal sex partners.[11] The man would not control the circumstances in which the partners had sex or the choice of positions or acts; the woman's preference would be counted equally. There would be no suggestion of a power play or conquest on the man's

---

[11]If it is a lesbian or male homosexual film, no one would play a caricatured male or female role. The reader has probably noticed that I have limited my discussion to heterosexual pornography, but there are many interesting analogies to be drawn with male homosexual pornography. Very little lesbian pornography exists, though lesbian scenes are commonly found in male-oriented pornography.

part, no suggestion that "she likes it when I hurt her." Sexual intercourse would not be portrayed as primarily for the purpose of male ejaculation—his orgasm is not "the best part" of the movie. In addition, both the man and woman would express their enjoyment; the man need not be cool and detached.

The film with a plot provides even more opportunity for nonsexist education. Today's pornography often portrays the female characters as playthings even when not engaging in sexual activity. Nonsexist pornography could show women and men in roles equally valued by society, and sex equality would amount to more than possession of equally functional genitalia. Characters would customarily treat each other with respect and consideration, with no attempt to treat men or women brutally or thoughtlessly. The local Pussycat Theater showed a film written and directed by a woman *(The Passions of Carol),* which exhibited a few of the features just mentioned. The main female character in it was the editor of a magazine parody of *Viva.* The fact that some of the characters treated each other very nicely, warmly, and tenderly did not detract from the pornographic features of the movie. This should not surprise us, for even in traditional male-oriented films, lesbian scenes usually exhibit tenderness and kindness.

Plots for nonsexist films could include women in traditionally male jobs (e.g., long-distance truckdriver) or in positions usually held in respect by pornography audiences. For example, a high-ranking female Army officer, treated with respect by men and women alike, could be shown not only in various sexual encounters with other people but also carrying out her job in a humane manner.[12] Or perhaps the main character could be a female urologist. She could interact with nurses and other medical personnel, diagnose illnesses brilliantly, and treat patients with great sympathy as well as have sex with them. When the Army officer or the urologist engage in sexual activities, they will treat their partners and be treated by them in some of the considerate ways described above.

In the circumstances we imagined at the beginning of [this part of the] paper, our nonsexist films could be appreciated in the proper spirit. Under these conditions the content of our new pornography would clearly be nonsexist and morally acceptable. But would the content of such a film be morally acceptable if shown to a typical pornography audience today? It might seem strange for us to change our moral evaluation of the content on the basis of a different audience, but an audience today is likely to see the "respected" urologist and Army officer as playthings or unusual prostitutes—even if our intention in showing the film is to counteract this view. The effect is that, although the content of the film seems morally acceptable and our intention in showing it is morally flawless, women are still degraded.[13] The fact that audience attitude is so important makes one wary of giving wholehearted approval to any pornography seen today.

The fact that good intentions and content are insufficient does not imply that one's efforts toward change would be entirely in vain. Of course, I could not deny that anyone who tries to change an institution from within faces serious difficulties. This is particularly evident when one is trying to change both pornography and a whole set of related attitudes, feelings, and institutions concerning sex and sex roles. But in conjunction with other attempts to change this set of attitudes, it seems preferable to try to change pornography

---

[12]One should note that behavior of this kind is still considered unacceptable by the military. A female officer resigned from the U.S. Navy recently rather than be court-martialed for having sex with several enlisted men whom she met in a class on interpersonal relations.

[13]The content may seem morally acceptable only if one disregards such questions as, "Should a doctor have sex with her patients during office hours?" More important is the propriety of evaluating content wholly apart from the attitudes and reactions of the audience; one might not find it strange to say that one film has morally unacceptable content when shown tonight at the Pussycat Theater but acceptable content when shown tomorrow at a feminist conference.

instead of closing one's eyes in the hope that it will go away. For I suspect that pornography is here to stay.[14]

QUESTIONS

1.   To what extent, if at all, is pornography morally objectionable on the grounds that it degrades women?
2.   Under what conditions, if any, could pornography be considered genuinely nonsexist and nondegrading?
3.   If it is true that most pornography is morally objectionable because it degrades women, is some form of censorship based on this consideration justifiable?

SUGGESTED ADDITIONAL READINGS

BERGER, FRED R.: *Freedom of Expression.* Belmont, Calif.: Wadsworth, 1980. This anthology, which addresses a number of issues related to freedom of expression, includes two notable selections relevant to the problem of pornography and censorship. The first selection, "The Moral Theory of Free Speech and Obscenity Law" (pp. 99–127), is by David A. J. Richards. The second selection, "Women Fight Back" (pp. 128–133), is an excerpt from Susan Brownmiller's *Against Our Will: Men, Women and Rape* (1975).

BERGER, FRED R.: "Pornography, Sex, and Censorship." *Social Theory and Practice,* vol. 4, Spring 1977, pp. 183–209. Berger argues that it is implausible to believe that unlimited access to pornography will produce the kinds of long-range social harms envisioned by many proponents of censorship. In his view, censorship constitutes an unjustifiable interference with freedom.

CLOR, HARRY M.: *Obscenity and Public Morality.* Chicago: University of Chicago Press, 1969. In this book, Clor develops an overall case for censorship. Especially useful are Chapter 4 (concerned with the effects of obscenity) and Chapter 5 (which suggests a rationale for censorship).

DEVLIN, PATRICK: *The Enforcement of Morals.* New York: Oxford University Press, 1965. Lord Devlin, a prominent English judge, is the foremost contemporary spokesman for the legitimacy of the principle of legal moralism. This short book contains seven of his essays.

DYAL, ROBERT: "Is Pornography Good for You?" *Southwestern Journal of Philosophy,* vol. 7, Fall 1976, pp. 95–118. Dyal argues that pornographic materials ought not to be subject to censorship. He also encourages individuals to loosen "autonomous controls" so as "to explore the aesthetic possibilities, cultural dimensions, and existential depths opened up by pornography."

FEINBERG, JOEL: *Social Philosophy.* Englewood Cliffs, N.J.: Prentice-Hall, 1973. Chapters 2 and 3 of this book provide a very helpful discussion of liberty-limiting principles.

---

[14] [Two] "final" points must be made:

1.   I have not seriously considered censorship as an alternative course of action. . . . Brownmiller . . . [is] not averse to it. But . . . other principles seem too valuable to sacrifice when other options are available. I believe that even if moral objections to pornography exist, one must preclude any simple inference from "pornography is immoral" to "pornography should be censored" because of other important values and principles such as freedom of expression and self-determination. In addition, before justifying censorship on moral grounds one would want to compare pornography to other possibly offensive material: advertising using sex and racial stereotypes, violence in TV and films, and so on.

2.   In discussing the audience for nonsexist pornography, I have focused on the male audience. But there is no reason why pornography could not educate and appeal to women as well.

HOLBROOK, DAVID, ed.: *The Case against Pornography.* New York: Library Press, 1973. In this anthology, Holbrook has collected nearly thirty selections, all of which develop (from various points of view) the case against pornography.

LEISER, BURTON M.: *Liberty, Justice and Morals,* 2d ed. New York: Macmillan, 1979. Part I of this book features a broad-based discussion of the enforcement of morals. Chapter 1 critiques the views of Lord Devlin. Successive chapters center on homosexuality, contraception and abortion, freedom of the press and censorship, and obscenity and pornography.

The Report of the Commission on Obscenity and Pornography. Washington, D.C.: U.S. Government Printing Office, 1970. This famous report, whose findings are frequently referred to in contemporary discussions of censorship, contains a wealth of valuable material. Part Three, Section II centers on the effects of erotic material.

SIMONS, G. L.: *Pornography without Prejudice.* London: Abelard-Schuman, 1972. In this short and highly readable book, Simons provides a vigorous defense of pornography and develops an overall case against censorship. Chapter 2 contains responses to a number of arguments commonly made against pornography.

MENTAL ILLNESS AND INDIVIDUAL LIBERTY

8

Mental illness poses both personal and social problems.[1] On the personal level, mental illness often disrupts family relationships, severely incapacitates individuals, and makes everyday living a hazardous, torturous affair. Mentally ill individuals who are severely disoriented or deluded may be unable to care for their routine needs, and may thus pose a serious risk to their own well-being. Those who are sufficiently depressed may run the risk of committing suicide. Those who are extremely agitated or confused may pose a threat of serious harm not just to themselves but to their families as well. On a wider social level, the mentally ill may be nuisances, disrupt social activities, and engage in serious antisocial behavior. In light of all this, questions arise concerning the state's legitimate role regarding those classified as mentally ill. Should we have laws which give representatives of the state, such as judges and psychiatrists, the power to control the behavior of those diagnosed as mentally ill? This power is exercised when patients are committed to mental institutions against their ''will'' or when they are subjected to some form of therapy either without their consent or with ''consent'' which is given only because acceptance of therapy is a necessary condition for release. The central question explored in this chapter can be posed as follows: Does the state have the right and/or duty to use coercion to institutionalize and/or treat mentally ill individuals against their will?

THE CONCEPT OF MENTAL ILLNESS

Explorations of the moral correctness of state interference in the lives of the mentally ill are complicated by the difficulty of defining ''mental illness.'' In modern physiological medicine, patients diagnosed as suffering from a condition such as diabetes are said to have a certain pathological condition, a physical disease. They are considered physically ill. Analogously, in modern psychiatry, patients diagnosed as suffering from some condition such as schizophrenia are said to have a certain psychopathological condition, a mental disease. They are considered mentally ill. As Willard Gaylin in this chapter points out, however, labels such as ''insane'' and ''mentally ill'' are applied so widely today that psychiatrists themselves are unable to provide a definition of ''mental illness.'' If psychiatrists and other mental health professionals had access to a firmly entrenched theory of mental illness, they would be on firmer ground when making their diagnoses. But that is just the problem. Mental health professionals subscribe to widely varying theories of mental illness. To add to the confusion, psychiatrists of the same school of thought often find it difficult to agree whether or not a certain diagnostic label is applicable to an individual case.

How then should we think of mental illness? We cannot disregard this question since the diagnosis of mental illness is a crucial link in justifications advanced for state interference with the mentally ill. But there is no simple answer. Miriam Siegler and Humphrey

---

[1]For the sake of simplicity, the expressions ''mental illness'' and ''mentally ill'' will be used throughout this introduction. This usage is not intended, however, to prejudge questions about the correct use of such expressions.

Osmond in this chapter present us with *eight* competing models of "madness." In presenting these models, they bring out the assumptions and potential policy implications of eight very different conceptions of mental illness. The disagreements among some of the other writers in this chapter concerning the morally correct treatment of the mentally ill (e.g., those between Thomas S. Szasz and Paul Chodoff) are due in part to fundamental disagreements concerning the correct conception of mental illness.

LIBERTY-LIMITING PRINCIPLES AND INVOLUNTARY CIVIL COMMITMENT

Explorations of the morality of *involuntary civil commitment* procedures usually involve implicit or explicit discussion of some of the liberty-limiting principles discussed in Chapter 7. Should those classified as mentally ill be committed to a mental institution on any of the following grounds?

1.   To keep them from harming others.

2.   To prevent them from offending others.

3.   To prevent them from harming themselves.

4.   To benefit them. (This would involve the principle of *extreme* paternalism. Whereas the principle of legal paternalism would justify limiting an individual's liberty to keep him or her from harming himself or herself, the principle of extreme paternalism would justify limiting individual liberty in order to benefit that individual.)

In assessing attempted justifications of involuntary civil commitment practices, we must keep two other questions in mind: (a) Which of the above principles are morally acceptable liberty-limiting principles? (b) Which principle is actually being used (explicitly or implicitly) to justify commitment? In regard to (a), for example, if the principles of paternalism are *not* acceptable liberty-limiting principles, involuntary civil commitment cannot be justified on paternalistic grounds. In regard to (b), critics of involuntary civil commitment often argue as follows: It is not uncommon to commit individuals to institutions simply because their behavior is offensive; but the attempt to justify their commitment is made on other inapplicable grounds, such as their supposed dangerousness. Much of the behavior which earns the mentally ill the label of dangerous is at most *offensive* to others. Shouting harangues on street corners and other bizarre behaviors, although offensive to some, pose no threat of serious harm. If offensive behavior is the real basis for committing someone to a mental institution, then the justifying ground would have to be provided by the offense principle and not the harm principle. But few of us would hold that offensive behavior alone is a sufficient ground for the deprivation of liberty. Therefore, exposing the actual reasons for commitment in certain cases may lead to the conclusion that interference in these cases is not justified.

Dangerousness and the Harm Principle

Since the harm principle is a widely accepted liberty-limiting principle, that principle alone would provide a strong ground for the involuntary civil commitment of mentally ill individuals *if* the mentally ill pose a serious threat of harm to others. It is not surprising, therefore, that the harm principle is often invoked, implicitly or explicitly, to justify involuntary civil commitment procedures. But are the mentally ill so dangerous that their commitment is necessary to protect others from harm? To answer this question it is necessary to distinguish between different kinds of cases.

In some cases there is very little doubt that those labeled mentally ill are dangerous and pose a *serious threat of physical harm to others*. Take an individual, classified as schizophrenic perhaps, who attempts to carry out the commands of a disembodied voice ordering the execution of parents or siblings. Persons of this sort certainly pose a serious imminent threat to others. Or take another individual, labeled paranoid perhaps, who has a history of violent and apparently irrational acts, and who gives every indication of repeating such acts. Persons of this sort might also be correctly perceived as dangerous. Thus, in cases involving either imminent potential physical violence or actual physical violence, involuntary civil commitment would certainly seem to be justified by the harm principle. Not everyone would agree with this conclusion. Thomas S. Szasz, for example, wants no special treatment for those considered mentally ill. If they perform acts which are forbidden by law, they should be subject to the same legal sanctions as anyone else, Szasz argues. But if they break no laws, the state has no moral right to interfere with their freedom.

Even if Szasz is wrong, however, and the harm principle is correctly invoked in justifying *some* involuntary civil commitments, it does not follow that it justifies the commitment of everyone who is labeled both mentally ill and dangerous. Mental health workers often diagnose individuals as mentally ill when their behavior seems inexplicable, bizarre, or threatening. They then make predictions about their dangerousness. The purported dangerousness of *most of those* diagnosed as mentally ill, however, is unsupported by actual evidence. Studies have shown either that mental patients as a group are no more dangerous than others[2] or that, if they are, the differences are so small that they allow very little success in prediction.[3] If a psychiatrist's prediction of dangerousness is accepted as sufficient justification for involuntary commitment, the uncertainty of those predictions would result in the commitment of a very large number of nondangerous people. For every actually dangerous person detained, many innocent, nondangerous people, who had committed no violent acts and broken no laws, would also be deprived of their freedom. This certainly seems morally unacceptable. Suppose social psychologists provided sound studies showing that a certain percentage of the inhabitants of a particular neighborhood would eventually commit a violent crime. Most of us would agree that it would be morally unacceptable to incarcerate all the inhabitants of that neighborhood, on the basis of statistical predictions, in order to prevent violent acts by some. Consistently with this, we would have to agree that it would be morally unacceptable to incarcerate all those classified as mentally ill and dangerous on the basis of similar sorts of statistical predictions. If this conclusion is correct, then the harm principle can at most justify only the involuntary civil commitment of those who have actually caused serious physical harm or pose an imminent threat of doing so. And this would exclude most of the mentally ill.

Paternalism

Like the harm principle, the paternalism principles are frequently invoked to justify state interference in the lives of the mentally ill. Before we can determine whether these principles do provide good grounds for involuntary civil commitment, we must answer two questions. (1) Is paternalistic interference ever justified? (2) If yes, under what conditions do paternalistic grounds constitute good reasons for depriving individuals of liberty? In considering the justifiability of paternalistic interventions, it is a good idea to keep in mind the difference between the legal paternalism principle and the extreme paternalism principle.

---

[2]Jonas R. Rappeport, ed., *The Clinical Evaluation of the Dangerousness of the Mentally Ill* (Springfield, Ill.: Charles C Thomas, 1967), pp. 72–80.
[3]Alan A. Stone, *Mental Health and Law: A System in Transition* (Rockville, Md.: Center for Studies of Crime and Delinquency, National Institute of Mental Health, DHEW Publication No. (ADM) 75-176, 1975).

The latter could apply to paternalistic actions whose intent is to benefit individuals and would be especially applicable in discussions of a mental patient's right to treatment. The former could apply to paternalistic actions whose intent is to keep individuals from harming themselves and would be especially applicable to involuntary civil commitment.

John Stuart Mill provides the classical utilitarian statement on the illegitimacy of paternalistic interventions. This statement is often cited in court opinions concerning the right of self-determination in medical matters. (It is included in a reading by Mill in the preceding chapter.)

> . . . one very simple principle [is] entitled to govern absolutely the dealings of society with the individual in the way of compulsion and control, whether the means used be physical force in the form of legal penalties, or the moral coercion of public opinion. That principle is, that the sole end for which mankind are warranted, individually or collectively, in interfering with the liberty of action of any of their number, is self-protection. That the only purpose for which power can be rightfully exercised over any member of a civilized community, against his will, is to prevent harm to others. His own good, either physical or moral, is not sufficient warrant. He cannot rightfully be compelled to do or forbear because it will be better for him to do so, because it will make him happier, because, in the opinion of others, to do so would be wise, or even right.

In this statement, Mill asserts that while prevention of harm to others is sometimes sufficient justification for interfering with another's liberty of action, the individual's good never is. Mill rejects paternalistic interventions because of the high utility value that he assigns to individual liberty. In assigning it such a high value, Mill assumes that individuals are, on the whole, better judges of their own interests than anyone else, so that minimizing paternalistic interventions will maximize human happiness. Mill himself qualifies the strong rejection of paternalism, stating:

> . . . this doctrine is meant to apply only to human beings in the maturity of their faculties. We are not speaking of children, or of young persons below the age which the law may fix as that of manhood or womanhood. Those who are still in a state to require being taken care of by others, must be protected against their own actions as well as external injury.

Mill assumes that in the kinds of cases he cites, people are justified in acting paternalistically because they *are* better judges of an individual's interests than is the individual himself or herself. Arguing in this way, Mill seems to open the door for the justification of paternalistic interventions in the lives of those who are not competent enough to make rational decisions about their own actions.

Many contemporary thinkers concerned with justifying paternalistic state interferences in the lives of the mentally ill adopt a similar approach. We condemn most paternalistic interventions, they argue, because they constrain an individual's freedom of choice and action. But what about those individuals who are incapable (either temporarily or permanently) of understanding the ramifications of their decisions and actions? Are their choices and actions really *free* ones? Take as an extreme example people who act under the influence of hallucinogenic drugs. Suppose that while in a hallucinogenic state people believed that they (like Superman) could fly. Suppose that, acting on that belief, they attempted to leap out of twentieth-floor windows in order to get home more quickly. We know their belief is grossly inconsistent with the best available inductive evidence about what happens to people who jump out of twentieth-floor windows. We also know that the drugged individuals are not freely choosing to die or injure themselves when they "choose" to leap out of windows. If we prevent them from jumping, we do temporarily interfere with their actions, but we do so on the assumption that they are not choosing to bring about the inevitable results of those actions. We have reason to believe that the inevitable, apparently irrational, self-harming results are not those intended by the would-be jumpers, and we assume that they would not choose those results if their mental competence had not been severely constrained by drugs. Take a less extreme case—a severely retarded individual, incapable of understanding traffic signals, who decides to go out alone in a busy city. Individuals in this condition can also be perceived as not quite competent enough to make decisions resulting in freely chosen actions. They may be completely unaware of the kinds of risks they would be running by going out alone, and if they understood those risks, they would not choose to run them. In both these kinds of cases, there is good reason to think that the people involved are incapable, whether temporarily or permanently, of the level of reasoning requisite for sufficiently free choices. Paternalistic interventions seem to be justified here in light of the high value placed on life *and* the permanent or temporary inability of the individuals involved to understand that acting on their decisions could be fatal.

Now take individuals who reject commitment or psychiatric help because their present condition renders them incapable of realizing that these are in their own long-term interest. If they were thinking more clearly, if they were not confused or severely depressed by their illnesses, would they not want the benefits involved? Would they not want others to keep them from running the risks to their physical and mental well-being that they will continue to run if they are not committed? Would they not want the treatment which would restore their competency for rational decision-making—a competency which is presently limited by delusions, compulsions, or other factors associated with mental illness? Those who argue in this way often use the words "autonomy" and "diminished autonomy" in stating their positions. In the ethically significant sense of *autonomy,* an *autonomous individual* can be defined as one who is capable of making rational, unconstrained decisions and acting accordingly. An individual *exercises autonomy* when he or she acts without constraint on the basis of such decisions. In keeping with this, an individual's autonomy can be *diminished* in various ways both when his or her actions are interfered with and when the ability to make decisions is constrained by the kinds of factors discussed above. The mentally ill individual, then, is perceived as someone with diminished autonomy, and paternalistic intervention in the lives of the mentally ill is perceived as justified when autonomy is sufficiently diminished so that serious risk-running behavior results.

The conclusion of this line of argument is that paternalistic interventions are justified when they are necessary either (1) to keep persons with severely diminished autonomy from doing themselves serious, irrevocable harm or (2) to temporarily constrain persons from acting to bring about *presumably* irrational self-harming ends until it can be determined whether the individuals are acting autonomously. This kind of position, often called "weak paternalism," is consistent with the position of those who agree with Mill's criticism of paternalism. The interventions are not seen as infringements on individual freedom. Rather, they are seen as attempts either to prevent individuals from seriously harming themselves when they are acting nonautonomously or to prevent them from harming themselves until it can be determined whether their actions are in fact freely chosen ones.

Further support for the justifiability of some instances of paternalism rests on a prudential argument which itself appeals to the importance of individual autonomy. We are aware that we often act in ignorance and that we are often tempted to act in ways incompatible with what we ourselves see as our long-term interests. Acting in ignorance, or too weak-willed to resist temptation, we may do ourselves serious irreversible harm of a sort which would severely diminish our autonomy. We are also aware that accidents, illnesses, diseases, and emotional pressures may diminish our ability for rational decision-making and thus our autonomy. We should be willing, therefore, to accept those paternalistic acts, laws, and practices intended either to protect our autonomy from being severely diminished or, if it has already been diminished, to restore it. This argument is sometimes advanced in order to justify laws allowing courts and psychiatrists to commit the mentally ill to institutions against their will in order to provide them with curative treatment intended to restore their autonomy or to keep them from the kind of self-harm which might further reduce it.

In a different vein, *opposition* to "paternalistic" interferences with the liberty of the mentally ill comes from certain sociologists, psychologists, and other social theorists whose analyses attempt to explain the recent emphasis on antipaternalism in American society. They attribute much of this recent antipaternalism to a growing awareness of the class differences in our society and of the fact that those who perform paternalistic acts (e.g., psychiatrists, judges, and the administrators and staffs of mental institutions) are usually members of the upper middle class, while those whose liberty is being limited are usually members of the poorer, less-privileged classes. An awareness of this class difference, and of related differences in interests and values, gives rise to serious doubts about both the ability and the willingness of those wielding paternalistic authority to act in the interests of those whose liberty they typically constrain. On this analysis, it is not the moral legitimacy of the principle of paternalism which is really at issue when "paternalistic" acts and practices are increasingly rejected. Rather, what is at issue are the abuses resulting from so-called paternalistic acts which do not in fact serve to benefit (or keep from harm) the individuals constrained, but which do in fact serve the ends of the members of the professions wielding paternalistic authority and of the middle and upper social classes to which they belong. This line of argument is intended to point out that the current antipaternalistic stress is probably not the result of conscious deliberation about the legitimacy of central ethical principles but a rejection of what passes as justified paternalism in a class society in which the "constrainers" are neither knowledgeable nor altruistic enough to perceive correctly the interests of those whose freedom they limit. However, the factual claims, if correct, tend to support a Mill-like claim that unless the interests and values of constrainers and constrainees coincide, individual self-interest, including the interest of those diagnosed as mentally ill, is better served in the long run if paternalism is rejected than if it is accepted.

In summary, a number of questions must be answered before a decision can be made to allow involuntary civil commitment on paternalistic grounds. First, is paternalism ever morally acceptable? Second, if it is acceptable when individuals lack a certain level of competence in decision-making, at what point are individuals to be presumed sufficiently incompetent to make decisions about their own welfare? Third, is the practice really intended to either benefit the mentally ill or keep them from self-harm or is the preferred paternalistic rationale simply a mask for a practice which deprives the mentally ill of liberty while serving others' interests?

THE RIGHT TO TREATMENT

One common rationale for committing the mentally ill to hospitals is that they badly need and will benefit from the treatment available in such institutions. In fact, some landmark judicial opinions regarding the mentally ill assert that those who are involuntarily committed have a constitutional right to treatment. In *Wyatt v. Stickney,* for example, the Federal District Court in Alabama ruled that the involuntarily committed "unquestionably have a constitutional right to receive such individual treatment as will give each of them a realistic

---

[4] *Wyatt v. Stickney,* 325 F. Supp. 781 (1971), p. 784.

opportunity to be cured or to improve his or her mental condition."[4] In the *O'Connor v. Donaldson* case reprinted in this chapter, failure to provide appropriate treatment was of crucial importance in determining the lower court's finding that Donaldson's constitutional right of liberty had been violated. From a moral standpoint, the acceptability of the need-for-treatment rationale hinges in part on the legitimacy of the extreme paternalism principle. But here again conceptual and factual questions become important. Is enforced treatment simply disguised punishment, as Lee Coleman and Trudy Solomon in this chapter argue? At what point are individuals to be judged incompetent to make their own decisions about possible treatment? Do psychiatrists actually know enough to consistently benefit those they are treating? The readings by Chodoff, Coleman, and Solomon deal with some of these questions.

Jane S. Zembaty

WILLARD GAYLIN

IN MATTERS MENTAL OR EMOTIONAL, WHAT'S NORMAL?

◼◼◼◼◼

Willard Gaylin, a psychiatrist, is the president of the Institute of Society, Ethics, and the Life Sciences, usually called the Hastings Center. He is also professor of psychiatry at Columbia College of Physicians and Surgeons. Gaylin's coedited books include *The Teaching of Medical Ethics* (1973) and *Operating on the Mind* (1975). He is the author of *Feelings: Our Vital Signs* (1979) and of many articles, including "On the Borders of Persuasion: A Psychoanalytic Look at Coercion."

Gaylin offers a brief overview of the changes that have occurred in the definition of mental illness since the mid-nineteenth century. He concludes that psychiatry today is incapable of defining mental illness.

◼◼◼◼◼

. . . In the 19th century it did not take a psychiatrist or a careful diagnostic standard to decide who was mentally ill. "Crazy," "lunatic," "insane" were synonymous words interchangeably used by the layman and the physician. The mentally ill were irrational and bizarre, different from you and me. The definition, while no longer the mystical-religious one of an earlier age, was closer to the concept of "possession" than the concept of sickness.

Still, in some ways there was an exact analogy between mental and physical illness. Both were seen as intruders in the normal human condition; both were seen as organ deteriorations, caused genetically or — with the evolution of the germ theory — by the occupation of an organ by a harmful external agent. Since the leading cause of psychosis in the 19th century was advanced syphilis, it was not a bad concept. But it was an all-or-none concept. You either had syphilis or you didn't. You were mentally ill or you were not. And if you were mentally ill it was because of an unnatural and external occupation of the self.

With Freud, of course, all the rules changed and the idea of mental illness became much more ambiguous. Freud understood episodes of aberrant behavior—a peculiar phobia, a handwashing ritual, an obsessional recurring idea, a hysterical paralysis of the arm—as symptoms of specific neurosis rather than total possession or dementia, and he recognized that such aberrance could occur within the healthy, functioning framework of "normal" people. The aberrant behavior, so understood, was not caused by invading disease, but was formed in a person's early development. It was woven into the total personality, and the function of the psychiatrist was to tease out the threads of the aberrant development in the otherwise healthy fabric.

But that was only the beginning. From that original point of departure at the turn of the century, definitions of mental illness have expanded to include progressively milder disorders; in that process, inevitably, the number of people that can be termed "mentally ill" has increased. Confusion was bound to follow.

For example, if unusual behavior can indicate mental illness, then so too can the absence of normal behavior, and one of the early additions to the list of mental malfunctions was the concept of nonfunctioning or inhibitions. But this development implied a standard of normality in the field of mental activity and emotions, indeed, in the field of behavior. It suggested that there are things that a person ought to feel or do, and that if he can't, it is the job of the therapist to help him develop the capacity. But the whole idea of normality is subject to serious question in the area of mental health. It is one thing to establish 98.6 degrees Fahrenheit as a normal body temperature; it is quite another to establish a "normal" standard of integrated behavior; biases are automatically introduced and objective standards seem particularly corruptible by personal values.

The direction of psychiatry and psychoanalysis in the 20th century only compounded the confusion. For interest began to shift from "symptom" neurosis to "character" neurosis. To those who think in terms of character neurosis, an individual need not exhibit any bizarre behavior, any specific symptoms of mental abnormality. Instead, the very nature of his developed character could itself be abnormal. All individuals—all healthy individuals—have character qualities that can be called paranoid, obsessive, hysterical, depressive or narcissistic; these traits can dictate the shape of one's pleasures, the shape of one's life. But some people are so dominated by them that they will severely limit, dominate or restrict the person's capacity for a full life. In these people it is the developed character itself, the personality, that becomes identified as the malfunctioning agent. Modern psychiatry and psychoanalysis are today so preoccupied with the idea of character neurosis that, proportionally, symptom neurosis has become rare; at any specific time, a typical psychoanalyst will not have one in treatment.

Finally, while psychiatry was expanding its own borders, the field of medicine was redirecting and assigning certain medical problems to the psychiatrist's domain, even though, at first, psychiatry was unwilling to accept them. These were the psychosomatic conditions. It was the internist who first recognized the enormous importance of emotional factors in such conditions as peptic ulcer, asthma, ulcerative colitis, etc. This created a peculiar new category of mental illness. A person could now be mentally ill but have no mental symptoms. The mental illness, rather than showing in alterations of behavior, perception, ideation, affect, reason or emotion would simply show in the functioning of bowels, gastric juices, bronchial tree.

As the psychiatric community's understanding of mental illness has developed and expanded in these ways, public attitudes toward it have changed radically. Today it is likely that everyone knows someone who is "sick." More important, the word "sick" has become part of the common parlance, often implying no more than misbehavior.

When, however, you come to that point where everybody is a little sick, you are not far from that point where nobody is sick. This is now a respectable, indeed a fashionable, position in some circles. One sees it in the writings of Thomas Szasz, whose most famous book is called "The Myth of Mental Illness." Here Dr. Szasz is concerned with the unparalleled and incredible violations of the civil rights of the insane. Beyond this, however, is that covey of contemporary writers who, sensing the general disillusionment with contemporary society and exploiting the national insecurity fed by such institutionalized irrationalities as the Vietnam war, have made a modern cliché out of the dubious thesis that the lunatics have taken over the running of the asylum, or that the sane people are those within the institutions for the insane. Such romantic illusions have encouraged a growing attitude, particularly among the young, that it may be ridiculous to attempt to define crazy in a crazy world—or, further, that crazy may be better than sane. When someone with the poetic image of R. D. Laing comes along, he tends to encourage this somewhat simplistic view of the problems of life.

The unfortunate result of all this is that psychiatry itself is not at a stage where it is capable of defining mental illness. . . .

QUESTIONS

1. What criteria, on your view, can be used to distinguish the mentally healthy from the mentally ill?
2. If psychiatrists cannot even define what mental illness is, are there any good reasons to think that they can provide "cures" for it?

**MIRIAM SIEGLER
and HUMPHREY OSMOND**

MODELS OF MADNESS, MODELS OF MEDICINE

Humphrey Osmond is professor of psychiatry at the University of Alabama at Birmingham. He is an elected member of London's Royal College of Physicians. Miriam Siegler, who has an M.A. in family life education, has held a variety of positions, including that of advisor to Schizophrenics Anonymous, a self-help group. Siegler and Osmond are joint authors of many articles, including "The Three Medical Models," "Models of Drug Addiction," and "Aesculapian Authority." These articles provided the raw material on which their book *Models of Madness, Models of Medicine* (1974) was based. They are also the authors of *Patienthood: The Art of Being a Responsible Patient* (1979). Osmond, in addition, is the author of numerous other articles, including "Psychiatry Under Siege: The Crisis Within."

Siegler and Osmond agree with Gaylin that the situation in psychiatry is confusing. Because different theories, notions, and ideologies compete for acceptance, those in psychiatry work with a hodgepodge composed of bits and pieces of very different, and often inconsistent, theories. Hoping to bring some order into this chaos, Siegler and Osmond develop eight models of madness which bring out the different assumptions and implications of the competing conceptions of mental illness.

. . . Any intelligent and critical person allowed to overhear conferences in most psychiatric centers, in this or other countries today, would be profoundly puzzled, not merely by the differences of opinion but by the lack of common ground among the discussants. Conversations can be heard which strongly resemble the Mad Hatter's tea party, and even when clearcut differences of opinion occur which might result in rational confrontation and serious debate, the contestants are likely, after a few rhetorical statements, to ride off in all directions. The question, What are they arguing about? was one which any critical observer might have raised, but perhaps the real question is: Why was that particular answer made? . . .

CONSTRUCTING THE MODELS

We have evolved a method for constructing models in an attempt to explain and perhaps alleviate the confusion in psychiatry, which nowadays resembles the Tower of Babel. Our pychiatric situation is perhaps even more chaotic than that of the legendary tower, for in that famous example of failed communication, each person was presumably speaking one language consistently, although not the same language as his fellow tower-builders. What we have in psychiatry is worse: each person uses a hodgepodge of bits and pieces of ideas, theories, notions, and ideologies in order to engage in a supposedly common enterprise with others similarly confused.

A common enterprise: that is the key. For if concerted action was never required, what difference would it make whether one were consistent or not? Very few of us always hold a clear and consistent view of this complex, puzzling, and ever-changing universe. Each of us collects scraps and shreds of theories about politics, economics, art, religion, philosophy, science, child psychology, etc., and so long as we are not asked to take any responsible action, we are content to live in a state of chronic, undifferentiated model-muddle. We know dimly that somewhere there is someone who has gone to the trouble of discovering the connection (or lack of connection) between the gold standard, low tariffs and the single tax, between free will and evolution, between thumbsucking and school performance, and we are grateful for these grand efforts on our behalf, but we also know that we will probably never understand them and that it probably doesn't matter very much.

However, when we are confronted with suffering people and their families, who demand that we exert ourselves on their behalf because we have declared ourselves to be expert in the field of their suffering, then it does matter what we say and do, and what we do depends upon the theories or models which we hold regarding those misfortunes we are supposed to alleviate. That is why we look to those few who have worked out some consistent position to guide our stumbling efforts. To write a book or set up a program which consistently uses a particular theory of madness that can be differentiated from all other theories is an intellectual achievement, a step beyond our usual state of eclectic muddlement. Unluckily, those giants of thought and system, to whom we turn for guidance, frequently hold points of view which are irreconcilable with each other. If we chose clearly articulated theories, one might be proved "true" and all others "false," thus giving us generally acceptable grounds for action. Alas, that most desirable of solutions, an orthodoxy such as Freud commended to Jung in the earlier part of this century, is not at present open to us, for there is no psychiatric theory at the moment which is so good and so universally accepted that exemplary members of this profession are prepared to use it, to insist that it be used by their co-professionals and thus end the controversy. Indeed, we have come to suspect that this failure to reach agreement lies not in the theories themselves so much as in the philosophical implications of those theories.

What then are we to do? There are too many theories, no one theory has universal acceptance, those who hold consistent theories disagree with each other violently, while at our door those afflicted with madness wait in desperate hope to learn what we plan for them. To make sense of this chaos, we must first gather together the disparate points of view and sort them into some kind of preliminary groups or types. In short, we must make a classification system.

There are immediate advantages to any classification system, however crude. The most obvious is that it makes it much easier to remember and recognize large amounts of data if they have been classified in some way or other. If one had to learn to recognize large numbers of animals, then one would probably begin by sorting them into categories, using the Linnaean or some other system. In setting up a library there must be some basis for arranging the books, otherwise they would never be found when wanted. They could be arranged by color or by weight, but somehow we recognize instinctively that we require criteria for this kind of sorting which feel fundamental rather than accidental.

A classification system makes it easier for the user or consumer to choose intelligently. In a library one wants to know how to find the novels of one author rather than another, or to find books on hog-raising rather than on hair-styling. If the book jackets were all blank, then the only way would be to look through the pages of each book, an appalling and unnecessary chore. In psychiatry, too, the user or consumer has choices: is he or she looking for a doctor who specializes in psychiatric diseases, or is one really asking for a guru or guide to point one toward enlightenment? But in this library the covers are all blank and one has to leaf through many pages to see if one has obtained the right expert. This not only wastes time and money, but prolongs the suffering of the person seeking help. . . .

It is sometimes said that you cannot compare apples and oranges, but this is not so; you can if you are willing to call them both "fruit." Because our models lie in different disciplines (medicine, law, philosophy, psychology, religion, etc.), we have the apples-and-oranges problem, and so we must compare our models in terms of common qualities. All of our models presuppose that there is a "mad" person who believes himself, or whom others believe, to have difficulty in occupying a normal social role; that there is a practitioner of some sort with special knowledge of this kind of event; and that there is a family and a community which have some interest in defining the situation. All the models deal with the question of what sort of thing madness is, what should be done about it, and how those involved ought to behave. These common elements provide the dimensions of our models. In this book we shall concern ourselves with twelve dimensions: definition or diagnosis; etiology; behavior (how it is to be interpreted); treatment; prognosis or outcome; suicide; the function of the hospital or other institution; personnel (who the practitioners shall be); the rights and duties of the patient, client, etc.; the rights and duties of the family; the rights and duties of community or society; and the goal of the model.

A model, as we shall use the term in this book, is an arrangement of an ideology, theory, point of view, etc., in such a manner that it can be compared with other ideologies, theories, points of view, etc. Comparability is the essence of model-making. To be in the model-making business, you require at least two models of at least two dimensions each. For example, if you want to buy a boat or a refrigerator, you want to know many things about it in order to make an intelligent choice: its size, its cost, its reliability, its capacity, etc.; in other words, you want a model with a sufficient number of relevant dimensions.

TABLE 1
MODELS OF MADNESS

	Medical Model	Moral Model	Impaired Model	Psychoanalytic Model	Social Model	Psychedelic Model	Conspiratorial Model	Family Interaction Model
1. Definition/ diagnosis	Doctor determines disease; informs patient clearly; rules out other diseases. Diagnosis determines treatment and prognosis.	Moral practitioner determines extent of unacceptable, dysfunctional or immoral behavior.	Person is permanently handicapped or disabled; e.g., incurably insane.	A continuum of emotional difficulties from mild neurosis to severe psychosis. Diagnosis unimportant; each case unique.	Mental illness is a symptom of a "sick" society, another aspect of poverty and discrimination.	Madness is really a mind-expanding "trip"; things appear more clear than ordinarily possible.	Madness exists only in the eye of the beholder; the so-called madman is simply the victim of labeling.	The whole family is "sick"; the one brought for help is only the "index patient," who may be the healthiest member of the family.
2. Etiology	Etiology important but not always known. Natural causes are assumed.	Unimportant. Bad behavior was learned somewhere.	Unimportant how person became impaired; often from birth.	Very important. Must reconstruct analysand's life from dreams, free associations, history-taking.	Socially disadvantaged families produce psychological problems in their members. Rate of social change is too fast or not fast enough.	Schizophrenics have been driven mad by their families, who try to get them to conform.	People are identified as mentally ill because others conspire to label them; the conspirators cannot tolerate deviance.	Patient is "sick" because acts out family pathology; family is "sick" because parents came from "sick" families, etc.
3. Subject's behavior	Indicates patient's illness. May help diagnosis.	Taken at face value; measured, not interpreted.	Behavior interpreted as normal with allowances made for handicap.	Interpreted symbolically. Therapist must de-code it, find out what it really means.	Behavior symptomatic of social pathology.	An attempt to break the bind their families have put them in.	Stems directly from the way he is treated by those conspiring against him.	All behavior in the family consists of moves and maneuvers in the family game.
4. Treatment	Medical, surgical treatments, nursing care; specific to diagnosis if possible. Contraindications possible.	Important. Modify "bad" behavior with positive and negative sanctions.	No treatment for an impairment. Rehabilitative measures important.	A special one-to-one relation with therapist involving transference.	Improve social, economic, political status of mentally ill and their families.	A guided "trip" into madness and back again.	"Treatment" is really a kind of brain-washing to induce conformity.	Family therapy.

5. Prognosis	Important. Follows from diagnosis. Doctor cannot promise cure but usually offers some hope.	Good, if client cooperates and practitioner can construct workable sanctioning system or reinforcement schedule.	No change expected for better or worse.	...place on continuum, e.g., prognosis poor for psychotics. Depends on whether analysand really wants to get well.	...depends on social change.	may lead to enlightenment.	the more someone is treated as mentally ill, the more he will behave that way. A way out of the vicious circle.	is successful, family will give up games and index patient will give up symptoms. A final move in the family game by a member who sees no other moves open.
6. Suicide	A serious risk in many psychiatric disorders. Doctor must watch for signs that patient is at risk.	A choice or option which ends all further possibility of behavioral change.	Not expected if person accepts his handicap.	Aggression turned against the self, or unwillingness to face real problems.	A symptom of anomie, despair.	"Trips" are risky; there is no guarantee that a person won't commit suicide.		
7. Function of institution	Hospital is a place where patients are treated and cared for; patients never *live* there or work *for* the hospital.	Correctional institution where person stays until his behavior improves; voluntarily or involuntarily.	Home for impaired provides protection, care, work, rehabilitation.	Any place where analysand can be analyzed, away from family that made him "sick."	Asylum for the severely damaged; or storefront clinic; or headquarters for the social revolution.	To provide a good atmosphere for guided "trips."	All institutions for schizophrenics degrade and invalidate human beings.	Hospital antitherapeutic, unless whole family is treated there.
8. Personnel	Doctors treat the ill, nurses care for them, other staff rehabilitate them.	Moral practitioners possessing knowledge on how to alter behavior, e.g., behavior therapists, clergymen, ward attendants.	Personnel must be skilled at rehabilitation; must be kind to the impaired.	Psychoanalysts or psychotherapists. Must have undergone analysis themselves.	Social psychiatrists, social workers, storefront clinic social workers, social revolutionaries.	Guides who have been there and back.	Conspirators: all who conspire to label a person as mentally ill. Anticonspirators: all who combat this, e.g., civil liberties lawyers, writers of exposé articles, etc.	Family therapists, game analysts.
9. Rights and duties of subject	Right to the sick role: exemption from normal responsibilities; no blame; right to special care. Duty to try to get well; to seek help and cooperate with that help.	Right to expect a serious effort to restore him to society. Duty to cooperate in effort to change his behavior.	Right to be protected from abuse, exploitation, persecution. Duty to behave as much as possible like normal person, within limits of impairment.	Right to have his behavior seen as symbolic, not judged morally. Right to sympathy for his long-standing emotional problems. Duty to cooperate with the therapy.	Right to expect social reforms to remove any special disadvantages. Right to care as social victims. Duty to cooperate with social change.	Right to well-guided "trip" in setting conducive to inner exploration. Duty to accept restraint if he is too much for others.	In a total institution the inmate has no rights and no duties.	Right to expect other members of family to agree to be defined as "sick" and to cooperate with family therapy. Duty to cooperate with family therapy.

TABLE 1
MODELS OF MADNESS

	Medical Model	Moral Model	Impaired Model	Psychoanalytic Model	Social Model	Psychedelic Model	Conspiratorial Model	Family Interaction Model
10. *Rights and duties of families*	Right to sympathy; right to be informed about illness and progress. Duty to cooperate with treatment.	Right to expect that experts have better sanctioning system than they have. Duty to encourage their immoral members to seek behavior therapy.	Right to know degree of impairment; right to be spared unreasonable hope. Duty to encourage impaired person to live as normally as possible.	No rights, not even being informed of progress. Duty not to interfere with therapy.	Right to expect social reforms to prevent social pathology. Duty to cooperate with social change.	No rights. Duty to allow their mad member to go on voyage of self-healing. *No right to label him and send him to hospital.*	Forfeited its usual rights by labeling one member as mentally ill and acting against him. Duty not to do this.	Right to be treated as "sick." Duty to cooperate with family therapy.
11. *Rights and duties of society*	Right to be protected from ill people who are a danger to others. Duty to provide medical care in one form or another.	Right to defend itself from members who endanger others by violating social norms or laws. Duty to provide possibility of rehabilitation.	Right to be protected from dangers due to impairment (e.g., insane drivers). Duty to protect impaired from abuse, exploitation, persecution.	No rights. Duty to see immoral behavior of analysands as symptoms of emotional disturbance.	No rights. Duty to change, or stop changing, so social pathology is not transmitted to individuals via their families.	No rights in relation to mad people. Duty to allow more "breakthrough."	Right to lock up those who have broken laws, but not those who are merely socially deviant.	No rights. Possibly, duty to provide family therapy.
12. *Goal of model*	Treat patients for illnesses; restore them to health if possible; otherwise prevent illness from getting worse. Reduce blame by conferring sick role. Accumulate medical knowledge.	Alter behavior to bring person into line with acceptable social norms.	To protect and care for permanently impaired persons; to provide rehabilitation for those able to function at a reduced level.	To resolve the analysand's longstanding unconscious emotional conflicts.	To reform society and create a healthy environment in which families can raise children without mental illness.	To allow certain people, now seen as mad, to develop their potential for inner exploration and to change the world through their insights.	Conspirators: to maintain the status quo by punishing deviance. Anticonspirators: to champion the persecuted.	To restore pathological families to mental health. To understand family dynamics.

What you also want is two or more models, for no amount of information about one model will tell you whether or not some other model might not be better. A boat which is the right size might be too expensive, while one that is inexpensive might be too small. The same is true of the various models used in psychiatry. The psychoanalytic model can give a more complete account of etiology than any of the other models, but it is exceptionally poor at discussing the rights and duties of the family. The medical model, which has fairly clear and well-known directions for the family, is often hazy about etiology.

If all those who participate in psychiatric enterprises had used only one model, and had used it consistently, we would never have been put to the trouble of constructing these models, but since very few people are highly consistent and most are not at all, we have made the models to show what it would look like if they were used purely and consistently. Table 1 presents the models in this idealized form. . . .

QUESTIONS

1. Siegler and Osmond point out the different rights and duties which accrue to society on each of their models. Examine those rights and duties. Which of them do you see as justified by the harm principle? By the paternalism principles?

2. Which of the models provide the best framework for society's treatment of the "mentally ill"?

THOMAS S. SZASZ

INVOLUNTARY MENTAL HOSPITALIZATION: A CRIME AGAINST HUMANITY

Thomas S. Szasz, M.D., is professor of psychiatry at the State University of New York, Upstate Medical Center in Syracuse. A cofounder of the American Association for the Abolition of Involuntary Mental Hospitalization, he has long been an outspoken critic of contemporary psychiatric practice. Among his numerous published works are *The Myth of Mental Illness* (1961), *The Ethics of Psychoanalysis* (1965), *The Manufacture of Madness* (1970), and *Heresies* (1976).

Szasz attacks the practice of committing persons to mental institutions against their will. He calls such commitments "a crime against humanity" and condemns the use of coercive state power against the "mentally ill." Szasz criticizes those who maintain that such commitments (1) *benefit* the mentally ill and/or (2) *protect* the mentally healthy members of society. Against (1), Szasz cites medical, moral, historical, and literary "evidence" to support his view that commitment does not serve the patient's interests; rather it serves the interests of others. Against (2), Szasz again cites the same sorts of evidence to show that the "danger posed by mental patients" is usually vaguely defined (e.g., their behavior may merely be offensive to some). Underlying Szasz's arguments here is the conspiratorial model of mental illness.

I

For some time now I have maintained that commitment—that is, the detention of persons in mental institutions against their will—is a form of imprisonment;[1] that such deprivation of liberty is contrary to the moral principles embodied in the Declaration of Independence and the Constitution of the United States;[2] and that it is a crass violation of contemporary concepts of fundamental human rights.[3] The practice of "sane" men incarcerating their "insane" fellow men in "mental hospitals" can be compared to that of white men enslaving black men. In short, I consider commitment a crime against humanity.

Existing social institutions and practices, especially if honored by prolonged usage, are generally experienced and accepted as good and valuable. For thousands of years slavery was considered a "natural" social arrangement for the securing of human labor; it was sanctioned by public opinion, religious dogma, church, and state;[4] it was abolished a mere one hundred years ago in the United States; and it is still a prevalent social practice in some parts of the world, notably in Africa.[5] Since its origin, approximately three centuries ago, commitment of the insane has enjoyed equally widespread support; physicians, lawyers, and the laity have asserted, as if with a single voice, the therapeutic desirability and social necessity of institutional psychiatry. My claim that commitment is a crime against humanity may thus be countered—as indeed it has been—by maintaining, first, that the practice is beneficial for the mentally ill, and second, that it is necessary for the protection of the mentally healthy members of society.

Illustrative of the first argument is Slovenko's assertion that "Reliance solely on voluntary hospital admission procedures ignores the fact that some persons may desire care and custody but cannot communicate their desire directly."[6] Imprisonment in mental hospitals is here portrayed—by a professor of law!—as a service provided to persons by the state because they "desire" it but do not know how to ask for it. Felix defends involuntary mental hospitalization by asserting simply, "We *do* [his italics] deal with illnesses of the mind."[7]

Illustrative of the second argument is Guttmacher's characterization of my book *Law, Liberty, and Psychiatry* as " . . . a pernicious book . . . certain to produce intolerable and unwarranted anxiety in the families of psychiatric patients."[8] This is an admission of the fact that the families of "psychiatric patients" frequently resort to the use of force in order to control their "loved ones," and that when attention is directed to this practice it creates embarrassment and guilt. On the other hand, Felix simply defines the psychiatrist's duty as the protection of society: "Tomorrow's psychiatrist will be, as is his counterpart today, one of the gatekeepers of his community."[9]

These conventional explanations of the nature and uses of commitment are, how-

[1]Szasz, T. S.: "Commitment of the mentally ill: Treatment or social restraint?" *J. Nerv. & Ment. Dis.* 125:293–307 (Apr.–June), 1957.
[2]Szasz, T. S.: *Law, Liberty, and Psychiatry: An Inquiry into the Social Uses of Mental Health Practices* (New York: Macmillan, 1963), pp. 149–90.
[3]Ibid., pp. 223–55.
[4]Davis, D. B.: *The Problem of Slavery in Western Culture* (Ithaca, N. Y.: Cornell University Press, 1966).
[5]See Cohen, R.: "Slavery in Africa." *Trans-Action* 4:44–56 (Jan.–Feb.), 1967; Tobin, R. L.: "Slavery still plagues the earth." *Saturday Review*, May 6, 1967, pp. 24–25.
[6]Slovenko, R.: "The psychiatric patient, liberty, and the law." *Amer. J. Psychiatry*, 121:534–39 (Dec.), 1964, p. 536.
[7]Felix, R. H.: "The image of the psychiatrist: Past, present, and future." *Amer. J. Psychiatry*, 121:318–22 (Oct.), 1964, p. 320.
[8]Guttmacher, M. S.: "Critique of views of Thomas Szasz on legal psychiatry," *AMA Arch. Gen. Psychiatry*, 10:238–45 (March), 1964, p. 244.
[9]Felix, op. cit., p. 231.

ever, but culturally accepted justifications for certain quasi-medical forms of social control, exercised especially against individuals and groups whose behavior does not violate criminal laws but threatens established social values.

II

What is the evidence that commitment does not serve the purpose of helping or treating people whose behavior deviates from or threatens prevailing social norms or moral standards; and who, because they inconvenience their families, neighbors, or superiors, may be incriminated as "mentally ill"?

1. The Medical Evidence

Mental illness is a metaphor. If by "disease" we mean a disorder of the physiochemical machinery of the human body, then we can assert that what we call functional mental diseases are not diseases at all.[10] Persons said to be suffering from such disorders are socially deviant or inept, or in conflict with individuals, groups, or institutions. Since they do not suffer from disease, it is impossible to "treat" them for any sickness.

Although the term "mentally ill" is usually applied to persons who do not suffer from bodily disease, it is sometimes applied also to persons who do (for example, to individuals intoxicated with alcohol or other drugs, or to elderly people suffering from degenerative disease of the brain). However, when patients with demonstrable diseases of the brain are involuntarily hospitalized, the primary purpose is to exercise social control over their behavior,[11] treatment of the disease is, at best, a secondary consideration. Frequently, therapy is non-existent, and custodial care is dubbed "treatment."

In short, the commitment of persons suffering from "functional psychoses" serves moral and social, rather than medical and therapeutic, purposes. Hence, even if, as a result of future research, certain conditions now believed to be "functional" mental illnesses were to be shown to be "organic," my argument against involuntary mental hospitalization would remain unaffected.

2. The Moral Evidence

In free societies, the relationship between physician and patient is predicated on the legal presumption that the individual "owns" his body and his personality.[12] The physician can examine and treat a patient only with his consent; the latter is free to reject treatment (for example, an operation for cancer).[13] After death, "ownership" of the person's body is transferred to his heirs; the physician must obtain permission from the patient's relatives for postmortem examination. John Stuart Mill explicitly affirmed that " . . . each person is the proper guardian of his own health, whether bodily, or mental and spiritual."[14] Commitment is incompatible with this moral principle.

3. The Historical Evidence

Commitment practices flourished long before there were any mental or psychiatric "treatments" of "mental diseases." Indeed, madness or mental illness was not always a neces-

---

[10]See Szasz, T. S.: "The myth of mental illness." This volume [*Ideology and Insanity*] pp. 12–24; *The Myth of Mental Illness: Foundations of a Theory of Personal Conduct* (New York: Hoeber-Harper, 1961); "Mental illness is a myth." *The New York Times Magazine*, June 12, 1966, pp. 30 and 90–92.

[11]See, for example, Noyes, A. P.: *Modern Clinical Psychiatry*, 4th ed. (Philadelphia: Saunders, 1956), p. 278.

[12]Szasz, T. S.: "The ethics of birth control; or, who owns your body?" *The Humanist*, 20:332–36 (Nov.-Dec.), 1960.

[13]Hirsch, B. D.: "Informed consent to treatment," in Averbach, A. and Belli, M. M., eds., *Tort and Medical Yearbook* (Indianapolis: Bobbs-Merrill, 1961), Vol. I, pp. 631–38.

[14]Mill, J. S.: *On Liberty* [1859] (Chicago: Regnery, 1955), p. 18.

sary condition for commitment. For example, in the seventeenth century, "children of artisans and other poor inhabitants of Paris up to the age of 25, . . . girls who were debauched or in evident danger of being debauched, . . ." and other "misérables" of the community, such as epileptics, people with venereal diseases, and poor people with chronic diseases of all sorts, were all considered fit subjects for confinement in the Hôpital Général.[15] And, in 1860, when Mrs. Packard was incarcerated for disagreeing with her minister-husband,[16] the commitment laws of the State of Illinois explicitly proclaimed that " . . . married women . . . may be entered or detained in the hospital at the request of the husband of the woman or the guardian . . . , without the evidence of insanity required in other cases."[17] It is surely no coincidence that this piece of legislation was enacted and enforced at about the same time that Mill published his essay *The Subjection of Women*.[18]

4. The Literary Evidence
Involuntary mental hospitalization plays a significant part in numerous short stories and novels from many countries. In none that I have encountered is commitment portrayed as helpful to the hospitalized person; instead, it is always depicted as an arrangement serving interests antagonistic to those of the so-called patient.[19]

III
The claim that commitment of the "mentally ill" is necessary for the protection of the "mentally healthy" is more difficult to refute, not because it is valid, but because the danger that "mental patients" supposedly pose is of such an extremely vague nature.

1. The Medical Evidence
The same reasoning applies as earlier: If "mental illness" is not a disease, there is no medical justification for protection from disease. Hence, the analogy between mental illness and contagious disease falls to the ground: The justification for isolating or otherwise constraining patients with tuberculosis or typhoid fever cannot be extended to patients with "mental illness."

Moreover, because the accepted contemporary psychiatric view of mental illness fails to distinguish between illness as a biological condition and as a social role,[20] it is not only false, but also dangerously misleading, especially if used to justify social action. In this view, regardless of its "causes" — anatomical, genetic, chemical, psychological, or social — mental illness has "objective existence." A person either has or has not a mental illness; he is either mentally sick or mentally healthy. Even if a person is cast in the role of mental patient against his will, his "mental illness" exists "objectively"; and even if, as in the case

[15]Rosen, G.: "Social attitudes to irrationality and madness in 17th and 18th century Europe." *J. Hist. Med. & Allied Sciences,* 18:220–40 (1963), p. 223.
[16]Packard, E. W. P.: *Modern Persecution, or Insane Asylums Unveiled,* 2 Vols. (Hartford: Case, Lockwood, and Brainard, 1873).
[17]Illinois Statute Book, Sessions Laws 15, Section 10, 1851. Quoted in Packard, E. P. W.: *The Prisoner's Hidden Life* (Chicago: published by the author, 1868), p. 37.
[18]Mill, J. S.: *The Subjection of Women* [1869] (London: Dent, 1965).
[19]See, for example, Chekhov, A. P.: *Ward No. 6,* [1892], in *Seven Short Novels by Chekhov* (New York: Bantam Books, 1963), pp. 106–57; De Assis, M.: *The Psychiatrist* [1881–82], in De Assis, M., *The Psychiatrist and Other Stories* (Berkeley and Los Angeles: University of California Press, 1963), pp. 1–45; London, J: *The Iron Heel* [1907] (New York: Sagamore Press, 1957); Porter, K. A.: *Noon Wine* [1937], in Porter, K. A., *Pale Horse, Pale Rider: Three Short Novels* (New York: Signet, 1965), pp. 62–112; Kesey, K.: *One Flew Over the Cuckoo's Nest* (New York: Viking, 1962); Tarsis, V.: *Ward 7: An Autobiographical Novel* (London and Glasgow: Collins and Harvill, 1965).
[20]See Szasz, T. S.: "Alcoholism: A socio-ethical perspective," *Western Medicine,* 7:15–21 (Dec.), 1966.

of the Very Important Person, he is never treated as a mental patient, his "mental illness" still exists "objectively" — apart from the activities of the psychiatrist.[21]

The upshot is that the term "mental illness" is perfectly suited for mystification: It disregards the crucial question of whether the individual assumes the role of mental patient voluntarily, and hence wishes to engage in some sort of interaction with a psychiatrist; or whether he is cast in that role against his will, and hence is opposed to such a relationship. This obscurity is then usually employed strategically, either by the subject himself to advance *his* interests, or by the subject's adversaries to advance *their* interests.

In contrast to this view, I maintain, first, that the involuntarily hospitalized mental patient is, by definition, the occupant of an ascribed role; and, second, that the "mental disease" of such a person — unless the use of this term is restricted to demonstrable lesions or malfunctions of the brain — is always the product of interaction between psychiatrist and patient.

2. The Moral Evidence

The crucial ingredient in involuntary mental hospitalization is coercion. Since coercion is the exercise of power, it is always a moral and political act. Accordingly, regardless of its medical justification, commitment is primarily a moral and political phenomenon — just as, regardless of its anthropological and economic justifications, slavery was primarily a moral and political phenomenon.

Although psychiatric methods of coercion are indisputably useful for those who employ them, they are clearly not indispensable for dealing with the problems that so-called mental patients pose for those about them. If an individual threatens others by virtue of his beliefs or actions, he could be dealt with by methods other than "medical": if his conduct is ethically offensive, moral sanctions against him might be appropriate; if forbidden by law, legal sanctions might be appropriate. In my opinion, both informal, moral sanctions, such as social ostracism or divorce, and formal, judicial sanctions, such as fine and imprisonment, are more dignified and less injurious to the human spirit than the quasi-medical psychiatric sanction of involuntary mental hospitalization.[22]

3. The Historical Evidence

To be sure, confinement of so-called mentally ill persons does protect the community from certain problems. If it didn't, the arrangement would not have come into being and would not have persisted. However, the question we ought to ask is not *whether* commitment protects the community from "dangerous mental patients," but rather from precisely *what danger* it protects and by *what means?* In what way were prostitutes or vagrants dangerous in seventeenth century Paris? Or married women in nineteenth century Illinois?

It is significant, moreover, that there is hardly a prominent person who, during the past fifty years or so, has not been diagnosed by a psychiatrist as suffering from some type of "mental illness." Barry Goldwater was called a "paranoid schizophrenic";[23] Whittaker Chambers, a "psychopathic personality";[24] Woodrow Wilson, a "neurotic" frequently

---

[21]See, for example, Rogow, A. A.: *James Forrestal: A Study of Personality, Politics, and Policy* (New York: Macmillan, 1964); for a detailed criticism of this view, see Szasz, T. S.: "Psychiatric classification as a strategy of personal constraint." This volume [*Ideology and Insanity*] pp. 190–217.

[22]Szasz, T. S.: *Psychiatric Justice* (New York: Macmillan, 1965).

[23]"The Unconscious of a Conservative: A Special Issue on the Mind of Barry Goldwater." *Fact*, Sept.–Oct., 1964.

[24]Zeligs, M. A.: *Friendship and Fratricide: An Analysis of Whittaker Chambers and Alger Hiss* (New York: Viking, 1967).

"very close to psychosis";[25] and Jesus, "a born degenerate" with a "fixed delusional system," and a "paranoid" with a "clinical picture [so typical] that it is hardly conceivable that people can even question the accuracy of the diagnosis."[26] The list is endless.

Sometimes, psychiatrists declare the same person sane *and* insane, depending on the political dictates of their superiors and the social demand of the moment. Before his trial and execution, Adolph Eichmann was examined by several psychiatrists, all of whom declared him to be normal; after he was put to death, "medical evidence" of his insanity was released and widely circulated.

According to Hannah Arendt, "Half a dozen psychiatrists had certified him [Eichmann] as 'normal.' " One psychiatrist asserted, " . . . his whole psychological outlook, his attitude toward his wife and children, mother and father, sisters and friends, was 'not only normal but most desirable.' . . ." And the minister who regularly visited him in prison declared that Eichmann was "a man with very positive ideas."[27] After Eichmann was executed, Gideon Hausner, the Attorney General of Israel, who had prosecuted him, disclosed in an article in *The Saturday Evening Post* that psychiatrists diagnosed Eichmann as " 'a man obsessed with a dangerous and insatiable urge to kill,' 'a perverted, sadistic personality.' "[28]

Whether or not men like those mentioned above are considered "dangerous" depends on the observer's religious beliefs, political convictions, and social situation. Furthermore, the "dangerousness" of such persons—whatever we may think of them—is not analogous to that of a person with tuberculosis or typhoid fever; nor would rendering such a person "non-dangerous" be comparable to rendering a patient with a contagious disease non-infectious.

In short, I hold—and I submit that the historical evidence bears me out—that people are committed to mental hospitals neither because they are "dangerous," nor because they are "mentally ill," but rather because they are society's scapegoats, whose persecution is justified by psychiatric propaganda and rhetoric.[29]

4. The Literary Evidence

No one contests that involuntary mental hospitalization of the so-called dangerously insane "protects" the community. Disagreement centers on the nature of the threat facing society, and on the methods and legitimacy of the protection it employs. In this connection, we may recall that slavery, too, "protected" the community: it freed the slaveowners from manual labor. Commitment likewise shields the nonhospitalized members of society: first, from having to accommodate themselves to the annoying or idiosyncratic demands of certain members of the community who have not violated any criminal statutes; and, second, from having to prosecute, try, convict, and punish members of the community who have broken the law but who either might not be convicted in court, or, if they would be, might not be restrained as effectively or as long in prison as in a mental hospital. The literary evidence cited earlier fully supports this interpretation of the function of involuntary mental hospitalization.

[25]Freud, S. and Bullitt, W. C.: *Thomas Woodrow Wilson: A Psychological Study* (Boston: Houghton Mifflin, 1967).

[26]Quoted in Schweitzer, A.: *The Psychiatric Study of Jesus* [1913] transl. by Charles R. Joy (Boston: Beacon Press, 1956) pp. 37, 40–41.

[27]Arendt, H.: *Eichmann in Jerusalem: A Report on the Banality of Evil* (New York: Viking, 1963), p. 22.

[28]Ibid., pp. 22–23.

[29]For a full articulation and documentation of this thesis, see Szasz, T. S.: *The Manufacture of Madness: A Comparative Study of the Inquisition and the Mental Health Movement* (New York: Harper & Row, 1970).

IV

I have suggested that commitment constitutes a social arrangement whereby one part of society secures certain advantages for itself at the expense of another part. To do so, the oppressors must possess an ideology to justify their aims and actions; and they must be able to enlist the police power of the state to impose their will on the oppressed members. What makes such an arrangement a "crime against humanity"? It may be argued that the use of state power is legitimate when law-abiding citizens punish lawbreakers. What is the difference between this use of state power and its use in commitment?

In the first place, the difference between committing the "insane" and imprisoning the "criminal" is the same as that between the rule of man and the rule of law:[30] whereas the "insane" are subjected to the coercive controls of the state because persons more powerful than they have labeled them as "psychotic," "criminals" are subjected to such controls because they have violated legal rules applicable equally to all.

The second difference between these two proceedings lies in their professed aims. The principal purpose of imprisoning criminals is to protect the liberties of the law-abiding members of society.[31] Since the individual subject to commitment is not considered a threat to liberty in the same way as the accused criminal is (if he were, he would be prosecuted), his removal from society cannot be justified on the same grounds. Justification for commitment must thus rest on its therapeutic promise and potential: it will help restore the "patient" to "mental health." But if this can be accomplished only at the cost of robbing the individual of liberty, "involuntary mental hospitalization" becomes only a verbal camouflage for what is, in effect, punishment. This "therapeutic" punishment differs, however, from traditional judicial punishment, in that the accused criminal enjoys a rich panoply of constitutional protections against false accusations and oppressive prosecution, whereas the accused mental patient is deprived of these protections.[32] . . .

The social necessity, and hence the basic value, of involuntary mental hospitalization, at least for some people, is not seriously questioned today. There is massive consensus in the United States that, properly used, such hospitalization is a good thing. It is thus possible to debate *who* should be hospitalized, or *how,* or for *how long*—but not whether *anyone should* be. I submit, however, that just as it is improper to enslave anyone—whether he is black or white, Moslem or Christian—so it is improper to hospitalize anyone without his consent—whether he is depressed or paranoid, hysterical or schizophrenic. . . .

QUESTIONS

1. Is involuntary civil commitment "a crime against humanity" or a humane social practice intended to "help" those who cannot help themselves?

2. Is involuntary civil commitment of the "mentally ill" analogous to punishment? What are the similarities? What are the differences?

[30]Hayek, F. A.: *The Constitution of Liberty* (Chicago: University of Chicago Press, 1960), especially pp. 162–92.
[31]Mabbott, J. D.: "Punishment" [1939], in Olafson, F. A., ed., *Justice and Social Policy: A Collection of Essays* (Englewood Cliffs, N.J.: Prentice-Hall, 1961), pp. 39–54.
[32]For documentation, see Szasz, T. S.: *Law, Liberty, and Psychiatry: An Inquiry into the Social Uses of Mental Health Practices* (New York: Macmillan, 1963); *Psychiatric Justice* (New York: Macmillan, 1965).

MAJORITY OPINION IN *O'CONNOR v. DONALDSON*

A biographical sketch of Justice Potter Stewart, an associate justice of the Supreme Court of the United States since 1958, is found on p. 87.

In 1943, after Kenneth Donaldson had made a political comment, his fellow workers apparently knocked him unconscious. Following this incident, Donaldson's parents asked a judge to commit their thirty-four-year-old son to a mental institution for treatment. Once Donaldson was institutionalized and his reactions to what he perceived as injustices were diagnosed as pathological, he was given electro-convulsive therapy. After eleven weeks of ECT, he was released. In 1956, Donaldson visited his parents in Florida. During his visit, he made some complaints which led his father to request a sanity hearing for his son. The senior Donaldson argued that his son was suffering from a "persecution complex." As a result of this complaint, Donaldson was arrested, jailed, and diagnosed as "paranoid schizophrenic" by a sheriff and two physicians. The physicians, each of whom spoke to Donaldson for less than two minutes, were not psychiatrists. Later a judge visited him and informed him that he would be sent to Florida State Hospital. This decision was based on the physicians' conclusions. Donaldson's requests for a judicial hearing and a lawyer were granted; but the hearing was held in jail, the physicians did not attend, and Donaldson's lawyer left while Donaldson was still testifying. Donaldson was sent to the hospital for a "few weeks rest." He remained there for fifteen years, never seeing a judge and seeing a psychiatrist only a few times a year. During those fifteen years, Donaldson petitioned various courts eighteen times, asking for a hearing. All but one of these requests were dismissed on the basis of physicians' reports and his previous institutionalization. When his case was finally going to be heard in 1971, Donaldson was released and certified as "no longer incompetent." However, he continued his suit asking $100,000 in damages for the fifteen years he had been committed without treatment. He won his case against J. G. O'Connor, the superintendent of the institution, and a codefendant physician, although only $38,500 was granted in damages.

The case was ultimately appealed to the United States Supreme Court. In handing down its 1975 landmark decision, the Court ruled that a finding of mental illness alone is insufficient grounds for confining a nondangerous individual when that individual has the capacity to survive safely in freedom, either by himself or with the help of responsible and willing relatives or friends. Justice Potter Stewart wrote the majority opinion which is partially reprinted here.

I

Donaldson's commitment was initiated by his father, who thought that his son was suffering from "delusions." After hearings before a county judge of Pinellas County, Fla., Donaldson was found to be suffering from "paranoid schizophrenia" and was committed for "care, maintenance, and treatment" pursuant to Florida statutory provisions that have since been repealed. The state law was less than clear in specifying the grounds necessary for commitment, and the record is scanty as to Donaldson's condition at the time of the judicial hearing. These matters are, however, irrelevant, for this case involves no challenge to the initial commitment, but is focused, instead, upon the nearly 15 years of confinement that followed.

The evidence at the trial showed that the hospital staff had the power to release a

United States Supreme Court. 422 U.S. 563 (1975).

patient, not dangerous to himself or others, even if he remained mentally ill and had been lawfully committed. Despite many requests, O'Connor refused to allow that power to be exercised in Donaldson's case. At the trial, O'Connor indicated that he had believed that Donaldson would have been unable to make a "successful adjustment outside the institution," but could not recall the basis for that conclusion. O'Connor retired as superintendent shortly before the suit was filed. A few months thereafter, and before the trial, Donaldson secured his release and a judicial restoration of competency, with the support of the hospital staff.

The testimony at the trial demonstrated, without contradiction, that Donaldson had posed no danger to others during his long confinement, or indeed at any point in his life. O'Connor himself conceded that he had no personal or secondhand knowledge that Donaldson had ever committed a dangerous act. There was no evidence that Donaldson had ever been suicidal or been thought likely to inflict injury upon himself. One of O'Connor's codefendants acknowledged that Donaldson could have earned his own living outside the hospital. He had done so for some 14 years before his commitment, and immediately upon his release he secured a responsible job in hotel administration.

Furthermore, Donaldson's frequent requests for release had been supported by responsible persons willing to provide him any care he might need on release. In 1963, for example, a representative of Helping Hands, Inc., a halfway house for mental patients, wrote O'Connor asking him to release Donaldson to its care. The request was accompanied by a supporting letter from the Minneapolis Clinic of Psychiatry and Neurology, which a codefendant conceded was a "good clinic." O'Connor rejected the offer, replying that Donaldson could be released only to his parents. That rule was apparently of O'Connor's own making. At the time, Donaldson was 55 years old, and, as O'Connor knew, Donaldson's parents were too elderly and infirm to take responsibility for him. Moreover, in his continuing correspondence with Donaldson's parents, O'Connor never informed them of the Helping Hands offer. In addition, on four separate occasions between 1964 and 1968, John Lembcke, a college classmate of Donaldson's and a longtime family friend, asked O'Connor to release Donaldson to his care. On each occasion O'Connor refused. The record shows that Lembcke was a serious and responsible person, who was willing and able to assume responsibility for Donaldson's welfare.

The evidence showed that Donaldson's confinement was a simple regime of enforced custodial care, not a program designed to alleviate or cure his supposed illness. Numerous witnesses, including one of O'Connor's codefendants, testified that Donaldson had received nothing but custodial care while at the hospital. O'Connor described Donaldson's treatment as "milieu therapy." But witnesses from the hospital staff conceded that, in the context of this case, "milieu therapy" was a euphemism for confinement in the "milieu" of a mental hospital. For substantial periods, Donaldson was simply kept in a large room that housed 60 patients, many of whom were under criminal commitment. Donaldson's requests for ground privileges, occupational training, and an opportunity to discuss his case with O'Connor or other staff members were repeatedly denied.

At the trial, O'Connor's principal defense was that he had acted in good faith and was therefore immune from any liability for monetary damages. His position, in short, was that state law, which he had believed valid, had authorized indefinite custodial confinement of the "sick," even if they were not given treatment and their release could harm no one.

The trial judge instructed the members of the jury that they should find that O'Connor had violated Donaldson's constitutional right to liberty if they found that he had

confined [Donaldson] against his will, knowing that he was not mentally ill or dangerous or knowing that if mentally ill he was not receiving treatment for his alleged mental illness. . . .

Now, the purpose of involuntary hospitalization is treatment and not mere custodial care or punishment if a patient is not a danger to himself or others. Without such treatment there is no justification from a constitutional stand-point for continued confinement unless you should also find that [Donaldson] was dangerous to either himself or others.

The trial judge further instructed the jury that O'Connor was immune from damages if he

reasonably believed in good faith that detention of [Donaldson] was proper for the length of time he was so confined. . . .

However, mere good intentions which do not give rise to a reasonable belief that detention is lawfully required cannot justify [Donaldson's] confinement in the Florida State Hospital.

The jury returned a verdict for Donaldson against O'Connor and a codefendant, and awarded damages of $38,500, including $10,000 in punitive damages.

The Court of Appeals affirmed the judgment of the District Court in a broad opinion dealing with "the far-reaching question whether the Fourteenth Amendment guarantees a right to treatment to persons involuntarily civilly committed to state mental hospitals." The appellate court held that when, as in Donaldson's case, the rationale for confinement is that the patient is in need of treatment, the Constitution requires that minimally adequate treatment in fact be provided. The court further expressed the view that, regardless of the grounds for involuntary civil commitment, a person confined against his will at a state mental institution has "a constitutional right to receive such individual treatment as will give him a reasonable opportunity to be cured or to improve his mental condition." Conversely, the court's opinion implied that it is constitutionally permissible for a State to confine a mentally ill person against his will in order to treat his illness, regardless of whether his illness renders him dangerous to himself or others.

II

We have concluded that the difficult issues of constitutional law dealt with by the Court of Appeals are not presented by this case in its present posture. Specifically, there is no reason now to decide whether mentally ill persons dangerous to themselves or to others have a right to treatment upon compulsory confinement by the State, or whether the State may compulsorily confine a nondangerous, mentally ill individual for the purpose of treatment. As we view it, this case raises a single, relatively simple, but nonetheless important question concerning every man's constitutional right to liberty.

The jury found that Donaldson was neither dangerous to himself nor dangerous to others, and also found that, if mentally ill, Donaldson had not received treatment. That verdict, based on abundant evidence, makes the issue before the Court a narrow one. We need not decide whether, when, or by what procedures, a mentally ill person may be confined by the State on any of the grounds which, under contemporary statutes, are generally advanced to justify involuntary confinement of such a person—to prevent injury to the public, to ensure his own survival or safety, or to alleviate or cure his illness. For the jury found that none of the above grounds for continued confinement was present in Donaldson's case.

Given the jury's findings, what was left as justification for keeping Donaldson in continued confinement? The fact that state law may have authorized confinement of the harmless mentally ill does not itself establish a constitutionally adequate purpose for the confinement. Nor is it enough that Donaldson's original confinement was founded upon a constitutionally adequate basis, if in fact it was, because even if his involuntary confinement was initially permissible, it could not constitutionally continue after that basis no longer existed.

A finding of "mental illness" alone cannot justify a State's locking a person up against his will and keeping him indefinitely in simple custodial confinement. Assuming that that term can be given a reasonably precise content and that the "mentally ill" can be identified with reasonable accuracy, there is still no constitutional basis for confining such persons involuntarily if they are dangerous to no one and can live safely in freedom.

May the State confine the mentally ill merely to ensure them a living standard superior to that they enjoy in the private community? That the State has a proper interest in providing care and assistance to the unfortunate goes without saying. But the mere presence of mental illness does not disqualify a person from preferring his home to the comforts of an institution. Moreover, while the State may arguably confine a person to save him from harm, incarceration is rarely if ever a necessary condition for raising the living standards of those capable of surviving safely in freedom, on their own or with the help of family or friends.

May the State fence in the harmless mentally ill solely to save its citizens from exposure to those whose ways are different? One might as well ask if the State, to avoid public unease, could incarcerate all who are physically unattractive or socially eccentric. Mere public intolerance or animosity cannot constitutionally justify the deprivation of a person's physical liberty.

In short, a State cannot constitutionally confine without more a nondangerous individual who is capable of surviving safely in freedom by himself or with the help of willing and responsible family members or friends. Since the jury found, upon ample evidence, that O'Connor, as an agent of the State, knowingly did so confine Donaldson, it properly concluded that O'Connor violated Donaldson's constitutional right to freedom. . . .

QUESTIONS

1. Should we have laws which give representatives of the state, such as judges and psychiatrists, the power to control the behavior of those diagnosed as mentally ill?
2. Were there any *good* reasons for confining Donaldson for even a short period?

LEE COLEMAN
and TRUDY SOLOMON

PARENS PATRIAE "TREATMENT": LEGAL PUNISHMENT IN DISGUISE

Lee Coleman, a psychiatrist in private practice in California, is a cofounder of the Committee Opposing Abuse of Psychiatry. Trudy Solomon, a social psychologist, is a policy analyst for the National Science Foundation. They are the joint authors of both this article and "Big Brother Knows Best." Coleman's other articles include "Problem Kids and Preventive Medicine: The Making of an Odd Couple." Solomon's other articles include "Informed Consent for Mental Patients."

Coleman and Solomon's arguments are directed against the widely accepted premise that there is a valid distinction between criminal punishment and the state-ordered "treatment" which is purportedly justified by the doctrine of *parens patriae* (literally, "in the place of the parent"). *Parens patriae* is the paternalistic doctrine that the state has both a right and a duty to help and protect those who cannot help themselves. Coleman and Solomon briefly analyze the concepts of treatment and punishment. They argue that a correct understanding of these concepts supports the view that *parens patriae* treatment is a form of punishment. In order to support their claim that the purported "right" to treatment cannot qualify as a *bona fide* right, they briefly analyze the concept of a right.

The rationale of state intervention in individual affairs under the doctrine of parens patriae is that the state has a right and a duty to help and protect those who cannot help themselves. All measures taken under the doctrine are justified as intended ultimately for the individual's own good. Cast in the mold of the medical model, which has gained increasing influence since the end of the nineteenth century, this intervention has been denominated "therapy" or "treatment."

By the process termed divestment, many areas of the criminal law have been either abandoned outright, in favor of parens patriae civil interventions, or profoundly influenced in ways discussed below. Until recently, this divestment process has been almost universally applauded. Rather than meting out criminal sanctions, the state has promised treatment to wayward youth, the mentally disordered, drug addicts, and even many criminals. The due process concerns of the criminal sanction were ignored; one should not need protection from one's therapist. Such constraints would, in fact, amount to an outright interference with the treatment process.

The state's benevolence has been questioned in recent years. Case law indicates that the courts are abandoning their hands-off attitude, and have begun to realize that due process protections are important, even in allegedly therapeutic or rehabilitative interventions. Civil commitment statutes are being revised by state legislatures to reflect greater concern for civil liberties. Prison therapy and indeterminate sentencing are increasingly recognized as potentially powerful tools of control, rather than as instruments of rehabilitation. Benevolent intent is no longer an acceptable justification for the wholesale denial of due process for juveniles. In addition to this emphasis on constitutional rights, recent judicial decisions have developed a new doctrine, the "right to treatment," regarded by many as a welcome development.[1] In short, psychiatry and the law are gradually reflecting a greater awareness of the individual freedoms at stake in parens patriae interventions.

Have these limitations on the therapeutic sanction arisen from a re-evaluation of the actual *basis* of parens patriae? We think not, for the fundamental premise is still accepted *that there is a valid distinction between criminal punishment and state ordered "treatment."* The thesis presented here is that both psychiatry and the law have yet to confront the inherent and *irreconcilable* differences between bona fide treatment and state-sanctioned parens patriae intervention. Until this fundamental confrontation takes place, civil rights reforms, although necessary in and of themselves, only blunt our sensitivity while we proceed to replace old forms of benevolent control with new ones. For reasons discussed below, this exchange may be far more ominous than is generally recognized.

Our aim is to question the very roots of parens patriae, and the analysis of language

---

[1]After initially taking a defensive posture, the American Psychiatric Association (APA) has now come out in support of the doctrine. Psychiatric News, July 16, 1975, at 1, col. 1. In our view, this stems from the APA's belated recognition that the right to treatment doctrine lends support to involuntary psychiatric treatment. In addition, the promulgation of standards of treatment, such as those enunciated in Wyatt v. Stickney, 334 F. Supp. 1341 (M.D. Ala. 1971), encourages increased funding for mental hospitals.

Reprinted with permission of the publisher from *Hastings Constitutional Law Quarterly*, vol. 3, no. 2 (Spring 1976), pp. 345–362.

is a crucial element in achieving this end. Any effort by one individual to influence another is profoundly affected by what both parties believe to be the purpose of the effort; furthermore, this common understanding depends as much on the *words chosen* as on the practices themselves. Thus, despite recent judicial and legislative recognition of the civil rights questions inherent in parens patriae interventions, these interventions continue to be considered as benevolent treatment. In questioning this assumption and providing an alternative framework, we will first analyze, through language, the assumptions underlying state-sanctioned psychiatric "treatment." Historic examples of control viewed as benevolence, considered together with current developments of that view, provide a broad perspective within which to view the future dangers of the therapeutic sanction.

TREATMENT RECONSIDERED

If treatment is to justify either civil intervention in the absence of criminal conviction or vastly broadened discretionary power within the criminal sanction, a clear understanding of the concept of treatment is crucial. Surprisingly, the literature dealing with parens patriae has been virtually silent on this fundamental issue.

Clearly linked with medicine, the concept of treatment is defined as the "management in the application of remedies; medical or surgical application or service."[2] In the debate about whether psychiatric interventions should properly be designated as treatments, the controversy hinges on whether one considers emotional problems to be true diseases or emotional responses to problems of living. The denomination of mental problems as diseases and psychiatric interventions as treatments is unfortunate. But a far more compelling distinction between bona fide treatment and parens patriae treatment is the element of volition.

Both medical ethics and the law clearly differentiate between treatment and battery. The distinction disregards issues of effectiveness, side effects, skillfulness, and intent. The crucial point is whether voluntary consent precedes the physician's actions. Without consent, what would by all medical standards be considered treatment becomes unlawful activity. Thus, the psychiatry practiced as parens patriae intervention upon patients who do not consent to it cannot qualify as bona fide treatment. The careless acceptance of these interventions as treatment has led not only to the waiving of due process guarantees, but also to nonrecognition of the punitive quality of all parens patriae controls.

PUNISHMENT RECONSIDERED

The nature of punishment is the second element of the traditional treatment/punishment dichotomy at the logical core of parens patriae philosophy. According to the *Encyclopaedia Britannica,* punishment is:

> the infliction of some pain, suffering, loss, or social disability as a direct consequence of some action or omission on the part of the person punished. . . . [T]he agent of punishment must be in a position of legitimate authority over the punished. . . .[3]

---

[2] 11 THE OXFORD ENGLISH DICTIONARY 309 (1933).

[3] 15 ENCYCLOPAEDIA BRITANNICA: MACROPAEDIA 281 (15th ed. 1974). The concept of punishment has received much more attention than the concept of treatment, perhaps because punishment is generally recognized as an ethical question whereas treatment, which is usually left to physicians and scientists, has been considered beyond the review of lay commentaries. We have found that the *Britannica's* definition of punishment is generally mirrored by other commentators. *See* CONTEMPORARY PUNISHMENT: VIEWS, EXPLANATIONS, AND JUSTIFICATIONS (R. Gerber & P. McAnany eds. 1972), particularly Flew, *Definition of Punishment,* at 31–35. *See also* Bittner & Platt, *The Meaning of Punishment,* 2 ISSUES IN CRIMINOLOGY 79 (1966).

This definition speaks neither of intent nor of the professional identity of the agent of punishment. Instead, the emphasis is on *infliction* of something by one person upon another within the context of delegated state authority. We posit that the above definition of punishment provides a conceptual framework for the realistic analysis of state-sanctioned intervention.

While prosecutors, judges, and prison guards are assumed to be in the business of punishment, however fairly or unfairly administered, it is assumed that therapists, as humanitarian professionals, offer treatment. A marvelous circularity results. If your intent (however measured or defined) is benevolent, you are a therapist; if you are a therapist, your intent is prima facie benevolent, and whatever you do is therapy.

These false criteria — benevolent intent and professional identity — upon which the parens patriae distinction between punishment and treatment has been drawn, have become the cornerstones of the therapeutic sanction. In the early years of this century, George Ives formulated a philosophy of treatment which remains basically unchanged. His initial comment was that punishment is an irrational remedy;[4] his expressed hope was that,

> in the Future, when the Courts convict a prisoner, he will not merely disappear from view, to undergo a senseless, indiscriminating punishment. He will not, in fact, be punished more than any other patient; but he may have to undergo a course of treatment varied according to his special need, which may, or may not, be painful in its operation. The difference between the cut of the surgeon and the stab of the assassin lies mainly in the motive which made the wound. They will inflict no moment of unnecessary suffering; if they have to give any pain, there will be purpose in it, and a friendly purpose.[5]

Despite Ives and the century-old rationale of parens patriae, the crucial difference between the surgeon and the assassin lies neither in the motive nor in the degree of skill of each, but rather in the consent given the surgeon and denied the assassin. The surgeon, absent such consent, may be considered an assassin of sorts:

> Anglo-Saxon law does not recognize . . . nonconsensual treatment. . . . [A]n operation without the patient's consent . . . is not treatment but battery. . . . [U]nconsented surgery is, in the eyes of the law, tantamount to attack with a knife.[6]

PARENS PATRIAE TREATMENT AS PUNISHMENT

We have seen that the concept of parens patriae treatment is a semantic fiction since this treatment lacks the consent that is the *sine qua non* of bona fide treatment. Is state ordered "help" thus inherently punishment? In light of the elements of punishment, as discussed above, no valid distinction exists between parens patriae treatment and legal punishment. Pain, suffering, loss, and disability can be inflicted by the legal agent of punishment and can also result from bona fide treatment. But in bona fide treatment they are a side-effect of procedures undertaken to cure or alleviate an illness, whereas in parens patriae treatment they are inflicted because of some act or omission. Although in parens patriae treatment the agent has legitimate authority to intervene, the intervention is nonetheless coercive, whereas the agent of bona fide treatment intervenes only with the consent of the patient.

---

[4]G. IVES, A HISTORY OF PENAL METHODS 266 (1914).
[5]*Id.* at 335.
[6]G. Alexander & T. Szasz, *From Contract to Status via Psychiatry*, 13 SANTA CLARA LAW. 537, 548 (1973).

Parens patriae treatment involves not only the physical pain and suffering that may result from particular forced interventions, but also the psychological pain and suffering that may result from disculturation, isolation, dehumanization, and loss of freedom, all direct consequences of the intervention itself. Regardless of the manner in which it occurs or the intent with which it is done, forcing something on someone represents a loss of freedom of choice and frequently results in pain and suffering. When we add that this pain, suffering, loss, or disability is sanctioned by law and is justified by action or omission on the part of the subject, it becomes evident that all parens patriae treatment constitutes legal punishment.

The use of the word "punishment" to describe a therapist's best efforts, or of the word "prison" to describe a humanely appointed hospital facility, will strike many as unduly harsh. Words have had the power to comfort us, and have played and continue to play a major role in the deception inherent in parens patriae interventions. The California Welfare and Institutions Code provides a typical example:

> It is hereby declared that the provisions of this code reflect the concern of the Legislature that mentally disordered persons are to be regarded as patients to be provided care and treatment and not as inmates of institutions for the purposes of secluding them from the rest of the public.
>
> Whenever any provision of this code theretofore or hereafter uses the term "inmate," it shall be construed to mean "patient."[7]

Such linguistic manipulation is not new. A nineteenth century example of the power of words is the dialogue between Elizabeth Ware Packard, a critic of mental asylums, and her psychiatrist, following Packard's incarceration:

> [Doctor:] "I don't like your calling this place a prison so much; for it isn't so. . . . You may call it a place of confinement if you choose, but not a prison."
>
> . . . .
>
> [Packard:] "It is a prison to me. . . . I intend to clothe truth in its own drapery and to call things by their true names as I apprehend them."
>
> . . . .
>
> [Doctor:] "But you will acknowledge, Mrs. Packard, that the penitentiary inmates are on a different plane as prisoners, from what you are?"
>
> . . . .
>
> [Packard:] "The penitentiary is our government's place of punishing the guilty; insane asylums are our government's place of punishing the innocent. . . ."
>
> . . . .
>
> [Doctor:] "You would not, in writing a dictionary, describe each as alike, would you?"
>
> [Packard:] "I should say they are one and the same thing, as to being prisoners."[8]

We desperately need the kind of linguistic honesty that Packard advocated. Just as the misuse of words has, in the past, been a powerful element in the successful effort to disguise punishment as treatment, such misuse continues to hamper psychiatric and legal decisionmaking.

Prisons are now "medical facilities," prison guards are "correctional officers," and prisoners are "inmates" or "patients"; the list of such linguistic sleights-of-hand is long. This

---

[7] CAL. WELF. & INST'NS CODE § 4132 (West 1972).
[8] 2 E. PACKARD, MODERN PERSECUTION 132-35 (1873) (emphasis deleted).

commentary will focus on one example of the continuing power of language to sanitize policies that pose grave threats to free society, the emerging doctrine of the right to treatment.

A Strange New Right

The right to treatment has its legal roots in the relatively recent judicial finding that involuntary hospitalization without treatment does in fact constitute punishment.[9] The corollary is that involuntary hospitalization with treatment is not punishment. Such logic is fast becoming conventional wisdom among progressives, both psychiatric and legal. Any skepticism that has arisen focuses on the issue of effectiveness: whether psychiatric diagnosis and treatment is sufficiently quantifiable, and if so, whether there is evidence that the psychiatric interventions are actually effective enough to justify involuntary hospitalization. Repeated efforts to document effectiveness have shown the difficulty, if not the impossibility, of demonstrating the outcome of psychiatric therapy. This in no way proves that psychiatric interventions are ineffective, as some critics suggest, but simply that the use of effective treatment as a legal quid pro quo for deprivation of liberty is based more on pious hope than on proven results. Judge Johnson's recent mandate that there must be a "treatment available for the illness,"[10] is typical of the legal and judicial faith that, with adequate safeguards, psychiatric treatments may be sufficiently effective to form the basis for civil commitment. The bench continues to hold tenaciously to the century-old belief that psychiatry, as a legitimate branch of medicine, has specific and demonstrably effective treatments for reliably diagnosable diseases.

But what if we could prove, either now or in the future, that psychiatry is capable of specific diagnoses and effective treatments? Would the right to treatment then be a legally and ethically supportable doctrine? The preoccupation with effectiveness, on the part of the bench, the bar, and the psychiatrists, suggests that we have failed once again, to ask the fundamental questions: What is a right, and what is treatment?

As our previous discussion of the concept of treatment indicated, bona fide treatment requires a consenting patient; anything forced on an individual through the authority of the state as a result of unacceptable behavior is properly regarded as punishment. Under this analysis the right to treatment immediately presents basic contradictions. The treatment is said to be the quid pro quo for the deprivation of freedom, but since the treatment is coercive it is not really treatment at all, but punishment. Thus if words were used more

---

[9]The landmark decision in this area was Rouse v. Cameron, 373 F.2d 451 (D.C. Cir 1966). In his majority opinion, Judge Bazelon identified treatment as a necessary condition of incarceration for the mentally disordered. He noted that "[a]bsent treatment, the hospital is 'transform[ed] . . . into a penitentiary where one could be held indefinitely for no convicted offense. . . .'" *Id.* at 453, *quoting* Ragsdale v. Overholser, 281 F.2d 943, 950 (1960) (Fahy, J., concurring).

Because the opinion in *Rouse* is based on statutes enacted by Congress, D.C. Code §§ 21-501, 21-543, 21-561 to -564, 24-301 (Supp. V, 1966), its value as a precedent may be limited; at least one circuit judge suggested that later statutory interpretation by the same court of appeals has implicitly revised the holding of *Rouse. See* Dobson v. Cameron, 383 F.2d 519, 523 (D.C. Cir. 1967) (Burger, J., concurring). Nevertheless the impact of Judge Bazelon's decision in *Rouse* was that parens patriae considerations, which had permitted the confinement of individuals who had not been convicted of any crime, now required treatment for such individuals.

At least one circuit has gone even further by holding that "persons committed under what we have termed a *parens patriae* ground for commitment must be given treatment lest the involuntary commitment amount to an arbitrary exercise of government power proscribed by the due process clause." Donaldson v. O'Connor, 493 F.2d 507, 521 (5th Cir. 1974), *vacated,* 422 U.S. 563 (1975). The court claimed this right of treatment exists regardless of whether those to be treated were committed under a parens patriae or police power rationale. *Id.* Donaldson is a significant decision because it finds constitutional rather than statutory underpinnings for a right of treatment.

[10]Lynch v. Baxley, 386 F. Supp. 378, 391 (M.D. Ala. 1974).

honestly, the "right to treatment" would be the "right to punishment," the individual's right to be punished by the state for being mentally disturbed. However, we know of no mental patients or their advocates who have demanded that the state honor their right to be punished. Consequently the treatment to which incarcerated persons are said to have a right is at best a legal fiction.

The other half of the right to treatment is the concept of a right. According to the Oxford English Dictionary, a right is "[a] legal, equitable, or moral title or claim to the possession of property or authority, the enjoyment of privileges or immunities. . . ."[11] The key concept is the freedom to enjoy certain things, such as speech, and the freedom to be spared certain things, such as unreasonable search and seizure. It makes no sense whatever to label as a right anything forced on an individual, and we see no reason to allow coercive psychiatric treatment to be an exception.

If both the terms "right" and "treatment" in the phrase "right to treatment" involve the deceptive use of language, there may be something gained by seeking out the real meaning of this legal doctrine. If, as we have attempted to show, forced treatment is correctly termed punishment, a more honest term for right to treatment is *justification* for treatment. This label discloses the state's effort to rationalize, and to cast in the light of benevolence, its continuing punishment and control of deviants who might be difficult to process within the criminal justice system. The depiction of forced treatment as a right obfuscates the reality that the right to treatment is a justification for punishment.

Punishment is, of course, not new, but the doctrine of a right to treatment provides a justification for continued non-criminal punishment in the face of a growing recognition of both ethical and constitutional problems within the therapeutic sanction. It is quite common for apologists of involuntary psychiatric interventions, particularly the psychiatrists, to claim that if we were to stop incarcerating mental patients we would be abandoning them and depriving them of their right to treatment.

Some of the most knowledgeable critics have considered the right to treatment as a useful vehicle in the struggle against involuntary psychiatry. This view, we feel, will prove extremely short-sighted. The right to treatment may well become a rationale for new forms of parens patriae control. . . .

QUESTIONS

1. Which of the liberty-limiting principles, on your view, would justify the involuntary civil commitment of those considered mentally incompetent?

2. In a well-known legal case, *Tarasoff v. Regents of California,* the court ruled that a doctor or psychotherapist treating a mentally ill patient has a duty to warn third parties of threatened dangers arising out of a patient's violent intentions. (In this particular case, the patient killed the daughter of the Tarasoffs.) According to the court, the mental patient's right to privacy was subordinate to the public interest in safety from violent assault. In light of our limited knowledge about the "potential dangerousness" of some of those considered mentally ill, is this court ruling another example of the denial of rights to the mentally ill on the basis of insufficient empirical evidence?

[11]8 THE OXFORD ENGLISH DICTIONARY, 670 (1933).

PAUL CHODOFF

THE CASE FOR INVOLUNTARY HOSPITALIZATION OF THE MENTALLY ILL

████████

Paul Chodoff is clinical professor of psychiatry at George Washington University School of Medicine and associate editor of the *American Journal of Psychiatry*. Chodoff, who also maintains a private practice, is the author of numerous articles, including "The Diagnosis of Hysteria: An Overview," "The Effect of Third-Party Payment on the Practice of Psychotherapy," and "Psychiatry and Fiscal Third Party."

Chodoff is concerned with the question of the justifiability of involuntary civil commitment. He presents a number of cases as examples of behavior which most of us would agree differ significantly from the norm. He uses these cases as a background for his analysis and evaluation of three stances that are often taken toward involuntary civil commitment. The three stances are those of (1) abolitionists, (2) medical-model psychiatrists, and (3) civil liberties lawyers.

████████

I will begin this paper with a series of vignettes designed to illustrate graphically the question that is my focus: under what conditions, if any, does society have the right to apply coercion to an individual to hospitalize him against his will, by reason of mental illness?

Case 1 A woman in her mid 50s, with no previous overt behavioral difficulties, comes to believe that she is worthless and insignificant. She is completely preoccupied with her guilt and is increasingly unavailable for the ordinary demands of life. She eats very little because of her conviction that the food should go to others whose need is greater than hers, and her physical condition progressively deteriorates. Although she will talk to others about herself, she insists that she is not sick, only bad. She refuses medication, and when hospitalization is suggested she also refuses that on the grounds that she would be taking up space that otherwise could be occupied by those who merit treatment more than she.

Case 2 For the past 6 years the behavior of a 42-year-old woman has been disturbed for periods of 3 months or longer. After recovery from her most recent episode she has been at home, functioning at a borderline level. A month ago she again started to withdraw from her environment. She pays increasingly less attention to her bodily needs, talks very little, and does not respond to questions or attention from those about her. She lapses into a mute state and lies in her bed in a totally passive fashion. She does not respond to other people, does not eat, and does not void. When her arm is raised from the bed it remains for several minutes in the position in which it is left. Her medical history and a physical examination reveal no evidence of primary physical illness.

Case 3 A man with a history of alcoholism has been on a binge for several weeks. He remains at home doing little else than drinking. He eats very little. He becomes tremulous and misinterprets spots on the wall as animals about to attack him, and he complains of "creeping" sensations in his body, which he attributes to infestation by insects. He does not

The American Journal of Psychiatry, vol. 133, no. 5 (May 1976), pp. 496–501. Copyright © 1976, the American Psychiatric Association. Reprinted by permission.

seek help voluntarily, insists there is nothing wrong with him, and despite his wife's entreaties he continues to drink.

Case 4 Passersby and station personnel observe that a young woman has been spending several days at Union Station in Washington, D.C. Her behavior appears strange to others. She is finally befriended by a newspaper reporter who becomes aware that her perception of her situation is profoundly unrealistic and that she is, in fact, delusional. He persuades her to accompany him to St. Elizabeths Hospital, where she is examined by a psychiatrist who recommends admission. She refuses hospitalization and the psychiatrist allows her to leave. She returns to Union Station. A few days later she is found dead, murdered, on one of the surrounding streets.

Case 5 A government attorney in his late 30s begins to display pressured speech and hyperactivity. He is too busy to sleep and eats very little. He talks rapidly, becomes irritable when interrupted, and makes phone calls all over the country in furtherance of his political ambitions, which are to begin a campaign for the Presidency of the United States. He makes many purchases, some very expensive, thus running through a great deal of money. He is rude and tactless to his friends, who are offended by his behavior, and his job is in jeopardy. In spite of his wife's pleas he insists that he does not have the time to seek or accept treatment, and he refuses hospitalization. This is not the first such disturbance for this individual; in fact, very similar episodes have been occurring at roughly 2-year intervals since he was 18 years old.

Case 6 Passersby in a campus area observe two young women standing together, staring at each other, for over an hour. Their behavior attracts attention, and eventually the police take the pair to a nearby precinct station for questioning. They refuse to answer questions and sit mutely, staring into space. The police request some type of psychiatric examination but are informed by the city attorney's office that state law (Michigan) allows persons to be held for observation only if they appear obviously dangerous to themselves or others. In this case, since the women do not seem homicidal or suicidal, they do not qualify for observation and are released.

Less than 30 hours later the two women are found on the floor of their campus apartment, screaming and writhing in pain with their clothes ablaze from a self-made pyre. One woman recovers; the other dies. There is no conclusive evidence that drugs were involved (1).

Most, if not all, people would agree that the behavior described in these vignettes deviates significantly from even elastic definitions of normality. However, it is clear that there would not be a similar consensus on how to react to this kind of behavior and that there is a considerable and increasing ferment about what attitude the organized elements of our society should take toward such individuals. Everyone has a stake in this important issue, but the debate about it takes place principally among psychiatrists, lawyers, the courts, and law enforcement agencies.

Points of view about the question of involuntary hospitalization fall into the following three principal groups: the "abolitionists," medical model psychiatrists, and civil liberties lawyers.

THE ABOLITIONISTS

Those holding this position would assert that in none of the cases I have described should involuntary hospitalization be a viable option because, quite simply, it should never be resorted to under any circumstances. As Szasz (2) has put it, "we should value liberty more highly than mental health no matter how defined" and "no one should be deprived of his freedom for the sake of his mental health." Ennis (3) has said that the goal "is nothing less than the abolition of involuntary hospitalization."

Prominent among the abolitionists are the "anti-psychiatrists," who, somewhat surprisingly, count in their ranks a number of well-known psychiatrists. For them mental illness simply does not exist in the field of psychiatry (4). They reject entirely the medical model of mental illness and insist that acceptance of it relies on a fiction accepted jointly by the state and by psychiatrists as a device for exerting social control over annoying or unconventional people. The anti-psychiatrists hold that these people ought to be afforded the dignity of being held responsible for their behavior and required to accept its consequences. In addition, some members of this group believe that the phenomena of "mental illness" often represent essentially a tortured protest against the insanities of an irrational society (5). They maintain that society should not be encouraged in its oppressive course by affixing a pejorative label to its victims.

Among the abolitionists are some civil liberties lawyers who both assert their passionate support of the magisterial importance of individual liberty and react with repugnance and impatience to what they see as the abuses of psychiatric practice in this field—the commitment of some individuals for flimsy and possibly self-serving reasons and their inhuman warehousing in penal institutions wrongly called "hospitals."

The abolitionists do not oppose psychiatric treatment when it is conducted with the agreement of those being treated. I have no doubt that they would try to gain the consent of the individuals described earlier to undergo treatment, including hospitalization. The psychiatrists in this group would be very likely to confine their treatment methods to psychotherapeutic efforts to influence the aberrant behavior. They would be unlikely to use drugs and would certainly eschew such somatic therapies as ECT.* If efforts to enlist voluntary compliance with treatment failed, the abolitionists would not employ any means of coercion. Instead, they would step aside and allow social, legal, and community sanctions to take their course. If a human being should be jailed or a human life lost as a result of this attitude, they would accept it as a necessary evil to be tolerated in order to avoid the greater evil of unjustified loss of liberty for others (6).

THE MEDICAL MODEL PSYCHIATRISTS

I use this admittedly awkward and not entirely accurate label to designate the position of a substantial number of psychiatrists. They believe that mental illness is a meaningful concept and that under certain conditions its existence justifies the state's exercise, under the doctrine of parens patriae, of its right and obligation to arrange for the hospitalization of the sick individual even though coercion is involved and he is deprived of his liberty. I believe that these psychiatrists would recommend involuntary hospitalization for all six of the patients described earlier.

The Medical Model

There was a time, before they were considered to be ill, when individuals who displayed the kind of behavior I described earlier were put in "ships of fools" to wander the seas or were left to the mercies, sometimes tender but often savage, of uncomprehending communities that regarded them as either possessed or bad. During the Enlightenment and the

Editors' note: Electroconvulsive therapy (ECT) involves direct intervention into the brain. In ECT, electric currents applied to the front of the patient's head induce convulsions and unconsciousness.

early nineteenth century, however, these individuals gradually came to be regarded as sick people to be included under the humane and caring umbrella of the Judeo-Christian attitude toward illness. This attitude, which may have reached its height during the era of moral treatment in the early nineteenth century, has had unexpected and ambiguous consequences. It became overextended and partially perverted, and these excesses led to the reaction that is so strong a current in today's attitude toward mental illness.

However, reaction itself can go too far, and I believe that this is already happening. Witness the disastrous consequences of the precipitate dehospitalization that is occurring all over the country. To remove the protective mantle of illness from these disturbed people is to expose them, their families, and their communities to consequences that are certainly maladaptive and possibly irreparable. Are we really acting in accordance with their best interests when we allow them to "die with their rights on" (1) or when we condemn them to a "preservation of liberty which is actually so destructive as to constitute another form of imprisonment" (7)? Will they not suffer "if [a] liberty they cannot enjoy is made superior to a health that must sometimes be forced on them" (8)?

Many of those who reject the medical model out of hand as inapplicable to so-called "mental illness" have tended to oversimplify its meaning and have, in fact, equated it almost entirely with organic disease. It is necessary to recognize that it is a complex concept and that there is a lack of agreement about its meaning. Sophisticated definitions of the medical model do not require only the demonstration of unequivocal organic pathology. A broader formulation, put forward by sociologists and deriving largely from Talcott Parsons' description of the sick role (9), extends the domain of illness to encompass certain forms of social deviance as well as biological disorders. According to this definition, the medical model is characterized not only by organicity but also by being negatively valued by society, by "nonvoluntariness," thus exempting its exemplars from blame, and by the understanding that physicians are the technically competent experts to deal with its effects (10).

Except for the question of organic disease, the patients I described earlier conform well to this broader conception of the medical model. They are all suffering both emotionally and physically, they are incapable by an effort of will of stopping or changing their destructive behavior, and those around them consider them to be in an undesirable sick state and to require medical attention.

Categorizing the behavior of these patients as involuntary may be criticized as evidence of an intolerably paternalistic and antitherapeutic attitude that fosters the very failure to take responsibility for their lives and behavior that the therapist should uncover rather than encourage. However, it must also be acknowledged that these severely ill people are not capable at a conscious level of deciding what is best for themselves and that in order to help them examine their behavior and motivation, it is necessary that they be alive and available for treatment. Their verbal message that they will not accept treatment may at the same time be conveying other more covert messages—that they are desperate and want help even though they cannot ask for it (11).

Although organic pathology may not be the only determinant of the medical model, it is of course an important one and it should not be avoided in any discussion of mental illness. There would be no question that the previously described patient with delirium tremens is suffering from a toxic form of brain disease. There are a significant number of other patients who require involuntary hospitalization because of organic brain syndrome due to various causes. Among those who are not overtly organically ill, most of the candidates for involuntary hospitalization suffer from schizophrenia or one of the major affective disorders. A growing and increasingly impressive body of evidence points to the presence of an important genetic-biological factor in these conditions; thus, many of them qualify on these grounds as illnesses.

Despite the revisionist efforts of the antipsychiatrists, mental illness *does* exist. It does not by any means include all of the people being treated by psychiatrists (or by non-psychiatrist physicians), but it does encompass those few desperately sick people for whom involuntary commitment must be considered. In the words of a recent article, "The problem is that mental illness is not a myth. It is not some palpable falsehood propagated among the populace by power-mad psychiatrists, but a cruel and bitter reality that has been with the human race since antiquity" (12, p. 1483).

Criteria for Involuntary Hospitalization

Procedures for involuntary hospitalization should be instituted for individuals who require care and treatment because of diagnosable mental illness that produces symptoms, including marked impairment in judgment, that disrupt their intrapsychic and interpersonal functioning. All three of these criteria must be met before involuntary hospitalization can be instituted.

1. Mental Illness   This concept has already been discussed, but it should be repeated that only a belief in the existence of illness justifies involuntary commitment. It is a fundamental assumption that makes aberrant behavior a medical matter and its care the concern of physicians.

2. Disruption of Functioning   This involves combinations of serious and often obvious disturbances that are both intrapsychic (for example, the suffering of severe depression) and interpersonal (for example, withdrawal from others because of depression). It does not include minor peccadilloes or eccentricities. Furthermore, the behavior in question must represent symptoms of the mental illness from which the patient is suffering. Among these symptoms are actions that are imminently or potentially dangerous in a physical sense to self or others, as well as other manifestations of mental illness such as those in the cases I have described. This is not to ignore dangerousness as a criterion for commitment but rather to put it in its proper place as one of a number of symptoms of the illness. A further manifestation of the illness, and indeed, the one that makes involuntary rather than voluntary hospitalization necessary, is impairment of the patient's judgment to such a degree that he is unable to consider his condition and make decisions about it in his own interests.

3. Need for Care and Treatment   The goal of physicians is to treat and cure their patients; however, sometimes they can only ameliorate the suffering of their patients and sometimes all they can offer is care. It is not possible to predict whether someone will respond to treatment; nevertheless, the need for treatment and the availability of facilities to carry it out constitute essential preconditions that must be met to justify requiring anyone to give up his freedom. If mental hospital patients have a right to treatment, then psychiatrists have a right to ask for treatability as a front-door as well as a back-door criterion for commitment (7). All of the six individuals I described earlier could have been treated with a reasonable expectation of returning to a more normal state of functioning.

I believe that the objections to this formulation can be summarized as follows.

1.   The whole structure founders for those who maintain that mental illness is a fiction.

2.   These criteria are also untenable to those who hold liberty to be such a supreme value that the presence of mental illness per se does not constitute justification for depriving an individual of his freedom; only when such illness is manifested by clearly dangerous behavior may commitment be considered. For reasons to be discussed later, I agree with those psychiatrists (13, 14) who do not believe that dangerousness should be elevated to primacy above other manifestations of mental illness as a sine qua non for involuntary hospitalization.

3.   The medical model criteria are "soft" and subjective and depend on the fallible judgment of psychiatrists. This is a valid objection. There is no reliable blood test for schizophrenia and no method for injecting grey cells into psychiatrists. A relatively small number of cases will always fall within a grey area that will be difficult to judge. In those extreme cases in which the question of commitment arises, competent and ethical psychiatrists should be able to use these criteria without doing violence to individual liberties and with the expectation of good results. Furthermore, the possible "fuzziness" of some aspects of the medical model approach is certainly no greater than that of the supposedly "objective" criteria for dangerousness, and there is little reason to believe that lawyers and judges are any less fallible than psychiatrists.

4.   Commitment procedures in the hands of psychiatrists are subject to intolerable abuses. Here, as Peszke said, "It is imperative that we differentiate between the principle of the process of civil commitment and the practice itself" (13, p. 825). Abuses can contaminate both the medical and the dangerousness approaches, and I believe that the abuses stemming from the abolitionist view of no commitment at all are even greater. Measures to abate abuses of the medical approach include judicial review and the abandonment of indeterminate commitment. In the course of commitment proceedings and thereafter, patients should have access to competent and compassionate legal counsel. However, this latter safeguard may itself be subject to abuse if the legal counsel acts solely in the adversary tradition and undertakes to carry out the patient's wishes even when they may be destructive.

Comment

The criteria and procedures outlined will apply most appropriately to initial episodes and recurrent attacks of mental illness. To put it simply, it is necessary to find a way to satisfy legal and humanitarian considerations and yet allow psychiatrists access to initially or acutely ill patients in order to do the best they can for them. However, there are some involuntary patients who have received adequate and active treatment but have not responded satisfactorily. An irreducible minimum of such cases, principally among those with brain disorders and process schizophrenia, will not improve sufficiently to be able to adapt to even a tolerant society.

    The decision of what to do at this point is not an easy one, and it should certainly not be in the hands of psychiatrists alone. With some justification thay can state that they have been given the thankless job of caring, often with inadequate facilities, for badly damaged people and that they are now being subjected to criticism for keeping these patients locked up. No one really knows what to do with these patients. It may be that when treatment has failed they exchange their sick role for what has been called the impaired role (15), which implies a permanent negative evaluation of them coupled with a somewhat less benign societal attitude. At this point, perhaps a case can be made for giving greater importance to the criteria for dangerousness and releasing such patients if they do not pose a threat to others. However, I do not believe that the release into the community of these severely malfunctioning individuals will serve their interests even though it may satisfy formal notions of right and wrong.

    It should be emphasized that the number of individuals for whom involuntary commitment must be considered is small (although, under the influence of current pressures, it may be smaller than it should be). Even severe mental illness can often be handled by securing the cooperation of the patient, and certainly one of the favorable efforts. However, the distinction between voluntary and involuntary hospitalization is sometimes more formal than meaningful. How "voluntary" are the actions of an individual who is being buffeted by the threats, entreaties, and tears of his family?

I believe, however, that we are at a point (at least in some jurisdictions) where, having rebounded from an era in which involuntary commitment was too easy and employed too often, we are now entering one in which it is becoming very difficult to commit anyone, even in urgent cases. Faced with the moral obloquy that has come to pervade the atmosphere in which the decision to involuntarily hospitalize is considered, some psychiatrists, especially younger ones, have become, as Stone (16) put it, "soft as grapes" when faced with the prospect of committing anyone under any circumstances.

THE CIVIL LIBERTIES LAWYERS

I use this admittedly inexact label to designate those members of the legal profession who do not in principle reject the necessity for involuntary hospitalization but who do reject or wish to diminish the importance of medical model criteria in the hands of psychiatrists. Accordingly, the civil liberties lawyers, in dealing with the problem of involuntary hospitalization, have enlisted themselves under the standard of dangerousness, which they hold to be more objective and capable of being dealt with in a sounder evidentiary manner than the medical model criteria. For them the question is not whether mental illness, even of disabling degree, is present, but only whether it has resulted in the probability of behavior dangerous to others or to self. Thus they would scrutinize the cases previously described for evidence of such dangerousness and would make the decision about involuntary hospitalization accordingly. They would probably feel that commitment is not indicated in most of these cases, since they were selected as illustrative of severe mental illness in which outstanding evidence of physical dangerousness was not present.

The dangerousness standard is being used increasingly not only to supplement criteria for mental illness but, in fact, to replace them entirely. The recent Supreme Court decision in *O'Connor v. Donaldson* (17) is certainly a long step in this direction. In addition, "dangerousness" is increasingly being understood to refer to the probability that the individual will inflict harm on himself or others in a specific physical manner rather than in other ways. This tendency has perhaps been carried to its ultimate in the *Lessard v. Schmidt* case (18) in Wisconsin, which restricted suitability for commitment to the "extreme likelihood that if the person is not confined, he will do immediate harm to himself or others." (This decision was set aside by the U.S. Supreme Court in 1974.) In a recent Washington, D.C., Superior Court case (19) the instructions to the jury stated that the government must prove that the defendant was likely to cause "substantial physical harm to himself or others in the reasonably foreseeable future."

For the following reasons, the dangerousness standard is an inappropriate and dangerous indicator to use in judging the conditions under which someone should be involuntarily hospitalized. Dangerousness is being taken out of its proper context as one among other symptoms of the presence of severe mental illness that should be the determining factor.

1. To concentrate on dangerousness (especially to others) as the sole criterion for involuntary hospitalization deprives many mentally ill persons of the protection and treatment that they urgently require. A psychiatrist under the constraints of the dangerousness rule, faced with an out-of-control manic individual whose frantic behavior the psychiatrist truly believes to be a disguised call for help, would have to say, "Sorry,

I would like to help you but I can't because you haven't threatened anybody and you are not suicidal." Since psychiatrists are admittedly not very good at accurately predicting dangerousness to others, the evidentiary standards for commitment will be very stringent. This will result in mental hospitals becoming prisons for a small population of volatile, highly assaultive, and untreatable patients (14).

2. The attempt to differentiate rigidly (especially in regard to danger to self) between physical and other kinds of self-destructive behavior is artificial, unrealistic, and unworkable. It will tend to confront psychiatrists who want to help their patients with the same kind of dilemma they were faced with when justification for therapeutic abortion on psychiatric grounds depended on evidence of suicidal intent. The advocates of the dangerousness standard seem to be more comfortable with and pay more attention to the factor of dangerousness to others even though it is a much less frequent and much less significant consequence of mental illness than is danger to self.

3. The emphasis on dangerousness (again, especially to others) is a real obstacle to the right-to-treatment movement since it prevents the hospitalization and therefore the treatment of the population most amenable to various kinds of therapy.

4. Emphasis on the criterion of dangerousness to others moves involuntary commitment from a civil to a criminal procedure, thus, as Stone (14) put it, imposing the procedures of one terrible system on another. Involuntary commitment on these grounds becomes a form of preventive detention and makes the psychiatrist a kind of glorified policeman.

5. Emphasis on dangerousness rather than mental disability and helplessness will hasten the process of deinstitutionalization. Recent reports (20, 21) have shown that these patients are not being rehabilitated and reintegrated into the community, but rather, that the burden of custodialism has been shifted from the hospital to the community.

6. As previously mentioned, emphasis on the dangerousness criterion may be a tactic of some of the abolitionists among the civil liberties lawyers (22) to end involuntary hospitalization by reducing it to an unworkable absurdity.

DISCUSSION

It is obvious that it is good to be at liberty and that it is good to be free from the consequences of disabling and dehumanizing illness. Sometimes these two values are incompatible, and in the heat of the passions that are often aroused by opposing views of right and wrong, the partisans of each view may tend to minimize the importance of the other. Both sides can present their horror stories — the psychiatrists, their dead victims of the failure of the involuntary hospitalization process, and the lawyers, their Donaldsons. There is a real danger that instead of acknowledging the difficulty of the problem, the two camps will become polarized, with a consequent rush toward extreme and untenable solutions rather than working toward reasonable ones.

The path taken by those whom I have labeled the abolitionists is an example of the barren results that ensue when an absolute solution is imposed on a complex problem. There are human beings who will suffer greatly if the abolitionists succeed in elevating an abstract principle into an unbreakable law with no exceptions. I find myself oppressed and repelled by their position, which seems to stem from an ideological rigidity which ignores that element of the contingent immanent in the structure of human existence. It is devoid of compassion.

The positions of those who espouse the medical model and the dangerousness approaches to commitment are, one hopes, not completely irreconcilable. To some extent these differences are a result of the vantage points from which lawyers and psychiatrists view mental illness and commitment. The lawyers see and are concerned with the failures and abuses of the process. Furthermore, as a result of their training, they tend to apply principles to classes of people rather than to take each instance as unique. The psychiatrists, on the other hand, are required to deal practically with the singular needs of individuals. They approach the problem from a clinical rather than a deductive stance. As physicians, they want to be in a position to take care of and to help suffering people whom they regard as sick patients. They sometimes become impatient with the rules that prevent them from doing this.

I believe we are now witnessing a pendular swing in which the rights of the mentally ill to be treated and protected are being set aside in the rush to give them their freedom at whatever cost. But is freedom defined only by the absence of external constraints? Internal physiological or psychological processes can contribute to a throttling of the spirit that is as painful as any applied from the outside. The "wild" manic individual without his lithium, the panicky hallucinator without his injection of fluphenazine hydrochloride and the understanding support of a concerned staff, the sodden alcoholic—are they free? Sometimes, as Woody Guthrie said, "Freedom means no place to go."

Today the civil liberties lawyers are in the ascendancy and the psychiatrists on the defensive to a degree that is harmful to individual needs and the public welfare. Redress and a more balanced position will not come from further extension of the dangerousness doctrine. I favor a return to the use of medical criteria by psychiatrists—psychiatrists, however, who have been chastened by the buffeting they have received and are quite willing to go along with even strict legal safeguards as long as they are constructive and not tyrannical.

REFERENCES

1. Treffert, D. A.: "The practical limits of patients' rights." *Psychiatric Annals* 5(4):91–96, 1971.

2. Szasz, T.: *Law, Liberty and Psychiatry,* New York, Macmillan Co., 1963.

3. Ennis, B.: *Prisoners of Psychiatry,* New York, Harcourt Brace Jovanovich, 1972.

4. Szasz, T.: *The Myth of Mental Illness,* New York, Harper & Row, 1961.

5. Laing, R.: *The Politics of Experience,* New York, Ballantine Books, 1967.

6. Ennis, B.: "Ennis on 'Donaldson'." *Psychiatric News,* Dec. 3, 1975, pp. 4, 19, 37.

7. Peele, R., Chodoff, P., Taub, N.: "Involuntary hospitalization and treatability. Observations from the DC experience." *Catholic University Law Review* 23:744–753, 1974.

8. Michels, R.: "The Right to Refuse Psychotropic Drugs." *Hastings Center Report,* Hastings-on-Hudson, NY, 1973.

9. Parsons, T.: *The Social System.* New York, Free Press, 1951.

10. Veatch, R. M.: "The medical model; its nature and problems." *Hastings Center Studies* 1(3):59–76, 1973.

11. Katz, J.: "The right to treatment—an enchanting legal fiction?" *University of Chicago Law Review* 36:755–783, 1969.

12. Moore, M.S.: "Some myths about mental illness." *Arch Gen Psychiatry* 32:1483–1497, 1975.

13. Peszke, M. A.: "Is dangerousness an issue for physicians in emergency commitment?" *Am J Psychiatry* 132:825–828, 1975.

14. Stone, A. A.: "Comment on Peszke, M. A.: Is dangerousness an issue for physicians in emergency commitment?" Ibid. 829–831.

15. Siegler, M., Osmond, H.: *Models of Madness, Models of Medicine.* New York, Macmillan Co., 1974.

16. Stone, A.: Lecture for course on The Law, Litigation, and Mental Health Services. Adelphi, Md., Mental Health Study Center, September 1974.

17. O'Connor v Donaldson, 43 USLW 4929 (1975).

18. Lessard v Schmidt, 349 F Supp 1078, 1092 (ED Wis 1972).

19. In re Johnnie Hargrove, Washington, DC, Superior Court Mental Health number 506-75, 1975.

20. Rachlin, S., Pam, A., Milton, J.: "Civil liberties versus involuntary hospitalization." *Am J Psychiatry* 132:189–191, 1975.

21. Kirk, S. A., Therrien, M. E.: "Community mental health myths and the fate of former hospitalized patients." *Psychiatry* 38:209–217, 1975.

22. Dershowitz, A. A.: "Dangerousness as a criterion for confinement." *Bulletin of the American Academy of Psychiatry and the Law* 2:172–179, 1974.

QUESTIONS

1. It is sometimes argued that some mentally ill individuals are not autonomous agents, since they are constrained by their own delusions and/or inabilities to formulate rational judgments about their own needs, actions, etc. Since they lack such autonomy, it is argued, and since autonomy is an important human value, involuntary treatment intended to restore that autonomy is sometimes justified. Is this a cogent argument?

2. Partly as a result of "right-to-treatment" legal decisions, a large number of institutionalized mental patients have been released from mental hospitals. Among those released, many greatly impaired persons have been "dumped" in large urban centers in "welfare hotels" located in run-down areas or in substandard facilities run for profit and providing few treatment resources. Is this a better solution for these patients than involuntary civil commitment? Are there better solutions?

SUGGESTED ADDITIONAL READINGS

BOORSE, CHRISTOPHER: "What a Theory of Mental Health Should Be." *Journal for the Theory of Social Behavior,* vol. 6, April 1976, pp. 61–84. Insisting on the need to develop a theory of mental health predicated upon an analogy between mental health and physical health, Boorse argues that the practice of clinical psychology and psychiatry may rightly be founded on the model of health and disease.

"Changing Social and Psychological Concepts of Mental Illness." *Journal of Contemporary Issues,* vol. 1, August 1973, pp. 31–56. This excellent review article examines a number of efforts to reevaluate both the nature of mental illness and the practice of psychiatry. A long and useful bibliography is also provided.

FORST, MARTIN L.: *Civil Commitment and Social Control.* Lexington, Mass.: Lexington Books, 1978. Forst offers an empirical investigation of the operation and functioning of one civil commitment statute [California's "Mentally Disordered Sex Offender (MDSO) Statute"] and its relation to the criminal justice system. He does a comparative study of the relationship between the civil and criminal commitment systems.

GOFFMAN, ERVING: *Asylums.* New York: Doubleday Anchor, 1961. Goffman provides an analysis of life in total institutions in general and in mental institutions in particular.

KATZ, JAY: "The Right to Treatment—An Enchanting Legal Fiction?" *University of Chicago Law Review,* vol. 36, Summer 1969, pp. 755–783. Katz discusses the implications of a United States Court of Appeals decision which involved the principle that individuals involuntarily confined to mental institutions have an "enforceable right to treatment."

LIVERMORE, JOSEPH M., CARL P. MALMQUIST, and PAUL E. MEEHL: "On the Justifications for Civil Commitment." *University of Pennsylvania Law Review,* vol. 117, November 1968, pp. 75–96. The authors explore the possible philosophical justifications for the involuntary civil commitment of the mentally ill. They reject the usual justifications because these premises are either false or too broad to support existing procedures.

MACKLIN, RUTH: "Mental Health and Mental Illness: Some Problems of Definition and Concept Formation." *Philosophy of Science,* vol. 39, September 1972, pp. 341–365. Macklin examines a number of difficulties associated with attempts to define mental health and mental illness. In Part 5 of this article, she directly addresses the views of Szasz, concluding that there is no compelling reason to adopt his view that mental illness is a myth.

ROSENHAN, D. L.: "On Being Sane in Insane Places." *Science,* vol. 179, January 19, 1973, pp. 250–258. This much-discussed article describes the results of an experiment in which sane people gained admittance to mental hospitals. Once inside the hospital, they were perceived as insane, leading Rosenhan to conclude that in psychiatric hospitals we cannot distinguish sane from insane.

ECONOMIC JUSTICE AND WELFARE

9

Should everyone in an affluent society be guaranteed a minimum income? Should people be required to work for that income even if they do not want to work? Should they be required to work at menial jobs they dislike in order to receive that income? Is it morally correct to tax the income of those who work in order to provide incomes for those who do not? Questions such as these fall in the domain of economic justice. Answering them requires theorizing about what constitutes an economically just society. And this in turn involves us with questions about the part that a just government ought to play in the economic sphere and about the justifiable limits of government interference with individual liberty.

AN ECONOMICALLY JUST SOCIETY

In a short story called "The Babylon Lottery," Jorge Luis Borges describes a society in which all societal benefits and obligations are distributed solely on the basis of a periodic lottery. An individual may be a slave at one period, an influential government official the following period, and a person sentenced to jail the third one, simply as the result of chance. When the temporary social and economic status of the individual is determined, no account is taken of the actual contribution the individual has made to society during a preceding period or of the individual's merit, effort, or need.[1] Such a situation strikes us as capricious. We are accustomed to think that there are some valid principles according to which economic goods are distributed within a society, even though we may disagree about what principles ought to be operative in an economically just society. In the United States, for example, aid to families with dependent children is sometimes said to be distributed on the basis of need; promotions in government offices and business firms are supposedly awarded on the basis of merit and achievement; and the higher incomes of physicians and lawyers are assumed to be due them on the basis of either the contribution they make to society or the effort they exert in preparing for their professions.

Whether, and to what extent, merit and achievement, need, effort, or productive contribution ought to be taken into account in the distribution of society's benefits are basic questions of economic justice. In responding to these questions, philosophers propose and defend various principles of economic justice. According to these philosophers, the wealth of society ought to be distributed on the basis of one or more of the following sorts of principles.

1. To each individual an equal share

2. To each individual according to that individual's needs

[1] Jorge Luis Borges, "The Babylon Lottery," in *Ficciones* (New York: Grove Press, 1956).

3. To each individual according to that individual's ability, merit, or achievement

4. To each individual according to that individual's effort

5. To each individual according to that individual's actual productive contribution

6. To each individual according to that individual's contribution to the total good

We will briefly discuss the first two principles since they are especially relevant to the readings in this chapter.

1. To Each Individual an Equal Share

On the strict equalitarian view, each individual in a society is entitled to the same portion of goods as every other individual. All human beings, just because they are human beings, have a right to an equal share in the wealth of their society. This strict equalitarian approach to economic justice leads to the paradoxical view that individual differences are to be ignored when the resources of a society are allocated. If you consider that these resources include food, shelter, and health care, as well as money, it appears absurd to maintain that each individual in society ought to receive a share identical to that of every other individual. Distribution strictly on the basis of the principle of equal sharing would seem to result in an unjust situation in which the 200-pound man receives the same amount of food as the 140-pound one and the diabetic and paraplegic receive no more health care than the healthy individual who needs neither insulin nor physical therapy. Since there are differences between individuals, it is apparently more equalitarian to distribute according to the principle of need. Equal distribution would then require not identical distribution but the equal satisfaction of needs.

2. To Each Individual According to That Individual's Needs

If distribution is to be made on the basis of needs, it is necessary to determine just what "needs" are to be considered. Are we to consider only essential or basic needs, such as the need for food, clothing, shelter, and health care? Or are we to consider also other human needs, such as the need for aesthetic satisfaction and intellectual stimulation? Whether the principle of need is accepted as the sole determinant of a just economic distribution within the society or as only one of those determinants, we need to select some way of ranking needs. If, on the one hand, the principle of need is the sole determinant of economic justice, we must first determine which needs take precedence — which needs must be satisfied before the satisfaction of other, less important needs is even considered. Then, if our society has the means to meet not only these basic needs but other less essential ones, we need to find some way of ranking the latter. (For example, does an artist's need for subsidy take precedence over a scientist's need to satisfy his or her intellectual curiosity about the existence of life on Mars?) If, on the other hand, the principle of need is to be taken as only one of the determinants of economic justice, we need to determine which needs must be satisfied before some other principle can be used as the basis for distributing the rest of society's wealth.

Note that if either or both of the first two principles are held to be the determinants of economic justice, the individual's own efforts, achievements, abilities, or productive contribution to society are not taken into account in determining that individual's benefits. When the claim is made, for example, that each family in a society ought to be guaranteed a minimum yearly income, the moral justification for this claim is often given either in terms of the principle of need or in terms of the conjunction of that principle and the principle of equal sharing: All human beings, just because they are human beings, are entitled to equal treatment in some important respects; they are entitled, for example, to have at least their most basic needs met by the society of which they are a part.

Philosophers, economists, and others vehemently disagree about whether the principle of need (or the principle of need in conjunction with the principle of equal sharing) is a morally acceptable principle of economic justice. Their disagreements stem in large measure from their different conceptions of the moral ideal around which the institutions of any just society ought to be organized. To understand three of the major positions on the relation between need and economic justice, it is necessary to understand the part played by certain moral ideals in theories about (1) the morally correct role of the government in economic activity and (2) the justifiable limits of government interference with individual liberty.

LIBERTY, EQUALITY, NEED, AND GOVERNMENT INTERFERENCE

Two moral ideals, liberty and equality, are of key importance in conceptions of justice in general, and economic justice in particular. A *libertarian* or *individualist* conception of justice, for example, holds *liberty* to be the ultimate moral ideal. A *socialist* conception of justice takes *social equality* to be the ultimate ideal; and a *liberal* (or *liberal-humanitarian*) conception of justice tries to combine both equality and liberty into one ultimate moral ideal.

The Libertarian Conception of Justice

On a libertarian view, individuals have certain *moral rights* to life, liberty, and property which any just society must recognize and respect. These rights are sometimes described as *warnings against interference:* If A has a right to X, no one should prevent A from pursuing X or deprive A of X, since A is entitled to it. According to a libertarian, the sole function of the government is to protect the individual's life, liberty, and property against force and fraud. Everything else in society is a matter of individual responsibility, decision, and action. Providing for the welfare of those who cannot or will not provide for themselves is not a morally justifiable function of government. To make such provisions, the government would have to take from some against their will in order to give to others. This is perceived as an unjustifiable limitation on individual liberty. Individuals own their own bodies and, therefore, the labor they exert. It follows, for the libertarian, that individuals have the right to whatever income or wealth their labor can earn in a free marketplace. Taxing some to give to others is analogous to robbery. John Hospers, who defends a libertarian position in this chapter, argues that taxing some in order to make provision for others is simply a form of legal, orderly, and systematic plunder.

The Socialist Conception of Justice

A direct challenge to libertarians comes from those who defend a socialist conception of justice. Although socialist views differ in many respects, one common element is a commitment to social equality and to government or collective measures furthering that equality. Since social equality is the ultimate ideal, limitations on individual liberty which are necessary to promote equality are seen as justified. Socialists attack the libertarian views on the primacy of liberty in at least two ways. First, they offer defenses of their ideal of social equality. These take various forms and will not concern us here. Second, they point out the meaninglessness of libertarian rights to those who lack adequate food, shelter, health care, etc. For those who lack the money to buy the food and health care needed to sustain life, the libertarian right to life is an empty sham. The rights of liberty, such as the right to freedom of speech, are a joke to those who cannot exercise those rights because of economic considerations. Where libertarians stress freedom from government interference, socialists stress freedom from want. Where libertarians stress *negative* rights (rights not to be interfered with), socialists stress *positive rights*—rights *to* food, health care, productive work, etc. Where libertarians criticize socialism for the limitations it imposes on liberty, socialists criticize libertarianism for allowing gross inequalities among those who are "equally human."

The Liberal Conception of Justice

Like the socialist, the liberal rejects the libertarian conception of justice since that conception does not include what liberals perceive as a fundamental moral concern. Any purported conception of justice which fails to incorporate the requirement that those who have more than enough must help those in need is morally unacceptable for the liberal. Like the socialist, the liberal recognizes the extent to which economic coercion in an industrial society actually limits the exercise of libertarian rights by those lacking economic power. Unlike the socialist, the liberal sees some of the negative rights of the libertarian as extremely important and advocates social institutions which will function to do both—ensure certain basic liberties for all (e.g., freedom of speech) and yet provide for the economic needs of the disadvantaged members of society. Furthermore, unlike the socialist, the liberal is not opposed to all social and economic inequalities. However, liberals disagree concerning both the morally acceptable extent of those inequalities and their correct justification. A utilitarian committed to a liberal position might hold that inequalities are justified to the extent that allowing them maximizes the total amount of good in a society. If, for example, increased productivity depends on giving workers a significantly higher income than that given to those collecting welfare,[2] and if such incentive-stimulated productivity increases the total amount of good in a society, then the inequalities between the assembly-line worker and the welfare recipient would be justified for the utilitarian. A different approach, argued for by John Rawls,[3] maintains that only those inequalities of social goods are justified which will contribute to raising the position of the *least*-advantaged groups in the society. Here the concern is not with the total amount of good in a society but with the good of the least advantaged. In this view, income inequalities necessary for productivity gains are justified only if the productivity gains work to the benefit of those in the lowest economic strata.

Practical Implications of the Three Theories

Some of the practical ramifications of the libertarian, socialist, and liberal conceptions of justice are brought out in Elizabeth Telfer's and Trudy Govier's articles in this chapter. Telfer is concerned with one important human need—the need for health care—and the correct government role in meeting that need. She discusses the advantages and disadvantages of libertarian, liberal, and socialist approaches to the role of government in health care delivery. Govier is concerned with the question, "Should the needy have a legal right to welfare benefits?" Criticizing the libertarian (individualist) position on welfare, she argues for a legal right to welfare based on utilitarian and justice considerations. Underlying some

---

[2]Just what constitutes *welfare* or a welfare program is a matter of dispute. Many would include a number of very different programs under this heading, e.g., unemployment benefits paid out of a fund supported by a mandatory payroll tax paid by employers, social security benefits paid out of a fund supported by a mandatory payroll tax on both employers and employees, Medicaid programs paid out of state and federal funds, and Aid to Families with Dependent Children paid out of state and federal funds. Usually, when what is at issue is a contrast between the incomes of workers and welfare recipients, the welfare in question includes such payments as Aid to Families with Dependent Children, food stamps, and Medicaid.

[3]John Rawls, *A Theory of Justice* (Cambridge, Mass.: Harvard University Press, 1971).

of her arguments for the superiority of a particular approach to welfare is the liberal conception of justice.

Marxist-Socialism and Welfare

A different position regarding welfare programs, worthy of consideration but not explicitly discussed in the readings in this chapter, is based on a Marxist-socialist analysis of the role that welfare programs play in a capitalist society. A Marxist-socialist, like the "utopian" socialist discussed above, is committed to the ultimate ideal of equalitarianism. However, the Marxist-socialist criticism of capitalist societies does not center primarily on the lack of economic equality in these societies. Rather, Marxist-socialists are critical of what they perceive as capitalism's failure to pay the worker in accordance with productive contribution. Workers under capitalism, on a Marxist analysis, receive only a part of the value of what they have produced. The rest, the *surplus value,* goes to capitalists who are then able to use it to support institutions which function to maintain the status quo and work against the interests of the worker. On a Marxist analysis, the political, legal, and social institutions in a capitalist society operate in the interests of the capitalist class. One of these interests is in the maintenance of a reserve industrial army which can be pulled into and pushed out of the work force in response to the capitalist's needs. On this analysis, welfare programs in capitalist societies provide one of the mechanisms for the maintenance of this army. As T. R. Young, a Marxist sociologist, puts it,

> In the United States, the surplus value of labor is used to make political donations by large corporations. These donations, in turn, are used to create the myth of the happy America, the prosperous America, the beneficent America by advertising agencies working on behalf of middle class politicians. Such is the view of Marx concerning the use of labor against the body of men who engage in productive work. Under this analysis, in such society the more one works, the stronger grows the apparatus of oppression. In some societies the technology of oppression centers around force, terror, and prison; in other societies, the technology of repression depends upon the smooth, sophisticated tactics of professional managers using what they know of psychology, of organizational theory, and of dramaturgy to control dissent and resistance. . . .
>
> . . . In the United States, the social welfare solution to poverty is to fashion a docile pool of surplus labor maintained at brute animal levels while large-scale organizations are heavily subsidized. American social welfare also fashions a set of rules which humiliate and infantilize the poor. . . . [S]ocial welfare practices in the U.S. provide industry with a well-managed group of poor people. In times of political unrest, welfare rolls are expanded and the rules relaxed. In times of economic trouble, the rolls are reduced and the rules stringently enforced. The poor are thereby depoliticized and deprived where they should be supplied in order to establish the preconditions for humanity: all this in the most affluent nation in history.[4]

In the last reading in this chapter, Joel Feinberg in effect briefly evaluates Marxist claims regarding the worker's productive contribution to the total value of the final product when he discusses the principle that productive contribution should be the basis for a just economic distribution. In considering a number of principles of economic justice, Feinberg seems to approach the issues from a liberal standpoint.

Jane S. Zembaty

---

[4]T. R. Young, "The Contributions of Karl Marx to Social Psychology," a paper in the Transforming Sociology Series (Red Feather, Colo.: Red Feather Institute for Advanced Studies in Sociology), pp. 2, 6.

MAJORITY OPINION IN *GOLDBERG v. KELLY*

A biographical sketch of Justice William Brennan is found on page 125.

A suit was brought against Jack R. Goldberg, Commissioner of Social Services of the City of New York, by residents of that city who were receiving financial aid under the federally assisted programs of Aid to Families with Dependent Children or under New York State's general Home Relief program. At issue was the right of the officials administering these programs to terminate aid without prior notice and hearing. Such termination, the plaintiffs charged, denied them due process of law. According to the Fourteenth Amendment to the Constitution, states are prohibited from depriving any person of life, liberty, or property without "due process of law." In using this clause in the amendment to attack the "right" of the officials to deny welfare recipients pretermination hearings, the claim is made that welfare payments are not "gratuities" charitably given, but more like "property" of which an individual cannot be deprived without due process of law. The lower court ruled in favor of the plaintiffs, and the United States Supreme Court upheld that decision. In this majority opinion, Justice Brennan argues that procedural process requires that pretermination evidentiary hearings be held before welfare payments are stopped. He stresses the fact that welfare payments are entitlements and not simply gratuities. For the purposes of this chapter, the case is interesting primarily because it involves a case where need alone is held to *entitle* the members of a society to at least a portion of the goods of that society.

The constitutional issue to be decided . . . is the narrow one whether the Due Process Clause requires that the recipient be afforded an evidentiary hearing before the termination of benefits. The District Court held that only a pre-termination evidentiary hearing would satisfy the constitutional command, and rejected the argument of the state and city officials that the combination of the post-termination "fair hearing" with the informal pre-termination review disposed of all due process claims. The court said: "While post-termination review is relevant, there is one overpowering fact which controls here. By hypothesis, a welfare recipient is destitute, without funds or assets. . . . Suffice it to say that to cut off a welfare recipient in the face of . . . 'brutal need' without a prior hearing of some sort is unconscionable, unless overwhelming considerations justify it." . . . The court rejected the argument that the need to protect the public's tax revenues supplied the requisite "overwhelming consideration." "Against the justified desire to protect public funds must be weighed the individual's overpowering need in this unique situation not to be wrongfully deprived of assistance. . . . While the problem of additional expense must be kept in mind, it does not justify denying a hearing meeting the ordinary standards of due process. Under all the circumstances, we hold that due process requires an adequate hearing before termination of welfare benefits, and the fact that there is a later constitutionally fair proceeding does not alter the result." . . .

Appellant does not contend that procedural due process is not applicable to the termination of welfare benefits. Such benefits are a matter of statutory entitlement for

United States Supreme Court. 397 U.S. 254 (1970).

persons qualified to receive them.[1] Their termination involves state action that adjudicates important rights. The constitutional challenge cannot be answered by an argument that public assistance benefits are "a 'privilege' and not a 'right'." . . . Relevant constitutional restraints apply as much to the withdrawal of public assistance benefits as to disqualification for unemployment compensation; . . . or to denial of a tax exemption; . . . or to discharge from public employment. The extent to which procedural due process must be afforded the recipient is influenced by the extent to which he may be "condemned to suffer grievous loss," . . . and depends upon whether the recipient's interest in avoiding that loss outweighs the governmental interest in summary adjudication. Accordingly, as we said in *Cafeteria & Restaurant Workers Union, etc. v. McElroy* (1961), . . . "consideration of what procedures due process may require under any given set of circumstances must begin with a determination of the precise nature of the government function involved as well as of the private interest that has been affected by governmental action." . . .

It is true of course, that some governmental benefits may be administratively terminated without affording the recipient a pre-termination evidentiary hearing.[2] But we agree with the District Court that when welfare is discontinued, only a pre-termination evidentiary hearing provides the recipient with procedural due process. . . . Thus the crucial factor in this context — a factor not present in the case of the blacklisted government contractor, the discharged government employee, the taxpayer denied a tax exemption, or virtually anyone else whose governmental entitlements are ended — is that termination of aid pending resolution of a controversy over eligibility may deprive an eligible recipient of the very means by which to live while he waits. Since he lacks independent resources, his situation becomes immediately desperate. His need to concentrate upon finding the means for daily subsistence, in turn, adversely affects his ability to seek redress from the welfare bureaucracy.

Moreover, important governmental interests are promoted by affording recipients a pre-termination evidentiary hearing. From its founding the Nation's basic commitment has been to foster the dignity and well-being of all persons within its borders. We have come to recognize that forces not within the control of the poor contribute to their poverty. This perception, against the background of our traditions, has significantly influenced the development of the contemporary public assistance system. Welfare, by meeting the basic demands of subsistence, can help bring within the reach of the poor the same opportunities that are available to others to participate meaningfully in the life of the community. At the same time, welfare guards against the societal malaise that may flow from a widespread

---

[1] It may be realistic today to regard welfare entitlements as more like "property" than a "gratuity." Much of the existing wealth in this country takes the form of rights that do not fall within traditional common-law concepts of property. It has been aptly noted that

> "Society today is built around entitlement. The automobile dealer has his franchise, the doctor and lawyer their professional licenses, the worker his union membership, contract, and pension rights, the executive his contract and stock options; all are devices to aid security and independence. Many of the most important of these entitlements now flow from government: subsidies to farmers and businessmen, routes for airlines and channels for television stations; long term contracts for defense, space, and education; social security pensions for individuals. Such sources of security, whether private or public, are no longer regarded as luxuries or gratuities; to the recipients they are essentials, fully deserved, and in no sense a form of charity. It is only the poor whose entitlements, although recognized by public policy, have not been effectively enforced."

Reich, *Individual Rights and Social Welfare: The Emerging Legal Issues*, 74 Yale L. J. 1245, 1255 (1965). See also Reich, *The New Property*, 73 Yale L. J. 733 (1964).

[2] One Court of Appeals has stated: "In a wide variety of situations, it has long been recognized that where harm to the public is threatened, and the private interest infringed is reasonably deemed to be of less importance, an official body can take summary action pending a later hearing."

sense of unjustified frustration and insecurity. Public assistance, then, is not mere charity, but a means to "promote the general Welfare, and secure the Blessings of Liberty to ourselves and our Posterity." The same governmental interests that counsel the provision of welfare, counsel as well its uninterrupted provision to those eligible to receive it; pre-termination evidentiary hearings are indispensable to that end.

Appellant does not challenge the force of these considerations but argues that they are outweighed by countervailing governmental interests in conserving fiscal and administrative resources. These interests, the argument goes, justify the delay of any evidentiary hearing until after discontinuance of the grants. Summary adjudication protects the public fisc by stopping payments promptly upon discovery of reason to believe that a recipient is no longer eligible. Since most terminations are accepted without challenge, summary adjudication also conserves both the fisc and administrative time and energy by reducing the number of evidentiary hearings actually held.

We agree with the District Court, however, that these governmental interests are not overriding in the welfare context. The requirement of a prior hearing doubtless involves some greater expense, and the benefits paid to ineligible recipients pending decision at the hearing probably cannot be recouped, since these recipients are likely to be judgment-proof. But the State is not without weapons to minimize these increased costs. Much of the drain on fiscal and administrative resources can be reduced by developing procedures for prompt pre-termination hearings and by skillful use of personnel and facilities. Indeed, the very provision for a post-termination evidentiary hearing in New York's Home Relief program is itself cogent evidence that the State recognizes the primacy of the public interest in correct eligibility determinations and therefore in the provision of procedural safeguards. Thus, the interest of the eligible recipient in uninterrupted receipt of public assistance, coupled with the State's interest that his payments not be erroneously terminated, clearly outweighs the State's competing concern to prevent any increase in its fiscal and administrative burdens. As the District Court correctly concluded, "the stakes are simply too high for the welfare recipient, and the possibility for honest error or irritable misjudgment too great, to allow termination of aid without giving the recipient a chance, if he so desires, to be fully informed of the case against him so that he may contest its basis and produce evidence in rebuttal."

QUESTIONS

1. In an affluent society such as ours, do all individuals who are unable to support themselves have a *moral* right to welfare?
2. Are welfare payments a form of charity?

MAJORITY OPINION IN *WYMAN v. JAMES*

A biographical sketch of Justice Harry Blackmun is found on page 5.

This case centers on the question, "Can a beneficiary of the Aid to Families with Dependent Children program (AFDC) refuse a home visit by a caseworker without risking the termination of benefits?" One such beneficiary, Barbara James, refused such a visit. When notified that refusal meant the termination of benefits, she brought a suit against the commissioner of the New York department of social services (Wyman) and others. James argued that a caseworker's visit constitutes a search and thereby violates Fourth and Fourteenth Amendment rights. (The Fourth Amendment asserts "the right of the people to be secure in their persons, houses, papers, and effects." The Fourteenth Amendment prohibits states from depriving any person of life, liberty, or property "without due process of law.") The District Court of New York ruled in favor of James. The case was appealed to the United States Supreme Court, which reversed the lower court's decision.

In ruling against James, the Court held that the home visitation in question is a *reasonable* administrative tool and does not violate any Fourth or Fourteenth Amendment rights. In presenting the factors which make it a reasonable tool, Justice Blackmun describes such payments as a form of charity. He stresses the public interest (1) in seeing that the money is utilized as those who supply the funds intend it to be and (2) in assisting and rehabilitating the beneficiary.

I

Plaintiff Barbara James is the mother of a son, Maurice, who was born in May 1967. They reside in New York City. Mrs. James first applied for AFDC assistance shortly before Maurice's birth. A caseworker made a visit to her apartment at that time without objection. The assistance was authorized.

Two years later, on May 8, 1969, a caseworker wrote Mrs. James that she would visit her home on May 14. Upon receipt of this advice, Mrs. James telephoned the worker that, although she was willing to supply information "reasonable and relevant" to her need for public assistance, any discussion was not to take place at her home. The worker told Mrs. James that she was required by law to visit in her home and that refusal to permit the visit would result in the termination of assistance. Permission was still denied.

On May 13 the City Department of Social Services sent Mrs. James a notice of intent to discontinue assistance because of the visitation refusal. The notice advised the beneficiary of her right to a hearing before a review officer. The hearing was requested and was held on May 27. Mrs. James appeared with an attorney at that hearing. They continued to refuse permission for a worker to visit the James home, but again expressed willingness to cooperate and to permit visits elsewhere. The review officer ruled that the refusal was a proper ground for the termination of assistance. His written decision stated:

"The home visit which Mrs. James refuses to permit is for the purpose of determining if there are any changes in her situation that might affect her eligibility to continue to receive Public Assistance, or

United States Supreme Court. 400 U.S. 309 (1971).

that might affect the amount of such assistance, and to see if there are any social services which the Department of Social Services can provide to the family."

A notice of termination was issued on June 2.

Thereupon, without seeking a hearing at the state level, Mrs. James, individually and on behalf of Maurice, and purporting to act on behalf of all other persons similarly situated, instituted the present civil rights suit. She alleged the denial of rights guaranteed to her under the First, Third, Fourth, Fifth, Sixth, Ninth, Tenth, and Fourteenth Amendments, and under Subchapters IV and XVI of the Social Security Act and regulations issued there-under. She further alleged that she and her son have no income, resources, or support other than the benefits received under the AFDC program. . . .

II

When a case involves a home and some type of official intrusion into that home, as this case appears to do, an immediate and natural reaction is one of concern about Fourth Amendment rights and the protection which that Amendment is intended to afford. Its emphasis indeed is upon one of the most precious aspects of personal security in the home: "The right of the people to be secure in their persons, houses, papers, and effects. . . ." This Court has characterized that right as "basic to a free society." And over the years the Court consistently has been most protective of the privacy of the dwelling. . . .

III

This natural and quite proper protective attitude, however, is not a factor in this case, for the seemingly obvious and simple reason that we are not concerned here with any search by the New York social service agency in the Fourth Amendment meaning of that term. It is true that the governing statute and regulations appear to make mandatory the initial home visit and the subsequent periodic "contacts" (which may include home visits) for the inception and continuance of aid. It is also true that the caseworker's posture in the home visit is perhaps, in a sense, both rehabilitative and investigative. But this latter aspect, we think, is given too broad a character and far more emphasis than it deserves if it is equated with a search in the traditional criminal law context. We note, too, that the visitation in itself is not forced or compelled, and that the beneficiary's denial of permission is not a criminal act. If consent to the visitation is withheld, no visitation takes place. The aid then never begins or merely ceases, as the case may be. There is no entry of the home and there is no search.

IV

If however, we were to assume that a caseworker's home visit, before or subsequent to the beneficiary's initial qualification for benefits, somehow (perhaps because the average ben-eficiary might feel she is in no position to refuse consent to the visit), and despite its inter-view nature, does possess some of the characteristics of a search in the traditional sense, we nevertheless conclude that the visit does not fall within the Fourth Amendment's pro-scription. This is because it does not descend to the level of unreasonableness. It is unrea-sonableness which is the Fourth Amendment's standard. . . .

There are a number of factors that compel us to conclude that the home visit pro-posed for Mrs. James is not unreasonable:

1. The public's interest in this particular segment of the area of assistance to the unfor-tunate is protection and aid for the dependent child whose family requires such aid for that child. The focus is on the *child* and, further, it is on the child who is *depen-*

dent. There is no more worthy object of the public's concern. The dependent child's needs are paramount, and only with hesitancy would we relegate those needs, in the scale of comparative values, to a position secondary to what the mother claims as her rights.

2. The agency, with tax funds provided from federal as well as from state sources, is fulfilling a public trust. The State, working through its qualified welfare agency, has appropriate and paramount interest and concern in seeing and assuring that the intended and proper objects of that tax-produced assistance are the ones who benefit from the aid it dispenses. Surely it is not unreasonable, in the Fourth Amendment sense or in any other sense of that term, that the State have at its command a gentle means, of limited extent and of practical and considerate application, of achieving that assurance.

3. One who dispenses purely private charity naturally has an interest in and expects to know how his charitable funds are utilized and put to work. The public, when it is the provider, rightly expects the same. It might well expect more, because of the trust aspect of public funds, and the recipient, as well as the caseworker, has not only an interest but an obligation.

4. The emphasis of the New York statutes and regulations is upon the home, upon "close contact" with the beneficiary, upon restoring the aid recipient "to a condition of self-support," and upon the relief of his distress. The federal emphasis is no different. It is upon "assistance and rehabilitation," upon maintaining and strengthening family life, and upon "maximum self-support and personal independence consistent with the maintenance of continuing parental care and protection. . . ." It requires cooperation from the state agency upon specified standards and in specified ways. . . .

5. The means employed by the New York agency are significant. Mrs. James received written notice several days in advance of the intended home visit.[1] . . .

6. Mrs. James, in fact, on this record presents no specific complaint of any unreasonable intrusion of her home. . . . She alleges only, in general and nonspecific terms, that on previous visits and, on information and belief, on visitation at the home of other aid recipients, "questions concerning personal relationships, beliefs and behavior are raised and pressed which are unnecessary for a determination of continuing eligibility." . . . What Mrs. James appears to want from the agency that provides her and her infant son with the necessities for life is the right to receive those necessities upon her own informational terms, to utilize the Fourth Amendment as a wedge for imposing those terms, and to avoid questions of any kind. . . .

V

Our holding today does not mean, of course, that a termination of benefits upon refusal of a home visit is to be upheld against constitutional challenge under all conceivable circumstances. The early morning mass raid upon homes of welfare recipients is not unknown. But that is not this case. Facts of that kind present another case for another day.

---

[1] It is true that the record contains 12 affidavits, all essentially identical, of aid recipients (other than Mrs. James) which recite that a caseworker "most often" comes without notice; that when he does, the plans the recipient had for that time cannot be carried out; that the visit is "very embarrassing to me if the caseworker comes when I have company"; and that the caseworker "sometimes asks very personal questions" in front of children.

We therefore conclude that the home visitation as structured by the New York statutes and regulations is a reasonable administrative tool; that it serves a valid and proper administrative purpose for the dispensation of the AFDC program; that it is not an unwarranted invasion of personal privacy; and that it violates no right guaranteed by the Fourth Amendment. . . .

QUESTIONS

1. Justice Blackmun sees private dispensation of charity as analogous to government dispensation of welfare monies. Is this a good analogy? Explain.
2. Are people like Barbara James expected to sacrifice certain important political rights for economic reasons? If yes, is this morally acceptable?

JUSTICE WILLIAM O. DOUGLAS

DISSENTING OPINION IN *WYMAN VS. JAMES*

William O. Douglas (1898–1980), who received his law degree from Yale Law School and taught law for a number of years, served as associate justice of the United States Supreme Court from 1939 to 1975. Justice Douglas is the author of many books, including *The Right of the People* (1958), *The Anatomy of Liberty* (1963), and *The Court Years: The Autobiography of William O. Douglas* (1980).

Justice Douglas asks whether "the government by force of its largesse has the power to 'buy up' rights' guaranteed by the Constitution." Citing various forms of government payments, Douglas sees it as inconsistent that the recipients of some of these payments are not subjected to "searches without warrant," but that the recipients of aid to families with dependent children are. He criticizes the view that the latter kind of aid is a form of charity whose recipients are rightfully subject to policing activities which deny them their constitutional rights.

We are living in a society where one of the most important forms of property is government largesse which some call the "new property." The payrolls of government are but one aspect of that "new property." Defense contracts, highway contracts, and the other multifarious forms of contracts are another part. So are subsidies to air, rail, and other carriers. So are disbursements by government for scientific research. So are TV and radio licenses to use the air space which of course is part of the public domain. Our concern here is not with those subsidies but with grants that directly or indirectly implicate the *home life* of the recipients.

In 1969 roughly 127 billion dollars were spent by the federal, state, and local governments on "social welfare." To farmers alone almost four billion dollars were paid, in

United States Supreme Court. 400 U.S. 309 (1971).

part for not growing certain crops. Almost 129,000 farmers received $5,000 or more, their total benefits exceeding $1,450,000,000. Those payments were in some instances very large, a few running a million or more a year. But the majority were payments under $5,000 each.

Yet almost every beneficiary whether rich or poor, rural or urban, has a "house" — one of the places protected by the Fourth Amendment against "unreasonable searches and seizures." The question in this case is whether receipt of largesse from the government makes the *home* of the beneficiary subject to access by an inspector of the agency of oversight, even though the beneficiary objects to the intrusion and even though the Fourth Amendment's procedure for access to one's *house* or *home* is not followed. The penalty here is not, of course, invasion of the privacy of Barbara James, only her loss of federal or state largesse. That, however, is merely rephrasing the problem. Whatever the semantics, the central question is whether the government by force of its largesse has the power to "buy up" rights guaranteed by the Constitution. But for the assertion of her constitutional right, Barbara James in this case would have received the welfare benefit. . . .

. . . In *See v. City of Seattle* (1967) we [decided] that the "businessman, like the occupant of a residence, has a constitutional right to go about his business free from unreasonable official entries upon his private commercial property." There is not the slightest hint in *See* that the Government could condition a business license on the "consent" of the licensee to the administrative searches we held violated the Fourth Amendment. It is a strange jurisprudence indeed which safeguards the businessman at his place of work from warrantless searches but will not do the same for a mother in her *home*.

Is a search of her home without a warrant made "reasonable" merely because she is dependent on government largesse?

Judge Skelly Wright has stated the problem succinctly:

> "Welfare has long been considered the equivalent of charity and its recipients have been subjected to all kinds of dehumanizing experiences in the government's effort to police its welfare payments. In fact, over half a billion dollars are expended annually for administration and policing in connection with the Aid to Families with Dependent Children program. Why such large sums are necessary for administration and policing has never been adequately explained. No such sums are spent policing the government subsidies granted to farmers, airlines, steamship companies, and junk mail dealers, to name but a few. The truth is that in this subsidy area society has simply adopted a double standard, one for aid to business and the farmer and a different one for welfare." Poverty, Minorities, and Respect For Law, 1970 Duke L. J. 425, 437–438.

If the welfare recipient was not Barbara James but a prominent, affluent cotton or wheat farmer receiving benefit payments for not growing crops, would not the approach be different? Welfare in aid of dependent children, like social security and unemployment benefits, has an aura of suspicion. There doubtless are frauds in every sector of public welfare whether the recipient be a Barbara James or someone who is prominent or influential. But constitutional rights — here the privacy of the *home* — are obviously not dependent on the poverty or on the affluence of the beneficiary. It is the precincts of the *home* that the Fourth Amendment protects; and their privacy is as important to the lowly as to the mighty. . . .

I would place the same restrictions on inspectors entering the *homes* of welfare beneficiaries as are on inspectors entering the *homes* of those on the payroll of government, or the *homes* of those who contract with the government, or the *homes* of those who work for those having government contracts. The values of the *home* protected by the Fourth Amendment are not peculiar to capitalism as we have known it; they are equally relevant

to the new form of socialism which we are entering. Moreover, as the numbers of function-
aries and inspectors multiply, the need for protection of the individual becomes indeed
more essential if the values of a free society are to remain. . . .

QUESTIONS

1.   At the beginning of his opinion, Justice Douglas lists various subsidy programs as examples of government largesse. Are the programs he lists analogous to the welfare program under which Barbara James
received funds? What are the similarities? What are the differences?

2.   Is it morally correct for those who receive what is traditionally called "welfare" (e.g., aid to dependent
children) to be subjected to attempts to "reform" their lives and to checkups by government
caseworkers?

JOHN HOSPERS

THE NATURE OF THE STATE

■■■■■■

John Hospers is professor of philosophy at the University of Southern California and editor of *Pacific
Philosophical Quarterly*. Specializing in aesthetics, ethics, and political philosophy, Hospers has written
a number of books, including *Human Conduct: Problems of Ethics* (1972), *Introduction to Philosophical
Analysis* (1967), and *Libertarianism: A Political Philosophy for Tomorrow* (1971).

Hospers, a defender of the libertarian conception of justice, argues that there are two methods for
obtaining goods which will satisfy one's needs and wants. The first is production and exchange of
goods and services (economic means). The second is plunder—when done by organized and legalized
looting, this involves the use of political means. In Hospers's view, the state systematically seizes the
"fruits of other men's labor, and through the use of force . . . renders secure the parasitic caste in
society." Hospers's arguments against social welfare programs are primarily consequentialist ones. He
identifies state interference in the economic sphere as the cause of increasing taxation, spiraling inflation, eventual dictatorship, depressions, and poverty. Giving primacy to individual liberty and to rights
of noninterference, Hospers agrees with those who assert a citizen's right to disassociate himself or
herself from the government—refusing to accept both its benefits and its liabilities.

■■■■■■

Most academicians, somewhat isolated from the marketplace which ultimately pays their
salaries, still appear to think of the State as a benevolent agent which may have gone
wrong in this way or that, but still to be trusted and admired (and in any case, used by
them). My own attitude toward the State, based on its workings and the experience of
myself and many others with its representatives, is very different.

It is difficult to communicate briefly an attitude toward the State which took many

Reprinted with permission of the author and the publisher from *The Personalist,* vol. 59, no. 4 (October 1978), pp. 398–404.

years of reading and reflection to develop. I shall begin with the thesis of Franz Oppenheimer's book *The State* (1908). There are, he said, two ways of obtaining the things one needs and wants: the first method is production and exchange—to produce something out of nature's raw materials or transform them into a product (or service) desired by others, and to take the surplus of one's own production of one thing and exchange it for another kind of surplus from the production of others. This method of survival, production and exchange, he called the *economic* means. But there is also a second means: not to produce anything at all but to seize by force the things that others have produced—the method of plunder. This he called the *political* means.

Not everyone, of course, can use the second means, since one cannot seize from others something they have not already created or produced. But some people can and do, siphoning off the fruits of other people's labor for themselves. In the end, the supply is destroyed if this means is used too extensively, since it does not add to but rather subtracts from the totality of production: the more that is used up by the predator, the more must be created by others to replenish the supply. And of course the systematic plunder of the goods that someone has produced considerably reduces his motivation for producing any more.

Now the State, said Oppenheimer, is *the organization of the political means*. It is the systematic use of the predatory process over a given territory. Crimes committed by individuals, e.g. murder and theft, are sporadic and uncertain in their outcome: the victims may resist and even win. But the State provides a legal, orderly, systematic channel for the seizure of the fruits of other men's labor, and through the use of force it renders secure the parasitic caste in society.

> The classic paradigm was a conquering tribe pausing in its time-honored method of looting and murdering a conquered tribe, to realize that the time-span of plunder would be longer and more secure, and the situation more pleasant, if the conquered tribe were allowed to live and produce, with the conquerors settling among them as the rulers exacting a steady annual tribute. One method of the birth of a State may be illustrated as follows: in the hills of southern Ruritania, a bandit group manages to obtain physical control over the territory, and finally the bandit chieftain proclaims himself "King of the sovereign and independent government of South Ruritania"; and, if he and his men have the force to maintain this rule for a while, lo and behold! a new State has joined the "family of nations," and the former bandit leaders have been transformed into the lawful nobility of the realm.[1]

The State cannot keep the process of extortion going indefinitely unless it also confers some benefits (people might sooner or later revolt). One such benefit is protection—protection against other tribes, and protection against aggressors within the tribe. The State seldom manages this efficiently (what *does* it do efficiently?)—e.g. it protects only heads of state, and with everyone else it punishes (if at all) only after the aggression has been committed. And of course it increases its levy on all citizens to pay for this protection. But the State well knows that people also desire other benefits, specifically economic benefits. And these the State endeavors to supply, if for no other reason than to keep them peaceful, and, in the case of a democracy, to win their votes.

But this presents a problem, for the State has no resources of its own with which to confer these benefits. It can give to one person only by first seizing it from another; if one person gets something for nothing, another must get nothing for something. But the citizen-

---

[1]Murray Rothbard, *Egalitarianism and Other Essays* (New York: Laissez Faire Press, 1973), p. 37. See also the opening pages of Richard Taylor, *Freedom, Anarchy and the Law* (Prentice-Hall, 1973).

voter's attention is so centered on the attractiveness of the things being promised that he forgets that the politician making the promises doesn't have any of these things to give — and that he will have none of them after he gets into office; he will seize the earnings of one special interest group and distribute those earnings to another such group (minus the government's 40% handling fee, of course). And thus

> . . . the promisees continue to give their votes to the candidate making the biggest promises. One candidate promises to get sufficient federal funds for urban transportation to maintain the artificially low-priced subway ride in New York City. Another promises sufficient funds to guarantee Kansas wheat farmers more income for less wheat than the open market gives. Both candidates win. They meet in the cloak room on Capitol Hill, confess their sins to each other, and each one pledges to help the other deliver on his promise.
>
> As the farmer collects the higher price for his wheat and the New Yorker enjoys his subsidized subway ride, each of them takes pride in the fine representative he has in Washington. As the farmer and the subway rider see it, each representative has just demonstrated that free servants are available, and that the honest citizen can get something for nothing if he will vote for the right candidate. The New Yorker fails to see that his own taxes have been increased in order to pay the Kansas farmer to cut down on his wheat production so the farmer can get a higher price for what he sells; so the New Yorker will have to pay a higher price for his bread. In like manner, the farmer doesn't seem to realize that his taxes have been increased in order to subsidize the urban transportation system, so the city dweller can enjoy a higher standard of living while lowering his own level of production; so the farmer will have the dubious privilege of paying the higher prices for the tools and machinery he has to buy. The farmer and the subway rider are expropriating each other's productive capacity and paying a handsome royalty to an unruly bureaucracy for the privilege of doing it. In the marketplace that would be called plundering. In the political arena it is known as social progress.[2]

Particularly profitable for the State is the "discovery" of scapegoats, those whose earnings it can systematically loot, and gain public approval for doing so through an incessant barrage of propaganda against them. Such scapegoats are not difficult to find: any person who wishes to be independent of the State; anyone who is a "self-made man," and most of all anyone who has produced and marketed something and attained wealth. Those who have not succeeded in open competition tend to envy those who have, and the State fans this envy.[3] Thus the majority of the population actually come to applaud the State for taking it away from those who have been more successful than they. Like those that killed the goose that laid the golden egg, they do not see ahead to the time when there will be no more eggs forthcoming. There will be little incentive to produce if years of effort are confiscated by the State, and many people who were employed before will now find themselves without work. The general standard of living of course will decline — most citizens do not see the inevitability of this, and some politicians do but don't mind, preferring to have a subservient and poverty-stricken population. In some States the process goes so far that the State itself becomes the sole owner of land, the sole employer of everyone (e.g., the Soviet Union); determining the profession and salary of every worker; and anyone who tries to save anything for himself, or earn anything other than through the State, is subject to interrogation, torture, and death by shooting or exile to the Gulag. Yet so successful, often, is the propaganda of the State on its own behalf, that even with this ultimate control over the life of every citizen, some people applaud the State as their protector and security ("the sanction of the victim"). As if the State could supply security, instead of (as it does)

---

[2]Bertel Sparks, "How Many Servants Can You Afford?" *The Freeman*, October 1976, p. 593.
[3]See Helmut Schoeck, *Envy*.

taking away from its subjects that much chance of ever taking steps to achieve their own security! But the process continues:

> As the competition for votes increases, each candidate finds it necessary to broaden his base. He must make more promises to more people. As these promises are fulfilled, more and more people find it advantageous to lower their own level of production so they can qualify for larger appropriations from the public till. Direct payments to farmers for producing less is an example of this. So are rent subsidies and food stamps for the lower income groups ... [And] some of the less skilled members of society learn that it is more profitable to them to cease production altogether and rely upon the relief rolls for everything. ... [Increasingly] the expectations of some special interest group have not been met, and the government is called upon to supply the shortage. That is to say, the government is called upon to supply some "free" services. Unfortunately, the government has nothing to give any special group except what it expropriates through taxation or otherwise from some other group.
>
> The contest becomes a contest between producers and non-producers, with the government aligned on the side of the non-producers. This result has nothing to do with whether government officials are honest or dishonest, wise or stupid. They are mere agents administering a system which the citizens, acting in their capacity as voters, have demanded. It is a system that includes in its own mechanism the seeds of its own destruction. The marginal producer, whether he is a laborer or a manager, cannot avoid seeing the advantages of allowing himself to fall below the survival line, cease his contributions to those who are still further below, and qualify for a claim upon his government, and through his government upon more successful competitors, for his own support. And each individual or business enterprise that takes that step will automatically draw the producer who is only slightly higher on the economic scale just a little closer to that same survival line. Eventually all are pulled below it and are faced with the necessity of beginning over again without any prosperous neighbors upon whom they can call for help, and without any backlog of capital they can use as a starting point.[4]

And thus does the State, once it goes into the business of conferring economic benefits, cause a state of splendidly equalized destitution for everyone. The State itself rises from the ashes more powerful than ever: with every economic crisis a new emergency is declared, giving the State more power with the full approval of the majority of its citizens ("only for the duration of the emergency"—whose end is never in sight), until it ends up in total control of everything and everyone—which of course is just what the State wanted all along. But by that time it is too late for anyone to object.

The full story is far too long even to outline here. I shall mention only a few chapter headings in the saga of The State:

1.   *Taxation.* It can usually be relied upon to increase until the point of total collapse ("take till there's nothing left to be taken").

2.   *Inflation.* Even high taxation is not enough to pay for what the politicians have promised the voters, so the State increases the money supply to meet the deficit. This of course decreases the value of each dollar saved, and ultimately destroys savings, penalizes thrift, wrecks incentive, bankrupts business enterprises and creates huge unemployment. But this is only the beginning:

3.   *Dictatorship.* As prices rise out of sight, demand for price controls increases. Price controls create shortages (men cannot continue to produce at a loss). Shortages create strikes, hunger riots, civil commotion as the shortages spread. From this arises a Caesar, to "take a firm hand" and "restore law and order." The economy is now

---

[4]Bertel Sparks, *op. cit.,* pp. 593–5.

totally controlled from the center (with all the inefficiency and waste that this implies), and each individual, including his wages and conditions of work (and what he may work at), is thoroughly regimented. Liberty has now been lost. Most of this scenario is probably inevitable for the U.S. in the next two decades.[5]

Other chapter headings along the way would include: (4) Depressions. The State, through its interventionist policies, is solely responsible for economic depressions.[6] (5) Poverty. The State is the cause of most of the poverty that there is in this country. If you want to eliminate poverty, eliminate State intervention in the marketplace.[7]—There are others, but the point is aptly summarized by Rose Wilder Lane, commenting on the slogan "Government should do for people what people can not do for themselves":

> Would persons who adopt such resolutions (and say the same thing again and again, all the time, everywhere) put that idea in realistic terms and say, "Government should do nothing but compel other persons, by force, to do what those persons do not want to do?" Because, obviously, if those other persons *want* to do it, they *will* do it, if it can possibly be done; so it will be done, if it can be—if they're simply let alone.
>
> "The people" have in fact done everything that *is* done; they built the houses and roads and railroads and telephones and planes, they organized the oil companies, the banks, the postal services, the schools—what didn't "the people" do? What happens is that, after they do it, the Government *takes* it. The Government takes the roads, the postal service, the systems of communications, the banks, the markets, the stock exchange, insurance companies, schools, building trades, telegraphs and telephones, *after* "the people" have done all these things for themselves.[8]

Small children are prolific with their spending proposals because their eyes are on the goodies to be attained, and they do not see the labor, the cost, the hardship and deprivation which their spending schemes would entail. Social planners are as a whole in the same category; they see the end but not the means.

These views have often been accused of being un-humanitarian. (Though President Ford is also among the big spenders—what else would you call a hundred billion dollar deficit in one year? which is more than all the profits of all American corporations put together—he occasionally vetoes a particularly virulent piece of legislation, and is accused of being un-humanitarian.) What is humanitarian about seizing other people's earnings and using them for purposes which *you* think they should be used for? While others think of the "great social gains" to be achieved (which will not occur anyway, since the State employees waste most of it—what poverty has been ended by poverty programs?), I think of the corner shopkeeper, already forced to the wall by confiscatory taxation, government inflation, and endless government regulation, trying to keep his head above water, and the effect of one government scheme after another to spend his money—what will be the effect of all this on him and others like him? Much more humanitarian are the words of the great French economist Frederic Bastiat, written in 1848:

> How is legal plunder to be identified? Quite simply. See if the law takes from some persons what belongs to them, and gives it to the other persons to whom it does not belong. See if the law benefits one citizen at the expense of another by doing what the citizen himself cannot do without committing a crime.[9]

---

[5]See Irwin Schiff, *The Biggest Con* (Arlington House, 1976), C. V. Myers, *The Coming Deflation* (Arlington House, 1976), Clarence B. Carson, *The War on the Poor* (Arlington House, 1970), and others.
[6]See, for example, Lionel Robbins, *The Great Depression,* and Murray Rothbard, *The Great Depression.*
[7]See, e.g., Clarence B. Carson, *The War on the Poor,* and Shirley Scheibla, *Poverty Is Where the Money Is.*
[8]Rose Wilder Lane, in Roger L. MacBride (ed.), *The Lady and the Tycoon* (Caxton Press, 1973), pp. 332-3.
[9]Frederic Bastiat, *The Law* (Foundation for Economic Education edition, p. 21).

The State, implemented by all the channels of communications which it controls, will use all its powers to resist such advice; and every economic incentive (and threat of deprivation) at its command will be used as well. But this in no way alters the fact that

> ... The State is no proper agency for social welfare, and never will be, for exactly the same reason that an ivory paperknife is nothing to shave with. The interests of society and of the State do not coincide; any pretense that they can be made to coincide is sheer nonsense. Society gets on best when people are most happy and contented, which they are when freest to do as they please and what they please; hence society's interest is in having as little government as possible, and in keeping it as decentralized as possible. The State, on the other hand, is administered by job-holders; hence its interest is in having as much government as possible. It is hard to imagine two sets of interests more directly opposed than these.[10]

Those who ignore these remarks, and seek to use the coercive power of the State to impose their ideas of welfare or utopia on others, must bear a heavy moral burden — the burden of the suffering they impose (however inadvertently) on others by their actions, of the incalculable loss in human well-being.

According to Rawls, man's primary social goods are "rights and liberties, opportunities and powers, income and wealth."[11] But some of these, when put into practice, would negate others. Rawls advocates (to take one example among many) government ownership of the means of production (though not necessarily all of them). This entails not only the inefficiency and waste and corruption that regularly characterize enterprises handled by the State, from the post office on down (or up?), but the huge bureaucracy required to administer it, which always seeks to increase its own numbers and power, and over which the citizen has no direct control.[12] When one spells out the full implications of all of this, very little is left of liberty; and the ostensible reason for placing such things in the hands of government — "so that everyone can have it" — ends up as its very opposite, "there's nothing left to distribute." Any resemblance between Rawls' theory and justice is strictly coincidental.

Dr. Burrill, like most of his colleagues, considers some ends so important that he would use the coercive apparatus of the State to enforce his ideals on everyone. He concludes that the marketplace is in need of improvement through State intervention (presumably along the lines of his own ideals), and that we need "a general justification of the entrepreneurial system as it stands." As it stands! As if there were anything left of the entrepreneurial system in this country but a mangled hulk, with a few crumbs thrown out by omnipotent government to produce and make money so that the State could confiscate it! as if this country still had a live and functioning "entrepreneurial system" instead of what we have now, a fascist-type State in which the State has a life-and-death stranglehold on every industry, every trade, every farm, every enterprise that exists! Is this battered ruin to be "improved" by still further interventions by the State? And what justifies one person in imposing *his* ideals on *everyone* through the coercive machinery of the State?[13]

It matters little whether Oppenheimer's account of the origins of the State is correct. (It surely is in most cases, but there are very significant differences in the case of the origin of the U.S.A.) It matters much more what the State is doing *now*. Whether the State was

---

[10]Albert Jay Nock, *Cogitations,* p. 40.

[11]John Rawls, *A Theory of Justice* (Harvard University Press, 1971), p. 91.

[12]For many examples of this, in the context of American history, see William Wooldridge, *Uncle Sam the Monopoly Man* (Arlington House, 1970).

[13]See John Hospers, *Libertarianism* (Nash, 1971); also Robert Nozick, *Anarchy, State, and Utopia* (Basic Books, 1975); Frederic Bastiat, *The Law;* Henry Hazlitt, *Economics in One Lesson* (Harper, 1946); Ludwig von Mises' books *Socialism; Bureaucracy, and Omnipotent Government* (all Yale University Press).

conceived and born in sin is less important than whether it is involved in sin now. And there is little doubt that, whatever its origin, sinning is currently its principal activity.

In a remarkably prescient letter to one H. S. Randall of New York, the British historian Thomas Macaulay wrote (May 23, 1857):

> The day will come when . . . a multitude of people will choose the legislature. Is it possible to doubt what sort of legislature will be chosen? On the one side is a statesman preaching patience, respect for rights, strict observance of the public faith. On the other is the demagogue ranting about the tyranny of capitalism . . . Which of the Candidates is likely to be preferred . . . ? I seriously apprehend that you will, in some season of adversity, do things which will prevent prosperity from returning; that you will act like some people in a year of scarcity: devour all the seed corn and thus make next year a year, not of scarcity but of absolute failure. There will be, I fear, spoliation. This spoliation will increase distress. The distress will produce fresh spoliation. There is nothing to stay you. Your Constitution is all sail and no anchor. When Society has entered on this downward progress, either civilization or liberty must perish. Either some Caesar or Napolean will seize the reins of government with a strong hand, or your Republic will be as fearfully plundered and laid waste by barbarians in the twentieth century as the Roman Empire in the fifth: with this difference, that the Huns and Vandals who ravaged the Roman Empire came from without, and that your Huns and Vandals will have been engendered within your country, by your own institutions.[14]

The State, says Robert Paul Wolff in his *In Defense of Anarchism,* wields great *power* over us—but whence derives its *authority* (the moral right to wield that power)? In a telling exposition of the distinction, he finds no basis for any such authority; nor does he succeed in solving this problem in the later (more pragmatic) sections of the book. (Even if a contract theory would help—and as Hume cogently argued, it wouldn't—there was in fact no such contract. Unlike other organizations such as churches and clubs, no one contracted to be ruled by the State.)

In all existing States, some individuals (through their representatives) get hold of the State apparatus to enforce their ideas of a good society on others, including those who find it useless, repellent, or immoral. A would like to impose his plan on B and C (they would be pawns on *his* chessboard); B would impose his plan on A and C; and so on. But, observed Bastiat,

> . . . by what right does the law force me to conform to the social plan of Mr. A or Mr. B or Mr. C? If the law has a moral right to do this, why does it not, then, force these gentlemen to submit to *my* plans? Is it logical to suppose that nature has not given *me* sufficient imagination to dream up a utopia also? Should the law choose one fantasy among many, and put the organized force of government at its service only?[15]

Am I then committed to anarchism? Not necessarily, though as it has been worked out in detail by numerous writers, with provisions for a system of private defense and courts, I consider it greatly preferable to the leviathan we have today.[16] One of the greatest and least appreciated of political philosophers, Herbert Spencer, was not an anarchist.[17]

[14]For similar predictions, see Alexis de Toqueville, *Democracy in America,* 1840.
[15]Bastiat, *The Law,* p. 71.
[16]See, for example, Morris and Linda Tannehill, *The Market for Liberty,* 1970; David Friedman, *The Machinery of Freedom* (Anchor Doubleday, 1973); Leonard Krimerman and Lewis Perry (eds.), *Patterns of Anarchy* (Anchor Doubleday, 1966); Lysander Spooner, *The Constitution of No Authority;* James J. Martin (ed.), *Men against the State* (De Kalb, Ill.: Adrian Allen Associates, 1953); also Chapter 11 of J. Hospers, *Libertarianism* (Nash, 1971).
[17]See his monumental work, *The Man versus the State* (1884; reprinted by Caxton Press, 1940).

He set forth "The Law of Equal Freedom": "Each man should be free to act as he chooses, provided he trenches not on the equal freedom of each other man to act as he chooses." Then he attempted to resolve the "problem of political authority" as follows, in the chapter "The Right to Ignore the State" (omitted from most subsequent editions) of his book *Social Statics:*

> ... we can not choose but admit the right of the citizen to adopt a condition of *voluntary outlawry.* If every man has freedom to do all that he wills, provided he infringes not on the equal freedom of any others, then he is free to *drop connection with the State*—to relinquish its protection and to refuse paying toward its support. It is self-evident that in so behaving he in no way trenches upon the liberty of others, for his position is a passive one, and while passive he cannot become an aggressor ... He cannot be compelled to continue one of a political corporation without a breach of the moral law, seeing that citizenship involves payment of taxes; and the taking away of a man's property against his will is an infringement of his rights. *Government being simply an agent employed in common by a number of individuals to secure to them certain advantages, the very nature of the connection implies that it is for each to say whether he will employ such an agent or not.* If any one of them determines to ignore this mutual-safety confederation, nothing can be said except that he loses all claim to its good offices and exposes himself to the danger of maltreatment—a thing he is quite at liberty to do if he likes. He cannot be coerced into political combination without breach of the Law of Equal Freedom; he *can* withdraw from it without committing any such breach, and he has therefore a right so to withdraw.[18]

These words of Spencer seem to me to contain the core of any political philosophy worthy of the name. No other provides sufficiently for voluntary consent and human liberty (or as Wolff says, autonomy), not to mention such other human values as individuality, enduring prosperity, creative opportunity, and peace.

QUESTIONS

1. Libertarians often argue that political freedom depends on economic freedom. Could one make a case for the claim that economic deprivation is a serious threat to political freedom?

2. Some libertarians argue that from a moral standpoint there is no difference between the actions of an ordinary thief and the government seizure of money from some in order to support others. They assume that if the first is wrong, then so is the other. Are they correct?

TRUDY GOVIER

THE RIGHT TO EAT AND THE DUTY TO WORK

Trudy Govier is associate professor of philosophy at Trent University, Ontario. Her areas of specialization are moral philosophy and logic. Govier's articles include "What Should We Do About Future People?" and "Is 'Are There External Objects' an Empirical Proposition?"

---

[18]Herbert Spencer, *Social Statics,* 1845, p. 185. Italics mine.

Govier focuses on issues arising out of the question, "Should the needy have a legal right to welfare benefits?" She first examines three positions which could be adopted in response to the question: (1) the individualist position; (2) the permissive position; and (3) the puritan position. She proceeds to evaluate the three positions' policies regarding welfare both on the basis of utilitarian considerations and on the basis of considerations of social justice. Govier concludes that permissivism is superior from both standpoints.

━━━━━━━━━━

Although the topic of welfare is not one with which philosophers have often concerned themselves, it is a topic which gives rise to many complex and fascinating questions — some in the area of political philosophy, some in the area of ethics, and some of a more practical kind. The variety of issues related to the subject of welfare makes it particularly necessary to be clear just which issue one is examining in a discussion of welfare. In a recent book on the subject, Nicholas Rescher asks:

> In what respects and to what extent is society, working through the instrumentality of the state, responsible for the welfare of its members? What demands for the promotion of his welfare can an individual reasonably make upon his society? These are questions to which no answer can be given in terms of some *a priori* approach with reference to universal ultimates. Whatever answer can appropriately be given will depend, in the final analysis, on what the society decides it should be.[1]

Rescher raises this question only to avoid it. His response to his own question is that a society has all and only those responsibilities for its members that it thinks it has. Although this claim is trivially true as regards legal responsibilities, it is inadequate from a moral perspective. If one imagines the case of an affluent society which leaves the blind, the disabled, and the needy to die of starvation, the incompleteness of Rescher's account becomes obvious. In this imagined case one is naturally led to raise the question as to whether those in power ought to supply those in need with the necessities of life. Though the needy have no legal right to welfare benefits of any kind, one might very well say that they ought to have such a right. It is this claim which I propose to discuss here.[2]

I shall approach this issue by examining three positions which may be adopted in response to it. These are:

(1)   *The Individualist Position:* Even in an affluent society, one ought not to have any legal right to state-supplied welfare benefits.

(2)   *The Permissive Position:* In a society with sufficient resources, one ought to have an unconditional legal right to receive state supplied welfare benefits. (That is, one's

---

[1]Nicholas Rescher, *Welfare: Social Issues in Philosophical Perspective,* p. 114.

[2]One might wish to discuss moral questions concerning welfare in the context of natural rights doctrines. Indeed, Article 22 of the United Nations Declaration of Human Rights states, "Everyone, as a member of society, has the right to social security and is entitled, through national effort and international cooperation and in accordance with the organization and resources of each State, to the economic, social and cultural rights indispensable for his dignity and the free development of his personality." I make no attempt to defend the right to welfare as a natural right. Granting that rights imply responsibilities or duties and that "ought" implies "can," it would only be intelligible to regard the right to social security as a natural right if all states were able to ensure the minimum well-being of their citizens. This is not the case. And a natural right is one which is by definition supposed to belong to all human beings simply in virtue of their status as human beings. The analysis given here in the permissive view is compatible with the claim that all human beings have a *prima facie* natural right to social security. It is not, however, compatible with the claim that all human beings have a natural right to social security if this right is regarded as one which is so absolute as to be inviolable under any and all conditions.

Reprinted with permission of the publisher from *Philosophy of the Social Sciences,* vol. 5 (1975), pp. 125–143.

right to receive such benefits ought not to depend on one's behaviour; it should be guaranteed).

(3) *The Puritan Position:* In a society with sufficient resources one ought to have a legal right to state-supplied welfare benefits; this right ought to be conditional, however, on one's willingness to work.

But before we examine these positions, some preliminary clarification must be attempted. . . .

Welfare systems are state-supported systems which supply benefits, usually in the form of cash income, to those who are in need. Welfare systems thus exist in the sort of social context where there is some private ownership of property. If no one owned anything individually (except possibly his own body), and all goods were considered to be the joint property of everyone, then this type of welfare system could not exist. A state might take on the responsibility for the welfare of its citizens, but it could not meet this responsibility by distributing a level of cash income which such citizens would spend to purchase the goods essential for life. The welfare systems which exist in the western world do exist against the background of extensive private ownership of property. It is in this context that I propose to discuss moral questions about having a right to welfare benefits. By setting out my questions in this way, I do not intend to endorse the institution of private property, but only to discuss questions which many people find real and difficult in the context of the social organization which they actually do experience. The present analysis of welfare is intended to apply to societies which (*a*) have the institution of private property, if not for means of production, at least for some basic good; and (*b*) possess sufficient resources so that it is at least possible for every member of the society to be supplied with the necessities of life.

1. The Individualist View

It might be maintained that a person in need has no legitimate moral claim on those around him and that the hypothetical inattentive society which left its blind citizens to beg or starve cannot rightly be censured for doing so. This view, which is dramatically at odds with most of contemporary social thinking, lives on in the writings of Ayn Rand and her followers.[3] The Individualist sets a high value on uncoerced personal choice. He sees each person as a responsible agent who is able to make his own decisions and to plan his own life. He insists that with the freedom to make decisions goes responsibility for the consequences of those decisions. A person has every right, for example, to spend ten years of his life studying Sanskrit — but if, as a result of this choice, he is unemployable, he ought not to expect others to labour on his behalf. No one has a proper claim on the labour of another, or on the income ensuing from that labour, unless he can repay the labourer in a way acceptable to that labourer himself. Government welfare schemes provide benefits from funds gained largely by taxing earned income. One cannot "opt out" of such schemes. To the Individualist, this means that a person is forced to work part of his time for others.

Suppose that a man works forty hours and earns two hundred dollars. Under modern-day taxation, it may well be that he can spend only two-thirds of that money as he chooses. The rest is taken by government and goes to support programmes which the working individual may not himself endorse. The beneficiaries of such programmes — those beneficiaries who do not work themselves — are as though they have slaves working for

---

[3]See, for example, Ayn Rand's *Atlas Shrugged, The Virtue of Selfishness,* and *Capitalism: the Unknown Ideal.*

them. Backed by the force which government authorities can command, they are able to exist on the earnings of others. Those who support them do not do so voluntarily, out of charity; they do so on government command.

> Someone across the street is unemployed. Should you be taxed extra to pay for his expenses? Not at all. You have not injured him, you are not responsible for the fact that he is unemployed (unless you are a senator or bureaucrat who agitated for further curtailing of business which legislation passed, with the result that your neighbour was laid off by the curtailed business). You may voluntarily wish to help him out, or better still, try to get him a job to put him on his feet again; but since you have initiated no aggressive act against him, and neither purposefully nor accidentally injured him in any way, you should not be legally penalized for the fact of his unemployment.[4]

The Individualist need not lack concern for those in need. He may give generously to charity; he might give more generously still, if his whole income were his to use, as he would like it to be. He may also believe that, as a matter of empirical fact, existing government programmes do not actually help the poor. They support a cumbersome bureaucracy and they use financial resources which, if untaxed, might be used by those with initiative to pursue job-creating endeavours. The thrust of the Individualist's position is that each person owns his own body and his own labour; thus each person is taken to have a virtually unconditional right to the income which that labour can earn him in a free market place.[5] For anyone to pre-empt part of a worker's earnings without that worker's voluntary consent is tantamount to robbery. And the fact that the government is the intermediary through which this deed is committed does not change its moral status one iota.

On an Individualist's view, those in need should be cared for by charities or through other schemes to which contributions are voluntary. Many people may wish to insure themselves against unforeseen calamities and they should be free to do so. But there is no justification for non-optional government schemes financed by taxpayers' money. . . .

2. The Permissive View

Directly contrary to the Individualist view of welfare is what I have termed the Permissive view. According to this view, in a society which has sufficient resources so that everyone could be supplied with the necessities of life, every individual ought to be given the legal right to social security, and this right ought not to be conditional in any way upon an individual's behaviour. *Ex hypothesi* the society which we are discussing has sufficient goods to provide everyone with food, clothing, shelter and other necessities. Someone who does without these basic goods is scarcely living at all, and a society which takes no steps to change this state of affairs implies by its inaction that the life of such a person is without value. It does not execute him; but it may allow him to die. It does not put him in prison; but it may leave him with a life of lower quality than that of some prison inmates. A society which can rectify these circumstances and does not can justly be accused of imposing upon the needy either death or lifelong deprivation. And those characteristics which make a person needy—whether they be illness, old age, insanity, feeblemindedness, inability to find paid work, or even poor moral character—are insufficient to make him deserve the fate to which an inactive society would in effect condemn him. One would not be executed for inability or failure to find paid work; neither should one be allowed to die for this misfortune or failing.

---

[4] John Hospers, *Libertarianism: A Political Philosophy for Tomorrow*, p. 67.
[5] I say virtually unconditional, because an Individualist such as John Hospers sees a legitimate moral role for government in preventing the use of force by some citizens against others. Since this is the case, I presume that he would also regard as legitimate such taxation as was necessary to support this function. Presumably that taxation would be seen as consented to by all, on the grounds that all "really want" government protection.

A person who cannot or does not find his own means of social security does not thereby forfeit his status as a human being. If other human beings, with physical, mental and moral qualities different from his, are regarded as having the right to life and to the means of life, then so too should he be regarded. A society which does not accept the responsibility for supplying such a person with the basic necessities of life is, in effect, endorsing a difference between its members which is without moral justification. . . .

The adoption of a Permissive view of welfare would have significant practical implications. If there were a legal right, unconditional upon behaviour, to a specified level of state-supplied benefits, then state investigation of the prospective welfare recipient could be kept to a minimum. Why he is in need, whether he can work, whether he is willing to work, and what he does while receiving welfare benefits are on this view quite irrelevant to his right to receive those benefits. A welfare recipient is a person who claims from his society that to which he is legally entitled under a morally based welfare scheme. The fact that he makes this claim licenses no special state or societal interference with his behaviour. If the Permissive view of welfare were widely believed, then there would be no social stigma attached to being on welfare. There is such a stigma, and many long-term welfare recipients are considerably demoralized by their dependent status.[6] These facts suggest that the Permissive view of welfare is not widely held in our society.

3. The Puritan View

This view of welfare rather naturally emerges when we consider that no one can have a right to something without someone else's, or some group of other persons', having responsibilities correlative to this right. In the case in which the right in question is a legal right to social security, the correlative responsibilities may be rather extensive. They have been deemed responsibilities of "the state." The state will require resources and funds to meet these responsibilities, and these do not emerge from the sky miraculously, or zip into existence as a consequence of virtually effortless acts of will. They are taken by the state from its citizens, often in the form of taxation on earned income. The funds given to the welfare recipient and many of the goods which he purchases with these funds are produced by other members of society, many of whom give a considerable portion of their time and their energy to this end. If a state has the moral responsibility to ensure the social security of its citizens then all the citizens of that state have the responsibility to provide state agencies with the means to carry out their duties. This responsibility, in our present contingent circumstances, seems to generate an obligation to *work*.

A person who works helps to produce the goods which all use in daily living and, when paid, contributes through taxation to government endeavours. The person who does not work, even though able to work, does not make his contribution to social efforts towards obtaining the means of life. He is not entitled to a share of the goods produced by others if he chooses not to take part in their labours. Unless he can show that there is a moral justification for his not making the sacrifice of time and energy which others make, he has no legitimate claim to welfare benefits. If he is disabled or unable to obtain work, he cannot work; hence he has no need to justify his failure to work. But if he does choose not to work, he would have to justify his choice by saying "others should sacrifice their time and energy for me; I have no need to sacrifice time and energy for them." This principle, a version of what Rawls refers to as a free-rider's principle, simply will not stand up to criticism.[7] To deliberately avoid working and benefit from the labours of others is morally indefensible.

[6]Ian Adams, William Cameron, Brian Hill, and Peter Penz, *The Real Poverty Report,* pp. 167–187.
[7]See *A Theory of Justice,* pp. 124, 136. Rawls defines the free-rider as one who relies on the principle "everyone is to act justly except for myself, if I choose not to," and says that his position is a version of egoism which is eliminated as a morally acceptable principle by formal constraints. This conclusion regarding the tenability of egoism is one which I accept and which is taken for granted in the present context.

Within a welfare system erected on these principles, the right to welfare is conditional upon one's satisfactorily accounting for his failure to obtain the necessities of life by his own efforts. Someone who is severely disabled mentally or physically, or who for some other reason cannot work, is morally entitled to receive welfare benefits. Someone who chooses not to work is not. The Puritan view of welfare is a kind of compromise between the Individualist view and the Permissive view. . . .

The Puritan view of welfare, based as it is on the inter-relation between welfare and work, provides a rationale for two connected principles which those establishing welfare schemes in Canada and in the United States seem to endorse. First of all, those on welfare should never receive a higher income than the working poor. Secondly, a welfare scheme should, in some way or other, incorporate incentives to work. These principles, which presuppose that it is better to work than not to work, emerge rather naturally from the contingency which is at the basis of the Puritan view: the goods essential for social security are products of the labour of some members of society. If we wish to have a continued supply of such goods, we must encourage those who work to produce them. . . .

APPRAISAL OF POLICIES: SOCIAL CONSEQUENCES AND SOCIAL JUSTICE

In approaching the appraisal of prospective welfare policies under these two aspects I am, of course, making some assumptions about the moral appraisal of suggested social policies. Although these cannot possibly be justified here, it may be helpful to articulate them, at least in a rough way.

Appraisal of social policies is in part teleological. To the extent that a policy, P, increases the total human welfare more than does an alternative policy, P', P is a better social policy than P'. Or, if P leaves the total human welfare as it is, while P' diminishes it, then to that extent, P is a better social policy than P'. Even this skeletal formulation of the teleological aspect of appraisal reveals why appraisal cannot be entirely teleological. We consider total consequences—effects upon the total of "human well-being" in a society. But this total is a summation of consequences on different individuals. It includes no judgements as to how far we allow one individual's well-being to decrease while another's increases, under the same policy. Judgements relating to the latter problems are judgements about social justice.

In appraising social policies we have to weigh up considerations of total well-being against considerations of justice. Just how this is to be done, precisely, I would not pretend to know. However, the absence of precise methods does not mean that we should relinquish attempts at appraisal: some problems are already with us, and thought which is necessarily tentative and imprecise is still preferable to no thought at all.

1. Consequences of Welfare Schemes

First, let us consider the consequences of the non-scheme advocated by the Individualist. He would have us abolish all non-optional government programmes which have as their goal the improvement of anyone's personal welfare. This rejection extends to health schemes, pension plans and education, as well as to welfare and unemployment insurance. So following the Individualist would lead to very sweeping changes.

The Individualist will claim (as do Hospers and Ayn Rand) that on the whole his non-scheme will bring beneficial consequences. He will admit, as he must, that there are people who would suffer tremendously if welfare and other social security programmes were simply terminated. Some would even die as a result. We cannot assume that spontaneously developing charities would cover every case of dire need. Nevertheless the Individualist wants to point to benefits which would accrue to businessmen and to working people and their families if taxation were drastically cut. It is his claim that consumption would rise, hence production would rise, job opportunities would be extended, and there would be an economic boom, if people could only spend all their earned income as they wished. This boom would benefit both rich and poor.

There are significant omissions which are necessary in order to render the Individualist's optimism plausible. Either workers and businessmen would have insurance of various kinds, or they would be insecure in their prosperity. If they did have insurance to cover health problems, old age and possible job loss, then they would pay for it; hence they would not be spending their whole earned income on consumer goods. Those who run the insurance schemes could, of course, put this money back into the economy — but government schemes already do this. The economic boom under Individualism would not be as loud as originally expected. Furthermore the goal of increased consumption-increased productivity must be questioned from an ecological viewpoint: many necessary materials are available only in limited quantities.

Finally, a word about charity. It is not to be expected that those who are at the mercy of charities will benefit from this state, either materially or psychologically. Those who prosper will be able to choose between giving a great deal to charity and suffering from the very real insecurity and guilt which would accompany the existence of starvation and grim poverty outside their padlocked doors. It is to be hoped that they would opt for the first alternative. But, if they did, this might be every bit as expensive for them as government-supported benefit schemes are now. If they did not give generously to charity, violence might result. However one looks at it, the consequences of Individualism are unlikely to be good.

Welfare schemes operating in Canada today are almost without exception based upon the principles of the Puritan view. To see the consequences of that type of welfare scheme we have only to look at the results of our own welfare programmes. Taxation to support such schemes is high, though not so intolerably so as to have led to widescale resentment among taxpayers. Canadian welfare programmes are attended by complicated and often cumbersome bureaucracy, some of which results from the interlocking of municipal, provincial and federal governments in the administration and financing of welfare programmes. The cost of the programmes is no doubt increased by this bureaucracy; not all the tax money directed to welfare programmes goes to those in need. Puritan welfare schemes do not result in social catastrophe or in significant business stagnation — this much we know, because we already live with such schemes. Their adverse consequences, if any, are felt primarily not by society generally nor by businessmen and the working segment of the public, but rather by recipients of welfare.

Both the Special Senate Committee Report on Poverty and the Real Poverty Report criticize our present system of welfare for its demoralization of recipients, who often must deal with several levels of government and are vulnerable to arbitrary interference on the part of administering officials. Welfare officials have the power to check on welfare recipients and cut off or limit their benefits under a large number of circumstances. The dangers to welfare recipients in terms of anxiety, threats to privacy and loss of dignity are obvious. According to the Senate Report, the single aspect shared by all Canada's welfare systems is "a record of failure and insufficiency, of bureaucratic rigidities that often result in the degradation, humiliation and alienation of recipients."[8] The writers of this report cite many instances of humiliation, leaving the impression that these are too easily found to be "inci-

[8] *Senate Report on Poverty*, p. 73.

dental aberrations.'"[9] Concern that a welfare recipient either be unable to work or be willing to work (if unemployed) can easily turn into concern about how he spends the income supplied him, what his plans for the future are, where he lives, how many children he has. And the rationale underlying the Puritan scheme makes the degradation of welfare recipients a natural consequence of welfare institutions. Work is valued and only he who works is thought to contribute to society. Welfare recipients are regarded as parasites and spongers—so when they are treated as such, this is only what we should have expected. Being on welfare in a society which thinks and acts in this fashion can be psychologically debilitating. Welfare recipients who are demoralized by their downgraded status and relative lack of personal freedom can be expected to be made less capable of self-sufficiency. To the extent that this is so, welfare systems erected on Puritan principles may defeat their own purposes.

In fairness, it must be noted here that bureaucratic checks and controls are not a feature only of Puritan welfare systems. To a limited extent, Permissive systems would have to incorporate them too. Within those systems, welfare benefits would be given only to those whose income was inadequate to meet basic needs. However, there would be no checks on "willingness to work," and there would be no need for welfare workers to evaluate the merits of the daily activities of recipients. If a Permissive guaranteed income system were administered through income tax returns, everyone receiving the basic income and those not needing it paying it back in taxes, then the special status of welfare recipients would fade. They would no longer be singled out as a special group within the population. It is to be expected that living solely on government-supplied benefits would be psychologically easier in that type of situation.

Thus it can be argued that for the recipients of welfare, a Permissive scheme has more advantages than a Puritan one. This is not a very surprising conclusion. The Puritan scheme is relatively disadvantageous to recipients, and Puritans would acknowledge this point; they will argue that the overall consequences of Permissive schemes are negative in that these schemes benefit some at too great a cost to others. (Remember, we are not yet concerned with the *justice* of welfare policies, but solely with their consequences as regards *total* human well-being within the society in question.) The concern which most people have regarding the Permissive scheme relates to its costs and its dangers to the "work ethic." It is commonly thought that people work only because they have to work to survive in a tolerable style. If a guaranteed income scheme were adopted by the government, this incentive to work would disappear. No one would be faced with the choice between a nasty and boring job and starvation. Who would do the nasty and boring jobs then? Many of them are not eliminable and they have to be done somehow, by someone. Puritans fear that a great many people—even some with relatively pleasant jobs—might simply cease to work if they could receive non-stigmatized government money to live on. If this were to happen, the permissive society would simply grind to a halt.

In addressing these anxieties about the consequences of Permissive welfare schemes, we must recall that welfare benefits are set to ensure only that those who do not work have a bearable existence, with an income sufficient for basic needs, and that they have this income regardless of why they fail to work. Welfare benefits will not finance luxury living for a family of five! If jobs are adequately paid so that workers receive more than the minimum welfare income in an earned salary, then there will still be a financial incentive

---

[9]The Hamilton Public Welfare Department takes automobile licence plates from recipients, making them available again only to those whose needs meet with the Department's approval. (*Real Poverty Report*, p. 186.) The *Globe and Mail* for 12 January 1974 reported that welfare recipients in the city of Toronto are to be subjected to computerized budgeting. In the summer of 1973, the two young daughters of an Alabama man on welfare were sterilized against their own wishes and without their parents' informed consent. (See *Time*, 23 July 1973.)

to take jobs. What guaranteed income schemes will do is to raise the salary floor. This change will benefit the many non-unionized workers in service and clerical occupations.

Furthermore it is unlikely that people work solely due to (i) the desire for money and the things it can buy and (ii) belief in the Puritan work ethic. There are many other reasons for working, some of which would persist in a society which had adopted a Permissive welfare system. Most people are happier when their time is structured in some way, when they are active outside their own homes, when they feel themselves part of an endeavour whose purposes transcend their particular egoistic ones. Women often choose to work outside the home for these reasons as much as for financial ones. With these and other factors operating I cannot see that the adoption of a Permissive welfare scheme would be followed by a level of slothfulness which would jeopardize human well-being.

Another worry about the Permissive scheme concerns cost. It is difficult to comment on this in a general way, since it would vary so much from case to case. Of Canada at the present it has been said that a guaranteed income scheme administered through income tax would cost less than social security payments administered through the present bureaucracies. It is thought that this saving would result from a drastic cut in administrative costs. The matter of the work ethic is also relevant to the question of costs. Within a Puritan framework it is very important to have a high level of employment and there is a tendency to resist any reorganization which results in there being fewer jobs available. Some of these proposed reorganizations would save money; strictly speaking we should count the cost of keeping jobs which are objectively unnecessary as part of the cost of Puritanism regarding welfare.

In summary, we can appraise Individualism, Puritanism and Permissivism with respect to their anticipated consequences, as follows: Individualism is unacceptable; Puritanism is tolerable, but has some undesirable consequences for welfare recipients; Permissivism appears to be the winner. Worries about bad effects which Permissive welfare schemes might have due to high costs and (alleged) reduced work-incentives appear to be without solid basis.

2. Social Justice under Proposed Welfare Schemes

We must now try to consider the merits of Individualism, Puritanism and Permissivism with regard to their impact on the distribution of the goods necessary for well-being. [Robert] Nozick has argued against the whole conception of a distributive justice on the grounds that it presupposes that goods are like manna from heaven: we simply get them and then have a problem—to whom to give them. According to Nozick we know where things come from and we do not have the problem of to whom to give them. There is not really a problem of distributive justice, for there is no central distributor giving out manna from heaven! It is necessary to counter Nozick on this point since his reaction to the (purported) problems of distributive justice would undercut much of what follows.[10]

There is a level at which Nozick's point is obviously valid. If A discovers a cure for cancer, then it is A and not B or C who is responsible for this discovery. On Nozick's view this is taken to imply that A should reap any monetary profits which are forthcoming; other people will benefit from the cure itself. Now although it cannot be doubted that A is a bright and hardworking person, neither can it be denied that A and his circumstances are the product of many co-operative endeavours: schools and laboratories, for instance. Because this is so, I find Nozick's claim that "we know where things come from" unconvincing at a deeper level. Since achievements like A's presuppose extensive social co-operation, it is morally permissible to regard even the monetary profits accruing from them as shareable by the "owner" and society at large.

[10]Robert Nozick, "Distributive Justice," *Philosophy and Public Affairs*, Fall 1973.

Laws support existing income levels in many ways. Governments specify taxation so as to further determine net income. Property ownership is a legal matter. In all these ways people's incomes and possibilities for obtaining income are affected by deliberate state action. It is always possible to raise questions about the moral desirability of actual conventional arrangements. Should university professors earn less than lawyers? More than waitresses? Why? Why not? Anyone who gives an account of distributive justice is trying to specify principles which will make it possible to answer questions such as these, and nothing in Nozick's argument suffices to show that the questions are meaningless or unimportant.

Any human distribution of anything is unjust insofar as differences exist for no good reason. If goods did come like manna from heaven and the Central Distributor gave A ten times more than B, we should want to know why. The skewed distribution might be deemed a just one if A's needs were objectively ten times greater than B's, or if B refused to accept more than his small portion of goods. But if no reason at all could be given for it, or if only an irrelevant reason could be given (e.g., A is blue-eyed and B is not), then it is an unjust distribution. All the views we have expounded concerning welfare permit differences in income level. Some philosophers would say that such differences are never just, although they may be necessary, for historical or utilitarian reasons. Whether or not this is so, it is admittedly very difficult to say just what would constitute a good reason for giving A a higher income than B. Level of need, degree of responsibility, amount of training, unpleasantness of work—all these have been proposed and all have some plausibility. We do not need to tackle all this larger problem in order to consider justice under proposed welfare systems. For we can deal here solely with the question of whether everyone should receive a floor level of income; decisions on this matter are independent of decisions on overall equality or principles of variation among incomes above the floor. The Permissivist contends that all should receive at least the floor income; the Individualist and the Puritan deny this. All would claim justice for their side.

The Individualist attempts to justify extreme variations in income, with some people below the level where they can fulfill their basic needs, with reference to the fact of people's actual accomplishments. This approach to the question is open to the same objections as those which have already been raised against Nozick's non-manna-from-heaven argument, and I shall not repeat them here. Let us move on to the Puritan account. It is because goods emerge from human efforts that the Puritan advances his view of welfare. He stresses the unfairness of a system which would permit some people to take advantage of others. A Permissive welfare system would do this, as it makes no attempt to distinguish between those who choose not to work and those who cannot work. No one should be able to take advantage of another under the auspices of a government institution. The Puritan scheme seeks to eliminate this possibility, and for that reason, Puritans would allege, it is a more just scheme than the Permissive one.

Permissivists can best reply to this contention by acknowledging that any instance of free-riding would be an instance where those working were done an injustice, but by showing that any justice which the Puritan preserves by eliminating free-riding is outweighted by *injustice* perpetrated elsewhere. Consider the children of the Puritan's free-riders. They will suffer greatly for the "sins" of their parents. Within the institution of the family, the Puritan cannot suitably hurt the guilty without cruelly depriving the innocent. There is a sense, too, in which Puritanism does injustice to the many people on welfare who are not free-riders. It perpetuates the opinion that they are non-contributors to society and this doctrine, which is over-simplified if not downright false, has a harmful effect upon welfare recipients.

Social justice is not simply a matter of the distribution of goods, or the income with which goods are to be purchased. It is also a matter of the protection of rights. Western societies claim to give their citizens equal rights in political and legal contexts; they also claim to endorse the larger conception of a right to life. Now it is possible to interpret these rights in a limited and formalistic way, so that the duties correlative to them are minimal. On the limited, or negative, interpretation, to say that A has a right to life is simply to say that others have a duty not to interfere with A's attempts to keep himself alive. This interpretation of the right to life is compatible with Individualism as well as with Puritanism. But it is an inadequate interpretation of the right to life and of other rights. A right to vote is meaningless if one is starving and unable to get to the polls; a right to equality before the law is meaningless if one cannot afford to hire a lawyer. And so on.

Even a Permissive welfare scheme will go only a very small way towards protecting people's rights. It will amount to a meaningful acknowledgement of a right to life, by ensuring income adequate to purchase food, clothing and shelter—at the very least. These minimum necessities are presupposed by all other rights a society may endorse in that their possession is a precondition of being able to exercise these other rights. Because it protects the rights of all within a society better than do Puritanism and Individualism, the Permissive view can rightly claim superiority over the others with regard to justice.

QUESTIONS

1. Which of the three approaches to welfare described by Govier (individualist, permissive, puritan) is found in our society?
2. Govier finds the permissive position superior to the others on the basis of both utilitarian and justice considerations. What arguments could an individualist offer to rebut Govier's arguments? What arguments could an advocate of the puritan position offer to counter Govier's?

ELIZABETH TELFER

JUSTICE, WELFARE, AND HEALTH CARE

Elizabeth Telfer teaches in the department of moral philosophy at the University of Glasgow (Scotland). She is the coauthor of *Respect for Persons* (1970) and "Automony," as well as the author of *Happiness* (1980) and "Friendship." The ideas in the article reprinted here are further developed in a forthcoming book, *Caring and Curing,* which Telfer coauthored with R. S. Downie.

Telfer is not concerned with the government's role regarding welfare in general. Rather, she focuses on one human need—the need for medical care. She assumes that the function of the government is to further the welfare of its citizens. From this it follows that the government has the responsibility to ensure that everyone who needs it is able to secure medical care (insofar as community resources permit). Given this starting point she discusses four ways in which a government could implement its obligation regarding health care: (1) laissez faire, (2) liberal humanitarian, (3) liberal socialist, and (4) pure socialist. She analyzes each system both for its content and for the views of its antagonists and protagonists in order to bring out some of the principles at issue in any discussion of socialized medicine.

In this paper I shall be examining some of the broad principles which are relevant to discussions as to the proper way to provide health care in the community. Such discussions have taken a very pointed turn in recent years, for example, in regard to the "pay beds" issue.* The state of that practical issue is changing all the time, so I shall not attempt to relate what I say at all closely to the present state of play. Rather I hope to elucidate some of the background of ideas against which the protagonists in that debate pursue their argument.

In my discussion I shall assume the principle that the state is responsible for the health of the citizens, in the sense that it is bound, insofar as the community's resources permit, to see that it is possible for everyone who needs it to secure medical care. The detailed analysis of this principle, whether in terms of needs, rights or justice, is a matter of controversy, but in broad outline the principle is entailed by any political philosophy which ascribes to a government the positive function of furthering the welfare of its citizens; and such a political philosophy is readily accepted by all but extremists at the present time. Assuming this principle, then, I shall examine the various ways in which a government might try to implement its obligation to see that everyone gets the opportunity of health care. There are of course many possibilities here, but I think four broad types can be distinguished, which I shall call respectively *laissez-faire,* liberal humanitarian, liberal socialist, and pure socialist. I shall briefly describe each system, and then discuss the pros and cons of each.

FOUR POSSIBLE SYSTEMS OF HEALTH CARE

The *laissez-faire* system leaves medical care entirely to private enterprise. Those who can afford it pay for their medical treatment on a business footing, either directly or through insurance schemes. The needy are looked after, if at all, by private charities. The government interferes only to the extent that it interferes in other commercial enterprises: that is to say, it enforces contracts, hears suits for damage and tries to prevent fraud — perhaps in this case by insisting on qualifications of some kind for medical practitioners. The liberal humanitarian system is a modification of this. Those who can afford it pay for themselves, as before. But the needy are looked after not by private charity but by the state, using funds obtained by taxing the less needy. The liberal socialist scheme is what we have in Britain today. Everyone, or everyone who is able, has to contribute to a state scheme which provides for his medical care. But he may if he wishes pay also for private medicine. There can of course be systems between the liberal humanitarian and the liberal socialist, whereby everyone may belong to the state system but anyone may instead if he wishes opt out both of benefiting from it and also from all or part of his share of paying for it. Lastly there is pure socialism, which is what some now advocate: the complete abolition by law of non-state medicine.

I shall take it that the *laissez-faire* system is agreed to be inadequate; indeed, under such a system the state would in my view be abrogating its responsibilities towards the

---

Editor's note: At issue in the "pay beds" controversy is whether National Health Service hospitals should have a certain number of beds or wards set aside for "private," i.e., paying, patients. The controversy stems partly from the fact that, for "public" patients, hospital admittance is based on medical priority. Public patients who do not need immediate care may wait much longer for treatment than private patients who need such treatment.

Reprinted with permission of the author and the publisher from *Journal of Medical Ethics,* vol. 2 (September 1976), pp. 107–111.

needy. It is true that the needy might be very well provided for if there were a strong enough tradition of charity of this kind. But it seems too haphazard a basis for such an important service. In any case, it might be said that the opportunity for health care is owed to everyone as a basic human right; if this is so, receiving it should not have to depend on people's goodwill, however forthcoming that goodwill is. Of course replacing a *laissez-faire* system with one of the others might mean a loss of that worthwhile thing, exercise of the motive of charity. But there are some things which are so important that getting them done properly is more important than getting them done inadequately from the right motive. In any case, scope would remain on any scheme for the exercise of charity. We have today, for example, charities which support medical research, and which may feel justified in pursuing projects with a high risk of failure which those bodies using taxpayers' extorted money feel unjustified in supporting.

I turn then to a consideration of the more plausible schemes. My strategy will be to mention first some of the advantages people have advanced in favour of liberal humanitarianism, and the criticisms made of it from a socialist point of view. then I shall turn to the advantages and disadvantages of socialism, considering the liberal and pure versions together for the time being. Finally I shall touch on the vexed and topical question of liberal *versus* pure socialism.

THE LIBERAL HUMANITARIAN SCHEME OF HEALTH CARE

The first advantage attributed to the liberal humanitarian scheme is that it meets everyone's needs with minimum coercion: people are constrained only to the extent of paying taxes for the needy and not made to contribute to their own good, a practice which smacks of unwarranted interference. Secondly, it is said that resources are more usefully distributed: state aid can be concentrated on those who really need special help, and those who are paying for their own services will have an incentive not to squander them, as they do not have under a state scheme.

The third and fourth advantages of the liberal humanitarian scheme are what may be called moral, rather than merely medical. The third is the advantage of preserved incentive. People are encouraged to work harder if they can get what they need only by working, and discouraged if extra work brings no extra reward. Having an incentive to work hard is a double advantage: it benefits the community by increasing prosperity and it cultivates industriousness in the individual's character. The fourth advantage is similarly one of development of character: to have to decide for oneself how to manage such an important department of one's life develops a sense of responsibility and powers of decision.

In criticising this system, the socialist can first point to the problem posed for the liberal humanitarian by those who are perfectly well able to provide for themselves, by means of private insurance, but neglect to do so. If they fall ill even the liberal humanitarian will have to admit that the state must look after them; it is unfair that they should receive this benefit without paying for it, but one cannot leave a man to die because he has been improvident. The socialist can say that for him there is no problem, because everyone has to pay his way.

The second socialist criticism is a denial that the medical needs of the average man can in fact be met by a non-coercive liberal scheme, on the ground that the average man, not just the needy man, could not afford to pay for modern medicine individually, even if he had in his control all that part of his money which at present the state takes from him for general medical care. This assertion, if true, would be a knock-down argument against liberal humanitarianism. I shall not discuss it in detail, as it depends on economic rather than philosophical arguments. One point in its favour is that the distinction on which the liberal humanitarian scheme really rests, between being and not being too poor to buy necessities, does not apply to medical care even roughly, because one person's basic necessities in medical care may be vastly more expensive than another person's luxuries. There may therefore be those who, although quite well off, will not be able to afford, or even necessarily afford the premiums to cover, what is medically necessary for them. At best, then, a scheme which really meets people's needs will require state subsidies not merely for the poorest but also for the illest; and this is already a departure from the basic liberal humanitarian scheme. Apart from this, the question whether a private system would be cheap enough for the consumer depends on such things as the way in which, and scale on which, it is organized; the level of doctor's fees in such a system; and so on. I shall say a little on the latter question shortly.

The third criticism is that to have some people recipients of state aid when the majority are paying for themselves creates an unfortunately sharp division between haves and have-nots, the independent and the dependent, which is more blurred when all are in a state scheme. However strongly one might insist on the human right to medical care, those who are given it without paying, when others pay, will feel they are recipients of charity; and this feeling is damaging to self esteem, and embittering to those who cannot help their dependent position.

The fourth socialist criticism of liberal humanitarianism is the most important and the most baffling, since it combines many different strands. It can be expressed by saying that the scheme makes medical care a commercial matter, and this is unsuitable. But why might it be thought to be unsuitable? Medicine is not like love, which logically cannot be bought. People say here that it is wrong to "traffick in," or to "exploit," people's need. This description might, however, apply equally well to those who sell food, or any needed commodity, and no-one suggests that they are immoral; a butcher or baker meets a need and in doing so meets his own needs too. There is, all the same, a difference in the medical case, which means that what may be called market safeguards do not protect the patient as well as they do the ordinary consumer. In general, the consumer is not actually suffering, as distinct from needy, and also he understands something of what he is buying; so he can "shop around" and look for cheap goods and services. But a patient will not want to wait and will not know how to judge, so he can very easily be exploited. Nor would an agreed "professional fee" system improve his position; on the contrary, if such fees were fixed at an over-high rate (as is perhaps the case with lawyers now) he would have no chance of finding the most favourable price for medical care.

The liberal humanitarian can agree with all these views, but points out that they do not constitute a special difficulty for his scheme as opposed to a socialist one. Given the urgency with which medical care is needed, doctors can on a socialist scheme also blackmail the consumers (here society at large) to pay them too much, so that again everyone suffers. The patient, he will go on, is best safeguarded by a private system, which will at least leave some room for "shopping around"; apart from that he is protected by the compassion and goodwill of the majority of the profession.

Here, however, the socialist tends to retort that the market system implicit in the liberal humanitarian scheme is deficient precisely in that it leaves no room for compassion or goodwill. Those partaking in a market economy (he goes on) are in business to make a profit, and as large a one as possible, just as the consumer is trying to pay as little as possible: that is what the market is all about. Greed, then, rather than compassion, is the motive of the doctor in a liberal humanitarian scheme.

This socialist doctrine is, however, a muddle. It is true that what we may call a pure market transaction can be defined as one in which each party seeks to do as well as possible. But this is an artificial abstraction from actual practice, where what goes on might be a product of all kinds of forces; doctor and patient will both be governed by many non-market considerations in arriving at a fee. It is also true as a matter of fact that the doctor in commercial medicine must make enough to live on if he is to remain in business; so the bottom end of his scale is fixed. But there is no practical necessity for him to be a pure marketeer, trying to make the largest possible profit, and therefore no reason why his main motive should not be compassion just as much as if he had private means and worked for nothing. Nor does compassion for a person's sufferings entail refusal to take any money from him, any more than sympathy for a stranded motorist entails refusal to accept payment for a gallon of petrol. Of course a doctor in a *laissez-faire* system has a problem if his patients are too poor to pay enough even to support him. But in a liberal humanitarian system such patients are subsidized by the state.

I think then that the claim that medicine should not be a commercial matter cannot be sustained in its crude form. But there is nevertheless a difficulty about commercial medicine which arises less obviously in a socialist system: considerations of cost, rather than of need, will obtrude too much into the doctor's medical thinking. Of course the National Health Service doctor also is constantly being urged to economize. But if he thinks a certain expensive drug or treatment is needed for a patient, not merely useful or beneficial, he can go ahead. With a private patient, however, he will have to think all the time, "Can this patient afford it?" and this must be very inhibiting to the process of making a balanced decision on treatment.

THE SOCIALIST SYSTEM OF HEALTH CARE

The strengths of the socialist position will already have emerged to some extent through their criticisms of the liberal humanitarian: a socialist scheme can offer very large resources to any individual who needs expensive treatment, in a way which avoids both the stigma suffered by the involuntary noncontributor and the unfair advantages enjoyed by the negligent one. It is also said that a socialist scheme avoids the self-interested motivation of a commercial scheme. But as we have seen there is no need for doctors participating in a commercial scheme to do so out of self interest. Moreover, there is no reason why doctors, and patients, should not be self interested in a state scheme: patients wanting more than their share of attention, doctors wanting more and more money. No doubt the philosophy behind the socialist scheme is "from each according to his capacity, to each according to his need"—a kind of fraternal spirit. But there is nothing in the system to ensure that participants in fact see it this way. No doubt they can see their National Insurance contributions and taxes as benefiting the community rather than themselves; but then the liberal humanitarian can see his taxes in that way too.

It is also maintained in favour of a socialist system that it ensures equal treatment for equal needs. This unqualified claim is probably rather optimistic. On a socialist scheme influence, aggressiveness and articulateness will to some extent win more attention and care than is fair, just as money may do on a commercial scheme. But to claim an advantage over liberal humanitarianism on grounds of equality the socialist has only to show that his scheme has more equal results than the liberal alternative; and this he can probably do. The question does arise, however, what importance is to be attached to achieving equality if everyone's basic needs are met; it might be maintained that above the level of basic needs the demands of equality are rather controversial. The real issue, then, is whether a socialist system meets people's needs more satisfactorily than its rivals. We have seen that where a large expenditure for one person is concerned this may be the case. But many would maintain that a socialist system is necessarily too wasteful of resources to be able to give a satisfactory routine service to all, on the grounds that the removal of any need to pay at the time encourages over-extravagant use. How far this common charge is borne out in practice is a question for the sociologist rather than for the philosopher. But it should be noted that "unnecessary" calls upon the doctor's time are often due to ignorance rather than to selfishness: an educated person does not think of calling in a doctor for a cold or 'flu or bleeding nose, not because he is too public-spirited, but because he himself knows what to do. It should therefore be possible for the socialist to lessen abuses without needing the deterrent of payment, by educating the public rather more than doctors at present seem to be willing to do.

I suggest then that the socialist might be able to escape the charge that his system is necessarily inefficient. But there are two other charges that are perhaps even more serious: that a socialist scheme is an unwarranted infringement of liberty, and that it under-mines individual responsibility. The first charge is not so easy to maintain as some of those who make it seem to think. Obviously the scheme is a curtailment of liberty; but it would presumably be justified nevertheless if it promoted a great common good that could be achieved in no other way. The issue of liberty, then, is partly the issue of whether the alternative liberal humanitarian system is economically viable. But even if it were, we must still ask whether the unhappiness of those who are stigmatized under it is a price worth paying for retaining greater freedom. And to this there is no easy answer.

The second criticism is that socialized medicine undermines individual responsibility for health. On a socialist system, it may be said, the state takes over that responsibility for health care which under a private system the individual possesses: the need to plan how his health care (and that of his family) is to be paid for, and to decide his priorities accord-ingly. Why is this said to be a bad thing? Many reasons are advanced. One is that the individual will come to think that all aspects of health care are now looked after by Them, and so cease to "take responsibility" for those things which on any system only he can provide: a sensible diet, adequate sleep and so on. Whether this happens in fact is an empirical question; it seems to me likely that those people who do take this kind of respon-sibility for themselves are too individualistic to be affected one way or the other.

A second reason for criticising the removal of responsibility is that it trivializes the individual's concern for his life: the more the important areas of life are taken over by the government, the more people see their main business in life as the contriving of amuse-ments. Instead of thinking about health and education, they think about clothes and holi-days. Now this is perhaps a tendentious description of the situation: if one were to say that state control of the utilities of life gives people more chance to cultivate their talents and develop their personal relationships, to think about things worthwhile in themselves rather than merely useful, the argument against state control would be less clear. But perhaps most people's capacity to achieve the aristocratic ideal of leisure, as opposed to mere amusements, is limited; if so, it might in general be true that too much socialism leads people to give trivial things undue importance in life.

The third and most important argument advanced against this kind of removal of responsibility is the claim that it saps character. On a liberal humanitarian scheme people have to make decisions and live with the results of them, whereas on a socialist scheme decisions are taken out of their hands. The argument is that a person who does not have to make decisions cannot express his individuality, because it is in making one's own choices, different from anyone else's, that individuality is both shown and fostered; and moreover he loses his autonomy, the capacity for self-determination which makes him a person in the full sense.

The socialist can reply that these considerations apply unqualifiedly only when every area of life is governed by the state; the nationalization of some aspects of life—such as education, housing, health—leaves plenty of scope for individual choice and decision. He might admit that there is even so a measure of deterioration in character, but think it amply compensated for by the increased benefits; or he might take the line that there is no need to assume that people's characters suffer at all. But even if he is right in this latter claim about what actually happens, the liberal can object on moral grounds: even supposing that character remains intact in a socialist world, is it appropriate to treat adults as though they were like children, capable of deciding only unimportant matters? This is where the liberty and responsibility arguments coincide; liberty, it might be said, is liberty in the exercise of responsibility. Treating people properly involves respecting their liberty, or treating them as responsible creatures. But, as I said earlier, even the claims of liberty may have to bow to those of utility, or of humanity to those who would suffer under a libertarian scheme.

THE LIBERAL SOCIALIST VERSUS THE PURE SOCIALIST SYSTEMS OF HEALTH CARE

I come now to the final section of my discussion: the issue of pure *versus* liberal socialism. At present our own system is a liberal version, which allows those who wish and are able to do so to buy extra services on a private basis. Many people now advocate that this should be forbidden by law, and pure socialized medicine imposed. The issue is very complex. In Great Britain the question is whether people should be allowed to supplement the services they can get under the National Health Service. But there is also the possibility of a system whereby people can opt out of the National Health Service altogether. I cannot go into the pros and cons of this latter system. Again, even in Great Britain there are two separate questions: whether private medicine in state hospitals should be forbidden, and whether private medicine should be forbidden altogether. I shall not be able to distinguish between these two positions with the exactness which they really require. A further complexity is that the degree of extra service which is available for private purchase varies very much. I shall assume that it consists only of earlier appointments and more leisurely consultations with general practitioners and specialists, freer choice of specialist, prompter hospital treatment for non-emergencies and more privacy in hospital. Private treatment is not necessarily better in any respect other than these, and the degree to which it is better even in these will vary from place to place.

The usual argument concerns the right to private treatment. But I would suggest that for some people on some occasions private treatment may be not merely a right but a duty. Whatever the arguments against it, they can surely on occasion be morally outweighed, for those who can manage to afford private treatment, by obligations to others: the obligation to be restored to full health quickly and not be a drag on family or colleagues; the obligation to arrange a hospital stay at the least difficult time for family or colleagues; the obligation to continue working in hospital and to secure the privacy which makes this possible. The fact that not everyone can afford private medicine does not absolve those who can from this kind of duty. It would sometimes be true to say, contrary to the normal view, that a person who insisted on public medicine when he could afford private was being selfish and unpublic spirited.

Of course the usual defense of private medicine is in terms not of duties but of rights. People have a right, it is said, to spend their money on what they like: some, it is often added, spend their spare money on bingo or drinking, why should I not spend mine on health insurance? This is basically an appeal to liberty. The mention of those who spend their money on smoking or drinking is an attempt to add considerations of equality. It is salutary to be reminded that there are now a great many ordinary people who could afford private treatment if they gave it high priority. But there are still some who could not, and while this is so, a man cannot claim the right to buy private treatment merely on grounds of equality. What he has to say instead is, Why is it thought that people should be free to spend far more than the poorest can spend on every other kind of goods, but not on medical care?

One reply might be that people should not be free to spend unequally in any sphere: in other words, wealth should be redistributed equally. I have already refused to enter into discussion of this general question and suggested that what is uncontroversial and of paramount importance is the meeting of needs. But this is precisely why some people who are by no means egalitarians in general are against private medicine. The public system, they maintain, does not at present meet people's basic needs, especially their need of reasonably prompt treatment. The so-called "extras" which private medicine provides are on this view not mere luxuries but basic necessities, open to the rich but too expensive for the poor. Assertions that we are free to buy everything other than medical care are thus beside the point, insofar as there is no other basic necessity beyond the reach of the poorest.

If this account is true, there are some medical necessities which can at present be got only by paying extra. But it does not follow that everyone's basic needs will more nearly be met if no one is allowed to pay extra. It is said that private patients use up a disproportionate amount of scarce resources; if they were done away with, queues would shorten and beds would multiply. But the extra services they receive are surely small in comparison with the extra money they pay; in other words, they are subsidizing the other patients. Without their money, resources would therefore be scarcer and queues longer, especially as some doctors would leave the profession, or the country, if there were no private patients. I suggest then that private medicine is one of those inequalities which are justified in that everyone, including the worst off, benefits from them.

The sensitive individual may still feel reluctant to avail himself of private medicine, even if he is convinced that the National Health Service can do with his money. I think this is to do with a sense of the fraternity of suffering: a wish not to cut oneself off from fellowsufferers by having an easier time, even if one's easier time is of use to them. Such a feeling is certainly likeable, just as is a person's reluctance to eat his Christmas dinner when he thinks of those who are starving. But if I am right about the value of the private patient's contributions he should ignore his feelings on this matter.

In this long paper I have reached few conclusions. As always in real-life issues, the philosophical aspect is too intertwined with the empirical, and the empirical too elusive in any case, to permit any dogmatism. What I have hoped to do is simply to bring out some of the principles at issue in any discussion of the rights and wrongs of socialized medicine.[1]

QUESTIONS

1. Should a government have as one of its functions the positive function of furthering the welfare of its citizens?
2. Telfer argues *against* the following claim: "A socialist scheme is an unwarranted infringement of liberty which undermines individual responsibility." Can you offer any arguments *for* that claim?

[1]This paper owes much to the following: Acton, H B (1971). *The Morals of Markets* (London, Longman Group), especially chapters III and IV, and Barry, Brian (1965). *Political Argument* (London, Routledge and Kegan Paul), chapter VII.

JOEL FEINBERG

ECONOMIC INCOME AND SOCIAL JUSTICE

Joel Feinberg is professor of philosophy at the University of Arizona. He has published many articles in the fields of ethics, philosophy of law, and social philosophy. He is also the author of *Doing and Deserving* (1970), *Social Philosophy* (1973), and *Rights, Justice, and the Bounds of Liberty* (1980). His edited works include *Reason and Responsibility* (1965; 5th ed., 1981) and *Moral Concepts* (1969), and his coedited ones include *Philosophy of Law* (1975) and *Philosophy and the Human Condition* (1980).

Feinberg discusses five principles of economic justice: equality, need, merit and achievement, contribution or due return, and effort. His discussion focuses on just distribution within an affluent society having a surplus to distribute even after the most basic needs of all its citizens are met. He concludes that need, contribution, and effort have the most weight as determinants of economic justice. However, the latter two criteria are applicable only after the basic needs of all the members of society are satisfied.

The term "distributive justice" traditionally applied to burdens and benefits directly distributed by political authorities, such as appointed offices, welfare doles, taxes, and military conscription, but it has now come to apply also to goods and evils of a nonpolitical kind that can be distributed by private citizens to other private citizens. In fact, in most recent literature, the term is reserved for *economic* distributions, particularly the justice of differences in economic income between classes, and of various schemes of taxation which discriminate in different ways between classes. Further, the phrase can refer not only to acts of distributing but also to de facto states of affairs, such as the *fact that* at present "the five percent at the top get 20 percent [of our national wealth] while the 20 percent at the bottom get about five percent."[1] There is, of course, an ambiguity in the meaning of "distribution." The word may refer to the *process* of distributing, or the *product* of some process of distributing, and either or both of these can be appraised as just or unjust. In addition, a "distribution" can be understood to be a "product" which is *not* the result of any deliberate distributing process, but simply a state of affairs whose production has been too complicated to summarize or to ascribe to any definite group of persons as their deliberate doing. The present "distribution" of American wealth is just such a state of affairs.

Are the 5 percent of Americans "at the top" really different from the 20 percent "at the bottom" in any respect that would justicize the difference between their incomes? It is doubtful that there is any characteristic — relevant or irrelevant — common and peculiar to all members of either group. *Some* injustices, therefore, must surely exist. Perhaps there are some traits, however, that are more or less characteristic of the members of the privileged group, that make the current arrangements at least approximately just. What could (or should) those traits be? The answer will state a standard of relevance and a principle of material justice for questions of economic distributions, at least in relatively affluent societies like that of the United States.

At this point there appears to be no appeal possible except to *basic attitudes*, but even at this level we should avoid premature pessimism about the possibility of rational

[1] "T. R. B. from Washington" in *The New Republic*, Vol. CLX, No. 12 (March 22, 1969), p. 4
Joel Feinberg, *Social Philosophy*, © 1973, pp. 107–117. Reprinted by permission of Prentice-Hall, Inc., New Jersey.

agreement. Some answers to our question have been generally discredited, and if we can see why those answers are inadequate, we might discover some important clues to the properties any adequate answer must possess. Even philosophical adversaries with strongly opposed initial attitudes may hope to come to eventual agreement if they share *some* relevant beliefs and standards and a common commitment to consistency. Let us consider why we all agree (that is the author's assumption) in rejecting the view that differences in race, sex, IQ, or social "rank" are the grounds of just differences in wealth or income. Part of the answer seems obvious. People cannot by their own voluntary choices determine what skin color, sex, or IQ they shall have, or which hereditary caste they shall enter. To make such properties the basis of discrimination between individuals in the distribution of social benefits would be "to treat people differently in ways that profoundly affect their lives because of differences for which they have no responsibility."[2] Differences in a given respect are *relevant* for the aims of distributive justice, then, only if they are differences for which their possessors can be held responsible; properties can be the grounds of just discrimination between persons only if those persons had a *fair opportunity* to acquire or avoid them. Having rejected a number of material principles that clearly fail to satisfy the "fair opportunity" requirement, we are still left with as many as five candidates for our acceptance. (It is in theory open to us to accept two or more of these five as valid principles, there being no a priori necessity that the list be reduced to one.) These are: (1) the principle of perfect equality; (2) the principle[s] of need; (3) the principles of merit and achievement; (4) the principle of contribution (or due return); (5) the principle of effort (or labor). I shall discuss each of these briefly.

(i) EQUALITY

The principle of perfect equality obviously has a place in any adequate social ethic. Every human being is equally a human being, and . . . that minimal qualification entitles all human beings equally to certain absolute human rights: positive rights to noneconomic "goods" that by their very natures cannot be in short supply, negative rights not to be treated in cruel or inhuman ways, and negative rights not to be exploited or degraded even in "humane" ways. It is quite another thing, however, to make the minimal qualification of humanity the ground for an absolutely equal distribution of a country's *material wealth* among its citizens. A strict equalitarian could argue that he is merely applying Aristotle's formula of proportionate equality (presumably accepted by all parties to the dispute) with a criterion of relevance borrowed from the human rights theorists. Thus, distributive justice is accomplished between A and B when the following ratio is satisfied:

$$\frac{A\text{'s share of } P}{B\text{'s share of } P} = \frac{A\text{'s possession of } Q}{B\text{'s possession of } Q}$$

Where P stands for economic goods, Q must stand simply for "humanity" or "a human nature," and since every human being possesses *that* Q equally, it follows that all should also share a society's economic wealth (the P in question) equally.

The trouble with this argument is that its major premise is no less disputable than its conclusion. The standard of relevance it borrows from other contexts where it seems very little short of self-evident, seems controversial, at best, when applied to purely economic contexts. It seems evident to most of us that merely being human entitles *everyone*—bad

---

[2]W. K. Frankena, "Some Beliefs About Justice," *The Lindley Lecture,* Department of Philosophy Pamphlet (Lawrence: University of Kansas, 1966), p. 10.

men as well as good, lazy as well as industrious, inept as well as skilled — to a fair trial if charged with a crime, to equal protection of the law, to equal consideration of his interests by makers of national policy, to be spared torture or other cruel and inhuman treatment, and to be permanently ineligible for the status of chattel slave. Adding a right to an equal share of the economic pie, however, is to add a benefit of a wholly different order, one whose presence on the list of goods for which mere humanity is the sole qualifying condition is not likely to win wide assent without further argument.

It is far more plausible to posit a human right to the satisfaction of (better: to an opportunity to satisfy) one's *basic* economic needs, that is, to enough food and medicine to remain healthy, to minimal clothing, housing, and so on. As Hume pointed out,[3] even these rights cannot exist under conditions of extreme scarcity. Where there is not enough to go around, it cannot be true that everyone has a right to an equal share. But wherever there is moderate abundance or better — wherever a society produces more than enough to satisfy the *basic needs of everyone* — there it seems more plausible to say that mere possession of basic human needs qualifies a person for the opportunity to satisfy them. It would be a rare and calloused sense of justice that would not be offended by an affluent society, with a large annual agricultural surplus and a great abundance of manufactured goods, which permitted some of its citizens to die of starvation, exposure, or easily curable disease. It would certainly be *unfair* for a nation to produce more than it needs and not permit some of its citizens enough to satisfy their basic biological requirements. Strict equalitarianism, then, is a perfectly plausible material principle of distributive justice when confined to affluent societies and basic biological needs, but it loses plausibility when applied to division of the "surplus" left over after basic needs are met. To be sure, the greater the degree of affluence, the higher the level at which we might draw the line between "basic needs" and merely "wanted" benefits, and insofar as social institutions create "artificial needs," it is only fair that society provide all with the opportunity to satisfy them.[4] But once the line has been drawn between what is needed to live a minimally decent life by the realistic standards of a given time and place and what is only added "gravy," it is far from evident that justice still insists upon absolutely equal shares of the total. And it is evident that justice does not require strict equality wherever there is reason to think that unequal distribution causally determines greater production and is therefore in the interests of everyone, even those who receive the relatively smaller shares.

Still, there is no way to *refute* the strict equalitarian who requires exactly equal shares for everyone whenever that can be arranged without discouraging total productivity to the point where everyone loses. No one would insist upon equal distributions that would diminish the size of the total pie and thus leave smaller slices for *everyone*; that would be opposed to reason. John Rawls makes this condition part of his "rational principle" of justice: "Inequalities are arbitrary unless it is reasonable to expect that they will work out to everyone's advantage. . . ."[5] We are left then with a version of strict equalitarianism that is by no means evidently true and yet is impossible to refute. That is the theory that purports to apply not only to basic needs but to the total wealth of a society, and allows departures from strict equality when, *but only when*, they will work out to everyone's advantage. Although I am not persuaded by this theory, I think that any adequate material principle will have to attach great importance to keeping differences in wealth within rea-

[3]David Hume, *Enquiry Concerning the Principles of Morals* Part III (LaSalle, Ill.: The Open Court Publishing Company, 1947). Originally published in 1777.
[4]This point is well made by Katzner, "An Analysis of the Concept of Justice," pp. 173–203.
[5]John Rawls, "Justice as Fairness," *The Philosophical Review*, LXVII (1958), 165.

sonable limits, even after all basic needs have been met. One way of doing this would be to raise the standards for a "basic need" as total wealth goes up, so that differences between the richest and poorest citizens (even when there is no real "poverty") are kept within moderate limits.

(ii) NEED

The principle of need is subject to various interpretations, but in most of its forms it is not an independent principle at all, but only a way of mediating the application of the principle of equality. It can, therefore, be grouped with the principle of perfect equality as a member of the equalitarian family and contrasted with the principles of merit, achievement, contribution, and effort, which are all members of the nonequalitarian family. Consider some differences in "needs" as they bear on distributions. Doe is a bachelor with no dependents; Roe has a wife and six children. Roe must satisfy the needs of eight persons out of his paycheck, whereas Doe need satisfy the needs of only one. To give Roe and Doe equal pay would be to treat Doe's interests substantially *more* generously than those of anyone in the Roe family. Similarly, if a small private group is distributing food to its members (say a shipwrecked crew waiting rescue on a desert island), it would not be fair to give precisely the same quantity to a one hundred pounder as to a two hundred pounder, for that might be giving one person all he needs and the other only a fraction of what he needs—a difference in treatment not supported by any relevant difference between them. In short, to distribute goods in proportion to basic needs is not really to depart from a standard of equality, but rather to bring those with some greater initial burden or deficit up to the same level as their fellows.

The concept of a "need" is extremely elastic. In a general sense, to say that S needs X is to say simply that if he doesn't have X he will be harmed. A "basic need" would then be for an X in whose absence a person would be harmed in some crucial and fundamental way, such as suffering injury, malnutrition, illness, madness, or premature death. Thus we all have a basic need for foodstuffs of a certain quantity and variety, fuel to heat our dwellings, a roof over our heads, clothing to keep us warm, and so on. In a different but related sense of need, to say that S needs X is to say that without X he cannot achieve some specific purpose or perform some specific function. If they are to do their work, carpenters need tools, merchants need capital and customers, authors need paper and publishers. Some helpful goods are not strictly needed in this sense: an author with pencil and paper does not really need a typewriter to write a book, but he may need it to write a book speedily, efficiently, and conveniently. We sometimes come to rely upon "merely helpful but unneeded goods" to such a degree that we develop a strong habitual dependence on them, in which case (as it is often said) we have a "psychological" as opposed to a material need for them. If we don't possess that for which we have a strong psychological need, we may be unable to be happy, in which case a merely psychological need for a functional instrument may become a genuine need in the first sense distinguished above, namely, something whose absence is harmful to us. (Cutting across the distinction between material and psychological needs is that between "natural" and "artificial" needs, the former being those that can be expected to develop in any normal person, the latter being those that are manufactured or contrived, and somehow implanted in, or imposed upon, a person.) The more abundant a society's material goods, the higher the level at which we are required (by the force of psychological needs) to fix the distinction between "necessities" and "luxuries"; what *everyone* in a given society regards as "necessary" tends to become an actual, basic need.

(iii) MERIT AND ACHIEVEMENT

The remaining three candidates for material principles of distributive justice belong to the nonequalitarian family. These three principles would each distribute goods in accordance, not with need, but with *desert;* since persons obviously differ in their deserts, economic goods would be distributed unequally. The three principles differ from one another in their conceptions of the relevant *bases of desert* for economic distributions. The first is the principle of *merit.* Unlike the other principles in the nonequalitarian family, this one focuses not on what a person has *done* to deserve his allotment, but rather on what kind of person he is—what characteristics he has.

Two different types of characteristic might be considered meritorious in the appropriate sense: skills and virtues. Native skills and inherited aptitudes will not be appropriate desert bases, since they are forms of merit ruled out by the fair opportunity requirement. No one deserves credit or blame for his genetic inheritance, since no one has the opportunity to select his own genes. Acquired skills may seem more plausible candidates at first, but upon scrutiny they are little better. First, all acquired skills depend to a large degree on native skills. Nobody is born knowing how to read, so reading is an acquired skill, but actual differences in reading skill are to a large degree accounted for by genetic differences that are beyond anyone's control. Some of the differences are no doubt caused by differences in motivation afforded different children, but again the early conditions contributing to a child's motivation are also largely beyond his control. We may still have some differences in acquired skills that are to be accounted for solely or primarily by differences in the degree of practice, drill, and perseverance expended by persons with roughly equal opportunities. In respect to these, we can propitiate the requirement of fair opportunity, but only by nullifying the significance of acquired skill as such, for now skill is a relevant basis of desert only to the extent that it is a product of one's own effort. Hence, *effort* becomes the true basis of desert (as claimed by our fifth principle, discussed below), and not simply skill as such.

Those who would propose rewarding personal *virtues* with a larger than average share of the economic pie, and punishing defects of character with a smaller than average share, advocate assigning to the economic system a task normally done (if it is done at all) by noneconomic institutions. What they propose, in effect, is that we use retributive criteria of distributive justice. Our criminal law, for a variety of good reasons, does not purport to punish people for what they are, but only for what they do. A man can be as arrogant, rude, selfish, cruel, insensitive, irresponsible, cowardly, lazy, or disloyal as he wishes; unless he *does* something prohibited by the criminal law, he will not be made to suffer legal punishment. At least one of the legal system's reasons for refusing to penalize character flaws as such would also explain why such defects should not be listed as relevant differences in a material principle of distributive justice. The apparatus for detecting such flaws (a "moral police"?) would be enormously cumbersome and impractical, and its methods so uncertain and fallible that none of us could feel safe in entrusting the determination of our material allotments to it. We could, of course, give roughly equal shares to all except those few who have *outstanding* virtues—gentleness, kindness, courage, diligence, reliability, warmth, charm, considerateness, generosity. Perhaps these are traits that deserve to be rewarded, but it is doubtful that larger economic allotments are the appropriate vehicles of rewarding. As Benn and Peters remind us, "there are some sorts of 'worth' for which rewards in terms of income seem inappropriate. Great courage in battle is recognized by medals, not by increased pay."[6] Indeed, there is something repugnant, as Socrates and the Stoics insisted,

---

[6]Benn and Peters, *Social Principles and the Democratic State,* p. 139.

in paying a man to be virtuous. Moreover, the rewards would offer a pecuniary motive for certain forms of excellence that require motives of a different kind, and would thus tend to be self-defeating.

The most plausible nonequalitarian theories are those that locate relevance not in meritorious traits and excellences of any kind, but rather in prior doings: not in what one is, but in what one has done. Actions, too, are sometimes called "meritorious," so there is no impropriety in denominating the remaining families of principles in our survey as "meritarian." One type of action-oriented meritarian might cite *achievement* as a relevant desert basis for pecuniary rewards, so that departures from equality in income are to be justicized only by distinguished achievements in science, art, philosophy, music, athletics, and other basic areas of human activity. The attractions and disadvantages of this theory are similar to those of theories which I rejected above that base rewards on skills and virtues. Not all persons have a fair opportunity to achieve great things, and economic rewards seem inappropriate as vehicles for expressing recognition and admiration of noneconomic achievements.

(iv) CONTRIBUTION OR "DUE RETURN"

When the achievements under consideration are themselves contributions to our general economic well-being, the meritarian principle of distributive justice is much more plausible. Often it is conjoined with an economic theory that purports to determine exactly what percentage of our total economic product a given worker or class has produced. Justice, according to this principle, requires that each worker get back exactly that proportion of the national wealth that he has himself created. This sounds very much like a principle of "commutative justice" directing us to *give back* to every worker what is really his own property, that is, the product of his own labor.

The French socialist writer and precursor of Karl Marx, Pierre Joseph Proudhon (1809–1865), is perhaps the classic example of this kind of theorist. In his book *What Is Property?* (1840), Proudhon rejects the standard socialist slogan, "From each according to his ability, to each according to his needs,"[7] in favor of a principle of distributive justice based on contribution, as interpreted by an economic theory that employed a pre-Marxist "theory of surplus value." The famous socialist slogan was not intended, in any case, to express a principle of distributive justice. It was understood to be a rejection of all considerations of "mere" justice for an ethic of human brotherhood. The early socialists thought it unfair, in a way, to give the great contributors to our wealth a disproportionately small share of the product. But in the new socialist society, love of neighbor, community spirit, and absence of avarice would overwhelm such bourgeois notions and put them in their proper (subordinate) place.

Proudhon, on the other hand, based his whole social philosophy not on brotherhood (an ideal he found suitable only for small groups such as families) but on the kind of distributive justice to which even some capitalists gave lip service:

> The key concept was "mutuality" or "reciprocity." "Mutuality, reciprocity exists," he wrote, "when all the workers in an industry, instead of working for an entrepreneur who pays them and keeps their prod-

---

[7]Traced to Louis Blanc. For a clear brief exposition of Proudhon's view which contrasts it with that of other early socialists and also that of Karl Marx, see Robert Tucker's "Marx and Distributive Justice," in *Nomos VI: Justice*, ed. C. J. Friedrich and J. W. Chapman (NewYork: Aldine-Atherton Press, 1963), pp. 306–25.

ucts, work for one another and thus collaborate in the making of a common product whose profits they share among themselves."[8]

Proudhon's celebrated dictum that "property is theft" did not imply that all *possession* of goods is illicit, but rather that the system of rules that permitted the owner of a factory to hire workers and draw profits ("surplus value") from *their* labor robs the workers of what is rightly theirs. "This profit, consisting of a portion of the proceeds of labor that rightfully belonged to the laborer himself, was 'theft.'"[9] The injustice of capitalism, according to Proudhon, consists in the fact that those who create the wealth (through their labor) get only a small part of what they create, whereas those who "exploit" their labor, like voracious parasites, gather in a greatly disproportionate share. The "return of contribution" principle of distributive justice, then, cannot work in a capitalist system, but requires a *fédération mutualiste* of autonomous producer-cooperatives in which those who create wealth by their work share it in proportion to their real contributions.

Other theorists, employing different notions of what produces or "creates" economic wealth, have used the "return of contribution" principle to support quite opposite conclusions. The contribution principle has even been used to justicize quite unequalitarian capitalistic status quos, for it is said that capital as well as labor creates wealth, as do ingenious ideas, inventions, and adventurous risk-taking. The capitalist who provided the money, the inventor who designed a product to be manufactured, the innovator who thought of a new mode of production and marketing, the advertiser who persuaded millions of customers to buy the finished product, the investor who risked his savings on the success of the enterprise — these are the ones, it is said, who did the most to produce the wealth created by a business, not the workers who contributed only their labor, and of course, these are the ones who tend, on the whole, to receive the largest personal incomes.

Without begging any narrow and technical questions of economics, I should express my general skepticism concerning such facile generalizations about the comparative degrees to which various individuals have contributed to our social wealth. Not only are there impossibly difficult problems of measurement involved, there are also conceptual problems that appear beyond all nonarbitrary solution. I refer to the elements of luck and chance, the social factors not attributable to any assignable individuals, and the contributions of population trends, uncreated natural resources, and the efforts of people now dead, which are often central to the explanation of any given increment of social wealth.

The difficulties of separating out causal factors in the production of social wealth might influence the partisan of the "return of contribution" principle in either or both of two ways. He might become very cautious in his application of the principle, requiring that deviations from average shares be restricted to very clear and demonstrable instances of unusually great or small contributions. But the moral that L. T. Hobhouse[10] drew from these difficulties is that *any* individual contribution will be very small relative to the immeasurably great contribution made by political, social, fortuitous, natural, and "inherited" factors. In particular, strict application of the "return of contribution" principle would tend to support a larger claim for the *community* to its own "due return," through taxation and other devices.

In a way, the principle of contribution is not a principle of mere *desert* at all, no

---

[8]Tucker, "Marx and Distributive Justice," p. 310.
[9]Tucker, "Marx and Distributive Justice," p. 311.
[10]L. T. Hobhouse, *The Elements of Social Justice* (London: George Allen and Unwin Ltd., 1922). See especially pp. 161–63.

matter how applied. As mentioned above, it resembles a principle of commutative justice requiring repayment of debts, return of borrowed items, or compensation for wrongly inflicted damages. If I lend you my car on the understanding that you will take good care of it and soon return it, or if you steal it, or damage it, it will be too *weak* to say that I "deserve" to have my own car, intact, back from you. After all, the car is *mine* or my due, and questions of ownership are not settled by examination of deserts; neither are considerations of ownership and obligation commonly outbalanced by considerations of desert. It is not merely "unfitting" or "inappropriate" that I should not have my own or my due; it is downright *theft* to withhold it from me. So the return of contribution is not merely a matter of merit deserving reward. It is a matter of a maker demanding that which he has created and is thus properly his. The ratio—A's share of X is to B's share of X as A's contribution to X is to B's contribution to X—appears, therefore, to be a very strong and plausible principle of distributive justice, whose main deficiencies, when applied to economic distributions, are of a practical (though severe) kind. If Hobhouse is right in claiming that there are social factors in even the most pronounced individual contributions to social wealth, then the principle of due return serves as a moral basis in support of taxation and other public claims to private goods. In any case, if A's contribution, though apparently much greater than B's, is nevertheless only the tiniest percentage of the total contribution to X (whatever that may mean and however it is to be determined), it may seem like the meanest quibbling to distinguish very seriously between A and B at all.

(v) EFFORT

The principle of due return, as a material principle of distributive justice, does have some vulnerability to the fair opportunity requirement. Given unavoidable variations in genetic endowments and material circumstances, different persons cannot have precisely the same opportunities to make contributions to the public weal. Our final candidate for the status of a material principle of distributive justice, the *principle of effort,* does much better in this respect, for it would distribute economic products not in proportion to successful achievement but according to the degree of effort exerted. According to the principle of effort, justice decrees that hard-working executives and hard-working laborers receive precisely the same remuneration (although there may be reasons having nothing to do with justice for paying more to the executives), and that freeloaders be penalized by allotments of proportionately lesser shares of the joint products of everyone's labor. The most persuasive argument for this principle is that it is the closest approximation to the intuitively valid principle of due return that can pass the fair opportunity requirement. It is doubtful, however, that even the principle of effort fully satisfies the requirements of fair opportunity, since those who inherit or acquire certain kinds of handicap may have little opportunity to *acquire the motivation* even to do their best. In any event, the principle of effort does seem to have intuitive cogency giving it at least some weight as a factor determining the justice of distributions.

In very tentative conclusion, it seems that the principle of equality (in the version that rests on needs rather than that which requires "perfect equality") and the principles of contribution and effort (where nonarbitrarily applicable, and only *after* everyone's basic needs have been satisfied) have the most weight as determinants of economic justice, whereas all forms of the principle of merit are implausible in that role. The reason for the priority of basic needs is that, where there is economic abundance, the claim to life itself and to minimally decent conditions are, like other human rights, claims that all men make with perfect equality. As economic production increases, these claims are given ever greater consideration in the form of rising standards for distinguishing basic needs from other wanted goods. But no matter where that line is drawn, when we go beyond it into the realm of economic surplus or "luxuries," nonequalitarian considerations (especially contribution and effort) come increasingly into play.

QUESTIONS

1. Assume that a society cannot meet even the most basic needs of *all* its citizens, such as the need for food and rudimentary shelter. Should that society adopt a system of distribution which would deny some the necessities of life to ensure the survival of the others?

2. Imagine a society in which all the economic benefits are distributed *solely* on the basis of the contributions made by individuals to the good of that society. Could such a society be an economically just society?

SUGGESTED ADDITIONAL READINGS

ARTHUR, JOHN, and WILLIAM SHAW, eds.: *Justice and Economic Distribution.* Englewood Cliffs, N.J.: Prentice-Hall, 1978. This collection of articles epitomizes the dominant current approach to distributive justice. That approach is highly abstract, pays little attention to practical applications, and is usually restricted to the intra-national level. The theories which dominate current discussion are those of John Rawls, Robert Nozick, and utilitarianism. The first part of the book presents selections by Rawls, Nozick, and utilitarians. The second part consists of selections which present positions offered in opposition to the dominant theories.

FEINBERG, JOEL: *Social Philosophy.* Englewood Cliffs, N.J.: Prentice-Hall, 1973. In Chapter 7 of this book, titled "Social Justice," Feinberg discusses in some detail formal and material principles of justice.

FREIDMAN, MILTON: *Capitalism and Freedom.* Chicago: University of Chicago Press, 1962. For Friedman, an economist and libertarian, the ethical principle governing the distribution of income in a free society is "to each according to what he or the instruments he owns produces." He sees economic freedom as a necessary condition for political freedom.

HAYEK, F. A.: *Law, Legislation and Liberty.* Vol. 2, *The Mirage of Social Justice.* Chicago: University of Chicago Press, 1976. Hayek, a libertarian, considers and criticizes the concept of "social justice." On Hayek's view the ideal of social justice (1) has no meaning, (2) is the harmful and dangerous cause of the misdirection of well-meant efforts, and (3) is a remnant of a closed society and incompatible with the individual freedom promised by an open society.

HELD, VIRGINIA, ed.: *Property, Profits, and Economic Justice.* Belmont, Calif.: Wadsworth, 1980. This is an excellent collection of readings centering on questions about our rights and interests in acquiring and holding property and in increasing or limiting profits.

NOZICK, ROBERT: *Anarchy, State, and Utopia.* New York: Basic Books, 1974. This book has engendered a great deal of discussion among philosophers concerned with distributive justice. Nozick, who endorses the libertarian conception of justice, holds the libertarian ideal to be exemplified by the principle, "from each as he chooses, to each as he is chosen."

RAWLS, JOHN: "Justice as Fairness." *Philosophical Review,* vol. 67, April 1958, pp. 164–194. In this article, Rawls offers a definition of justice in terms of two principles which he maintains all rational, self-interested persons would agree are in the equal interests of all. He argues (1) that everyone has the right to equal liberty, and (2) that differences of wealth and privilege are justified only if everyone is free to compete for them and if everyone benefits from them.

————: *A Theory of Justice.* Cambridge, Mass.: Harvard University Press, 1971. This is a more developed discussion of the position Rawls presents in the above article. It is a seminal work which has stimulated a great deal of discussion among philosophers.

RESCHER, NICHOLAS: *Distributive Justice.* Indianapolis: Bobbs-Merrill, 1966. Rescher discusses and critiques the utilitarian approach to distributive justice. Although difficult in parts, the book offers a useful discussion of the problems of distributive justice (Chapter 1) and the principles of distributive justice (Chapter 4). It also includes an extensive bibliography devoted solely to the problems of distributive justice (pp. 153–155).

STEINER, HILLEL: "The Just Provision of Health Care: A Reply to Elizabeth Telfer." *Journal of Medical Ethics,* vol. 2, 1976, pp. 185–189. Steiner examines the four positions offered by Elizabeth Telfer in the article reprinted in this chapter. He criticizes Telfer, and argues for a fifth position which incorporates the important elements of Telfer's two extreme positions—the laissez faire and pure socialist approaches to health care delivery. A brief reply by Telfer follows Steiner's article.

STERBA, JAMES P., ed.: *Justice: Alternative Political Perspectives.* Belmont, Calif.: Wadsworth, 1980. This book is divided into four major sections: (1) "The Concept of Justice"; (2) "Liberal Justice" (this includes defenses and critiques of both the contractual and utilitarian traditions); (3) "Libertarian Justice: Defenses and a Critique"; and (4) "Socialist Justice: Defenses and a Critique."

THUROW, LESTER: *The Zero Sum Society.* New York: Basic Books, 1980. Thurow, a professor of economics and management, analyzes the unprecedented economic predicament presently confronting the United States and discusses various policy prescriptions designed to solve our economic problems. In Thurow's view, the government must be willing to make equity decisions designed to achieve and maintain a just distribution of income.

VEATCH, ROBERT M., and ROY BRANSON, eds.: *Ethics and Health Policy.* Cambridge, Mass.: Ballinger, 1976. Included in this collection of articles are several dealing with justice and health care delivery. Those interested in John Rawls's theory of distributive justice will be especially interested in the article by Ronald M. Green, "Health Care and Justice in Contract Theory Perspective."

WORLD HUNGER

10

Widespread world hunger is an undeniable fact. Famines in Africa and Southeast Asia are commonplace. For many in places like Zaire, Haiti, Colombia, and Algeria malnutrition is an everyday fact of life. Very few of the victims of famine and malnutrition actually "die of hunger"; but they die of illnesses, such as flu and intestinal problems, which they could have survived if they had not been weakened by hunger. The victims are often very old or very young. Aftereffects for those who survive are often tragic and long-lasting. A large number of children are stunted in growth and suffer incapacitating brain damage as a result of malnutrition. Whole populations are permanently weakened, listless, and lethargic, lacking the energy for any economic advances which might help prevent future famines. What does morality dictate that affluent countries (or their people) *should* do to prevent such devastating hunger and malnutrition? What *can* they do? This chapter presents some recent attempts to answer these two inseparable questions. As the readings show, answers concerning the moral *obligations* of more affluent individuals and nations in regard to world hunger are intertwined with answers concerning the *causes of world hunger* and *effective ways of eliminating those causes.*

NEO-MALTHUSIANISM

One answer regarding the causes of world hunger is offered by people labeled "Neo-Malthusians." Following Thomas Robert Malthus (1766–1834), they identify the cause as *overpopulation.* For Malthus, unrestricted population growth necessarily outstrips economic growth, especially the growth in food supplies. This, in turn, *necessarily* results in famines. Uncontrolled fertility is the cause of poverty, and poverty is the cause of the miseries of the poor, including starvation. It has been shown that Malthus was wrong in certain respects, since in many countries the economic growth rate, including the growth in food supplies, has far outstripped the population growth rate. But contemporary Neo-Malthusians hold that the economic growth rate cannot be sustained. They offer different reasons in support of this view (e.g., political or technical ones), but they all agree that continued economic growth is impossible. Having identified overpopulation as *the cause* of scarcity, Neo-Malthusians locate the solution to problems of world hunger in population control. Optimistic Neo-Malthusians hold that birth-control measures can eventually succeed in curbing population growth sufficiently to avert future famines. Pessimistic Neo-Malthusians hold that serious political and psychological obstacles to planned population-control measures make famines inevitable in some countries. They predict that these famines will in turn effectively curb unmaintainable population growth unless those in more affluent countries intervene. Some pessimistic Neo-Malthusians, including Garrett Hardin in this chapter, use their Malthusian analyses of world hunger to support claims about what more affluent individuals and nations *ought* to do regarding the needs of potential famine victims. The expressions "ethics of triage" and "lifeboat ethics" are often applied to the ethical approaches advocated by pessimistic Neo-Malthusians.

The expression "method of triage" was first used to describe the French approach to their wounded in the First World War. The wounded were sorted into three categories. Those with the slightest injuries were given quick first aid. Those who could not be helped were simply allowed to die. Those in between received the most intensive medical care. Analogously, applying the method of triage to world food problems involves a three-way classification of countries/societies: (1) those which will survive even without aid; (2) those with serious food and population problems which will nevertheless survive if given enough aid because they are prepared to take the measures necessary to bring their food resources and populations into line—these ought to be given the necessary aid; (3) those whose problems are insoluble in the long run because they are not willing to adopt the necessary population-control measures—according to the ethics of triage, this last group should receive no help. Thus, the proponents of the ethics of triage argue that the affluent should help only those potential victims of famine and malnutrition who reside in countries which are effectively trying to bring population size into line with the country's food supply.[1]

The argument for the moral correctness of the ethics of triage is a consequentialist one and depends on the correctness of the following factual claim: Economic aid to countries with long-run "insoluble" problems is only a stopgap measure which in the long run will have highly undesirable consequences. Aid to societies in group 3, it is said, may alleviate current suffering, but it will cause more long-term suffering for the members of both the needy and affluent countries. Suffering will increase because economic aid will enable more people to survive and reproduce. If no real attempt is made to control population growth, the ever-increasing population will make ever-increasing demands on the world food supply. These demands will have a strong adverse effect on the quality of the life led by future members of today's more affluent societies. In time, it will be impossible even for the members of the once affluent countries to survive. If help is withheld from the countries in group 3, however, one of two things will follow. Either the needy countries will instigate measures to limit their populations in keeping with their own resources, or else nature itself through famine and disease will decimate the population to the appropriate level. In effect, those who argue in this way maintain that responsibilities and rights go hand in hand. People in the afflicted societies cause their own problems by having too many children. They are entitled to have their most basic needs met by more affluent individuals and societies only if they accept a crucial responsibility—the responsibility for limiting their fertility sufficiently so that they do not continue to place an ever-growing burden on the world's food resources.

Garrett Hardin's lifeboat-ethics argument echoes some of the major contentions of the ethics of triage. Comparing nations to boats, Hardin maintains that many countries have outstripped their "carrying capacity." He advances a consequentialist argument to support his claim that the affluent *ought not* to help those in the overpopulating countries. In Hardin's view, the long-range effects of food aid will not only be harmful but disastrous for everyone. They will be disastrous for countries whose fertility rates remain uncontrolled by either human planning or nature, since future generations in these countries will suffer massive starvation and profound misery. They will be disastrous for the human species as a whole, since the eventual outcome may be the elimination of the species. Hardin sees no real need to use the method of triage in making decisions about which countries should be given aid. If giving food to *any* overpopulated country does more harm than good, he argues, that food should not be given. For Hardin, "the question of triage does not even arise."[2]

NON-MALTHUSIAN ALTERNATIVES
Criticisms of Neo-Malthusianism take many forms. Some critics, for example, attack the *moral* claims of pessimistic Neo-Malthusians. Rejecting the consequentialist approach to

[1]See especially Paul and William Paddock, *Famine—1975!* (Boston: Little, Brown, 1968).
[2]Garrett Hardin, "Carrying Capacity as an Ethical Concept," in George R. Lucas, Jr., and Thomas W. Ogletree, eds., *Lifeboat Ethics* (New York: Harper & Row, 1976), p. 131.

the moral dilemma, they maintain that no matter what the long-term consequences might be, we have an obligation to meet the most basic need of *existing* persons — the need for food. The most prominent attacks against Malthusianism, however, center around rejections of some or all of the Malthusian claims regarding the causes and/or the inevitability of famine and malnutrition in needy, developing countries. The counter-analyses offered reject the Neo-Malthusian contention that the necessary economic growth is impossible. On these analyses, economic growth in the developing countries *themselves* is both possible and an essential part of the solution to problems of world hunger. Two major lines of argument emerge in these counter-analyses.

The first counter-analysis, exemplified by some of the arguments offered by William Murdoch and Allan Oaten in this chapter, focuses on identifying the causes of high fertility rates among the poor in developing countries. Only if we understand why the poor have high rates of reproduction can we help to instigate and support social practices which will tend to end the cycle of poverty, high birth rates, and starvation which Neo-Malthusians see as inevitable. Against the pessimistic Neo-Malthusians, proponents of this analysis argue that famines and malnutrition are not inevitable. Against the optimistic Neo-Malthusians, they argue that planned birth-control practices backed by government policies are not the solution. Ironically, the major factors influencing high fertility rates are identified as hunger and poverty. The Presidential Commission on World Hunger makes the point succinctly:

> Where hunger and poverty prevail, the population growth rate is more likely to increase than to decrease. Under inequitable social and economic conditions, a poor couple's desire for many children is a response to high infant mortality, the need for extra hands to help earn the family's daily bread, and the hope of support in old age. The key to reducing family size is to improve the social conditions which make large families a reasonable option.[3]

On this analysis, the eradication of famine and malnutrition would require social and economic changes in the developing countries themselves, changes which would eliminate some of the gross inequalities of wealth and property in these countries. Without the recommended changes, it is argued, economic growth, including growth in the food supply, will not take place, population growth will not be slowed, and the tragic cycle will be repeated indefinitely.

Some of those who utilize this first approach against Neo-Malthusians argue that the practices of members of more affluent nations prevent some of the poorest countries from increasing their own food supply. The identified culprits include multinational agribusinesses based in Western societies. It is charged that these multinationals have shifted the production of luxury items for the Western market from the highly industrialized countries to underdeveloped ones where cheap land and labor are available. As a result, the land in needy, underdeveloped countries is used to produce goods for members of the more affluent countries, while the food that is needed for the home market remains unproduced. In addition, it is argued that the international economic order favors the affluent, industrialized nations and is shaped by their needs. It is the affluent, industrialized societies which largely determine the prices for both the manufactured goods which developing nations must import and the agricultural products which the needy countries export. To the extent that the practices of those in affluent societies work against the potential self-sufficiency and real economic growth of the developing countries, they help create and perpetuate the cycle of poverty, high fertility rates, and hunger.

---

[3]The Presidential Commission on World Hunger, *Overcoming World Hunger: The Challenge Ahead* (1980), p. 26.

The second counter-analysis against Neo-Malthusianism comes from Marxist-socialists and incorporates some of the elements of the first counter-analysis. Marxist-socialists reject both the contention that overpopulation is the cause of scarcity in the world and the contention that the requisite economic growth is impossible. They identify capitalism as the major cause of worldwide scarcity. Agreeing with the kinds of claims just discussed concerning the negative impact of multinational corporations on the economic growth of developing countries, they see a Marxist-socialist economic system as the only solution to the problem of world hunger. Howard L. Parsons's article in this chapter exemplifies the Marxist-socialist position.

WHAT OUGHT WE TO DO?

What ought we as individuals to do in regard to potential and actual famine victims? As the above discussion shows, the answers for each of us may depend on what we take to be a correct analysis of the causes of famine and malnutrition in the world. But if we prescind from the kind of factual questions discussed above, we can still ask questions about the basis of *any* possible moral obligation that we as individuals might have to prevent starvation and malnutrition among the needy. Peter Singer in this chapter attempts to establish a foundation for such a moral obligation on the general principle, "Persons are morally required to prevent something bad from happening if they can do so without sacrificing anything of comparable moral significance." In his view, even a weaker version of this principle is sufficient to establish a moral obligation to aid the victims of severe famines. Other ethicists rely on one or more of the principles of economic justice discussed in the introduction to Chapter 9. Some, for example, extend claims based on the principle of need in conjunction with the principle of equal sharing to the international level. They maintain that all human beings, just because they are human beings, are entitled to equal treatment in some important respects; they are entitled, for example, to have at least their most basic needs, such as their need for food, met by other human beings who have more than enough to meet their own needs.

Jane S. Zembaty

THE PRESIDENTIAL COMMISSION ON WORLD HUNGER

WHY SHOULD THE UNITED STATES BE CONCERNED?

In 1978 President Jimmy Carter appointed a Presidential Commission on World Hunger, chaired by Ambassador Sol Linowitz. It included Dr. Jean Mayer, Dr. Stephen Muller, Dr. Norman Borlaug, David W. Brooks, Harry Chapin, John Denver, Senator Robert Dole, Dr. Walter P. Falcon, Orville Freeman, Representative Benjamin Gilman, Senator Patrick Leahy, Bess Myerson, Representative Richard Nolan, Dr. Howard A. Schneider, Dr. Adele Smith Simmons, Raymond Singletary Jr., Dr. Eugene L. Stockwell, Dr. Clifford Wharton, Mr. Thomas H. Wyman, and Daniel E. Shaughnessy. The Commission was charged with the following tasks: (1) to identify the basic causes of domestic and international hunger and malnutrition; (2) to assess past and present national programs and policies that affect hunger and malnutrition; (3) to review existing studies and research on hunger; (4) to recommend to the President and Congress specific actions to create a coherent national food and hunger policy; and (5) to help implement those recommendations and focus public attention on food and hunger issues. The selection appearing here is excerpted from the Commission's final report, *Overcoming World Hunger: The Challenge Ahead.*

The Commission's major recommendation is that the elimination of hunger should be the primary focus of the United States Government in its relationship with developing countries. In support of its recommendations the Commission offers the following reasons: (1) The moral obligation to overcome hunger, based on two universal values—respect for human dignity and social justice; (2) the dependence of national security on the economic well-being of the developing countries; and (3) the dependence of the economic vitality of the United States on a healthy international economy.

The major recommendation of the Presidential Commission on World Hunger is that the United States make the elimination of hunger the primary focus of its relations with the developing world—with all that implies for U.S. policy toward development assistance, trade, foreign investment and foreign affairs. In the Commission's view, there are significant reasons for the United States to place the elimination of hunger at the top of its list of global concerns.

MORAL OBLIGATION AND RESPONSIBILITY

Moral obligation alone would justify giving highest priority to the task of overcoming hunger. Even now, millions of human beings live on the edge of starvation—in conditions of subhuman poverty that, if we think about them at all, must fill us with shame and horror. We see this now most poignantly in famine conditions, but it is a fact of life every day for half a billion people. At least one out of every eight men, women and children on earth suffers malnutrition severe enough to shorten life, stunt physical growth, and dull mental ability.

Whether one speaks of human rights or basic human needs, the right to food is the most basic of all. Unless that right is first fulfilled, the protection of other human rights becomes a mockery for those who must spend all their energy merely to maintain life itself. The correct moral and ethical position on hunger is beyond debate. The major world religions and philosophical systems share two universal values: respect for human dignity and a sense of social justice. Hunger is the ultimate affront to both. Unless all governments begin now to act upon their rhetorical commitments to ending hunger, the principle that human life is sacred, which forms the very underpinnings of human society, will gradually but relentlessly erode. By concentrating its international efforts on the elimination of hunger, the United States would provide the strongest possible demonstration of its renewed dedication to the cause of human rights.

Moral obligation includes responsibility. In the Commission's view, the United States has a special capability and hence a special responsibility to lead the campaign against world hunger. The United States is by far the most powerful member of the world's increasingly interdependent food system. It harvests more than half the grain that crosses international borders. Its corporations dominate world grain trade. Its grain reserves are the largest on earth. Because of its agricultural productivity, its advanced food technology, and

Reprinted from *Overcoming World Hunger: The Challenge Ahead* (Washinton, D.C.: Government Printing Office, 1980).

its market power, the United States inevitably exerts a major influence on all aspects of the international food system.

Global interdependence in food means that two straight years of bad harvests in any of the major grain-producing nations of the world could precipitate another global food crisis like the one that occurred in 1972-74. Recurrent crises of this nature could bring widespread famine and political disorder to the developing countries and would severely disrupt a fragile world economy already weakened by energy shortages and rampant inflation. U.S. policies will have a major role in determining whether or not this scenario will be played out.

American policies and resources also hold the key to solving that continuing world food crisis embodied in the swelling ranks of the chronically malnourished. To these hungry millions, it makes no difference whether such policies are made by choice or inertia, by acts of commission or acts of omission. In view of the undeniable influence that this nation's actions will have on world hunger, the Commission urges immediate yet careful long-range planning to assure that U.S. policy truly helps rather than harms the world's hungry people. Delay will only make the same ends more difficult and expensive to accomplish, and will not lift responsibility from the United States.

The Commission does not mean to imply that the United States alone can solve the world hunger problem. All nations, including those of the developing world, must make the conquest of hunger a common cause. However, the Commission is persuaded that unless the United States plays a major role by increasing its own commitment and action toward this goal, no effective and comprehensive global program to combat hunger is likely to be undertaken in the foreseeable future. Moreover, once its own commitment is clear, the United States will be in a particularly strong position to encourage others to do more. The Commission believes that the United States is uniquely situated to influence the fate of millions who do not get enough to eat.

NATIONAL SECURITY

The Commission believes that promoting economic development in general, and overcoming hunger in particular, are tasks far more critical to the U.S. national security than most policymakers acknowledge or even believe. Since the advent of nuclear weapons most Americans have been conditioned to equate national security with the strength of strategic military forces. The Commission considers this prevailing belief to be a simplistic illusion. Armed might represents merely the physical aspect of national security. Military force is ultimately useless in the absence of the global security that only coordinated international progress toward social justice can bring. . . .

ECONOMIC INTEREST

The Commission also finds compelling economic reasons for the United States to focus on the elimination of hunger. The United States can maintain its own economic vitality only within a healthy international economy whose overall strength will increase as each of its component parts becomes more productive, more equitable and more internationally competitive. To sustain a healthy global economy, the purchasing power of today's poor people must rise substantially, in order to set in motion that mutually reinforcing exchange of goods, services and commodities which provides the foundation for viable economic partnership and growth. . . .

[Thus we conclude that there] are compelling moral, economic and national security reasons for the United States Government to make the elimination of hunger the central focus of its relations with the developing world. . . .

QUESTIONS

1. According to the Commission, there are compelling *economic* reasons for the United States to focus on the elimination of hunger in its relations with developing countries. If this is correct, what evidence can be given to support it?

2. It has been said that the United States cannot solve the problem of world hunger; it *is* the problem. What reasons could be offered to support such a contention?

PETER SINGER

FAMINE, AFFLUENCE, AND MORALITY

A biographical sketch of Peter Singer is found on p. 163.

Singer expresses concern over the fact that while members of the more affluent nations spend money on trivia, people in the needier nations are starving. He argues that it is morally wrong not to prevent suffering whenever one can do so without sacrificing anything morally significant. Giving aid to the victims of famine can prevent such suffering. Even if such giving requires a drastic reduction in the standard of living of the members of the more affluent societies, the latter are morally required to meet at least the basic need for food of people who will otherwise starve to death.

As I write this, in November 1971, people are dying in East Bengal from lack of food, shelter, and medical care. The suffering and death that are occurring there now are not inevitable, not unavoidable in any fatalistic sense of the term. Constant poverty, a cyclone, and a civil war have turned at least nine million people into destitute refugees; nevertheless, it is not beyond the capacity of the richer nations to give enough assistance to reduce any further suffering to very small proportions. The decisions and actions of human beings can prevent this kind of suffering. Unfortunately, human beings have not made the necessary decisions. At the individual level, people have, with very few exceptions, not responded to the situation in any significant way. Generally speaking, people have not given large sums to relief funds; they have not written to their parliamentary representatives demanding increased government assistance; they have not demonstrated in the streets, held symbolic fasts, or done anything else directed toward providing the refugees with the means to satisfy their essential needs. At the government level, no government has given the sort of

Peter Singer, "Famine, Affluence, and Morality," *Philosophy & Public Affairs* 1, no. 3 (Spring 1972). Copyright © 1972 by Princeton University Press. Reprinted by permission.

massive aid that would enable the refugees to survive for more than a few days. Britain, for instance, has given rather more than most countries. It has, to date, given £14,750,000. For comparative purposes, Britain's share of the nonrecoverable development costs of the Anglo-French Concorde project is already in excess of £275,000,000, and on present estimates will reach £440,000,000. The implication is that the British government values a supersonic transport more than thirty times as highly as it values the lives of the nine million refugees. Australia is another country which, on a per capita basis, is well up in the "aid to Bengal" table. Australia's aid, however, amounts to less than one-twelfth of the cost of Sydney's new opera house. The total amount given, from all sources, now stands at about £65,000,000. The estimated cost of keeping the refugees alive for one year is £464,000,000. Most of the refugees have now been in the camps for more than six months. The World Bank has said that India needs a minimum of £300,000,000 in assistance from other countries before the end of the year. It seems obvious that assistance on this scale will not be forthcoming. India will be forced to choose between letting the refugees starve or diverting funds from her own development program, which will mean that more of her own people will starve in the future.[1]

These are the essential facts about the present situation in Bengal. So far as it concerns us here, there is nothing unique about this situation except its magnitude. The Bengal emergency is just the latest and most acute of a series of major emergencies in various parts of the world, arising both from natural and from man-made causes. There are also many parts of the world in which people die from malnutrition and lack of food independent of any special emergency. I take Bengal as my example only because it is the present concern, and because the size of the problem has ensured that it has been given adequate publicity. Neither individuals nor governments can claim to be unaware of what is happening there.

What are the moral implications of a situation like this? In what follows, I shall argue that the way people in relatively affluent countries react to a situation like that in Bengal cannot be justified; indeed, the whole way we look at moral issues — our moral conceptual scheme — needs to be altered, and with it, the way of life that has come to be taken for granted in our society.

In arguing for this conclusion I will not, of course, claim to be morally neutral. I shall, however, try to argue for the moral position that I take, so that anyone who accepts certain assumptions, to be made explicit, will, I hope, accept my conclusion.

I begin with the assumption that suffering and death from lack of food, shelter, and medical care are bad. I think most people will agree about this, although one may reach the same view by different routes. I shall not argue for this view. People can hold all sorts of eccentric positions, and perhaps from some of them it would not follow that death by starvation is in itself bad. It is difficult, perhaps impossible, to refute such positions, and so for brevity I will henceforth take this assumption as accepted. Those who disagree need read no further.

My next point is this: if it is in our power to prevent something bad from happening, without thereby sacrificing anything of comparable moral importance, we ought, morally, to do it. By "without sacrificing anything of comparable moral importance" I mean without causing anything else comparably bad to happen, or doing something that is wrong in itself, or failing to promote some moral good, comparable in significance to the bad thing that we can prevent. This principle seems almost as uncontroversial as the last one. It requires us

---

[1]There was also a third possibility: that India would go to war to enable the refugees to return to their lands. Since I wrote this paper, India has taken this way out. The situation is no longer that described above, but this does not affect my argument, as the next paragraph indicates.

only to prevent what is bad, and not to promote what is good, and it requires this of us only when we can do it without sacrificing anything that is, from the moral point of view, comparably important. I could even, as far as the application of my argument to the Bengal emergency is concerned, qualify the point so as to make it: if it is in our power to prevent something very bad from happening, without thereby sacrificing anything morally significant, we ought, morally, to do it. An application of this principle would be as follows: if I am walking past a shallow pond and see a child drowning in it, I ought to wade in and pull the child out. This will mean getting my clothes muddy, but this is insignificant, while the death of the child would presumably be a very bad thing.

The uncontroversial appearance of the principle just stated is deceptive. If it were acted upon, even in its qualified form, our lives, our society, and our world would be fundamentally changed. For the principle takes, firstly, no account of proximity or distance. It makes no moral difference whether the person I can help is a neighbor's child ten yards from me or a Bengali whose name I shall never know, ten thousand miles away. Secondly, the principle makes no distinction between cases in which I am the only person who could possibly do anything and cases in which I am just one among millions in the same position.

I do not think I need to say much in defense of the refusal to take proximity and distance into account. The fact that a person is physically near to us, so that we have personal contact with him, may make it more likely that we *shall* assist him, but this does not show that we *ought* to help him rather than another who happens to be further away. If we accept any principle of impartiality, universalizability, equality, or whatever, we cannot discriminate against someone merely because he is far away from us (or we are far away from him). Admittedly, it is possible that we are in a better position to judge what needs to be done to help a person near to us than one far away, and perhaps also to provide the assistance we judge to be necessary. If this were the case, it would be a reason for helping those near to us first. This may once have been a justification for being more concerned with the poor in one's own town than with famine victims in India. Unfortunately for those who like to keep their moral responsibilities limited, instant communication and swift transportation have changed the situation. From the moral point of view, the development of the world into a "global village" has made an important, though still unrecognized, difference to our moral situation. Expert observers and supervisors, sent out by famine relief organizations or permanently stationed in famine-prone areas, can direct our aid to a refugee in Bengal almost as effectively as we could get it to someone in our own block. There would seem, therefore, to be no possible justification for discriminating on geographical grounds.

There may be a greater need to defend the second implication of my principle — that the fact that there are millions of other people in the same position, in respect to the Bengali refugees, as I am, does not make the situation significantly different from a situation in which I am the only person who can prevent something very bad from occurring. Again, of course, I admit that there is a psychological difference between the cases; one feels less guilty about doing nothing if one can point to others, similarly placed, who have also done nothing. Yet this can make no real difference to our moral obligations. Should I consider that I am less obliged to pull the drowning child out of the pond if on looking around I see other people, no further away than I am, who have also noticed the child but are doing nothing? One has only to ask this question to see the absurdity of the view that numbers lessen obligation. It is a view that is an ideal excuse for inactivity; unfortunately most of the major evils — poverty, overpopulation, pollution — are problems in which everyone is almost equally involved.

The view that numbers do make a difference can be made plausible if stated in this way: if everyone in circumstances like mine gave £5 to the Bengal Relief Fund, there would be enough to provide food, shelter, and medical care for the refugees; there is no reason why I should give more than anyone else in the same circumstances as I am; therefore I have no obligation to give more than £5. Each premise in this argument is true, and the argument looks sound. It may convince us, unless we notice that it is based on a hypothetical premise, although the conclusion is not stated hypothetically. The argument would be sound if the conclusion were: if everyone in circumstances like mine were to give £5, I would have no obligation to give more than £5. If the conclusion were so stated, however, it would be obvious that the argument has no bearing on a situation in which it is not the case that everyone else gives £5. This, of course, is the actual situation. It is more or less certain that not everyone in circumstances like mine will give £5. So there will not be enough to provide the needed food, shelter, and medical care. Therefore by giving more than £5 I will prevent more suffering than I would if I gave just £5.

It might be thought that this argument has an absurd consequence. Since the situation appears to be that very few people are likely to give substantial amounts, it follows that I and everyone else in similar circumstances ought to give as much as possible, that is, at least up to the point at which by giving more one would begin to cause serious suffering for oneself and one's dependents—perhaps even beyond this point to the point of marginal utility, at which by giving more one would cause oneself and one's dependents as much suffering as one would prevent in Bengal. If everyone does this, however, there will be more than can be used for the benefit of the refugees, and some of the sacrifice will have been unnecessary. Thus, if everyone does what he ought to do, the result will not be as good as it would be if everyone did a little less than he ought to do, or if only some do all that they ought to do.

The paradox here arises only if we assume that the actions in question—sending money to the relief funds—are performed more or less simultaneously, and are also unexpected. For if it is to be expected that everyone is going to contribute something, then clearly each is not obliged to give as much as he would have been obliged to had others not been giving too. And if everyone is not acting more or less simultaneously, then those giving later will know how much more is needed, and will have no obligation to give more than is necessary to reach this amount. To say this is not to deny the principle that people in the same circumstances have the same obligations, but to point out that the fact that others have given, or may be expected to give, is a relevant circumstance: those giving after it has become known that many others are giving and those giving before are not in the same circumstances. So the seemingly absurd consequence of the principle I have put forward can occur only if people are in error about the actual circumstances—that is, if they think they are giving when others are not, but in fact they are giving when others are. The result of everyone doing what he really ought to do cannot be worse than the result of everyone doing less than he ought to do, although the result of everyone doing what he reasonably believes he ought to do could be.

If my argument so far has been sound, neither our distance from a preventable evil nor the number of other people who, in respect to that evil, are in the same situation as we are, lessens our obligation to mitigate or prevent that evil. I shall therefore take as established the principle I asserted earlier. As I have already said, I need to assert it only in its qualified form: if it is in our power to prevent something very bad from happening, without thereby sacrificing anything else morally significant, we ought, morally, to do it.

The outcome of this argument is that our traditional moral categories are upset. The traditional distinction between duty and charity cannot be drawn, or at least, not in the place we normally draw it. Giving money to the Bengal Relief Fund is regarded as an act of charity in our society. The bodies which collect money are known as "charities." These organizations see themselves in this way—if you send them a check, you will be thanked for your "generosity." Because giving money is regarded as an act of charity, it is not thought that there is anything wrong with not giving. The charitable man may be praised, but the man who is not charitable is not condemned. People do not feel in any way ashamed or guilty about spending money on new clothes or a new car instead of giving it to famine relief. (Indeed, the alternative does not occur to them.) This way of looking at the matter cannot be justified. When we buy new clothes not to keep ourselves warm but to look "well-dressed" we are not providing for any important need. We would not be sacrificing anything significant if we were to continue to wear our old clothes, and give the money to famine relief. By doing so, we would be preventing another person from starving. It follows from what I have said earlier that we ought to give money away, rather than spend it on clothes which we do not need to keep us warm. To do so is not charitable, or generous. Nor is it the kind of act which philosophers and theologians have called "supereroga-tory"—an act which it would be good to do, but not wrong not to do. On the contrary, we ought to give the money away, and it is wrong not to do so.

I am not maintaining that there are no acts which are charitable, or that there are no acts which it would be good to do but not wrong not to do. It may be possible to redraw the distinction between duty and charity in some other place. All I am arguing here is that the present way of drawing the distinction, which makes it an act of charity for a man living at the level of affluence which most people in the "developed nations" enjoy to give money to save someone else from starvation, cannot be supported. It is beyond the scope of my argument to consider whether the distinction should be redrawn or abolished altogether. There would be many other possible ways of drawing the distinction—for instance, one might decide that it is good to make other people as happy as possible, but not wrong not to do so.

Despite the limited nature of the revision in our moral conceptual scheme which I am proposing, the revision would, given the extent of both affluence and famine in the world today, have radical implications. These implications may lead to further objections, distinct from those I have already considered. I shall discuss two of these.

One objection to the position I have taken might be simply that it is too drastic a revision of our moral scheme. People do not ordinarily judge in the way I have suggested they should. Most people reserve their moral condemnation for those who violate some moral norm, such as the norm against taking another person's property. They do not condemn those who indulge in luxury instead of giving to famine relief. But given that I did not set out to present a morally neutral description of the way people make moral judgments, the way people do in fact judge has nothing to do with the validity of my conclusion. My conclusion follows from the principle which I advanced earlier, and unless that principle is rejected, or the arguments shown to be unsound, I think the conclusion must stand, however strange it appears. . . .

The second objection to my attack on the present distinction between duty and charity is one which has from time to time been made against utilitarianism. It follows from some forms of utilitarian theory that we all ought, morally, to be working full time to increase the balance of happiness over misery. The position I have taken here would not lead to this conclusion in all circumstances, for if there were no bad occurrences that we could prevent without sacrificing something of comparable moral importance, my argument would have no application. Given the present conditions in many parts of the world, however, it does follow from my argument that we ought, morally, to be working full time to relieve great suffering of the sort that occurs as a result of famine or other disasters. Of course, mitigating circumstances can be adduced—for instance, that if we wear ourselves out through overwork, we shall be less effective than we would otherwise have been. Nevertheless, when all considerations of this sort have been taken into account, the conclusion remains: we ought to be preventing as much suffering as we can without sacrificing something else of comparable moral importance. This conclusion is one which we may be reluctant to face. I cannot see, though, why it should be regarded as a criticism of the position for which I have argued, rather than a criticism of our ordinary standards of behavior. Since most people are self-interested to some degree, very few of us are likely to do everything that we ought to do. It would, however, hardly be honest to take this as evidence that it is not the case that we ought to do it . . . .

The conclusion reached earlier [raises] the question of just how much we all ought to be giving away. One possibility, which has already been mentioned, is that we ought to give until we reach the level of marginal utility — that is, the level at which, by giving more, I would cause as much suffering to myself or my dependents as I would relieve by my gift. This would mean, of course, that one would reduce oneself to very near the material circumstances of a Bengali refugee. It will be recalled that earlier I put forward both a strong and a moderate version of the principle of preventing bad occurrences. The strong version, which required us to prevent bad things from happening unless in doing so we would be sacrificing something of a comparable moral significance, does seem to require reducing ourselves to the level of marginal utility. I should also say that the strong version seems to me to be the correct one. I proposed the more moderate version — that we should prevent bad occurrences unless, to do so, we had to sacrifice something morally significant — only in order to show that even on this surely undeniable principle a great change in our way of life is required. On the more moderate principle, it may not follow that we ought to reduce ourselves to the level of marginal utility, for one might hold that to reduce oneself and one's family to this level is to cause something significantly bad to happen. Whether this is so I shall not discuss, since, as I have said, I can see no good reason for holding the moderate version of the principle rather than the strong version. Even if we accepted the principle only in its moderate form, however, it should be clear that we would have to give away enough to ensure that the consumer society, dependent as it is on people spending on trivia rather than giving to famine relief, would slow down and perhaps disappear entirely. There are several reasons why this would be desirable in itself. The value and necessity of economic growth are now being questioned not only by conservationists, but by economists as well.[2] There is no doubt, too, that the consumer society has had a distorting effect on the goals and purposes of its members. Yet looking at the matter purely from the point of view of overseas aid, there must be a limit to the extent to which we should deliberately slow down our economy; for it might be the case that if we gave away, say, forty percent of our Gross National Product, we would slow down the economy so much that in absolute terms we would be giving less than if we gave twenty-five percent of the much larger GNP that we would have if we limited our contribution to this smaller percentage.

I mention this only as an indication of the sort of factor that one would have to take into account in working out an ideal. Since Western societies generally consider one percent of the GNP an acceptable level for overseas aid, the matter is entirely academic. Nor does it affect the question of how much an individual should give in a society in which very few are giving substantial amounts.

It is sometimes said, though less often now than it used to be, that philosophers have no special role to play in public affairs, since most public issues depend primarily on an assessment of facts. On questions of fact, it is said, philosophers as such have no special expertise, and so it has been possible to engage in philosophy without committing oneself to any position on major public issues. No doubt there are some issues of social policy and foreign policy about which it can truly be said that a really expert assessment of the facts is required before taking sides or acting, but the issue of famine is surely not one of these.

---

[2]See, for instance, John Kenneth Galbraith, *The New Industrial State* (Boston, 1967); and E. J. Mishan, *The Costs of Economic Growth* (London, 1967).

The facts about the existence of suffering are beyond dispute. Nor, I think, is it disputed that we can do something about it, either through orthodox methods of famine relief or through population control or both. This is therefore an issue on which philosophers are competent to take a position. The issue is one which faces everyone who has more money than he needs to support himself and his dependents, or who is in a position to take some sort of political action. These categories must include practically every teacher and student of philosophy in the universities of the Western world. If philosophy is to deal with matters that are relevant to both teachers and students, this is an issue that philosophers should discuss.

Discussion, though, is not enough. What is the point of relating philosophy to public (and personal) affairs if we do not take our conclusions seriously? In this instance, taking our conclusion seriously means acting upon it. The philosopher will not find it any easier than anyone else to alter his attitudes and way of life to the extent that, if I am right, is involved in doing everything that we ought to be doing. At the very least, though, one can make a start. The philosopher who does so will have to sacrifice some of the benefits of the consumer society, but he can find compensation in the satisfaction of a way of life in which theory and practice, if not yet in harmony, are at least coming together.

QUESTIONS

1. Think about the following claim: Contributing to famine relief is not a moral obligation which we must perform if we are to act in a morally correct way, but an act of charity which we may or may not perform. Can you offer any arguments to defend it?
2. Singer says, "We ought to be preventing as much suffering as we can without sacrificing something else of comparable moral importance." What moral considerations would outweigh the obligation Singer claims we have to aid famine victims?

GARRETT HARDIN

LIVING ON A LIFEBOAT

Garrett Hardin is professor of biology at the University of California at Santa Barbara. He is the author of many books, including *Population, Evolution, and Birth Control* (1969), *Exploring New Ethics for Survival* (1972), and *The Limits of Altruism: An Ecologist's View of Survival* (1977).

Hardin uses the metaphor of a lifeboat to argue that the time may have come to refuse aid in the form of food to needy countries which do not accept the responsibility for limiting their population growth. He argues that adherence to the principle "From each according to his ability; to each according to his need" will have strong adverse effects. Bolstered by our aid, needy countries will continue their irresponsible policies in regard to food production and population growth. Furthermore, he argues, the food we supply will enable these populations to continue to increase. This in the long run will jeopardize the survival of the human species.

No generation has viewed the problem of the survival of the human species as seriously as we have. Inevitably, we have entered this world of concern through the door of metaphor. Environmentalists have emphasized the image of the earth as a spaceship — Spaceship Earth. Kenneth Boulding (1966) is the principal architect of this metaphor. It is time, he says, that we replace the wasteful "cowboy economy" of the past with the frugal "spaceship economy" required for continued survival in the limited world we now see ours to be. The metaphor is notably useful in justifying pollution control measures.

Unfortunately, the image of a spaceship is also used to promote measures that are suicidal. One of these is a generous immigration policy, which is only a particular instance of a class of policies that are in error because they lead to the tragedy of the commons (Hardin 1968). These suicidal policies are attractive because they mesh with what we unthinkingly take to be the ideals of "the best people." What is missing in the idealistic view is an insistence that rights and responsibilities must go together. The "generous" attitude of all too many people results in asserting inalienable rights while ignoring or denying matching responsibilities.

For the metaphor of a spaceship to be correct the aggregate of people on board would have to be under unitary sovereign control (Ophuls 1974). A true ship always has a captain. It is conceivable that a ship could be run by a committee. But it could not possibly survive if its course were determined by bickering tribes that claimed rights without responsibilities.

What about Spaceship Earth? It certainly has no captain, and no executive committee. The United Nations is a toothless tiger, because the signatories of its charter wanted it that way. The spaceship metaphor is used only to justify spaceship demands on common resources without acknowledging corresponding spaceship responsibilities.

An understandable fear of decisive action leads people to embrace "incrementalism" — moving toward reform in tiny stages. As we shall see, this strategy is counterproductive in the area discussed here if it means accepting rights before responsibilities. Where human survival is at stake, the acceptance of responsibilities is a precondition to the acceptance of rights, if the two cannot be introduced simultaneously.

LIFEBOAT ETHICS

Before taking up certain substantive issues let us look at an alternative metaphor, that of a lifeboat. In developing some relevant examples the following numerical values are assumed. Approximately two-thirds of the world is desperately poor, and only one-third is comparatively rich. The people in poor countries have an average per capita GNP (Gross National Product) of about $200 per year; the rich, of about $3,000. (For the United States it is nearly $5,000 per year.) Metaphorically, each rich nation amounts to a lifeboat full of comparatively rich pople. The poor of the world are in other, much more crowded lifeboats. Continuously, so to speak, the poor fall out of their lifeboats and swim for a while in the water outside, hoping to be admitted to a rich lifeboat, or in some other way to benefit from the "goodies" on board. What should the passengers on a rich lifeboat do? This is the central problem of "the ethics of a lifeboat."

First we must acknowledge that each lifeboat is effectively limited in capacity. The land of every nation has a limited carrying capacity. The exact limit is a matter for argument, but the energy crunch is convincing more people every day that we have already exceeded the carrying capacity of the land. We have been living on "capital" — stored petroleum and coal — and soon we must live on income alone.

Let us look at only one lifeboat—ours. The ethical problem is the same for all, and is as follows. Here we sit, say 50 people in a lifeboat. To be generous, let us assume our boat has a capacity of 10 more, making 60. (This, however, is to violate the engineering principle of the "safety factor." A new plant disease or a bad change in the weather may decimate our population if we don't preserve some excess capacity as a safety factor.)

The 50 of us in the lifeboat see 100 others swimming in the water outside, asking for admission to the boat, or for handouts. How shall we respond to their calls? There are several possibilities.

One. We may be tempted to try to live by the Christian ideal of being "our brother's keeper," or by the Marxian ideal (Marx 1875) of "from each according to his abilities, to each according to his needs." Since the needs of all are the same, we take all the needy into our boat, making a total of 150 in a boat with a capacity of 60. The boat is swamped, and everyone drowns. Complete justice, complete catastrophe.

Two. Since the boat has an unused excess capacity of 10, we admit just 10 more to it. This has the disadvantage of getting rid of the safety factor, for which action we will sooner or later pay dearly. Moreover, *which* 10 do we let in? "First come, first served?" The best 10? The neediest 10? How do we *discriminate*? And what do we say to the 90 who are excluded?

Three. Admit no more to the boat and preserve the small safety factor. Survival of the people in the lifeboat is then possible (though we shall have to be on our guard against boarding parties).

The last solution is abhorrent to many people. It is unjust, they say. Let us grant that it is.

"I feel guilty about my good luck," say some. The reply to this is simple: *Get out and yield your place to others.* Such a selfless action might satisfy the conscience of those who are addicted to guilt but it would not change the ethics of the lifeboat. The needy person to whom a guilt-addict yields his place will not himself feel guilty about his sudden good luck. (If he did he would not climb aboard.) The net result of conscience-stricken people relinquishing their unjustly held positions is the elimination of their kind of conscience from the lifeboat. The lifeboat, as it were, purifies itself of guilt. The ethics of the lifeboat persist, unchanged by such momentary aberrations.

This then is the basic metaphor within which we must work out our solutions. Let us enrich the image step by step with substantive additions from the real world.

REPRODUCTION

The harsh characteristics of lifeboat ethics are heightened by reproduction, particularly by reproductive differences. The people inside the lifeboats of the wealthy nations are doubling in numbers every 87 years; those outside are doubling every 35 years, on the average. And the relative difference in prosperity is becoming greater.

Let us, for a while, think primarily of the U.S. lifeboat. As of 1973 the United States had a population of 210 billion people, who were increasing by 0.8% per year, that is, doubling in number every 87 years.

Although the citizens of rich nations are outnumbered two to one by the poor, let us imagine an equal number of poor people outside our lifeboat—a mere 210 million poor people reproducing at a quite different rate. If we imagine these to be the combined populations of Colombia, Venezuela, Ecuador, Morocco, Thailand, Pakistan, and the Philippines, the average rate of increase of the people "outside" is 3.3% per year. The doubling time of this population is 21 years.

Suppose that all these countries, and the United States, agreed to live by the Marxian ideal, "to each according to his needs," the ideal of most Christians as well. Needs, of course, are determined by population size, which is affected by reproduction. Every nation regards its rate of reproduction as a sovereign right. If our lifeboat were big enough in the beginning it might be possible to live *for a while* by Christian-Marxian ideals. *Might.*

Initially, in the model given, the ratio of non-Americans to Americans would be one to one. But consider what the ratio would be 87 years later. By this time Americans would have doubled to a population of 420 million. The other group (doubling every 21 years) would now have swollen to 3,540 million. Each American would have more than eight people to share with. How could the lifeboat possibly keep afloat?

All this involves extrapolation of current trends into the future, and is consequently suspect. Trends may change. Granted: but the change will not necessarily be favorable. If—as seems likely—the rate of population increase falls faster in the ethnic group presently inside the lifeboat than it does among those now outside, the future will turn out to be even worse than mathematics predicts, and sharing will be even more suicidal.

RUIN IN THE COMMONS

The fundamental error of the sharing ethics is that it leads to the tragedy of the commons. Under a system of private property the man (or group of men) who own property recognize their responsibility to care for it, for if they don't they will eventually suffer. A farmer, for instance, if he is intelligent, will allow no more cattle in a pasture than its carrying capacity justifies. If he overloads the pasture, weeds take over, erosion sets in, and the owner loses in the long run.

But if a pasture is run as a commons open to all, the right of each to use it is not matched by an operational responsibility to take care of it. It is no use asking independent herdsmen in a commons to act responsibly, for they dare not. The considerate herdsman who refrains from overloading the commons suffers more than a selfish one who says his needs are greater. (As Leo Durocher says, "Nice guys finish last.") Christian-Marxian idealism is counterproductive. That it *sounds* nice is no excuse. With distribution systems, as with individual morality, good intentions are no substitute for good performance.

A social system is stable only if it is insensitive to errors. To the Christian-Marxian idealist a selfish person is a sort of "error." Prosperity in the system of the commons cannot survive errors. If *everyone* would only restrain himself, all would be well; but it takes *only one less than everyone* to ruin a system of voluntary restraint. In a crowded world of less than perfect human beings—and we will never know any other—mutual ruin is inevitable in the commons. This is the core of the tragedy of the commons. . . .

WORLD FOOD BANKS

In the international arena we have recently heard a proposal to create a new commons, namely an international depository of food reserves to which nations will contribute according to their abilities, and from which nations may draw according to their needs. Nobel laureate Norman Borlaug has lent the prestige of his name to this proposal.

A world food bank appeals powerfully to our humanitarian impulses. We remember John Donne's celebrated line, "Any man's death diminishes me." But before we rush out to see for whom the bell tolls let us recognize where the greatest political push for international granaries comes from, lest we be disillusioned later. Our experience with Public Law 480 clearly reveals the answer. This was the law that moved billions of dollars worth of U.S. grain to food-short, population-long countries during the past two decades. When

P.L. 480 first came into being, a headline in the business magazine *Forbes* (Paddock 1970) revealed the power behind it: "Feeding the World's Hungry Millions: How it will mean billions for U.S. business."

And indeed it did. In the years 1960 to 1970 a total of $7.9 billion was spent on the "Food for Peace" program, as P.L. 480 was called. During the years of 1948 to 1970 an additional $49.9 billion were extracted from American taxpayers to pay for other economic aid programs, some of which went for food and food-producing machinery. (This figure does *not* include military aid.) That P.L. 480 was a give-away program was concealed. Recipient countries went through the motions of paying for P.L. 480 food—with IOU's. In December 1973 the charade was brought to an end as far as India was concerned when the United States "forgave" India's $3.2 billion debt (Anonymous 1974). Public announcement of the cancellation of the debt was delayed for two months: one wonders why. . . .

What happens if some organizations budget for emergencies and others do not? If each organization is solely responsible for its own well-being, poorly managed ones will suffer. But they should be able to learn from experience. They have a chance to mend their ways and learn to budget for infrequent but certain emergencies. The weather, for instance, always varies and periodic crop failures are certain. A wise and competent government saves out of the production of the good years in anticipation of bad years that are sure to come. This is not a new idea. The Bible tells us that Joseph taught this policy to Pharaoh in Egypt more than 2,000 years ago. Yet it is literally true that the vast majority of the governments of the world today have no such policy. They lack either the wisdom or the competence, or both. Far more difficult than the transfer of wealth from one country to another is the transfer of wisdom between sovereign powers or between generations.

"But it isn't their fault! How can we blame the poor people who are caught in an emergency? Why must we punish them?" The concepts of blame and punishment are irrelevant. The question is, what are the operational consequences of establishing a world food bank? If it is open to every country every time a need develops, slovenly rulers will not be motivated to take Joseph's advice. Why should they? Others will bail them out whenever they are in trouble.

Some countries will make deposits in the world food bank and others will withdraw from it: there will be almost no overlap. Calling such a depository-transfer unit a "bank" is stretching the metaphor of *bank* beyond its elastic limits. The proposers, of course, never call attention to the metaphorical nature of the word they use.

THE RATCHET EFFECT

An "international food bank" is really, then, not a true bank but a disguised oneway transfer device for moving wealth from rich countries to poor. In the absence of such a bank, in a world inhabited by individually responsible sovereign nations, the population of each nation would repeatedly go through a cycle of the sort shown in Figure 1. P_2 is greater than P_1, either in absolute numbers or because a deterioration of the food supply has removed the safety factor and produced a dangerously low ratio of resources to population. P_2 may be said to represent a state of overpopulation, which becomes obvious upon the appearance of an "accident," e.g., a crop failure. If the "emergency" is not met by outside help, the population drops back to the "normal" level—the "carrying capacity" of the environment—or even below. In the absence of population control by a sovereign, sooner or later the population grows to P_2 again and the cycle repeats. The long-term population curve (Hardin 1966) is an irregularly fluctuating one, equilibrating more or less about the carrying capacity.

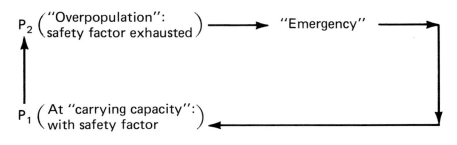

$$P_2 \left(\begin{array}{l} \text{"Overpopulation":} \\ \text{safety factor exhausted} \end{array} \right) \longrightarrow \text{"Emergency"} \longrightarrow$$

$$P_1 \left(\begin{array}{l} \text{At "carrying capacity":} \\ \text{with safety factor} \end{array} \right) \longleftarrow$$

Fig. 1

A demographic cycle of this sort obviously involves great suffering in the restrictive phase, but such a cycle is normal to any independent country with inadequate population control. The third century theologian Tertullian (Hardin 1969) expressed what must have been the recognition of many wise men when he wrote: "The scourges of pestilence, famine, wars, and earthquakes have come to be regarded as a blessing to overcrowded nations, since they serve to prune away the luxuriant growth of the human race."

Only under a strong and farsighted sovereign — which theoretically could be the people themselves, democratically organized — can a population equilibrate at some set point below the carrying capacity, thus avoiding the pains normally caused by periodic and unavoidable disasters. For this happy state to be achieved it is necessary that those in power be able to contemplate with equanimity the "waste" of surplus food in times of bountiful harvests. It is essential that those in power resist the temptation to convert extra food into extra babies. On the public relations level it is necessary that the phrase "surplus food" be replaced by "safety factor."

But wise sovereigns seem not to exist in the poor world today. The most anguishing problems are created by poor countries that are governed by rulers insufficiently wise and powerful. If such countries can draw on a world food bank in times of "emergency," the population *cycle* of Figure 1 will be replaced by the population *escalator* of Figure 2. The input of food from a food bank acts as the pawl of a ratchet, preventing the population from retracing its steps to a lower level. Reproduction pushes the population upward, inputs from the world bank prevent its moving downward. Population size escalates, as does the absolute magnitude of "accidents" and "emergencies." The process is brought to an end only by the total collapse of the whole system, producing a catastrophe of scarcely imaginable proportions.

Such are the implications of the well-meant sharing of food in a world of irresponsible reproduction. . . .

To be generous with one's own possessions is one thing; to be generous with posterity's is quite another. This, I think, is the point that must be gotten across to those who would, from a commendable love of distributive justice, institute a ruinous system of the commons. . . .

If the argument of this essay is correct, so long as there is no true world government to control reproduction everywhere it is impossible to survive in dignity if we are to be guided by Spaceship ethics. Without a world government that is sovereign in reproductive matters mankind lives, in fact, on a number of sovereign lifeboats. For the foreseeable future survival demands that we govern our actions by the ethics of a lifeboat. Posterity will be ill served if we do not.

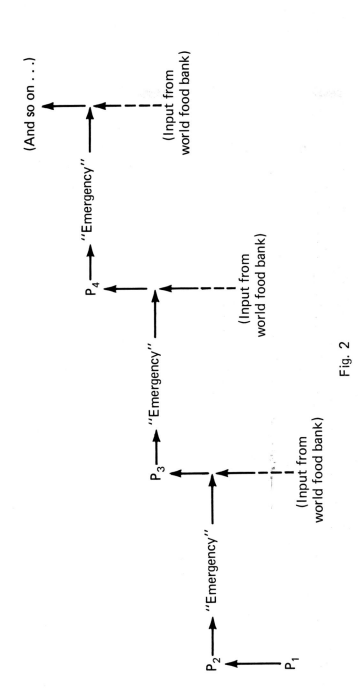

Fig. 2

REFERENCES

Anonymous. 1974. *Wall Street Journal* 19 Feb.

BOULDING, K. 1966. The economics of the coming spaceship earth. In H. Jarrett, ed. *Environmental Quality in a Growing Economy*. Johns Hopkins Press, Baltimore.

HARDIN, G. 1966. Chap. 9 in *Biology: Its Principles and Implications*, 2nd ed. Freeman, San Francisco.

————. 1968. The tragedy of the commons. *Science* 162: 1243–1248.

————. 1969. Page 18 in *Population, Evolution, and Birth Control*, 2nd ed. Freeman, San Francisco.

MARX, K. 1875. *Critique of the Gotha program*. Page 388 in R. C. Tucker, ed. *The Marx-Engels Reader*, Norton, N.Y., 1972.

OPHULS, W. 1974. The scarcity society. *Harpers* 248 (1487): 47–52.

PADDOCK, W. C. 1970. How green is the green revolution? *Bioscience* 20: 897–902.

QUESTIONS

1. What evidence is available to support the claim that the resources of the world will not be able to save all the poor countries? If it cannot be conclusively proved that all the poor countries cannot be saved, can a moral justification be given for refusing to aid famine victims in all those countries?
2. Suppose that it is highly unlikely that all the nations in the world can be saved. Which would be the better moral choice:
    (a) to deliberately cut off aid to those least likely to survive in order to ensure the survival of the others or
    (b) to continue our aid despite our awareness of the consequences which will probably follow?

WILLIAM W. MURDOCH
and ALLAN OATEN

POPULATION AND FOOD: METAPHORS AND THE REALITY

William W. Murdoch is professor of biological science at the University of California at Santa Barbara. His research centers on population and community dynamics of organisms. He is the editor of *Environment-Resources, Pollution and Society* (2d ed., 1975). Allan Oaten is associate professor of biological science at the University of California at Santa Barbara. His areas of specialization are mathematical biology and statistics.

Murdoch and Oaten begin by pointing out several weaknesses in Garrett Hardin's lifeboat, commons, and ratchet metaphors. They then bring out various factors other than food supply which affect population growth. These factors include parental confidence about the future, low infant mortality rates, literacy, widely available rudimentary health care, increased income and employment, and an adequate diet above subsistence levels. For Murdoch and Oaten, if the bulk of a population does not share in the increased social and economic benefits which result from significant national progress, fertility rates in poor and relatively poor countries are unlikely to fall.

████ ██

MISLEADING METAPHORS

[Hardin's] "lifeboat" article actually has two messages. The first is that our immigration policy is too generous. This will not concern us here. The second, and more important, is that by helping poor nations we will bring disaster to rich and poor alike:

> Metaphorically, each rich nation amounts to a lifeboat full of comparatively rich people. The poor of the world are in other, much more crowded lifeboats. Continuously, so to speak, the poor fall out of their lifeboats and swim for a while in the water outside, hoping to be admitted to a rich lifeboat, or in some other way to benefit from the "goodies" on board. What should the passengers on a rich lifeboat do? This is the central problem of "the ethics of a lifeboat." (Hardin, 1974, p. 561)

Among these so-called "goodies" are food supplies and technical aid such as that which led to the Green Revolution. Hardin argues that we should withhold such resources from poor nations on the grounds that they help to maintain high rates of population increase, thereby making the problem worse. He foresees the continued supplying and increasing production of food as a process that will be "brought to an end only by the total collapse of the whole system, producing a catastrophe of scarcely imaginable proportions" (p. 564).

Turning to one particular mechanism for distributing these resources, Hardin claims that a world food bank is a commons—people have more motivation to draw from it than to add to it; it will have a ratchet or escalator effect on population because inputs from it will prevent population declines in over-populated countries. Thus "wealth can be steadily moved in one direction only, from the slowly-breeding rich to the rapidly-breeding poor, the process finally coming to a halt only when all countries are equally and miserably poor" (p. 565). Thus our help will not only bring ultimate disaster to poor countries, but it will also be suicidal for us.

As for the "benign demographic transition" to low birth rates, which some aid supporters have predicted, Hardin states flatly that the weight of evidence is against this possibility.

Finally, Hardin claims that the plight of poor nations is partly their own fault: "wise sovereigns seem not to exist in the poor world today. The most anguishing problems are created by poor countries that are governed by rulers insufficiently wise and powerful." Establishing a world food bank will exacerbate this problem: "slovenly rulers" will escape the consequences of their incompetence—"Others will bail them out whenever they are in trouble"; "Far more difficult than the transfer of wealth from one country to another is the transfer of wisdom between sovereign powers or between generations" (p. 563).

What arguments does Hardin present in support of these opinions? Many involve metaphors: lifeboat, commons, and ratchet or escalator. These metaphors are crucial to his thesis, and it is, therefore, important for us to examine them critically.

The lifeboat is the major metaphor. It seems attractively simple, but it is in fact simplistic and obscures important issues. As soon as we try to use it to compare various policies, we find that most relevant details of the actual situation are either missing or distorted in the lifeboat metaphor. Let us list some of these details.

Most important, perhaps, Hardin's lifeboats barely interact. The rich lifeboats may drop some handouts over the side and perhaps repel a boarding party now and then, but generally they live their own lives. In the real world, nations interact a great deal, in ways that affect food supply and population size and growth, and the effect of rich nations on poor nations has been strong and not always benevolent.

First, by colonization and actual wars of commerce, and through the international marketplace, rich nations have arranged an exchange of goods that has maintained and even increased the economic imbalance between rich and poor nations. Until recently we have taken or otherwise obtained cheap raw material from poor nations and sold them expensive manufactured goods that they cannot make themselves. In the United States, the structure of tariffs and internal subsidies discriminates selectively against poor nations. In poor countries, the concentration on cash crops rather than on food crops, a legacy of colonial times, is now actively encouraged by western multinational corporations (Barraclough 1975). Indeed, it is claimed that in famine-stricken Sahelian Africa, multinational agribusiness has recently taken land out of food production for cash crops (Transnational Institute 1974). Although we often self-righteously take the "blame" for lowering the death rates of poor nations during the 1940s and 1950s, we are less inclined to accept responsibility for the effects of actions that help maintain poverty and hunger. Yet poverty directly contributes to the high birth rates that Hardin views with such alarm.

Second, U.S. foreign policy, including foreign aid programs, has favored "pro-Western" regimes, many of which govern in the interests of a wealthy elite and some of which are savagely repressive. Thus, it has often subsidized a gross maldistribution of income and has supported political leaders who have opposed most of the social changes that can lead to reduced birth rates. In this light, Hardin's pronouncements on the alleged wisdom gap between poor leaders and our own, and the difficulty of filling it, appear as a grim joke: our response to leaders with the power and wisdom Hardin yearns for has often been to try to replace them or their policies as soon as possible. Selective giving and withholding of both military and nonmilitary aid has been an important ingredient of our efforts to maintain political leaders we like and to remove those we do not. Brown (1974b), after noting that the withholding of U.S. food aid in 1973 contributed to the downfall of the Allende government in Chile, comments that "although Americans decry the use of petroleum as a political weapon, calling it 'political blackmail,' the United States has been using food aid for political purposes for twenty years—and describing this as 'enlightened diplomacy.'"

Both the quantity and the nature of the supplies on a lifeboat are fixed. In the real world, the quantity has strict limits, but these are far from having been reached (University of California Food Task Force 1974). Nor are we forced to devote fixed proportions of our efforts and energy to automobile travel, pet food, packaging, advertising, corn-fed beef, "defense" and other diversions, many of which cost far more than foreign aid does. The fact is that enough food is now produced to feed the world's population adequately. That people are malnourished is due to distribution and to economics, not to agricultural limits (United Nations Economic and Social Council 1974).

Hardin's lifeboats are divided merely into rich and poor, and it is difficult to talk about birth rates on either. In the real world, however, there are striking differences among the birth rates of the poor countries and even among the birth rates of different parts of single countries. These differences appear to be related to social conditions (also absent from lifeboats) and may guide us to effective aid policies.

Hardin's lifeboat metaphor not only conceals facts, but misleads about the effects of his proposals. The rich lifeboat can raise the ladder and sail away. But in real life, the problem will not necessarily go away just because it is ignored. In the real world, there are armies, raw materials in poor nations, and even outraged domestic dissidents prepared to sacrifice their own and others' lives to oppose policies they regard as immoral.

No doubt there are other objections. But even this list shows the lifeboat metaphor to be dangerously inappropriate for serious policy making because it obscures far more than it reveals. Lifeboats and "lifeboat ethics" may be useful topics for those who are shipwrecked; we believe they are worthless—indeed detrimental—in discussions of food-population questions.

The ratchet metaphor is equally flawed. It, too, ignores complex interactions between birth rates and social conditions (including diets), implying as it does that more food will simply mean more babies. Also, it obscures the fact that the descrease in death rates has been caused at least as much by developments such as DDT, improved sanitation, and medical advances, as by increased food supplies, so that cutting out food aid will not necessarily lead to population declines.

The lifeboat article is strangely inadequate in other ways. For example, it shows an astonishing disregard for recent literature. The claim that we can expect no "benign demographic transition" is based on a review written more than a decade ago (Davis 1963). Yet, events and attitudes are changing rapidly in poor countries: for the first time in history, most poor people live in countries with birth control programs; with few exceptions, poor nations are somewhere on the demographic transition to lower birth rates (Demeny 1974); the population-food squeeze is now widely recognized, and governments of poor nations are aware of the relationship. Again, there is a considerable amount of evidence that birth rates can fall rapidly in poor countries given the proper social conditions (as we will discuss later); consequently, crude projections of current population growth rates are quite inadequate for policy making.

THE TRAGEDY OF THE COMMONS

Throughout the lifeboat article, Hardin bolsters his assertions by reference to the "commons" (Hardin 1968). The thesis of the commons, therefore, needs critical evaluation.

Suppose several privately owned flocks, comprising 100 sheep altogether, are grazing on a public commons. They bring in an annual income of $1.00 per sheep. Fred, a herdsman, owns only one sheep. He decides to add another. But 101 is too many: the commons is overgrazed and produces less food. The sheep lose quality and income drops to 90¢ per sheep. Total income is now $90.90 instead of $100.00. Adding the sheep has brought an overall loss. But Fred has gained: *his* income is $1.80 instead of $1.00. The gain from the additional sheep, which is his alone, outweighs the loss from overgrazing, which he shares. Thus he promotes his interest at the expense of the community.

This is the problem of the commons, which seems on the way to becoming an archetype. Hardin, in particular, is not inclined to underrate its importance: "One of the major tasks of education today is to create such an awareness of the dangers of the commons that people will be able to recognize its many varieties, however disguised" (Hardin 1974, p. 562) and "All this is terribly obvious once we are acutely aware of the pervasiveness and danger of the commons. But many people still lack this awareness . . ." (p. 565).

The "commons" affords a handy way of classifying problems: the lifeboat article reveals that sharing, a generous immigration policy, world food banks, air, water, the fish populations of the ocean, and the western range lands are, or produce, a commons. It is also handy to be able to dispose of policies one does not like and "only a particular instance of a class of policies that are in error because they lead to the tragedy of the commons" (p. 561).

But no metaphor, even one as useful as this, should be treated with such awe. Such shorthand can be useful, but it can also mislead by discouraging thought and obscuring important detail. To dismiss a proposal by suggesting that "all you need to know about this proposal is that it institutes a commons and is, therefore, bad" is to assert that the proposed commons is worse than the original problem. This might be so if the problem of the commons were, indeed, a tragedy—that is, if it were insoluble. But it is not.

Hardin favors private ownership as the solution (either through private property or the selling of pollution rights). But, of course, there are solutions other than private ownership; and private ownership itself is no guarantee of carefully husbanded resources.

One alternative to private ownership of the commons is communal ownership of the sheep—or, in general, of the mechanisms and industries that exploit the resource—combined with communal planning for management. (Note, again, how the metaphor favors one solution: perhaps the "tragedy" lay not in the commons but in the sheep. "The Tragedy of the Privately Owned Sheep" lacks zing, unfortunately.) Public ownership of a commons has been tried in Peru to the benefit of the previously privately owned anchoveta fishery (Gulland 1975). The communally owned agriculture of China does not seem to have suffered any greater over-exploitation than that of other Asian nations.

Another alternative is cooperation combined with regulation. For example, Gulland (1975) has shown that Antarctic whale stocks (perhaps the epitome of a commons since they are internationally exploited and no one owns them) are now being properly managed, and stocks are increasing. This has been achieved through cooperation in the International Whaling Commission, which has by agreement set limits to the catch of each nation.

In passing, Hardin's private ownership argument is not generally applicable to nonrenewable resources. Given discount rates, technology substitutes, and no more than an average regard for posterity, privately owned nonrenewable resources, like oil, coal and minerals, are mined at rates that produce maximum profits, rather than at those rates that preserve them for future generations. . . .

BIRTH RATES: AN ALTERNATIVE VIEW

Is the food-population spiral inevitable? A more optimistic, if less comfortable, hypothesis, presented by Rich (1973) and Brown (1974a), is increasingly tenable: contrary to the "ratchet" projection, population growth rates are affected by many complex conditions beside food supply. In particular, a set of socioeconomic conditions can be identified that motivate parents to have fewer children; under these conditions, birth rates can fall quite rapidly, sometimes even before birth control technology is available. Thus, population growth can be controlled more effectively by intelligent human intervention that sets up the appropriate conditions than by doing nothing and trusting to "natural population cycles."

These conditions are: parental confidence about the future, an improved status of women, and literacy. They require low infant mortality rates, widely available rudimentary health care, increased income and employment, and an adequate diet above subsistence levels. Expenditure on schools (especially elementary schools), appropriate health services (especially rural paramedical services), and agricultural reform (especially aid to small farmers) will be needed, and foreign aid can help here. It is essential that these improvements be spread across the population; aid can help here, too, by concentrating on the poor nations' poorest people, encouraging necessary institutional and social reforms, and making it easier for poor nations to use their own resources and initiative to help themselves. It is *not* necessary that per capita GNP be very high, certainly not as high as that of the rich countries during their gradual demographic transition. In other words, low birth rates in poor countries are achievable long before the conditions exist that were present in the rich countries in the late 19th and early 20th centuries.

Twenty or thirty years is not long to discover and assess the factors affecting birth rates, but a body of evidence is now accumulating in favor of this hypothesis. Rich (1973) and Brown (1974a) show that at least 10 developing countries have managed to reduce their birth rates by an average of more than one birth per 1,000 population per year for periods of 5 to 16 years. A reduction of one birth per 1,000 per year would bring birth rates in poor countries to a rough replacement level of about 16/1,000 by the turn of the century, though age distribution effects would prevent a smooth population decline. We have listed these countries in Table 1, together with three other nations, including China, that are poor and yet have brought their birth rates down to 30 or less, presumably from rates of over 40 a decade or so ago.

These data show that rapid reduction in birth rates is possible in the developing world. No doubt it can be argued that each of these cases is in some way special. Hong Kong and Singapore are relatively rich; they, Barbados, and Mauritius are also tiny. China is able to exert great social pressure on its citizens; but China is particularly significant. It is enormous; its per capita GNP is almost as low as India's; and it started out in 1949 with a terrible health system. Also, Egypt, Chile, Taiwan, Cuba, South Korea, and Sri Lanka are quite large, and they are poor or very poor (Table 1). In fact, these examples represent an enormous range of religion, political systems, and geography and suggest that such rates of decline in the birth rate can be achieved whenever the appropriate conditions are met.

TABLE 1

DECLINING BIRTH RATES AND PER CAPITA INCOME IN SELECTED DEVELOPING COUNTRIES. (THESE ARE CRUDE BIRTH RATES, UNCORRECTED FOR AGE DISTRIBUTION.)

		Births/1,000/Year		
Country	**Time Span**	**Avg. Annual Decline in Crude Birth Rate**	**Crude Birth Rate 1972**	**$ per Capita per Year 1973**
Barbados	1960–69	1.5	22	570
Taiwan	1955–71	1.2	24	390
Tunisia	1966–71	1.8	35	250
Mauritius	1961–71	1.5	25	240
Hong Kong	1960–72	1.4	19	970
Singapore	1955–72	1.2	23	920
Costa Rica	1963–72	1.5	32	560
South Korea	1960–70	1.2	29	250
Egypt	1966–70	1.7	37	210
Chile	1963–70	1.2	25	720
China			30	160
Cuba			27	530
Sri Lanka			30	110

"The common factor in these countries is that the *majority* of the population has shared in the economic and social benefits of significant national progress. . . . [M]aking health, education and jobs more broadly available to lower income groups in poor countries contribute[s] significantly toward the motivation for smaller families that is the prerequisite of a major reduction in birth rates" (Rich 1973).

The converse is also true. In Latin America, Cuba (annual per capita income $530), Chile ($720), Uruguay ($820), and Argentina ($1,160) have moderate to truly equitable distribution of goods and services and relatively low birth rates (27, 26, 23, and 22, respectively). In contrast, Brazil ($420), Mexico ($670), and Venezuela ($980) have very unequal distribution of goods and services and high birth rates (38, 42, and 41, respectively). Fertility rates in poor and relatively poor nations seem unlikely to fall as long as the bulk of the population does not share in increased benefits. . . .

. . . As a disillusioning quarter-century of aid giving has shown, the obstacles of getting aid to those segments of the population most in need of it are enormous. Aid has typically benefitted a small rich segment of society, partly because of the way aid programs have been designed but also because of human and institutional factors in the poor nations themselves (Owens and Shaw 1972). With some notable exceptions, the distribution of income and services in poor nations is extremely skewed—much more uneven than in rich countries. Indeed, much of the population is essentially outside the economic system. Breaking this pattern will be extremely difficult. It will require not only aid that is designed specifically to benefit the rural poor, but also important institutional changes such as decentralization of decision making and the development of greater autonomy and stronger links to regional and national markets for local groups and industries such as cooperative farms.

Thus, two things are being asked of rich nations and of the United States in particular: to increase nonmilitary foreign aid, including food aid, and to give it in ways, and to governments, that will deliver it to the poorest people and will improve their access to national economic institutions. These are not easy tasks, particularly the second, and there is no guarantee that birth rates will come down quickly in all countries. Still, many poor countries have, in varying degrees, begun the process of reform, and recent evidence suggests that aid and reform together can do much to solve the twin problems of high birth rates and economic underdevelopment. The tasks are far from impossible. Based on the evidence, the policies dictated by a sense of decency are also the most realistic and rational.

REFERENCES

BARRACLOUGH, G. 1975. The great world crisis I. *The N.Y. Rev. Books* **21**: 20–29.

BROWN, L. R. 1974a. In the Human Interest. W. W. Norton & Co., Inc., New York. 190 pp.

——. 1974b. By Bread Alone. Praeger, New York. 272 pp.

DAVIS, K. 1963. Population. *Sci. Amer.* **209**(3): 62–71.

DEMENY, P. 1974. The populations of the underdeveloped countries. *Sci. Amer.* **231**(3): 149–159.

GULLAND, J. 1975. The harvest of the sea. Pages 167–189 in W. W. Murdoch, ed. Environment: Resources, Pollution and Society, 2nd ed. Sinauer Assoc., Sunderland, Mass.

HARDIN, G. 1968. The tragedy of the commons. *Science* **162**: 1243–1248.

——. 1974. Living on a lifeboat. *BioScience* **24**(10): 561–568.

OWENS, E., and R. SHAW. 1972. Development Reconsidered. D. C. Heath & Co., Lexington, Mass. 190 pp.

RICH, W. 1973. Smaller families through social and economic progress. Overseas Development Council, Monograph #7, Washington, D.C. 73 pp.

TEITELBAUM, M. S. 1975. Relevance of demographic transition theory for developing countries. *Science* **188:** 420–425.

Transnational Institute. 1974. World Hunger: Causes and Remedies. Institute for Policy Studies, 1520 New Hampshire Ave., NW, Washington, D.C.

United Nations Economic and Social Council. 1974. Assessment present food situation and dimensions and causes of hunger and malnutrition in the world. E/Conf. 65/Prep/6, 8 May 1974.

University of California Food Task Force. 1974. A hungry world: the challenge to agriculture. University of California, Division of Agricultural Sciences. 303 pp.

QUESTIONS

1. Suppose that Murdoch and Oaten are correct in their analysis of the causes of high fertility rates. What changes should our government make in its treatment of those developing countries which have the most serious food problems?
2. Murdoch and Oaten hold that there are solutions other than private ownership to the "problems of the commons." They suggest a possible alternative—the communal ownership of the mechanisms and industries that exploit the resource, combined with communal planning for management. Just what would this alternative require from the United States? From you?

HOWARD L. PARSONS

MALTHUSIANISM AND SOCIALISM

Howard L. Parsons is professor of philosophy at the University of Bridgeport. He is a founding sponsor of the American Institute for Marxist Studies. Parsons's books include *Ethics in the Soviet Union Today* (1967), *Man East and West: Essays in East-West Philosophy* (1975), and *Marx and Engels on Ecology* (1977).

Parsons rejects the analysis of the causes of scarcity offered by Neo-Malthusians such as Garrett Hardin. For Parsons, the primary cause of scarcity lies in the private ownership, management, and direction of the means of production and reproduction. Capitalism, and the multinational corporations it has spawned, are responsible for world scarcities. In Parsons's view, those who offer a Neo-Malthusian analysis of the problems are interested in preserving capitalism and the privileges of those who benefit from it, and not in the satisfaction of the human needs of all people, including those of the Third World. Parsons see Marxist-socialism as the best Third World response to the problems of scarcity.

Like their mentor, Neo-Malthusians write as if the blind forces of natural and political economy determine the destiny of mankind. What they mean but hide by humanitarian computer language is that capitalism does and ought to determine that destiny and that a no-growth policy is capitalism's only way to survive. Modern Malthusians, armed with a computer, take, from the viewpoint of needs, a conservative, timid attitude toward natural and social economy. They do not challenge it with humankind's collective imagination, ingenuity, and effort. They emphasize limitation and restraint. They take scarcity to be a consequence of impersonal forces like technology (while population is, as Malthus argued, the "responsibility" of individual persons). But when they speak of scarcity they mean continued scarcity for large masses of people and continued exploitation and affluence for the ruling groups. They do not intend to save mankind. They intend to save themselves. While they are busy gobbling up the world's resources, they call on the world's people to stop propagating.

Capitalism cannot solve the scarcity problem. It limits production according to profit and market standards. It generates a surplus product that it cannot dispose of. It creates chronic unemployment. It is fearful of established communist economies and imminent Third World socialism. Therefore it cries out to the masses: We have enough people! Stop reproducing! Control your appetites for sex, food, fuel, etc.!

NEO-MALTHUSIAN CAPITALISM AND SOCIALISM
The philosophical views of Neo-Malthusian capitalism on nature, man, and political economy, in opposition to Marxist-socialist views, may be summarized as follows:

1) Nature is *severely limited* (scarce) in its resources for man and the laws it imposes on man, vs.: nature is *not so severely limited.*

2) Man is *either over nature or under nature*, vs.: man is *with nature.*

3) Man has *relatively little freedom* to control nature, vs.: man has *relatively much freedom* to control nature.

4) The limits of nature and man's freedom require *scarcity economics*, vs.: the potentialities of nature and man's freedom make possible *abundance economics.*

5) Nature should be controlled primarily by and for *a ruling class*, vs.: nature should be controlled by and for *the people.*

6) The growth of population and production should be *arrested* in accordance with the demands of the preservation of *capitalism* and its ruling class, vs.: population and production should be *developed* in accordance with the demands of a system serving human need, i.e., *socialism.*

7) There ought to be a *class division* between the capitalists who control the resources of nature and society and the people who control their sex and propagation, vs.: there ought to be a *classless society* in which all the people collectively control their lives in their social and natural environment.

The primary cause of scarcity in the modern world centers in the private ownership, management, and direction of the means of production and reproduction. Where industrial

Reprinted with permission of the publisher from *Revolutionary World*, Special Issue, "Self, Global Issues, and Ethics," vols. 21/22 (1977).

factories and techniques, machines, tools, and money are owned by a capitalist class, managed by their hirelings, and directed to the maximizing of profit for the owners, then the class of wage earners working for that class will live in absolute and relative scarcity, and those not working will be bordering on or in a state of starvation. An industrial capitalist enterprise if it is successful produces goods for consumption but also a certain portion of wealth which is returned to the enterprise in the form of investment in new means of production. The result is increased production, hence increased investment, and so on. This is industrial growth—in contemporary parlance, a positive feedback loop. Marx called it accumulation, a basic feature of capitalism. Accumulation is made possible because the capitalist appropriates the "free gifts" of nature[1]—the soil, the raw materials, the water, the wind and water power, etc.—and then the surplus product of laborers after they are paid a wage. . . .

[Such exploitation] generates wealth, but it also concentrates the wealth and the control of the wealth-creating process in the hands of a few. Nature and labor create wealth or value; a capitalist class organizes nature and labor so as to expand wealth and simultaneously restrict its expansion. The restriction occurs because the capitalist does not return to nature the soil-nutrients and vegetation that it strips from nature, defiling it with pollutants;[2] because the laborer is not paid enough to buy back his product; and because the growth and centralization of capital and the improvement of technology and labor-power produce a growing "industrial reserve army." A few become rich, most become poor. The accumulation of wealth is also the accumulation of misery. Capitalism engenders the "paradox" of "overproduction" and "underconsumption." The creativity of the laboring masses is both released and inhibited. This contradiction shows itself in the periodic rhythm of the boom and bust of capitalism.

Scarcity, which is an insufficiency of goods and services to meet the generic human needs of all the people, is a function of both the means of production and the size of the population. In what it produces capitalism is restricted in both quantity and kind because its obsessive drive is toward the greatest amount of surplus-value, accumulation, profitable production, and market expansion.[3] For example, U.S. capitalism does not use one-fourth of its industrial machinery. Capitalism is not organized primarily to produce goods and services directed to the fulfillment of generic human needs—food, clothing, housing, fuel, safety, medical care, family life, education, vocational skill, recreation, play, art, a fit ecological environment, love, creativity, old age security, etc. U.S. capitalism devotes much capital to the technology of war, the petroleum and automotive industries, banking, junk merchandise, and sales. In 1970 $44 billion were spent on public education, $77 billion on the military establishment. Advertising c ısumed $20 billion in 1971. Between 10 and 20 million U.S. people are chronically hungry.

This economy is anarchic and arbitrary with respect to its ends. In 1968, 100 of the biggest industrial firms owned about half of the total assets of the nation's 1.5 million corporations.[4] These monopolies exercise a tight control over investment, production, price, employment, competition, and innovation. Moreover, the system is very inefficient and wasteful on its own grounds, i.e., in the misemployment and underemployment of natural and human resources; the shunting of human energies, skills, and talents into profitable but

[1] Karl Marx, *Capital, A Critique of Political Economy*, Vol. III. Ed. by Frederick Engels. Translated from the first German edition by Ernest Untermann. Chicago: Charles H. Kerr, 1909, p. 865.

[2] Thus the prime cause of pollution is not individuals but corporations. See Gus Hall, *Ecology: Can We Survive Under Capitalism?* New York: International, 1972.

[3] Paul A. Baran and Paul M. Sweezy have emphasized the giant corporation's problem of utilizing rising surplus by private consumption and investment, sales, civilian government, militarism, and imperialism. *Monopoly Capital.* New York: Monthly Review, 1966.

[4] Robert L. Heilbroner et al., *In the Name of Profit.* New York: Doubleday, 1972.

humanly unproductive activities; the distribution of goods and services by means of commerce, competition, production, employment, wage, and demand; the distribution of income by ownership of the means of production; and the employment of parasitic, unproductive labor. Examples of unproductive laborers (as given by Paul A. Baran) are those engaged in armament manufacture, and in the making of items of luxury, conspicuous display, and social distinction; government officials; members of the military; clergymen; lawyers; tax evasion specialists; public relations experts; advertising agents; brokers; merchants; speculators.[5] An economy organized to serve humanistic ends by rational means would eliminate millions of such unproductive workers, and the scarcity which they now perpetuate would be overcome by productive employment directed to the fulfillment of generic human needs. Such workers now live off the surplus product of capital; they do not contribute to the production of wealth but serve to facilitate and solidify a system whose main ingredient is scarcity. . . .

A primary cause of the scarcity in the capitalist world is U.S. multinational corporations. The U.S. economy accounts for nearly half of the world capitalist industrial output and for 60 percent of the global total of foreign investment.[6] In 1968 the investments in Asia and Africa yielded more than 40 percent of all direct private foreign investment.[7] From 1961 to 1971 U.S. direct investors extracted a net balance of $30 billion from foreign countries.[8] During the decade of the 1950s, when they controlled 40 percent of the total GNP of Latin America, they invested more than $6 billion and took home more than $11 billion.[9] In manufacturing in Latin America, 78 percent of multinational foreign investments are financed from domestic savings; more than half of the profits made from these monies leave the country.[10] So there is a parasitic draining of the resources of these poor countries to the rich ones, pre-eminently the United States.

It is now public knowledge that these multinational investments have been protected on a world scale by intelligence agencies of the U.S. government, in collaboration with the Armed Forces and other official agencies. They have, in foreign countries, assisted in the overthrow of governments, initiated or sided in efforts at the kidnapping and assassination of government leaders in the Congo, Cuba, the Dominican Republic, and Chile,[11] bribed officials, blown up refineries, bridges, and railroads, bribed newspaper employees, corrupted scientists and Christian missionaries, and counterfeited currencies. (I omit here comparable crimes committed by these agencies at home.) The democratic governments overthrown—in Iran, Guatemala, Brazil, Uruguay, Chile—were replaced by fascistic, repressive, murderous regimes protecting multinational corporations[12] in collusion with local capitalists.

The principal perpetrators and perpetuators of scarcity and poverty, of oppression and suffering among the peoples of the world, are these multinational capitalists, their government agents, and their reactionary ideologues, who strive to block the people's progress, abundance, democracy, and socialism at every turn.

---

[5] *The Political Economy of Growth*. New York: Monthly Review, 1957, pp. 32–33.
[6] *Multinational Corporations*. A compendium of Papers Submitted to the Subcommittee on International Trade of the Committee on Finance of the United States Senate. Washington, D.C.: U.S. Government Printing Office, 1973, p. 44.
[7] Gus Hall, *Imperialism Today*. New York: International, 1972, p. 56.
[8] *Multinational Corporations*, p. 112.
[9] William Appleman Williams, *The Great Evasion*. Chicago: Quandrangle, 1964, p. 63.
[10] Ronald Müller, "The Multinational Corporation and the Underdevelopment of the Third World," in Charles K. Wilber, ed., *The Political Economy of Development*. New York: Random House, 1973, pp. 138–139.
[11] *Alleged Assassination Plots Involving Foreign Leaders*. An Interim Report of the Select Committee to Study Governmental Operations with Respect to Intelligence Activities United States Senate. Washington, D.C.: U.S. Government Printing Office, 1975.
[12] The subversion of these governments has now been established by sworn testimony. See Herbert Aptheker, "U.S. Imperialism and Its Intelligence Agencies," *Political Affairs*, Vol. LIV, No. 11 (November, 1975), pp. 54–55.

The new Malthusianism of our time gets support from two groups both of whom side with capitalism and oppose socialism: (1) the liberals, who for partially humanitarian reasons are distressed about the "excess" population and "scarce" means of subsistence in the world and want to moderate the scarcity; and (2) the conservatives, who are openly partisan toward the preservation of capitalism and against communism and the rising Third World. . . .

QUESTIONS

1. Is Marxist-socialism the solution to problems of scarcity?
2. Is capitalism the cause of the problems of world hunger and overpopulation? Explain.

SUGGESTED ADDITIONAL READINGS

AIKEN, WILLIAM, and HUGH LAFOLLETTE, eds.: *World Hunger and Moral Obligation*. Englewood Cliffs, N.J.: Prentice-Hall, 1977. With the exception of Joseph Fletcher, a theologian, and Garrett Hardin, a biologist, all the authors in this collection are philosophers. The writers examine various issues raised by the central question, "What moral responsibility do affluent nations (or the people in them) have to the starving masses?" The article by Peter Singer which is reprinted in this chapter is also reprinted in this volume and is followed by a postscript in which Singer (1) presents some later thoughts on the topic and (2) responds to some critics.

BERELSON, BERNARD: "Beyond Family Planning." *Science*, vol. 163, February 7, 1969, pp. 533–543. Berelson wrote this article while he was president of the Population Council. He provides an exhaustive categorization of proposals that go "beyond family planning" for the sake of "solving" the population problem. He then appraises these proposals in terms of technological readiness, political viability, administrative feasibility, economic capability, ethical acceptability, and presumed effectiveness.

BROWN, PETER G., and HENRY SHUE, eds.: *Food Policy*. New York: Free Press, 1977. This book is designed to provide a foundation for a reflective appraisal of questions about the moral obligation of the agriculturally affluent in regard to world hunger. The articles, which were all written specifically for this volume, are divided into four sections: (1)"Needs and Obligations"; (2) "Responsibilities in the Public Sector"; (3)"Responsibilities in the Private Sector"; and (4) "Reducing Dependence."

EBERSTADT, NICK: "Myths of the Food Crisis." *New York Review of Books*, February 19, 1976, pp 32–37. Eberstadt attacks the myths about world hunger which distort our perception of the problems and lead to the pessimism exemplified by Garrett Hardin.

GUSSOW, JOAN DYE: *The Feeding Web: Issues in Nutritional Ecology*. Palo Alto, Calif.: Bull Publishing Co., 1978. Gussow, a nutritionist, provides a collection of readings accompanied by her interpretations of those readings. She is concerned with "what the facts about the present state of the world" imply for "living human organisms completely dependent on complex foodstuffs for survival." The readings examine the biological, technical, social, scientific, and commercial matrices in which the production, purchasing, and consumption of food are embedded.

KUTZNER, PATRICIA L., CHRISTIAN MILLER, and MARK LEWY: *Who's Involved with Hunger: An Organizational Guide*. World Hunger Education Service, 1979. This is a list of various organizations which are concerned with hunger. The list includes government organizations and private agencies. The private agencies are subdivided according to their focus—global, national, and regional.

LAPPÉ, FRANCES MOORE, and JOSEPH COLLINS: *Food First: Beyond the Myth of Scarcity*, rev. ed. New York: Ballantine Books, 1978. Lappé and Collins reject the Neo-Malthusianism represented by Garrett Hardin. They try to dispel the "myths" which surround the world hunger issue and argue that the obstacles to overcoming world hunger are put up in our name, using our tax money, by corporations based in our economy.

LUCAS, GEORGE R., JR., and THOMAS OGLETREE, eds: *Lifeboat Ethics*. New York: Harper & Row, 1976. Most of the articles in this anthology appeared initially in *Soundings*. The articles are written by ethicists (many of whom are theologians) and scientists and grew out of concerns stemming from the advocacy of triage as a methodological response to world hunger.

RACHELS, JAMES: "Killing and Starving to Death." *Philosophy,* vol. 54, April 1979, pp. 159–171. Rachels, attacking the view that killing is worse than letting die, argues that letting die is just as bad as killing. For Rachels our duty not to let people die from starvation is as strong as our duty not to kill them.

WOGAMAN, J. PHILIP, ed: *The Population Crisis and Moral Responsibility.*Washington, D.C.: Public Affairs Press, 1973. This anthology emphasizes theological perspectives but contains articles by ethicists and population experts as well. The various articles are collected in four separate sections: (1) the moral basis of policy objectives; (2) the moral responsibility of government; (3) moral analysis of policy proposals; (4) moral responsibility of religious communities.

ANIMALS AND THE ENVIRONMENT

11

Humankind is not alone on this planet. We live among a multitude of animals, plants, and natural (inanimate) objects. Our interactions with these nonhuman forms of life and with the environment as a whole raise a number of moral prolems. Some of the most prominent of these problems are explored in this chapter.

OUR TREATMENT OF ANIMALS

In a now well-known book, *Animal Liberation* (1975), Peter Singer forcefully calls attention to the suffering that humankind routinely inflicts upon (nonhuman) animals.[1] For one thing, in order to ensure a steady supply of meat at our tables, we raise animals in such a way (the intensive rearing methods of "factory farming") that their short lives are dominated by pain and suffering. For another, in order to obtain scientific information whose value is often questionable, we devise experiments which entail the infliction of intense pain on animals, our experimental subjects. Because Singer finds humankind so willing to subordinate important animal interests to much less important human interests, he charges the human community with "speciesism." "Experimenting on animals, and eating their flesh, are perhaps the two major forms of speciesism in our society."[2]

Singer employs the term "speciesism" in order to emphasize similarities with racism and sexism. Just as black liberation entails the eradication of racism and women's liberation entails the eradication of sexism, animal liberation entails the eradication of speciesism. According to Singer,

> The racist . . . [gives] greater weight to the interests of members of his own race, when there is a clash between their interests and the interests of another race. Similarly the speciest allows the interests of his own species to override the greater interests of members of other species.[3]

We share a common moral conviction that it is wrong to treat a human being "like a guinea pig." In the face of Singer's attack on speciesism, we are encouraged to wonder if it might be wrong to treat a guinea pig "like a guinea pig."

It seems clear that we do, by and large, treat animals as means to our own ends. Is our underlying attitude toward animals justifiable? As soon as reflection begins on this topic, the questions seem to multiply rapidly. What is the difference between human life and animal life? To what extent, and on what grounds, is human life of greater worth than

---

[1]Peter Singer, *Animal Liberation* (New York: New York Review, 1975).
[2]Peter Singer, "All Animals are Equal," *Philosophic Exchange*, vol. 1 (Summer 1974), p. 111.
[3]Ibid., p. 108.

animal life? Do animals have rights, perhaps even a right to life? Are animal interests rightly accorded equal consideration with human interests, as Singer believes? Or, perhaps, are animal interests rightly subordinated, at least to some extent, to human interests? In one of this chapter's selections, Martin Benjamin suggests that the difference between human beings and animals is by and large the difference between beings who possess reflective-consciousness (persons) and those who possess only simple consciousness. Since he considers the former to have greater worth than the latter, he believes that it is not wrong to attribute more weight to human interests than animal interests. In his view, however, animal interests must not be disregarded. They may not be sacrificed for the sake of "trivial (human) tastes or desires," but they may be sacrificed in order to meet "important (human) needs."

Is the human interest in eating meat sufficiently important to justify our practice of raising and slaughtering animals? Intertwined with this question is the issue of a vegetarian diet. Advocates of vegetarianism offer diverse arguments to support their position. Some advocate a vegetarian diet simply because they believe it to be superior in terms of health benefits. If a vegetarian diet does offer special health advantages (a controversial claim), then each individual, as a matter of personal prudence, would be well advised to adopt it. Apart from this *prudential argument,* many vegetarians advance *moral arguments* in defense of their diet. One common moral argument, closely related to the considerations developed in Chapter 10, is based on the fact that hunger, malnutrition, and starvation seriously threaten many people in our world. It is morally indefensible, the argument goes, to waste desperately needed protein by feeding our grain to animals whom we then eat. Eight pounds of protein in the form of grain are necessary on the average to produce one pound of protein in the form of meat. Since this process is so inefficient, we are morally obliged to adopt a vegetarian diet so that our protein resources in the form of grain can be shared with those who desperately need help. Though this particular moral argument is not without force, it would seem that it does not establish a need for a completely vegetarian diet. It may well be that world hunger could effectively be alleviated if people in affluent countries simply consumed *less* meat.

The most important moral arguments advanced in defense of a vegetarian diet are those which take account of the impact of meat production on the animals themselves. Two lines of argument in this category may be distinguished. (1) Though it is not necessarily wrong to kill animals for food (assuming the killing is painless), it is morally indefensible to subject them to the cruelty of "factory farming." Since the meat available in our society is produced in just this way, we are morally obliged not to eat it. (2) It is morally wrong to kill animals for food, however painless the killing; animals, like human beings, have a right to life. In the opening selection of this chapter, James Rachels explicitly advances the first line of argument and is strongly inclined to accept the second as well.

THE ENVIRONMENT AND THE HUMAN COMMUNITY

We live now in a time not infrequently called the "age of ecology." There is an increasing awareness of and dissatisfaction with a number of tendencies in our society: (1) the tendency to produce material goods with little regard for the extent to which the by-products of industrial technology serve to pollute and degrade the environment; (2) the tendency to "develop" the land with little regard for the preservation of wilderness areas as well as endangered plant and animal species; (3) the tendency to exploit natural resources with little regard for conservation.

What moral obligations do we have with regard to the environment? In the rest of this section, we will consider only those moral obligations which are related to and predicated upon human needs and interests. As will be made clear in the following section, however, it is a controversial matter whether an adequate "environmental ethic" can be predicated solely upon a consideration of *human* interests.

The Duty Not to Pollute the Environment

It seems clear, by reference to human needs and interests, that we can make out a prima facie duty not to pollute the environment. That is, in the absence of overriding moral considerations, we are morally obliged not to pollute. Human welfare, in fact human life, crucially depends on such necessities as breathable air, drinkable water, and eatable food. Thus, in the absence of overriding moral considerations, pollution is morally unacceptable precisely because it is damaging to the public welfare. On an alternative construal, the prima facie duty not to pollute may be understood as being based upon a basic human right, the right to a livable environment. Still, however confident we are in positing a prima facie duty not to pollute, we are left with the problem of weighing the collective human interest in a nonpolluted environment against competing human interests, often economic in nature.

The following schematic example illustrates some of the complexities that confront us when environmental interests clash with economic interests. An industrial plant, representing a (small, large, massive) financial investment, producing a product that is (unessential, very desirable, essential) to society, and providing a (small, large, enormous) number of jobs, pollutes the environment in a (minor, substantial, major) way. In which of these several cases is the continued operation of the plant morally unacceptable? Certainly the general public interest in the quality of the environment must be recognized. But what of the economic interests of the owner, the employees, and potential consumers? In sum, how is the collective human interest in a nonpolluted environment to be equitably weighed against competing economic interests? At this point, many are inclined to appeal to the kind of cost/benefit analyses that are characteristic of utilitarian thinking.

The Duty to Preserve the Environment

If human interests provide a viable foundation for a moral obligation not to pollute, it may also be possible to recruit them in support of a more generalized moral obligation to preserve our natural environment. Ecology teaches us that human life is crucially intertwined with the ecosystem as a whole, yet ecologists frequently emphasize how little we actually know about the complicated multileveled interaction of life forms. If we destroy one part of the ecosystem, we may unwittingly trigger a chain of events that ultimately culminates in substantial detriment to human well-being. Hence, a serious regard for human welfare seems to necessitate our making every effort to preserve our natural environment.

The Duty to Preserve Endangered Species and Wilderness Areas

Are we morally obliged to preserve endangered animal and plant species? Are we morally obliged to preserve (at least some) wilderness areas? In many ways the continued existence of endangered species and wilderness areas brings enjoyment to or has utility for people. Hence, it can be argued, a moral obligation to preserve both endangered species and wilderness areas can be firmly based on the interests of the human community. In one of this chapter's selections, Joel Feinberg emphasizes the interests of future generations and argues that we have a duty to future generations to preserve endangered species.

Duties to Future Generations

In speaking of duties *to* future generations, we imply that future generations have rights which we are morally obligated to respect. Yet some philosophers contend that it does not make sense to speak of future generations as having rights: How can something that does not even exist have rights? Feinberg defends the view that it makes sense to speak of future generations as having rights. In providing such a defense, he enters upon a difficult but enlightening analysis of the concept of a right. Along the way, he draws conclusions as to whether or not individual animals, individual plants, and whole species (of plants and animals) may be said to have rights. Such conclusions are relevant in assessing whether or not, with regard to environmental matters, we have moral obligations *to* nonhuman forms of life.

Both the presently existing generation and future generations, it would seem, have a serious interest in the minimization of pollution, the preservation of the environment in general, and the preservation of endangered species and wilderness areas in particular. With regard to the conservation of natural resources, however, our interests (i.e., those of the present generation) may very well conflict with those of posterity. Thus we find John Passmore in this chapter concerned with the following question: To what extent, if at all, do we have a duty to future generations to conserve natural resources?

Broadly speaking, two approaches to this important question may be distinguished.

(1) Approaches Minimizing the Duty to Future Generations Here the optimistic argument is made that science and technology will develop to the point that future generations will easily find substitutes for natural resources that we find essential. At any rate, the needs of future generations are so uncertain and unforeseeable that we ought not to bother about conservation at all.

(2) Approaches Maximizing the Duty to Future Generations Here it is contended that, despite inevitable uncertainties about the needs of future generations, we are relatively certain of some of these needs. At any rate, we must act responsibly on the facts as we see them. Thus it is our duty to future generations to conserve the planet's natural resources, to cut excess consumption, and to recycle as effectively as possible.

DO WE NEED A NONANTHROPOCENTRIC ETHIC?

Our morality can be called *anthropocentric* in that we ordinarily presume that moral obligation is essentially a function of *human* interests. In recent years, however, it has frequently been suggested that an anthropocentric morality cannot provide an adequate foundation for an understanding of our moral obligations with regard to the environment. In this spirit, we have heard proposals for the development of a "new ethic," an "ecological ethic," an "environmental ethic." The extension of moral consideration to the nonhuman community is the thread that links all such proposals. Aldo Leopold (1887–1948), whose essay "The Land Ethic" has encouraged many to take seriously the possibility of developing a nonanthropocentric ethic, writes:

> The land ethic simply enlarges the boundaries of the community to include soils, waters, plants, and animals, or collectively, the land. . . . In short, a land ethic changes the role of *Homo sapiens* from conqueror of the land-community to plain member and citizen of it. It implies respect for his fellow-members, and also respect for the community as such. . . . A thing is right when it tends to preserve the integrity, stability, and beauty of the biotic community. It is wrong when it tends otherwise.[4]

In one of this chapter's selections, William Godfrey-Smith considers the value of wilderness. He maintains that wilderness has substantial *instrumental* value (for humankind)

---

[4]Aldo Leopold, "The Land Ethic," in *A Sand County Almanac* (New York: Oxford University Press, 1966), pp. 219, 220, 240.

but insists that it has *intrinsic* value as well. In the spirit of Leopold, Godfrey-Smith calls for the development of a nonanthropocentric ethic and briefly explores its possibilities.

Thomas A. Mappes

JAMES RACHELS

VEGETARIANISM

A biographical sketch of James Rachels is found on page 52.

The primary reason why cruelty to animals is wrong, Rachels argues, is that tortured animals *suffer,* just as tortured humans suffer. Inflicting pain on animals can sometimes be justified, he maintains, but we must have a sufficiently good reason for doing so. The fact that we enjoy the way meat tastes is a reason that "will not even come close to justifying the cruelty" that is part and parcel of contemporary meat production. Moreover, he contends, since humanely produced meat would be prohibitively expensive for most of us, a vegetarian diet is, for all practical purposes, a moral demand. Rachels considers the theoretical possibility of obtaining meat by painlessly killing humanely raised animals. In his view, even this option is morally problematic. Reluctant to dismiss the view that animals have a "right to life," he insists that we must abandon "the Kantian attitude that animals are nothing more than things to be used for our purposes."

. . . One of my conclusions will be that it is morally wrong for us to eat meat. Many readers will find this implausible and even faintly ridiculous, as I once did. After all, meat eating is a normal, well-established part of our daily routines; people have always eaten meat; and many find it difficult even to conceive of what an alternate diet would be like. So it is not easy to take seriously the possibility that it might be wrong. Moreover, vegetarianism is commonly associated with Eastern religions whose tenets we do not accept, and with extravagant, unfounded claims about health. A quick perusal of vegetarian literature might confirm the impression that it is all a crackpot business: tracts have titles like "Victory Through Vegetables" and promise that if one will only keep to a meatless diet one will have perfect health and be filled with wisdom. Of course we can ignore this kind of nonsense. However, there are other arguments for vegetarianism that must be taken seriously. . . .

I

The wrongness of cruelty to animals is often explained in terms of its effects on human beings. The idea seems to be that the animals' interests are not *themselves* morally important or worthy of protection, but, since cruelty to animals often has bad consequences for *humans,* it is wrong to make animals suffer. In legal writing, for example, cruelty to animals is included among the "victimless crimes," and the problem of justifying legal prohibitions is seen as comparable to justifying the prohibition of other behavior, such as homosexuality or the distribution of pornography, where no one (no human) is obviously hurt. Thus, Louis Schwartz says that, in prohibiting the torturing of animals:

> It is not the mistreated dog who is the ultimate object of concern . . . Our concern is for the feelings of other human beings, a large proportion of whom, although accustomed to the slaughter of animals for food, readily identify themselves with a tortured dog or horse and respond with great sensitivity to its sufferings.[1]

Philosophers also adopt this attitude. Kant, for example, held that we have no direct duties to nonhuman animals. "The Categorical Imperative," the ultimate principle of morality, applies only to our dealings with humans:

> The practical imperative, therefore, is the following: Act so that you treat humanity, whether in your own person or in that of another, always as an end and never as a means only.[2]

And of other animals, Kant says:

> But so far as animals are concerned, we have no direct duties. Animals are not self-conscious, and are there merely as means to an end. That end is man.[3]

He adds that we should not be cruel to animals only because "He who is cruel to animals becomes hard also in his dealings with men."[4]

Surely this is unacceptable. Cruelty to animals ought to be opposed, not only because of the ancillary effects on humans, but because of the direct effects on the animals themselves. Animals that are tortured *suffer,* just as tortured humans suffer, and *that* is the primary reason why it is wrong. We object to torturing humans on a number of grounds, but the main one is that the victims suffer so. Insofar as nonhuman animals also suffer, we have the *same* reason to oppose torturing them, and it is indefensible to take the one suffering but not the other as grounds for objection.

Although cruelty to animals is wrong, it does not follow that we are never justified in inflicting pain on an animal. Sometimes we are justified in doing this, just as we are sometimes justified in inflicting pain on humans. It does follow, however, that there must be a *good reason* for causing the suffering, and if the suffering is great, the justifying reason must be correspondingly powerful. As an example, consider the treatment of the civet cat, a highly intelligent and sociable animal. Civet cats are trapped and placed in small cages inside darkened sheds, where the temperature is kept up to 110°F by fires.[5] They are confined in this way until they finally die. What justifies this extraordinary mistreatment? These animals have the misfortune to produce a substance that is useful in the manufacture of perfume. Musk, which is scraped from their genitals once a day for as long as they can survive, makes the scent of perfume last a bit longer after each application. (The heat

[1]Louis B. Schwartz, "Morals Offenses and the Model Penal Code," *Columbia Law Review,* 63 (1963); reprinted in Joel Feinberg and Hyman Gross, eds., *Philosophy of Law* (Encino, Calif.: Dickenson Publishing Company, Inc., 1975), p. 156.
[2]Immanuel Kant, *Foundations of the Metaphysics of Morals,* trans. Lewis White Beck (Indianapolis: The Bobbs-Merrill Co., Inc., 1959), p. 47.
[3]Immanuel Kant, *Lectures on Ethics,* trans. Louis Infield (New York: Harper Torchbooks, 1963), p. 239.
[4]Ibid., p. 240.
[5]Muriel the Lady Dowding, "Furs and Cosmetics: Too High a Price?" in Stanley and Rosling Godlovitch and John Harris, eds., *Animals, Men and Morals* (New York: Taplinger Publishing Co., Inc., 1972), p. 36.

increases their "production" of musk.) Here Kant's rule—"Animals are merely means to an end; that end is man"—is applied with a vengeance. To promote one of the most trivial interests we have, thousands of animals are tormented for their whole lives.

It is usually easy to persuade people that this use of animals is not justified, and that we have a moral duty not to support such cruelties by consuming their products. The argument is simple: Causing suffering is not justified unless there is a good reason; the production of perfume made with musk causes considerable suffering; our enjoyment of this product is not a good enough reason to justify causing that suffering; therefore, the use of animals in this way is wrong. At least my experience has been that, once people learn the facts about musk production, they come to regard using such products as morally objectionable. They are surprised to discover, however, that an exactly analogous argument can be given in connection with the use of animals as food. Animals that are raised and slaughtered for food also suffer, and our enjoyment of the way they taste is not a sufficient justification for mistreating them.

Most people radically underestimate the amount of suffering that is caused to animals who are raised and slaughtered for food.[6] They think, in a vague way, that slaughterhouses are cruel, and perhaps even that methods of slaughter ought to be made more humane. But after all, the visit to the slaughterhouse is a relatively brief episode in the animal's life; and beyond that, people imagine that the animals are treated well enough. Nothing could be further from the truth. Today the production of meat is Big Business, and the helpless animals are treated more as machines in a factory than as living creatures.

Veal calves, for example, spend their lives in pens too small to allow them to turn around or even to lie down comfortably—exercise toughens the muscles, which reduces the "quality" of the meat, and besides, allowing the animals adequate living space would be prohibitively expensive. In these pens the calves cannot perform such basic actions as grooming themselves, which they naturally desire to do, because there is not room for them to twist their heads around. It is clear that the calves miss their mothers, and like human infants they want something to suck: they can be seen trying vainly to suck the sides of their stalls. In order to keep their meat pale and tasty, they are fed a liquid diet deficient in both iron and roughage. Naturally they develop cravings for these things, because they need them. The calf's craving for iron is so strong that, if it is allowed to turn around, it will lick at its own urine, although calves normally find this repugnant. The tiny stall, which prevents the animal from turning, solves this "problem." The craving for roughage is especially strong since without it the animal cannot form a cud to chew. It cannot be given any straw for bedding, since the animal would be driven to eat it, and that would spoil the meat. For these animals the slaughterhouse is not an unpleasant end to an otherwise contented life. As terrifying as the process of slaughter is, for them it may actually be regarded as a merciful release.

Similar stories can be told about the treatment of other animals on which we dine. In order to "produce" animals by the millions, it is necessary to keep them crowded together in small spaces. Chickens are commonly kept eight or ten to a space smaller than a newspaper page. Unable to walk around or even stretch their wings—much less build a nest—the birds become vicious and attack one another. The problem is sometimes exacerbated because the birds are so crowded that, unable to move, their feet literally grow around the wire floors of the cages anchoring them to the spot. An "anchored" bird cannot escape attack no matter how desperate it becomes. Mutilation of the animals is an efficient solu-

---

[6]By far the best account of these cruelties is to be found in Chapter 3 of Peter Singer's *Animal Liberation* (New York: New York Review Books, 1975). I have drawn on Singer's work for the factual material in the following two paragraphs. *Animal Liberation* should be consulted for a thorough treatment of matters to which I can refer here only sketchily.

tion. To minimize the damage they can do to one another, the birds' beaks are cut off. The mutilation is painful, but probably not as painful as other sorts of mutilations that are routinely practiced. Cows are castrated, not to prevent the unnatural "vices" to which overcrowded chickens are prone, but because castrated cows put on more weight, and there is less danger of meat being "tainted" by male hormones.

> In Britain an anesthetic must be used, unless the animal is very young, but in America anesthetics are not in general use. The procedure is to pin the animal down, take a knife and slit the scrotum, exposing the testicles. You then grab each testicle in turn and pull on it, breaking the cord that attaches it; on older animals it may be necessary to cut the cord.[7]

It must be emphasized that the treatment I am describing—and I have hardly scratched the surface here—is not out of the ordinary. It is typical of the way that animals raised for food are treated, now that meat production is Big Business. As Peter Singer puts it, these are the sorts of things that happened to your dinner when it was still an animal.

What accounts for such cruelties? As for the meat producers, there is no reason to think they are unusually cruel men. They simply accept the common attitude expressed by Kant: "Animals are merely means to an end; that end is man." The cruel practices are adopted not because they are cruel but because they are efficient, given that one's only concern is to produce meat (and eggs) for humans as cheaply as possible. But clearly this use of animals is immoral if anything is. Since we can nourish ourselves very well without eating them, our *only reason* for doing all this to the animals is our enjoyment of the way they taste. And this will not even come close to justifying the cruelty.

II

Does this mean that we should stop eating meat? Such a conclusion will be hard for many people to accept. It is tempting to say: "What is objectionable is not *eating* the animals, but only making them suffer. Perhaps we ought to protest the way they are treated, and even work for better treatment of them. But it doesn't follow that we must stop eating them." This sounds plausible until you realize that it would be impossible to treat the animals decently and still produce meat in sufficient quantities to make it a normal part of our diets. As I have already remarked, cruel methods are used in the meat-production industry because such methods are economical; they enable the producers to market a product that people can afford. Humanely produced chicken, beef, and pork would be so expensive that only the very rich could afford them. (*Some* of the cruelties could be eliminated without too much expense—the cows could be given an anesthetic before castration, for example, even though this alone would mean a slight increase in the cost of beef. But others, such as overcrowding, could not be eliminated without really prohibitive cost.) So to work for better treatment for the animals would be to work for a situation in which most of us would *have* to adopt a vegetarian diet.

Still, there remains the interesting theoretical question: *If* meat could be produced humanely, without mistreating the animals prior to killing them painlessly, would there be anything wrong with it? The question is only of theoretical interest because the actual choice we face in the supermarket is whether to buy the remains of animals that are *not* treated humanely. Still, the question has some interest, and I want to make two comments about it.

First, it is a vexing issue whether animals have a "right to life" that is violated when we kill them for trivial purposes; but we should not simply assume until proven otherwise

[7]Singer, *Animal Liberation*, p. 152.

that they *don't* have such a right.[8] We assume that humans have a right to life—it would be wrong to murder a normal, healthy human even if it were done painlessly—and it is hard to think of any plausible rationale for granting this right to humans that does not also apply to other animals. Other animals live in communities, as do humans; they communicate with one another, and have ongoing social relationships, killing them disrupts lives that are perhaps not as complex, emotionally and intellectually, as our own, but that are nevertheless quite complicated. They suffer, and are capable of happiness as well as fear and distress, as we are. So what could be the rational basis for saying that we have a right to life, but that they don't? Or even more pointedly, what could be the rational basis for saying that a severely retarded human, who is inferior in every important respect to an intelligent animal, has a right to life but that the animal doesn't? Philosophers often treat such questions as "puzzles," assuming that there must be answers even if we are not clever enough to find them. I am suggesting that, on the contrary, there may not be any acceptable answers to these questions. If it seems, intuitively, that there *must* be some difference between us and the other animals which confers on us, but not them, a right to life, perhaps this intuition is mistaken. At the very least, the difficulty of answering such questions should make us hesitant about asserting that it is all right to kill animals, as long as we don't make them suffer, unless we are also willing to take seriously the possibility that it is all right to kill people, so long as we don't make them suffer.

Second, it is important to see the slaughter of animals for food as part of a larger pattern that characterizes our whole relationship with the nonhuman world. Animals are wrenched from their natural homes to be made objects of our entertainment in zoos, circuses, and rodeos. They are used in laboratories, not only for experiments that are themselves morally questionable,[9] but also in testing everything from shampoo to chemical weapons. They are killed so that their heads can be used as wall decorations, or their skins as ornamental clothing or rugs. Indeed, simply killing them for the fun of it is thought to be "sport."[10] This pattern of cruel exploitation flows naturally from the Kantian attitude that animals are nothing more than things to be used for our purposes. It is this whole attitude that must be opposed, and not merely its manifestation in our willingness to hurt the animals we eat. Once one rejects this attitude, and no longer regards the animals as disposable at one's whim, one ceases to think it all right to kill them, even painlessly, just for a snack.

But now let me return to the more immediate practical issue. The meat at the supermarket was not produced by humane methods. The animals whose flesh this meat once was were abused in ways similar to the ones I have described. Millions of other animals are being treated in these ways now, and their flesh will soon appear in the markets. Should one support such practices by purchasing and consuming its products?

It is discouraging to realize that no animals will actually be helped simply by one person ceasing to eat meat. One consumer's behavior, by itself, cannot have a noticeable impact on an industry as vast as the meat business. However, it is important to see one's behavior in a wider context. There are already millions of vegetarians, and because they don't eat meat there *is* less cruelty than there otherwise would be. The question is whether one ought to side with that group, or with the carnivores whose practices cause the suffering. Compare the position of someone thinking about whether to buy slaves in the year

[8]It is controversial among philosophers whether animals can have any rights at all. See various essays collected in Part IV of Tom Regan and Peter Singer, eds., *Animal Rights and Human Obligations* (Englewood Cliffs, N.J.: Prentice-Hall, 1976). My own defense of animal rights is given in "Do Animals Have a Right to Liberty?" pp. 205–223, and in "A Reply to VanDeVeer," pp. 230–32.
[9]See Singer, *Animal Liberation*, Chap. 2.
[10]It is sometimes said, in defense of "non-slob" hunting: "Killing for pleasure is wrong, but killing for food is all right." This won't do, since for those of us who are able to nourish ourselves without killing animals, killing them for food *is* a form of killing for pleasure, namely, the pleasures of the palate.

1820. He might reason as follows: "The whole practice of slavery is immoral, but I cannot help any of the poor slaves by keeping clear of it. If I don't buy these slaves, someone else will. One person's decision just can't by itself have any impact on such a vast business. So I may as well use slaves like everyone else." The first thing we notice is that this fellow was too pessimistic about the possibilities of a successful movement; but beyond that, there is something else wrong with his reasoning. If one really thinks that a social practice is immoral, that *in itself* is sufficient grounds for a refusal to participate. In 1848 Thoreau remarked that even if someone did not want to devote himself to the abolition movement, and actively oppose slavery, ". . . it is his duty, at least, to wash his hands of it, and, if he gives it no thought longer, not to give it practically his support."[11] In the case of slavery, this seems clear. If it seems less clear in the case of the cruel exploitation of nonhuman animals, perhaps it is because the Kantian attitude is so deeply entrenched in us. . . .

QUESTIONS

1. Are we morally obligated to adopt a vegetarian diet?
2. Do animals have a right to life?
3. Is hunting a morally justifiable practice?

MARTIN BENJAMIN

ETHICS AND ANIMAL CONSCIOUSNESS

Martin Benjamin is professor of philosophy at Michigan State University. He is especially interested in the application of philosophical analysis and theory to questions of social policy. He is the coauthor of *Ethics and Nursing* (1981) and the author of such articles as "Pacifism for Pragmatists," "Moral Agency and Negative Acts in Medicine," and "Can Moral Responsibility be Collective and Non-Distributive?"

Benjamin focuses attention on three historically important philosophical positions regarding the "nature and extent of ethical restrictions on the human use and treatment of nonhuman animals"—"indirect obligation" theories, "no obligation" theories, and "direct obligation" theories. Rejecting each of these positions as inadequate, he nonetheless identifies in each a "kernel of truth" which he incorporates into a fourth position. According to this alternative position, it is important to distinguish beings possessing reflective-consciousness from those possessing only simple consciousness. The former (identified as persons) may justifiably be thought to have a higher status or greater worth than the latter. By virtue of the higher status or greater worth of persons, their important needs (but not their "trivial tastes or desires") are considered sufficient to justify the infliction of pain and suffering on beings possessing only simple consciousness.

[11]Henry David Thoreau, *Civil Disobedience* (1848).

INTRODUCTION

Are there any ethical restrictions on the ways in which human beings may use and treat nonhuman animals? If so, what are they and how are they to be justified? In what follows, I will first review three standard responses to these questions and briefly indicate why none of them is entirely satisfactory. Next I will identify what I take to be the kernel of truth in each of the three responses and then I will attempt to blend them into a fourth, more adequate, position. In so doing, I hope to suggest the importance, from an ethical point of view, of further inquiry into the nature and extent of consciousness in nonhuman animals.

THREE STANDARD POSITIONS

Historically, Western philosophers have responded to questions about the nature and extent of ethical restrictions on the human use and treatment of nonhuman animals in three ways. First, those who hold what I label "Indirect Obligation" theories maintain that ethical restrictions on the use and treatment of animals can be justified *only if* they can be derived from direct obligations to human beings. The second type of response, which I label "No Obligation" theories, holds that there are no restrictions whatever on what humans may do to other animals. And the third type of response, which I label "Direct Obligation" theories, maintains that ethical restrictions on the use and treatment of animals can sometimes be justified solely for the sake of animals themselves. I will not elaborate each of these positions.

I. Indirect Obligation

Among the most noted philosophers in the Western tradition, St. Thomas Aquinas (1225–1274) and Immanuel Kant (1724–1804) have acknowledged restrictions on human conduct with regard to the use and treatment of nonhuman animals, but these restrictions are, in their view, ultimately grounded upon obligations to other human beings. Blending views that can be traced both to the Bible and Aristotle, Aquinas held a hierarchial or means-end view of the relationship between plants, animals, and humans, respectively:

> There is no sin in using a thing for the purpose for which it is. Now the order of things is such that the imperfect are for the perfect . . . things, like plants which merely have life, are all alike for animals, and all animals are for man. Wherefore it is not unlawful if men use plants for the good of animals, and animals for the good of man, as the Philosopher states (*Politics*, i , 3).
>
> Now the most necessary use would seem to consist in the fact that animals use plants, and men use animals, for food, and this cannot be done unless these be deprived of life, wherefore it is lawful both to take life from plants for the use of animals, and from animals for the use of men. In fact this is in keeping with the commandment of God himself (*Genesis* i, 29, 30 and *Genesis* ix, 3).[1]

Nevertheless, it does not follow, for Aquinas, that one can do anything to an animal. For example, one is still prohibited from killing another person's ox: "He that kills another's ox, sins, not through killing the ox, but through injuring another man in his property. Wherefore this is not a species of the sin of murder but of the sin of theft or robbery." And there may

---

[1]St. Thomas Aquinas, *Summa Theologica,* literally translated by the English Dominican Fathers (Benziger Brothers, 1918), Part II, Question 64, Article 1. Reprinted in Tom Regan and Peter Singer, eds., *Animal Rights and Human Obligations* (Prentice-Hall, 1976), p. 119.

even be similarly *indirect* grounds for not harming animals who are no one's property. Thus, Aquinas explains,

> if any passages of Holy Writ seem to forbid us to be cruel to dumb animals, for instance to kill a bird with its young: this is either to remove man's thoughts from being cruel to other men, and lest through being cruel to animals one become cruel to human beings: or because injury to an animal leads to the temporal hurt of man, either of the doer of the deed, or of another.[2]

Kant, too, held that insofar as humans are obligated to restrain themselves in their dealings with animals, it is due to their obligations to other humans. Thus,

> so far as animals are concerned, we have no direct duties. Animals are not self-conscious and are there merely as a means to an end. That end is man. . . . Our duties towards animals are merely indirect duties towards humanity. Animal nature has analogies to human nature, and by doing our duties to animals in respect of manifestations of human nature, we indirectly do our duty to humanity. . . . If . . . any acts of animals are analogous to human acts and spring from the same principles, we have duties towards the animals because thus we cultivate the same duties towards human beings. If a man shoots his dog because the animal is no longer capable of service, he does not fail in his duty to the dog, for the dog cannot judge, but his act is inhuman and damages in itself that humanity which it is his duty to show towards mankind. If he is not to stifle his human feelings, he must practice kindness towards animals, for he who is cruel to animals becomes hard also in his dealings with men.[3]

Thus Aquinas and Kant both hold what I have labeled "Indirect Obligation" theories with regard to ethical restrictions on the use and treatment of animals. Although they agree that we have obligations *with regard* to animals, these obligations are *not,* at bottom, *owed to* the animals themselves but rather they are owed to other human beings.

There are, nonetheless, significant problems with Aquinas's and Kant's positions, at least in their present forms. First, insofar as Aquinas assumes that it is necessary for humans to use animals for food and thus to deprive them of life, his position must be reconsidered in the light of modern knowledge about nutrition. It has been maintained, for example, that a perfectly nutritious diet may require little or no deprivation of animal life and, even if it does, that the average American consumes twice as much animal protein as his or her body can possibly use.[4] Insofar as we continue to consume large quantities of animal foodstuff requiring pain and the deprivation of life, then, we do so, not so much to serve vital nutritional demands, but rather to indulge our acquired tastes. Secondly, insofar as Aquinas's view is based upon a hierarchial world-view and assumes that those lower in the order or less perfect are to serve the good of those higher or more perfect, it is open to a serious theoretical objection. It is, unfortunately, not difficult to imagine a group of beings—perhaps from another part of the universe—who are more rational and more powerful than we. Assuming that such beings are more perfect than we are, it seems to follow, if we adopt the principles underlying Aquinas's view, that we ought to acquiesce in their using us for whichever of their purposes they fancy we would serve. But do we want to agree with the rightness of this? And if we take Aquinas's view, would we have any grounds on which to disagree?

---

[2]St. Thomas Aquinas, *Summa Contra Gentiles,* literally translated by the English Dominican Fathers (Benziger Brothers, 1928), Third Book, Part II, Chap. CXII. Reprinted in Regan and Singer, p. 59.
[3]Immanuel Kant, "Duties to Animals and Spirits," in *Lectures on Ethics,* translated by Louis Infield (Harper and Row, 1963). Reprinted in Regan and Singer, p. 122.
[4]Francis Moore Lappé, "Fantasies of Famine," *Harper's,* 250 (February 1975), p. 53.

As for Kant's view, the main difficulties have to do first with his emphasis on self-consciousness as a condition for being the object of a direct obligation, and second with his assumption that all and only human beings are self-conscious. I will postpone consideration of the first difficulty until later. For the moment, let me simply develop the second. Even supposing that being self-conscious is a necessary condition for being the object of a direct obligation, it does not follow either that *all* human beings are the objects of direct obligations or that *no* animal can be the object of such an obligation. First, advances in medical knowledge, techniques, and technology have, among other things, preserved and prolonged the lives of a number of human beings who are severely retarded or otherwise mentally impaired due to illness or accident and the irreversibly comatose (e.g., Karen Ann Quinlan). In our day, then, if not in Kant's, one cannot assume that all human beings are self-conscious. Second, some contemporary researchers have suggested that at least some non-human animals have a capacity for becoming self-conscious that has, until recently, been undetected or ignored by humans. Thus, even if we follow Kant and accept self-consciousness as a condition for being the object of direct obligations, it does not follow that *all* and *only* humans satisfy this condition. Some humans, it may turn out, will not be the objects of direct obligations and some animals will.

2. No Obligation

If animals are not conscious—that is, if they are not sentient and have no capacity for pleasure, pain, or any other mental states—they may not even be the objects of indirect obligations. Insofar as Aquinas says that it is possible to be "cruel to dumb animals" and Kant says that "he who is cruel to animals becomes hard in his dealings with men," each presupposes that animals, unlike plants and machines, are sentient and are thereby capable of sensation and consciousness. Thus it is surprising to find René Descartes (1596–1650), a renowned philosopher, mathematician, and scientist, comparing animals to machines. Nonetheless, this is just what he did in his influential *Discourse on Method* when he compared machines made by the hand of man with human and nonhuman animal bodies made by the hand of God: "From this aspect the body is regarded as a machine which, having been made by the hands of God, is incomparably better arranged, and possesses in itself movements which are much more admirable than any of those which can be invented by man."[5] Living *human* bodies were, for Descartes, distinguished from living *animal* bodies by the presence of an immortal soul which was a necessary condition for mental experiences. Without a soul, a living biological body was a natural automaton, "much more splendid," but in kind no different from those produced by humans.

For Descartes, the criterion for distinguishing those living bodies which were ensouled from those which were not was the capacity to use language. The former, he believed, included all and only human beings. Among humans, he maintained,

> there are none so depraved and stupid, without even exempting idiots, that they cannot arrange different words together, forming of them a statement by which they make known their thoughts; while on the other hand, there is no other animal, however perfect and fortunately circumstanced it may be, which can do the same.[6]

Insofar as nonhuman animals do appear to do some things better than we do, Descartes added, "it is nature which acts in them according to the disposition of their organs, just as

---

[5]René Descartes, *Discourse on Method*, in *Philosophical Works of Descartes*, translated by E. S. Haldane and G. R. T. Ross (Cambridge University Press), Vol. I. Reprinted in Regan and Singer, p. 61.
[6]*Ibid.*

a clock, which is only composed of wheels and weights is able to tell the hours and measure the time more correctly than we can do with all our wisdom."[7] As for the ethical implications of his view, Descartes, in a letter to Henry More, noted that his "opinion is not so much cruel to animals as indulgent to men . . . since it absolves them from the suspicion of crime when they eat or kill animals."[8]

Insofar as Descartes's position presupposes that all and only human beings have the capacity to use language, it is open to the same sort of criticisms and objections that we raised against Kant. That is, advances in medicine are providing more nonlinguistic humans and advances in science are suggesting that at least some nonhuman animals have more linguistic facility or capacity than we previously supposed. Moreover, even if Descartes were correct in believing that the capacity to use language is uniquely human, why should this, rather than the capacity to feel pain and experience distress, be the principal criterion for determining the nature and extent of ethical restrictions on the use and treatment of animals? It is this objection which sets the stage for positions which hold that humans have direct obligations to at least some animals.

3. Direct Obligation

Jeremy Bentham (1748-1832), the father of modern utilitarianism, held that pain and pleasure were what governed behavior and that any ethical system which was founded on anything but maximizing the net balance of pleasure over pain, dealt in "sounds instead of sense, in caprice instead of reason, in darkness instead of light." Every action, for Bentham was to be assessed in terms of its likelihood of maximizing the net balance of happiness. But, he noted, if the capacity to experience pleasure and pain was what qualified one to be taken into account in estimating the effects of various courses of action, then nonhuman as well as human animals would have to be taken into account insofar as they, too, had the capacity to experience pleasure and pain. Thus, for Bentham, it is sentience, or the capacity for pleasure and pain, that determines whether a being qualifies for moral consideration.

> What else is it that should trace the insuperable line? Is it the faculty of reason, or perhaps the faculty of discourse? But a full-grown horse or dog is beyond comparison a more rational, as well as a more conversable animal than an infant of a day or a week or even a month old. But suppose they were otherwise, what would it avail? The question is not, Can they *reason* nor Can they *talk?* but, *Can they suffer?*[9]

The question now is, what grounds do we have to believe that animals *can* suffer, can feel pain, or can experience distress? If a being lacks the capacity to convey his suffering, pain, or distress linguistically how do we know that it actually has such experiences and isn't a rather splendid automaton going through the motions?

In response to such skepticism, one holding a utilitarian direct obligation theory must show why he or she believes that nonhuman animals are conscious. There are a number of ways one might go about this. First, one could stress behavioral similarities between human and nonhuman animals in their respective responses to certain standard pain- and pleasure-producing stimuli. Comparing the behavior of nonhuman animals wth human infants would

---

[7] *Ibid*, p. 62.

[8] René Descartes, Letter to Henry More, in *Descartes: Philosophical Letters,* translated and edited by Anthony Kenny (Oxford University Press, 1970). Reprinted in Regan and Singer, p. 66.

[9] Jeremy Bentham, *The Principles of Morals and Legislation* (1789), Chapter XVII, Section 1. Reprinted in Regan and Singer, p. 129.

be especially forceful here. Second, we could stress relevant neurophysiological similarities between humans and nonhumans. After making these comparisons we may then be inclined to agree with Richard Sergeant when he claims that:

> Every particle of factual evidence supports the contention that the higher mammalian vertebrates experience pain sensations at least as acute as our own. To say that they feel less because they are lower animals is an absurdity; it can easily be shown that many of their senses are far more acute than ours— visual acuity in certain birds, hearing in most wild animals, and touch in others; these animals depend more than we do on the sharpest possible awareness of a hostile environment.[10]

So, if Sergeant is correct in this, at least some animals are conscious and hence, on utilitarian grounds, qualify as the objects of direct obligation.

There are, nonetheless, significant limitations to this view. First, although utilitarianism takes nonhuman animals directly into account in determining ethical obligations, there is no guarantee that animals will, in fact, fare better on this view than they will on an Indirect Obligation view like that of Aquinas or Kant. Contemporary animal welfare advocates who find utilitarianism hospitable to their position have not fully appreciated utilitarianism's indifference to any outcome apart from the maximization of happiness. Thus, for example, on utilitarian grounds, a policy which causes a great amount of pain to animals which also causes an even greater amount of offsetting pleasure to humans, would appear to be ethically justified. Second, one who adopts utilitarianism because it takes direct account of animal suffering, must recognize all of its implications. One of the standard objections to utilitarianism is that it seems, on the face of it, more suited to animals than it is to human beings. Thus Bentham's version was initially caricatured as philosophy for swine because it seemed to imply that it was better to be a satisfied pig than a dissatisfied human; or better to be a fool satisfied than Socrates dissatisfied.

A FOURTH POSITION

Although none of the positions we have examined is entirely satisfactory, each, I believe, has something to recommend it. *Indirect Obligation* theories are correct to stress the difference between what I will call "simple consciousness" and "reflective-consciousness," but they have not adequately characterized the difference nor have they fully appreciated its ethical significance. *No Obligation* theories, at least that of Descartes, are correct in emphasizing the relationship between the use of language and the development of reflective-consciousness. And, finally, *Direct Obligation* theories are correct in noting that the possession of simple consciousness (or sentience) in human or nonhuman animals is, by itself, sufficient to give them independent standing in the ethical deliberations of beings who are reflectively-conscious. I will now, very briefly, outline each of these fundamental insights and suggest how they may be integrated into a fourth, more adequate position.

The fundamental insight of *Indirect Obligation* theories is their recognition of a difference between simple and reflective consciousness. Beings having only simple consciousness can experience pain, have desires, and make choices. But they are not capable of reflecting upon their experiences, desires, and choices and altering their behavior as a result of such self-conscious evaluation and deliberation. Beings who can do this I will, fol-

---

[10]Richard Sergeant, *The Spectrum of Pain* (London, Hart-Davis, 1969), p. 72. Cited by Peter Singer in Tom Regan, ed., *Matters of Life and Death* (Random House, 1980), p. 225.

lowing John Locke (1632-1704), label "persons." A person, in Locke's view, is "A thinking intelligent being that has reason and reflection and can consider itself as itself, the same thinking thing, in different times and places."[11] Although they were mistaken in believing that the class of persons fully coincided with the class of human beings, *Indirect Obligation* theorists were correct to emphasize the special status of persons. For only persons are capable of tracing the consequences and implications of various courses of action and then deliberating and deciding to embark on one rather than another on grounds other than self-interest. To do this is part of what it means to have a morality, and it is the capacity for taking the moral point of view (that is, voluntarily restricting one's appetite or desires for the sake of others) that gives the persons their special worth.

The fundamental insight of Descartes's *No Obligation* theory was to recognize the connection between the development and exercise of personhood and the development and exercise of language. As Stuart Hampshire has recently pointed out, although people often associate the use of language primarily with communication, "language's more distinctive and far-reaching power is to bring possibilities before the mind. Culture has its principal source in the use of the word 'if,' in counterfactual speculation."[12] Only language, then, gives us the power to entertain complex unrealized possibilities. "The other principal gift of language to culture," Hampshire continues, "is the power to date, and hence to make arrangements for tomorrow and to regret yesterday."[13] Thus a being cannot become a person and, in Locke's words, "consider itself as itself, the same thinking thing, in different times and places," without the use of language.

Finally, the fundamental insight of *Direct Obligation* theories was to note that one needn't be a person to be the object of a moral obligation. Simple consciousness or sentience is sufficient to entitle a being to be considered *for its own sake* in the ethical deliberations of persons. If, for example, the capacity to feel pain is sufficient ground for a *prima facie* obligation not to cause gratuitous pain to persons, why is it not also a sufficient ground for a similar obligation not to cause pain to beings having simple consciousness? With regard to the evil of avoidable and unjustifiable pain, the question is, as Bentham emphasized, not "Can they reason nor Can they talk? but, Can they suffer?"

Putting all of this together, we may say that persons, who are characterized as possessing reflective consciousness, may have a higher status than beings having only simple consciousness. Their special worth is a function of the extent to which they use language "to bring possibilities before the mind" and then restrain their more trivial desires for the sake of not harming others whom they recognize, from the moral point of view, as their equals in certain respects. Among the beings whose interests must be taken into account *for their own sake* in the moral deliberations of persons are beings possessing only simple consciousness. To the extent that persons reluctantly cause pain, suffering, and even death to beings possessing simple consciousness in order to meet *important needs,* what they do may be justified by appeal to their higher status or greater worth. But, to the extent that persons inflict avoidable pain and suffering on such beings merely to satisfy certain *trivial tastes or desires,* they pervert their greater capacities. In so doing, they ironically undermine their claim to higher status or worth and thereby weaken any justification they may have had for sacrificing beings having only simple consciousness for important ends.

---

[11]John Locke, *Essay Concerning Human Understanding,* ed. by John Yolton (J. M. Dent & Sons, 1961), Vol. One, Book II, Ch. XXVII, p. 281.
[12]Stuart Hampshire, *"Human Nature,"* New York Review of Books, XXVI (December 6, 1979), Special Supplement, p. d.
[13]*Ibid.*

Whether something is to be classified as an "important need" or a "trivial taste or desire" will frequently be a matter of debate and uncertainty. Yet we should not allow disputes over difficult cases to blind us to the existence of relatively easy cases. There is, for example, little doubt that well-designed, nonduplicative research on animals aimed at preventing or treating disease serves an important need. And it seems just as certain that causing pain to animals in order to test the toxicity of "new and improved" floor polishes or cosmetics serves trivial tastes or desires. And even cases that are not so immediately clear may be resolved by a bit of thoughtful investigation. Thus I suspect that most people who care to learn something about human nutrition and the treatment of animals on modern "factory farms" will be strongly inclined to conclude that factory farming causes pain and suffering to animals for the sake of trivial tastes and desires.[14]

FURTHER INQUIRY

The foregoing is at best a sketch or outline of a position on the ethical significance of animal awareness. A number of refinements need to be made and a number of questions need to be answered before we can confidently use it to make particular judgments and decisions about the use and treatment of nonhuman animals. First, we must do more in the way of spelling out the crucial distinction between simple consciousness and reflective consciousness. In addition, we must determine the extent to which *various degrees* of both types of consciousness are distributed or realized within members of various classes of human and nonhuman animals. It is important to note here that since there is nothing in the distinction between simple and reflective consciousness that requires it to follow species lines, the investigations in question will involve infants and severely retarded and severely brain-damaged human beings, as well as nonhuman animals.

Among the important questions we must ask is whether, and if so, to what extent, beings who lack reflective consciousness can experience things other than pain and pleasure. For example, can chimps, dogs, pigs, or chickens experience sadness, boredom, loneliness, frustration, apprehensiveness, disappointment, anxiety, and other states that are not as closely identified with determinate behavioral responses as is pain? If so, how would we know? Questions of this kind will, I hope, be soon addressed by philosophers of mind, ethologists, psychologists, neurophysiologists, and others. My principal aim has been to show why, from an ethical point of view, they are important questions.

QUESTIONS

1. Benjamin rejects the "indirect obligation" theories of both Aquinas and Kant, the "no obligation" theory of Descartes, and the "direct obligation" theory of Bentham. Is any of these theories essentially defensible?
2. Does human life have greater worth than animal life? If so, on what grounds?
3. What human needs, if any, are sufficiently important to warrant the infliction of pain and suffering on animals?

[14]See, for example, Peter Singer, *Animal Liberation* (New York: New York Review, 1975); and Jim Mason and Peter Singer, *Animal Factories* (New York: Crown Publishers, 1980).

JOEL FEINBERG

THE RIGHTS OF ANIMALS AND UNBORN GENERATIONS

A biographical sketch of Joel Feinberg is found on p. 343.

Feinberg provides a detailed analysis of the concept of a right. He undertakes such an analysis for the *proximate purpose* of showing that it is conceptually possible to ascribe rights to unborn generations and for the *ultimate purpose* of providing support for the view that unborn generations have rights against us—rights which entail the moral demand that those of us now living protect the environment. On Feinberg's analysis, only the sorts of beings who are capable of having interests can meaningfully be said to have rights. In the light of this principle, he argues that individual animals may be said to have rights but individual plants may not be said to have rights. Likewise, he contends, a *species* of animals (or plants) cannot be said to have rights. (Feinberg interprets the duty to protect a threatened species as a duty to future human beings rather than as a duty to the threatened species itself.) With regard to unborn generations, he contends, it is clear that they will have interests when they eventually come to exist. Feinberg argues that the rights of unborn generations are *contingent*; he denies that they have a right to be born, but given the fact that some persons will in fact be born, they have the right to be born into a world which is not "a used up garbage heap."

Every philosophical paper must begin with an unproved assumption. Mine is the assumption that there will still be a world five hundred years from now, and that it will contain human beings who are very much like us. We have it within our power now, clearly, to affect the lives of these creatures for better or worse by contributing to the conservation or corruption of the environment in which they must live. I shall assume furthermore that it is psychologically possible for us to care about our remote descendants, that many of us in fact do care, and indeed that we ought to care. My main concern then will be to show that it makes sense to speak of the rights of unborn generations against us, and that given the moral judgment that we ought to conserve our environmental inheritance for them, and its grounds, we might well say that future generations *do* have rights correlative to our present duties toward them. Protecting our environment now is also a matter of elementary prudence, and insofar as we do it for the next generation already here in the persons of our children, it is a matter of love. But from the perspective of our remote descendants it is basically a matter of justice, of respect for their rights. My main concern here will be to examine the concept of a right to better understand how that can be.

THE PROBLEM

To have a right is to have a claim[1] *to* something and *against* someone, the recognition of which is called for by legal rules or, in the case of moral rights, by the principles of an enlightened conscience. In the familiar cases of rights, the claimant is a competent adult human being, and the claimee is an officeholder in an institution or else a private individual,

---

[1]I shall leave the concept of a claim unanalyzed here, but for a detailed discussion, see my "The Nature and Value of Rights," *Journal of Value Inquiry* 4 (Winter 1971): 263–277.

Reprinted with permission of the publisher from *Philosophy & Environmental Crisis*, edited by William T. Blackstone, pp. 43–68. Copyright © 1974 by the University of Georgia Press.

in either case, another competent adult human being. Normal adult human beings, then, are obviously the sorts of beings of whom rights can meaningfully be predicated. Everyone would agree to that, even extreme misanthropes who deny that anyone in fact has rights. On the other hand, it is absurd to say that rocks can have rights, not because rocks are morally inferior things unworthy of rights (that statement makes no sense either), but because rocks belong to a category of entities of whom rights cannot be meaningfully predicated. That is not to say that there are no circumstances in which we ought to treat rocks carefully, but only that the rocks themselves cannot validly claim good treatment from us. In between the clear cases of rocks and normal human beings, however, is a spectrum of less obvious cases, including some bewildering borderline ones. Is it meaningful or conceptually possible to ascribe rights to our dead ancestors? to individual animals? to whole species of animals? to plants? to idiots and madmen? to fetuses? to generations yet unborn? Until we know how to settle these puzzling cases, we cannot claim fully to grasp the concept of a right, or to know the shape of its logical boundaries.

One way to approach these riddles is to turn one's attention first to the most familiar and unproblematic instances of rights, note their most salient characteristics, and then compare the borderline cases with them, measuring as closely as possible the points of similarity and difference. In the end, the way we classify the borderline cases may depend on whether we are more impressed with the similarities or the differences between them and the cases in which we have the most confidence.

It will be useful to consider the problem of individual animals first because their case is the one that has already been debated with the most thoroughness by philosophers so that the dialectic of claim and rejoinder has now unfolded to the point where disputants can get to the end game quickly and isolate the crucial point at issue. When we understand precisely what *is* at issue in the debate over animal rights, I think we will have the key to the solution of all the other riddles about rights.

INDIVIDUAL ANIMALS

Almost all modern writers agree that we ought to be kind to animals, but that is quite another thing from holding that animals can claim kind treatment from us as their due. Statutes making cruelty to animals a crime are now very common, and these, of course, impose legal duties on people not to mistreat animals; but that still leaves open the question whether the animals, as beneficiaries of those duties, possess rights correlative to them. We may very well have duties *regarding* animals that are not at the same time duties *to* animals, just as we may have duties regarding rocks, or buildings, or lawns, that are not duties *to* the rocks, buildings, or lawns. Some legal writers have taken the still more extreme position that animals themselves are not even the directly intended beneficiaries of statutes prohibiting cruelty to animals. During the nineteenth century, for example, it was commonly said that such statutes were designed to protect human beings by preventing the growth of cruel habits that could later threaten human beings with harm too. Prof. Louis B. Schwartz finds the rationale of the cruelty-to-animals prohibition in its protection of animal lovers from affronts to their sensibilities. "It is not the mistreated dog who is the ultimate object of concern," he writes. "Our concern is for the feelings of other human beings, a large proportion of whom, although accustomed to the slaughter of animals for food, readily identify themselves with a tortured dog or horse and respond with great sensitivity to its sufferings."[2] This seems to me to be factitious. How much more natural it is

---

[2]Louis B. Schwartz, "Morals, Offenses and the Model Penal Code," *Columbia Law Review* 63 (1963): 673.

to say with John Chipman Gray that the true purpose of cruelty-to-animals statutes is "to preserve the dumb brutes from suffering."[3] The very people whose sensibilities are invoked in the alternative explanation, a group that no doubt now includes most of us, are precisely those who would insist that the protection belongs primarily to the animals themselves, not merely to their own tender feelings. Indeed, it would be difficult even to account for the existence of such feelings in the absence of a belief that the animals deserve the protection in their own right and for their own sakes.

Even if we allow, as I think we must, that animals are the intended direct beneficiaries of legislation forbidding cruelty to animals, it does not follow directly that animals have legal rights, and Gray himself, for one,[4] refused to draw this further inference. Animals cannot have rights, he thought, for the same reason they cannot have duties, namely, that they are not genuine "moral agents." Now, it is relatively easy to see why animals cannot have duties, and this matter is largely beyond controversy. Animals cannot be "reasoned with" or instructed in their responsibilites; they are inflexible and unadaptable to future contingencies; they are subject to fits of instinctive passion which they are incapable of repressing or controlling, postponing or sublimating. Hence, they cannot enter into contractual agreements, or make promises; they cannot be trusted; and they cannot (except within very narrow limits and for purposes of conditioning) be blamed for what would be called "moral failures" in a human being. They are therefore incapable of being moral subjects, of acting rightly or wrongly in the moral sense, of having, discharging, or breeching duties and obligations.

But what is there about the intellectual incompetence of animals (which admittedly disqualifies them for duties) that makes them logically unsuitable for rights? The most common reply to this question is that animals are incapable of *claiming* rights on their own. They cannot make motion, on their own, to courts to have their claims recognized or enforced; they cannot initiate, on their own, any kind of legal proceedings; nor are they capable of even understanding when their rights are being violated, of distinguishing harm from wrongful injury, and responding with indignation and an outraged sense of justice instead of mere anger or fear.

No one can deny any of these allegations, but to the claim that they are the grounds for disqualification of rights of animals, philosophers on the other side of this controversy have made convincing rejoinders. It is simply not true, says W. D. Lamont,[5] that the ability to understand what a right is and the ability to set legal machinery in motion by one's own initiative are necessary for the possession of rights. If that were the case, then neither human idiots nor wee babies would have any legal rights at all. Yet it is manifest that both of these classes of intellectual incompetents have legal rights recognized and easily enforced by the courts. Children and idiots start legal proceedings, not on their own direct initiative, but rather through the actions of proxies or attorneys who are empowered to speak in their names. If there is no conceptual absurdity in this situation, why should there be in the case where a proxy makes a claim on behalf of an animal? People commonly enough make wills leaving money to trustees for the care of animals. Is it not natural to speak of the animal's right to his inheritance in cases of this kind? If a trustee embezzles money from the animal's account,[6] a proxy speaking in the dumb brute's behalf presses the animal's claim, can he not be described as asserting the animal's *rights*? More exactly, the animal itsef claims its rights through the vicarious actions of a human proxy speaking

---

[3] John Chipman Gray, *The Nature and Sources of the Law,* 2d ed. (Boston: Beacon Press, 1963), p. 43.
[4] And W. D. Ross for another. See *The Right and The Good* (Oxford: Clarendon Press, 1930), app. 1, pp. 48–56.
[5] W. D. Lamont, *Principles of Moral Judgment* (Oxford: Clarendon Press, 1946), pp. 83–85.
[6] Cf. H. J. McCloskey, "Rights," *Philosophical Quarterly* 15 (1965): 121, 124.

in its name and in its behalf. There appears to be no reason why we should require the animal to understand what is going on (so the argument concludes) as a condition for regarding it as a possessor of rights.

Some writers protest at this point that the legal relation between a principal and an agent cannot hold between animals and human beings. Between humans, the relation of agency can take two different forms, depending upon the degree of discretion granted to the agent, and there is a continuum of combinations between the extremes. On the one hand, there is the agent who is the mere "mouthpiece" of his principal. He is a "tool" in much the same sense as is a typewriter or telephone; he simply transmits the instructions of his principal. Human beings could hardly be the agents or representatives of animals in this sense, since the dumb brutes could no more use human "tools" than mechanical ones. On the other hand, an agent may be some sort of expert hired to exercise his professional judgment on behalf of, and in the name of, the principal. He may be given, within some limited area of expertise, complete independence to act as he deems best, binding his principal to all the beneficial or detrimental consequences. This is the role played by trustees, lawyers, and ghost-writers. This type of representation requires that the agent have great skill, but makes little or no demand upon the principal, who may leave everything to the judgment of his agent. Hence, there appears, at first, to be no reason why an animal cannot be a totally passive principal in this second kind of agency relationship.

There are still some important dissimilarties, however. In the typical instance of representation by an agent, even of the second, highly discretionary kind, the agent is hired by a principal who enters into an agreement or contract with him; the principal tells his agent that within certain carefully specified boundaries "You may speak for me," subject always to the principal's approval, his right to give new directions, or to cancel the whole arrangement. No dog or cat could possibly do any of those things. Moreover, if it is the assigned task of the agent to defend the principal's rights, the principal may often decide to release his claimee, or to waive his own rights, and instruct his agent accordingly. Again, no mute cow or horse can do that. But although the possibility of hiring, agreeing, contracting, approving, directing, canceling, releasing, waiving, and instructing is present in the typical (all-human) case of agency representation, there appears to be no reason of a logical or conceptual kind why that *must* be so, and indeed there are some special examples involving human principals where it is not in fact so. I have in mind legal rules, for example, that require that a defendant be represented at his trial by an attorney, and impose a state-appointed attorney upon reluctant defendants, or upon those tried *in absentia*, whether they like it or not. Moreover, small children and mentally deficient and deranged adults are commonly represented by trustees and attorneys, even though they are incapable of granting their own consent to the representation, or of entering into contracts, of giving directions, or waiving their rights. It may be that it is unwise to permit agents to represent principals without the latters' knowledge or consent. If so, then no one should ever be permitted to speak for an animal, at least in a legally binding way. But that is quite another thing than saying that such representation is logically incoherent or conceptually incongrous—the contention that is at issue.

H. J. McCloskey,[7] I believe, accepts the argument up to this point, but he presents a new and different reason for denying that animals can have legal rights. The ability to make claims, whether directly or through a representative, he implies, is essential to the possesion of rights. Animals obviously cannot press their claims on their own, and so if they have rights, these rights must be assertable by agents. Animals, however, cannot be represented, McCloskey contends, not for any of the reasons already discussed, but rather

---

[7]Ibid.

because representation, in the requisite sense, is always of interest, and animals (he says) are incapable of having interests.

Now, there is a very important insight expressed in the requirement that a being have interests if he is to be a logically proper subject of rights. This can be appreciated if we consider just why it is that mere things cannot have rights. Consider a very precious "mere thing"—a beautiful natural wilderness, or a complex and ornamental artifact, like the Taj Mahal. Such things ought to be cared for, because they would sink into decay if neglected, depriving some human beings, or perhaps even all human beings, of somethng of great value. Certain persons may even have as their own special job the care and protection of these valuable objects. But we are not tempted in these cases to speak of "thing-rights" correlative to custodial duties, because, try as we might, we cannot think of mere things as possessing interests of their own. Some people may have a duty to preserve, maintain, or improve the Taj Mahal, but they can hardly have a duty to help or hurt it, benefit or aid it, succor or relieve it. Custodians may protect it for the sake of a nation's pride and art lovers' fancy; but they don't keep it in good repair for "its own sake," or for "its own true welfare," or "well-being." A mere thing, however valuable to others, has no good of its own. The explanation of that fact, I suspect, consists in the fact that mere things have no conative life: no conscious wishes, desires, and hopes; or urges and impulses; or unconscious drives, aims, and goals; or latent tendencies, direction of growth, and natural fulfillments. Interests must be compounded somehow out of conations; hence mere things have no interests. A fortiori, they have no interests to be protected by legal or moral rules. Without interests a creature can have no "good" of its own, the achievement of which can be its due. Mere things are not loci of value in their own right, but rather their value consists entirely in their being objects of other beings' interests.

So far McCloskey is on solid ground, but one can quarrel with his denial that any animals but humans have interests. I should think that the trustee of funds willed to a dog or cat is more than a mere custodian of the animal he protects. Rather his job is to look out for the interests of the animal and make sure no one denies it its due. The animal itself is the beneficiary of his dutiful services. Many of the higher animals at least have appetites, conative urges, and rudimentary purposes, the integrated satisfaction of which constitutes their welfare or good. We can, of course, with consistency treat animals as mere pests and deny that they have any rights; for most animals, especially those of the lower orders, we have no choice but to do so. But it seems to me, nevertheless, that in general, animals *are* among the sorts of beings of whom rights can meaningfully be predicated and denied.

Now, if a person agrees with the conclusion of the argument thus far, that animals are the sorts of beings that *can* have rights, and further, if he accepts the moral judgment that we ought to be kind to animals, only one further premise is needed to yield the conclusion that some animals do in fact have rights. We must now ask ourselves for whose sake ought we to treat (some) animals with consideration and humaneness? If we conceive our duty to be one of obedience to authority, or to one's own conscience merely, or one of consideration for tender human sensibilities only, then we might still deny that animals have rights, even though we admit that they are the kinds of beings that *can* have rights. But if we hold not only that we ought to treat animals humanely but also that we should do so for the animals' own sake, that such treatment is something we owe animals as their due, something that can be claimed for them, something the withholding of which would be an injustice and a wrong, and not merely a harm, then it follows that we do ascribe rights to animals. I suspect that the moral judgments most of us make about animals do pass these phenomenological tests, so that most of us do believe that animals have rights, but are reluctant to say so because of the conceptual confusions about the notion of a right that I have attempted to dispel above.

Now we can extract from our discussion of animal rights a crucial principle for tentative use in the resolution of the other riddles about the applicability of the concept of a right, namely, that the sorts of beings who *can* have rights are precisely those who have (or can have) interests. I have come to this tentative conclusion for two reasons: (1) because a right holder must be capable of being represented and it is impossible to represent a being that has no interest, and (2) because a right holder must be capable of being a beneficiary in his own person, and a being without interests is a being that is incapable of being harmed or benefitted, having no good or "sake" of its own. Thus, a being without interests has no "behalf" to act in, and no "sake" to act for. My strategy now will be to apply the "interest principle," as we can call it, to the other puzzles about rights, while being prepared to modify it where necessary (but as little as possible), in the hope of separating in a consistent and intuitively satisfactory fashion the beings who can have rights from those which cannot.

VEGETABLES

It is clear that we ought not to mistreat certain plants, and indeed there are rules and regulations imposing duties on persons not to misbehave in respect to certain members of the vegetable kingdom. It is forbidden, for example, to pick wildflowers in the mountainous tundra areas of national parks, or to endanger trees by starting fires in dry forest areas. Members of Congress introduce bills designed, as they say, to "protect" rare redwood trees from commercial pillage. Given this background, it is surprising that no one[8] speaks of plants as having rights. Plants, after all, are not "mere things"; they are vital objects with inherited biological propensities determining their natural growth. Moreover, we do say that certain conditions are "good" or "bad" for plants, thereby suggesting that plants, unlike rocks, are capable of having a "good." (This is a case, however, where "what we say" should not be taken seriously: we also say that certain kinds of paint are good or bad for the internal walls of a house, and this does not commit us to a conception of walls as beings possessed of a good or welfare of their own.) Finally, we are capable of feeling a kind of affection for particular plants, though we rarely personalize them, as we do in the case of animals, by giving them proper names.

Still, all are agreed that plants are not the kinds of beings that can have rights. Plants are never plausibly understood to be the direct intended beneficiaries of rules designed to "protect" them. We wish to keep redwood groves in existence for the sake of human beings who can enjoy their serene beauty, and for the sake of generations of human beings yet unborn. Trees are not the sorts of beings who have their "own sakes," despite the fact that they have biological propensities. Having no conscious wants or goals of their own, trees cannot know satisfaction or frustration, pleasure or pain. Hence, there is no possiblity of kind or cruel treatment of trees. In these morally crucial respects, trees differ from the higher species of animals.

Yet trees are not mere things like rocks. They grow and develop according to the laws of their own nature. Aristotle and Aquinas both took trees to have their own "natural ends." Why then do I deny them the status of beings with interest of their own? The reason is that an interest, however the concept is finally to be analyzed, presupposes at least rudimentary cognitive equipment. Interests are compounded out of *desires* and *aims*, both of which presuppose something like *belief*, or cognitive awareness. . . .

WHOLE SPECIES

The topic of whole species, whether of plants or animals, can be treated in much the same way as that of individual plants. A whole collection, as such, cannot have beliefs, expectations, wants, or desires, and can flourish or languish only in the human interest-related

[8]Outside of Samuel Butler's *Erewhon*.

sense in which individual plants thrive and decay. Individual elephants can have interests, but the species elephant cannot. Even where individual elephants are not granted rights, human beings may have an interest — economic, scientific or sentimental — in keeping the species from dying out, and *that* interest may be protected in various ways by law. But that is quite another matter from recognizing a right to survival belonging to the species itself. Still, the preservation of a whole species may quite properly seem to be a morally more important matter than the preservation of an individual animal. Individual animals can have rights but it is implausible to ascribe to them a right to life on the human model. Nor do we normally have duties to keep individual animals alive or even to abstain from killing them provided we do it humanely and nonwantonly in the promotion of legitimate human interests. On the other hand, we do have duties to protect threatened species, not duties to the species themselves as such, but rather duties to future human beings, duties derived from our housekeeping role as temporary inhabitants of this planet. . . .

FUTURE GENERATIONS

We have it in our power now to make the world a much less pleasant place for our descendants than the world we inherited from our ancestors. We can continue to proliferate in ever greater numbers, using up fertile soil at an even greater rate, dumping our wastes into rivers, lakes and oceans, cutting down our forests, and polluting the atmosphere with noxious gases. All thoughtful people agree that we ought not to do these things. Most would say we have a duty not to do these things, meaning not merely that conservation is morally required (as opposed to merely desirable) but also that it is something due our descendants, something to be done for their sakes. Surely we owe it to future generations to pass on a world that is not a used up garbage heap. Our remote descendants are not yet present to claim a livable world as their right, but there are plenty of proxies to speak now in their behalf. These spokesmen, far from being mere custodians, are genuine representatives of future interests.

Why then deny that the human beings of the future have rights which can be claimed against us now in their behalf? Some are inclined to deny them present rights out of a fear of falling into obscure metaphysics, by granting rights to remote and unidentifiable beings who are not yet even in existence. Our unborn great-great-grandchildren are in some sense "potential" persons, but they are far more remotely potential, it may seem, than fetuses. This, however, is not the real difficulty. Unborn generations are more remotely potential than fetuses in one sense, but not in another. A much greater period of time with a far greater number of causally necessary and important events must pass before their potentiality can be actualized, it is true; but our collective posterity is just as certain to come into existence "in the normal course of events" as is any given fetus now in its mother's womb. In that sense the existence of the distant human future is no more remotely potential than that of a particular child already on its way.

The real difficulty is not that we doubt whether our descendants will ever be actual, but rather that we don't know who they will be. It is not their temporal remoteness that troubles us so much as their indeterminacy — their present facelessness and namelessness. Five centuries from now men and women will be living where we live now. Any given one of them will have an interest in living space, fertile soil, fresh air, and the like, but that arbitrarily selected one has no other qualities we can presently envision very clearly. We don't even know who his parents, grandparents, or great-grandparents are, or even whether he is related to us. Still, whoever these human beings may turn out to be, and whatever they might reasonably be expected to be like, they will have interests that we can affect, for better or worse, right now. That much we can and do know about them.

The identity of the owners of these interests is now necessarily obscure, but the fact of their interest-ownership is crystal clear, and that is all that is necessary to certify the coherence of present talk about their rights. We can tell, sometimes, that shadowy forms in the spatial distance belong to human beings, though we know not who or how many they are; and this imposes a duty on us not to throw bombs, for example, in their direction. In like manner, the vagueness of the human future does not weaken its claim on us in light of the nearly certain knowledge that it will, after all, be human.

Doubts about the existence of a right to be born transfer neatly to the question of a similar right to come into existence ascribed to future generations. The rights that future generations certainly have against us are contingent rights: the interests they are sure to have when they come into being (assuming of course that they will come into being) cry out for protection from invasions that can take place now. Yet there are no actual interests, presently existent, that future generations, presently nonexistent, have now. Hence, there is no actual interest that they have in simply coming into being, and I am at a loss to think of any other reason for claiming that they have a right to come into existence (though there may well be such a reason). Suppose then that all human beings at a given time voluntarily form a compact never again to produce children, thus leading within a few decades to the end of our species. This of course is a wildly improbable hypothetical example but a rather crucial one for the position I have been tentatively considering. And we can imagine, say, that the whole world is converted to a strange ascetic religion which absolutely requires sexual abstinence for everyone. Would this arrangement violate the rights of anyone? No one can complain on behalf of presently nonexistent future generations that their future interests which give them a contingent right of protection have been violated since they will never come into existence to be wronged. My inclination then is to conclude that the suicide of our species would be deplorable, lamentable, and a deeply moving tragedy, but that it would violate no one's rights. Indeed if, contrary to fact, all human beings could ever agree to such a thing, that very agreement would be a symptom of our species' biological unsuitability for survival anyway.

CONCLUSION

For several centuries now human beings have run roughshod over the lands of our planet, just as if the animals who do live there and the generations of humans who will live there had no claims on them whatever. Philosophers have not helped matters by arguing that animals and future generations are not the kinds of beings who can have rights now, that they don't presently qualify for membership, even "auxiliary membership," in our moral community. I have tried in this essay to dispel the conceptual confusions that make such conclusions possible. To acknowledge their rights is the very least we can do for members of endangered species (including our own). But that is something.

QUESTIONS

1. What rights, if any, do animals have? Do all animals have the same rights? (For example, do mosquitos have the same rights as chimpanzees? Do pets perhaps have special rights?)
2. What rights, if any, do future generations have? In particular, do future generations have a right to come into existence?
3. Do we have a moral obligation to protect an animal or plant species threatened with extinction? If so, on what grounds?

JOHN PASSMORE

CONSERVATION AND POSTERITY

John Passmore is professor of philosophy at Australian National University (Canberra, Australia). His published works include *Hume's Intentions* (1952), *A Hundred Years of Philosophy* (1957), *Philosophical Reasoning* (1961), and *Science and Its Critics* (1978). *Man's Responsibility for Nature* (1974), from which this selection is excerpted, is a book dedicated entirely to ecological themes.

Passmore reviews the question of the extent to which we can be certain that our successors will need certain natural resources. He concludes that uncertainties in this regard are difficult to eradicate. Yet, he argues, to the extent that there is a reasonable certainty that our successors will need certain resources, we are obliged not to waste them. On Passmore's view, we ought to be prepared to sacrifice certain forms of enjoyment for the sake of conservation, but we ought not to sacrifice the continued development of our cultural heritage. To allow human "loves" (art, science, friendship, etc.) to languish in the name of conservation, he argues, is not in the true interest of posterity.

The conservationist programme confronts us with a fundamental moral issue: ought we to pay any attention to the needs of posterity? To answer this question affirmatively is to make two assumptions: first, that posterity will suffer unless we do so; secondly that if it will suffer, it is our duty so to act as to prevent or mitigate its sufferings. Both assumptions can be, and have been, denied. To accept them does not, of course, do anything to solve the problem of conservation, but to reject them is to deny that there is any such problem, to deny that our society would be a better one — morally better — if it were to halt the rate at which it is at present exhausting its resources. Or it is to deny this, at least, in so far as the arguments in favour of slowing-down are purely conservationist in character — ignoring for the moment, that is, such facts as that the lowering of the consumption-rate is one way of reducing the incidence of pollution and that a high rate of consumption of metals and fossil fuels makes it impossible to preserve untouched the wildernesses in which they are so often located.

To begin with the assumption that posterity will suffer unless we alter our ways, it is still often suggested that, on the contrary, posterity can safely be left to look after itself, provided only that science and technology continue to flourish. This optimistic interpretation of the situation comes especially from economists and from nuclear physicists. . . . If these scientists, these economists, are right, there simply is no "problem of conservation."

Very many scientists, of course, take the opposite view, especially if they are biologists. Expert committees set up by such scientific bodies as the American National Academy of Sciences have, in fact, been prepared to commit themselves to definite estimates of the dates at which this resource or that will be exhausted. This is always, however, on certain assumptions. It makes a considerable difference whether one supposes or denies that rates of consumption will continue to increase exponentially as they have done since 1960; it makes a very great — in many cases an overwhelming — difference whether one supposes or denies that substitutes will be discovered for our major resources. The Academy's extrapolations are best read as a *reductio ad absurdum* of the supposition that our present patterns of resource consumption can continue even over the next century.

The possibility that substitutes will be discovered introduces a note of uncertainty into the whole discussion, an uncertainty which cannot be simply set aside as irrelevant to our moral and political decisions about conservation, which it inevitably and properly influences. At the moment, for example, the prospect of developing a fuel-cell to serve as a substitute for petrol is anything but bright; confident predictions that by 1972 nuclear fusion would be available as an energy source have proved to be unrealistic. But who can say what the situation will be in twenty years time? The now commonplace comparison of earth to a space-ship is thus far misleading: the space-ship astronaut does not have the facilities to invent new techniques, nor can he fundamentally modify his habits of consumption. Any adequate extrapolation would also have to extrapolate technological advances. But by the nature of the case — although technologists have a bad habit of trying to persuade us otherwise — we cannot be at all certain when and whether those advances will take place, or what form they will assume, especially when, unlike the moonshots, they involve fundamental technological innovations such as the containing of nuclear fusion within a magnetic field.

No doubt, the space-ship analogy is justified as a protest against the pronouncements of nineteenth-century rhetoricians that the earth's resources are "limitless" or "boundless." (It was often supposed, one must recall, that oil was being produced underground as fast as it was being consumed.) Fuel-cells, nuclear fusion reactors, machinery for harnessing solar energy all have to be built out of materials, including, as often as not, extremely rare metals. Men can learn to substitute one source of energy or one metallic alloy for another, the more plentiful for the less plentiful. But that is the most they can do. They cannot harness energy without machines, without radiating heat, without creating wastes. Nor can they safely presume that no source of energy, no metal, is indispensable; there is nothing either in the structure of nature or in the structure of human intelligence to ensure that new resources will *always* be available to replace old resources. Think how dependent we still are on the crops our remote agriculture-creating forefathers chose to cultivate; we have not found substitutes for wheat, or barley, or oats, or rice. Nor have we domesticated new animals as beasts of burden. So, quite properly, the conservationist points out.

The uncertainties, however, remain. We can be confident that some day our society will run out of resources, but we do not know when it will do so or what resources it will continue to demand. The Premier of Queensland recently swept aside the protests of conservationists by arguing that Queensland's oil and coal resources should be fully utilised now, since posterity may have no need for them. This is not a wholly irrational attitude. One can readily see the force of an argument which would run thus: we are entitled, given the uncertainty of the future, wholly to ignore the interests of posterity, a posterity whose very existence is hypothetical — granted the possibility of a nuclear disaster — and whose needs, except for such fundamentals as air and water, we cannot possibly anticipate. . . .

We are called upon not to waste those resources our successors will certainly need. But we ought not to act, out of concern for posterity's survival, in ways which are likely to destroy the civilised ideals we hope posterity will share with us. We should try so to act that our successors will not be wholly without electricity, but we need not, should not, close down our civilisation merely in the hope that a remote posterity will have some hope of surviving. . . .

But what sort of sacrifices ought we to make? It follows from what I have already said that we ought not to be prepared, in the supposed interests of posterity, to surrender our loves or the freedom which makes their exercise possible, to give up art, or philosophy, or science, or personal relationships, in order to conserve resources for posterity. Posterity will need our loves as much as we need them; it needs chains of love running to and through it. . . . Those who urge us to surrender our freedom and to abandon our loves so that posterity can enjoy a "true freedom" and a "true love" ought never to be trusted. No doubt, as individuals, we might sometimes have to sacrifice our freedom or certain of our loves. But only to ensure their maintenance and development by others. And this is true, I should argue, even if they can be maintained only at the cost of human suffering— although there is in fact no evidence to suggest that we shall save posterity from suffering by surrendering our freedoms.

The surrender of forms of enjoyment is a different matter. What we would be called upon to do, at this level, is to reduce the consumption of certain goods—those which depend on raw materials which cannot be effectively recycled—and to recycle whenever that is possible, even although the costs of doing so would involve the sacrifice of other goods. That is the kind of sacrifice we ought to be prepared to make, if there is a real risk that it is essential for the continued existence of a posterity able to carry on the activities we love. . . .

QUESTIONS

1. To what extent can we be certain about the needs of posterity for natural resources?
2. Do we have any significant moral obligations to posterity with regard to the conservation of natural resources?

THE VALUE OF WILDERNESS

William Godfrey-Smith teaches in the deparment of philosophy at Australian National University (Canberra, Australia). His major philosophical interests include environmental philosophy and the metaphysics of time. These interests are reflected in such articles as "The Rights of Non-Humans and Intrinsic Values," "Beginning and Ceasing to Exist," and "Special Relativity and the Present."

Godfrey-Smith investigates the kinds of justification that might come into play in making a case for the preservation of wilderness. He begins by calling attention to a characteristic assumption of Western moral thought: "Value can be ascribed to the nonhuman world only insofar as it is good for the sake of the well-being of human beings." In the light of this "decidedly anthropocentric bias," he contends, only *instrumental* justifications for preserving wilderness are deemed acceptable. Though Godfrey-Smith maintains that a powerful case for the preservation of wilderness can be founded on its instrumental value (i.e., its value for humankind), he believes that we must develop an ecologically based morality which recognizes natural systems as possessing their own intrinsic value. In the spirit of Aldo Leopold, Godfrey-Smith argues that the boundaries of the moral community should be extended. In his view, we must learn to extend moral consideration to "items treated heretofore as matters of expediency."

Wilderness is the raw material out of which man has hammered the artifact called civilization.

Aldo Leopold[1]

The framework which I examine is the framework of *Western* attitudes toward our natural environment, and wilderness in particular. The philosophical task to which I shall address myself is an exploration of attitudes toward wilderness, especially the sorts of justification to which we might legitimately appeal for the preservation of wilderness: what grounds can we advance in support of the claim that wilderness is something which we should *value*?

There are two different ways of appraising something as valuable. It may be that the thing in question is good or valuable *for the sake* of something which we hold to be valuable. In this case the thing is not considered to be good in itself; value in this sense is ascribed in virtue of the thing's being a *means* to some valued end, and not as an *end in itself*. Such values are standardly designated *instrumental* values. Not everything which we hold to be good or valuable can be good for the sake of something else: our values must ultimately be *grounded* in something which is held to be good or valuable in itself. Such things are said to be *intrinsically* valuable. As a matter of historical fact, those things which have been held to be instrinsically valuable, within our Western traditions of thought, have nearly always been taken to be states or conditions of *persons*, e.g., happiness, pleasure, knowledge, or self-realization, to name but a few.

It follows from this that a very central assumption of Western moral thought is that value can be ascribed to the nonhuman world only insofar as it is good for the sake of the well-being of human beings.[2] Our entire attitude toward the natural environment, therefore, has a decidedly anthropocentric bias, and this fact is reflected in the sorts of justification which are standardly provided for the preservation of the natural environment.

A number of thinkers, however, are becoming increasingly persuaded that our anthropocentric morality is in fact inadequate to provide a satisfactory basis for a moral philosophy of ecological obligation. It is for this reason that we hear not infrequently the claim that we need a "new morality." A new moral framework—that is, a network of recognized obligations and duties—is not, however, something that can be casually conjured up in order to satisfy some vaguely felt need. The task of developing a sound biologically based moral philosophy, a philosophy which is not anthropocentrically based, and which provides a satisfactory justification for ecological obligation and concern, is, I think, one of the most urgent tasks confronting moral philosophers at the present. It will entail a radical reworking of accepted attitudes—attitudes which we currently accept as "self-evident"—and this is not something which can emerge suddenly. Indeed, I think the seminal work remains largely to be done.

In the absence of a comprehensive and convincing ecologically based morality we naturally fall back on *instrumental* justifications for concern for our natural surroundings, and for preserving wilderness areas and animal species. We can, I think, detect at least four main lines of instrumental justification for the preservation of wilderness. By *wilderness* I understand any reasonably large tract of the Earth, together with its plant and animal communities, which is substantially unmodified by humans and in particular by human technology. The natural contrast to *wilderness* and *nature* is an *artificial* or *domesticated* environment. The fact that there are borderline cases which are difficult to classify does not, of course, vitiate this distinction.

[1]Aldo Leopold, *A Sand County Almanac* (New York: Oxford University Press, 1949), p. 188.
[2]Other cultures have certainly included the idea that nature should be valued for its own sake in their moral codes, e.g., the American Indians, the Chinese, and the Australian Aborigines.

Reprinted, as a shortened version prepared by the author, from "The Value of Wilderness," *Environmental Ethics*, vol. 1 (Winter 1979), pp. 309–319. Copyright © by William Godfrey-Smith.

The first attitude toward wilderness espoused by conservationists to which I wish to draw attention is what I shall call the "cathedral" view. This is the view that wilderness areas provide a vital opportunity for spiritual revival, moral regeneration, and aesthetic delight. The enjoyment of wilderness is often compared in this respect with religious or mystical experience. Preservation of magnificent wilderness areas for those who subscribe to this view is essential for human well-being, and its destruction is conceived as something akin to an act of vandalism, perhaps comparable to — some may regard it as more serious than[3] — the destruction of a magnificent and moving human edifice, such as the Parthenon, the Taj Mahal, or the Palace of Versailles.

Insofar as the "cathedral" view holds that value derives solely from human satisfactions gained from its contemplation it is clearly an instrumentalist attitude. It does, however, frequently approach an *intrinsic value* attitude, insofar as the feeling arises that there is importance in the fact that it is there to be contemplated, whether or not anyone actually takes advantage of this fact. Suppose for example, that some wilderness was so precariously balanced that *any* human intervention or contact would inevitably bring about its destruction. Those who maintained that the area should, nevertheless, be preserved, unexperienced and unenjoyed, would certainly be ascribing to it an intrinsic value.

The "cathedral" view with respect to wilderness in fact is a fairly recent innovation in Western thought. The predominant Graeco-Christian attitude, which generally speaking was the predominant Western attitude prior to eighteenth-and nineteenth-century romanticism, had been to view wilderness as threatening or alarming, an attitude still reflected in the figurative uses of the expression *wilderness*, clearly connoting a degenerate state to be avoided. Christianity, in general, has enjoined "the transformaton of wilderness, those dreaded haunts of demons, the ancient nature-gods, into farm and pasture,"[4] that is, to a domesticated environment.

The second instrumental justification of the value of wilderness is what we might call the "laboratory" argument. This is the argument that wilderness areas provide vital subject matter for scientific inquiry which provides us with an understanding of the intricate interdependencies of biological systems, their modes of change and development, their energy cycles, and the source of their stabilities. If we are to understand our own biological dependencies, we require natural systems as a norm, to inform us of the biological laws which we transgress at our peril.

The third instrumentalist justification is the "silo" argument which points out that one excellent reason for preserving reasonable areas of the natural environment intact is that we thereby preserve a stockpile of genetic diversity, which it is certainly prudent to maintain as a backup in case something should suddenly go wrong with the simplified biological systems which, in general, constitute agriculture. Further, there is the related point that there is no way of anticipating our future needs, or the undiscovered applications of apparently useless plants, which might turn out to be, for example, the source of some pharmacologically valuable drug — a cure, say, for leukemia. This might be called, perhaps, the "rare herb" argument, and it provides another persuasive instrumental justification for the preservation of wilderness.

The final instrumental justification which I think should be mentioned is the "gymnasium" argument, which regards the preservation of wilderness as important for athletic or recreational activities.

---

[3]We can after all *replace* human artifacts such as buildings with something closely similar, but the destruction of a wilderness or a biological species is irreversible.
[4]John Passmore, *Man's Responsibility for Nature* (London: Duckworth, 1974; New York: Charles Scribner's Sons, 1974), p. 17; cf. chap. 5.

An obvious problem which arises from these instrumental arguments is that the various activities which they seek to justify are not always possible to reconcile with one another. The interests of the wilderness lover who subscribes to the "cathedral" view are not always reconcilable with those of the ordinary vacationist. Still more obvious is the conflict between the recreational use of wilderness and the interests of the miner, the farmer, and the timber merchant.

The conflict of interest which we encounter here is one which it is natural to try and settle through the economic calculus of cost-benefit considerations. So long as the worth of natural systems is believed to depend entirely on instrumental values, it is natural to suppose that we can sort out the conflict of interests within an objective frame of reference, by estimating the human satisfactions to be gained from the preservation of wilderness, and by weighing these against the satisfactions which are to be gained from those activities which may lead to its substantial modification, domestication, and possibly even, destruction.

Many thinkers are liable to encounter here a feeling of resistance to the suggestion that we can apply purely economic considerations to settle such conflicts of interest. The assumption behind economic patterns of thought, which underlie policy formulation and planning, is that the values which we attach to natural systems and to productive activities are commensurable; and this is an assumption which may be called into question. It is not simply a question of the difficulty of quantifying what value should be attached to the preservation of the natural environment. The feeling is more that economic considerations are simply out of place. This feeling is one which is often too lightly dismissed by tough-minded economists as being obscurely mystical or superstitious; but it is a view worth examining. What it amounts to, I suggest, is the belief that there is something *morally* objectionable in the destruction of natural systems, or at least in their wholesale elimination, and this is precisely the belief that natural systems, or economically "useless" species, do possess an *intrinsic* value. That is, it is an attempt to articulate the rejection of the anthropocentric view that all value, ultimately, resides in *human* interest and concerns.

A feeling persists that cost-benefit analyses tend to overlook important values. One consideration which tends to be discounted from policy deliberations is that which concerns *economically* unimportant species of animals or plants. A familiar subterfuge which we frequently encounter is the attempt to invest such species with spurious economic value, as illustrated in the rare herb argument. A typical example of this, cited by Leopold, is the reaction of ornithologists to the threatened disappearance of certain species of songbirds: they at once came forward with some distinctly shaky evidence that they played an essential role in the control of insects.[5] The dominance of economic modes of thinking is again obvious: the evidence has to be economic in order to be acceptable. This exemplifies the way in which we turn to instrumentalist justifications for the maintenance of biotic diversity.

The alternative to such instrumentalist justifications, the alternative which Leopold advocated with great insight and eloquence, is to widen the boundary of the moral community to include animals, plants, the soil, or collectively *the land*.[6] This involves a radical shift in our conception of nature, so that land is recognized not simply as property, to be dealt with or disposed of as a matter of expediency: land in Leopold's view is not a commodity which belongs to us, but a community to which we belong. This change in conception is far-reaching and profound. It involves a shift in our metaphysical conception of nature — that is, a change in what sort of thing we take our natural surroundings to *be*.

[5] Aldo Leopold, "The Land Ethic," in *Sand County Almanac*, p. 210.
[6] Cf. Aldo Leopold, "The Conservation Ethic," *Journal of Forestry* 31 (1933): 634–43, and "The Land Ethic," *Sand County Almanac*.

The predominant Western conception of the natural world is largely a legacy of the philosophy of Descartes. This philosophy has alienated man from the natural world through its sharp ontological division between conscious minds and mechanically arranged substances which, for Descartes, constitute the rest of nature. An adequate environmental ethic must, *inter alia*, replace the world-view which emerges from Cartesian metaphysics.

This will involve a shift from the piecemeal reductive conception of natural items, to a *holistic* or systemic view in which we come to appreciate the symbiotic interdependencies of the natural world. On the holistic or total-field view, organisms—including man—are conceived as nodes in a biotic web of intrinsically related parts.[7] That is, our understanding of biological organisms requires more than just an understanding of their structure and properties; we also have to attend seriously to their interrelations. Holistic or systemic thinking does not deny that organisms are complex physicochemical systems, but it affirms that the methods employed in establishing the high-level functional relationships expressed by physical laws are often of very limited importance in understanding the nature of biological systems.

The holistic conception of the natural world contains, I think, the possibility of extending the idea of community beyond human society. And in this way biological wisdom does, I think, carry implications for ethics. Just as Copernicus showed us that man does not occupy the physical center of the universe, Darwin and his successors have shown us that man occupies no *biologically* privileged position. We still have to assimilate the implications which this biological knowledge has for morality.

Can we regard man and the natural environment as constituting a community in any morally significant sense? Passmore, in particular, has claimed that this extended sense of community is entirely spurious.[8] Leopold, on the other hand, found the biological extension of community entirely natural.[9] If we regard a community as a collection of individuals who engage in cooperative behavior, Leopold's extension seems to me entirely legitimate. An ethic is no more than a code of conduct designed to ensure cooperative behavior among the members of a community. Such cooperative behavior is required to underpin the health of the community, in this biologically extended sense, *health* being understood as the biological capacity for self-renewal,[10] and *ill-health* as the degeneration or loss of this capacity.

Man, of course, cannot be placed on "all fours" with his biologically fellow creatures in all respects. In particular, man is the only creature who can act as a full-fledged moral agent, i.e., an individual capable of exercising reflective rational choice on the basis of principles. What distinguishes man from his fellow creatures is not the capacity to *act*, but the fact that his actions are, to a great extent, free from programming. This capacity to modify our own behavior is closely bound up with the capacity to acquire knowledge of the natural world, a capacity which has enabled us, to an unprecedented extent, to manipulate the environment, and—especially in the recent past—to alter it rapidly, violently, and globally. Our hope must be that the capacity for knowledge, which has made ecologically hazardous activities possible, will lead to a more profound understanding of the delicate biological interdependencies which some of these actions now threaten, and thereby generate the wisdom for restraint.

To those who are skeptical of the possibility of extending moral principles, in the manner of Leopold, to include items treated heretofore as matters of expediency, it can be pointed out that extensions have, to a limited extent, already taken place. One clear—

---

[7]Cf. Arne Naess, "The Shallow and the Deep, Long-Range Ecology Movement," *Inquiry* 16 (1973):95–100.
[8]Passmore, *Man's Responsibility for Nature*, chap. 6; "Attitudes to Nature," p. 262.
[9]Leopold, "The Land Ethic."
[10]*Ibid.*, p. 221.

if partial—instance, is in the treatment of animals. It is now generally accepted, and this is a comparatively recent innovation,[11] that we have at least a *prima facie* obligation not to treat animals cruelly or sadistically. And this certainly constitutes a shift in moral attitudes. If—as seems to be the case—cruelty to animals is accepted as intrinsically wrong, then there *is* at least one instance in which it is *not* a matter of moral indifference how we behave toward the nonhuman world.

More familiar perhaps are the moral revolutions which have occurred within the specific domain of human society—witness the progressive elimination of the "right" to racial, class, and sex exploitation. Each of these shifts involves the acceptance, on the part of some individuals, of new obligations, rights, and values which, to a previous generation, would have been considered unthinkable.[12] The essential step in recognizing an enlarged community involves coming to see, feel, and understand what was previously perceived as alien and apart: it is the evolution of the capacity of *empathy*.

We can, however, provide—and it is important that we can provide—an answer to the question: "What is the *use* of wilderness?" We certainly ought to preserve and protect wilderness areas as gymnasiums, as laboratories, as stockpiles of genetic diversity, and as cathedrals. Each of these reasons provides a powerful and sufficient instrumental justification for their preservation. But note how the very posing of this question about the *utility* of wilderness reflects an anthropocentric system of values. From a genuinely ecocentric point of view the question "What is the *use* of wilderness?" would be as absurd as the question "What is the *use* of happiness?"

The philosophical task is to try to provide adequate justification, or at least clear the way, for a scheme of values according to which concern and sympathy for our environment is immediate and natural, and the desirability of protecting and preserving wilderness self-evident. When once controversial propositions become platitudes, the philosophical task will have been successful.

I will conclude, nevertheless, on a deflationary note. It seems to me (at least much of the time) that the shift in attitudes which I think is required for promoting genuinely harmonious relations with nature is too drastic, too "unthinkable," to be very persuasive for most people. If this is so, then it will be more expedient to justify the preservation of wilderness in terms of instrumentalist considerations; and I have argued that there *are* powerful arguments for preservation which can be derived from the purely anthropocentric considerations of human self-interest. I hope, however, that there will be some who feel that such anthropocentric considerations are not wholly satisfying, i.e., that they do not really do justice to our intuitions. But at a time when *human* rights are being treated in some quarters with a great deal of skepticism it is perhaps unrealistic to expect the rights of nonhumans to receive sympathetic attention. Perhaps, though, we should not be too abashed by this: extensions in ethics have seldom followed the path of political expediency.

QUESTIONS

1. Does wilderness have only instrumental value?
2. Is it true, as Godfrey-Smith maintains, that our anthropocentric morality is "inadequate to provide a satisfactory basis for a moral philosophy of ecological obligations"?

[11]Cf. Passmore, "The Treatment of Animals," *Journal of the History of Ideas* 36 (1975): 195–218.
[12]Cf. Christopher D. Stone, "Should Trees Have Standing? Toward Legal Rights for Natural Objects," *Southern California Law Review* 45 (1972): 450–501.

DISSENTING OPINION IN *SIERRA CLUB v. MORTON*

A biographical sketch of Justice William O. Douglas is found on page 316.

This case developed when Walt Disney Enterprises, Inc., was awarded a permit from the U.S. Forest Service to construct a $35 million recreational complex in the Mineral King Valley, a wilderness area in the Sierra Nevada Mountains of California. The Sierra Club, an organization with a well-known interest in environmental preservation, opposed the "development" of Mineral King Valley and brought suit against the Secretary of the Interior (Rogers C. B. Morton) in an effort to block it. Though the Sierra Club was successful in obtaining a preliminary injunction from the District Court, the Ninth Circuit Court of Appeals reversed. The United States Supreme Court, by a four-to-three margin (two justices not participating), upheld the reversal. The Court's decision was predicated entirely upon the contention that the Sierra Club lacked *standing* to bring suit in such a case. For an organization to have standing to bring suit, the Court said, it is necessary that it be "adversely affected" or "aggrieved"; it is not sufficient that it simply have a special "interest in a problem."

Justice Douglas, in his dissenting opinion, directly addresses the issue of standing. He argues that environmental objects themselves must be granted legal standing, thereby becoming capable of suing for their own preservation. "Those who have an intimate relation with the inanimate object about to be injured, polluted, or otherwise despoiled are its legitimate spokesmen." Thus, he suggests, the Sierra Club should be recognized as speaking in the name of Mineral King Valley.

. . . The critical question of "standing" would be simplified and also put neatly in focus if we fashioned a federal rule that allowed environmental issues to be litigated before federal agencies or federal courts in the name of the inanimate object about to be despoiled, defaced, or invaded by roads and bulldozers and where injury is the subject of public outrage. Contemporary public concern for protecting nature's ecological equilibrium should lead to the conferral of standing upon environmental objects to sue for their own preservation.[1] This suit would therefore be more properly labeled as *Mineral King v. Morton.*

Inanimate objects are sometimes parties in litigation. A ship has a legal personality, a fiction found useful for maritime purposes. The corporation sole—a creature of ecclesiastical law—is an acceptable adversary and large fortunes ride on its cases.[2] The ordinary corporation is a "person" for purposes of the adjudicatory processes, whether it represents proprietary, spiritual, aesthetic, or charitable causes.[3]

So it should be as respects valleys, alpine meadows, rivers, lakes, estuaries, beaches, ridges, groves of trees, swampland, or even air that feels the destructive pressures of modern technology and modern life. The river, for example, is the living symbol of all the life

---

[1] See Stone, Should Trees have Standing? Toward Legal Rights for Natural Objects, 45 S. Cal. L. Rev. 450 (1972).

[2] At common law, an office holder, such as a priest or the King, and his successors constituted a corporation sole, a legal entity distinct from the personality which managed it. Rights and duties were deemed to adhere to this device rather than to the office holder in order to provide continuity after the latter retired. The notion is occasionally revived by American courts.

[3] Early jurists considered the conventional corporation to be a highly artificial entity. Lord Coke opined that a corporation's creation "rests only in intendment and consideration of the law." Mr. Chief Justice Marshall added that the device is "an artificial being, invisible, intangible, and existing only in contemplation of law." Today suits in the names of corporations are taken for granted. United States Supreme Court. 405 U.S. 727 (1972).

it sustains or nourishes—fish, aquatic insects, water ouzels, otter, fisher, deer, elk, bear, and all other animals, including man, who are dependent on it or who enjoy it for its sight, its sound, or its life. The river as plaintiff speaks for the ecological unit of life that is part of it. Those people who have a meaningful relation to that body of water—whether it be a fisherman, a canoeist, a zoologist, or a logger—must be able to speak for the values which the river represents and which are threatened with destruction.

I do not know Mineral King. I have never seen it nor travelled it, though I have seen articles describing its proposed "development." . . . The Sierra Club in its complaint alleges that "One of the principal purposes of the Sierra Club is to protect and conserve the national resources of the Sierra Nevada Mountains." The District Court held that this uncontested allegation made the Sierra Club "sufficiently aggrieved" to have "standing" to sue on behalf of Mineral King.

Mineral King is doubtless like other wonders of the Sierra Nevada such as Tuolumne Meadows and the John Muir Trail. Those who hike it, fish it, hunt it, camp in it, or frequent it, or visit it merely to sit in solitude and wonderment are legitimate spokesmen for it, whether they may be a few or many. Those who have intimate relation with the inanimate object about to be injured, polluted, or otherwise despoiled are its legitimate spokesmen.

The Solicitor General . . . takes a wholly different approach. He considers the problem in terms of "government by the Judiciary." With all respect, the problem is to make certain that the inanimate objects, which are the very core of America's beauty, have spokesmen before they are destroyed. It is, of course, true that most of them are under the control of a federal or state agency. The standards given those agencies are usually expressed in terms of the "public interest." Yet "public interest" has so many differing shades of meaning as to be quite meaningless on the environmental front. Congress accordingly has adopted ecological standards . . . and guidelines for agency action have been provided by the Council on Environmental Quality of which Russell E. Train is Chairman.

Yet the pressures on agencies for favorable action one way or the other are enormous. The suggestion that Congress can stop action which is undesirable is true in theory; yet even Congress is too remote to give meaningful direction and its machinery is too ponderous to use very often. The federal agencies of which I speak are not venal or corrupt. But they are notoriously under the control of powerful interests who manipulate them through advisory committees, or friendly working relations, or who have that natural affinity with the agency which in time develops between the regulator and the regulated. As early as 1894, Attorney General Olney predicted that regulatory agencies might become "industry-minded," as illustrated by his forecast concerning the Interstate Commerce Commission:

"The Commission is or can be made of great use to the railroads. It satisfies the public clamor for supervision of the railroads, at the same time that supervision is almost entirely nominal. Moreover, the older the Commission gets to be, the more likely it is to take a business and railroad view of things." M. Josephson, The Politicos 526 (1938).

Years later a court of appeals observed, "the recurring question which has plagued public regulation of industry [is] whether the regulatory agency is unduly oriented toward the interest of the industry it is designed to regulate, rather than the public interest it is supposed to protect."

The Forest Service—one of the federal agencies behind the scheme to despoil Mineral King—has been notorious for its alignment with lumber companies, although its mandate from Congress directs it to consider the various aspects of multiple use in its supervision of the national forests.

The voice of the inanimate object, therefore, should not be stilled. That does not mean that the judiciary takes over the managerial functions from the federal agency. It merely means that before these priceless bits of Americana (such as a valley, an alpine meadow, a river, or a lake) are forever lost or are so transformed as to be reduced to the eventual rubble of our urban environment, the voice of the existing beneficiaries of these environmental wonders should be heard.

Perhaps they will not win. Perhaps the bulldozers of "progress" will plow under all the aesthetic wonders of this beautiful land. That is not the present question. The sole question is, who has standing to be heard?

Those who hike the Appalachian Trail into Sunfish Pond, New Jersey, and camp or sleep there, or run the Allagash in Maine, or climb the Guadalupes in West Texas, or who canoe and portage the Quetico Superior in Minnesota, certainly should have standing to defend those natural wonders before courts or agencies, though they live 3,000 miles away. Those who merely are caught up in environmental news or propaganda and flock to defend these waters or areas may be treated differently. That is why these environmental issues should be tendered by the inanimate object itself. Then there will be assurances that all of the forms of life which it represents will stand before the court—the pileated woodpecker as well as the coyote and bear, the lemmings as well as the trout in the streams. Those inarticulate members of the ecological group cannot speak. But those people who have so frequented the place as to know its values and wonders will be able to speak for the entire ecological community.

Ecology reflects the land ethic; and Aldo Leopold wrote in A Sand County Almanac 204 (1949), "The land ethic simply enlarges the boundaries of the community to include soils, waters, plants, and animals, or collectively, the land."

That, as I see it, is the issue of "standing" in the present case and controversy.

QUESTIONS

1. Suppose someone made the following objection to Justice Douglas: "Since an inanimate object has no interests of its own, it is simply impossible for anyone to 'speak in its name.'" Would this be a justifiable criticism?

2. Does the wilderness have a moral right to exist?

SUGGESTED ADDITIONAL READINGS

Environmental Ethics. This journal, identifying itself as "An Interdisiplinary Journal Dedicated to the Philosophical Aspects of Environmental Problems," began publication in 1979. It is an invaluable source of material relevant to the issues under discussion in this chapter.

GOODPASTER, K. E., and K. M. SAYRE, eds.: *Ethics and Problems of the 21st Century.* Notre Dame, Ind.: University of Notre Dame Press, 1979. This collection of original essays is generally relevant. Part One features three papers under the heading, "Broadening the Concept of Morality." Also especially notable are papers by Richard T. DeGeorge, "The Environment, Rights, and Future Generations" (pp. 93–105), and Peter Singer, "Not for Humans Only: The Place of Nonhumans in Environmental Issues" (pp. 191–206).

LEOPOLD, ALDO: "The Land Ethic." In *A Sand County Almanac* (New York: Oxford University Press, 1966), pp. 217–241. In this essay, a frequent reference point of contemporary discussions, Leopold calls for an extension of the ethical community beyond its traditional anthropocentric limits.

REGAN, TOM: "The Moral Basis of Vegetarianism." *Canadian Journal of Philosophy*, vol. 5, October 1975, pp. 181–214. Regan sets out to show that "a vegetarian way of life can be seen, from the moral point of view, to have a rational foundation." He objects to the nontrivial, undeserved pain that animals typically suffer when subjected to intensive rearing methods but insists that "it is the killing of animals, and not just their pain, that matters morally."

————, ed.: *Matters of Life and Death*. New York: Random House, 1980. Two of the long essays in this collection are especially relevant. In "Animals and the Value of Life" (pp. 218–259), Peter Singer directly confronts the issue of the justifiability of killing animals. In "The Search for an Environmental Ethic" (pp.299–335), William T. Blackstone identifies and discusses a host of issues related to the development of an adequate environmental ethic.

————, and PETER SINGER, eds.: *Animal Rights and Human Obligations*. Englewood Cliffs, N.J.: Prentice-Hall, 1976. This very useful anthology provides readings organized in four categories: (I) "Contemporary Realities," (II) "Animal and Human Nature," (III) "Do Humans Have Obligations to Other Animals?" and (IV) "Do Animals Have Rights?"

ROLSTON, HOLMES, III: "Is There an Ecological Ethic?" *Ethics*, vol. 85, January 1975, pp. 93–109. In analyzing the notion of an ecological ethic, Rolston distinguishes between a *secondary* ecological ethic (in which an underlying classical moral principle or system is simply applied to generate moral conclusions with regard to the environment) and a *primary* ecological ethic (in which a basic moral principle or system itself emerges from ecological considerations). He finds the latter, the more radically ecological ethic, to be the more attractive option.

SAGOFF, MARK: "On Preserving the Natural Environment." *Yale Law Journal*, vol. 84, December 1974, pp. 205–267. In this expansive article, Sagoff ultimately proposes "a nonutilitarian rationale for preserving the natural environment." He develops the view that "the obligation to preserve nature . . . is an obligation to our cultural tradition."

SINGER, PETER: *Animal Liberation*. New York: New York Review, 1975. Singer advances a vigorous critique of our present attitudes toward animals and our dealings with them. He also provides a wealth of relevant factual material.

STONE, CHRISTOPHER: *Should Trees Have Standing?* Los Altos, Calif.: Kaufmann, 1974. This short book bears the subtitle, "Toward Legal Rights for Natural Objects." Stone develops in great depth the line of argument relied on by Justice Douglas in *Sierra Club v. Morton* (1972).